# Stratusphunk

*The Life and Works of George Russell*

Duncan Heining

**Jazz Internationale**
Framlingham, Suffolk, UK
2020

Published by Jazz Internationale.

Copyright © 2010, 2020 Duncan Heining

All rights reserved. No part of this book may be reproduced in any form or by any electronic or mechanical means, including information storage and retrieval systems, without written permission from the publisher, except by a reviewer who may quote passages in a review.

The publisher can be contacted at jazzinternationale@gmail.com

Dedicated to Jock Millgårdh, his wife Manda
and their children Maja, Kalle and Max.
George loved you all very much.

# Contents

| | | |
|---|---|---|
| | Acknowledgments | vii |
| | Introduction | ix |
| Chapter 1 | From Such Beginnings... | 1 |
| Chapter 2 | On Class and Culture | 23 |
| Chapter 3 | Cincy Blues | 43 |
| Chapter 4 | New York, N.Y. or in Search of the Lost Chord | 59 |
| Chapter 5 | A Bird in Igor's Yard | 74 |
| Chapter 6 | Ballad of Hix Blewitt | 97 |
| Chapter 7 | Space Music | 125 |
| Chapter 8 | You Are My Sunshine | 141 |
| Chapter 9 | Norwegian Blues - Pining for the Fjords? | 175 |
| Chapter 10 | Listen to the Silence | 193 |
| Chapter 11 | Living Time at New England Conservatory | 213 |
| Chapter 12 | Playing the African Game | 233 |
| Chapter 13 | Live in a European Time Spiral | 247 |
| Chapter 14 | It's About Time | 265 |
| Chapter 15 | On Conceptual Thinking | 277 |
| | Bibliography | 301 |
| | Interviews | 313 |
| | Appendix A: Recordings | 314 |
| | Appendix B: Tour Dates, 1982–2005 | 326 |
| | Index | 335 |
| | About the Author | 345 |

# Acknowledgements

I would like to thank all of the musicians and interviewees who gave their time and help in creating this book. I particularly wish to thank Hans Koller (Head of Jazz, Trinity Laban) and Ingrid Monson (Quincy Jones Professor of African-American Music, Harvard) for assistance in clarifying issues relating to the Lydian Concept. Finally, the greatest debt is owed to my partner, Annie, for her unstinting intellectual, emotional, and financial support. George Russell has had a number of wonderful women in his life, none more so than his wife Alice. I have been especially fortunate in having just one.

# Introduction

"Will I then have to lose myself in this abyss of freedom? To what shall I cling in order to escape the dizziness that seizes me before the virtuality of this infinitude? However, I shall not succumb. I shall overcome my terror and shall be reassured by the thought that I have the seven notes of the scale and the chromatic intervals at my disposal, that strong and weak accents are within my reach, and that in all of these I possess solid and concrete elements that offer me a field of experience just as vast as the upsetting and dizzying infinitude that that had just frightened me. It is into this field that I shall sink my roots, fully convinced that combinations which have at their disposal twelve sounds within each octave and all *possible* rhythmic varieties *promise* me *riches that* all *the activity of* human genius will never exhaust." *Igor* Stravinsky (Original italics) [1]

## STRATUSPHUNK

*George Russell: The Story of an American Composer* was my first book. It was published by Scarecrow Press in 2010. Though it received favourable reviews, priced around $80, it hardly troubled the *Guardian* or *New York Times* bestseller lists.

Reading it through for this revised paperback and digital edition, I am pleased with my efforts. I felt at the time and feel now that I had done my subject proud. It had been a labour of love and took me to places I might not have visited and introduced me to many incredible and talented people, whom I otherwise would not have met, not all of them musicians. And quite a few of those individuals would merit a book of their own.

When I started my biography of George Russell in Autumn 2003, I had recently retired from my career in the British probation and prison services due to illness. The therapeutic benefits of researching and writing the book at that time were great indeed. And yet, going through it page by page in preparation for this edition also reminded me of the trials and difficulties of dealing with the publishing industry. Let us just say that it involved a set of experiences and frustrations I would prefer not to repeat.

In 2003 self-publishing was something for vanity projects. In 2020, the publishing industry (or at least substantial sections of it) seems unable to adjust to the digital age in a way that makes sense to any but the most successful authors. In such circumstances, self-publishing is not only logical but now stigma-free.

*Stratusphunk* offers the reader a book about one of the most important, if often overlooked, figures in jazz and does so in a form substantially revised compared to the first edition. Since the publication of *George Russell: The Story of an American Composer*, I have written two other books, studied for a PhD by published work and studied music theory formally through the ABSRM (Associated Boards of the Royal Schools of Music). I think I am now able to a better job in presenting George Russell and his life's work to the world and hope readers of *Stratusphunk* will agree.

The changes I have made vary from the small to the large. Corrections of various errors have been made, several long, complex chapters have been broken up and the syntax at certain points improved to clarify key points. I think it now flows much better than before.

Three reviewers made specific comments in their reviews that I felt warranted attention and I have responded to those comments. The first, by the eminent British writer and broadcaster Alyn Shipton, concerned the absence of a (relatively) concise outline of the Lydian Chromatic Concept of Tonal Organisation, George Russell's major contribution to jazz theory.[2] As the Lydian Concept was central to Russell's life and work, discussion of aspects of the Lydian Concept continue throughout the text. However, I have sought to address Shipton's valid criticism in Chapter Four by providing a summary of key points relating to the theory. I give full credit to the sources I have drawn upon in this summary in the text.

The second reviewer, Fernando Ortiz de Urbina, found the final chapter of the first edition "convoluted and arid" and suggested it added little to the rest of the narrative. De Urbina was not the only reviewer to make this criticism.[3] Grego Applegate Edwards writing in Canadian magazine *Cadence* used the same terms to describe that section. I rather agree with both de Urbina and Applegate Edwards.[4]

In my defence, by that point and with little in the way of editorial support from the publishers, I had been working on the book for five years and struggled with that chapter. In response to these criticisms, the key points that I had wished to make are now addressed within the main text, while I have dropped certain arguments that now seem of less importance. The new concluding chapter is more straightforward focusing on reviewing Russell's achievements and contextualising his ideas and beliefs, musical and philosophical.

De Urbina does, however, raise a couple of points with which I disagree. He picks me up for noting that a large number of jazz writers accepted and replicated Russell's account of his origins without question, namely that he was the product of a liaison between a white music professor and an African-American music student at Oberlin College. De Urbina then refers to a number of my own errors in the text, such as my reference to "trumpeter John Carisi".[5]

I accept that my point could have been clearer in the first edition but the accounts given by predominantly white journalists of Russell's birth narrative, placing the emphasis upon the white music professor father (for whose existence there is no evidence) is of a different order of magnitude. At worst, it is indicative of colour and gender blindness on the part of those writers.

For this reason, I deal with this issue in some detail below and more briefly in the main text. I have chosen to do it in this way to cover the issue fully but avoid disrupting the main narrative. Applegate Edwards also raised the issue of race and racism pointing out that though this was addressed in relation to Russell's early life in Cincinnati such questions were largely abandoned in the rest of the book. Again, I agree with this criticism, if not with an apparent undertone to the reviewer's comments in this respect. Hopefully, he will now feel that such questions are foregrounded rather than backgrounded in *Stratusphunk*.[6]

## *STRATUSPHUNK*: A BRIEF WORD ON METHODOLOGY

From the outset with *George Russell: The Story of an American Composer*, my aim was to write what is best described as a 'critical biography' of George Russell. The biographer, Paul Murray Kendall, noted,

> Assembling a string of facts in chronological order does not constitute the life of a person; it only gives an outline of events. The biographer therefore seeks to elicit from his materials the motives for his subject's actions and to discover the shape of his personality.[7]

As Kendall points out critical biographies emphasise research, evidencing, academic standards of referencing, "proofs" supported by evidence and require that conjecture is "duly labelled" as such. In writing *George Russell: The Story of an American Composer*, inevitably, I drew upon my academic background in the social sciences, including in psychology and sociology. I also drew upon my professional training as a social worker, in terms of my interviewing and assessment skills but also in terms of the background it gave me in relating theory to practice.

Both my academic and professional backgrounds involved a high degree of normative training in the development of a critical, self-reflective practice. In the case of academic work, this required a respect for both academic standards and ethical research practice. In terms of my work as a social worker/probation officer, this involved respect for the person and a commitment to their welfare and to their personal integrity as a human being.

Two methodological approaches, in particular, link my past professional activities, my academic background and my writings on music. The first is General Systems Theory (GST), first developed by the theoretical biologist Ludwig von Bertalanffy in the 1940s but later extended to other areas of scientific and social scientific practice.[8] For my purposes, GST allows the exploration of relationships between individuals and their wider systems of engagement. In some respects, GST is less a 'theory' in the fullest sense and more a means of organising information through the creation of relational 'models' from the data.[9]

The second approach is known as Social Diagnosis. The term originated with the remarkably prescient American social work pioneer, Mary Richmond (1861-1928). She described this as, "the attempt to arrive at as exact a definition as possible of the social situation and personality of a given client."

> Investigation, or the gathering of evidence begins the process, the critical examination and comparison of evidence follow and last come its interpretation and the definition of the social difficulty.[10]

The point is that the individual biographer brings to bear their own specific range of skills and experience to the task. Had my academic and professional backgrounds been in literature, music history, music, social anthropology or cultural studies, then *George Russell: The Story of an American Composer* would have been a different book. Russell's story would have remained the same but the way the material was presented and the emphasis in interpretation would have differed.

In his review of *George Russell: The Story of an American Composer*, Fernando Ortiz de Urbina also found my "reflections on the psychological background of the musician" too speculative.[11] Returning to Paul Murray Kendall's definition of the function of biography, such a comment misses the very point of the activity. As to the word "speculative," so is theoretical physics but that hardly invalidates the exercise. Moreover, compared to Sheldon Cooper's field of expertise, in terms of access to the subject under examination, in my case access was somewhat more direct and immediate.

The biographer's responsibility is to do their research to the fullest extent that is realistic and possible, to marshal their evidence and locate it within an explanatory framework appropriate to it. With *George Russell: The Story of an American Composer*, I feel that that is what I had achieved. The reader only needs to refer to the list of eighty interviews undertaken, including seven with Russell himself, and the extensive bibliography to realise the lengths to which I went to offer a very comprehensive account of his life and work.

But de Urbina's comment also raises issues of competence. I am not going to suggest that jazz biographers, writers and historians should only draw upon those academic and professional fields in which they are proficient. However, in reflecting upon a subject's "psychological background," a writer must be very careful that they do have at least some degree of competence in that area.

De Urbina is right to be concerned in that respect. This is particularly the case where the subject is long deceased and where the author has not interviewed them personally. Any conclusions in such circumstances are inevitably based only on second- and third-hand accounts of the individual. Where the writer is of a different racial, ethnic, gender or class background from their subject, there is a danger that the writer will draw inferences from such accounts of an individual's behaviour without full knowledge of the socio-cultural context in which that behaviour takes place. In cases such as that, it is better that the writer be very circumspect in their comments.

However, here my subject was still alive and I had ready access to him and those close to him. I interviewed musician colleagues, students, friends and lovers and I read dozens of articles and interviews with the subject. To that material, I was able to bring the range of skills and theoretical knowledge located in my training. Moreover, that training also emphasised the importance of sensitivity to the individual subject's own racial and class background in ways that, sadly, fall outside the training required in many other areas of work, including journalism.

I stand by my "reflections upon the psychological background" in *George Russell: The Story of an American Composer* and, here, in *Stratusphunk*. They are grounded in research and grounded within an appropriate theoretical framework, itself rooted in an understanding of developmental psychology.

There was one other issue I deliberately avoided in the original text. While undertaking research for *George Russell: An American Composer*, Russell had begun to experience symptoms associated with dementia – most notably, difficulty in organising his thoughts. My reason for not revealing this was simple. Russell continued to work with the support of his partner Alice and certain band-members, such as Pat Hollenbeck. Enabling Russell to continue to do so was more than a financial issue. It helped him to cope with the condition and he lived for those moments on stage. I have no problem with my decision.

As to how his capacity to respond to my questions affected my interviews with him, this clearly did have implications for my research. It was here that my training as a social worker again came into its own, not least training in interviewing skills. Over the years, I have interviewed and reported upon thousands of people, often individuals for whom telling their story as a coherent narrative was even more difficult than was the case with Russell in those later years. In all such instances, one needs to allow the account to unfold in its own time, using questions more to clarify and help provide a loose structure to assist the respondent in their narrative rather than simply to elicit information. Most of all, one must be patient.

As a writer, I tape all of my interviews and transcribe them in full. In the main, I was surprised how much information I gained even from the very last of my interviews with Russell. And, of course, no piece of information stands on its own and must be set against other sources, the process of doing so known as triangulation. The researcher is responsible for checking and cross-checking information and I have done just that with my biography of George Russell to the best of my ability.

What I describe here are conscious, deliberate practices, processes and research strategies born of training and study. "Too speculative?" Here, I defend my corner.

## *STRATUSPHUNK*: MYTHS AND LEGENDS

One of the tasks of a biographer is to sort out myth from reality and fact from fantasy. In certain respects, the way George Russell told his story to journalists and jazz writers contained a number of mythological elements. I do not think this was in any degree intentional on Russell's part but many of the written accounts of his background have been unhelpful in placing him and his achievements in the real context of his life.

In our culture, and indeed across others as the Jungian author Joseph Campbell has shown, the life stories of exceptional individuals and/or heroic figures are frequently given a particular shape and form. Campbell refers to this as the "hero myth" and saw it as something that varied across cultures but was based on a common "monomyth". The form itself is rooted in our collective unconscious but reflects particular, even elemental, patterns and themes. It purports to explain but, instead, results in the mythologizing of its subject. Myths may tell the most wonderful stories but they make for lousy history. [12]

It is easy to understand the temptation for journalists seeking an angle upon which to hang their subject's story. If nothing else, this can be essential if one wants to please one's editor. But the danger is that the angle becomes the story or worse ends up consuming it, while a more interesting and exciting story is hidden from the reader. It is not simply that I believe in telling the truth, as best I can. Rather, it is the fact that I find the true story far more enlightening, rewarding and uplifting than the all-consuming, fabricated angle.

While he was a man of great integrity and honesty, George Russell did tend to muddy the waters when it came to discussing his own origins, understandably re-telling the story he was told, in his mid-teens by his adoptive mother. But Russell went further than merely repeating the story told to him of his birth. He often attached it to discussion of what he saw as the most important element in his life's work, that is the Lydian Concept. On occasion, it seemed as if the account of his own origins helped explain the origins of the Concept. This had the effect of adding the gloss of myth to that tale.

Given that Russell came to be seen as a kind of *éminence grise* behind more fêted jazz cardinals such as Miles Davis, John Coltrane and others, a further spin is given to his story. With a subtle twist, Russell becomes a shadowy, almost magical figure behind the scenes.

In the introduction to a stand-alone BBC Radio Three programme on Russell, musician, writer and broadcaster Ian Carr noted,

> [George Russell is] one of the most mysterious and unorthodox figures in jazz. His ideas have been hugely influential, yet he has been for the most part a shadowy presence on the side-lines. It may be that his covert genius has its roots in the secrecy surrounding his birth in Cincinnati in 1923. [13]

The title given by Carr to that programme was *The Invisible Guru*, while the title of the series of eight half-hour programmes written and presented by Carr for BBC Radio Three was *The Trail Blazer*. Similar hyperbole could be found in the titles of any number of articles upon Russell over the years. These have included such descriptions of Russell as "Jazz Visionary," "Jazz Prophet,", "St. George and the Chord,", "The Lydian Pioneer," and "The Mathematical Musician." [14] Such epithets might have been written by the writers' editors but they arose from the way these journalists had sought to tell Russell's story, which in turn grew out of his account of himself and his life. The picture these all paint is of a lonely but heroic figure forging ever forward but never achieving their due recognition. And it is a tale that begins with assumptions about "the secrecy surrounding his birth".

Russell was neither an enigma, nor a legend. Those two labels bedevil so much jazz writing and, all too often, are used in an attempt to sneak some second-division jazz musician into the pantheon. Nor were his life or origins mysterious in any way – most definitely far from ordinary but there is no mystery involved.

He was not a 'legend' because his music and ideas were both real and concrete and had real and concrete influence. That he and his life's work are less-well known and less well-understood than they might be is unfortunate but do not justify the use of the kind of heroic language above. Indeed, I wrote this biography in the hope that it might redress that imbalance.

His life story is intriguing and fascinating. It is a picture of an African-American artist, who rose from lowly and even unpromising beginnings to achieve status as a composer, theorist and educator. But it also tells that story as a parable of the struggles faced by people from minority groups, everywhere, in the face of racism and discrimination.

We would be wrong to find too much comfort in George Russell's successes. And we are wrong to mythologize him. Researching and writing this book was hard work but the information needed to tell his story and place his work in the context of his life and world was there to be discovered.

Another even more problematic issue arises in connection with Russell's account of his origins. Although this is covered in Chapters One and Two, I will spend a little time exploring this issue further here.

Russell was adopted as a baby and brought up in Cincinnati, Ohio by Bessie and Joseph Russell, a respectable African-American working-class couple. Bessie was a nurse and Joseph a cook on the B&O railroad. Russell only discovered that he was adopted in his mid-teens and after Joseph's death. At some point, he was given a school photograph and his mother, who is in the picture pointed out to him. He treasured that photograph. Russell would refer affectionately in his telling of the story to his natural parents as 'the kids', whose love was forbidden by intolerance and racism.

A number of articles, otherwise well-written and generally accurate, have made much in their account of Russell's background of his putative biological father, "the white professor of music" at Oberlin and little of his mother, a music student at the college.[15] When one starts to unpack this, however, a number of points emerge from these accounts. Firstly, they suggest some kind of belief on the authors' parts in the genetic inheritance of musical talent – in itself, perhaps justifiable or not. Secondly, these accounts clearly focus on the putative father, ignoring the possibility that such talents might have been inherited from the biological mother, "an African-American music student".

From my research, it seems highly likely that Russell was the child of Kathleen George, who studied music at Oberlin College, and an unidentified white male. Kathleen left her course around the time that she would have been pregnant with Russell. Prior to attending Oberlin, she had lived with her uncle and family in West Virginia and had completed high school at the Bluefield Colored Institute, Bluefield, WV. This is the school in Russell's photograph of his mother and fellow students. I have, however, found no evidence for the existence of the "white music professor" to whom Russell referred in various interviews.[16]

Russell talked readily of his white music professor father and, perhaps, unconsciously, believed that the association gave his ideas a certain status in some way. However, he would always mention his "biological mother" at the same time, seeing them very much as a unity, albeit one that was not tolerated by society at the time.

And Kathleen George, a young African-American from one of the Southern states where segregation was still very much in force, must have been a quite remarkable young woman. That she studied at the prestigious Oberlin Conservatory of Music, as a woman and as an African-American woman in those years, is surely evidence of real ability and achievement in itself. If we accept the possibility that Russell might have inherited his gifts through genetic transmission, then surely we must also credit his "biological mother".

But I have other problems with this stress upon the "white professor of music" and on biology for it downplays the influences of home and community. In his adoptive parents Bessie and Joseph, George Russell found loving, caring parents who set boundaries for him and taught him right from wrong. Theirs was a home filled with music, where musicians on tour, including from Duke Ellington's band, sometimes stayed. From Russell's account, and from my research, the wider community, too, was filled with music and rich in cultural and social values and offering strong role models, both male and female.

Nor should one overlook Russell's description of his adoptive father Joseph's eccentric piano playing. Joseph loved to play the piano but, as Russell told one interviewer, he knew little about harmony or melody but would just let his fingers fall wherever they might. Or as Russell put it, "like Cecil Taylor before Cecil Taylor." I was not alone in finding in that description parallels with Russell's own playing of the instrument. [17] This casual emphasis on Russell's "white music professor" father fails to acknowledge the many positive influences offered by African-American parents and communities to their young ones, often in the face of the greatest obstacles. Russell was raised in an such a community by Bessie and Joseph Russell and no "white music professor" played any part in that.

But there seems to be something else at play here. Think for a moment of how jazz is frequently understood as a marriage of African rhythms and European harmony, of Africa meeting Europe. As Gunther Schuller noted in his book *Early Jazz* (1968) "Jazz writing abounds with such oversimplifications as that jazz rhythm came by way of Africa, while jazz harmonies are exclusively based on European practices..." Schuller saw the appropriations of elements of western harmony by African-American jazz musicians as being highly selective and was keen to stress the very different cultural basis of African and European musics. And, yet, when Schuller states, "One thing is clear: any discussion of harmony in jazz must begin with the realization that in the beginning African-American music had no harmony," it is easy to see how such oversimplifications came to dominate. [18] André Hodeir in *Jazz: Its Evolution and Essence* (1958) referred to the European influences on jazz in the following terms,

> These elements, all of Anglo-Saxon or French origin – hymns, songs, and, later, popular dances and military marches – gave jazz some of its principal characteristics: its tonal system, its form, the four-beat measure, the four-bar unit of construction, a kind of syncopation, and so forth. [19]

While, a few pages later, he adds, "The European element did in a sense corrupt Negro folklore, but it made it productive at the same time." [20] I admire both individuals greatly, Schuller particularly so. Both Schuller and Hodeir clearly saw African-Americans as the primary actors in these selective borrowings. However, in both cases and that of many other authors, I cannot help but detect an underlying assimilationist assumption in their understanding of cultural processes, one that mirrors liberal American assumptions about how racial and social progress in the USA can be achieved. [21]

In a way, Russell's birth narrative and the way it has been received by jazz journalists seem to offer a parallel to the way in which jazz is presented as a music that crossed the racial divide. "The white male music professor" plus the "African-American female music student" equates to a marriage of European art music and African rhythm made, not in heaven, but in the racially segregated world of 1920s USA.

While this is not the place to discuss these issues in depth, such an over-simplified equation fits too easily into notions of "jazz as democracy" and, by extension, of American exceptionalism, of America as the land of opportunity and freedom. As disc jockey Wills Conover once proclaimed on his show, *Voice of America Jazz Hour*, "Only in such a society – and ours is the best example I know - could jazz have developed." [22] Similar assumptions, though less explicitly stated (frequently with much greater acknowledgement of the evils of slavery, Jim Crow and race discrimination) can certainly be found in the writings of several white liberal North American critics. [23]

Two major debates around race and jazz in America have occurred over the years – the "Crow-Jim" debacle around *DownBeat* magazine in the early/mid-sixties and the furore around efforts by Wynton Marsalis, Albert Murray and Stanley Crouch to position jazz as an essentialist African-American art form in the nineties.

Briefly, in the first period, white *DownBeat* journalists (and it seems some white jazz musicians) accused African-American musicians such as Max Roach, Abbey Lincoln, Cecil Taylor and others of practicing "Crow-Jim" in their unwillingness to hire white musicians, reflecting their own assimilationist stance with regard to jazz – a charge rebuffed in turn by Roach *et al* with allegations of discrimination by the largely white media, promoters and club owners. [24]

In the second period, Marsalis/Murray/Crouch sought to secure an agenda built upon an exclusionary definition of the jazz tradition based upon canonical works and the pressurising of cultural institutions and funding bodies to reflect that definition. [25] In this second period, opposition to the Marsalis camp came both from both white and African-American critics and musicians. Yet, there were discernible differences in the criticisms offered by African-American musicians such as David Murray and Lester Bowie, who disputed the Marsalis *et al* definition of the jazz tradition and whose work was excluded from that definition, and white critics such as Gene Lees and Eric Nisenson, whose arguments, it can be argued, again reflected an assimilationist perception of race and jazz. [26]

More than anything else, these debates have revealed the absence of any coherent understanding of issues of race, racism and jazz within large sectors of both the jazz establishment – promoters, arts funding bodies, the media – and the jazz audience. Such discussions have largely revolved around questions of ownership, about whether or not white jazz musicians can truly play authentic jazz and around the creation of a limited and limiting jazz tradition based upon the blues and the notion of swing. Important work by black and white writers on these issues – John F. Szwed, Ralph Ellison, Amiri Baraka, Ingrid Monson, Paul Austerlitz, A. B. Stellman, Ben Sidran, Fumi Okiji and others – has often remained peripheral to discussion.

At the heart of the issue in both debates and periods has been a contest over control of the narrative of jazz as a music and its history, if the first time as tragedy, the second has been as farce. On the one hand, there is the conflation of jazz, America, democracy and freedom, leaving one with the impression that slavery and the decades of brutality and liberal prevarication that followed were an aberration to be (eventually) rectified by the democratic promise of the constitution. By that token, jazz is seen as a safe space for "cats of any colour" representing the "real America," waiting only for the "unhip" to finally catch on.

The positions taken by African-American artists such as Roach, Lincoln, Taylor and others in the earlier debates arose from very real economic and cultural grievances of jazz musicians but were also were clearly linked to the wider struggles for civil and economic rights of African-Americans. By contrast, it is harder to discern in the position taken by the Marsalis/Murray/Crouch camp in the nineties a political agenda beyond an attempt to force mainstream cultural bodies in the USA to acknowledge and promote African-American cultural achievement. As to any wider strategic goals, I can only discern the vaguest, neo-liberal notion that some trickle-down process might result in an improved cultural and social position for African-Americans more generally as a result.

Were I an African-American musician, I would find the very notion that jazz offered a safe space for black musicians alongside their white colleagues insulting. The idea is belied by the history of the music, certainly into the sixties. That white musicians experienced much the same pressures abounding in the world of jazz clubs as black musicians does not alter this. The money was often poor, the hours long, work precarious, segregation in many states a reality, drug and alcohol dependency a constant danger, infiltration by organized crime of the club scene and hassles from the police and city and state licensing authorities a fact of life. By contrast, it does seem entirely reasonable to suggest that the uncertain and hazardous working environment of African-American (and white) jazz musicians was a direct consequence of the lower status jazz occupied in the country of its birth compared to that of classical music or its lower value in terms of market return compared to pop, rock and country music. In turn, that lower status can be seen to derive from racist assumptions regarding the value and worth of African-Americans and of their cultural products.

The "cats-of-any-color" perspective of Gene Lees and others seems to me a very rose-tinted, ahistorical view indeed. It is one that ignores that gains made by African-Americans have been won not through command of democratic, electoral processes but by peaceful, and sometimes, violent direct action in the face of organized white resistance and, indeed, backsliding and equivocation on the part of white politicians. Paul Austerlitz, both a professional musician and an ethnomusicologist, has noted bluntly in response to such notions,

> A fundamental difference between whites and blacks in American music that while whites have played what they wished, segregation kept black musicians behind fences. [27]

That surely is a crucial part of the lived experience of every African-American, now or in the past, musician or non-musician. It is a part of the history of the music that cannot be wished away, set aside or forgotten. It is part and parcel of telling the story of jazz honestly, not least in a context where for many, in America and elsewhere, white lives are seen to matter so much more than those of people of colour. As Fumi Okiji has pointed out recently, jazz developed in a context where African-Americans were denied full human subjectivity. She notes, in relation to the 'jazzocracy' argument,

> What is most striking here is the contradiction between black expression (jazz) being the bearer of the liberal democratic ideal and black life being devoid of human quality.[28]

To suggest that jazz expresses the America beloved of white liberals ignores African-American experience. As Fumi Okiji argues, black America "by way of its expression in jazz, poses a direct challenge to the understanding of the terms *America, freedom* and *democracy*."[29] Even more specifically, in *Black and Blur* (2017), Fred Moten locates the phenomenon of jazz as an art form in the context of the history of slavery and segregation, the latter not understood as an historical event or as a series of events or even as a legacy of such events but as a "durational field." That is to say that slavery and segregation without redress and reconciliation can never be over. As Moten notes, "Jazz does not disappear the problem; it is the problem, and will not disappear." See in this way, jazz derives its critical moment from the contradictions in its relationship wider American culture and society.[30]

The African-American sociologist and civil rights activist, W.E.B. Dubois used the term "double consciousness" to describe the dual and conflicting identity of African-Americans, based simultaneously in the African-American in-group but related to, if more problematically, the mainstream of American culture. Paul Austerlitz has extended Dubois' concept to talk in terms of the need for a jazz consciousness" that would "situate the music in the overlapping contexts of the United States, the African diaspora, and the larger world."[31] As he notes,

> The story of the strife attendant to the five-hundred-year legacy of the forced migration of Africans to the Americas is inextricable from jazz consciousness.[32]

Furthermore, this jazz consciousness acknowledges jazz as a music that was created in the USA by African-Americans syncretically, that is transforming with those tools available to them a range of musical resources of various origins. So doing, what was created essentially Africanised or, perhaps better, African-Americanised those musical resources, creating something that was entirely new. Of equal importance is the stress that Austerlitz places on the influences of what he calls "Latino" musics but which I would prefer to describe as "Afro-Latino." This is, however, entirely consistent with Austerlitz' point in this regard. As an aside, the reader will note that Afro-Latin influences continued to surface in George Russell's music throughout his career.

The arguments put forward by Austerlitz are in the best sense utopian. They express not some idealized "jazzocracy" but a universalism that, itself, reflects how the jazz musicians he quotes from Duke Ellington and Billy Taylor to Anthony Braxton and Milford Graves saw/see jazz as a music. Jazz consciousness does not deny the special place in the music for its African-American creators and innovators but nor does it deny musicians of other backgrounds a place in jazz. As an idea, it lies a long way from the trivialisations of white liberals and distances itself from the exclusionary position-taking of the Marsalis/Murray/Crouch axis.

Though Austerlitz does not say this specifically, it is not a matter of ownership but one of emotional, spiritual, psychological and cultural connection.

I was born in a rural community in Britain I sang at primary/junior school from collections of English folk song compiled by Cecil Sharp and attended Anglican church services, singing hymns that often drew upon those same musical traditions. As a child and adolescent, I heard music by Edward Elgar, Ralph Vaughan Williams, Sir Hubert Parry, Benjamin Britten and Gustav Holst, all of whom found inspiration in the folk musics of these islands. Perhaps my deepest emotional and psychological musical connection lies in the cadences of English/British folk music. This fact does not stop me loving jazz, blues, so-called world musics or European Art Music. I simply have to acknowledge that when I hear guitarist Martin Carthy sing "Scarborough Fair" or Sandy Denny sing "Tam Lin" or Vaughan Williams' *The Lark Ascending* my reaction can only be described as profound and spiritual.

These things are built into my musical DNA. It does not stop other musics making their way into my consciousness and affecting me in ways that are just as spiritually uplifting but rather that my musical journey began with those cadences in English folk music. I do not deny any singer, African-American, Chinese, Serbian or Indonesian the right to sing those songs just as well as Martin Carthy or Sandy Denny. Nor do I deny any violinist of whatever nationality or ethnic group the right to play *The Lark Ascending* and move me with their interpretation. But nor do I have any desire to deny to African-American jazz musicians or fans, or Afro-British jazz musicians or fans, a different connection to jazz from mine. I do not share the same cultural experiences and those cultural experiences include the experience of discrimination and white racism.

How we tell the music's story needs to acknowledge those contradictions, understand how these may have shaped the music and how, through its marginal cultural position, jazz might provide one mechanism, among others, of examining critically the persistent divisions of both class and race that persist across America, Britain, France and other liberal democratic societies. Some readers may feel I have strayed somewhat from my original point about the way George Russell's story has been told in the past. I would simply say in response that the way of its telling tells us more about the ideological and cultural assumptions of those doing the telling than it does about George Russell or about jazz.

## *STRATUSPHUNK*: A LIFE WELL-LIVED

George Russell was a unique figure in African-American music. He was a theoretician, a composer of note, a working musician, and an educator. Over a decade before his first record, *The George Russell Smalltet - Jazz Workshop* (1956), he had begun his life's work developing the Lydian Chromatic Concept of Tonal Organization. One of a rare breed of thinker-musicians, he has had - through his ideas and music – a major influence on the development of jazz after 1950. From his early composition with Dizzy Gillespie of "Cubano-Be, Cubano-Bop," through the changes wrought by modal jazz as a consequence of his ideas, to his impact on the Scandinavian and European scenes, his achievements are among the most outstanding in the music.

His life story weaves its way through modern jazz intersecting with the lives of many of its most colourful and significant figures. Charlie "Bird" Parker, Dizzy Gillespie, Miles Davis, John Coltrane, Bill Evans, Gerry Mulligan, John Lewis, Gil Evans, Eric Dolphy, Ornette Coleman, Don Cherry and Carla Bley were not just Russell's contemporaries. They were his peers, his colleagues and his friends. He touched their lives and music and, in turn, was encouraged by them.

Born to a young African-American woman in 1923, George Russell was given up for adoption and he was brought up by a working-class African-American couple in Cincinnati, Ohio. It was not an auspicious start in life. However, fostered by the love and care of his adoptive parents Bessie and Joseph Russell and the encouragement and support of a local community determined to do its best by its children, his abilities and talents emerged.

At the same time, we should not ignore the fact that his tale is one of a potential realized despite obstacles of birth, discrimination, ill health, poverty, and neglect. For, Russell's early life and career were acted out against the dramatic landscape of America's racial divide. It is an important part of American mythology that the United States is the land of opportunity - where, if you have it in you, you can and will succeed. Seen from certain angles, Russell's life would seem to bear this out. The truth is always more complex, however.

Though his struggle has often been more concerned with developing the Lydian Concept than with seeking recognition for his music, his success has come despite the American Dream rather than because of it. An African-American child born in an inner city experiences a very different world from a WASP born with a trust fund in place, let alone the scion of an oil dynasty. The novelist Ross MacDonald once wrote,

> In a puritanical society, the poor and fatherless, suffering the quiet punishments of despair, may feel themselves permanently and justifiably damned for crimes they can't remember having committed. [33]

As MacDonald suggests, in holding out its promise, the American Dream makes those who fail to achieve its promise responsible for their failure, never the wider inequalities and injustices of American society. Russell succeeded because of his talents, discovering ways of negotiating the race and class boundaries that society might have imposed upon him and escaping those "quiet punishments of despair". Many others from similar backgrounds did not and do not do so. And from his adoption by Bessie and Joseph Russell onwards, he was confronted by racism in his native Cincinnati and beyond.

Some writers have found the whole circumstances of his birth and adoption "mysterious," and the story Russell was told about his origins has achieved an almost mythic significance in reference to his work. As will I hope be realised, the truly remarkable story concerns what Russell made of his life and talents and where these came from *in fact*, rather than in fantasy.

By his twenties and despite suffering from two bouts of tuberculosis, he had established himself in New York within the core of the Jazz Bloomsbury that gathered in Gil Evans's apartment on West 55th Street. It was in the course of a now-famous conversation with Miles Davis that the idea of an overarching musical concept was born. Asked what his musical aims were, Davis replied, "Learning all the changes." Knowing Davis knew the changes already, Russell realized he meant something else,

> I think everybody then who knew about Miles knew he knew how to play the changes. So it occurred to me to look for a new way to relate to chords.[34]

And so a lifelong study began that would lead Russell to question the musical and philosophical basis of Western music and propose instead a system based on the relationships between scales and chords. The theory would lead jazz into modal playing and would even anticipate the jazz-rock of the sixties and seventies. He would call it the Lydian Chromatic Concept of Tonal Organization.

"Cubano-Be, Cubano-Bop," written in 1947 for Dizzy Gillespie and His Orchestra, fused Afro-Cuban rhythms with jazz. Generally accepted as the first avowedly modal piece in jazz, it was followed by "A Bird in Igor's Yard," written for Buddy DeFranco and His Orchestra. Perhaps considered by the record company to be far ahead of its time, the track wasn't released until 1970, though New York DJ Symphony Sid played a tape of the recording repeatedly on his radio show. From the late forties into the mid-fifties, Russell also wrote and arranged for Earl Hines, Charlie Ventura, Artie Shaw, Dizzy Gillespie, Claude Thornhill, Ella Fitzgerald, singer Lucy Reed, Teddy Charles, Hal McKusick and Lee Konitz.

But the Lydian Concept proved a demanding mistress. In fact, although he published his thesis in 1953, it wasn't until 1956 that Russell made his first record, *Jazz Workshop*, an astonishing album full of unusual textures and rhythms. Working on and refining his Lydian Concept, Russell put the principles of his theory into practice with his own music. A series of ground-breaking recordings followed that included *Jazz in the Space Age*, *New York, N.Y.*, and six albums for the Riverside label, including the brilliant *Ezz-thetics* with Eric Dolphy. By then his Lydian Concept was acknowledged for its impact on the emergence of modal jazz, not least upon the music of Miles Davis. Davis had by then released *Kind of Blue*, while John Coltrane was forging his own take on modal approaches to jazz. The direction Russell had initiated had become preeminent in modern jazz.

By 1965 Russell had become increasingly alienated by both the aggressively political stance of the Free Jazz movement and by America's increasing involvement in Southeast Asia. He accepted an invitation to work in Sweden and his influence there proved decisive for a new generation of musicians in Scandinavia and beyond, including Jon Christensen, Palle Mikkelborg, Terje Rypdal, Arild Andersen and a very young Jan Garbarek. In Scandinavia, his music continued to develop and produced a number of recordings, the significance of which are only now being realised.

He also had a child by a Swedish woman but despite his success in northern Europe he could not settle. In 1969 Russell took up composer Gunther Schuller's offer to teach in the newly created Jazz Department of the New England Conservatory. Since then, he taught some of the most able and searching musicians. Players like Don Byron, Ricky Ford, Marty Ehrlich and John Medeski have studied the Concept, and others, like Randy and Michael Brecker, studied Russell's ideas through his former student and musical colleague, Dave Baker. From the eighties onwards, he worked and recorded with his Living Time Orchestra for Blue Note, Soul Note, and Label Bleu and toured North America, Japan and Europe. In some ways, he was more feted abroad than at home but any disregard Stateside did not stand in the way of both Guggenheim and MacArthur fellowships. George Russell wrote both short and extended works for jazz orchestras and groups. He wrote ballets and choral works and his influence continues to be felt.

This biography will explain why George Russell is perhaps less well known and less highly regarded than his achievements deserve. It will examine a career that was sustained over seven decades without any loss of artistic integrity and without the rewards sometimes received by lesser talents. So where does he belong in the jazz firmament? This biography hopes to restore some balance and will weigh Russell's gifts and contributions to jazz. And perhaps at the end, readers will agree that George Russell has earned his place in the pantheon.

## *STRATUSPHUNK*: A FINAL POINT

In effect, it feels as if I have written this book twice. Writing it has been a voyage of discovery into George Russell's music and into his thinking about music and life. But getting to write it twice has advanced my own thinking about jazz as a music and reflects changes in my own understanding of the cultural values and meaning of jazz. The process has prompted a more radical way of understanding jazz, not just as an art form but also, as a repository of different ways of confronting aesthetic and ethical issues as these pertain to all the arts.

More and more, I come to the conclusion that the way jazz is presented by the jazz establishments of the world misses the very things that might connect it to wider audiences, namely its roots in gospel, blues and rhythms that make you want to move and be part of the music. Even in his eighties, when the Living Time Orchestra was really cookin', George would start to dance and he was a great dancer. One time at the New England Conservatory, I heard a group of students discussing the terpsichorean abilities of various faculty members. They all agreed that George Russell was the best dancer on the staff. And Russell also understood how music might connect us with something beyond ourselves; through our own personal essence, perhaps, but with something greater. It is a lesson that has been too long in the learning but I thank you, George, for teaching me that.

## Notes

1. Igor Stravinsky, *Poetics of Music in Six Lessons*, (Cambridge, MA: Harvard University Press, 1974) p.64
2. Alyn Shipton, review of *George Russell: The Story of an American Composer*, *Jazzwise*, March 2010???
3. Fernando Ortiz de Urbina, review of *George Russell: The Story of an American Composer*, *Cuardernos de Jazz* website, May 2011.
4. Grego Applegate Edwards, review of *George Russell: The Story of an American Composer*, *Cadence*, July-September 2010, pp. 60-63.
5. De Urbina, op cit.
6. Applegate Edwards, op cit.
7. Paul Murray Kendall, Biography entry in Online Encyclopedia Britannica 2013 at http://www.britannica.com/EBchecked/topic/65924/biography; see also Kendall, *The Art of Biography*, (London: George Allen & Unwin, 1973).
8. Debora Hammond, *The Science of Synthesis: Exploring the Social Implications of General Systems Theory* (Boulder, CO: University of Colorado Press, 2003)
9. K. Boulding, "General Systems Theory: The Skeleton of Science," Management Science, 2, 3 (pp.197-208) Apr. 1956
10. Mary Richmond, *Social Diagnosis*, Russell, New York, NY: Sage Foundation 2017; see also Eric Sainsbury, 1970 *Social Diagnosis in Casework*, Abingdon: RKP
11. De Urbina, op cit.
12. Joseph Campbell, *The Hero with a Thousand Faces*, London: Fontana, 1993
13. Ian Carr, *The Trail Blazer* BBC Radio Three (eight half-hour programmes broadcast July 4 – August 22, 1994 and "The Invisible Guru" BBC Radio Three July 1, 1994.
14. Robert Palmer, "A Jazz Visionary Eyes the Evolution of Life on Earth." *New York Times*, April 28, 1985; R. DiNardo, "Jazz Prophet." *Boston Globe Sunday Magazine*, June 12, 1983, Gary Giddens, " St. George and the Chord" *Village Voice*, March 24, 1975; Peter Gamble "George Russell the Lydian Pioneer Takes Stock with Peter Gamble," *Jazz Journal*, July 1992; Howard Mandel, "The Mathematical Musician." *Washington Post*, September 27, 1987. N.B. I make no apologies for the title of my article on Russell for *Avant* Magazine – "A Meeting with a Remarkable Man". Firstly, Russell was remarkable. Secondly, we had spoken about his interest in the teachings of George Gurdjieff, who had written a book on his travels and spiritual quests entitle *Meetings with Remarkable Men*. The allusion should be clear. Duncan Heining, "A Meeting with a Remarkable Man," *Avant* 7 (Summer 1998).
15. See for example, Robert Dinardo, "Jazz Prophet", *Boston Globe*, October 6th, 1983; Bob Claypool, "Blazing the fusion trail," *Houston Post*, October 8, 1983; Max Harrison, "George Russell: Rational Anthems," *The Wire*, issue 3, Spring 1983, p.30-31; Howard Mandel, "The Mathematical Musician: George Russell and His Concept on Chords", *Washington Post*, September 27, 1987.
16. It seems unlikely that in 1930's America, a white professional (perhaps married) who had fathered an 'illegitimate' child by a black woman would actually check on his well being. Even had the natural father been so named, he would not have been granted access to such confidential information. Until recently, all adoptions were closed.
17. See *Stratusphunk* Chapter One; Robert E. Moore, "George Alan Russell: Jazz's First Theorist" *Trotter Institute Review*, 2 (Summer 1988), p.15-19. Moore also noted Joseph's unusual approach to harmony and, when interviewed, remarked that it reminded him of Charles Ives' "Country Band March" and the story behind it. Misspelling in original.
18. Gunther Schuller, *Early Jazz: Its Roots and Musical Development*, (Oxford: OUP, 1968), p.4; p.38.
19. André Hodeir, *Jazz: Its Evolution and Essence*, (London: Jazz Book Club, 1958) p.40;
20. Op cit, p.44

21. Much more recently, Alyn Shipton, *A New History of Jazz*, London: Continuum, 2001 offers a more dynamic, sociological interpretation locating the origins of jazz in cultural and racial milieu of New Orleans. Shipton's account is what I would call a 'systems' approach as opposed to the more traditional, linear historical account offered by Hodeir and Schuller.
22. Quoted in Fumi Okiji, *Jazz as Critique: Adorno and Black Expression Revisited*, (Stanford, CA: Stanford University Press, 2018), p.16.
23. For example, Gary Giddens, *Visions of Jazz: The First Century*, (Oxford: OUP, 1998); John A. Kouwenhoven, *Made in America: The Arts in Modern American Civilisation*,( New York: W. W. Norton & Co, 1967 - originally published in 1948). Kouwenhoven wrote, "In this one artistic form, if nowhere else, Americans have found a way to give expression to the Emersonian ideal of a union which is perfect only 'when all the uniters are isolated.' By its resolution of this basic conflict jazz relates itself intimately with the industrial society out of which it evolved." In this bizarre and telling section, Kouwenhoven likens the organization of the jazz group to the principles of scientific management outlined by F. W. Taylor; Marshall Stearns, "Jazz is America", Program notes Newport Jazz Festival 1955, p.56-59 - "Tomorrow, with proper study and encouragement, jazz can be a fabulous influence – on the most personal level – to foster friends of democracy everywhere." (p.59); Kabir Sehgal, *Jazzocracy: Jazz, Democracy, + The Creation of a New American Mythology*, (Mishawaka, IN: Better World Books, 2008) - "Jazz is an idea writ in sound, color and imagination: it is iconoclastic, democratic and fiercely innovative." (p.9)
24. See Ingrid Monson, *Freedom Sounds: Civil Rights Call Out to Jazz and Africa*, (Oxford: OUP, 2007), pp. 238-251.
25. See Albert Murray, *Stomping the Blues*, (New York: McGraw-Hill, 1976). Also https://wyntonmarsalis.org/news/entry/art-is-about-elegant-form-an-interview-with-albert-murray-by-wynton-marsalis; For example, see Nat Chinen, "Wynton Marsalis: The Once and Future King of Jazz at Lincoln Center" https://www.nytimes.com/2006/08/27/arts/music/27chin.html
26. See Kabir Sehgal, op cit; Gene Lees, *Cats of Any Color: Jazz Black and White*, (London: Da Capo, 2001); Eric Nisenson, *Blue: The Murder of Jazz*, (New York: St. Martin's Press, 1997). For a contrasting perspective see Jon Panish, *The Color of Jazz: Race and Representation in Postwar American Culture*, (Jackson, MS: University of Mississippi Press, 1997). Panish examines critically how white assumptions regarding the desirability of assimilation of people of colour is reflected in writing on jazz.
27. Paul Austerlitz, *Jazz Consciousness: Music, Race, and Humanity*, (Middletown, CT: Wesleyan University Press, 2005), p.13
28. Okiji, 2018, p.17.
29. Ibid.
30. Fred Moten, *Black and Blur*, (Durham, NC: Duke University Press 2017), p.xii.
31. Austerlitz, (Original italics) p.x
32. Op cit, p.xi
33. R. MacDonald, "Writing the Galton Case," in *On Crime Writing* (Santa Barbara, CA: Capra Press, 1973).
34. *George Russell – A Jazz Portrait*, WGBH Radio, Boston.

CHAPTER ONE

## From Such Beginnings . . .

George Russell was clearly upset. We were at 'Stone Mill' in the Berkshires where Jimmy and Juanita Giuffre lived. Juanita had been married to George back in the fifties and I was interviewing her for this biography. They had remained friends, after their divorce and Alice and George Russell were staying with the Giuffres that weekend. Jimmy suffered from Parkinson's Disease, so I was unable to talk to him but I was looking forward to speaking with Juanita.

As I waited for Juanita to finish attending to Jimmy, Russell started talking about something that had happened in Cincinnati, when he was a young man just starting out as a professional musician. He'd told me the story before and that was the problem. Now he did not want it in the book. It concerned a young white bassist, whom Russell and his mother had befriended and who was severely beaten one night by two white men. Russell had told me that the two men were police officers and had beaten his friend for fraternizing with African-Americans. Sixty years later and Russell was expressing his fears about how white citizens and officials in Cincinnati might react in response to the suggestion should it appear in this book.

For me, the story was pivotal in Russell's life. It indicated the cost for someone such as him of growing up as an African-American in a racist society and also revealed what it meant for him as an individual, as someone who was an unusually sensitive human being. But more than that, it explained how he finally came to leave the Mid-West and head for New York. We talked and eventually reached what seemed a mutually acceptable compromise.

Reflecting later, I wondered what had disturbed Russell so much. I had just returned from Cincinnati, where I had been undertaking research for his biography, bringing pictures from his life back in the Mid-West. Photos from childhood taken at a school where he had been bitterly unhappy, including some of a childhood friend who had been in the same TB ward as he and who had later died of tuberculosis. A report card from that same school where he had experienced discrimination and felt constantly worthless and undermined. These were all reminders of difficult times and of a place from which he had chosen to escape as soon as he could. It was not surprising that the issue Russell picked to express his discomfort concerned events that lead to his leaving home. As Alice Norbury-Russell would later say when she and I talked about this, "George doesn't like to look back. He likes to go forward. He's happy to reminisce but that's different. He just doesn't like to dwell on things that for him lie in the past."[1]

This was a reminder that biography could be both a flattering and a threatening process for its subject. It could evoke positive memories and experiences but equally negative ones half-repressed or happily consigned to oblivion. And it raised the question, 'Who owns a life?' The subject? The biographer? The fans and other readers?

The story of someone in Russell's position extends beyond them. He could not own it entirely or the manner of its telling. What our lives say about us, they also say about others and their potential. They talk about universal forces and themes much greater than us or the subject of a biography.

I understood Russell's discomfort both in terms of his fear about what might be said about him and in terms of his concern that he might lose control of his own story. Someone else was walking around in his life and memories. But, as to the themes that dominated his life or the external forces that might have shaped it, these were never under his control. Yet, it was important to be sensitive to his discomfiture, to respect his feelings and to maintain his confidence.

For Russell, his discovery of the Lydian Chromatic Concept of Tonal Organization, his ground-breaking contribution to jazz and music theory, had to be central to the book. That, rather than half-forgotten events from his past, was ultimately what mattered to him. But writing a biography has to be about the whole life, if the life's work and the individual who created that work are to be understood.

Obviously, I had no intention of ignoring Russell's major contribution to jazz theory. But, in writing George Russell's biography, I also needed to concern myself with how he developed this new way of thinking about the music and jazz improvisation. New ways of thinking, whether about human psychology, physics, biology, politics or culture do not arise in splendid isolation. In Russell's case, as in that of many others who have influenced our world in greater or less great ways, his thinking evolved through the complex interaction of his life and personality, his relationships, his environment and wider social, economic and cultural forces. And, in his case, one of those wider forces was racism both in its systemic, political sense and at the very personal level of individual experience.

But there were also themes that emerge about what is or is not jazz and where its place lies in modern culture. There are themes about influence and the transmission of ideas, both in terms of the influences on Russell himself and in terms of his influence on others and on the development of jazz. There are questions to be addressed about education and jazz and how jazz or any creative enterprise can be taught. And perhaps most important of all there runs through all of this the history of a truly beautiful and remarkable art and the place of George Russell in its story.

George Russell came into the world at 8:00 p.m. on June 23, 1923. He was born in an apartment at Helena Flats, 1339 Lincoln Avenue in the Walnut Hills district of Cincinnati. The block housed some eleven African-American families.[2] It is unclear in which precise apartment Russell was born and there is no apparent connection between his or his birth mother's name and the names that appear on census records for the block. The doctor certifying the birth was Louis A. Cornish, MD. Russell's mother gave her name as Mary Smith and her place of birth as West Virginia. She was nineteen and single, and the birth certificate records her as "Coloured." The space for the father's name is left blank. Russell's name is given as "George Allen Smith" on the certificate.

Research confirms that "Mary Smith" was an alias given to Dr. Cornish. The doctor was either quite happy not to pursue this further or saw no reason to question her identity. Since there are no apparent connections by name to other residents at 1339 Lincoln Avenue, it seems a reasonable assumption that "Mary" was staying with friends or relatives with a different surname. Perhaps she was estranged from her own family or sent away to give birth due to her family's desire to retain an image of respectability. Speculation perhaps, but it would certainly fit the story Russell was told much later about his birth and origins.

On January 23, 1924, George was adopted by Mr. Joseph A. and Mrs. Bessie O. Russell. He had been with his adoptive parents since June 25, two days after his birth, according to the adoption petition. The mother's consent form gives her name this time as "Grace Smith" and the witness's name was given as "J. H. George." The adoption certificate states that "George Allen, an illegitimate male child" was, with the consent of his mother, adopted by the Russells. With this document, signed by probate judge William H. Leeds, secured in the public record, George Allen Smith became George Allen Russell. It would not be until he was in his mid-teens that Russell would learn about his origins. Even then, he would never see any reason to pursue his birth mother or birth father or seek any connection with their families.

Mrs. Bessie Russell—she always insisted on that form of address from strangers—was a nurse who worked for Dr. Eli Miller. Miller was a very well-respected physician who would later play a leading role in the Planned Parenthood movement in Cincinnati.[3] She was an active member of the African Methodist Episcopal Mount Zion Church in Walnut Hills. This was one of the most significant of the black churches in Cincinnati, and its minister, Reverend Gilbert,[4] one of its most important community leaders and spiritual figures. As a woman of some standing in her own community, and with her work for Dr. Miller, it seems likely that Mrs. Russell would have insisted that correct procedures for the adoption be followed.

Joseph and Bessie Russell wed on Christmas Day, 1916, in St. Louis, Missouri, so they had been married for six and a half years when they adopted George. They were childless, though whether this was due to an inability on their part to conceive or some other reason is unclear. How the adoption came about is unclear. Certainly, there is no reason to assume that Mrs. Russell attended "Mary Smith" during her pregnancy in a professional capacity. Nevertheless, the potential connections are there. From my research, there is no reason to suppose that the Russells would have known "Mary/Grace" or her family, though they might have known the family with whom she was staying. However, it seems at least possible that the connection might have come through Dr. Miller. It is a reasonable assumption that two white doctors working in the African-American community would have known each other and Dr. Miller would have known that the Russells were looking to adopt. Alternatively, Mrs. Russell might have known the nurse attending "Mary/Grace." But there are other reasons to wonder about a connection between the Russells and George Russell's natural mother and also about the possible part Dr. Miller might have played in the adoption. Melbourne Terrace, where the Russells lived, was just a few blocks from Lincoln Avenue, where Russell was born. It also leads into Reading Road, close to Miller's practice. It is therefore possible that although Cornish attended the delivery, "Mary/Grace" might have come under Miller's care during her pregnancy. Whatever the connection might have been, this is now lost and, as noted, George never felt a need to know.

During the nineteenth century, Walnut Hills was a fairly wealthy area of the city, attracting bankers, merchants and lawyers to its elegant streets. Cable cars arrived in the 1880s, followed by faster and more reliable electric streetcars in 1898. The increased accessibility of the area from downtown both reduced its exclusivity and brought the development of less expensive housing for middle-income families and, from the 1890s to the 1920s, there was an expansion of row houses, apartment buildings, and modest single-family dwellings. While the 1930s brought a greater influx of African-American families into the area, some people of colour had been living there since the 1860s. Although at one point the area seems to have become quite run-down, its days of decline appeared to have been behind it and, by the time, of Russell's birth, it was a respectable neighbourhood that attracted African-Americans who had good jobs and who were keen to see certain standards of propriety maintained. [5]

Lieutenant Commander Dwight McPheeters, a childhood friend of George Russell's and later one of the Tuskegee Airmen, recalled,

> It was an all-black neighbourhood apart from a couple of grocery stores. There was one on Kerper and the lane leading to Washington Terrace and another at the end of Kerper Avenue but those were the only white people who—not lived—but were in that neighbourhood. But I'll tell you one thing, we didn't have any crime in that neighbourhood. People watched out for one another. It wasn't well-to-do or upper-middle-class. It was a whole bunch of folks that were struggling but at the same time they were very disciplined about their families and their neighbourhood. We had a couple of good policemen who used to be around there that everybody understood and respected. [6]

William R. Davis, until retirement a teacher at Loyola University, Chicago, also knew Russell and lived in the area. "It was very close. The people at that time, everyone knew each other. We might live a block away or two blocks away but you knew each other." Though it was not an affluent neighbourhood, in Davis's words,

The people in neighbourhood, the men worked. Most of the women that were able to, if the father had a good job, could stay at home and take care of the children. My mother was a domestic worker. I had an aunt that did live across the court from us that did never have to work because her husband had a better job but then we had people who were just postmen, we had people who were railroad Pullman porters and we had people who worked for the U.S. Postal Service delivering the mail. We had a few teachers and a few social workers in the neighbourhood and those were the people who had had the opportunity to go to college and become teachers and social workers, etc. Most of the people there in the neighbourhood were just plain ordinary working people, blue-collar more or less.[7]

Mrs. Bessie O. Russell was born in St. Louis in 1883 and, according to Russell, she was one of the first nurses of colour in Cincinnati.[8] Mr. Joseph Russell was born in 1879 and was a chef on the B&O Railroad. He and Bessie were both in their forties when they adopted George. Given their age and childless status, it is a little surprising that they had not adopted a baby sooner. This might suggest that it was the opportunity to adopt George himself that presented itself to the Russells and again that there might have been some family connection between one of the Russells and "Mary/Grace." Though he does not know why his parents were childless, Russell says that theirs was not a happy marriage. They had separate bedrooms and, in Russell's words, Joseph's "marriage to Bessie had most of the time been strained." Describing his father, Russell said, "He was an intelligent man. He had street knowledge. He didn't need any official colleges or high schools. He was a gentleman and he could talk well and [was] a good man but they had a bad relationship. I never saw them kiss or hug or sleep together."[9]

Bessie's work for Dr. Miller also became a source of dissention in the marriage.

> He still supported us—as my mother did—but at one point he asked my mother to stop working for Dr. Miller and I think that had to do with their marriage, you know. And she had to stop working for Dr. Miller. Nurse that she could be—she was probably the best nurse in Cincinnati. She knew her nursing up and down because I saw her save lives of people.[10]

It seemed that Joseph was threatened by her working for Miller rather than her working per se.

> The relationship between my mother and Dr. Miller was very tight. I don't know how tight because Dr. Miller was married and he was a man of scruples and they both were. My father might have thought something was going on there because "she's not giving it to me." If there was a fight, my mother would win. She had muscles. She was a strong lady. Once there was . . . she had a gun, so he started crying and went to his room.[11]

From all his comments, it is clear that Russell loved and admired both his parents deeply. But there is also a powerful vein of sadness that runs through his account of their marriage. "He'd come in, he'd lay down the food he'd gotten, the great food he'd gotten from the train that he hadn't used and he'd go up stairs and start playing the races. He played the races a lot."[12] And:

I was sad that they didn't have a happy life together, that there wasn't more of a rapport between them. You kind of felt the distance between these two wonderful people. Both were wonderful. My father went to the third grade. My mother graduated, was the first black woman to graduate from Mihara University from Atlanta, Georgia, in nursing. My father used to . . . I played cards with him a lot. I loved cards. He loved cards. When he was sick I played cards with him. He'd fix me, I forget the name of the drink but it had ginger ale and whisky and sugar. What's that called? Boilermaker or something. We'd have fun playing but it got so that getting down the stairs must've been an ordeal and he slept upstairs. But he left me with a lot. [13]

Being a railroad man, Joseph was frequently away, though he sometimes took George on trips with him. Bessie was, however, perhaps the more constant and significant figure in his life. Dwight McPheeters remembered her fondly, "She had the sweetest disposition you ever saw and I think she spoiled George. That was my opinion. But she was a very, very nice lady. I never met his father." [14]

William R. Davis has a similar recollection, "His mother and my mother were friends. We all belonged to the same church. All I remember was that she was one of the nicest people in the block. You see, the families were very close in that neighbourhood, especially those that belonged to the church." [15] At that time, the Russells were living on Kerper Avenue, and although their area of Walnut Hills was predominantly African-American, Russell spoke about Bessie's German origins on her mother's side. He also had early recollections of a family friend, "Aunt Nee," who had blonde hair and was married to a "black feller." These memories suggest that the racial divisions in Cincinnati were sometimes less clear-cut than might be assumed. He recalled, "Because my mother had a number of friends, people who were white people, I knew white people better than I knew coloured people." [16]

Russell told Vivian Perlis in a 1993 interview for the American Music Series that as a child he would often bring "some little ragamuffin home" and Bessie would take care of him. "[M]y mother would kind of adopt him, as a friend of mine, sometimes for long times, or some kid whose home life was horrible, she'd take him in and he'd become a playmate. But not for a terribly long time, maybe for a year even, she'd do that." [17]

One of Russell's earliest memories is from when he was five. Bessie had sent him to get a haircut at the barber's across the road from Dr. Miller's surgery. "I went to the barbershop. Came out, I didn't see any cars. One car turns a corner and slams into me and ran over my face." [18] He was carried to Dr. Miller's surgery, where one patient—a Mrs. Tannenbaum, a member of the Jewish-German family who owned Cincinnati's main department store—rushed him in her car to the hospital nearby.

It was a Jewish hospital and in Cincinnati at that time blacks were not allowed into that hospital. She got to [the] Jewish hospital and the attendants kept saying . . . I don't know how they could tell what kind of race I was, but she must've said, "I have this little coloured boy with me." They said, "Coloured boy? He's not going in here." She said, "The hell he isn't." *(laughs)* She said, "You get the hell out of the way." She got me to the operating room and the doctor said to the assistants there, "Get your ass moving. We got to help this kid." That was beautiful. I guess they had to sew on my ear. For some years, I had the streaks where the car had run over me, the impressions it made. [19]

It was a lucky escape for Russell and he was in hospital for some weeks. He recalled being treated well by the hospital staff despite being "the first person of colour to be admitted" to the hospital. "The cook made special dishes for me and they treated me royally. I hated it when they dismissed me because they'd done all they could do. My mother was visiting all the time. I had the time of my life and I almost cried the day they took me home, because they celebrated me." [20]

The accident seems to have set Russell back at school and held back his physical development. "The next impression I had was of Hoffman School, Kindergarten. I'm not sure I have this right but I must've started Kindergarten a year later than the average person. My age thing got all messed up with the accident." [21] Dr. Robert Moore, an academic and tenor saxophonist who began research for a biography of George Russell in the eighties, spoke to a number of people in Cincinnati who had known Russell as a child.

> [W]hen he was very young the kids nicknamed him Kelly. I guess that as a result of that accident, of being hit by a car, I guess maybe naturally that he wasn't as gifted or as physically adept as some of his playmates and he'd always be the last one picked to play baseball or whatever and he was rather awkward physically. They nicknamed him Kelly because of a baseball player for the Cincinnati Reds—I think his name was Red Kelly—who wasn't particularly good, who was usually cited as a problem on the team. So that name followed him and George spoke of this in the context of his getting an interest in playing the drums. In the Boy Scout troop he was the second best drummer and he took great pride in that and that became his thing to excel in. [22]

The incident at the hospital also made Russell aware that his colour set him aside from other parts of the world he lived in. "The negativity of the world begins to start with incidents like this. However, being unconscious and everything, it doesn't make a deep impression until you're able to go back on it. While it's happening you don't think anything of it." [23] He had also begun to appreciate that there were differences between life at home and life on the street.

> I did have an impression that things on the street weren't exactly like things in your house. Things on the street were disconnected from your house. It was a separate language to survive. For example, my mother, beautiful Bessie, growing up and being Dr. Miller's nurse, she used technical terms like "rectum." This is your *rectum*. This is your . . . whatever. Kids being kids, one day one guy kicked me right in the ass. I said, "You've kicked me in my rectum! *(laughs)*" All the kids around said, "What?" And they broke out laughing. That taught me. That was the beginning of something else in me I suppose. It's a different language in the street, so I began to learn street survival and street language. [24]

At Kindergarten, Russell says the first thing he did the first day was to kiss the girls—

white or black. It was a mixed school, as were many of the city's schools. In racist societies, people of colour need to develop special skills to negotiate the different worlds with which they must have contact. There are different codes, different ways of speaking—and, as he noted, Russell seems to have begun to learn this quite young.[25]

> So, the impression between home and the street was just beginning to grow. Especially when the guys did the rectum thing. That started in me a new compulsion to speak the language of the street until I could finally speak it better than they could. And still today, if I lose something I say, "Where the fuck . . . ?" The part of you that cares about protecting you, the red light goes on between the streets and your own essence. At home I felt relatively safe. In the streets, even when things got normal and everything was done, the same day I realised the differences, not to the extent that . . . well, [I suppose] it did mess with my psychology that I was different but not as formidably as it did later on. I mean a little later on. Like, my father was from Georgia, went to the third grade in school but he was a third-degree Mason. He was an intelligent man, chef-cook on the railroad. I remember him meeting a cracker, a fucking policeman, who said, "Boy, what you doin' wearing that pin?" My father just said, "Oh!" Took the pin off, or else.[26]

This sense of difference, of being in an alien environment, was fostered by Russell's experiences of school. Cincinnati had begun to integrate the school system—or at least to allow schools to integrate their pupils—in the twenties. As William R. Davis recalled,

> "The high schools were always integrated. You went to the high school for the district you lived in. If you went to the high school that I went to you had to take an examination at the sixth-grade level, and for Walnut Hills at the seventh-grade level. If you passed the exam and [then you could] go [on] through the twelfth grade. Walnut Hills had a reputation of being one of the better high schools in the nation. I had the opportunity to go there."[27]

And yet in most other respects *de facto* segregation was the day-to-day order of life. Ohio had been a free state since its inception. However, it bordered on Indiana and, more importantly, Kentucky, which was a slave state and had fought on the side of the Confederacy. This left its legacy long after the Civil War. Describing the postbellum situation in the Midwest, C. Vann Woodward noted in *The Strange Career of Jim Crow*,

> Generally speaking, the farther west the Negro went in the free states the harsher he found the proscription and segregation. Indiana, Illinois and Oregon incorporated in their constitutions provisions restricting the admission of Negroes to their borders.[28]

Moreover, informal segregation in so-called 'free states' could be almost as vicious as in slave states. As early as the 1830s, Alexis de Tocqueville was shocked by depth of racial bias he saw in the North, writing that "the prejudice of race appears to be stronger in the states that have abolished slavery than in those states where it still exists; and nowhere is it so intolerant as in those states where servitude has never been known."[29]

It's a point made eloquently by Dwight McPheeters: "Cincinnati is a bigoted town and it's barely underneath the surface at this time. These people are one step away from Dixie." [30] William R. Davis echoed this comment.

> It has always been that way. Racism is a very strong factor in the life there and although they have organizations that have tried and are still trying to alleviate some of the friction between the races, there is something there that I would say—having been gone for fifty years, I'm still in contact [and] I have four sisters that are there—most of the people are still alienated against one another. That may be because of the influence of southern Indiana and Kentucky, which is immediately across the river from Cincinnati. A lot of the traffic that you get coming into Cincinnati for buying goods, trading and entertainment comes from Kentucky and Indiana and Tennessee. Some of them come from as far away as Tennessee just to see a baseball game. We have those kind[s] of influences that are still there and it's difficult to change the mores of people who have been brought up with those kinds of differences in their minds. [31]

Russell went from the Kindergarten to Hoffman Elementary and was one of the small minority of African-American students attending the school. Hoffman had been recently desegregated and, although the option of him attending a blacks-only school existed, Bessie Russell rejected this for her son. As a professional woman who seems to have had the ability to function effectively in both black and white worlds, she appears to have wanted Russell to be able to do the same. On balance, he seems to have felt that was the right choice, as he later told Vivian Perlis:

> I could have gone to any of the other schools. Some schools weren't desegregated. But my mother insisted that I go to Hoffman, which was an integrated school. So in a way we were—we few who went to the school, the integrated school—were much more faced with the reality of things—which is good— than the kids who didn't go to the integrated schools. [32]

At the same time, it was clearly not a happy experience and he felt constantly undermined and undervalued because of his colour.

> I think what finished me at Hoffman in the eighth grade, the teacher who had a book and she had different people reading it. It was a book about slavery— one of the famous books—the word "Nigger" was all through the book, and she pointed at me and asked me to read the book to the class. I read maybe five words that had "Nigger" in and slammed the book down and left the class. [33]

Such insensitivity was commonplace and when he was fourteen, Russell was chosen for a part in the school play. It was *Gone with the Wind* and his role was that of Aunt Jemima.

> Dwight could've killed me. I tried to explain to him. He said, "What the hell did you do that for? It's a disgrace." I'm smart enough to act Aunt Jemima. I'm smart enough to see the pattern. [But] I too, of course, felt belittled. [34]

McPheeters remembered the event well, though his view had softened over the years.

> Yeah. I really panned him. I think maybe our friendship suffered because of that. I didn't think that George should do that. I thought that he was degrading himself and all of us by doing that but like Hattie McDaniel in the movies, we did the same—kind of ridicule of her—but she paved the way for a lot of us to get into the movies. [35]

Russell described another incident that took place on a field trip, which perhaps reveals the complexity of thoughts and feelings that go through a young African-American's mind in a world of such divisions.

> It's things like—when you're in a class with whites and you feel that they're special or something. Even incidents like the eighth-grade class, which made me thirteen or fourteen or so, going out on a nature thing and being on a mountain and this girl slipped and I happened to be there at the drop-off of the mountain and I caught her and her arms were around me. I associated that with, "Let's see how the crowd reacts?" You know? Would they appreciate what I'd just done? My teacher did, because he was Jewish, but would the others or would they want to say, "What are your arms doing around that white woman?" I was saving her life. [36]

If the divisions in Cincinnati, and Ohio as a whole, were marked, as a young boy Russell was still surprised by his first experience of traveling south with Bessie to visit Joseph's family.

> The big one was when we took a train, my mother and I going south to see his family. The train was nice. The food was nice on the train. After we left Cincinnati, we went to the next town in Kentucky. Nothing happened there, but then at the next stop further south we had to go, my mother and I, both light-skinned, had to go to the back of the train, which was full of black people. Then I said, "Oh, I get it." So it grew on me, this difference, because of these incidents. [37]

He was seven at the time, and he recalled being told very clearly not to leave the family's farm under any circumstances. He was too young to understand what precisely they feared might happen to him but remembers the palpable sense of danger the warning implied. Returning to the North, or rather the Midwest, he understood for the first time the implications of segregation: "Then when I got back north and all the theatres were segregated. I understood all that then. I understood I was really different." [38]

It's hard even now to understand what this means for a young African-American, growing up in a world where the routine humiliations of everyday discrimination demean but where in some situations those same racist impulses can place physical safety in jeopardy. There is a story from their time in high school, that both Russell and McPheeters told, that illustrates this very well. Russell remembered it as a Boy Scout trip to Indiana, while McPheeters recalled that they were at a YMCA camp in the state. Though there are other differences in their recollection, the substance of their accounts remained the same. Their teacher or scout leader was an African-American man named J. Harvey Kearns. As McPheeters told it,

> So we stopped in Liberty, Indiana, and they were having a street carnival there and, before we could get out of the car, a state trooper came up and said to Mr. Kearns, "What do you boys want?" Mr Kearns said, "We want to see the carnival." And the state trooper said, "Well they don't allow coloured people in this town after 6 o'clock." So, Mr Kearns said, "This is America and I'm going to see the carnival." I was scared to death and so was everybody else. So was George. Everybody was scared but J. Harvey Kearns. He was like a banty rooster. The crowd started following us and there was this thing with this sledgehammer; you were supposed to hit it and ring the bell. This guy sees us and he blocked our way. He was the concession owner. He said, "Want to try this thing, boy?" So he gives the hammer to Mr. Kearns and he hit it a couple of times and it didn't go up. Kearns was a little guy. Then one of the people in the crowd walked up and says, "Hey boy, let me show you how to do it." And he showed him and Mr. Kearns hit it again and rang the bell and the concession owner grabbed a cigar and shoved it in his mouth and he didn't smoke. *(laughs)* Then we went to get something to eat and all you could hear was, "Nigger. Nigger. Nigger." I tell you, I wanted to get out of that place. I didn't want to hang around. And so we went into this restaurant and the waitress wanted to know what we wanted and we said we'd like to have something to eat. So, she didn't know what to do and went over to talk to the manager and the manager took us and put us at a table right by the kitchen door. Boy, they were washing dishes and clanging pots and pans in the kitchen, so you couldn't hear yourself talk or think. But they served us. And the crowd gathered outside and I said to myself, "Oh God, I don't know if we're ever going to get out of here alive or not." But we went out the back door, got in the car and went on back to the retreat. But those were the days, and anybody who says, "Those were the good old days" is a damn liar. [39]

As Russell remembered it, they were told to get out of town for their own safety. "One man said, 'You better leave town.' I think it was a policeman. I think that was the home of the KKK. So we did. We left." [40] He told musician, broadcaster, and writer Ian Carr in 1992:

> I saw them humiliate this beautiful man, who was very much a gentleman and very much a soft-spoken, very sensitive individual. You know, "Hit it, boy!" But he picked up the hammer . . . one of those things you hit, a hammer and a bell, to see if you can get the iron ball up to hit the bell. And he nearly shot that bell up through the [top] when they called him "boy." And they called him other things you know that were not very nice, you know. [41]

On the one hand, one might wonder at the risks that Mr. Kearns took with his young charges. They hardly bear thinking about.

It is not clear whether this J. Harvey Kearns is the same man, who also worked for the civil rights organisation the National Urban League. It does seem, however, quite likely that it was the same individual. Certainly, the J. Harvey Kearns that McPheeters and

Russell remember was very active in African-American politics and community activities in Cincinnati. [42]

Any confusion around this issue lies in two different spellings used for the surname (both "Kearns" and "Kerns") and the fact that the NUL activist of that name moved around different parts of the U.S.A. during his life. Either way, it is clear that Kearns was determined to show Russell, McPheeters and their friends that this was their country and that in order to have any hope of sharing in its ownership, they would have to stand up to violence and bigotry. That long march to freedom has still many miles to go but no-one should underestimate how such quiet but determined acts of defiance as that shown by Kearns to these young people helped pave the road. The lesson he taught that day was certainly not lost upon Russell or Dwight McPheeters. As the latter told me six decades later,

> I've been determined for practically all my adult life that any unwritten law which was made for me or mine is going to be broken. I will not accept those kinds of things. [43]

Their mutual friend, William R. Davis, spent part of his career working as a specialist lecturer to underprivileged, bright-but-failing young people. Davis made a similar point and one that he sought continually to communicate to his students,

> There is opportunity, which I always vouchsafed to the students and children there when I was working in Cincinnati, being prepared as well as anybody else is prepared regardless of your race or religion or whatever and if the opportunity is there you can grab it. [44]

But despite the prejudice of many, there were also children and adults who felt able to cross America's Great Divide of race and colour. Russell remembered a small but, for him, puzzling and even touching incident at Hoffman.

> This eighth-grade student—his name was Bentley—passed a note to me and the note was from the girl who was considered one of the smartest girls in the class—Marion Laing—and she was very beautiful and the note said, "I've always loved you." She had given it to Bentley to give it to me. I just understood that because—I think she was German—I was on the football team. [45]

And how did the other football players react to him being black? "Oh, we didn't have any problems." [46]

Russell went from Hoffman to Withrow High, as did Dwight McPheeters. William R. Davis, on the other hand, went to Walnut Hills, a more prestigious establishment. McPheeters had also been intended for Walnut Hills, "I had missed going to Walnut Hills High School. They had a test for people to be eligible to go there but I had the measles when they were giving that test. I don't know if I would have passed it or not. The Walnut Hills kids came from all over town depending on if they passed the test." [47]

For Russell, and also for McPheeters, Withrow High held few happy memories. A homeroom photograph in the 1939 yearbook shows Russell crouching at one side, six feet from the rest of his contemporaries. It seemed to echo his feelings about the experience.

> I really didn't belong to that except for the grace of one good kid. I remember him still today. His sister was the story lady on the radio. She told stories for kids. Wendell Gabrick was his name. Wendell and I were real tight because he loved cooking and I loved cooking. This all happened at Withrow. It ended up with us being the two guys in the room with the rest being thirty women, with the average ignorant shit coming from people, "Oh you sissies!" I was used to being degraded. Wendell wasn't but he'd come home with me, by himself, and he'd go back by himself. In the black neighbourhoods at the time the blacks were scared to do anything to white people. In white neighbourhoods, it was much more scary for black people. [48]

The stupidity of the informal but overt discrimination and segregation that operated was something that did not escape all white children. As William R. Davis remembered: "I was in the Boy Scouts and we were doing some merit badge projects and I had three friends who were white and we would go hide in the woods near school to do these projects and nobody knew what was happening until they were all done and the inspectors would come to check them out." [49] This contrasts markedly with Dwight McPheeters's experience of trying to attend a Scout Jamboree at the Civic Centre in Cincinnati. "I heard about it and I was a Boy Scout, so I thought I'd put on my Scout uniform and go down. I went to the door and this white man said, 'What are you doing here?' I said, 'I'm a Boy Scout and I'm here for the Jamboree.' He said, 'This is for whites. Go have your own black Scout Jamboree.'" [50]

It was not that children could not be cruel or reflect the prejudices of their parents. As Russell told Ian Carr, "They were all under the same thing too. I mean they were given roles to play in life, you know, but without realizing they're just roles." [51] But for some white children, like Wendell Gabrick, the differences just didn't accord with their own experiences of the world. And not all adults were quite so ignorant either. Dwight McPheeters spoke about a teacher named Mr. Surdo, who ran the Withrow Special Chorus and Glee Club.

> Surdo was a little man who wore a toupee but he was a tyrant and he was as fair and square and straight as an arrow. I know I was invited along with everybody in the Special Chorus to Mr. Surdo's house for a party he was having. Well, I didn't go and I think that Leonard Williams was also invited and we didn't go. When I went back to school the following week, Mr. Surdo called me to his office and wanted to know why I didn't come to his party. I told him that I didn't think that I would be welcome. Well, he gave me what for and he told me that his house was open to all of his students and he says, "Your colour doesn't mean a thing to me. As far as I'm concerned, you're a part of the group of children that I teach and I don't teach colour one way or the other. I teach music. When I have a party, I want all the students that I teach to be there." [52]

Sadly, Surdo left shortly after and his replacement was, in McPheeters's words, "a latent bigot but it showed." [53] But both he and Russell recalled teachers and lessons that did offer some inspiration. For McPheeters it was English with Miss Atkins and for Russell it was government. "I only cared about a course called government. I got A in that and Ds in everything else."[54] Russell also sang in the Boys' Glee Club and the school's A Cappella Choir, though in a photograph of the former his name appears as "George Russel" and he does not seem to have been physically present. He did not take any other formal musical training at Withrow and his academic record was, to say the least, undistinguished. As he said, Ds and C-minuses predominate on his report cards, though physical geography also stands out as one of his better subjects. He told Ian Carr, "The school didn't like me and I didn't like it, you know."[55] Though the school was integrated, Russell remembered that out of several thousand pupils fewer than twenty were black. According to him, his lack of any more formal musical training, despite his involvement in the Boy Scouts drum and bugle band, was in part due to one of the teachers, "The music teacher there, Mr. Smithee, told me that I'd never be allowed in the band, you know, and that I didn't belong in music."[56]

And some white teachers made no effort to hide their racist attitudes, as Dr. Robert Moore recounted in an article he wrote on Russell for the *Trotter Institute Review*,

> Racism and racial discrimination played a most important part in Russell's life, as it did in the lives of most of his peers. Interviews conducted with some of his early associates—musical and others—revealed that racism cut quite deeply into all of their lives. Every interviewee had a collection of horror stories to tell. George recalls being pushed down the hall by the gym teacher at the Hoffman School who yelled at him, "You ain't nothing but a Nigger." He was discouraged from participating in the high school band.[57]

A sense grew in Russell that there was a gap between what he experienced and saw and felt and what he was being taught at school. Again talking with Carr in 1992, he noted, "At an early, very early age, I had a feeling that I wasn't hearing the whole story and I was hearing a coloured story. *(laughs)* Coloured in favour of the people who were the dominant race [who] were running the culture as they saw it. So there was already a cultural clash."[58]

Such feelings could only be reinforced in Russell by experience. "Dwight and I were in the Hoffman choir when the YMCA in Cincinnati invited the choir to come and swim except for me and Dwight. *(laughs)* Everybody in the class must've been fifty people. The Young Men's Christian Association! That woke me up to religion."[59]

If the issue about mixed-race swimming sounds laughable, then it should be noted that throughout the high schools in Cincinnati, African-American students always swam last period on Fridays. The pool was then cleaned. Both McPheeters and William R. Davis recalled this vividly, nearly seventy years on. McPheeters's voice shook with fury as he said,

> To show you what we were up against to some extent, and this is just to some extent, they allowed the black students to swim on the last period on Friday and after they swam they would drain the pool and . . . yeah, they would drain the pool.[60]

And Davis, who was on the Walnut Hills swimming team, laughed at the absurdity:

On occasion you find a great deal of integration—some things we did interracially that showed how ridiculous more or less the segregation idea was. I had a very good friend by the name of Reginald Brown. Reginald Brown and I were swimmers and track men. I played football, ran on the track team, played basketball and swam. Reggie and I were swimming in a competition with our homeroom, which was all-white. The African-American students' regular swimming periods at that time were the last period on Friday. Over the weekend they cleaned the swimming pool. We used to laugh at that and some of the white boys laughed too because we were swimming together every afternoon after school and yet we couldn't swim in class with them during the week. It was stupid but there were grown people that controlled the thing—we didn't. [61]

Home life and community offered one set of experiences growing up. School and the white world was a whole other universe of often—or even mainly— negative events. For some— Russell, McPheeters and Davis—it presented a set of challenges to overcome. For others, perhaps these challenges were just too overwhelming.

Russell was sixteen when his father, Joseph, died. It was Russell himself who found him on September 12, 1939.

He was done in. I don't know if you've ever experienced negativity, serious negativity. It pulls you down, you know. So, one morning, for some reason, I got up early and I walked in his room. And he was sitting like this *(demonstrates posture: one knee raised pulled against his chest with both arms around it)* looking right in my eyes, but dead. I looked at him for a long time, you know. I said, "Mom"—they slept in different rooms—"Mom, I think that Dad is dead." He was holding his frickin' leg . . . because he was in terrible pain. He had arthritis, rheumatism, all of it together and he wasn't hollering or crying. He didn't do that. I think that was due to his being a Mason. And my mother screamed. So that made me the man. Mom took up [child] nursing. People wanted to take a vacation, she'd take care of their children. She did that most of her life, the rest of her life. [62]

As to what Russell gained or learned from Joseph, he identified an important kind of knowledge—"He gave me an idea of what I cannot be, and he was a real father." [63] But Joseph also loved music, and when in his teens Russell was playing drums with a neighbourhood orchestra, he would come and listen to them practice, very much the proud father. And there was something in both the quiet dignity and the caution Russell describes about Joseph that he has also perhaps developed. When a "cracker" sheriff Down South tells you to take off your Masonic Pin, it's foolhardy to argue. Dignity and self-respect, after all, lie within.

By the time of Joseph's death, things at Withrow were deteriorating. As he explained to Ian Carr, "You know that feeling of the way the dominant class was thinking, that there was something suspect in it was born early on . . . And it made a rebel out of me. A quiet one, but a rebel." [64] And he qualified this very slightly, adding, "If you wanted me to act a certain way and it's life-threatening, I'll act that way, you know. If you want me to say 'Yessa boss,' I'll say 'Yessa boss'—if it's life-threatening, you know. But I'll get you somewhere up the line."⁶⁵ His rebellion at Withrow High took the form of an increasing extracurricular involvement in playing jazz and absenting himself from school, both physically and psychologically.

> The music... I talk about that in something I'm writing about the past and how it grew. For the instant I heard jazz music, I said, "I have to have a part in that," and that was actually in high school—Withrow High School in Cincinnati... I attended school but I wasn't really there with the type of material the school was talking about... and I, in a sense, rejected the academic knowledge and went for instinctive knowledge from the very beginning. My aim was to somehow live a spiritual life. That was a big help that saved me.⁶⁶

His rejection of the school's white cultural values also involved a sartorial assault on the school's informal dress code. As he recalled, "I was rebellious to begin with and I probably set off the fashion period down there because I wore high-draped pants and shoes that were oh so mellow."⁶⁷ And as he told Carr, "I began to have troubles when the principal would call me in his office quite regularly and ask me why I was wearing those high chequered pants and purple pants with red checks in them and why am I wearing that goatee to school?"⁶⁸

The school's initial response was to refer him to a psychologist for the usual panoply of assessments and Rorschach tests but "psychologizing" the "problem" he presented clearly didn't work. Russell remembered, "And them sending me to a psychiatrist for a Rorschach test, which I managed to make as ugly as possible. I mean you just play that game, all of that crap."⁶⁹ Or, as he told Vivian Perlis in 1993, "[T]hey managed at school to send me for one Rorschach test too many. Even then I thought it was idiotic, and I still think they're absolutely idiotic. [Because] I would say anything weird just to shock the person administering the test."⁷⁰

For Russell, from his early encounters of racism at Hoffman Elementary to his even more humiliating experiences at Withrow High, his sense of alienation from and antagonism toward education grew. He described it to Perlis as "a creative conflict with the establishment." Up to that point, he had not really identified with any ethnic group, feeling that he had been "well-protected, insulated from all of that." Increasingly he saw himself as "anti-establishment" and his admiration for others he saw as being against the system increased, whether they were musicians, artists, or gangsters. He was determined not to fit the mould that he felt education was shaping for him.

> I knew—I knew that I felt inside a revolution; that I wanted to revolt. I felt a strong feeling of revolting. And that's really what I did. *(laughs)* I wanted to rebel, the result of those experiences has made me a rebel. In some way I wanted to rebel against this kind of stupid ethnocentricity, which I didn't know anything about that word at the time. I just knew the feeling of being called a "Nigger" or being the butt of stupid jokes and remarks and the feeling that if you were white you had a natural right to a mind and, well, most of those minds hadn't had an original thought, ever. They never had the imagination to be a rebel at all. They were cogs in the wheel.⁷¹

But Russell's rebellion largely seems to have reflected the qualities of resilience, caution, self-reliance and respect for self that he learnt from his father, Joseph, rather than suggest something more confrontational and aggressive. He certainly could be abrasive and antagonistic should the need arise but there was also a subtlety and subversive character to Russell's response to the iniquities he had to confront in his life.

It is worth taking a moment to think in more depth about the processes Russell, Dwight McPheeters and William R. Davis describe. The social psychologists Peter Berger and Thomas Luckmann suggest that where "acutely discrepant worlds are mediated in primary socialisation, the individual is presented with a choice of profiled identities apprehended by him as genuine biographical possibilities." They continue, "[T]here may be a socially concealed asymmetry between 'public' and 'private' biography."

Russell, like his peers McPheeters and Davis, developed a strong sense of himself from his life at home with Joseph and Bessie and within the rich community life of Walnut Hills. This is broadly what Berger and Luckmann mean by primary socialization. As they note, "The original reality of childhood is 'home' and all later realities are 'artificial' in comparison." Secondary socialization refers to those forces such as education that ideally build upon "successful" primary socialization and mirror it to a greater or lesser extent. By contrast in racist societies, such as 1930s USA, the social "knowledge" imparted by the education system clearly devalued and denigrated individuals such as Russell, McPheeters and Davis, in severe contrast to the positive experiences of home and community. What Berger and Luckmann describe above as a failure of effective socialization must, in the context of Russell's experience, be an "effective" adaptation. [72]

Adaptation and socialization in the context of inequality and racism are hugely complicated matters. In George Russell's situation, he told me that he was brought up knowing as many white people as black, and by a mother he describes as "seventy percent German." With considerable skill, he became adept at negotiating difficult situations where race and colour were potential sources of conflict. For example, he developed a strategy for dealing with police officers who would stop him at night with the demand, "What are you, boy?" He would say, "I'm Greek-Italian," and with his "swarthy" complexion duly registered and noted, they would let him pass. Writing about the impact of attributions upon an individual where there is a severe disjunction between how one is perceived and how one sees oneself, psychiatrist R. D. Laing noted,

> It is an achievement to realize one is not necessarily who others take one to be. Such awareness of discrepancy between self-identity, being-for-oneself, and being-for-others, is painful. There is a strong tendency to feel guilt, anxiety, anger or doubt if self-attributions are disjunctive with attributions made about self by others, particularly when attributions are taken as injunctions. [73]

Interestingly, Berger and Luckmann also look at the additional "socialization" needed by priests, revolutionaries, and musicians (!). [74] Extending the point they are making but slightly, it is a reasonable supposition that from the age when Russell began playing jazz professionally, the most positive and "effective" secondary socialization he experienced was through the community of musicians in which he moved. This perhaps provided a psychological, emotional, and social counter to the negative experiences of mainstream education. Music made sense in a world that did not.

And by the time he was fourteen, Russell was playing drums regularly in a nightclub with a pianist backing a singer, and the clothes—purple high-waisters, zoot suits, set off with a goatee and moustache—he wore for school reflected the demimonde he inhabited. The periodic summonses to the principal's office continued and Russell remembered that he was on the verge of expulsion. It was possibly on the last such occasion that something peculiar happened. The principal, Mr. Peoples, told him,

> that he had gotten a call from my father asking how I was doing in school and how he hates to have to tell him that, you know, I'm on the verge of being expelled. Well, that was rather strange. That was a strange day in my life because my father had been dead a year, you know.[75]

Or, as he later recalled,

> The last dealing I had with Withrow was the president [principal] Mr. Peoples saying, "Your father called." My father probably did call. I guess he's from West Virginia but he wasn't the father I knew. I never saw him in my life and Mr. Peoples telling me that they were letting me go from school because they didn't like the way I dressed—long drape pants. It was too "out" for them.[76]

It is unclear whether the principal's comment was simply malicious and made out of ignorance or whether Russell's biological father was actually following his progress "from afar." Either way, it was this that led to his discovery that he was adopted.

Russell admitted he had suspicions that Bessie and Joseph were not his birth parents. A "cousin" had let something slip when he was twelve. "Actually, my mother protected me from finding out and we had a little suggestion when I was twelve in the Boy Scouts drum and bugle corps in Cincinnati. That probably came from my cousin, Juanita, who was, I believe, adopted by another family, but we used to play as cousins but weren't really cousins."[77] And, "I suspected but the truth came out when . . . she said, 'I'm not your real mother.' I said, 'You are because you have been.' And she remains my mother, with no hard feelings against what I call 'the kids.'"[78]

Following the confrontation with the Withrow principal, Bessie told him the story of his origins, namely that he was the "love child" of a white music professor at Oberlin College and a light-skinned African-American student from a wealthy background in Kentucky. Some children might have reacted badly to such news. Bessie and Joseph had, after all, kept the truth from him for sixteen years. Some children might have felt that their biological mother—and father—had abandoned or disowned them. But any anger he felt seems only to have been directed immediately toward the school principal but primarily to a system that would not allow his biological parents to be together. He spoke of "the kids,"

That was a pretty huge shock for me because that really even before my mother said "I'm not your real mother"—although in my experience she's the only . . . she was totally a real mother—but the "kids" she was standing in for didn't have a chance because she did come from an upper-income family [who] made sure that her decisions were as close to white as could be at the time. [79]

Even late in life, Russell still seemed genuinely touched that his biological father might have contacted his school to express an interest in his progress. "So, my father, a white music professor, had that much of an interest, but the times were really rough. The rules were absurd. *(laughs)*" [80]

In the dining area of the Russells' home in Boston, there was a photograph of a group of African-American students. In the front row, a light-skinned black woman is sitting on the ground. "It's funny that picture has about three tiers to sit on and my mother was in the front row and if I show it to people they usually pick her out pretty easily." [81] The resemblance is striking.

On the front of the photograph is written "Class 1920 B.C.I." During research for this book, two names were found on the back of the photograph— Lettie E. George (written underneath "Class Philo . . . 1920") and Kathaleen (sic) George. The latter were only revealed when Russell's wife, Alice, removed the photograph for copying in connection with this biography.

From this information, it proved possible to trace "BCI" and identify the school as Bluefield Colored Institute, Bluefield WV, a school for African-American children in West Virginia. The 1920 U.S. Census shows that Nannie K. (Kathleen) George was the daughter of James H. and Lettie W. George, and that Lettie E. was their niece, who lived with them in Northfork, West Virginia. J. H. George was, of course, the witness to the consent to adopt. Further research, with assistance from archivists at Oberlin College, confirmed that Nannie Kathleen George attended Oberlin in 1922–23 but left during her first year. She was a student of music and the annual catalogue of Oberlin students 1922-23 gives her address as 181 Pleasant Street, Northfork WV. The fact that J. H. George witnessed the consent seems to confirm that Nannie Kathleen was in fact George Russell's mother.

With regard to the belief that Russell's father was a 'white music professor' at Oberlin, there is no evidence to confirm this. However, what Russell made of this story is intriguing. In a way, the story of his origins, far from leaving him feeling abandoned or betrayed, gave him a sense of identity and security in a world that was becoming increasingly insecure. In a positive sense, it was as if his origins as a "love-child" of a white man and a black woman allowed him to inhabit both the white and black worlds. The lack of bitterness he seemed to feel was quite remarkable, even in respect to the insensitive and indiscreet way in which the school principal dealt with him and which led to his discovering that he was adopted. It is as if the stability and love that Bessie and Joseph gave him allowed him to have a relationship in phantasy with his biological parents, "the kids," as he termed them.

Russell recounted this account of his origins on many occasions to various writers and interviewers and in their accounts the 'white music professor' father looms large. [82] The assumption seems to be that Russell might, therefore, have inherited his musical gifts from this source. One of the earliest pieces to emphasize the latter was a 1960 biographical article for Broadcast Music Inc. by Nat Hentoff.[83]

Somewhat forgotten in the process is the 'black' mother, Nannie Kathleen George, a woman talented enough in her own right to gain a place in an era of formal and informal segregation to a prestigious conservatoire. Russell was clearly, in part at least, responsible for the creation of this myth but its uncritical repetition by so many writers can be reasonably criticised for both colour- and gender-blindness. As I have argued earlier at greater length, this story presented in this way parallels, and conveniently so, the conventional narrative of the origins of jazz, as a marriage of African and European elements.

That aside, the way in which Russell dealt with this knowledge is characteristic of a pattern in his life where he would transcend potentially negative occurrences, turning them into positive learning experiences with these being seen (if only in hindsight) pivotal life-changing events. It was true of his childhood car accident, of the way he handled Bessie and Joseph's emotional coldness toward each other, of how he learned to manage the differences between street and home and between the white world and the black. It is evidence of an attitude to life—involving simultaneously a kind of spiritual certainty and also an intellectual and emotionally intelligent questioning—that seems to have sustained him.

## Notes

1. Interview with Norbury-Russell, November 2004.
2. The apartments' residents listed in the Cincinnati City Directory for 1923 were Stanley Cohen, Wendell E. Mitchell, Edward Turner, Sally Dowlin, John W. Hodges, Ernest Montgomery, Clifford W. Reid, Hosie Hand, Matty Gibbs, James Jones, and G. W. Byrd.
3. Dr. Elizabeth Campbell, a pioneer in the area of sexual hygiene and birth control in Cincinnati, also had her residence on Reading Road, where Dr. Miller's office was located. See Marguerite Wykoff Zapoleon, "Cincinnati Citizens: Elizabeth Campbell (1862–1945) and M. Edith Campbell (1875–1962)," *Queen City Heritage* 43, no. 4 (Winter 1985): 4–20.
4. See Wendell P. Dabney, *Cincinnati's Colored Citizens* (Cincinnati, OH: Dabney Publishing, 1926).
5. Geoffrey J. Giglierano and Deborah A. Overmyer, with Frederic L. Propas, *The Bicentennial Guide to Greater Cincinnati: A Portrait of Two Hundred Years* (Cincinnati, OH: Cincinnati Historical Society, 1988).
6. Interview with Dwight McPheeters, June 2004.
7. Interview with William R. Davis, August 2004.
8. Interestingly, Dabney does not include Bessie Russell in his list of "colored" health professionals. He does, however, note Joseph Russell and his profession. See Dabney, *Cincinnati's Coloured Citizens*.
9. Interview with George Russell, June 2004.
10. Ibid.
11. Ibid.
12. Ibid.
13. Ibid.
14. Interview with McPheeters.
15. Interview with W. Davis.

16. Interview with G. Russell, June 2004.
17. Vivian Perlis, interview with George Russell, American Music Series, December 8, 1993, Oral History Project of American Music, sponsored and supported by the National Endowment for the Arts Special Jazz Projects.
18. Interview with G. Russell, June 2004.
19. Ibid.
20. Ibid.
21. Ibid.
22. Interview with Robert Moore, July 2004. Moore refers here to George Kelly, who played somewhat unsuccessfully for the Cincinnati Reds from 1927-1930.
23. Interview with G. Russell, June 2004.
24. Ibid.
25. G. John and D. Humphrey, *Because They're Black* (Harmondsworth, UK: Penguin, 1971).
26. Interview with G. Russell, June 2004.
27. Interview with W. Davis.
28. C. Vann Woodward, *The Strange Career of Jim Crow* (New York: Oxford University Press, 1966), p. 19.
29. Quoted in ibid., p. 20.
30. Interview with McPheeters.
31. Interview with W. Davis.
32. Perlis, interview with G. Russell.
33. Interview with G. Russell, June 2004.
34. Ibid.
35. Interview with McPheeters.
36. Interview with G. Russell, June 2004.
37. Ibid.
38. Ibid.
39. Interview with McPheeters.
40. Interview with G. Russell, June 2004.
41. Ian Carr, interview with George Russell, June 1992.
42. Cincinnati Public Library has a photograph on its "West End Stories Project" site of Kearns giving an award to a group of young African-American women. The picture of Kearns fits Dwight McPheeters' description of him as a "banty rooster" to a tee. (https://blog.cincinnatilibrary.org/Blog/wesp); see also *Cincinnati Enquirer*, October 12, 1938, p.11 "Lecture Series Planned;" *The Jewish Post* July 28, 1939 p.2 "Cincinnati Plans Series of Anti-Coughlin Radio Programmes." The latter is of considerable interest. Father Charles Coughlin was Catholic priest who used his radio show in support of his near-fascist and anti-Semitic political views. It is clear that J. Harvey Kearns was one of those cited by *The Jewish Post* as being involved in these anti-Coughlin broadcasts.
43. Interview with McPheeters.
44. Interview with W. Davis.
45. Interview with G. Russell, June 2004.
46. Ibid.
47. Interview with McPheeters.
48. Interview with G. Russell, June 2004.
49. Interview with W. Davis.
50. Interview with McPheeters.
51. Carr, interview with G. Russell, June 1992.
52. Interview with McPheeters.
53. Ibid.
54. Carr, interview with G. Russell, June 1992.
55. Ibid.

56. Ibid.
57. Robert E. Moore, "George Alan Russell: Jazz's First Theorist," *Trotter Institute Review* 2 (Summer 1988): 15–19.
58. Carr, interview with G. Russell, June 1992.
59. Interview with G. Russell, June 2004.
60. Interview with McPheeters.
61. Interview with W. Davis.
62. Interview with G. Russell, June 2004.
63. Ibid.
64. Carr, interview with G. Russell, June 1992.
65. Ibid.
66. Interview with George Russell, June 2003.
67. Ibid.
68. Carr, interview with G. Russell, June 1992.
69. Ibid.
70. Perlis, interview with G. Russell.
71. Ibid.
72. P. Berger and T. Luckmann, *The Social Construction of Reality* (Harmondsworth, UK: Penguin, 1981), particularly pp. 149–88; also K. B. Clark and M. P. Clark, "Racial Identification and Preferences in Negro Children," in *Readings in Social Psychology*, edited by E. E. Maccoby, T. M. Newcomb, and E. L. Hartley (New York: Holt, Rinehart & Winston, 1958); W. Oliver, "Black Males and Social Problems: Prevention through Afro-Centric Socialization," *Journal of Black Studies* 20, no. 1 (1989): 1–19.
73. R. D. Laing, *Self and Others* (Harmondsworth, UK: Penguin, 1975): 152.
74. Berger and Luckmann, *The Social Construction of Reality*, 164–65.
75. Carr, interview with G. Russell, June 1992.
76. Interview with G. Russell, June 2004. N.B. Interviewed by Bob Daughtry for the Smithsonian Jazz Oral History Program NEA in May 2004, Russell made additional remarks regarding the conversation with Withrow High's Principal. In the interview, he makes reference to the Principal telling him that his biological father was teaching music at a school in a city, the name of which Russell could no longer recall, "near Cincinnati, on the high river?" This interview was not on line when I was writing the first edition of this biography. There is little chance now of identifying whether there is any evidence to support Russell's beliefs regarding his natural father.
77. Interview with G. Russell, June 2003.
78. Ibid.
79. Ibid.
80. Ibid. N.B. See note 16. Introduction, p. xxiv
81. Interview with G. Russell, June 2003.
82. See, for example, Max Harrison, "George Russell—Rational Anthems (Phase 1)," *Wire* (Spring 1983): 30–31; Robert DiNardo, "Jazz Prophet," *Boston Globe Sunday Magazine*, June 12, 1983; Ian Carr, program Notes for a Contemporary Music Network tour (1992); Ian Carr, *The Invisible Guru*, BBC Radio Three broadcast, July 1, 1994; Bob Claypool, "Blazing the Fusion Trail: Russell on the road conducting startling brand of jazz," *Houston Post*, October 8, 1983; Howard Mandel, "The Mathematical Musician," *Washington Post*, September 27, 1987; John Fordham, "Send Off the Clones," *Guardian* (Manchester), March 5, 1998, and "King George's Gold Blend," *Guardian* (Manchester), September 1, 1989. I repeated the same story, myself, in an article I wrote in 1998. See Duncan Heining, "A Meeting with a Remarkable Man," *Avant* 7 (Summer 1998).
83. Nat Hentoff, "George Russell," *Broadcast Music Inc.* (1960).

CHAPTER TWO

# On Class and Culture

This world of daily humiliations that was life in the Midwest for African-Americans had economic, political, social, cultural and psychological implications. It would leave emotional scars even on those who eventually transcended its imposed limitations but many others less talented, resilient or resourceful would remain trapped in its grip. Some, though by no means all, would to some degree internalize the image of themselves that the dominant white culture imposed upon them. As George Russell put it to me,

> [It] made me feel inferior and it made actually the race feel inferior because we used to berate each other. "Oh, nigger you can't do that." You know. It was stupid; we were beginning to accept the fact that we were stupid when we weren't. But I guess we grew more stupid by believing that there was no way out.[1]

Here, Russell was describing a psychological process that functions at both individual and broader socio-cultural levels. The capacity to impose such definitions on others—sometimes in the face of opposition—requires the power and authority, as well as the mechanisms, to do so. School, the education system, control of the means of mass communication and, ultimately and more directly, the offices of enforcement and repression—all these were in the hands of white people and in particular those with wealth and political influence. But Russell's point goes a step further in its insights. The fostering among African-Americans of a self-image of inferiority was then reinforced within their communities themselves. Sadly, this is a story that is all too common and is documented and examined extensively in the academic literature of sociology and psychology.[2]

Such images of African-Americans held by white people—and, as Russell suggests, by some black people as well—were in sharp contrast to the richness of cultural activity in the Walnut Hills area where George Russell, Dwight McPheeters and William R. Davis lived. In his interview with Vivian Perlis, Russell looked back with some fondness to a childhood that in cultural terms was far from underprivileged. "Anyway, as much and as boring as Cincinnati could be, and I look back on it now, and as much as one would think I was born into an underprivileged situation, I was born into an overprivileged situation. I had culture booming out of every nook and cranny of that town and in my neighbourhood."[3]

First of all, there were those activities centred around the church. In Russell's and Davis's case, that was the African Methodist Episcopal Mount Zion Church. As William R. Davis remembered,

> At the time that we were in the church, George sang in the boys' choir. We had a wonderful choirmaster there who organized this boys' choir. We had forty-seven boys in that choir. At that time I was seven years old, so George was about six. We stayed in that boys' choir until our voices began to change during our mid-teenage years. At that time we were probably going to high school, so we sang in the chancel choir with the adults after that point. But George was a good singer.[4]

Mount Zion had at that time a very forward-thinking minister in Rev. Gilbert and the church was a focus for the community in a number of ways. For one thing, it had indoor recreational facilities, as Davis recalled. "One of the things that happened at the church was that we had a full-size gymnasium in the basement. That church and one of the schools, Douglas School, were the only places you could go for indoor recreation in Walnut Hills, that particular section of the city."[5]

Sports were as—or more—important than music within the African-American community in Walnut Hills. Russell had been on the football team at Hoffman and William R. Davis was a football player, swimmer and track star. And within the area, there were those whose sporting success motivated the young men in the community. Davis's vivid memory again noted,

> There were various playgrounds throughout the city. We had one young man who was the 1924 broad jump champion in the Olympics who lived right behind us and he would come down to the little playground in our neighbourhood and show us things about running and jumping. He was one of some very good track people in that neighbourhood. His name was DeHart Hubbard. His record stood from 1924 until Jesse Owens won the broad jump in 1936. That's how long his record for the broad jump—the long jump as they call it now—lasted. But we had people like that in the neighbourhood. We had some football and baseball players who were inspirational to us as well.[6]

Russell remembered Mount Zion well and told me that his mother insisted that he attend services. But he was more drawn to another church, probably Pentecostal, two blocks away.

I used to sneak down there without my mother knowing. It was near a big hole, a deep hole, like a working pit. And the people lived down there - it was a pretty rough place. They used to have these Holy Roller services. It was shocking sometimes. They went into trances and things. I used to lie on my stomach and look in the windows. But the rhythm was incredible, man, and that's what influenced me. [7]

And as he told Ian Carr:

In the traditional Baptist churches, they had very good gospel music. And the sanctified music I heard because there were churches in what was called "the hollow," which was kind of a ravine that was close to our house and down in this hollow there was a sanctified church. And there'd be storefront churches. When I did venture downtown in what they called the "Black Bottom" there would be these storefront churches and this enormous rhythmic thing would be coming out. [8]

At some point Russell's mother also turned toward a more fundamental "Holy Roller" Christianity and became a follower of Bishop Mary Mack.

What I remember about Bishop was her weight—she weighed nearly four hundred pounds. She was big and fiercely black. She owned a Rolls-Royce, with accommodations in the back for a throne. She owned two mansions very close to us. She had a chauffeur. My mother and Bishop became very good friends. My mother was consulting with Bishop when she was going through troubled times. And I do remember Bishop and I became good friends with Bishop's grandkid. His name was Sam. So, they were going to the World's Fair in 1933 and I was ten. And so, they took me along—it was a big thing for me in the Rolls-Royce with the chauffeur, Marvin.

He continued,

In the meantime, she owned churches all over the United States—I'm not kidding—and in Hawaii. She was touring her churches at the same time we visited the World's Fair. I had to go to services with her in her own church; she had her own network of churches. What happened in those churches was that she healed people; the music was incredible. It was the music that affected me. [9]

Asked to describe the music by Vivien Perlis, Russell said it was "more primitive than gospel," though clearly gospel-based with "fierce rhythms," and members of the congregation "would get the tongue and faint and have water thrown on them." [10] Robert Moore's research confirmed that the family attended "Mount Zion African Methodist Evangelical Church," as did "a number of Cincinnati's Black Elite." He also noted that Bessie and George Russell also travelled and attended revival meetings with Mack, though Moore noted that it was Mary Mack's son, rather than her grandson, whom Russell befriended. [11] Again, the attraction for Russell lay more in the music than in the religious experience itself. He hinted, in fact, in his interview with Perlis that by the time he was sixteen he had had experiences with Mack's church that discouraged him from "becoming a devout believer as I was on my way to being." Unfortunately, Perlis did not pursue this line of inquiry in the interview.

And there were plenty of opportunities to hear and make music in Walnut Hills. Dwight McPheeters and his sister both took music lessons.

> George was more interested in music. I was interested in music too. My sister and I were both given music lessons. I was too stubborn, stupid, or whatever to take it because I had an ear for music because when I was given piano lessons my piano teacher would play a piece over [and] I could play it right behind him. But when it came to reading the notes, that was out. I didn't want to practice. After piano lessons I was given violin lessons and I did not practice and did something or other to the bow and the bow went to pieces and my father said, "That's the last music lesson you're gonna get out of this house." But I always had a good voice. I had a baritone voice and I sang in the choruses at Withrow High School and so did George.[12]

Russell had also had music lessons with a Professor Ryder, a very strict teacher, when he was about seven or eight. It had not been a happy experience for the young and sensitive boy. He described Ryder as a "knuckle-cracker" who responded to wrong notes with a sharp crack on the back of a child's hands with a ruler. That was pretty much it for Russell as far as any formal musical education was concerned, at that time at least.[13]

But jazz was all around Cincinnati and Walnut Hills. Cincinnati was, after all, at a crossroads in the Midwest. Musicians would pass through and head on to St. Louis or Kansas City, north to Chicago, and on to New York. Or maybe west to Los Angeles and San Francisco or southeast to New Orleans. And there were the riverboats that headed up and down the Ohio river en route to the Mississippi and the Missouri. Many of those passenger steamers featured bands. Bessie Russell loved music and took her son on trips on the boats and it was on one of those trips that he first heard jazz.

Years later he recollected that it was Fate Marable's band he had seen and that it was the drummer that most held his attention.[14] Many articles have noted Marable's significance in Russell's very early musical development.[15] While this makes for a charming tale, any influence was probably far less important than the cumulative effect of seeing the various riverboat orchestras. There were others Russell recalled with just as much clarity. When he spoke with Carr of these riverboat trips, it was Noble Sissle who stuck out in his memory and it was again his drummer who made the greatest impression—and not only for his musical skills.

> Cincinnati was very music conscious and my mother used to take me on these riverboats that used to pass. It usually'd start in New Orleans and go up the Mississippi to St. Louis, then on to the Ohio, up to Cincinnati and Cairo and then Pittsburgh, you know. Bringing culture all the way. I know I heard the Noble Sissle band because—I forgot his name—but the drummer and my cousin had an affair . . . but he was a dandy. I was impressed by all this, you know. These guys were very glamorous to me. And they dressed beautifully and

they looked beautiful and they got all the women. So I thought, this [is] it—you know, this is the life for me. [16]

Russell also talked to Perlis about the impact of hearing and seeing these riverboat jazz bands. Again, it was Sissle he remembered and the rhythm of the drums.

> **GR:** They were the boat bands. So, you know, that's a real part of Americana. They were transplanting this music wherever they went, and of course by 1923 jazz had really established itself as an art form in America, although it wasn't taken seriously, you know. Here it was taken seriously, in Europe . . . and I was always impressed with the drummers. Drums became my first instrument . . .
> **VP:** Was it a lot of early Dixieland jazz and ragtime also, or ?
> **GR:** It was pretty organized big-band jazz. It really wasn't [Dixieland] - the musicians were reading arrangements. So these were schooled musicians; I know one of the bands was Noble Sissle. Noble Sissle was a legend. [17]

Of at least as much importance was a man by the name of Zack Whyte. Whyte had an orchestra with the wonderful name the Chocolate Beau Brummels. William R. Davis recalls that Whyte was a near neighbour of the Russells.

> Further down on that porch was a gentleman by the name of Zack Whyte who had his own orchestra, the Chocolate Beau Brummels. They all lived right there in close proximity, not more than twenty or thirty yards apart. Those kind[s] of things could have been an influence on him because those people were right there. [18]

Or, as Russell himself recalled, "[In] my neighbourhood [was] Zack Whyte, one of the first people to have a band on a riverboat that went from Cincinnati up the Ohio to St. Louis and then down to New Orleans. It was bands like that that really began to get to me. They were really attractive and the music was attractive." [19]

Though, the riverboat orchestras played New Orleans-inspired jazz, as Russell remembered it, it had clearly by then developed into a sophisticated big-band form of the music. [20] Swing had not yet arrived, or at least had not crossed that far into the mainstream. Cincinnati jazz historian Bill Lawless Jones echoes this point in his sleeve notes for two CDs featuring Cincinnati jazz of the modern era:

> [T]he 20's saw the expansion of the normally small jazz band of 5 to 7 pieces, which played "Dixieland Style," into the big band of 10 to 12 instruments with arranged scores. Fletcher Henderson of NYC's Roseland Ballroom is generally credited with having organized the first big band. Well, perhaps Mr. Henderson was a year ahead of anyone else, or maybe he got the publicity virtue of being in America's largest city. Anyway, right here in Cincinnati in 1927, a man by the name of Zack Whyte organized a big band. [21]

One of Whyte's musicians was Melvin James "Sy" Oliver, who proved influential both as a trumpeter and as an arranger, first for Whyte and later for Jimmie Lunceford and

Tommy Dorsey. Lawless Jones adds that, while with Whyte, Oliver "composed such tunes as 'Stomp It Off' and 'Dream of You' and arranged traditional melodies like 'Swanee River' and 'Dear Old Southland.'" [22] This was music, it seems, that was already in a process of transformation as it continued its spread across the U.S.A. Many of the musicians were readers, as James Lincoln Collier notes about Fate Marable. When Marable took the then young "unschooled" Louis Armstrong into his band, it was essentially an exception in his usual hiring policy. [23] This was the kind of music that fired Russell's imagination. It was full of glamour and excitement and it moved with the rhythms of the popular dances of the time.

It is not surprising that it was the drums Russell was attracted to and his first opportunity to develop that interest in rhythm came through playing in the Boy Scouts marching band.

> And, of course, the other drummers—some of them were quite good—and they, even if they played the orthodox march music, they played it in a way that was . . . had something else in it, had this rhythm, you know. And it was this rhythm that really stuck with me. This Americanized African rhythm will always intrigue me and that being the most obvious kind of musical impression that weighed on me heavily, I turned to playing drums and started off with just sort of youth bands. [24]

He acquired his first drum set through Dwight McPheeters, who had got them from his godparents.

> I said, "Yes, I'd like to have them." My mother was not really favourable to that. It was a set of trap drums. They weren't regular band drums. Anyhow the noise that I made around the house drove my mother up the wall and so she decided on her own, and since I was not taking any lessons regarding the drums, that she would get rid of them. So, she called Mrs. Russell—she called her "Sweets," that was her nickname—and she asked if George wanted the drums and Mrs. Russell said, "Yes, George would like to have the drums." So, she gave my mother five dollars for the drums and those were the first set of drums that George ever had. I like to think that I was responsible *(laughs)* for everything that followed. [25]

William R. Davis also remembered the drum set, "I remember when she bought George that drum set and I don't remember who influenced her to buy him a drum set, maybe it was because he was in the Boy Scouts and they had a drum and bugle corps. George and my brother and others were playing these snare drums and blowing bugles for parades and things like that." [26]

One of the most important local musicians living in Walnut Hills was tenor saxophonist Jimmy Mundy. Mundy played with Paul Whiteman, Earl Hines and Benny Goodman, though his greatest claim to fame was that he wrote "Travelin" Light" for Billie Holiday. He lived a couple of doors down from Russell's family and his return from a tour was always a source of excitement in the neighbourhood.

> Jimmy had written for all the bands. We were going so fast, that I forgot to mention that

Jimmy was a great inspiration. I told you how he'd come home in his big car, park it out in front of his door—and these are just little houses built for . . . I forget what they call them, but they've got a name for them—but for people with just modest incomes. As soon as Mrs. Critten and his mother saw him, she'd throw a fit—"Jimmy's here." Then he'd go up and put on his bedroom shoes and his fancy nightwear and drive his car to Kerper Avenue to the main street and go to one of the bars and have a drink and everybody would know that Jimmy's in town. [27]

It was Mundy who first suggested that Russell might pursue a career in music. "I didn't know how great Jimmy was but Jimmy was a great, great guy and he wanted me to go to a Battle of Music with Benny Goodman. My mother wouldn't let me go because I was sixteen years old, so I didn't hear that, but Jimmy said, 'I'll go over and talk to your mother.' He told her, 'Look George belongs in music.'" [28]

William R. Davis also remembered Mundy very well. "But right next to George on that same row of apartments in that building, there was another family and the man in the family was the son of a lady about Mrs. Russell's age who became the arranger for Benny Goodman, and that was Jimmy Mundy and he may have been one of the influences that inspired George to go into music." [29]

The great African-American jazz pianist Art Tatum had a cousin with the wonderful name of Spaulding Givens (later known by his Muslim name, Nadi Qamar), who lived nearby, and Tatum would play locally when he was in town, as did Fats Waller. Once again, from William R. Davis's impeccable memory, "There were other entertainers that came by there in the neighbourhood. We all used to go round and listen to them. Fats Waller used to come there and play at a speakeasy that was not far from there, right down the hill from where George would live." [30]

Nelson Burton, a drummer and stalwart of the Cincinnati scene, tells in his memoirs how Waller lived and worked in Cincinnati during the Great Depression. [31] As well as his own show on "The Nation's Station," Cincinnati-based Radio WLW, Waller played organ on the schmaltzy *Moon River* show. It was a performance on the latter that got Waller fired from the station. Supposed to play suitably nocturnal accompaniment for host Peter Grant's poetry recitation, an inebriated Waller swung the hell out of his Wurlitzer. The next day after Waller had gone, the cleaners found a pile of gin bottles in the back of the instrument.

Russell's mother actually got him on a bill with Waller at the YMCA, singing "Moon Over Miami" accompanied by "some lame piano player," as he told Carr. "I must've been nine years old and I was always a very naive person, but I wasn't naive enough to know that this was a very corny thing for me to be doing, to be singing 'Moon Over Miami,' you know." [32] One writer, Francis Davis, recounts this tale with wonderful embellishment and has Fats Waller, "a friend of the family," accompanying Russell, but sadly, as so often is the case, the truth was more mundane. [33]

William R. Davis also spoke about Peg Leg Bates, the dancer. "He wasn't a musician. He was a one-legged dancer, a one-legged tap dancer. That was his nomer because he had one peg leg and one normal. He had a cousin that lived in the neighbourhood too." [34]

Traveling musicians with limited access to hotels because of formal and informal segregation would often stay with black families when on tour and Russell's family was no exception. And from time to time Russell's mother would leave him with friends who took in itinerant performers. "This brings up something that I didn't focus on, but one thing with my mother being a nurse, [she] had to board me with people and many times they were musicians. So I was born sort of sleeping with musicians, so guys used to tell me things."[35]

But there were other influences around. Russell spoke of how Nadi Qamar/Spaulding Givens brought some records to his house one day. "It was this *Festivals of Debussy*. That may have been the first time I really heard what struck me as modern symphonic music. And I was very impressed. And I didn't let it go. I pursued it from then on, you know."[36]

William R. Davis offered further support to the idea that culture and talent in the neighbourhood extended beyond jazz.

> We had some very talented people. And in our church we had this Mr. N. W. Ryder who was a very, very good leader, a good composer, a good conductor, a good choirmaster. We had two violin players that played with our choir. Emile Burbanks ended up playing with the Cincinnati Symphony Orchestra. Those kind[s] of people were around us where we grew up.[37]

As well as singing in the Glee Club and choir at Withrow, Russell and Dwight McPheeters were in a semi-professional vocal group together. "George and I sang in a quartet. The person who played for us and arranged our music was a lady by the name of Marie Gerard. There was George Russell, Leonard Williams, George Bassard and myself. We tried to model our singing after the Modernaires and that group that Tommy Dorsey had and we sang those songs."[38]

But even then, racism intruded.

> Well, Marie and a couple of people from the YMCA made arrangements for us to sing before a group of politicians, of Republicans in this town. They told Marie that we were not to sing any modern songs. We were told to sing only spirituals. So Marie began to give us some music and we sang spirituals but we always thought that with the group that we had if we hadn't been black we could have been as famous as the Modernaires because we were good. We were very good. We didn't have a name but when we were called on to go to these places, Marie would call us and tell us that we'd got to go to this place or that, so we did.[39]

By his teens Russell was working regularly as a drummer and McPheeters's mother commented often to her son about the late nights he was keeping.

> He was in his mid-teens. My mother used to say that he ought to be home in bed. He's out all night and he has to go to school the next day. He's going to get sick. He probably was on that road but we didn't run around together. We knew each other. We were good friends but we seldom were in the same group because he was always working. George has worked in music practically all of his life.[40]

According to McPheeters, by then most of Russell's friends were in the music business. "He was very, very loyal to the music world," he remembered, "and everything else was secondary." [41] Russell's aptitude for music had developed as much through his associations as by his application and practicing but he had reached the point where his skills had advanced sufficiently for him to work regularly around Cincinnati. His closest associates were guitarist Teddy Weatherford (clearly not the pianist and bandleader of that name, who took jazz to India and the Far East) and the Gaston brothers, Harold and Roger, and according to McPheeters, the group, though still in school, was making a regular income from music. William R. Davis also remembers Roger Gaston as a track star but the whole Gaston family seems to have been very talented.

Photographs from the Withrow High School yearbook for 1939 reveal a smiling, handsome young Harold Gaston. It is not hard to see character and intelligence in that face and a real self-assurance as well. Other pictures show him performing in the orchestra and with the choir and playing double bass in the Minstrel Show band. There is, of course, no irony or sense of the ridiculous in the yearbook reviewer's comments,

> Tapping toes, smiling ponies, greasepaint, the strains of a hit tune, Smittie's grin of delight, costumes galore, the query, "Do I look alright?," idiotic end-men in their colourful array—these phrases spell Minstrel Show. To the expectant audience of amazed parents and more amazed teachers, the Minstrel means more than all these: it means an appreciation of hard work, of the numerous beautiful costumes, of the professional appearance throughout, of the fact that a high school can produce a hit to a full house for five nights. And to the Minstreleers themselves, the show symbolizes abundant fun, new friendships made, pleasant memories, and, at the end, a sigh of satisfaction. [42]

And white people dress as black people and mug a grotesque caricature for the mainly white adult audience and black students still get to swim last period Friday afternoon, after which the pool gets cleaned. But Harold Gaston is there, as if the chance to play music is much more important in the long run and any fresh insult is just another among many. And if that were his rationale, he was probably right, because everything Russell, Davis and McPheeters remember about him suggests that Harold was a quite remarkable individual. It was he who would famously teach Russell "the rudiments of music theory" a few years later, when they were both in a sanatorium suffering from tuberculosis. Harold was the effective leader of the group of semi-professional young African-American musicians of which Russell was the youngest member. As William R. Davis recalled,

> Then in the neighbourhood we had a group of very talented high school young men who were musicians. They had a club called the Rhythm Club—we called the band the Rhythm Club. And they were all accomplished musicians while they were in high school. George ended up playing drums with them before he went with one of the other orchestras. They played high school dances and other kinds of events around the city of Cincinnati but then they ended up having to get into the union. The union people didn't want them to play certain places because they were not union musicians but they all ended up being in the

union. The Rhythm Club began to break up because of the war and I know George got that job with another band and began to travel and that.[43]

The Rhythm Club had more than its share of bright young talents, as Davis told me.

We had another man there who played piano for this Rhythm Club by the name of Andrew Johnson. Andrew Johnson was the only person that Duke Ellington let rehearse his band when he came to Cincinnati. Andrew Johnson was a most talented young man but he never left the city of Cincinnati. He married and began to raise a family and though he had opportunities to go away, he never did. George grew up around a bunch of very talented young men. Ralph Green—did he mention Ralph Green? Ralph Green lived in the same building that I lived in. Ralph Green was a high school track star, football player, he played the trombone and the piano. He played the trombone and the piano in this Rhythm Club that they had. There was another boy by the name of Oliver McLean. Now, Oliver played with the Lionel Hampton Band when it came to Cincinnati and did not have a tenor sax player. Oliver McLean belonged to our church, and he was another musician that George grew up with. Oliver played every reed instrument you could name, including the oboe. He was an excellent musician. These guys were a little bit older than us but we used to go and listen to them. They would let us listen to them rehearse on Tuesday afternoons. There was another young man by the name of Charles Lewis who was an excellent trumpet player and Charles left Cincinnati to go to New York. I don't know what happened after he went to New York but every time Louis Armstrong came to Cincinnati they had this trumpet contest and Charlie would win the trumpet, he'd win the trumpet every time. They would give a trumpet to the winner of the contest. And they were the people that George was associated with as a youngster. That's the thing that I see that contributed in helping him to want to be a good musician, because the guys that we grew up with were all good. I mean they were exceptional, very much so.[44]

By then Russell was quite confident in his abilities as a drummer and was working six nights a week backing a singer in a club. His schoolwork and attendance were, as already noted in the previous chapter, clearly suffering, but as he put it later to Vivian Perlis, "In the meantime I had felt music, especially drums, very strongly." Describing Harold Gaston as an "African" and "a star in their school orchestra, both the symphony orchestra, and any other kind of orchestra," he talked about rehearsing with the jazz band Harold had formed.

And he asked me to play drums with that orchestra. [So] I'm going to rehearsals of a, let's say, young, very excellent orchestra that impressed me very much, young orchestra, it was called the Rhythm Club, and they rehearsed in my neighbourhood so I used to go and listen to their rehearsals. In the meantime, I am sneaking down to the Cotton Club at Six and Mound, and listening to the bands that come through and feeling more and more that music is what I want. The regular school was not going good. When I went to high school I was really only good in one subject. I'd learned what I'd wanted to learn from school and . . . I read in a magazine about Hemingway, and he said, "If you want to be a writer, you don't need to go to school." That impressed me very much, and the whole thing was building up to make music the number-one priority in my life, and so that's all I can say.[45]

Russell took Hemingway's maxim to heart, not least, because it made perfect sense to a young African-American by then completely alienated by an education system that treated him as if his were a second-class mind being prepared for a life sitting at the back of the bus. Though Hemingway's words rang true, Harold Gaston's impact on Russell's life would, in some ways, prove both more direct and lasting.

According to Nelson Burton, Gaston studied at the Cosmopolitan School of Music founded in Cincinnati by pianist Artie Matthews, composer of "Weary Blues" and other early blues and ragtime pieces. Burton notes that blacks could attend the uptown white conservatory only if they were light enough "to pass" and Matthews set up the Cosmopolitan School of Music to provide young African-Americans with "an equal chance to get their formal musical training." He adds that back then, black areas of Cincinnati held a greater mix within them of people and that "teachers, tradesmen, ministers, and well-respected figures like Dr. Matthews provided role models for the children." Saxophonist and Basie Orchestra leader Frank Foster was apparently another student who attended the school.[46] Burton's comments about Harold Gaston (or Gastonia, as he refers to him) reveals the impression the young man made on those that knew him.

> Many fine musicians, educators and choral directors came out of the Cosmopolitan School of Music, including a bass player, Harold Gastonia, who caught Duke Wellington's [sic] eye at age seventeen. Gastonia died of tuberculosis before he got the chance to join the Duke. TB was a common disease back then. Penicillin wasn't invented yet so they didn't know how to treat it other than to put patients in a sanatorium. Even though Gastonia died young, memories of his great playing still linger in my mind.[47]

Russell's recollections of Gaston also remained very vivid after so many years. "I was there when Jimmy Blanton died, Ellington's bass player and I was playing with the band as a drummer. That band was so good, and it was conducted by a dear friend of mine, Harold Gaston."[48]

And again, a year earlier, he remembered,

> [W]hen Jimmy Blanton died at twenty-one [sic], a wonderful bass player, it was Harold Gaston that got the message from Ellington. That's how good he was. His family was, his entire family, first of all they were artistic. They had a very African kind of appearance, very tall . . . Watusi tall and dignified. Harold was like that. He's the only black guy who played . . . they had the good sense to have him play with the Cincinnati Symphony Orchestra.[49]

Burton is quite correct when he notes the direct influence that Harold Gaston had on his younger sanatorium roommate. In fact, it is a debt Russell always acknowledged. He told Ian Carr in 1992 about the time they were hospitalized together: "And he being in the hospital too, he could pass the time teaching me the elements of music, chords and basics ... intervals, basic techniques of writing, you know." [50]

Burton's memories of Russell are less kind. However, his comments are interesting in the distinction he makes between Gaston's influence on Russell in teaching him music and the distinct differences in the music Gaston wrote and that which Russell would later compose.

> George Russell, now a famous jazz innovator, was Gusto's roommate, and I suspect that some of the music Gastonia left in his trunk helped Russell get his foot in the door in Cincinnati. Once Russell got to New York, his music took off into a different orbit. It was, and still is, way out there, real strange and progressive, and nothing like Gusto's. [51]

Additionally, Burton's clearest recollections of Russell are not about his music at all. They refer instead to another aspect of the young man's personality and behaviour.

> In those early years, I remember more about Russell's personal style and natty dressing than I do about his music, which didn't seem so outstanding. He never wore hats because he had such nice wavy hair. Everything always matched— scarves, gloves, shoes and all. Look at him now. He's a star and people can say, "Yeah, George Russell. He came from these parts." [52]

Robert Moore told another story that arose in an interview he did with Nadi Qamar:

> Nadi was a little older than George but they did play a few gigs in Cincinnati. There was one particular occasion George talks about when they were playing at some little club and they started without any preparation, just started playing in a generally free manner, something that was out of the ordinary and I remember Nadi telling me about that particular evening. They were playing the changes to "Rosetta" and Nadi said he did not remember too much about that night because he had come across some kind of intoxicant which led him to play things that he'd never played before. [53]

Russell said something similar to Vivian Perlis in 1993. "We played at this place in a sort of poor white neighbourhood. And every night what we sort of... we just improvised, that's what we did. We were improvising, and we'd get into some pretty wild stuff and when we'd get too wild, fights would break out in the audience." [54]

As already noted, Qamar introduced Russell to Debussy and symphonic music, sparking what proved to be a life-long interest in European Art Music, and Russell remained in touch with his friend. Although never one of the more well-known names in jazz, Qamar has his own place in jazz history in several respects. Firstly, he played piano with Charles Mingus. The bass/piano duets (as well as a few trio sides with Max Roach) they recorded were released on the Mingus Debut Records box set. Secondly, Qamar was something of a pioneer of world jazz and he developed an interest in African percussion instruments such as the kalimba or thumb piano. Saxophonist T. K. Blue, who has played with Abdullah Ibrahim and Randy Weston, speaks of encountering Nadi Qamar and Don Cherry on the

New York downtown scene in the seventies and says that Qamar influenced him to take up the kalimba.[55] Though Qamar's own history in jazz falls far behind that of Russell's, his achievements do suggest that his significance within the music world Russell inhabited goes far beyond that of being simply Art Tatum's less well-known cousin. Rather, he was a part of the rich cultural milieu in which Russell moved in Cincinnati.

Qamar told WKCR's Ben Young in 1998, in a tribute to Russell on his seventy-fifth birthday, about life in Cincinnati.

> We were just completely surrounded by good musicians, both black and white, even though there was... the colour line was there in the conservatories and things but the musicians, black musicians had musicians who were capable of teaching other black musicians anything they wanted to learn. So George and myself were surrounded by very fine musicians.

He also mentions relatives and others who were "very musical in both European classical and jazz" and speaks of a community that was "well evolved into African-American and European cultural influences."[56]

And there was one other musical influence that rarely gets acknowledged in the telling of this story. Given that some writers assume he was influenced in some way by a biological father and professor of music whom Russell had never known, it is ironic that the more direct influence of his adopted father, Joseph, should be ignored. As Russell recalled to Carr:

> [W]hen he came home his chief love was to play the piano, you know. But he didn't have... he had a left hand but he didn't care what he hit in the left hand. He played stride but he didn't *(laughing)* care about what the chord was. So he came up with some pretty incredible music, 'cause he would sing along with this very, very outgoing piano.[57]

At other times, Russell has jokingly referred to his father's playing as being "like Cecil Taylor before Cecil Taylor." The strange thing about Russell's description of Joseph's piano style is that it could almost describe the sound of his own highly rhythmic approach. It is a point that was not lost on Robert Moore.

> Did George mention that Joseph Russell liked to play the piano? He was not a trained musician. Did he tell you about his particular style of playing, which kind of reminds me of a similar story I think I heard, a similar story with Ives, with the composer Ives, whose father played in a similar fashion? Very chromatic! *(laughs)* The impression I got was that he played a kind of Stride. The important thing is to keep the rhythm happening. If you play things with a certain confidence, no matter what your playing skills, it's going to be valid in some way. *(laughs)*[58]

And did it strike him that if the "amateurish" tag was removed it could be a description of Russell's playing as well? "Exactly. Exactly. I think so."

Russell made a very similar point to Vivian Perlis.

**GR:** One of his delights was to play—I'm sort of thinking of Ives in this situation, I think Ives's father played a kind of pretty, I don't like the term "dissonant," but dissonant piano that influenced Ives's harmonic sense, you know?

**VP:** Yes, he even talked about "piano drums," which amused me, because I think you did that a little later on too?

**GR:** Yes, my father played and sang. He might have been lucky with one or two notes of a melody. About as close as he came to the melody in accompanying himself was to, was actually his singing of the melody, because he hit very few notes in the melody in the right hand that corresponded to the song he was singing. And the left hand was totally, totally anything. Just wherever the fingers fell, playing stride piano. So he influenced . . . my sense of the seed of being progressive was planted within. He was just having a good time. He didn't know anything about harmony or melody or anything. He liked the sound of the piano and he kind of let the fingers fall wherever they happened to be.[59]

One other aspect of life in Cincinnati in Russell's early and formative years needs to be considered, namely how the city's race-political divisions were reflected in its music scene. Cincinnati was—like the United States itself—a mass of contradictions. Its integrated schools enforced all manner of informal segregations and, even though it had always been a "free" state, de facto and formal separation of the races operated throughout the city, including in its jazz and nightclubs. Vine Street, a long stretch that runs from east to west in the city, was the effective dividing line. In many ways it still is, though it now separates the ghetto of the Over-the-Rhine district from prosperous downtown. Back in the thirties, the East Side was set aside for white musicians belonging to Union Local 1 and club owners operated a policy of "Only Caucasians Need Apply." Inevitably, the economic implications of this segregation for black musicians were severe. As Nelson Burton notes, if you were not a big star among white audiences or working at the Cincy Cotton Club, "you'd be scuffling."[60]

But as Bill Lawless Jones points out, Cincinnati loved music and loved jazz. Because of its unique geographical position, Cincinnati was at a crossroads for travelling musicians, white and black. Lawless Jones notes the irony that "segregated" Cincinnati had an integrated Cotton Club, while "liberal" New York's more famous club of the same name did not allow black patrons and made its black artists use the servants' entrance. And it was, of course, located in Harlem![61]

Cincinnati's Cotton Club always allowed black and white musicians and fans to fraternize. Musicians from touring bands would fetch up there for after-hours sessions of drinking, carousing and music making. As Burton writes, when you got the call from the Cotton Club, you knew you had arrived as far as Cincy was concerned. And from time to time, Russell got the call. Once again the glamorous life of the jazz musician was spread out before him, with all the current and past sounds and styles of jazz. As Robert Moore explains:

> By the age of 14, Russell's interest in music, coupled with his adolescent interest in exploring the adult world, took him far beyond the boundaries of Walnut Hills. He began making the long four mile trek down Gilbert Avenue to downtown Cincinnati and the

Cotton Club. Although "Cotton Clubs" were to be found in just about every American city with a sizeable black population, Cincinnati's was known throughout the black entertainment world. Jimmy Lunceford, Cab Calloway, Earl Hines, Andy Kirk and others of that stature appeared there. The Cotton Club became school for George as his attendance at Withrow High School dropped precipitously. Finally, at the age of 16, George dropped out of high school and began working at a downtown department store in the day and playing at night.[62]

Russell has described the Cotton Club as "his school" and he played there as a "dep" on several occasions. In a letter to me, Russell wrote,

> Situated in what was called the "Black Bottom," (deep downtown) of Cincinnati, the club was noted as the "Graveyard of Bands," due to the ever-present demands of audiences to hear something hot and new. If a band lacked something new and lacked that spark, it didn't last long with the Cincy audience. It was located on the ground floor of the Hotel Sterling. Lee Morgan, the black owner, was married to a white woman who sometimes worked at the club. It was a hang for the Cincinnati police (black and white) who managed to maintain law and order. The bands were mainly middle-sized groups that had made a name as river bands coming up from New Orleans to Kansas City, St Louis, Cincinnati and up the Ohio River to Pittsburgh; these were historically important bands such as Noble Sissle, Zack Whyte, McKinney's Cotton Pickers, Andy Kirk, the Sweethearts of Rhythm (all girl band) and the Chick Webb Band. I first played there as a sub with the Alabama State Collegians and then was hired when other bands came through needing a drummer.[63]

So it was that by the age of sixteen, Russell had committed himself to a career in music. As Robert Moore has noted, it was a hard life. His days were spent working in a department store and nights into the early hours passed playing jazz. Joseph was dead and school was behind him. The life Russell had first observed on the riverboats was opening up before him.

Returning to the question of Russell's musical influences, with the rich musical and cultural milieu that was the community of Walnut Hills, it seems quite unnecessary to focus on the occupation of his biological father in explaining his talent. By contrast, evidence of significant and positive influences from within his community is extensive. Even though identifying influence can be a tricky business, there is more than enough in Russell's story itself, and in his own insights into his life, to allow us to focus on some key individuals and factors in his development as an individual and as an artist.

Harold Gaston would certainly give Russell something very valuable in teaching him the rudiments of musical theory but his contribution would seem to have been much broader than that. By all accounts he was not only very gifted, he was also dedicated and committed to his music. As an older boy, Gaston took Russell into his circle and even seems to have acted as a mentor to him. His influence was perhaps also as much by example as in what he actually taught Russell.

We have also noted how Nadi Qamar introduced Russell to Debussy and symphonic music. Russell considered this important enough to include it in his biography for the French Record company Label Bleu, for whom he recorded two albums in the eighties and nineties. [64] Additionally, Russell played drums in a trio with Qamar, including on the night where they discovered the possibility of improvisation that did not rely in some way on chord progressions. It is also important to note the impression made by those other members of the Rhythm Club mentioned by William R. Davis—pianist Andrew Johnson, [65] trombonist Ralph Green, saxophonist Oliver McLean and trumpeter Charles Lewis - as well as the impact of the wild, ecstatic gospel music he heard in "the hollow" and "Black Bottom" areas of Cincinnati.

And then there is the broader influences of musicians within the community, people like Zack Whyte and Jimmy Mundy, who offered both positive role models, and, in Mundy's case, direct encouragement to Russell. They also promoted a sense of adult glamour. As Russell has said, they looked great, the girls loved them and they commanded respect. Russell identified powerfully with these men and in Burton's description of him and his attention to detail in his mode of dress, we have a graphic illustration of that process of identification.

These influences would seem to have promoted in Russell an open-minded, questing attitude to music and culture, albeit one that was also quite selective in what he took from his observations.

And there were the positive cultural values he encountered in Walnut Hills and the broader black community in which he lived. As we have heard, this was a blue-collar to lower-middle-class area, but one that also contained its share of black professional people such as teachers and social workers. It was a "respectable" neighbourhood with low crime rates and a strong sense of community. Religion and Christian values were clearly important within it, as was the desire for self-improvement and, to some degree, mutual encouragement and mentorship, whether by the likes of athlete DeHart Hubbard, the African Methodist Episcopalian Church's provision of indoor recreation facilities, in the formation and pooling of resources of the Rhythm Club and in the altruistic acts of Harold Gaston in sharing his musical knowledge with others, including Russell. Such influences contrasted markedly with the racism experienced in most of his dealings with white society and it is to these influences that Russell owed much of his sense of identity as an African-American.

As for the negative effects of white racism, these have been detailed in the previous chapter at length to show the obstacles placed in Russell's way by the highly stratified society into which he was born and to emphasize his achievements. But their inclusion is also intended to show Russell's own response to racism. In various ways, he made something distinctly personal from these events. They inspired in him an understandable hatred of racism and racists but not of white people or of America. It gave him a hatred of intolerance, authoritarianism and totalitarianism and made him a questioner of authority. The contrast to Bessie's reaction to his expulsion from school to Russell's own illustrates this well: "The getting expelled from school made my mother feel, 'Well, this child is disturbed.' . . . but I took it as a badge of honour." [66]

And what of his origins and upbringing? Russell learned quite late that Bessie and Joseph were not his biological parents. Yet far from reacting with any sense of betrayal, abandonment or loss of identity, he transformed this experience into a positive one. He talked of "the kids" who were kept apart by society's rules and describes himself as a "love-child." He made it work for him and turned a potential negative into a powerful positive.

In some ways, Russell gave the impression of a self-assured and self-confident individual. In others, he seemed to share with many other adopted children the sense of displacement, dislocation and insecurity that the knowledge of "abandonment" can cause. He would describe himself as a "loner" and his single-minded focus on the Lydian Concept and his own spiritual searching suggest a desire to make connections with something greater than himself. Yet even if this assessment is accurate, his adjustment was both remarkably successful and creative in its outcomes for him and for his music. Again, this was the observable pattern of Russell's life: He would turn potentially negative experiences into positive ones and crises into opportunities.

## Notes

1. Interview with George Russell, June 2004.
2. There's a huge body of literature within what is generally described as phenomenological or interactionist psychology and sociology that explores these same processes. See, for example, R. D. Laing, *The Divided Self* (Harmondsworth, UK: Penguin, 1971) and *Self and Others* (Harmondsworth, UK: Penguin 1975); E. Goffman, *Stigma* (Harmondsworth, UK: Penguin, 1968); and H. S. Becker, *The Outsiders Studies in Sociology of Deviance* (New York: MacMillan, 1966). There is also a body of literature in psychology that deals with the experience of concentration camp victims (Bruno Bettelheim), hostages (the term "Stockholm Syndrome" was coined by psychologist Nils Bejerot to describe the behaviour of those held captive during the famous Norrmalmstorg bank robbery of August 1973; the syndrome develops out of the victims' attempts to relate to their captor or gain the kidnapper's sympathy; in this case, the victims kept on defending their captors even after their six-day physical detention was over, and they showed reticent behaviour in the legal procedures that followed), and of victims of colonialism (see F. Fanon, *The Wretched of the Earth* [Harmondsworth, UK: Penguin, 1969] and *Toward the African Revolution* [Harmondsworth, UK: Penguin, 1970]) and the way in which the oppressed internalize a debased image of themselves through identification with their oppressors.
3. Vivian Perlis, interview with George Russell, American Music Series, December 8, 1993, Oral History Project of American Music, sponsored and supported by the National Endowment for the Arts Special Jazz Projects.
4. Interview with William R. Davis, August 2004.
5. Ibid.
6. Ibid.
7. Interview with George Russell, December 2003.
8. Ian Carr, interview with George Russell, June 1992.
9. Perlis, interview.
10. Ibid.
11. Robert E. Moore, "George Alan Russell: Jazz's First Theorist," *Trotter Institute Review* 2 (Summer 1998): 18.
12. Interview with Dwight McPheeters, June 2004.
13. This would have been Noah Walker Ryder, rather than his somewhat more famous son, Noah Francis Walker. The latter, born in 1914 would have been just seven years older than Russell.

Noah Francis did, however, live with his family in Walnut Hills and, like, William R. Davis attended Walnut Hills High School. Marjorie Johnson, "Noah Francis Ryder: Composer and Educator." *The Black Perspective in Music* 6, no. 1 (1978), pp.19-31.

14. Most notable here is George Russell's response to a questionnaire sent in preparation of Leonard Feather's 1960 edition of *The Encyclopedia of Jazz*, where it notes, "First infatuated with Jazz when mother took him on River Boat Excursion featuring Fate Marble [sic] Orchestra from St. Louis. Was especially intrigued with drummer."
15. See, for example, Moore, "George Alan Russell"; Robert Palmer, "A Jazz Visionary Eyes the Evolution of Life on Earth," *New York Times*, April 28, 1985.
16. Carr, interview with G. Russell, June 1992.
17. Perlis, interview.
18. Interview with W. Davis.
19. Interview with George Russell, June 2003.
20. Interview with George Russell, June 2004. See also Nelson Burton, *My Life in Jazz* (Cincinnati: Clifton Hills Press, 2000).
21. Bill Lawless Jones, sleeve notes to *Cincinnati Jazz Collection Volume I* (1998), J Curve Records J71098. Whyte's line-up for two 1929 recording sessions was William Benton (d), Floyd Brady (tb), Herman Chittison (p), Montgomery Morrison (tba), Sy Oliver, Bubber Whyte, Henry Savage (t), Clarence Paige, Ben Ricardson, Earl Tribble (as), Al Sears (ts, bs), and Zack Whyte (bj, ldr).
22. Ibid.
23. James Lincoln Collier, *The Making of Jazz—A Comprehensive History* (Basingstoke, UK: Papermac, 1981), p. 145. See also Wikipedia entry for Marable. Fate Marable (December 2, 1890–January 16, 1947) was a jazz pianist and bandleader. Marable was born in Paducah, Kentucky, and learned piano from his mother. At the age of seventeen he began playing on the steamboats plying the Mississippi River. He soon became bandleader for boats on the Strekfus Line, which ran several paddle wheelers that held dances and excursions along the river from New Orleans, Louisiana, to Minneapolis, Minnesota. Marable appreciated the new "jazz" sound being played by the New Orleans musicians, and the bulk of his band members were recruited from that city. Members of Marable's bands were expected to be able to play a wide variety of music, from hot numbers to light classics; to play both by head and from sheet music; and above all to keep the dancers happy. Noted musicians who spent time in Marable's bands included Red Allen, Louis Armstrong, Baby Dodds, Johnny Dodds, Pops Foster, Al Morgan, and Zutty Singleton, among others. In addition to piano and bandleading, Marable played the boats' steam calliope, a contraption that could be heard for miles up and down the river and poured down so much water from condensing steam that Marable performed wearing a raincoat and hood. Marable died of pneumonia in Saint Louis, Missouri. See also A. Shipton, *A New History of Jazz* (London: Continuum, 2001), pp. 111–14; and G. Schuller, *The Swing Era* (Oxford: Oxford University Press, 1989), pp. 785–87.
24. Carr, interview with G. Russell, June 1992.
25. Interview with McPheeters.
26. Interview with W. Davis.
27. Interview with G. Russell, June 2004.
28. Ibid.
29. Interview with W. Davis.
30. Ibid.
31. Burton, *My Life in Jazz*.
32. Carr, interview with G. Russell, June 1992.
33. Francis Davis, "George Russell: The Intellect of the Heart," *Jazz Times*, December 12, 1984.
34. Interview with W. Davis.
35. Interview with G. Russell, June 2004.
36. Carr, interview with G. Russell, June 1992.

37. Interview with W. Davis. See note 13 above.
38. Interview with McPheeters.
39. Ibid.
40. Ibid.
41. Ibid.
42. Withrow High School yearbook, 1939.
43. Interview with W. Davis.
44. Ibid.
45. Perlis, interview with G. Russell.
46. Burton, *My Life in Jazz*, chap. 10. 46.
47. Ibid., pp. 62–63.
48. Interview with G. Russell, June 2004.
49. Interview with G. Russell, June 2003.
50. Carr, interview with G. Russell, June 1992.
51. Burton, *My Life in Jazz*, p. 64.
52. Ibid.
53. Moore, "Jazz's First Theorist," p. 18.
54. Perlis, interview with G. Russell.
55. See the T. K. Blue Official Web Site, www.tkblue.com.
56. Ben Young, interview with Nadi Qamar, WKCR Radio, New York, 1998.
57. Carr, interview with G. Russell, June 1992.
58. Interview with Robert E. Moore, July 2004.
59. Perlis, interview with G. Russell.
60. Burton, *My Life in Jazz*, p. 64.
61. Lawless Jones, sleeve notes to *Cincinnati Jazz Collection Volume I*; also sleeve notes to *Cincinnati Jazz Collection Volume II* (1999), J Curve Records J7005; Lawless Jones, sleeve notes to *Cincinnati Jazz Collection Volume I* and *Cincinnati Jazz Collection Volume II*.
62. Moore, "Jazz's First Theorist," p. 18.
63. George Russell, letter to author, October 13, 2004. Russell's memory may be faulty regarding McKinney's Cotton Pickers. The group apparently disbanded in 1934, when George was only eleven.
64. The Label Bleu Web site notes, "Still in Cincinnati, a pianist among his friends, Spaulding Givens (who will work with Charles Mingus and will be called later Nadi Qamar) lets him hear Debussy's records, preceding his discovery of Stravinsky." See http://www.label-bleu.com/artist.php?lng=e&artist_id=46.
65. Lawless Jones mentions Andrew Johnson in relation to the access or lack of access for black students to music colleges and the development in the black community of "professors" who taught piano or other instruments. Johnson's father was one such, as were Noah Ryder and Wendell P. Dabney. See also Burton, *My Life in Jazz*.
66. Perlis, interview with G. Russell.

CHAPTER THREE

# Cincy Blues

How did it feel for sixteen-year-old George Russell, walking those streets free of the school he hated and now a part of the adult world in fact, if not by virtue of age of majority? We can guess it felt exhilarating, exciting and full of possibility. Home was becoming increasingly a place to refuel and recharge. It was not that Bessie was irrelevant. She was the only mother Russell knew and he loved her. However, it would be surprising if she had much more influence over her son than most parents, then or today, have over their teenage children. She was a disciplinarian with strong moral values. She was, nevertheless, by one account—that of Dwight McPheeters and his mother—somewhat indulgent of her child.[1] Did she know where George was and what he was doing, even half of the time? She would be an unusual parent if she did and, with her involvement with Bishop Mack's ministry, she was not always around.

But there is another issue. Entry to manhood was anyway achieved at a younger age for African-American males than for whites. Young George was working, which any mother would expect and hope, and was probably not that different from his peers within his race and class. He worked by day as a lift operator in a department store in Cincinnati. In fact, George, given his background, was never afraid of hard, "blue-collar" work. Later he would work whenever he needed to but never to the point that it got in the way of his more important activities in music. He had been a semi-professional musician from the age of fourteen or fifteen. Now, every night he could, he played the drums.

> As I said, I got kicked out of school and began doing night gigs with singers in clubs and not getting paid much money but learning all the time. Anyway, the kids, especially the

black kids and to the lesser degree the whites, they wanted jazz. We had some fabulous musicians come into that town. The era . . . was amazing.[2]

It was hardly a healthy lifestyle and Russell blamed this and the experience of playing in smoky jazz clubs for his first bout of tuberculosis. "I was working nine to five at Klein's in Cincinnati, the department store. I would come home, get a little food down and go to work in a night club four or five blocks from my house with my mother, yeah. When we were working between something like nine-thirty and two and coming back home and then getting up too early to have a decent breakfast."[3]

It was around this time that Russell was invited to Wilberforce University, about fifty miles north of Cincinnati, to audition for the school's Collegians jazz band. According to Russell, the reason he got the call was due both to the school's need for a drummer and the positive reputation he was building in the clubs around town. Students from the college came to Cincinnati and heard him in the Cotton Club. "Students told the Collegians, 'Hey, this guy can play.' I got a letter from Wilberforce. They asked me to come up and that's what I did."[4]

At that time, he was playing in a club "across the river" in Kentucky owned and run by the mob, "a Dillinger," as Russell told me. Nelson Burton confirms that "across the river was a common expression on both sides of the Ohio but it had different meaning depending on the direction." He describes crossing the river as a "Jekyll-and-Hyde sort of thing."[5] "Mobsters knew they no longer had the law in their pockets when they crossed to Cincinnati, so their behaviour was beyond reproach." However, "[b]y keeping the prostitutes and the gamblers on the other side of the river, Cincinnati had a clear conscience on the surface of being the goody-goody-two-shoes that she wasn't."[6]

Here the story becomes a little confused, due to both the distance in time and Russell's memory. Certainly, things did not work out at Wilberforce first time. Whether Russell failed the audition, as Ernie Wilkins, a Collegian at the time, told Robert Moore,[7] or whether, as Russell remembers, he was asked to return later because the band leader was initially unhappy with his playing, is uncertain. According to Russell's recollection, "The first semester I really wasn't playing that well" and "they weren't satisfied with my playing."[8] Wilkins has suggested that part of the reason Russell failed at Wilberforce the first time stemmed from the kit Russell was using,[9] which was the one his mother had bought him as a child. This seems quite possible, as that set was subsequently lost in a fire around this period, forcing Russell and his mother to replace it. However, when school started in the fall semester of 1940, Russell was again invited to join the Collegians. He celebrated the night before his departure, playing blackjack with his older bandmates in "the Dillinger's" club. He told me he believed it was his mob-connected employer who encouraged the band to let him win the money back[10] but he gave Vivian Perlis a slightly less elaborate version before talking more generally about his time at Wilberforce.

> **GR:** So, I was again working both in the day and at night in some joint across the river from Cincinnati owned by some gangster in Newport, Kentucky. I had managed to save up a little money, I would guess, certainly, and then I took all the money—I needed some money, just a small bit to register—and I gambled that night, the night before I was going

to Wilberforce and lost it all in a blackjack game *(laughing)* but with other musicians. They must have known, because they stayed on, and they sort of let me win it back. And I not only won it back but I had money to spare. The next day I drove up to Wilberforce and registered. Wilberforce was to be my home then, really, from the time I was seventeen or eighteen, until . . . not seventeen, sixteen to about nineteen, playing in their world-class college orchestra with other musicians who would become very well known, like Ernie Wilkins. This was a band, its roster read like a Who's Who in American jazz. So that was quite an experience.

**VP:** Was it necessary for you to study other things in order to get through?

**GR:** Yes, a lot of other things. Wilberforce was kind of a prep school for upper-middle-class blacks, especially for the kids who tended to get in trouble, especially older kids. So it had a number of older, really, they were men, there, who were all taking business administration. Most of them eventually practiced it in the underworld, what they learned at Wilberforce. *(laughing)*.[11]

Russell always minimized any influence on or benefit to him from formal education, a tendency that perhaps stems from his negative experiences at Withrow. He has always portrayed himself as essentially an autodidact. At that time, Wilberforce, still today a private African-American college, had a university and a high school. As Russell had not completed his elementary education, he attended the high school, studying the general academic curriculum. His report card made troubling reading for Bessie Russell. Out of 206 days, Russell was absent 34 and tardy 31. Apart from a couple of Bs in music, Cs predominate, and there's more than a spattering of Ds and Es! As for "effort," that was graded as "D," "below average, unsatisfactory but passing."

There is a rather poignant letter on his course record from Bessie to one of the teachers, Mr. B. H. Heard.

Dear Sir,

I received my son's Report Card / Geo Allan Russell/ I can't say I am any more pleased than you are with it. But there is a slight improvement from the first one and we hope he will continue to make more or better improvement than the last one. I do know he had dental trouble and I do hope he can hold up until school is over to have the rest of the work attended to. As soon as I can make it convenient I will come up and have a talk with you. I have been very sick since the Boy was home. Enclosed Mr Heard you will find two dollars, $1.65 for Physical Geography Text and Laboratory Field Manual and weekly periodical scholastic and please give him balance left which is 35c. I do thank you for your patience and interest shown him and I will continue to ask please help and encourage him for my sake. I want him to finish school above all things.

Respectfully Yours
Bessie O. Russell [12]

Her wish would not be granted. The first semester, Russell continued to live in Cincinnati and commuted to Wilberforce, working at the same time in the department store.[13] During the second semester, though resident on campus, he continued to trek back to Cincinnati for gigs. He recalls that he was also at the time working at Wright-Patterson Air Base to earn money.[14] How he actually found time to do any studying at all during his eighteen months at the college is in itself remarkable. It was obvious, anyway, that his only real interest was playing in the Collegians and in the clubs of Cincinnati.

How much Russell actually gained from his studies at Wilberforce is a matter of conjecture. Interestingly, Dr. Anna M. Terry was his teacher of music at the school and she would later serve on the Board of Trustees of New England Conservatory (NEC), where Russell taught from 1969 until 2004. When Ian Carr asked Russell about Terry, an educator of some standing, Russell minimized what he learned at school, instead referring to his later period in hospital due to TB with Harold Gaston. "She [Terry] helped me out in talking to me but I still didn't learn music formally from her. I learned music formally in a hospital."[15]

I suspect Russell underestimated what he had gained from Dr. Terry at Wilberforce. It seems more plausible that by the time he came to learn "the rudiments of arranging," as he has put it, from Harold Gaston in the tuberculosis sanatorium, he had sufficient knowledge and understanding to take advantage of what Gaston had to teach. Also, there are those Bs and Cs in music at Wilberforce, suggesting that he learned a little more at Wilberforce than he has since allowed.

I am not alone in this assumption. Robert Moore interviewed Terry for his *Trotter Institute Review* article on Russell. He wrote, "It was at Wilberforce that he received his first formal instruction in music from Professor Anna Terry, mentor to a long list of distinguished African-Americans. About Russell, Professor Terry related: 'When he came to me he didn't know a thing... what a staff was. I had to teach him all of the fundamentals.'"[16]

Two photographs of the Collegians in the 1942 and 1943 college yearbooks show Russell dressed in bolero-jacketed uniform, white shirt and straight dark tie behind a kit with "Wilberforce Collegians" written on the bass drum. Oliver McLean, the Collegians' alto player, was highly regarded in Cincinnati and the Midwest. However, aside from McLean, Russell and tenor saxophonist/arranger Ernie Wilkins were the only members of that band to make careers of note in jazz.

Having worked on his drumming between his first and second invitations to Wilberforce, it was playing with the Collegians that Russell really enjoyed about his time at the college. "In the meantime, I had—in that six months—I had really learned how to play drums. So when they got me back it was wonderful. You know, we had just a great time."[17]

Recalling the band's roll call of past stars—inaccurately, as it happens, including in error Fletcher Henderson and Coleman Hawkins[18]—Russell pointed out that all the black universities of the period had "incredibly exciting jazz orchestras."

> And one of our most enjoyable tasks was to follow the football team around in the fall, they going on their bus and we going on ours to these various universities. And on Saturday the football team would play the football team and then at night there'd be this battle of the bands between... with the Wilberforce Collegians and, let's say, the Alabama State Collegians, with Lucky Thompson and... oh, Willie... you know, Willie Cook.[19]

At that point, for Russell, playing jazz mattered more than anything, even more than clothes, cars or girls or any of the things that drive an eighteen-year-old young man. Although "handsome" George Russell, as he is dubbed in one of the yearbook photos, clearly already had an eye for the women who were attracted to jazzmen and their lives.

On December 8, 1941, following the Japanese attack on Pearl Harbor, the United States declared war on Japan. As Russell recalled, "It was around '41 that I was called up for the draft. In that . . . at the draft you know, the World War II thing, I volunteered for the Marines 'cause they told me I'd be playing in the Marine Band. Hardy har, har, har, you know." [20]

Russell wanted to fight and was swept up in the patriotic fervour that followed Pearl Harbor, though with hindsight he wondered if he would have been up to demands of the Corps.

I wanted to [fight] . . . not knowing all of the things I would have had to go through if I'd made it, because in those days the Marine Corps demands were rough, very rough. I was with a friend, a pianist, and we were in a room of three thousand people, naked men, who had taken these examinations and then I heard my name called. But before that we had told a Marine colonel that we wanted to join and he was delighted and he showed us the way to where they examined me. They took my friend but they told me I had tuberculosis; saved my life in a lot of ways. [21]

As he told Carr, "But they spared me a few, a few of their most interesting parties—Iwo Jima, Guadalcanal." [22]

Russell remembered meeting his pianist friend, who was drafted, in Chicago a few years later. "He was a piano player but couldn't play piano when he got back. Just had this look on his face. If you saw it you would never forget it. That was a knockout blow for me to see him in that state. Didn't speak. Just the way he looked." [23]

Russell was admitted to the Branch Hospital in Cincinnati. He described it as a "good hospital, wonderful hospital," where he had a private room with a veranda; it was nevertheless a segregated facility. Harold Gaston, Russell's school friend and colleague in the Rhythm Club, was also a patient. In a broadcast for WGBH Radio in Boston, Russell summarized his six months in the hospital.

I went into the hospital and one of the patients was Harold Gaston. We used to pass the time with him coming in and teaching me music, the rudiments of music. Harold and I were part of a group that began to protest the segregated policies in the hospital lunchroom. The chief doctor said, "I think you are both well enough to be dismissed." I was glad to hear it, even though it was a big lie. [24]

That is the expurgated version. The real story tells something about the racial fault lines in American society. There are always those who, whatever their reasons, will explore the margins of social divisions and will sometimes cross the line far beyond what was considered acceptable. Prescribed six months of bed rest, Russell's experience was surely not what his doctor had in mind.

Each patient had their own room with a beautiful view, but whites on one floor, blacks on another. There had to be some nurses that liked that, and one of them—the head nurse—used to come in the room and look at me and not ask me what's wrong but just look at me for a long time. Finally, a nurse came in who was from Kentucky and she did it all. I sucked her breast. [25]

And: "The nurses had infiltrated to the patients . . . and this is a segregated facility . . . and the guys, the black guys used to get visits at night from some of the nurses and I managed to do that just in time before the hospital clamping down on any kind of integration." [26]

In some ways, what is most amazing is less the fact that white nurses were having sex with black patients but that they were doing so with patients who had tuberculosis! As he told me in 2004,

At the same time, this woman from Kentucky, she was a nurse and she took a liking to me . . . she was white . . . as did a number of nurses there who made boyfriends of the patients. And the head nurse walks in in the middle of the night and catches me at it. [27]

Gaston and Russell passed the time—when not engaged in other such therapeutic and recreational activities—with Gaston teaching Russell music theory and arranging. "And from him I learned the elements of music—chords and basics, intervals, basic techniques of writing, you know." [28]

The senior nurse who caught Russell *in flagrante delicto* had not kept matters to herself. With Gaston and Russell trying to desegregate the hospital in other ways, it was more than the hospital administration could bear. "We were being rebels and trying to integrate the food facility there at the hospital. They would have none of that. But Gaston was a rebel, got kicked out of the hospital. The hospital changed president [director] and the new president came from Mississippi and that was it. He released us." [29]

Neither he nor Gaston was cured of the disease and it is with a bitter tone in his voice that Russell recalled that this amounted to a death sentence for his friend. Although Russell recognized that his lifestyle may have contributed to his contracting tuberculosis, the disease was rife across America, in particular in poorer areas where people lived in close proximity. [30]

Gaston and his entire family, apparently, died of the disease. In Gaston's case, he would never fulfil the promise offered by those musical gifts that led to the call to replace the great Jimmy Blanton in Duke Ellington's orchestra shortly before his final illness. Both Russell and Burton have referred to this, though Russell has elsewhere mentioned Lionel Hampton as the bandleader calling on Gaston's services. [31] It is one of those cases of "what might have been" had that doctor from Mississippi followed his oath rather than his prejudices. Given that Russell played with Gaston and no doubt visited his home, it is possible that this was where he caught tuberculosis, though that too is conjecture. Like many such diseases, tuberculosis is no respecter of class, race, gender or religion.

Russell's two stints in the hospital for tuberculosis figure significantly in interviews he has given over the years. There is no doubt that these illnesses were genuinely life-threatening and life-changing events. In one interview, he actually noted specifically that when talking about his periods in hospital, "I'm just mentioning a few of the things that shaped my life."³² It was during his second bout of tuberculosis that Russell first elaborated his Lydian Concept. But it is worth considering for a moment Russell's experiences in relation to the way he and others have told his story. Such considerations say something about the rather formalized and archetypal form in which such stories are told in our culture.

In his 1993 work, *The Hero with a Thousand Faces*, the Jungian writer Joseph Campbell describes in detail common themes from myths and biography that recur in the telling of the lives of exceptional individuals. He suggests that there is an unspoken and unconscious format to which such stories must conform. According to Campbell, symbolic rites of passage, chance encounters, perilous journeys, isolation and misunderstanding, difficult trials, secret helpers, atonement with the father—all of these often feature in "hero" biographies.

Through these "transformative" events, the "hero" emerges a changed person, "possessing the power to bestow great benefits upon his fellow man."³³ Virgin or mysterious birth origins also feature. It is not about questioning "the frequent kernel of biographical truth," to use Frank J. Sulloway's phrase about another "hero," Sigmund Freud.³⁴ It is how life stories told in this way are understood that requires thought. Overreliance on such archetypical forms may cause the biographer – or jazz journalist - to miss important issues and fresh insights.

Here, it suffices to note again Russell's origins. For example, in his program for the BBC on Russell, Ian Carr slipped into this mythologizing narrative,

> [George Russell is] one of the most mysterious and unorthodox figures in jazz. His ideas have been hugely influential, yet he has been for the most part a shadowy presence on the side-lines. It may be that his *covert genius has its roots in the secrecy surrounding his birth* in Cincinnati in 1923. (my italics)³⁵

Having dealt with any number of individuals who have been adopted in the course of a career in social work, I can find no mystery or even great "secrecy" here. Carr has extrapolated from Russell's account of his birth and constructed a narrative that does not stand scrutiny and, worse, which mystifies rather than informs.

As I have shown, there is a "kernel of biological truth" in Russell's account of his origins. It is not an uncommon American story of its time—an attractive, talented and respectable young woman of colour is seduced by—here we assume—an older, white authority figure. Nannie Kathleen would have been about eighteen years old. Assuming, in the absence of evidence, that Russell's father was a 'professor of music,' he would have been at least a decade older than her. Even when Russell was conceived, by the standards of that time, this man would have been said to have 'taken advantage' of his young charge. By today's standards, at most educational institutions, his behaviour would have been a sackable offence. That their association, given the social and political culture of the time, was taboo states the obvious but by following Russell's account – and even elaborating upon it – Carr and other writers miss the opportunity to explain what this might mean as far as Russell himself was concerned.

I have already stressed that the construction Russell made of the story is of much greater importance in understanding him as an individual and as a black artist working within the confused racial mix of American jazz than the story itself. To that I would add that, in telling his story in this way, Russell was conforming to the kind of mythologizing that Joseph Campbell describes. The account fits the hero myth of a kind of virgin birth, for, to all intents and purposes, his biological father is the shadowy, (holy) ghostlike figure here.

In turn, Russell's bouts of tuberculosis are his perilous journeys. His experiences at Withrow High, in racially divided Cincinnati, and in its jazz clubs are his rites of passage. But, as we shall see, even more pertinent is the inward journey Russell would later take, as we shall see, in the hospital when he "discovered" the Lydian Concept. It is that voyage of (self-)discovery that also predominates within the hero myth.

To tell a story of a life requires a willingness to read the narrative critically, not to accept the information at face value but to contextualise it in order that a fuller, richer picture can emerge. Such mythologizing clouds our understanding and appreciation. Russell's life was, in reality, fascinating enough and his achievements significant enough that it neither requires or benefits from such a telling.

At a more down-to-earth level, for the teenage Russell, the experience of being in the hospital—of having sex with nursing staff, of challenging the system and of learning the "rudiments of music"—was both exhilarating and liberating. It was, in all senses, a "rite of passage." Tuberculosis saved him from fighting and, even as it threatened his life, it possibly saved him.

The regret at having to leave is obvious in his comment: "The hospital became like a school to me and it was a hard thing to be fired from a hospital and being a patient who was actually not cured." [36] At the same time, there is an understandable anger in his voice as he notes that this was, for Gaston, a death sentence. As he also told Vivian Perlis, "Harold was actually on his way. When I came back three months after that he was dead. And all of this was really completely needless, it was murder, actually, 'cause the doctor knew he wasn't gonna live. So, I'm getting more and more radicalized." [37]

From the hospital, Russell returned to work and to the jazz clubs of Cincinnati and Kentucky. In the hospital, he had written his first composition, "New World" and he sold it to A. B. Townsend, leader of the house band at the Cincinnati Cotton Club. Around this time, Nadi Qamar, who had been living in Los Angeles, returned to Cincinnati. Some fifty-plus years later, Qamar recalled playing with "one of his [Russell's] small bands on Central Avenue in Downtown Cincinnati Ohio."

Interviewed by Ben Young in 1998 for a programme dedicated to Russell, Qamar's memories were still quite clear, "We didn't really play anything together until I went to the West Coast. I was out there for a while and met Charles Mingus and, when I came back to visit my mother in Ohio, we got together and started doing some things around Cincinnati, Ohio—not too many." [38] What surprises most of all is what he appears to be saying about Russell's music back in Cincinnati.

> When I saw him again, he was, to me, he was totally into himself. He wasn't playing drums with other people's music, he was playing with his own quintet or writing, when I saw him

again. But he was very open too. You could bring in arrangements and the band would try 'em out. You know, like that he was really into himself, what he wanted to do and what he wanted to write. To me, he remained that way all through the years.[39]

Qamar continued in his interview with Young to suggest that Russell's music, even then, involved "very complex rhythms and scales and harmonic clusters."

Russell also told Ian Carr about the period after his hospitalization:

**GR:** And [I] concentrated on writing when I came out of the hospital because then I had found something that I knew I could do well, you know.
**IC:** What? Arranging?
**GR:** Arranging, composing . . .
**IC:** How long did it take you to realize that you could do them well? I mean . . .
**GR:** Well, right away, because when I wrote my first arrangement, I wrote it in the hospital with no piano and the person who got the arrangement he bought it, you know. So that . . . that was always a sign that you were doing something right, if they paid you, you know.[40]

By this point, Russell had clearly advanced considerably as a musician and as a composer/arranger. Qamar's comments are of interest because they suggest a more consistent and coherent history of Russell's musical development than he himself offered. Clearly, Harold Gaston's help was significant and seemed to trigger an advance in Russell's confidence and competence. With that encouragement, building no doubt upon his studies at Wilberforce, Russell had sold his first composition. What is more, it was barely five years later that Russell composed the remarkably advanced "Cubano-Be, Cubano-Bop" for Dizzy Gillespie and two years later the even more startling "A Bird in Igor's Yard" for Buddy DeFranco.

By this point, around 1943, Russell had begun to outgrow Cincinnati. His first break came through bandleader and saxophonist Benny Carter, as he told Ian Carr, "It was a time when drummers were scarce and Benny Carter came through and he had heard about my drumming. He hired me."[41]

Trombonist J. J. Johnson was Russell's roommate and they quickly became friends. Russell told me of one occasion when he and Johnson missed the whole first set of a gig. They had been smoking marijuana and were completely stoned. One of the band had needed to deputize for Russell, and Carter, by all accounts a tolerant man, was understandably unhappy.[42]

The tour took in New York and Russell heard bebop for the first time in the clubs of Manhattan and, as a drummer, he was particularly struck by the playing of Max Roach.

"There was a new music developing on 52nd Street and it was bebop. I went down to the street and heard this really fantastic music. And the drummer was Max Roach. I'm looking at Max and he just moved his wrist and got all this energy and I had to really swing to get all that, to really fire up a big band, a professional big band."[43]

Of his own playing at the time, Russell recalled later for WGBH Boston, "I could play time really beautifully but I wasn't a show drummer. I couldn't throw the sticks. I wasn't a great solo drummer. There was this exciting music on 52nd Street and I remember going down to hear Dizzy and Bird and Max and I heard Max play and I said, 'There's a drummer. There's really a drummer.'" [44]

While Russell enjoyed the experience of playing gigs like the Apollo Theatre in Harlem, he noted to Vivian Perlis that he felt, for the first time, "a disenchantment with drums."

It seemed that Benny Carter had a similar disenchanting experience on that tour.

During that tour in Boston, Benny called me in and said, "I hate to tell you this but I found a drummer." *(laughs)* I was shocked in a way and relieved in a way. I was tired of carrying those drums around. I said, "Who's the drummer?" He said, "Max Roach." *(laughs)* So that was just about the beginning of my writing career. [45]

And:

Benny called me into the room at the Apollo Theatre in Harlem, where we were, and he said, "George, I have to give you two weeks' notice. *(laughs)* I've a new drummer coming in." He'd been to 52nd Street, heard Max play and knew that he had to have that drummer—and I agreed with him! *(laughs)* Once I heard Max I realized I'd never be anywhere near as good a drummer as him. [46]

Asked about Benny Carter, he says, "I didn't really know Benny. We weren't chummy. He wanted a job done. He wanted it done well and with me he wanted it done well enough to get by. And I did that. I filled that spot for the time he needed me and I agreed with him with the two weeks' notice." [47]

The band played the Howard Theatre in Washington and two weeks later Roach took over the drum chair. Russell did the only thing he could. He headed home. "I got out as fast as I could and took the train back home and began to do what I should be doing, which was write. I started writing, then, maybe the first day I got back home." [48]

And to Perlis:

So after the two weeks at the Howard, I left and went back to Cincinnati and dove headfirst into writing music, and actually writing for the Benny Carter Orchestra, the piece was called "New World." I didn't know when or where I'd see him. And then I also started playing with a band around. First this "New World" piece, I tried it out with the band at the Cotton Club and it sounded great. So I said, "I'll put a big band arrangement on this for Benny Carter." [49]

Though aware of the new jazz being played in New York, there was one particular tune he had heard on the radio that encapsulated these developments for Russell. That tune was Thelonious Monk's "Round Midnight." He later told Ian Carr that it was this song that had made him want to head for the Big Apple. "That struck me as incredibly . . . as an incredibly profound new piece of music or new music, you know." [50]

There was also one particular incident that subsequently precipitated his leaving Cincinnati, heading first to Chicago and then to New York. That incident seemed to crystallize all his negative feelings towards his home town. A young white bass player called Fitz had arrived in the town, had lodged with Bessie Russell and her son and sometimes played in a trio with Russell and Qamar at a downtown club with mainly white clientele.

> One night this guy comes down and sits in with us and he said he noticed two rather big men in the back of the club, white men. He wondered why they were watching him. This is all because he was living with us. One night after we had packed up, Fitz was taken out by these two guys that were Cincinnati police detectives and about four in the morning there was a knock on the door ... about four or five ... a kind of weak knock on the door, and there before you stood the most bloody, beaten person. He said, "They threatened to throw me in the river." He said, "They kept asking me ..."—they asked him either whether he was black or white. He said, "I'm white." [51]

Russell and Nadi Qamar tried to raise this issue within the community and in wider Cincinnati but without success. As he told Vivian Perlis about this "ghastly story," "Incidents happened, not really worth discussing, made me realize I had to get out of Cincinnati. The hatred there was just unbelievable." [52]

Speaking to me in 2003, Russell remembered, "Cincinnati got to be unliveable, so I went to Chicago and started out playing with a band in Chicago—the Paradise Ballroom Band—and that held me over. That was maybe three or four months later that Benny came through Chicago, where I was living at the time. I told him I had worked on a piece for the band. He took the band down in the basement of the theatre and said, 'George has a piece. Let's hear it.' It was called 'New World.' He bought it. He loved the piece. He didn't give me a lot of money but I was off to writing." [53]

It was the same tune he had already sold to A. B. Townsend. According to Russell, "New World" in this incarnation "was rather impressionistic, beautiful chords and put together in a nice way. Benny liked it and gave me $25.00 for it! I was living with a girl in Chicago and that helped enormously." [54]

In fact, Russell kept on rearranging that piece and selling it to a number of different band leaders, including Cab Calloway, Earl Hines and Dizzy Gillespie. Fortunately for Russell, none of the four or more bands to whom he sold the piece recorded it. Had they done so, not only would his subterfuge have been exposed but a valuable source of income would have been lost!

> I sold that piece many times. That piece kept me alive when I went back to New York. Because we didn't have any money. Three of us lived in a hotel room in Harlem on 125th Street and Lennox Avenue. We had gotten out of Chicago and were living in New York but it got more and more difficult because we were barely surviving. But we made it in our own way. [55]

In late 1944-early 1945 and still in Chicago, Russell got work writing for Earl Hines.

They had opened up a new club at the big hotel there on 63rd Street in what was then the black community of Chicago, right in the centre. They were presented by the Panther Room of the Hotel Shermann in downtown Chicago, which was at the time mostly a white audience, and they had a show. It was opening night and it [the club and the scene in Chicago] was mostly run by gangsters and they [Hines and his manager] asked me to write music for the show. I took from here to there. I stayed up four nights—took from this thing and that thing, a little Debussy, a little Ravel—and wrote the show music. The point was, I was really tired. I didn't go to bed for four nights—but I wasn't the only one who was tired because when the band started playing the music it sounded absolutely ridiculous, just terrible. For one hour, with the gangsters looking on. It was one day before the club opened but they were looking a little angry, I should say. One good thinking person in the band said, "What key is this in?" Well, the copyist had put the wrong key signature. I was really worried, because those guys were for real. We played the music and it was beautiful enough to get a very good review in a Chicago newspaper. I think it was the *Tribune*. [56]

Russell told the story slightly differently to Ian Carr. In that telling the "lavish nightclub" was the El Grotto in the Hotel Pershing, and it was an uptown take on the downtown, white Panther Room. This would be the correct version. The Hotel Sherman was on Clerk and Randolph. The Hotel Pershing was on 64th and Cottage Grove. Hines took his band into the El Grotto in early March 1945, prior to which he was on tour. [57]

Russell described the initial rehearsal as being like "a combination of Webern, Ran Blake and Charles Ives" and says that it was the longest hour of his life as the gangster owners looked on. The copyist had transposed the music correctly but had failed to put the transposed key signatures required by different instruments on the sheets. [58]

The point he makes about Debussy and Ravel is important to note. Speaking to Ian Carr, Russell is quite specific about the influence and refers to the Debussy's *Nocturnes* (1897–99), an orchestral piece in three sections, which Russell names correctly as "Nuages," "Fêtes," and "Sirenes." Just two years after his discharge from the hospital, this was clearly quite sophisticated music. By this point, he was already drawing upon an unusual range of sources and upon music to which Nadi Qamar had introduced him in his teens.

It is worth taking a moment to consider what Russell might have heard in this suite that he could use as a jazz composer. Debussy's concern was to convey ordinary, everyday emotions—the feeling one might get watching clouds, for example ("Nuages")—primarily using the tone colours and harmonies of an orchestra or a single instrument. The second section of *Nocturnes* draws on Gamelan and uses a pentatonic scale in its simple tune. That section is also rather static in the way the orchestra is used, with only flute and harp suggesting movement. Key centres are implied rather than fixed in Debussy's music and he tends to use muted brass to create softer textures. Then there is Debussy's extensive use of percussion, almost to the point, in "Fetes," of suggesting a sense of swing. He also used percussion to create additional colours and textures. [59] Considered in this way, it is not hard to understand what composers such as Duke Ellington, Billy Strayhorn, Gil Evans and Russell might have found in the music of Debussy and Ravel. Their ability to use the resources of a jazz orchestra in similar ways could and did open up new possibilities in jazz. And in Russell's case such possibilities coincided with how he came to understand the relationship between chords and scales and the different ways of using time in music.

So, as Russell would later explain to Ian Carr, he now felt ready for the Big Apple. "And that was it, you know. Then I had my ticket, you know." For many musicians of his generation, New York was the big pull, and, like them, Russell was willing to accept any amount of hardship to try and make it in what had become the home of the new jazz era.

> Then after hanging around Chicago for a year, and I had heard a little bebop when I was in New York with Benny, but I had two young friends, Little Diz and Little Bird—Robert Gay and Henry Pryor—and they played Bird and Monk until I really heard it. And especially Monk I heard. Then I said, "It's time to move on to New York." So, we had fifteen dollars between us and we all jumped on a bus for New York.[60]

## Notes

1. Interview with Dwight McPheeters, June 2004.
2. Interview with George Russell, June 2003.
3. Ibid.
4. Ibid.
5. Nelson Burton, *My Life in Jazz* (Cincinnati, OH: Clifton Hills Press, 2000), p. 33.
6. Ibid.
7. Interview with Robert Moore, July 2004.
8. Interview with G. Russell, June 2003.
9. Interview with Moore.
10. Interview with G. Russell, June 2003.
11. Vivian Perlis, interview with George Russell, American Music Series, December 8, 1993, Oral History Project of American Music, sponsored and supported by the National Endowment for the Arts Special Jazz Projects.
12. Letter from Bessie O. Russell to Mr. B. H. Heard, March 3, 1941.
13. Ian Carr, interview with George Russell, June 1992; also interview with G. Russell, June 2003.
14. Interview with G. Russell, June 2003.
15. Carr, interview with G. Russell, June 1992.
16. Robert E. Moore, "George Alan Russell: Jazz's First Theorist," *Trotter Institute Review* 2 (Summer 1988): 18.
17. Carr, interview with G. Russell, June 1992.
18. Ibid. Horace, Fletcher's brother, formed the Collegians, and Benny Carter was also in the orchestra at that time as Russell rightly notes. Fletcher, however, attended Clark University and then took his masters at Columbia in chemistry. However, he found his job prospects in chemistry to be very restricted due to his race and turned to music for a living. (See Frank Driggs, liner notes in *The Fletcher Henderson Story*, Columbia CL419.) Coleman Hawkins attended Washburn College. See J. Chilton, *Song of the Hawk* (London: Quartet, 1990).
19. Carr, interview with G. Russell, June 1992.
20. Ibid.
21. Interview with George Russell, June 2004.
22. Carr, interview with G. Russell, June 1992.
23. Interview with George Russell, October 2003.
24. *George Russell—A Jazz Portrait*, WGBH Radio, Boston.

25. Interview with G. Russell, June 2004.
26. Ibid.
27. Ibid.
28. Carr, interview with G. Russell, June 1992.
29. Interview with G. Russell, June 2004.
30. Burton, *My Life in Jazz*, p. 62. Although Burton is wrong regarding when penicillin was discovered, which was in 1928, the drug was not synthesized effectively until the late thirties or available in injectable form until 1941. (See R. Bud, *Penicillin—Triumph and Tragedy* [Oxford: Oxford University Press, 2007].)
31. Interview with G. Russell, June 2003.
32. Interview with G. Russell, June 2004.
33. Joseph Campbell, *The Hero with a Thousand Faces* (London: Fontana, 1993); Frank J. Sulloway, *Freud, Biologist of the Mind* (London: Fontana, 1980), p. 447.
34. Frank J. Sulloway, *Freud, Biologist of the Mind*. Bungay, Suffolk: Fontana, 1980, p.446.
35. Ian Carr, *George Russell—The Invisible Guru*, BBC Radio 3 broadcast, July– August 1994.
36. Interview with G. Russell, June 2003.
37. Perlis, interview with G. Russell.
38. Ben Young, interview with Nadi Qamar, WKCR Radio, New York, 1998. See also Dom Cerulli, "George Russell," *DownBeat*, May 29, 1958. Discussing his second hospitalization, Russell states, "I had experimented scantily with polytonality before but on the piano in the library of the hospital, I really began an intensive research into tonality." This suggests a greater degree of continuity in Russell's musical development than the composer has sometimes acknowledged and provides some confirmation of Qamar's recollections.
39. Young, interview with Qamar.
40. Carr, interview with G. Russell, June 1992.
41. Carr, interview with G. Russell, June 1992; interview with Moore.
42. Russell told this story over dinner in a club in Boston in October 2003 in my presence.
43. Perlis, interview with G. Russell.
44. *George Russell—A Jazz Portrait*.
45. Ibid.
46. Interview with G. Russell, October 2003. Interestingly, J. J. Johnson described Russell as "a fine big-band drummer, with excellent time and imagination." See Burt Korall, "Who Is George Russell?" *DownBeat*, February 16, 1961.
47. Interview with G. Russell, October 2003.
48. Ibid.
49. Perlis, interview with G. Russell.
50. Carr, interview with G. Russell, June 1992.
51. Interview with G. Russell, June 2003.
52. Perlis, interview with G. Russell.
53. Ibid.
54. Interview with G. Russell, October 2003.
55. Ibid.
56. Ibid.
57. Charles A. Sengstock *That Toddlin' Town: Chicago's White Bands and Orchestras*, (Urbana and Chicago: University of Illinois Press 2004), p.177; wardellgray.org.
58. Carr, interview with G. Russell, June 1992.
59. See, for example, D. J. Grout and C. V. Palisca, *A History of Western Music* (New York: Norton, 1996), pp. 681–82; also K. Anderson, sleeve notes for Debussy—Prélude à l'après-midi d'un faune, Nocturnes, La Mer (1990), Naxos CD 8.550262.
60. Carr, interview with G. Russell, June 1992. Robert Gay was brother of the famous Chicago gospel trio, The Gay Sisters, who performed with Mahalia Jackson and who had a hit record with "God Will Take Care of You" in 1951. Robert Gay played trumpet, hence the nickname,

and later played with Dizzy Gillespie and Sonny Rollins. See Mark Burford, *Mahalia Jackson and the Black Gospel Field*, (New York, NY: Oxford University Press, 2019), p.117; Henry Pryor was probably Henry Lee Pryor and is referred to by pianist Sadik Hakim as a "great unknown saxophonist" in an interview for *Jazz Journal International*. Hakim notes that Pryor was "killed by police while breaking into a church to get money for dope. See Sadik Hakim, "Reflections of an Era: My Experiences with Bird and Prez," *Jazz Journal International* [London], Vol. 49, No. 8, August 1996, p.18. See also, "Shot to death trying to loot S. Side church," *Chicago Tribune*, April 24, 1951, p.5.

CHAPTER FOUR

# New York, N.Y. or In Search of the Lost Chord

It was May 1945, the war was still on, bebop was at its height in New York, and George Russell and his two friends Little Bird and Little Diz had just arrived in the city. With fifteen dollars in their collective pocket, they faced a simple choice. Two of them could get a room but the third was out on the streets. So they moved into the Hotel Barada, right behind the Apollo at 125th Street and 7th Avenue and Russell would sneak in after dark to share the room. After a week the money had run down to five dollars and, to make it last, they moved into a cheaper room at the Braddock Hotel, on 134th Street, one without windows. It was high summer, which in New York is about as humid and sticky as it gets in the Northern Hemisphere and Russell decided he would be more comfortable sleeping in nearby Gracie Park.[1]

In the telling, Russell made it all sound quite jolly, one of those experiences that was hell at the time but looking back was character-forming. The trio ate at a local Catholic Mission for fifty cents. Then, even that got too expensive. But Russell, always very fastidious about his personal hygiene, was able to keep himself clean by using the rest rooms of a nearby hotel.

> Mrs. Kramer was a lady who owned some big hotels in town and what she must have thought of people like me, down-and-outers, who would use those lovely lush bathrooms. So you could stay clean, scrape a little here and there and eat at the automat. About the third night, I began to realize that I wasn't up for this kind of adventure for too long.[2]

Back in Ohio, it must have been late 1942 or more likely 1943, Russell had gone to Dayton to see the Duke Ellington Band. Several of the musicians could not find a hotel, due to "colour bar" problems, and so Russell invited Ray Nance, Betty Roche, Al Hibbler and Skippy Williams to stay at his home with the redoubtable and always welcoming Bessie. Now in New York, Russell was able to call in a favour.

> And Skippy said, 'If you're ever down and out in New York, give me a call.' That's what I did. He said, 'George, I remember you, come on over.' I stayed with him and took my arrangement of 'New World' over to Dizzy. He said, 'I'm glad to get this because I'm starting a big band now, I'll try this.' They tried it and Dizzy gave me like $25 or $30. [3]

In fact, Russell has telescoped events slightly here. By other accounts he has given, to Ian Carr and to me, he had by that point met up with Max Roach. The drummer seems to have adopted Russell as a protégé and introduced him to Bird, Diz and everyone on "the Street." As he said in another interview, "When I was in New York with Skippy, I don't know what got into Max, because he didn't have to do it, but he introduced me to everybody as an arranger."[4] It was Roach's introduction and the credibility that went with that that provided Russell with the opportunity to sell Gillespie "New World," and, as Russell remembers, "it was kind of my passport into the group of musicians that were doing this fantastic . . . that were part of this incredible revolution."[5]

What is striking about Russell's account, and that of others such as Gil Evans and Gerry Mulligan, is the openness of that group.[6] Bebop was a virtuoso music, rhythmically and harmonically adventurous and often played at breakneck tempos that discouraged all but the most confident and able. Yet, despite the cool, the hip vernacular, the drugs, the clothes and the attitude—all meant to exclude the straight world—genuine ability, black or white, was welcomed. As Russell noted, "The one entrée to the group was talent. So people who later on were talented were welcomed."[7] And musicians shared their ideas and knowledge, which was great for someone like the twenty-two-year-old Midwesterner, as Russell told Carr: "It didn't last but it was the prevailing feeling at the time, a feeling of great openness, you know."[8]

Much of that spirit Russell attributes to Charlie Parker. "I don't know what the cause of that was particularly, but, one thing, it was like Charlie Parker was the centre of that. And I think it was his spirit, and generous spirit, that encouraged very much this community feeling around what was happening mainly because of him."[9]

Though not much, back then the money from selling "New World" was enough to get Russell his own room.

> With the money, I moved to my own place on 48th near 6th Avenue, just one room. There's all these guys working the Street, nobody had thought to rent a room or anything. I had Bird in my room, well, a lot of other people too. The landlady was going crazy. She said, 'I don't like all of those strange people coming in here.' I said, 'They're just like me.' *(laughs)* I think she didn't know I was black or something. [10]

Although he had only been "on the Street" a few months, Russell had by now met

Miles Davis as well and, by his account, had been invited to join Charlie Parker's quintet on drums. His room on 48th Street was used by just about everyone playing the clubs around 52nd Street. Charlie Parker would come by between sets to cook up and shoot heroin.

> Bird used to ask me, "George, do you want some of this [Heroin]?" I said, "Bird, I don't think I can take it." He said, "Okay." I knew that people like Fats Navarro—talented people—losing a hundred pounds in weight and just getting eaten up from the inside with these drugs, and Bird himself. Dizzy stayed pretty free of that, though. I just knew that I didn't have the stamina to take that. Something wanted more of me than to just come have a nice time, an interesting time for half a life, and die. [11]

Russell did, however, drink quite heavily during the forties and fifties. He was never an alcoholic but attitudes toward alcohol were somewhat different back then. According to Russell's wife, Alice, he told her that he would open a fifth of scotch in the morning and drink his way through it during the day. In the evening, he would go to a club and drink some more. He also smoked a pipe despite having had tuberculosis. Again, the association between tobacco and health problems was less well known then. And Russell also enjoyed smoking pot. Dwight McPheeters remembered a car ride up to Harlem with Russell and some other guys.

> I remember when I was going to photo school in New York, George asked me if I wanted to go up Minton's Playhouse and so I said, "Yes." So I jumped in this car with George and about three or four other guys and it was really cold and they had all the windows shut. Even with all these guys in the car and the car would heat up with all these bodies in it but they wanted the windows shut. The reason why they wanted the windows shut was because they didn't want the smell of pot to get out onto the street. George asked me, "You coppin'?" I said, "Uh-uh!" I got a big headache out of it, that's all, so I never got into pot. I smoked a lot of cigarettes in my life but I tried smoking pot once but it did nothing for me. [12]

Russell seems to have got on particularly well with Miles Davis. Davis, was three years his junior and, still a student at Juilliard, was playing in Charlie Parker's quintet at night.

> Miles and I hit it off really good. He'd invite me to a one-room apartment, in the West Nineties or something, and we'd sit down and play chords. He liked my harmonic sense and I loved his harmonic sense and we tried to see what kind of chords we'd come up [with]. [13]

It was in the course of one such visit to Davis's apartment and one such conversation that Russell discovered his course in life. Russell has told this story many times over the years. It has become one of those little legends or myths, true though it may be, that life and jazz thrive upon, almost acquiring a Zenlike truth, a story that encapsulates something universal. [14]

We were having a session, you know, where musicians trade off ideas. He'd play a chord, "How do you like that?" "I like that." I played some chords and he, I think he liked my harmonic sense, and, of course, he was extraordinary, you know. But I said, "What's your aim musically, what do you really wanna do?" And he said, "I wanna learn all the changes." [15]

Knowing that Davis was already a highly gifted melodic improviser whose grasp of the changes was second to none, Russell was presented with a paradox. "I think everybody then who knew about Miles knew he knew how to play the changes. So it occurred to me to look for a new way to relate to chords." [16]

In 1958, Davis was interviewed by Nat Hentoff for *Jazz Review*. In the interview, he spoke of his dissatisfaction with the then dominant approach based upon chord changes in jazz. It is clear from their discussion just how much the trumpeter had taken from Russell regarding other ways of approaching harmony and melody. As he noted, "Bill Evans knows too what can be done with scales. All chords, after all, are relative to scales and certain chords make certain scales."

What follows in the interview is a neat summation by Davis of the practicalities of a modal approach in opening up jazz improvisation.

When you go this way, you can go on forever. You don't have to worry about changes and you can do more with the line. It becomes a challenge to see how melodically inventive you are. When you're based on chords, you know at the end of 32 bars that the chords have run out and there's nothing to do but repeat what you've just done – with variations. I think a movement in jazz is beginning away from the conventional string of chords and a return to emphasis on melodic rather than harmonic variation. There will be fewer chords but infinite possibilities as to what to do with them. [17]

For some reason Russell was unable to keep the apartment on 48th, probably because he could not make the rent. So he moved in with a couple of other musicians who had a place over on the West Side of Manhattan, around the Seventies. "We lived on Cream of Wheat every morning. We lived on Riverside Drive in a huge apartment but we didn't have any money. I remember laying out in the sun one day on Riverside Drive and this big [gurgling] in my chest started." [18]

Russell had already been to the doctor with a nagging cough that had been diagnosed as a "bad cold." It was, however, his uncured tuberculosis flaring up and that gurgling sensation was "a haemorrhage coming on." [19]

It was, by now, late summer of 1945. In just a few months in the city, Russell had established himself within that group of musicians who were shaping the new jazz but now he was really in a bad way. He was admitted to St. Joseph's Hospital in the Bronx and that was to be his home for the next fifteen months. This time there was no private room and this time the nurses—mainly elderly nuns—reserved their hands for more strictly medical procedures. With fifteen chronically and critically ill men on the ward, Russell would turn over in his corner bed, face the wall and go deep inside his own thoughts. And that puzzle that Davis had set for him kept coming back to him.

I went to the hospital at 143rd and Brook Avenue, St. Joseph's and it was a very dreary Catholic hospital. At the first opportunity I got a chance—it was a room with fifteen patients—I got a chance to get a bed in a corner where I had no one next to me, at least on one side, and made a little cosy pad for myself and then focused on what Miles had said— he'd wanted to learn all the changes. So I had a lot of time in bed to think about it. In the meantime, they are coming and visiting me, Dizzy, Miles, Max, which was nice, and J. J. I reasoned that if there just could be a scale that sounded, projected the sound of a chord and not in the way the major scale projects the sound of a C-major chord. The scale of an almost harmonic unity.[20]

Or as he told Ian Carr,

Traditional music [theory] gave us the key signature and from this arbitrary key signature it builds chords up from the tonic. I had a feeling that there must be another way to approach playing chordally, that's all. And the first impression I got was that for every chord there had to be a scale that sounded a unity with that chord and that, more so than any other scale, it projected the sound of that chord.[21]

The first six months in hospital involved complete bed rest, but, after those six months, Russell was able to get up and, using the piano in the solarium, began to test his ideas. Unfortunately for the other patients who had nowhere else to go, those experiments involved fairly interminable explorations of the C-major chord, the C-major scale and the latter with a raised fourth. After a couple of days of this, the patients revolted and started hurling the remains of the lunchtime meal and their loved ones' gifts of grapes and other fruit in Russell's direction. Fortunately, one of the sisters of mercy came to his—or rather, his fellow patients'—aid and moved him into the library, where he could experiment to his heart's desire.

In repeatedly playing these scales, it was as if Russell was engaged in a scientific experiment, weighing notes against each other, examining sounds and tones in the most minute detail and testing their correspondence to each other. Again speaking with Ian Carr, he explained how his thinking developed.

And I finally decided that the major scale just doesn't cut it. It doesn't make it, you know. It doesn't sound a unity with its major chord. And then I began to look for reasons why it didn't. And then I found it wasn't a ladder of fifths. It wasn't a ladder of perfect fifths like the Lydian on the tonic, because the Lydian did sound a unity. But the major scale always sounded this effortful feeling of striving for the tonic, striving to become a unity.[22]

To his apparent surprise, as he told Vivian Perlis, the G-major scale with its first tetra chord (i.e. G-A-B-C) actually sounded "closer to the tonality of a C-major chord than the C-major scale." And, as a result of his experiments, he concluded,

I said, "I don't care what anybody says; this isn't just the Lydian mode of the G-major scale, this is the C-Lydian scale, the closest scale to the C-major chord."[23]

That is, drawing upon the circle of fifths – C, G, D, A, E, B, F♯/G♭, C♯/D♭, A♭, E♭, B♭, F – Russell's research led him to the conclusion that the Lydian scale, containing the raised fourth (F♯), was a better expression of the C major triad (C-E-G) than the C major scale. [24]

Russell expressed this concisely and eloquently in the 1959 edition of the Lydian Concept, in relation to the emergence of the major scale in Western music,

> The major scale probably emerged as the predominating scale of Western music, because within its seven tones lies the most fundamental harmonic progression of the classical era... the tonic major chord on C... the subdominant major chord on F... the dominant seventh chord on G—thus, the major scale *resolves* to its tonic major chord. The Lydian scale *is* the sound of its tonic major chord. [25]

Russell would use the term "chord-mode" to define this relationship between a chord and the scale it expressed.

Providing a simple, lay explanation of the Lydian Concept is not easy. However, in a wide-ranging article on the Lydian Chromatic Concept, "Born out of jazz...Yet embracing all music," Professor Eric Porter provides a useful description,

> The Concept is a theory that allows an improviser or composer to identify a series of scales that can be used to express a chord or other harmonic framework (e.g., a series of resolving chords or the key of a piece of music). [26]

From his starting point with the C Lydian Scale, Russell goes on to identify "parent scales" that best express other chord values, for example a minor seventh chord. In turn, five additional scales, identified by Russell, may be used by the composer or improviser, alone or together, "to express any chord or harmonic framework, although they do so with increasing dissonance." [27] The value of the Concept lies in the scope it grants an improviser in terms of their note selection, as Porter explains,

> Thus Russell's system ultimately allows an improvising musician to play any note in the tempered scale, although one is to do so while maintaining an awareness of the "tonal gravity" (i.e., the relative relationship to the parent scale) of the notes one is playing. [28]

In other words, all twelve tones were available in the chromatic scale - hence, the use of the term 'chromatic' in the title of Russell's book, *Lydian Chromatic Concept of Tonal Organization*.

In this sense, the Concept offers a qualified freedom to musician and composer. It is both highly practical and non-prescriptive. It increases the range of musical choices for improviser and composer and, perhaps most importantly, it was based on observation of the actual practice of jazz musicians. Focusing on the functionality of the Lydian Concept, Ian Carr offers a helpful summation,

> The basic point about this concept is that it encourages improvisers to convert chord

symbols into the scales that best convey the sound of the chords. The next stage is the idea of the superimposition of one scale on another, which leads to pan-tonality, the presence of more than one key centre, but occurring within a dominant tonality. In other words, the music is not atonal (in no particular key), but it can accommodate some polytonality. [29]

Carr goes on to quote Russell himself, who emphasises that "jazz is a music rooted in folk scales." The implication of this is that atonality, the negation of tonal centres simply would not, for example, support the blues scale, so important to jazz, with its implied tonic centre. [30]

The notion of 'tonal gravity' has been central to Russell's thinking from the late forties onwards. As Andy Wasserman, an ex-student of Russell and now himself a teacher of the Lydian Concept puts describes the idea on his website,

Tonal gravity is the heart of the Lydian Chromatic Concept. Simply put, the basic building block of tonal gravity is the interval of the perfect fifth.

And:

Since the interval of the perfect fifth is the building block of tonal gravity, a seven-tone scale created by successive fifths establishes the most vertically unified harmonic order whereby the gravity falls down each fifth back to the singular Lydian tonic. [31]

Hence, the Lydian scale takes the seven ascending consecutive intervals of the circle of fifths – C, G, D, A, E, B, F# - and arranges these within a single octave. [32]

Russell has told a number of interviewers over the years – Ian Carr, Vivian Perlis, Ingrid Monson and myself, amongst others - that, early on in his researches, he was already aware that his ideas challenged traditional Western musical theory or at least its ubiquity and that it represented, if not new knowledge, knowledge that had been lost. At this point, however, while emphasising intuition against (or at least as much as) intellect and that his discovery was rooted in nature, Russell turned to physics and mathematics for a scientific basis to the Concept.

In this respect and as an autodidact in this regard at least, Russell seems to have drawn upon discussions with a scientist friend, George Endrey. [33] The desire to locate the theory within the field of physics is understandable given the period. When Russell first developed his ideas, physics was very much the dominant field of scientific research. Russell's argument was that, since gravity affects all things in the universe, music and tones must therefore be similarly subject to the laws of physics.

I do not wish to make too much of this point but it does raise questions regarding Russell's scientific claims for the Concept. Here we must note that, while Russell appended the words "for Improvisation" to his book's title in the earlier 1959 edition, the final 2001 edition was subtitled, "The Art and Science of Tonal Gravity." Indeed, Russell always thought of the Concept in these terms. Russell was incorrect in his understanding of gravity.

In fact, tones, as sounds, are not affected by gravity at all. Two tones emitted from the same source and location but at different high and low frequencies may sound different. It may appear that they come from different points. However, these occupy the same area in space. Sound itself remains entirely unaffected by the force of gravity. In space, no one can hear you scream. [34] Any scientific explanation for 'tonal gravity' is more likely to lie within the field of neuropsychology with its capacity to explain how our brains process music.

If, however, Russell's understanding of how science might offer validation for the Concept was flawed, the way Russell went about researching the relationship between chords and scales, as he has described to various interviewers, does have much in common with the way scientific (and social scientific) theories are tested. That is that an initial hypothesis is generated from observation and this is then tested in an attempt to disprove (rather than prove) the hypothesis. Should the hypothesis fail refutation, it can be accepted. [35]

Russell is also correct in his understanding of the relationship between music and mathematics. For example, in the 2001 edition of Russell's book, an ex-student Reed Gratz uses the frequency ratios for each of the twelve intervals of the chromatic scale to show "the strong relationship between the tonic note and the raised fourth," in contrast to the less strong relationship of the natural fourth. [36]

Moreover, as a descriptor or metaphor for the way we hear music in relation to the way other notes in a scale seem to be drawn to the tonic, the term 'tonal gravity' does have a value. Russell used the term helpfully as a means of describing what he saw as the three main approaches to jazz improvisation. Initially, these were "vertical" where tonal gravity is inferred by the chord and horizontal where tonal gravity is inferred by the scale. With the arrival on the scene of Ornette Coleman, he would add a third – "supra-vertical". The examples of musicians he employed to explain this idea were Coleman Hawkins (vertical), Lester Young (horizontal) and, again, Ornette Coleman (supra-vertical). [37] These are offered in his book both graphically and, by listening, to suggested examples one is able to hear the differences of approach Russell outlines.

Nor should Russell's error in terms of his understanding of physics detract from the wider intentions and implications of his project. Eric Porter quotes Ingrid Monson, herself an ex-student of Russell's, to show how this had a bi-polar focus that sought to bring together a command of musical theory, deriving from scientific and rationalist discourse, and romantic, artistic notions of soul and spiritual essence. Hence, "art" and "science".

Monson's point is highly important here. She stresses how African-American jazz musicians, (along with other African-American intellectuals, political and religious leaders) saw the struggle for emancipation in both political and spiritual terms. The latter is seen in the way that many black musicians turned to Islam, the likely religion of their forebears in West Africa, or looked further east to religions far older still. Whether seeking to locate musical practices scientifically or philosophically, musicians such as Russell and Coltrane shared, Monson argues, a wider determination to demonstrate and celebrate the validity and legitimacy of those practices against the racist tropes underpinning white ideas regarding jazz, whether those of white supremacists or more mainstream assumptions about black people. [38]

In his claims for the Concept, as both Porter and Monson show, Russell sought to retain romantic notions of music and art as spiritual transcendence but also to harness those notions to the "rationalist tools of music theory" [39] and, to what Porter calls, "black music technologies." [40] In so doing, Russell challenges racist ideas around jazz as a music of the unschooled. And, as Russell would tell *DownBeat* writer Burt Korall in a 1961 interview, "You can retain the funk." [41]

In fact, Russell went further and more articulately than many of his contemporaries in this regard. He was quite clear that he saw western musical theory as being restrictive of musical creativity and, as such, saw parallels in this regard with wider social and racial exclusions. While he accepted the primacy of equal temperament as the underpinning of all music, he argued that traditional musical theory was an ideological reflection of Western liberal values based upon rights of property and definitions of good and bad. In place of that ideology, Russell saw, or at least came to see, the Concept as reflecting a notion of music as a part of the natural world, perhaps one also unsullied such materialistic values. [42] In later years, Russell would come to relate his discovery to an even deeper and more personal view of the world and his – and others' – place in it, as he told Ian Carr,

> And that had something to do with, in a way, this feeling that had always bothered me about life, you know, that I was having to adopt a way of being and a way of thinking that was put on me by the church, by education, you know, that didn't conform to my essence.

And he added,

> I didn't make any philosophical associations with it early on, but I was very curious that the Lydian Scale was a ladder of fifths and the major scale wasn't. [43]

In the period between his 'discovery' and the first publication of the Lydian Chromatic Concept (1953), such considerations seem to have been at most embryonic in Russell's mind. His four/five years in Scandinavia in the 1960s and involvement in a Gurdjieffian circle in Norway were the factors that led to this way of thinking about music and its relationship to nature and the individual.

But, aside from such philosophical considerations, that conversation with Miles Davis around 1945 would, in turn, lead to a major shift or series of shifts in jazz practice. The process initiated that afternoon would take several years to unravel from Russell's hospitalisation, through the performance and recording of his piece "Cubano Be, Cubano Bop" (arguably the first modal composition in jazz), to the first and second publications of the *Lydian Chromatic Concept of Tonal Organisation* (1953 and 1959) to the later emergence of modal jazz as one of the major compositional, improvisational and educational approaches in jazz. And, in numerous ways, Russell's ideas have continued to influence jazz practice, if frequently under-acknowledged and with their greater potential to do so as yet unfulfilled.

As Russell later told Vivian Perlis, he was very lucky to survive. One of the other patients on the ward Russell befriended was Eddie Roane, a trumpeter who had played with Louis Jordan. Roane died of tuberculosis in Russell's arms. Apparently, at one point,

Russell himself was so ill that a priest came to give him the last rites; he shouted at him that he was an atheist and told him to get lost.[44] But those months in hospital were also both life-saving and life-affirming and, most significantly, transformative for his thinking about music and how to pursue his own musical goals.

Russell came out of hospital around Christmas 1946 and went to stay with Max Roach and his family. Keeping track of Russell's living arrangements from the late forties into the early fifties is a demanding activity in itself. However, for much of the next period, he lived variously with Roach and, at one point, with Roach's mother. Living conditions were quite squalid, according to Russell, but he was forever grateful for Roach's support and generosity. He was in all respects treated as a member of the family.

> Well, when I got out of the hospital, Max invited me to stay in Brooklyn with him and I stayed at his house on Monroe Street for about nine months. And it was back there, when you got out of hospital, there was a program in place run by the New York Welfare Department where you got subsidized and they even sent you to school or something. It's through that program that I started to study with Stefan Wolpe in New York. But they took care of the . . . you know, paying Mrs. Roach for my lodging and food. And so when I hear people put down the welfare system, you know, I think that's ridiculous because I know I'm a product of that.[45]

Stefan Wolpe was a German socialist composer who had worked with Hans Eisler and who fled his homeland in 1933 to escape Nazi persecution both as a socialist and a Jew. Having studied with Webern in Vienna, he went first to Palestine and then, in 1938, to New York. As a teacher, friend or colleague, Wolpe was a huge influence on the whole post-war generation of American composers, including Elliott Carter, John Cage (who was president of the Stefan Wolpe Society at one point), Morton Feldman, Christian Wolff and Milton Babbitt. Trumpeter John Carisi, arrangers Eddie Sauter and Bill Finnegan, clarinettist Tony Scott, and film composer Elmer Bernstein also studied with him.[46]

According to Austin Clarkson in his 2003 collection, *On The Music of Stefan Wolpe*, it was Gil Evans who suggested to Russell that he might study with Wolpe.[47] Gil Evans himself was not, apparently, one of Wolpe's students. However, as author Brigid Cohen has pointed out, Wolpe's significance for the group of jazz musicians clustered around Gil Evans was actually greater than just his role as teacher to Russell and a handful of other jazz musician/composers. In fact, he seems to have been, at least, an occasional member of the group that met and exchanged ideas in Evans' midtown apartment, while many of that group were often to be found at Wolpe's home. Indeed, through Wolpe, these musicians were connected with wider intellectual and avant-garde circles in New York. As Cohen has noted,

> His home was a rare space that drew the varied likes of Franz Kline, Gil Evans, Yoko Ono, George Russell, Willem and Elaine de Kooning, Leonard Meyer, Robert Creeley, and the Juilliard String Quartet.[48]

The attraction felt by these jazz musicians to Wolpe was reciprocated and it seems that their ideas may well have impacted on the composer. As Cohen argues, Wolpe's approach was dialogic. He would explore with students how his compositional and theoretical approaches might connect with their own.

> As Gil Evans reportedly put it, "You would go to [Wolpe] as a jazz arranger, and you would come back a jazz arranger."[..] Sustained by carefully preserved disciplinary and cultural distinctions (especially the difference between improvisation and non-improvisation), a crossover of attitudes and techniques flourished in these musicians' sound-worlds. [49]

What Russell drew from Wolpe was both the older man's life experience and his knowledge of contemporary music theory.

> He knew I was a kid who didn't know much about anything and didn't know a lot about life. My interest was in talking to him chiefly about life but I wanted to know his principal concepts of music. The two things that impressed me, that caused me to think in a new way, were his theory of the rate of chromatic circulation as a means of destroying any tonical integrity and the principle of the thirdless sound. [50]

In fact, in the interview above with Vivian Perlis, Russell is quite specific in identifying the *Jazz Workshop* album, "Lydian M-1," and *All About Rosie* as examples of compositions that used Wolpe's ideas. Along with a host of other composers and musicians, Russell also provided his comments for a centennial memorial publication on Wolpe. Even allowing for the fact that such remarks are invariably fulsome in their praise of the dear departed, Russell's final words are quite touching and seem to reflect very genuinely what the young man found in Wolpe at a more personal level.

> Wolpe's overall effect on me was immensely positive. I felt a living, breathing force in this man that was extremely life-positive. You couldn't be around him without that force entering you. To that extent Wolpe and the two principles that stuck with me and his forceful being are part of *me* now, and they always have been, and always will be. He's alive in those of us that he touched. [51]

As Brigid Cohen has argued,

> Russell studied Wolpe's post-tonal methods while developing his own. His modal jazz highlighted slow-moving, mode-based harmonies—usually articulated by drones and vamps—over which soloists could improvise drawing from an expanded harmonic vocabulary that included prominent non-triadic "thirdless sounds." These more open harmonic, textural, and rhythmic frameworks invited the allusions to non-Western sounds associated with the genre—exemplified as early as Russell's "CubanaBe/CubanaBop" and further elaborated in later works like John Coltrane's "India" and "Africa." [52]

However, Cohen actually goes further, suggesting that the "connections between

Wolpe's mid-century aesthetic and Russell's work exceed their similarity of harmonic language." Cohen cites, in particular, Wolpe's *Quartet for Saxophone, Trumpet, Percussion and Piano* (1950) as a specific example of their "deeper shared identifications," which "turned on questions of self-representation and human recognition." This is a very important insight into both Wolpe and Russell and their music. Both in different ways – Wolpe as a Jew, refugee and Marxist fleeing Nazi Germany and Russell an African-American growing up in segregated, Jim Crow America – had been denied their own humanity by oppressive regimes. And both in their respective ways would use their music to embody the "desire to self-represent and to be recognised." [53]

In fact, one way of understanding the work of composers and bandleaders such as Jelly Roll Morton, Duke Ellington, Billy Strayhorn, Benny Carter and others is to see this as the slow but steady reclaiming of the dignity and humanity of a people through the cultural achievements of jazz. This was all the more admirable given that this took place in spite of the violent, corrosive racism of many white Americans and the often primitivist and exoticist tropes placed on the music by would-be critics and supporters. If anything, bebop and its musicians merely made such claims explicit, as Russell,

> The legacy of bebop lay in its challenge to this whole feeling of blacks as an inferior intellect, you know...I think it was a very muscular drive that bebop represented. To convince – to try again to convince small-minded people that if have any kind of sensitivity at all, you can see that this music does not come from someone who lacks complexity. [54]

It will be apparent that Russell had used his first couple of years in New York, despite the inconvenience of severe illness, very purposefully. However, his activities to this point focused almost entirely on developing his own ideas. Max Roach might have introduced Russell to his peers as an "arranger". Yet, to date, his only contribution to the city's music had been a piece he had written back in Cincinnati in the hospital and had sold at least four or five times already. It was certainly too early for his Lydian Concept to have achieved anything other than "work in progress" status. A pattern had already emerged where Russell would compose only when he had someone or something to write for. Otherwise his work would, from this point on, focus on the Concept. However, now out of the hospital, Russell was about to produce something that would cement his reputation even outside the bebop inner circle.

> Dizzy approached me one day and he said that he was getting very interested in Afro-Cuban drumming and music, and there was this wonderful drummer in town, Chano Pozo, and he had a theme and maybe it would be possible for me to put a suite around it, you know, encompass it in a suite. And it was a beautiful theme. So it didn't take long for me to get the idea of what to do with it and the whole introduction then was modal. [55]

The use of modes had been around in jazz and in other musical forms for ages. However, what Russell did with "Cubano-Be, Cubano-Bop" was to use modes consciously and, through this and his subsequent work, both as a theorist and as a composer, he made the jazz community aware of modes and their potential in jazz. Also, as he himself put it,

"It was the first application of modality using the Concept. The 'Cubano-Be, Cubano-Bop' thing sort of got the reputation rolling." [56]

More than that, Afro-Cuban musical practice was well-suited to Russell's new approach, as Paul Austerlitz has noted,

> The static harmonies of Cuban music made their way into jazz through these compositions, influencing modal improvisation, which uses scales, rather than chords, as building blocks, and which became a standard technique in jazz beginning in the 1950s. [57]

Premiered at Carnegie Hall at a concert promoted by British-born critic Leonard Feather under the banner – "A Celebration of the New Jazz" on September 29, 1947, Russell conducted Dizzy Gillespie's Big Band in front of a capacity crowd. Charlie Parker played with Gillespie in a quintet at the same gig but sat in the audience for Russell, Gillespie, and Pozo's number and also for John Lewis's "Toccata for Trumpet." Ella Fitzgerald also sang with Gillespie and, as *DownBeat*'s headline put it, "Despite Bad Acoustics, Gillespie Concert Offers Some Excellent Music." Critic Michael Levin saw "Cubano-Be, Cubano-Bop" as a definite "stand-out," writing, "The crowd unquestionably liked the 'Cubano-Bop' number with its added bongo and congo [sic] drum soloists the best, illustrating a point the Beat has often made that there is much jazz can pick up on from the South American and Afro-Cuban rhythm styles." [58]

After Carnegie Hall, the band took the show up to Boston's Symphony Hall and Russell travelled with the band. He recalls that Chano Pozo was sitting at the back and began this African chanting. "I said, 'Dizzy, you know, you should open the whole middle section up, bring Chano out front, let him do this.' We built a whole thing out of it, you know." [59]

This account would seem to be confirmed by Gillespie in his autobiography, *To Be or Not To Bop* (2009). More importantly, when the Gillespie Orchestra came to record the piece, the chant section was at its heart. [60]

The African-American contingent in the audience, however, was embarrassed by this. Looking back on the incident, Russell identifies this as a consequence of the way black people were taught to be ashamed of their culture and later, in his conversation with Ian Carr, he related this directly to a process of ethnocentricity that is "literally messing up the planet,"

> The black people in the audience were very noticeable because they started to laugh when Chano came out on stage in his native costume. It's like Louis [Armstrong] when they sent him to Africa, you know. Louis said, 'Damn, these people really do climb trees like monkeys.' *(laughing)*" [61]

Whilst it is hard to know how far Russell and Gillespie articulated to themselves at the time their purpose in including this section in the performance, it does seem that their intention was to celebrate Africanness and the origins of jazz. For example, Gillespie's biographer, Alyn Shipton draws attention to the trumpeter's subsequent adoption of African clothes and stress upon the connections of his music with the "Afro-Cuban rhythmic tradition". Shipton clearly views this and Gillespie's other Afro-Cuban collaborations as the beginning of this process of Africanisation in Gillespie's work and life.[62] In a way, and several decades before Afrocentrism emerged as an important element in American education, it was clearly an attempt to say to an audience, "This is something special and something of which we should be proud." It was an early attempt to take a stereotype and transform it by framing it in a positive rather than a negative context. In a sense, it links with Russell's disagreement with his friend Dwight McPheeters over his playing Aunt Jemima in their school play *Gone with the Wind*.

Whatever the audience's reaction, "Cubano-Be, Cubano-Bop" was Russell's first significant contribution to jazz composition, and it remains a marvellous piece and was, as Gillespie noted, a wonderful collaborative effort. "That was a collaboration. That was a collaboration of all three. I think that was the most successful collaboration I've ever seen with three people. I can see what I wrote. I can see what George wrote and I can see the contribution of Chano Pozo and then George Russell came back and spread out what I had written and what Chano had done."[63] The fact that these three potentially disparate elements hang together so well is a tribute to Russell, as Gillespie appears to acknowledge in that last sentence.

Recorded in the studio on December 22, 1947, it remains a highly symphonic work, with "harshly incantatory ensemble passages," "its juxtaposition of very different textures and types of motion," and the "disconcertedly independent of convention" ways it used the "jazz orchestra's resources," as Max Harrison has noted. He adds, "It is consistent but accords with laws then unfamiliar."[64] Ingrid Monson's detailed analysis of the piece in the *International Dictionary of Black Composers* is also well worth reading by students of music. Her final paragraph, however, suffices for our purposes:

> Fifty years after its first performance, 'Cubano-Be, Cubano-Bop' remains a model of innovative writing for Big Band. Its collaborative genesis, a synthesis of Afro-Cuban rhythms and Bebop and its imaginative use of modes 12 years before the emergence of the term "modal jazz," collectively explain why George Russell must be included in the first rank of composers writing for jazz orchestra.[65]

Anyone doubting the significant advance represented by this piece should hear it followed by Gillespie and Pozo's "Manteca," written around that time and in a similar vein. However well this stands on its own, compared to "Cubano-Be, Cubano-Bop" it sounds frankly ordinary.[66]

## Notes

1. Vivian Perlis, interview with George Russell, American Music Series, December 8, 1993, Oral History Project of American Music, sponsored and supported by the National Endowment for the Arts Special Jazz Projects.
2. Ibid.
3. Ibid.
4. Carr, interview with G. Russell, June 1992.

5. Ibid.
6. Stephanie Stein Crease, Gil Evans—Out of the Cool (Chicago: A Cappella, 2002). See also M. Harrison, "Gerry Mulligan," in These Jazzmen of Our Time, ed. R. Horrocks (London: Jazz Book Club, 1959).
7. Interview with George Russell, October 2003.
8. Carr, interview with G. Russell, June 1992.
9. Ibid.
10. George Russell—A Jazz Portrait, WGBH Radio, Boston.
11. Interview with George Russell, June 2003.
12. Interview with Dwight McPheeters, June 2004.
13. Perlis, interview with G. Russell.
14. J. Campbell, The Hero with a Thousand Faces (London: Fontana, 1993).
15. Ian Carr, interview with George Russell for BBC Radio 3 broadcast The Trailblazer—George Russell, July 1994.
16. George Russell—A Jazz Portrait.
17. Nat Hentoff, "An Afternoon with Miles Davis," Jazz Review, Dec. 1958, p.12.
18. Perlis, interview with G. Russell.
19. George Russell—A Jazz Portrait.
20. Perlis, interview with G. Russell.
21. Carr, interview with G. Russell, June 1992.
22. Ibid.
23. Perlis, interview with G. Russell.
24. Porter, Eric "'Born out jazz...but embracing all music': Race, Gender, and Technology in George Russell's Lydian Chromatic Concept" in Rustin, Nichole. T. and Tucker, Sherrie Big Ears: Listening for Gender in Jazz Studies. (Durham, N.C.: Duke University Press, 2008), p.214; also Ingrid Monson, Freedom Sounds: Civil Rights Call Out to Jazz and Africa. (Oxford: OUP, 2007), p.288.
25. George Russell, The Lydian Chromatic Concept of Tonal Organization (New York, N.Y.: Concept 1959), p.xx
26. Porter op cit, p.214-215.
27. Porter op cit, p.215.
28. Ibid.
29. Carr, Ian; Fairweather, Digby; and Priestley, Brian, The Rough Guide to Jazz: The Essential Companion to Artists and Albums (London: Rough Guides, 2004), p.688.
30. Carr, ibid.
31. Andy Wasserman, https://andywasserman.com/music-theory/george-russell-s-lydian-chromatic-concept.
32. Ibid.
33. Notes to New York, N.Y. CD reissue Impulse IMP 12782.
34. M. Nelkon, Principles of Physics (Harlow, UK: Longman, 1981), chaps. 22 and 23; I. S. Grant and W. R. Phillips, The Elements of Physics (Oxford: Oxford University Press, 2001), pp. 245–72. The difference between "sound" waves and electromagnetic wave phenomenon, such as light and radio waves, relates to mass. Sound has no mass upon which gravity can act. This is why sound requires another medium, such as air or water, through which it can travel. Unlike light waves, which consist of tiny particles called photons, sound cannot travel where there is no atmosphere. By contrast, light and radio waves can travel through space. See also J. Gribbin, Get a Grip on the New Physics (London: Weidenfeld & Nicholson, 1999), pp. 82–90.
35. See, for example, R. G. A. Dolby, "The Sociology of Knowledge in Natural Science," Science Studies 1, no. 1 (1971); and K. Popper, The Logic of Scientific Discovery (New York: Basic, 1959).
36. Reed Gratz, "An Historical Perspective of the Lydian and Major Scales." Appendix 1 in Lydian Chromatic Concept of Tonal Organization, by George Russell. Brookline, MA: Concept, 2001. p.244.

37. George Russell, *The Lydian Chromatic Concept of Tonal Organization* (New York, N.Y.: Concept 2001), p.56
38. Monson, op cit. See Chapter 8.
39. Monson, op cit, p.156.
40. Porter, op cit, p.222
41. George Russell, "Where Do We Go From Here?" in *The Jazz Word*, ed. D. Cerulli, B. Korall, and M. Nasatir (London: Ballantine, 1960), p. 185.
42. George Russell, *The Lydian Chromatic Concept of Tonal Organization* 2001. See Chapter VIII.
43. Carr, interview with G. Russell, June 1992.
44. Perlis, interview with G. Russell.
45. Carr, interview with G. Russell, June 1992.
46. Brigid Cohen, *Stefan Wolpe and the Avant-Garde Diaspora*. Cambridge, UK: CUP, 2016. p.232.
47. A. Clarkson, ed. *On the Music of Stefan Wolpe* (New York: Pendragon, 2003).
48. Brigid Cohen. "Diasporic Dialogues in Mid-Century New York: Stefan Wolpe, George Russell, Hannah Arendt, and the Historiography of Displacement." *Journal of the Society for American Music*, Volume 6, No. 2, 2012. p.144.
49. Cohen, op cit. p.149.
50. Perlis, interview with G. Russell.
51. A. Clarkson, http://www.wolpe.org/page10/page10.html#George%20Russell
52. Cohen, op cit. pp.154-155.
53. Brigid Cohen, *Stefan Wolpe and the Avant-Garde Diaspora*, Cambridge: Cambridge University Press, 2012, p.242.
54. Ingrid Monson. "Oh Freedom—George Russell, John Coltrane and Modal Jazz." In *In the Course of Performance*, edited by B. Nettl and M. Russell. London: University of Chicago Press, 1998, p.157.
55. Carr, interview with G. Russell, June 1992. NB. Pozo's real name was Luciano Gonzales.
56. George Russell—*A Jazz Portrait*.
57. Paul Austerlitz, *Jazz Consciousness: Music, Race and Humanity* (Middletown, CT: Wesleyan University Press. 2005) p.74.
58. Michael Levin, "Despite Bad Acoustics, Gillespie Concert Offers Some Excellent Music," *Chicago Tribune*, October 22, 1947. Russell also arranged 'Relaxin' at Camarillo' for Gillespie's band for the concert. Part of the concert, including both 'Cubano-Be, Cubano-Bop' and 'Relaxin' at Camarillo', as well as five numbers performed by Gillespie with Charlie Parker, have been issued by Blue Note as Diz N' Bird at Carnegie Hall (724385706127).
59. Carr, interview with G. Russell, June 1992.
60. Gillespie, Dizzy (with Al Fraser). *To Be or Not To Bop* (Minneapolis, MN: University of Minneapolis Press. 2009) p.324.
61. Carr, interview with G. Russell, June 1992.
62. Alyn Shipton. *Groovin' High: The Life of Dizzy Gillespie*. (New York, NY: OUP. 1999) p.201.
63. Dizzy Gillespie, quoted in *The Invisible Guru*, BBC Radio 3, July 1994.
64. Max Harrison, "George Russell—Rational Anthems," *Wire* (Spring 1983). p.30.
65. Ingrid Monson, "George Russell," in *International Dictionary of Black Composers*, ed. S. A. Floyd Jr. (Chicago: Fitzroy Dearborn, 1999).
66. Dizzy Gillespie, *Dizziest*, Bluebird Records 5785-1-RB (Double LP).

CHAPTER FIVE

## A Bird in Igor's Yard

When "Cubano-Be, Cubano-Bop" received its premiere at Carnegie Hall, Russell was just twenty-four years old. On one level, given the critical acclaim received by his first major composition, it was a remarkable achievement. While Russell was clearly an insider amongst the musicians grouped around Gil Evans, Dizzy Gillespie, Charlie Parker and Max Roach, he was largely unknown outside those circles. On another level, his payment from Gillespie for "Cubano-Be, Cubano-Bop" was small and the amount of work as a composer/arranger that its critical success brought with it was hardly life-changing. Asked by Ian Carr whether Russell did other arrangements for Gillespie's band, Juanita Giuffre, Russell's first wife, noted, "He didn't. He didn't work that steadily. He wrote 'Cubano-Be, Cubano-Bop' for him and I think Dizzy gave him a very nominal amount of money for it. It was a big success."[1]

It was certainly a hand-to-mouth existence and Russell did what he had done back in Cincinnati. He took occasional jobs in stores or in catering but, whereas in Ohio there was regular work playing drums to supplement his earnings and relieve the drudgery, several patterns began to emerge that would mark Russell's approach to his career for the next ten years—and, in fact, for the rest of his life. The first of these was that his pursuit of the Lydian Concept would become his overriding concern. Second, Russell was never afraid of work—Joe and Bessie had instilled that virtue in him—and he would take menial jobs when necessary to survive, albeit only as long as absolutely essential to pay the bills. Third, as stated previously, he would compose only when he had something or someone to write for. Composing would always take second place to the Concept. Despite his pride in works like *The African Game*, *Jazz in the Space Age* and *All About Rosie*, the sense one got from talking with him is that such achievements were almost incidental to the main feature - the Lydian Concept. Of course, he welcomed the income from composing for others and from making records. From time to time, in the fifties and sixties, a record date could mean enough money to live on for up to six months or even a year. But, just as importantly, it provided an opportunity to test out his ideas. Speaking about his contract with Riverside Records in the early sixties, Russell told Ben Young of WKCR,

> I was thirty-five years old before I could say I was earning money from music. That all started with the RCA Victor album [*Jazz Workshop*], and things were touch and go in between. So the offer from Riverside meant a few months of being able to pay the bills and also a chance to create. Well, the offer from Riverside stretched out not only into one album but into two or three or four albums and that was good for a couple of years of security and at the same time being able to test, because I always was working at the Concept, and being able to test the new ideas coming from the Concept in music, check them out and I would never let anything go without being satisfied with it aesthetically.[2]

This pattern continued throughout his life, albeit with a full-time teaching post and occasional grant replacing income from recording. As he said above, the money from a recording meant that he could live on it for several months and be free to work on the Concept. For, as Russell also explained to Young, the Concept had a life of its own almost separate from the music-making process.

> Well, for me the Lydian Chromatic Concept was an obligation that I took on and I took it on . . . rather than just use it as an instrument for me becoming a composer ten years ahead of his time or something and being able to afford all the pleasurable, creamy and delightful things that money can buy. I didn't choose that way at all because I knew I had something to offer and, as I said, I debated about whether I should really part with it. The thing that convinced me is that it does deal with gravity and it deals with gravity behaving and controlling music and therefore you can't keep gravity a secret without really going against nature. So I'm obligated and have been obligated to take time away from the music to work on the Concept. I'm always working on the Concept. Like this time, for example, the book has to be finished now, so I don't want or need any commissions. They do interfere. I don't have time for that. The book is very important to get out there. So we're working very hard on that. And all through my musical life, and the Concept was the beginning of it in 1945— the Lydian Concept—I've dropped composing from time to time to devote to that. But then with having worked on it and having worked it up to another level, I use that level to then compose from it and, if I have to drop it for a while, I'll do it and work it up to another level.[3]

Or on a more prosaic level, as Russell told Carr, "When I was with Max, his mother told him, 'Max, this boy never sleeps, you know. He's always working on the theory.'"[4]

But, in a sense, it must be understood that neither the Concept, nor "Cubano-Be, Cubano-Bop" sprang fully-formed from Russell's brow. Rather both emerged from and reflected those milieux that Russell had encountered both in "Gil Evans's Church of the Aesthetic," as Russell described it to Carr, and in the intellectual circles around Stefan

Wolpe. This was the late forties and, having led jazz into the post-war era with bebop, the musicians centred around Evans were looking to see how much further they could push the boundaries of jazz. With Wolpe, the concerns were even broader taking in a range of other arts, as well as social and political ideas, concerns that certainly also touched these forward-thinking jazz musicians.

Moreover, however advanced "Cubano-Be, Cubano-Bop" might have been, it had to have a context in which it could be appreciated. This required an articulate and progressive audience of musicians, critics, and fans. This had been prepared not only by bebop but by the open-mindedness of the previous generation of musicians, both black and white.

It is far too simplistic to suggest that jazz prior to bebop was somehow conservative and mainstream. One only has to think of Duke Ellington and Billy Strayhorn, of Russell's erstwhile employers Benny Carter and Earl Hines, of Fletcher Henderson or of white bandleaders like Claude Thornhill, Benny Goodman, Artie Shaw and Stan Kenton. These musicians were quite familiar with modern composers such as Copland, Stravinsky, Milhaud and Ravel, many of whom were themselves influenced by jazz. And Russell was, as noted, one of a number of jazz musicians who chose to study with Wolpe.[5] Nor was the influence in one direction in Wolpe's case. Brigid Cohen has pointed very specifically in her writing on Wolpe on the ways in which the new jazz influenced the composer.[6]

Moreover, these cultural advances grew out of a particularly fertile historical context. The Second World War had been, in many ways, both a portent for social, cultural and political changes and their progenitor. It had amplified both conservative and progressive currents that had come into existence in the thirties but also created contexts in which both could flourish.

J. Ronald Oakley has described the 1950s as 'a period of puzzling paradoxes,'[7] within which optimism for the future and belief in progress contrasted with nagging fears about nuclear war and communism. In post-WWII America, rigid conservative and reactionary cultural, social and political impulses contrasted with other more progressive, if less powerful forces. And within the space between these two conflicting currents, possibilities arose artistically and socially, if less so in the arenas of politics and economics. If, as Martin Halliwell suggests, the fifties would later be vilified in the sixties "by those who saw themselves as its victims," the post-war years also saw the birth of what was later described as the counter-culture and the first skirmishes in the battle against segregation.[8]

Nor were jazz musicians, promoters, writers and fans – black and white – unaffected by the struggles for civil rights. Ingrid Monson in *Freedom Sounds: Civil Rights Callout to Jazz and Africa* (2007) reveals a picture of ongoing struggle to break down 'Jim Crow' segregation in the music business. Such activism focused not only on the refusal of black and, some, white artists and band leaders to play segregated or whites-only venues but also on direct activism, for example to desegregate the American Federation of Musicians and the broadcaster NBC. Monson argues that such struggles were intimately bound up with wider African-American civil rights activism.[9]

Though, the 1950s and 1960s were the years when the struggles of Black America for full emancipation were at their height, those struggles had their roots in the expectations raised in African-Americans during the Second World War. Many African-Americans served during the war, often visiting countries where their race and colour did not bar them entry into the wider white world. Many other African-Americans, due to the war effort, found paid employment in jobs that had previously largely been reserved for white people and at wage levels they had not experienced before. Come the war's end, it was back to business as usual as black ex-soldiers found their service unrewarded and black workers were laid off to make way for returning white service men.[10] This was the beginning of and antecedent to new phases in campaigning for civil rights and the rise of both a new Black Nationalism. And these struggles were inevitably reflected in African-American music and literature. Black avant-garde jazz musicians and their poet/writer *confrères* represented the most radical and politicised sections of African-America. Writing of the later liberation struggles in the 1960s, W. S. Tkweme has argued that African-American jazz musicians in the late fifties-early sixties connected with all aspects of African-American arts, including poetry, and both initiated, pioneered and were "the harbingers of the shifts in black consciousness seen in the work of 1960s Artists and African-Americans in general."[11] I would simply suggest that signs of such developments were already present from the late forties onwards.

In other respects, jazz also provided a soundtrack to the kinds of, often, radical intellectual discourse of these years. Readers will be aware of the connection between the Beat poets and jazz but the connections between jazz and literature were much wider than that embracing genuine political radicals such as Kenneth Rexroth, ruth wolf, Kenneth Patchen, Ralph Ellison, Langston Hughes and Lawrence Ferlinghetti. More than that, jazz connected with art and literature – and comedy – through what Stephen R. Duncan describes as 'rebel cafes' such as the Village Vanguard (which opened in 1935 and was a cabaret club before it became a jazz venue) and Café Society (1938-1948) in New York and the Black Cat Café in San Francisco (1933-1963).[12] And, of course, one of the attractions of jazz for many young Americans lay in its rebellious, outsider image and stance, one that in and of itself questioned the dominant culture and white bourgeois American values.

At the same time, the war years had also seen a different set of behaviours, more assertive of personal and group affiliations, emerge within the African-American and Latino communities. Groups of black and pachuco youths, who identified strongly with jazz as dance music, marked themselves as outsiders through the clothes that they chose to wear, primarily the zoot suit. There had been "zoot suit riots" in Los Angeles and other centres along the West Coast, involving black and Mexican youths and the predominantly white U.S. servicemen stationed along the coast. These riots had spread to other urban centres, including Detroit, Pittsburgh, and New York. Stuart Cosgrove in his article "The Zoot-Suit and Style Warfare" suggests that one consequence of the recruitment of men into the armed forces and women into the defence industries was a reduction of the extent of parental supervision of black and Mexican youth. At one point, Cosgrove notes there were as many as 15 million civilians engaged directly in "war work" and 12 million military personnel "on the move" in the United States.[13] By any standards this was a major social upheaval for any society and its consequences were both negative in terms of heightening racial divisions and positive in terms of their longer-term consequences in creating the potential for social change and greater equality.

And, while bebop did break with past jazz in significant respects, it is better to see it as the outcome of a series of merging aesthetic, social, and economic currents rather than a "revolution" or a "divide." In this context, Houston Baker Jr.'s term, "cultural matrix" is particularly helpful, which he defines as a "point of ceaseless input and output, a web of intersecting, crisscrossing impulses always in productive transit."[14]

Furthermore, the musicians who gathered around Gil Evans were a highly literate and articulate bunch and were progressive on social issues as well. As Russell noted to WKCR's Ben Young,

> [T]he company I was keeping at that time . . . was Gil Evans's 55th Street conclave with John Lewis, Johnny Carisi, Miles, and Gerry Mulligan and myself being sort of the . . . forming the particular spearhead of that group and, of course, Gil Evans being the patron saint of that way. We used to listen to all kinds of music in that little one-room apartment and, as the title insinuates, I think one of our favourite pieces was *Sacré du Printemps*, and I was particularly amazed at that piece and still am, and at the same time Bird being in the same company because Bird used to frequent that 55th Street one-room apartment of Gil's under the St. Regis Hotel in the basement with a cat named Becky.[15]

Russell also mentioned Arnold Schoenberg's demanding, non-tonal early work, his song-cycle *Pierrot Lunaire*, as another piece that the group listened to extensively. In addition, the group would often visit the nearby Juilliard School and listen to pre-concert rehearsals of music by composers such as Stravinsky and Paul Hindemith. Moreover, this was a group that shared ideas but in a self-critical and challenging way:

> [A]nd I was always attracted to people who came along and were and are some of this music's greatest innovators and I learned from them and I had this intensity to experiment. I was in the right circle to do that. Mulligan did it in his way. Miles did it in his way and John [Lewis], of course, with the Modern Jazz Quartet but it helped being in that environment. And something always saw to it that I was in an environment that goaded me into not being satisfied with the latest work but to take it further and not to experiment on the audience but to only release that that I had in essence thought was my very best at that time.[16]

As for Evans himself, Russell describes him in the following terms: "He was the father, the patron. He was the head, the body, the heart and the spirit of those times. The wise man." And the "wise man" held open house day and night.

> It was a big room in the basement and with practically every musician in New York coming in at any time after the gig at maybe 4 o'clock in the morning and it would still be available and we'd talk with Gil and that was the place where the "Cool" was born. Mulligan and I, many times, we worked all night on pieces. Gil was, as I said, he was the caretaker there to see that some beautiful music was made. He wouldn't let go and we would march up to Juilliard if a classical composer like Hindemith was going to give a concert He did a piece called *History of the Soldier* there. We attended the rehearsals a couple of days before that.

> We could sit in on the rehearsals at Juilliard. I watched Hindemith's assistant put the piece together. If it was Stravinsky, we'd be there. We played it down in the basement. We played all kinds of music. [17]

Maybe it is just the benefit of hindsight but Russell said that he felt that history was being made down in that basement.

> Well, I personally thought I was part of that history. I was accepted, certainly but that idea was a living fact. Yeah, there was no way it could be otherwise. The music had to go somewhere and it came out of that basement. He had Miles Davis, Gerry Mulligan, John Carisi, John Lewis, the Modern Jazz Quartet there every night practically. So there was something came out of that. Plus Gil himself and his band and his writing. Music was the thing that we did and every aspect of life was devoted to music. I think we thought of ourselves as a kind of club and they were good days. [18]

It was an elite circle but not elitist. Anyone with talent was welcome. However, Russell was still scuffling a living. Nor did he seem to be keen to sell himself. As he told Carr, "Well, I was really practicing that legendary art that I think many artists are forced to get acquainted with and that is living off the graces of a nice lady, you know." Russell told Carr that he lived with a woman and her husband on Park Avenue, and when Carr described her as his "patron," Russell concurred. However, in a more recent interview, he explained the situation in more detail, "I did live with . . . there was this woman who took a liking to me. She lived on Park Avenue, Anita Kushner. She was very much involved in the arts. She had a husband and they were very nice people. When I came into the picture I lived with them." [19]

Asked if this were *une ménage a trois*, Russell replied,

> It sounds like that and it was like that. *(laughs)* I don't want to say anything damaging about her. She was a wonderful woman. She took a liking to me and she wanted me there. Her husband went along with it. That lasted maybe a year. She had a good piano and I wrote "A Bird in Igor's Yard," it's one of the things I wrote on her piano for Buddy DeFranco. [20]

When that came to an end, Russell moved in with the lyricist Jack Segal, writer of the popular songs "Scarlet Ribbons" and "When Sunny Gets Blue." Their apartment also became a hangout for the members of Gil Evans's circle as well as other artists like Harry Belafonte and Tony Bennett. Segal, it seems, was interested in the ideas of psychologist Wilhelm Reich and, according to Russell, actually had an "orgone box" in his living room. [21]

While it hardly constituted a major change in Russell's circumstances, he did succeed in selling two compositions and an arrangement between April 1949 and January 1950. The first of these was "A Bird in Igor's Yard." Buddy DeFranco had just formed his own big band. DeFranco was more than just a fine clarinet player. An established player with the big bands of Tommy Dorsey, Gene Krupa, and Boyd Raeburn, he was equally at home with the new sounds of bebop and had played with Miles Davis, Lee Konitz, Bud Powell, Max Roach and J. J. Johnson. At the time, DeFranco had a vision for his new band that encompassed both the new music and the "progressive" sounds of Stan Kenton. "A Bird in Igor's Yard" should have fitted perfectly into that vision.

Featuring a band that included Konitz, Al Cohn, Serge Chaloff and Oscar Pettiford, it did not, however, prove quite the heaven-made match anticipated. Four tracks were recorded for Capitol, Stan Kenton's label, by the band, including Russell's. The others, arranged by Gerry Valentine and Manny Albam, included "The Boy Next Door" and "This Time the Dream's on Me." "A Bird in Igor's Yard" stands out from the other tracks both in terms of the complexity of its arrangement and the unusual sonorities it pioneered. Russell's attempt to make Stravinsky dance with Bird would receive a better and more convincing reading seven years later on his own *Jazz Workshop* date. That said, the DeFranco performance is a fascinating slice of modernist, forward-looking jazz.

In fact, a myth grew up in jazz circles that the piece was so far advanced and ahead of its time that Capitol refused to release it. This seems improbable. Firstly, the label had little apparent difficulty with some of Kenton's "progressive" jazz at that time. It seems unlikely that the label would have rejected the performance on those grounds alone. Secondly, none of the pieces recorded at that date were actually released until much later and one could hardly claim that the other three pieces were in any sense that "advanced." Third, the recording itself is not that well balanced and the opening ensembles sound rather frayed. Finally, DeFranco seems to have been rather unhappy with the result and his own playing. As he told *DownBeat* in 1951, "That was one attempt at pioneering I never should have made." [22]

An acetate of the piece was obtained by the DJ Symphony Sid and broadcast regularly on his show. This no doubt helped to fuel the myth surrounding "A Bird in Igor's Yard." What does matter about "A Bird in Igor's Yard" is what it says about Russell's ambition, even this early in his career. He was drawing on composers like Stravinsky, Debussy, Schoenberg and Ravel quite consciously and was deliberately bringing their ideas and harmonic language into jazz and into contact with improvisation. In doing so, he emphasized the written elements of jazz in creating a symphonic sound for the jazz orchestra, just as he would later stress the chamber elements of the small jazz group. This was years before John Lewis and Gunther Schuller coined the term "Third Stream." Russell might not have been alone in wishing to expand the scope of jazz in this respect. Gil Evans had already taken such steps with Claude Thornhill, Ellington and Strayhorn had stretched the vocabulary of jazz and Kenton had pressed its case for a place in the concert hall as well as the dance hall. And classical composers like Gershwin, Copland, and Stravinsky had taken bold steps toward jazz. Nevertheless, a case can be made that "A Bird in Igor's Yard" is perhaps the most "advanced" and coherent such statement up to that point. What is more, its statement of intent is unequivocal and explicit.

Another Russell piece, "Similau," was recorded by Artie Shaw during that period and he also did an arrangement of Duke Ellington/Juan Tizol's "Caravan" for Charlie Ventura. Both were big-band recordings. Shaw's band of 1949 (the recording was actually made early in 1950) was known as his Bebop Band and included players like Zoot Sims, Al Cohn and guitarist Jimmy Raney, just as earlier Shaw bands had contained the talents of Barney Kessel, Georgie Auld and pianist Dodo Marmarosa. Two points should be made here. First, like fellow clarinettist DeFranco, Shaw was an adventurous and forward-thinking musician who reacted positively to bebop. Second, his attempts to meet the challenge of the new music were met by commercial failure. That emphasizes a further point that what happens in New York or out on the West Coast does not necessarily catch on with Middle America.

"Similau" is qualitatively different from the other fifteen or so sides Shaw recorded with this band around 1949. The listener need only contrast it with John Bartee's "Afro-Cubano," clearly a tip of the cap to "Cubano-Be, Cubano-Bop" or bop pianist/composer Tadd Dameron's "So Easy." While these tunes are delightful examples of big-band playing, with Shaw frighteningly good on his instrument, they are of their time and genre. "Similau" seems to have as much in common with Stravinsky or Schoenberg as it does with many other examples of big band writing and arranging of the period. It has a truly filmic quality with discordant brass and its dark and sombre mood. If that were how it sounds now to us, how at odds would it have sounded to the listening public brought up on Miller and Dorsey? [23]

Russell's recalled that he approached Shaw with the piece he had written.

At the time I was just very relieved that he was such a gentleman, you know, such a nice guy. I can't say I was close with Artie, but afterward, when he had recorded "Similau," I would see him in different places, once on a horse in upstate New York. He said, "Hello." I didn't recognize him but I finally saw the smile and that was Artie. People question me about it but I really didn't know the chap. [24]

Interviewed by Ben Young for WKCR, Russell recalled that the Charlie Ventura performance of "Caravan," like that of "A Bird in Igor's Yard," was held back by the record company. In the same interview, he also spoke of an arrangement he had done for Ella Fitzgerald of "How High the Moon."

Charlie Ventura asked me to arrange "Caravan," just as Ella Fitzgerald asked me to arrange "How High the Moon." She came out with that record about 1948, actually, and they both suffered the same fate because Ella ended up in the Decca studios; I had overwritten, overextended myself and had written some things for her to sing. She just took the first chorus of it and Ray Brown quickly came up with some kind of ending, not my ending, but the chorus, I mean, the first chorus of it is my arrangement. So she was very, very annoyed at me in the studio, you know, but later on, about five or six months later I bumped into her on the street—she and Ray. She said, "I want to take you to dinner." The record sold something like 10 million copies with a fragment of my arrangement. So the same thing with Charlie Ventura, turned out to be. They weren't angry because they knew it was the best I could do and it was a good, exciting arrangement but it wasn't . . . the company decided it wasn't commercial enough. That happened with "A Bird in Igor's Yard," so "Caravan" was released twenty, thirty years after it was written. [25]

Assuming the Russell arrangement is the one actually used in part by Brown and

Fitzgerald, the recording session took place in December 1947. Russell's memory is close enough for jazz, as they say. It appeared as the 'b' side of "Someone Like You", which was released in 1949. With regard to the fate of his arrangement of "Caravan," it was recorded as part of a December 1949 session for a box set of three 78rpm discs of Duke Ellington and Billy Strayhorn pieces, released under the title *Charlie Ventura Plays Duke Ellington for Dancing*. "Caravan" was not included in that release and was held back until it appeared on an EP, "For Boppers Only" in 1955. As to why Russell's arrangement did not make it onto the box set, one suspects the clue is in the titles – ". . . for Dancing" against "For Boppers . . ." Russell's take on the Ellington/Tizol tune is at odds with the other pieces from that session such as the quick step of "Take the 'A' Train" and the slow fox-trot of "Prelude to a Kiss." With its at times dissonant harmonies, subtle rhythmic shifts and, halfway in, dramatic change of tempo, it would challenge many amateur terpsichoreans! That said, it sounds like the band, and Ventura in particular, had a ball of their own with Russell's arrangement.

Asked if he liked what Ventura had done with his arrangement of "Caravan," Russell replied, "I liked everything that I gave to people. I liked it. Especially the things I gave to people at that level." In terms of payment, as he acknowledges, "I can't say I made money. After a piece was gone, I can't say I kept up with it. I'm not a business man, so I can't follow up these things and see if I'm getting cheated or not." [26]

This would lack of attention to the business side would continue, at least until the seventies when his third wife, Alice Norbury Russell, began to take care of this for Russell. Not only did he rarely compose without a commission or recording date, he showed a lack of concern for material gain or pursuit of fame. His work on the Concept and its expression in his music from time to time was enough, it seemed.

At this point in the late forties/early fifties, jazz was beginning to move on from its bebop phase in new directions that should have suited Russell's talents. Miles Davis had met Gil Evans towards the end of 1947 when Evans had asked the trumpeter's permission to orchestrate Davis's "Donna Lee" for the Claude Thornhill Band. [27] Already impressed with Evans's ideas and chafing at the simple arrangements that bop relied upon—in contrast with the demanding soloing required—Davis began pushing Evans and his circle to put their ideas to test. Hiring halls and calling up the musicians, Davis proved the catalyst and driving force that would lead to the famous *Birth of the Cool* sessions. Rehearsals continued through 1948, leading to live performances at the Royal Roost on Broadway in September. The personnel changed according to availability, but Davis, altoist Lee Konitz, Gerry Mulligan, Max Roach, John Lewis and Gil Evans were fairly constant. The line-up drew heavily from the Thornhill band, with Mulligan, Lewis, Evans and trumpeter John Carisi writing and arranging the material. [28]

According to Robert Moore, bassist Red Mitchell told him that Mulligan had told him that Russell had provided a couple of tunes but that these had not been used as they were considered "too difficult." [29] Though not perhaps part of that circle, Mitchell played with Mulligan a few years later. Russell himself has no recollection of this. Gunther Schuller, who played French horn on one of the sessions, believes this may have been the case, as his son George noted,

Gunther does have a vague memory of George having written something for the Birth of the Cool band but he's not sure if that was something written specifically for one of the three sessions or if it was a chart that was rehearsed prior to those sessions. Gunther was in the last session. Gunther also said that perhaps whatever George wrote for the band might have resulted in a later composition like "Lydian M1" or one of those pieces he wrote for the small group RCA recordings. [30]

Certainly Pete Welding's liner notes for the first CD reissue mention Russell as part of the pool working on the material and Gerry Mulligan's memories from 1971 note Russell as one of the regulars at Gil's, "George Russell, our resident innovator. (Wrote a couple of fine, interesting charts for Claude Thornhill's band that I suppose there's no trace of now.)" [31]

It is easy to overestimate the immediate impact of these sessions. It was not a regular working band and, apart from a couple of 78s issued from the sessions, it was not until 1954 that eight tracks were released on a 10-inch LP and another three years before all twelve made it on to an album. They were, however, influential within the jazz community—in New York at least— in terms of the expansion of the possibilities for jazz composition and arranging. Perhaps they also began to open up an audience for what, unsatisfactorily, became known as "Cool Jazz." Lee Konitz was already working with blind Italian American pianist Lennie Tristano and a group of like-minded musicians such as guitarist Billy Bauer and tenor player Warne Marsh. In the early fifties Lewis would form the Modern Jazz Quartet and Gerry Mulligan would debut his piano-less quartet with trumpeter Chet Baker. The music of these groups and others would frequently be referred to as "cool jazz" and such musicians would also help to create a small audience for Russell when he finally recorded in his own right in the mid-fifties.

However, it seems fair to say that—at that time, at least—neither the record companies nor the record buying public seemed ready for such experimentation. French horn player and composer Gunther Schuller met the young composer during this period. Their meeting would prove important for Russell's future in several respects over the years.

> I met George Russell about three weeks after I'd met John Lewis, which was 1948. We went to George's apartment and as I entered the place I was hearing Alexander Scriabin's *Prometheus* on the record turntable. Well, I was bowled over because jazz musicians didn't listen generally to Scriabin's *Prometheus* or any . . . some people listened to classical music but it was still a rarity in those days. So, I realized almost immediately that George was obviously a broad-gauged composer, musician and thinker. Anyway we got on wonderfully and then he told me already at that time he was embarking on this attempt to create a theoretical concept for jazz, which as we all know he has spent the rest of his life on and is about to embark on another edition. [32]

Around that same period, Russell had met Juanita Odjenar (later Juanita Giuffre), a beautiful young woman of Irish, Mulatto, Cherokee, and Filipino extraction. She was about nineteen and had met Dizzy Gillespie at a gig. The trumpeter had phoned her and visited her at her parents' home. Reluctantly her parents and grandmother, protective of their only child, agreed that she could go with Dizzy to meet "his arranger" in Jamaica, Long Island. That was John Lewis. They took the cab that Gillespie had left outside, its meter running, while Dizzy played the family piano and chatted.

> So we went out and John was not at home and Dizzy walked in and yelled for John and we heard a voice in the bathroom. "I'm here but it's not John." And I had to go to the bathroom so badly at the time, that Dizzy said, "You go on in." There sat George in the tub with depilatory on his face because he was so delicate with shaving burns. He didn't like that and had something wrapped around his head. Well, all of a sudden I didn't have to go to the bathroom. I just bounced back I was so shocked. He said, "Hello, how are you?" That's how I met George Russell, under those circumstances. [33]

It was a couple of years later before Russell introduced himself properly. They began dating and Juanita became pregnant. As she explained, "Then, in 1950, we got married. It was like one of those funny little marriages that took place because I was pregnant. So it was something my family didn't know. They weren't particularly happy about this musician who walks in to my grandmother and says, 'Do you have a flair for drama? We're getting married.' My grandmother said, 'You have a flair for what? How much money do you have? My granddaughter's been well taken care of.' She brought him to tears." [34]

Despite their concerns, her parents gave their permission and Russell married for the first time. Juanita was working for an insurance company but also studying art part-time. From the outset, Juanita took on the role of provider. As Russell told Ian Carr, "In the early part of that marriage we had this deal that I should work on the music." [35] Partly to prove to herself—but mainly to her parents—that "money wasn't that important" and that love conquers all, Juanita did so gladly. She also had a sense that George had an important contribution to make to music and the world.

> Even as a young person, I knew that there was something important he had to do and say and so that became *our* goal. It wasn't just his goal; it was *our* goal at that point to see this thing to fruition, whatever it was. We didn't know if it would be just composing; the Concept was always there in some form or another. In a sketchy sense it was always there. I knew without even understanding what it was that there was something very deep he was reaching for and I felt as though this is a goal that should be accomplished. [36]

It was, however, a situation Russell found conflicting. His upbringing with Joseph and Bessie had taught him different standards. He told Ian Carr that he felt after a time that he should work as well. He also acknowledged his frustration at the lack of progress of his career in music. "I was twenty-three when I conducted Dizzy in Carnegie Hall, you know. So, I had to contend with this feeling. I felt I'd reached a certain plateau." [37]

Life was certainly a struggle for Russell and his young wife. They were living in a one-room apartment in the Beechwood Hotel down on 23rd St between Lexington and 3rd Avenue. They shared bathroom and kitchen facilities with the other residents. All human life was there, as Juanita Giuffre remembered,

> There were all kinds of people at this hotel, starting with hookers who were really pretty decent women. There was a sailor who would always come home to this place. You would have to put your food and lock it up in this community refrigerator. The stove that everybody used had cockroaches jumping out of it. But I'd never ever lived like that before. It was like an adventure for me. Even though I was embarrassed about it, this was a learning experience I never would have gotten any other way about people. There was one guy, a doctor, and he was working for the Mafia and he would disappear. We would hear him walking down the hall at night. He would disappear and it turned out that when he was studying, he was on internship and wasn't ready to practice yet, he'd operated on his wife, some emergency thing he just had to take care of himself and she died and he lost his license. He ended up with the Mafia going out digging out bullets or whatever you do for the Mafia. We had a stripper there that was quite fond of George. [38]

Juanita had a miscarriage not long after the marriage and also developed lupus, which damaged her kidneys. As a result, she was never able to have children. With hindsight, Juanita realized how problematic it would have been had she carried the baby to full-term and beyond.

> And not only that, George didn't want children at that time. Later it was different. But then he really didn't want children and luckily for the children neither of us felt that we were capable of handling it. Were we going to take a child into the Beechwood Hotel and who knows? There are just some people that are just not meant to be parents and if they admit it at the beginning that's all well and good. I think it's that much better for the children that might have been in that kind of relationship. I've seen relationships where that would happen, where the woman would kind of force the man or the man will force it if they want children very badly. In this case, nobody was terribly anticipating that it would be a good idea. Because you'd have the extra trauma of trying to make a living in music, which is already bad enough. It's as big enough a child as it is. Then to bring a child into that kind of uncertainty is kind of crazy. [39]

According to Russell, initially they lived "in an apartment that was by the river, a very nice apartment." They could not make the rent one time and did a moonlight flit. "The rent was a little high, so . . . we had to move one night. We just had to get out. We were down to the last penny and we ended up in the Hotel Beechwood, which was another trip because that was one step away from the Bowery but we made it nice." [40]

Russell recalled that one day, Juanita ran down a hill near their apartment and the next day started haemorrhaging and then lost the baby. As he put it, "She had enough babies to watch over, you know. *(laughing)*" [41]

Russell's contact with Lee Konitz through the *Birth of the Cool* sessions did, however, yield a further commission. In early 1951 Konitz was recording a session with a group that contained fellow Tristano alumni Sal Mosca on piano, Arnold Fishkin on bass and Billy Bauer. Max Roach was on drums and the trumpeter was Miles Davis. Interviewed for this book, Konitz noted that the word "commission" suggested a degree of greater formality than was really the case. As he put it, "Somehow he knew that I was doing this date and he made them available and I was very pleased to try to play them. George had written at least two tunes that were very challenging to play. Miles wasn't on top form at that time but I was very grateful that he was willing to be a sideman with me. George's pieces were very original and very interesting to play and very difficult." [42]

The two pieces were "Odjenar," after Juanita's maiden name, and "Ezz-Thetic." It was the latter that really stood out for Konitz.

> Yeah, "Ezz-Thetic" after a boxer named Ezzard Charles and it was based pretty much on the standard "Love for Sale" and it was a very difficult line at that fast tempo and I think Miles had borrowed a trumpet for the date and he was really kind of on his toes trying to get all the notes. So I was concerned with getting my notes right and I was praying that he got his right and it came out pretty good, I think. But those were some interesting times and George certainly contributed to that. [43]

In fact, difficult though "Ezz-Thetic" might have been, it was "Odjenar" that was unusual as a jazz recording for the time. It is a strange, ominous piece beginning with unaccompanied alto and trumpet that moves, some might say uneasily, between classical and jazz styles.

Brigid Cohen, in a highly perceptive article on Stefan Wolpe, which examines the composer's wider intellectual affiliations as well as his associations with modern jazz, sees "Odjenar" as "testifying to Wolpe and Russell's exchange." She notes that the tune shows how far Russell had progressed towards a more open harmonic and rhythmic framework and how the "rate of chromatic circulation" and "principle of the thirdless sound," concepts Russell credited to Wolpe, are already in play.

> The tune announces its eccentricity from the beginning. Lee Konitz smoothly plays a melodically off-kilter, but rhythmically straight oscillating line that ends a half-step higher than where it began. Many segments of the line belong to one diatonic collection or another and create the impression of tonal allusion, but taken together the whole line can hardly be understood as establishing any key. Indeed, within such a short span of time as Konitz's first phrase, Russell makes use of all but four notes of the chromatic scale. Davis's subsequent entrance fills in the last four pitch classes (C, Bb, Ab, and E) completing the circulation of all twelve pitch classes in a line full of difficult dissonant leaps, landing on an E4 that clashes with the D#4 in the saxophone. [44]

As Cohen also points out slightly later in the article,

> The hallmarks of George Russell's modal jazz—repeated vamps and ostinatos—provide rhythmic and harmonic foundations for Konitz's and Davis's later improvisations. Russell used similar atonal techniques to those in "Odjenar" in compositions like "Jack's Blues" and "Livingstone, I Presume" released on the album *Jazz Workshop* in 1956, which Russell described as showing the specific influence of his exchanges with Wolpe. [45]

"Odjenar" would certainly have sat very easily alongside the other pieces recorded for

Russell's first album, *Jazz Workshop*. It reveals just as strongly as his other compositions, Russell's ability to take ideas and practices from contemporary composition, transforming these effectively within a jazz context.

Davis's playing here has always disappointed Russell, as it was the only time the trumpeter actually played one of Russell's compositions. He was, however, badly strung out on heroin at the time and actually tried to leave the session at one point. Juanita, who was present, made him stay. Russell recalls, "As he was going out the door she ran over and grabbed him by the back of the neck, the collar and drug him back in. And she said, 'You're staying here until you finish this and I'm going to see to it.' He wasn't in much of a condition to do battle. *(laughing)*" [46]

Davis cannot even manage the tricky melody line on "Ezz-Thetic," playing only a counter line. Konitz, however, is quite astonishing both in the speed and fluidity of his performance and in the way he builds his solo. Of the rest of the sextet, Roach swings and drives the music on and Billy Bauer and Sal Mosca are on fine form. It is just a shame that Davis needed to score more than he wanted to play. It is also sad that Charlie Parker, who played "Ezz-thetic" at gigs, did not record the piece. There is apparently a score for strings in existence, which may have been intended for the *Bird with Strings* album but which obviously came to nothing. [47]

After six years in New York, Russell had had four compositions and one arrangement recorded, plus another half if we include Ella Fitzgerald's recording of "How High the Moon." "New World" had not made it into the studio and "A Bird in Igor's Yard" lay in Capitol's vaults, while RCA had yet to release his arrangement of "Caravan" written for and performed by Charlie Ventura. Though he was still working on the Concept, money was tight and Russell realized he had to find some work, preferably work that would not interfere too much with his musical research. Macy's, the department store, provided the answer. "Because Juanita was pulling in all the money and, you know, I couldn't get away with saying, 'Well, let's have a deal and, when I make it, then you can lay back and relax.' It really isn't that way, anyway. So I did take the job at Macy's." [48]

Working in the store's wallpaper department was undemanding but Russell was less happy when he was switched to men's toiletries. However, it was then that he realized that nobody knew or cared that much where he was. It also meant that he could avoid the embarrassment of seeing people he knew from the business, like the time he had to serve his friend MJQ bassist Percy Heath.

"So I'd walk in. I'd get there on time in the morning. Punch the clock and go home and work on the Concept all day, you know. That seemed fair. Then, I'd walk in about five minutes of nine at night." [49] One day, Juanita came home from work unexpectedly. "He swore I was from Macy's until he saw my smiling face and such fear as you've never seen before! *(laughs)* He would do little odd jobs here and there just to keep us paying this small rent at this hotel." [50]

Other jobs included working as both a counterman and a cook in various diners around the five boroughs. In his scrapbooks, there is a note from those times with details of his work schedule. Interestingly, it is scribbled on a copy of the review of the Gillespie Carnegie Hall concert, acting as both a message about the ironies of life and a reminder not to forget where he came from.

Russell published the first edition of *The Lydian Chromatic Concept of Tonal Organization* privately in 1953. It was a mimeographed affair bound in a ring binder. As Russell told Ben Young, it was not a best seller. In fact, it did not even get into double figures. Quite how Russell's ideas spread through the jazz community is therefore in part speculation. A comment Russell made to Young, however, suggests both a gradual filtering process initially and one that perhaps led to some misunderstanding of his intentions.

> When I completed the Concept in the first edition in 1953, what it had to say became available by osmosis practically. "Oh, George uses modes. He doesn't use chords." Okay, that's a mistake because I always use chords but chords are modes. Chords come from modes, which wasn't really perceived at that time. So this idea is released in the jazz community and not only in the jazz community but in modern music. It was released that you've got to take modes seriously because, if you have a scale, you have modes, because modes are simply the scale begun and ended in its natural order in any one of the scale tones.[51]

He continued, "So, that information got disseminated in 1953 and then I came out with the 1959 publication, and by that time I had a conversation with Miles about it before he did 'Milestones.'"[52]

Russell did have a few students in that period but this fact alone cannot account for the spread of his ideas. His comments in a WGBH radio broadcast from 1998 on the subject offer a partial explanation.

> In 1953 I published the Lydian Concept. I think I sold one book. Not everybody had $120. Somehow the knowledge itself was spread by word of mouth—you know, "Hey, man have you heard of that book? That George is into something else." That's how it spread and became what Archie Shepp called "The Bible of the Avant-garde." The writing was simply an expression of the Concept and if I couldn't integrate the writing and the Concept I would work and work and work until I could because that's what made the Concept grow.[53]

"Word of mouth" as a description of the dissemination of Russell's ideas actually becomes more accurate and convincing if one bears in mind the context. Four points need to be noted here. First, there was, as we have noted amongst musicians a hunger for new ideas. What is more, there was widespread interest in how jazz was going to develop among musicians and critics. This is evident from even a cursory read of *DownBeat* circa 1949–1953. Second, the jazz community—at least in terms of the number of musicians—was actually quite small. Most of the players knew each other and connected via gigs, clubs, and hangout joints. Third, Russell's connection with and important role within that grouping of the most forward-thinking musicians in New York provided a mechanism for his ideas to spread, even if only truncated form. Finally, Russell's ideas, at least to his more perceptive peers, drew on the practice of jazz musicians. It is a point John Lewis made to Ian Carr in 1992 when asked whether he considered the Lydian Concept to be a significant breakthrough: "It was, but not for me and not for the same generation that he and I both belonged to because the things he was using were the way we both played and thought. This was really for the next generation of people." [54]

Pianist/composer and close friend of Russell, John Benson Brooks amplified this point in a *Jazz Review* article on Russell's Lydian Concept.

> The boppers of the 'forties inherited the jazz scale—natural major with traditional options on the flat 3rd, flat 7th and flat 9th (or flat 2nd) and put the blue note, freedom squawk, or fly in the ointment (a feature absolutely essential to jazz's life) on the so-called flatted fifth, of F# in the scale of C. Notice that the last two options in the history of the scale are enharmonically tonic and fifth of the F# scale.
>
> Inevitably this soon had everybody playing around with polytonality and if you were blowing in a C gravity while the bass was in F# then, crazy. And why worry, since the circle of perfect fifths was an equilibrium with a magic gravity that would carry you through?

Benson Brooks then referred briefly to the contribution of Joseph Schillinger and the Schillinger Method to jazz theory, continuing,

> Tunes which had chord circles with several tonic stations (like "How High . . . ," "All the Things . . ." etc.) were the thing and everybody was trying to work out a chromatic mobility (12 tonics) that would make melodic sense. It is to George Russell's everlasting credit that he did it. [55]

Russell has never hidden his debt to the musicians he observed. This is clear from his analysis of the different melodic approaches of Coleman Hawkins, Lester Young, John Coltrane and Ornette Coleman in chapter IV of *The Lydian Chromatic Concept of Tonal Organization* (2001) and his examinations of solos by Miles Davis ("Four"), Eric Dolphy ("245"), and John Coltrane ("Giant Steps") in chapter V. [56]

Given the closeness of the group—Evans, Mulligan, Miles, Carisi, Lewis, Schuller *et al.*—Benson Brooks' contextualisation of Russell's ideas seems a fair assessment. Theirs was a world in which ideas and practices were discussed and shared and the Concept, not only drew on musicians' actual practise but, had practical application. There is also an issue of sequence to be considered. Russell first published the Lydian Concept six years after "Cubano-Be, Cubano-Bop" and it would be another five years before Miles recorded the classic "Milestones." It is therefore very likely that, ultimately, Russell's own recordings in the fifties and his writing for others did more to disseminate the use of modes, if not his deeper theoretical concerns, than the book itself.

Interviewed in 1958 by Dom Cerulli for a major article in *DownBeat*, Russell talked about this period and how he was exploring the Concept and its compositional applications.

> I'd usually compose for a short period then run into a problem that couldn't be explained, and I'd have to retreat into research again for the answer. It was frustrating, but I'd always find the answer. And following each of these revolutions, I'd find that the theory was more manipulative and easier to handle. And it placed more resources at my disposal.

And later,

> "My cycles of composing became longer and longer in duration, to the point where they are no longer interrupted by besieging problems, and I am free to grapple with the more subtle elements of music, such as taste . . . I think for the first time I had some inkling of what I was going after: a concept with a soul, born out of jazz and its needs, yet embracing all music created in the equal temperament system. I finished the thesis in 1953. [57]

It would be another three years before Russell got what turned out to be his most significant break so far. Vibraphonist Teddy Charles was recording an album for Ahmet Ertegun for Atlantic Records and had commissioned a number of writers to provide material. Gil Evans arranged "You Got to My Head," saxophonist Jimmy Giuffre provided "The Quiet Time" and Russell contributed "Lydian M-1." Featuring a ten-piece band with four saxes, trumpet, and a five-piece rhythm section, the album was in the modernist vein of the times. Highly arranged, well prepared, and beautifully played, its seven tracks sound much of a piece and bear comparison with the MJQ, *Birth of the Cool*, and the music Mulligan and Chet Baker were making. Unsurprisingly, the pieces commissioned from Evans, Giuffre, and Russell provided the meat of the record, and "Lydian M-1" revealed how far Russell's writing had progressed, albeit in the absence of any real recording or performance outlet. As Teddy Charles recalled, "I felt his 'Cubano-Be, Cubano-Bop' for Dizzy was a breakthrough to new music and a new harmonic, tonal, and rhythmical territory. Again, "Lydian M-1" was extraordinarily challenging. His personality was very different from our contemporaries." [58]

"Lydian M-1" was also one of the only Russell recordings that underwent major editing, as Russell told Ben Young of WKCR. It seems the band struggled with the music, and the engineer, Tom Dowd apparently, then battled to achieve a satisfactory cut.

> **GR:** "Lydian M-1," which was the piece that enabled me to . . . sort of put me on the map in terms of getting record dates, either to compose music for other people or featuring my own group, that piece "Lydian M-1" had . . . now I forget the engineer but he worked for Atlantic and he's very famous, Tom . . .
> **BY:** Tom Dowd?
> **GR:** Tom Dowd, his hair turned grey practically overnight because there were fifty-six splices on the piece, lasting just six minutes long. *(laughs)*
> **BY:** Were there problems putting it together? Were the musicians goofing up the solos?
> **GR:** Yeah, to have it turn out right, it took that and he was completely immersed in tape. He had tape attached to his belt, around his neck. Sometimes he looked like Tarzan.
> **BY:** Were you directing the edit?
> **GR:** Well, I was with him and wouldn't let him get away with anything in terms of shortcuts. Actually, it worked out. It doesn't really sound that way but Tom really sweated that. [59]

*Time* magazine liked Charles's album, noting, "Vibraphonist Charles, not content with rhythmic exploration, exploits harmonic possibilities developed by Duke Ellington, uses dissonance to create colour and mood rather than sheer shock. The album ranges from familiar ('Nature Boy') to far-out ('Lydian M-1')."[60] Teo Macero, later Miles Davis's producer, commented in *Metronome*, "'Lydian M-1' was by George Russell. This is my first association with his work. I felt that the composition did not come up to the level of [Gigi] Gryce or Charles' compositions but that it was well-worth hearing. He has potential as a composer but needs more of a 'classical' approach in developing his musical ideas."[61]

One hates to disagree with someone like Teo Macero but the piece has more ideas running through it than many a jazz LP of the time. The intricacy of the horn lines and the way they intersect with Charles' vibes is hugely impressive and, despite its complexity, "Lydian M-1" really swings.

It was heard by a young alto player called Hal McKusick. Apart from his involvement with Russell, McKusick has been largely overlooked as a musician but he made some fine records in his own name, with a sound somewhere between Paul Desmond and Lee Konitz. McKusick was doing a date for RCA Victor and had a budget that allowed him to recruit a number of writers for the project. The altoist had been working with a quartet of Barry Galbraith on guitar, Milt Hinton on bass and Osie Johnson on drums. Apparently, he had met Russell in the street and asked him to write something for his group. Eight months later, Russell rang him and told him the piece, "Lydian Lullaby," was ready.

McKusick knew Gil Evans from their time with the Thornhill band and Evans gave him "Blues for Pablo," later made famous by Miles Davis, and "Jambangle." For the rest, the record carried a couple of Jimmy Giuffre tunes, others by Johnny Mandel and Al Cohn and featured a quartet on some tracks and an octet on the remainder. The octet, incidentally, included Jimmy Raney on guitar and Sol Schlinger on baritone, both of whom had been on the Teddy Charles album. *Hal McKusick - Jazz Workshop* is a remarkable record. It is imaginative and forward-looking and is as concerned with the role of composition in jazz as it is with improvisation.

In the end, Russell contributed three tunes, "Lydian Lullaby," played by the quartet; "Miss Clara," performed by the octet; and "The Day John Brown Was Hanged" with the quartet and Russell himself on drums. (He also contributed tambourine on Evans's "Blues for Pablo"). On "Lydian Lullaby" the interplay between McKusick and Galbraith is marvellous but the tune then shifts abruptly into a second, slower, bluesy movement and from there into a swinging third section before returning to its opening theme. Its suite-like quality, with Russell using the quartet more as a classical composer might, creates a sense of thematic development. It is a quality that Stephanie Stein Crease has described as Russell's "advanced structural sensibility."[62] That same sensibility is even more evident on "The Day John Brown Was Hanged." As Russell later noted,

> "That was the period when I wrote short pieces. Each one's a little vignette. I like to think of it as a play that says something, that has different moods and different doors and different atmospheres, you know. From then on it was set."[63]

Each of its three movements has its own subtitle. The first—"The Day John Brown Was Hanged"—features Galbraith playing the melody of the "Battle Hymn of the

Republic" while McKusick wails a mournful spiritual in the distance, contrasting the formal, stately expression of loss with perhaps the more immediate grief felt by those left unfree. The second section—"Some Did a Dance"—is unironic with its gaily dancing alto over a swaying rhythm accompaniment. The third section—"Some Wailed the Blues"— builds to a mournful blues before the piece returns to a partial restatement of the opening theme.

This composition is Russell's second great contribution—after "Cubano-Be, Cubano-Bop"—to jazz and to American music generally. Two things stand out instantly. First, Russell has deliberately created a programmatic piece of music. Though others had done so before in jazz—notably Ellington, on compositions such as "Harlem Airshaft" as well as larger-scale works like *Black, Brown and Beige*—Russell's piece reveals an elaborate set of intentions. It is a highly political work, though not in any simplistic, "agitprop" sense. It is a quintessentially American work using American forms and subject matter and derived from an American sensibility. It acknowledges division, past and current, on racial matters, in particular in its second section. It notes the ambivalence in which Brown as a historical figure is held, despite his partial appropriation by the political establishment. Russell is perhaps suggesting that so radical a figure cannot be contained within the status quo implied by the "Battle Hymn." Its sophistication lies in the fact that Russell does not state his own position but implies those held by others—slaves and emancipated Negroes, southerners, Republicans and the north-eastern liberal political elite. He asks instead that listeners consider their own position in relation to those implied above. In these respects "The Day John Brown Was Hanged" goes far beyond anything before and much since in jazz. The second point that stands out is that Russell is again utilizing complex materials and techniques from jazz and classical music and bringing these together in a conscious and coherent form. However, here he is not writing for big band but for small jazz ensemble. [64]

"Miss Clara" sits uneasily in this company. It is, in comparison, a trifle— almost a throwaway. Described in the original sleeve notes as the kind of intentional "satire, in jazz terms, that might be associated with Fred Allen or Bob and Ray," [65] it plays with styles. There is a little bit of Dixieland interaction between the horns, a touch of blues; it sounds like an "out-of-towner's" expectation of his first night in a big-city jazz club. Like many musical jokes, it falls a little flat.

"Miss Clara" was recorded in April 1956, four weeks after "Lullaby" and "John Brown." By that time, fate had intervened in the lives of Russell and his young wife, in the avuncular form of Jack Lewis, RCA's head of jazz, as Russell told Ian Carr,

> And Jack was doing the Hal McKusick date and he liked what I was doing, you know. So one day we invited him to lunch in our one-room suite at the Beechwood. He took one look around. He said, "Oh man!" He said, "You know, you can't live like this." He said, "I'll get you your own record date and you can charge what you want to." So he did, you know. And that ... that was the RCA *Jazz Workshop* record, which came out of this Hal McKusick date, you know. And with the Workshop album we were able to move out of that place and move over to Bank Street. [66]

*DownBeat* even carried a short news item in its March 21, 1956, issue noting that Russell was working for RCA Victor on his own album and on McKusick's, although it mentions Kenny Dorham as the trumpeter they would use rather than Art Farmer, who actually played the dates. The short item also notes that McKusick's record would include "a six-minute suite by Russell titled 'John Brown'" and refers to Russell's inactivity on the scene since 1951 and the Konitz-Davis session, which had just been reissued as part of a 12-inch Prestige LP, *Conception*. [67]

Around this time, Russell also arranged a set of standards for the Hal McKusick Quartette— McKusick, Galbraith, Hinton, Johnson—a remarkable and innovative pianoless group. Recorded at the Brooklyn Academy of Music in November 1956, *Jazz at the Academy* was released on Coral and featured a stunning "Over the Rainbow" as a showcase for Hinton as well as beautiful versions of "These Foolish Things" and "Out of this World."

As Leonard Feather wrote at the time,

> That jazz and the academy are not incompatible, that their fusion does not have to produce a hybrid or reduce the authenticity of the resultant performance, can clearly be discerned in the present efforts of the Hal McKusick Quartette. They are the work of a skilled and well-trained leader, a compatible group of sideman, and a composer-arranger noted for his originality and resourcefulness. [68]

McKusick would continue to work with Russell through the fifties on other projects. He appeared on both *New York, N.Y.* (1959) and *Jazz in the Space Age* (1960), as well as on Russell's "All About Rosie" from the famous/infamous *Birth of the Third Stream* (1957) record, evidence of the Russell's loyalty to those whose work he admired. As an aside, I finally located McKusick after my original biography of the composer appeared. UK-based German composer/pianist Hans Koller, himself an admirer of Russell's work, got in touch with the saxophonist hoping to use his distinctive and delicate alto saxophone on one of his own recordings. Before that could happen, McKusick had died. Although his own career might have taken place in the margins of jazz history, the few records he made are a joyful reminder that there are still treasures to be rediscovered in jazz by those willing to search.

## Notes

1. Ian Carr, interview with Juanita Giuffre for BBC Radio 3 Broadcast George Russell—The Invisible Guru, July 1994.
2. Ben Young, broadcast devoted to George Russell in celebration of his seventy-fifth birthday, WKCR Radio, New York, June 23, 1998.
3. Ibid.
4. Ian Carr, interview with George Russell, June 1992.
5. See A. Clarkson, ed., *On the Music of Stefan Wolpe* (New York: Pendragon, 2003).
6. Cohen, "Diasporic Dialogues in Mid-Century New York: Stefan Wolpe, George Russell, Hannah Arendt, and the Historiography of Displacement," pp. 156-159.

7. J. Ronald Oakley, *God's Country: America in the Fifties*, (New York, NY: Dember Books, 1986), p.x.
8. Martin Halliwell, *American Culture in the 1950s* (Edinburgh: Edinburgh University Press, 2007); Stephen R. Duncan, *The Rebel Café: Sex, Race, and Politics in Cold War America's Nightclub Underground* (Baltimore, MD: John Hopkins, 2018)
9. Ingrid Monson. *Freedom Sounds: Civil Rights Callout to Jazz and Africa* (New York, NY: OUP. 2007) pp.29-65.
10. William T. Martin Riches, *The Civil Rights Movement: Struggle and Resistance*, (Basingstoke: Palgrave Macmillan, 2010), pp.10-18; Ralph F. de Bedts, *Recent American History: 1933 Through World War II*, (Homewood, IL: Dorsey, 1973), pp.334-337.
11. Tkweme, W. S. 2008 'Blues in Stereo: The Texts of Langston Hughes in Jazz Music' *African American Review* (AAR) 2008 Fall-Winter; 42 (3-4): 503-512.
12. Café Society was where Billie Holiday popularized the protest song "Strange Fruit." See Stephen R. Duncan. *The Rebel Café: Sex, Race and Politics in Cold war America's Nightclub Underground*. (Baltimore, MY: John Hopkins Press. 2018)
13. Stuart Cosgrove, "The Zoot-Suit and Style Warfare," *History Workshop Journal* 18 (Autumn 1984), pp. 77–91.
14. Houston R. Baker Jr., H. 1984 *Blues, Ideology and Afro-American Literature* (Chicago: University of Chicago Press), p.3.
15. Young, broadcast devoted to George Russell.
16. Ibid.
17. Interview with George Russell, April 2003.
18. Ibid.
19. Carr, interview with G. Russell, June 1992.
20. Interview with George Russell, June 2004
21. Carr, interview with G. Russell, June 1992.
22. Leonard Feather, "Dance Biz Needs Younger Leaders: DeFranco," *DownBeat*, March 9, 1951.
23. See Mike Baillie's sleeve notes in *The Artistry of Artie Shaw*, Fresh Sound FSR-CD397.
24. Interview with George Russell, October 2003.
25. Young, broadcast devoted to George Russell.
26. Interview with George Russell, October 2003.
27. Stein Crease. *Gil Evans: Out of the Cool*. (Chicago: A Cappela. 2002), pp.152-154.
28. Ibid. p.158-159.
29. Interview with Robert Moore, July 2004.
30. E-mail interview with George Schuller, May 2006.
31. See sleeve notes to *Miles Davis—The Complete Birth of the Cool*, Capitol 724349455023. NB. One of these would seem to be the ubiquitous "New World."
32. Interview with Gunther Schuller, October 2003.
33. Interview with Juanita Giuffre, June 2004.
34. Ibid.
35. Carr, interview with G. Russell, June 1992.
36. Interview with Giuffre.
37. Carr, interview with G. Russell, June 1992.
38. Interview with Giuffre.
39. Ibid.
40. Interview with G. Russell, October 2003.
41. Ibid.

42. Interview with Lee Konitz, April 2004.
43. Ibid. As a side note, Lee Konitz took part in a *DownBeat* "Blindfold Test" in 1957 and one track he reviewed was Russell's "Ye Hypocrite, Ye Beelzebub" from Russell's *Jazz Workshop* LP. "I like the written part of this very much. Sounds like something George Russell might have done." That said, Konitz was less impressed with the players and gave it three and a half stars out of a possible five. Lee Konitz, "Blind Date," *DownBeat*, July 11, 1958.
44. Brigid Cohen, "Diasporic Dialogues in Mid-Century New York: Stefan Wolpe, George Russell, Hannah Arendt, and the Historiography of Displacement," pp. 155-156.
45. Ibid. p. 156.
46. Conversation with George Russell, October 2006.
47. See Dom Cerulli, "George Russell," *DownBeat*, May 29, 1958, p. 16.
48. Carr, interview with G. Russell, June 1992.
49. Ibid.
50. Carr, interview with Giuffre, July 1994.
51. Young, broadcast devoted to George Russell.
52. Ibid.
53. George Russell—A Jazz Portrait, WGBH Radio, Boston.
54. Ian Carr, interview with John Lewis, The quote is taken from Carr's notebooks.
55. John Benson Brooks, "George Russell," *Jazz Review*, February 1960, p. 38.
56. See Dom Cerulli, "George Russell," *DownBeat*, May 29, 1958, p. 16.
57. George Russell, *Lydian Chromatic Concept of Tonal Organization* (Brookline, MA: Concept, 2001).
58. Interview with Teddy Charles, October 2007.
59. Young, broadcast devoted to George Russell.
60. Review of Teddy Charles Tentet, *Same* (Atlantic 1229), *Time*, May 21, 1956.
61. Teo Macero, Review of Teddy Charles Tentet, *Same* (Atlantic 1229), *Metronome*, June 1956. Ironically, Macero was given the same track to review in *DownBeat*'s "Blindfold Test," March 6, 1957. He notes that Russell is "a very talented composer" but that here, "[h]e didn't do anything with what he had. It was all at the same level, I think."
62. Stephanie Stein Crease, quoted by A. Kramer, sleeve notes to *George Russell—The Complete Bluebird Recordings*, Lonehill LHJ10177.
63. Young, broadcast devoted to George Russell.
64. See Max Harrison, "George Russell—Rational Anthems (Phase 1, 2, 3)," *Wire* (Spring/Summer/Autumn 1983): 31.
65. John S. Wilson, sleeve notes to *Hal McKusick—Jazz Workshop*, RCA Victor LPM1366.
66. Carr, interview with G. Russell, June 1992.
67. "Russell Writing for Victor Jazz," *DownBeat*, March 21, 1956.
68. Quoted in sleeve notes to *Hal McKusick Quartet—The Complete Barry Galbraith, Milt Hinton and Osie Johnson Recordings*, Lonehill LHJ10176. *High Fidelity* magazine was less impressed: "Jazz at the Academy is in the rather monotonous vein that McKusick had escaped from in the RCA Victor (Jazz Workshop) disc." No date but probably early 1957.

CHAPTER SIX

## Ballad of Hix Blewitt

The Russells' new address on Bank Street lay in Greenwich Village, which was still hip at that time but far from chichi. It was still a real step up from the Beechwood. Jack Lewis had acted as quickly as he had promised and Russell was in the studio recording the first of three sessions that would lead to his first album before Hal McKusick's record was actually finished. McKusick played alto and flute, Barry Galbraith guitar, Milt Hinton bass and Joe Harris drums. To these four were added trumpeter Art Farmer and pianist Bill Evans. Evans would prove to be one of two musicians, significant in themselves in jazz history, whose names would be forever associated with Russell. The other is Jan Garbarek, the Norwegian saxophonist.

Russell had met Evans through Lucy Reed, a singer he had known in Chicago and perhaps had had a relationship with. Russell would go on to work with Reed on her LP, *This Is Lucy Reed* (1957 Fantasy). The singer was performing in New York with Evans as her accompanist, at that time a role low on the food chain for a jazz musician. As Juanita Giuffre explained,

> Oh, Bill was a dear friend. He really was. He was a sweetheart and he looked like [a] minister's son. When we first met him, we went out on a ferry ride with a girl who had very much a big crush on George, but she brought Bill Evans anyway, and we went out on this ferry thing around New York City and Billy's standing there by the rail looking very studious and anything but a jazz musician and this girl was saying, "He plays very well and he's quite a nice piano player"—because he at that time was accompanying her, which to us was just like accompanying—we didn't think much of it.[1]

Russell's own recollection of the experience continues:

> A singer who lived in Chicago knew me—a very sweet singer—and she brought Bill up to the 24th Street hang where Juanita and I first lived with the one room. There wasn't anything to do on Sunday in New York, it was summertime and New York is like a desert. So she introduced me to her friend and he seemed very detached like a businessman, like he belonged to a bank, worked in a bank. He didn't seem to be very joyful. So I said in desperation, "Let's take the Staten Island Ferry," which we did, came back and Lucy said, "This man's a piano player. Ask him to play." That's one thing we had in the place—a piano. "Yeah, why don't we ask him to play. Why not, you know?" Expecting to hear a bank teller doodle on the piano. *(whistles)* It was one of those times when you feel like you're being blown up in witnessing a very special kind of adventure, as he played piano like nobody I ever heard. I didn't expect that outta him. All that self-reserve thing, you could see in his music there was much more to him. He and I became very good friends. I got him onto Victor. I wouldn't have anybody else. I knew who I wanted to play piano on the Victor album.[2]

Evans could evoke that kind of surprise despite his quiet and unassuming appearance and could do so without resorting to grandstanding or pyrotechnics. Pianist Jack Reilly, who later studied with both Russell and Lennie Tristano, first met Evans in the early fifties.

> I was at the Navy School of Music in Washington, D.C. I heard this piano playing coming from this room and I said, "What is that?" This guy said, "It's Bill." Shearing, Teddy Wilson, Bud Powell—everything but with a notch above and a synthesis already in his playing of all three. I said, "Oh my god!" Such fluency. I got to play with him. Then, of course, I got all his recordings; I got all the ones with George especially.[3]

With the support of Jack Lewis, Russell's *Jazz Workshop* took much of 1956 to prepare, rehearse and record. That painstaking care and attention to detail paid off, resulting in one of the great jazz albums of all time. On March 31 the sextet Russell had chosen went into the studio and recorded four sides—"Ye Hypocrite Ye Beelzebub," "Jack's Blues," "Livingstone I Presume," and "Ezz-Thetic." Four days later Russell was back in the studio with Hal McKusick and an octet to record "Miss Clara" for the saxophonist's own date. Though "Ezz-Thetic" had obviously been composed five years earlier, it is unclear whether the other three pieces were already written or whether Russell finished these between Lewis's offer of a contract and the date itself. The latter seems the more likely possibility. There was then a gap of seven months before the second session took place in October and the final four tunes were finished just before Christmas 1956.

During these gaps in recording, the musicians rehearsed every Sunday at Milt Hinton's place, as Russell recalled,

> It was wonderful because we did something that a lot of groups didn't do—we practiced

because Milt Hinton opened the door to his house in Jamaica Plain. I had done all the writing of the music, twelve songs, and Milt insisted we come out every Sunday and rehearse. So we were a well-rehearsed band, thanks to Milt, when we walked in that studio. Art Farmer, Bill Evans, you know, Milt Hinton, Barry Galbraith, especially Barry. Things were gradually working, I can't see why, for me. They gradually put me on the scene. We must have done something right. [4]

Milt Hinton offers a slightly different take on events. Describing the stressful nature and pace of studio work in his autobiography, he talks of the way he and his friends would relieve the stress with weekend jam sessions. "There really wasn't much of a chance to play jazz during the week and none of us were willing to give up sessions for a steady job in a club. So getting together and letting loose was a great way to unwind." As Hinton noted, it also allowed players to keep up with their peers and before long his house on Ruscoe Street became a "regular weekend hang-out." He continues, "After a while, some of us even put thirty-five dollars apiece in a kitty so we could pay a couple of composers and arrangers we knew to write for us. We contacted people like Manny Albam, George Russell and Gil Evans and they were overjoyed." [5]

Either way, this meant that when Russell's group got into the studio they knew the material inside out. Art Farmer told Ian Carr that it was the intricacy of Russell's tunes that demanded this regime:

We would rehearse every Sunday if everybody was available, and then we would take the music home and study it. It was hard and by the time we felt we were ready—or he felt we were ready—we would go in the studio and do two or three or four numbers because they were short numbers and so we could get around twelve tunes or something like that [on an album]. It wasn't easy. I think he was writing more intricate then because whatever the structure of the song was, well, that was what you really had to improvise on. It wasn't like writing one piece and then opening the thing up to improvise. If he had a 6/4 bar in the melody then you had to deal with that when you improvised. He had these chords. Sometimes he didn't know what to call them himself. I remember one time he had the guitarist, Barry Galbraith, he said, "Barry, what would you call this chord?" He played a chord on the piano. Playing the guitar, Barry's very used to leaving out notes. So he said, "I would call this such-and-such a chord with the fifth taken out" or something. [6]

But, as Farmer also told Carr, rehearsing to this extent meant the musicians were able to contribute more in their playing and enhance and even extend the compositions.

I remember, though, that some of the things on George's record when I was playing, when I was playing solo, I had worked with the music so closely that some of the things that sounded like they were part of the piece were actually my solo. We really did take some time on that but, ironically, no matter how much time you spent on it, when you got in the studio that's where you really learned it. *(laughs)* If you were thinking you were just going to go out there and coast, well, it wasn't like that at all. Anyway, it turned out very good and I was very proud to be a part of it. [7]

The album acted as a herald for the extensive use of modes in jazz not only as a compositional tool but primarily as a means of opening up improvisation. It is one of the records that many musicians instantly refer to when Russell is mentioned. In the nineties, when pianist/ composer Ran Blake got a petition together to request that RCA reissue the album, he had no problem getting signatures from hundreds of the major figures in the music. Two years before Miles Davis and *Kind of Blue* raised the bar still higher, the album set new standards for small group playing and writing. Each of its twelve tracks is a mini-drama, complete unto itself and the listener is instantly drawn into an almost filmic evocation of images of jazz clubs, city life and constant movement.

"Ezz-Thetic" received a remarkably assured reading, with a sparkling solo from Evans and some sharp playing from the rest of the band, while "Livingstone I Presume" is a witty and playful picture complete with jungle sounds. However, it is with "Concerto for Billy the Kid" that the album really takes off. Paul Motian replaced Joe Harris on drums for this session. He remembered it only vaguely when interviewed but recalled that it was not typical of the jazz record sessions that he was used to.

> It was very different from what I expected or what I had experienced up to that time. It seemed like it was really different. It was kind of a small group of seven or eight musicians, something unusual for me. I don't really know about that, but I did my best and it sounds pretty good now. Bill Evans sounds incredible on that. Milt Hinton was the bass player, I recall. [8]

On "Concerto," Motian's opening cymbal ride creates an immediate sense of urgent expectation. First Farmer and McKusick and then Evans and Galbraith grab the attention with a series of repeating phrases, extending or doubling its complex lines. Evans takes his solo in two parts, split by a unison section with the horns and guitar. It swings, races, twists and turns before Farmer takes a short chorus. This is Evans's first great solo in recorded jazz and one of the album's high points. The second, unused version of this number from the session lacks the energy of the one chosen for release but there are people who think that Evans's second solo is even better than the first, with its well-chosen quote from Thelonious Monk's "Well You Needn't."

"Round Johnny Rondo" has a fugue-like quality and uses quite dissonant counterpoint between the horns to create a sense of movement and tension. "Witch Hunt" is a helter-skelter pursuit that returns at the end to its starting point. Whether Russell was making a political point, given the tenor of the times, with its title is unclear. Beyond the nagging, babel-like introduction there is little to suggest such a connection. Indeed, its middle-section and solos are warm, bright and confident in mood. However, it is the four pieces from the final session in December that seem in some ways the most ambitious. On that occasion, Osie Johnson on drums and Teddy Kotick on bass replaced Motian and Hinton.

"Ballad of Hix Blewitt" requires some explanation, because Russell has always published his music under the name of Russ-Hix. The composer's own notes refer to the "memory of a friend with a legendary quality." Russell goes on to describe a man who combined "the West, the Blues and good Dixie humour in his character." According to

Russell's third wife, Alice, he knew Hix Blewitt from his and Juanita's time at the Beechwood Hotel.

> Hix was a Texan. He played clarinet with [I believe] the Bob Crosby Orchestra. Hix left the Orchestra because he left his dentures in a hotel room in Chicago and couldn't afford to replace them. In New York, he found a gig transcribing tunes for a wealthy man who thought himself a songwriter. Although he couldn't read music, he would sing the melody and lyrics and Hix would write it all down. He was a dedicated alcoholic who was fond of saying "Hix Blewitt and no one heard it." [9]

This appropriately elegiac composition sets McKusick's lovely flute playing against a soft, delicate guitar and piano accompaniment before the rest of the group comes in. It plays around with the overall tonality and seems to move between keys, its classical, pastoral feel recalling something of Copland and Ives. The ballad indicates Russell's capacity for empathy with people often from very different worlds and experiences than his own and illustrates how their histories feed into his own vision and art.

"Knights of the Steamtable" doffs its hat respectfully to Russell's former colleagues in the catering industry and to his friend Gerry Mulligan, who had written a tune called "Knights of the Turntable," dedicated to New York's jazz DJs. It is marked by the way it uses polytonality as Farmer's trumpet solo improvises in A-minor against the overall key of the piece in B-flat minor. "Sad Sergeant" draws on an old spiritual but adds a martial feel to what is essentially a blues number. Like several of the compositions on the album, it has an episodic quality, with Russell creating a series of short, dynamic movements within the short space of the tune.

The most surprising piece on the record, however, is "Fellow Delegates." Featuring Russell's only recorded percussion solo, its middle section comprises a part-improvised duet with Osie Johnson using wood-blocks and Russell himself performing on chromatically tuned drums (Boo-Bams) made by "David Wheat's Musical Engineering Associates of Sausalito, California."

David "Buck" Wheat was a jazz and folk musician, who came to fame with the Kingston Trio. However, he and his business partner Bill Loughborough were also instrument makers, who had created musical instruments for the maverick hobo composer Harry Partch. Boo-Bams were made from Bamboo, hence the name, and it is their distinctive sound that served to make "Fellow Delegates" into something quite unique in jazz. Indeed, when the rest of the group return to play the polytonal theme, the sense is less of jazz rather than something much more akin to the advanced contemporary composition being created in Europe and America. To my ears, there are distinct parallels with Partch's music, perhaps also with Louis "Moondog" Hardin and the music that Steve Reich would later create in terms of the structure of the piece and its cyclical movement. It remains one of the most unusual pieces Russell has written and recorded.

*Jazz Workshop* was the only album Russell made for RCA. According to him, Jack Lewis was not popular among the suits at the company and the knives were out for him. The group featured on the record was, with the exception of a TV broadcast for NBC (*The Subject Is Jazz*, broadcast on June 28, 1958), a studio band and never did any gigs. In fact, it was not till the sixties that Russell had a regular working band. Still, as a "nonperformer" and with no real wish to be in the spotlight, why would he have wanted to form his own ensemble?

Both the McKusick and Russell records were released in 1957. *DownBeat* gave McKusick five stars and Nat Hentoff commented, "I was most moved by Russell, Evans and Giuffre, particularly by Russell's extraordinarily evocative, functionally dramatic 'John Brown', the longest work in the set." The *Washington Post* also singled out the same tune as the "most ambitious and successful" track in its review, on an album where "improvisation is subordinated to very well-written compositions, which are far superior to the usual jazz originals." Fred Sherman in the *Miami Herald* called "John Brown" "superlative" and C. H. Garrigues in the *San Francisco Examiner* described it as "as bitter and as topical a piece as Ellington ever wrote." [10]

Don L. McIver in the *Fort Lauderdale Sunday News* provided one dissenting voice.

> Then comes George Russell with "The Day John Brown Was Hanged", "Miss Clara" and "Lydian Lullaby." Russell's billed as a "formulator of a new set of tonal principles based on the Lydian mode" whatever that means. The result leaves the reviewer cold. If anyone had bothered to check, Russell's "new" principles can be found in the arranging system formulated by Schillinger in the early part of the century and used extensively by every modern-day composer from Hindemith through Bernstein and by such jazz luminaries as Eddie Sauter and Bill Finegan. [11]

We can be certain that Russell had never intended to cause such offence! There is inevitably overlap between Russell's ideas and those of Schillinger, given the common territory they were exploring. Both were interested in the scientific and mathematical underpinnings of music and, in Schillinger's case, he proposed that certain patterns were common to music and the very structure of the human nervous system. Neither system is prescriptive and both lay claim to universality. It is also worth noting that McIver is wrong about when and where Schillinger's method was developed and who it influenced. Among his pupils were many from jazz and popular music, including Benny Goodman and Tommy Dorsey and from classical music George Gershwin and from film Carmine Coppola. However, Sauter and Finnegan were not, it seems, among them. Hindemith derived his own set of principles and ideas quite separately. For a time Schillinger's biggest source of influence came through Lawrence Berk, who went on to found the Berklee School of Music, where Schillinger's system was taught up to the 1960s.

However, perhaps the simplest way of defining the differences between Russell and Schillinger is to note that Russell developed his ideas from study of the circle of fifths and the overtone series and the application in music of the relationship between chords and scales. Schillinger's intention was much more pedagogical in its focus and concerned with developing the range of resources available to the composer through an understanding of the relationship between mathematics and music. The other point of significant difference is in terms of compositional outcome. Russell has proved himself a composer of note and distinction, while Schillinger's own works are largely dismissed.

*Metronome* expressed perhaps the majority opinion and did so articulately.

Most impressive of the writing is that of George Russell and Gil Evans. Russell, especially on "Lydian Lullaby," "John Brown" and "Miss Clara" seems to have that unique ability to portray the varieties of feeling in a given situation. It's much like turning a stone about in the sun and noticing the multiple variations of design and reflection that come to the eye. [12]

With regard to Russell's own debut album, The *Village Voice* carried a short interview by Bob Reisner with Russell in its July 10, 1957, issue, in which Russell says, "The jazz composer is no different from the classical composer except that he uses the rhythmic and tonal language of jazz. He also leaves little gaps for improvisation. The best jazz composition, in fact, does not sound written but improvised." This echoes the point that Art Farmer made above, when interviewed by Ian Carr. Russell was reiterating remarks he had already made in the intelligent, if grandiloquent, sleeve notes he wrote for his own *Jazz Workshop* release, from which both Nat Hentoff in the *Saturday Review* and the uncredited writer in *Jazz Today* quoted extensively in their reviews of the record. However, the point Russell makes in those notes is a useful one—the jazz composer draws on the jazz tradition of improvisation and holds this in focus not just in presenting material for the soloist to improvise but by utilizing the vitality and practice of "its strongest improvisers" and by conveying that improvisatory, dynamic spirit within the written material. There were also further interview pieces in the *Cincinnati Post*, *Jazz Today*, and the magazine of Russell's union, the *RWDSU Record*. [13]

However, in those same notes, and in discussion of his achievements by critics, Russell may have inadvertently set up a further obstacle to the reception of his music. Polly Cochran's heartfelt piece in the *Indianapolis Star* reflected a certain sense of alienation. While she clearly appreciated Russell's music, she commented, "There is much to enjoy and admire about this LP." However, she also noted, "But one look at the complicated liner notes and comes the feeling that your pleasure and/or disappointments are those of a retarded mind. You're not hip." This is no cultural Philistine talking. Rather, Cochran presents the dilemma facing the "ordinary fan," that modern jazz had advanced to a stage where it sometimes seemed that one could not truly understand or appreciate it without a degree in music and unless one was one of the chosen of an esoteric minority. She continued, "Still, these are growing pains jazz must suffer. And composers such as Russell help to nurture that growth." [14]

Others were less equivocal, however, about Russell's *Jazz Workshop*. C. H. Garrigues, again in the *San Francisco Examiner*, spoke of Russell taking jazz "out of the realm of casual improvisation and into that of serious composition." Noting Russell's intentions as expressed in his notes, *Hi-Fi Low-Down* commented, "We feel that Russell has accomplished this purpose to an amazing degree." In *DownBeat*, Leonard Feather was even more enthusiastic. Awarding the LP five stars, he noted that Russell had succeeded in extending the harmonic possibilities of jazz without resorting to atonality or the "Schoenberg mathematics of the juggled twelve-tone row." In this regard, Feather commented, "Russell has succeeded in lifting his album to a unique status and stature." [15]

Such comments were echoed in *Cash Box*, which called it a "fascinating, expertly performed jazz platter," while *Billboard* commented on Russell's ability to close the gap between written and improvised jazz and called him "one of the more original composing minds in contemporary music." Memphis's *Commercial Appeal*—and what an ironic title that is in this context—on the other hand, did not like the album, calling it "dull and unswinging."[16]

However fulsome such praise from Feather et al, in a sense, these critics indirectly illustrated Polly Cochran's lament. Perhaps Russell would have been better served if his supporters in the media had emphasized the sense of swing and enthusiasm that pervades these performances. They could have noted how the material creates startling and exciting opportunities for the musicians. They could have pointed out how Russell draws on the blues, spirituals and jazz to reaffirm jazz as a music as much indebted to folk music as it is to European classical forms. They might also have stressed the drama, good humour and wit that these twelve tunes convey. In fairness, Hentoff, Feather and others did mention these things and more than in passing. But somehow it got lost in the desire to grasp a music that challenged as much as it confirmed, to have a jazz that was Art with a capital A.

One of the most touching items I discovered in George Russell's personal scrapbook was a letter from Ernest Green, a sixteen-year-old African-American student at Central High School in Little Rock, Arkansas. For a short time in 1957, the world watched as nine black children were determined to exercise their right to attend the school of their choice, despite the threats and jeers of white supremacists and the opposition of the state governor, Orville Faubus. So extreme and awful were the TV and newspaper reports that President Dwight D. Eisenhower called out the troops to ensure the children were safely escorted into the school building, as was their legal right. As the veteran (white) radical commentator I. F. Stone wrote at the time, perhaps just a little presumptuously but with understandable rage and passion,

> When a station wagon guarded by army jeeps took little Negro children to and from school instead of leaving them to run the gauntlet of hate alone, the Negro felt that for the first time in American history he was being treated like a first-class citizen, that for a wonderful moment he was no longer on the outside, wistfully looking in.[17]

Ernest was the oldest and "leader" of the nine and a newspaper clipping in Russell's files describes him as a jazz fan. Russell responded to this by sending him a copy of the *Jazz Workshop* album. Ernest's reply reads, "When I received your album I was so thrilled I hardly knew what to do." Later, he says, "I really dig your writings and the titles are the absolute *end*." Given Russell's own experiences as an adolescent at school in Cincinnati, the reader may justifiably surmise that no review ever meant as much to the composer.[18]

The reviews of *Jazz Workshop* provide a sense of jazz at a turning point, moving away from its place as entertainment or dance music to something more rarefied, intellectual and serious—a music more at home in the concert hall than in the club or speakeasy. In reality, both the exoticist images that surrounded jazz and those that would see it as an unsophisticated folk music were always ideological and social constructions that denied it status and value. Jazz was bound to develop and with the (chronically slow, perhaps) breaking down of racial barriers would come a broader intellectual and social acceptance of African-Americans and their cultural contributions. Sadly, admission to the Academy always comes at a price. Jazz could never be innocent again—if ever it was.

With *Jazz Workshop* Russell had finally arrived, and two other records helped heighten his profile on the scene during this period, as well as replenishing his and Juanita's finances. They were both albums by women singers. The first, *Moody Marilyn Moore* (Bethlehem BCP 73), was by saxophonist Al Cohn's then wife. Russell contributed three arrangements to the record. "If Love is Trouble" and "Born to Blow the Blues," were both songs with lyrics by Jack Segal, with whom Russell had once shared an apartment. The other Russell track is Alec Wilder's "Trouble is a Man." Moore was a singer who wore her debt to Billie Holiday on her sleeve and Russell's settings work well with this in mind. However, it is Bob Russell and Jack Segal's "Born to Blow the Blues" that is most obviously Russell's work, with its intriguing tone colours and the way the different instruments relate to each other and to Moore herself. The record received a five-star review in *DownBeat* from Leonard Feather, who singled out "Born to Blow the Blues" as a "little-known and valuable" choice of material. [19]

The second album to which Russell, and Gil Evans, contributed at that time was *This Is Lucy Reed* (Fantasy 3243). The record was made partly in New York and partly in Chicago. The Chicago tracks featured a completely different band and arrangements by pianist Eddie Higgins.

In comparison with Evans's and Russell's efforts, the tracks recorded in Chicago are ordinary girl singer fare, as is the one other arrangement from Jack English. [20] Evans's take on Cole Porter's "Love for Sale" is a delight, as is "No Moon At All," with its Thornhill-like easy-going swing. Of Russell's three tracks, "Born to Blow the Blues" is given a somewhat different, almost operatic arrangement compared to the Mandy Moore version. It features Art Farmer on trumpet, who shadows Reed's voice perfectly, while guitarist Barry Galbraith and bassist Milt Hinton offer fine support. Sol Schlinger, who also played on the Teddy Charles session, was on baritone sax and bass clarinet and Romeo Penque played flute and English horn, while Don Abney is on piano and Russell himself on drums. His arrangement of "This Is New," from Kurt Weill and Ira Gershwin, is a rich confection indeed, and, like Evans, he succeeds in creating a really full orchestral sound from so small an ensemble. However, the standout track is "In the Wee Small Hours of the Morning."

Given the defining quality of the Sinatra-Riddle version of two years earlier, it might almost seem an affront to attempt it. But Russell and Reed transform it into a subtle, quiet, yet cinematic little gem. Taken even slower than Sinatra's version, Russell locates Reed's voice in the centre of the ensemble, which he uses sparingly. Those points when some instruments drop out—for example, where just Galbraith, Hinton, and Russell are heard behind the voice—are spine-tingling. Such moments heighten the drama when the whole group is heard and Galbraith is quite astonishing. Russell would later describe him as his "orchestra." This performance explains why.

Asked around this time by a *Village Voice* journalist what the difference between arranging and composing was, Russell replied, "It's around 95 cents. Union scale is $4.60 per four-bar page for composition and $3.65 for arrangement." [21]

Russell was being only partly facetious. Talking to Ian Carr, Russell said, "I never would get a lot of work but I'd always get enough work to pay the bills." Russell referred back to his connection with Hal McKusick. "McKusick again would get a couple of albums. And he did get a couple and but this time for Decca. So, I wrote some things for him—like 'Stratusphunk' came out of one of his Decca Recordings. That was in '58. I did a whole Brooklyn Academy record for him. And that was living money." [22]

Maybe Russell had been slow to make an impact on the jazz scene. He and Juanita had struggled—but now, with the help of the renowned Milt Gabler, his fortunes were about to take a turn for the better and his critical and artistic standing would at last begin to reflect the expectations his friends had for him.

Early in 1957, an even more significant break had come Russell's way. In its April 4, 1957, issue, *DownBeat* carried a short news item, "Six Works of Jazz Commissioned by Brandeis University." Brandeis was the first academic institution to commission a series of "jazz and jazz-influenced compositions." Each composer was paid $350 and three classical composers—Gunther Schuller, Milton Babbitt and Harold Shapero—were asked to compose classical pieces making reference to jazz, while three writers from jazz were to compose pieces for jazz orchestra. The three jazz musicians, chosen by Schuller and critic Nat Hentoff, were Jimmy Giuffre, Charles Mingus and George Russell. The concert was scheduled for June as part of the Brandeis Creative Artists Festival. [23]

Schuller is generally credited with coining the term "Third Stream" to describe music coming either from the jazz or the classical genre that drew heavily on both traditions at a symposium following the concert. In 1955 he and John Lewis had formed the Modern Jazz Society to promote "difficult" music that was rarely heard properly rehearsed and performed in concert venues and this subsequently became the Jazz and Classical Music Society. That same year, a concert was given by the society at New York's Town Hall featuring music from Lewis, Jimmy Giuffre, and J. J. Johnson. A second concert was planned for 1956 to feature a piece by Schuller, *Symphony for Brass and Percussion*. However, this would have clashed with another performance of the work in New York and plans were shelved. That concert finally went ahead at Brandeis in Waltham, Massachusetts, on June 6, 1957, though featuring a different Schuller composition.

Of the jazz works, all three seem to have been well received. Writing in *DownBeat*, Reverend Norman O'Connor, chaplain at Boston University and a great friend to many in the jazz world, was generous in his comments about the three jazz compositions but critical of Babbitt and Shapero's efforts—"All Set" and "On Green Mountain," respectively—and diplomatic about Schuller's "Transformation." His verdict was that Russell's *All About Rosie* "was the most successful of the material by jazz personalities" and described it as "quite taut and with strong rhythmic tension." He added, "For the jazz listener, the entire program lacked the fire and excitement of good jazz. Strangely, these most valuable characteristics of jazz were the most neglected in the concert." [24] Pianist, Richard Katz, writing in *Jazz Today*, was hesitant when considering whether jazz could achieve equal status with classical music in the near future, at least in America. However, he was full of enthusiasm for all of the music, except Babbitt's twelve-tone "All Set," calling it a "brainwasher." He described *All About Rosie* as "a stunning work" that "really caught fire and was extremely well-received." With Giuffre's "Suspensions," Katz noted "the charm of the deceptively simple folk-blues tinged melodies" and in Mingus's "Revelations" he drew attention to its "almost Wagnerian, brooding-like intensity." But of most importance about his comments was Katz's sense that it was an "event of far-reaching significance." If he were to have added that it would have consequences that its progenitors had not intended, he would have been seriously prescient. [25]

Among the band members were the now usual suspects Hal McKusick, Bill Evans, Art Farmer, Barry Galbraith and Teddy Charles. Schuller conducted the orchestra, except on "All About Rosie," which Russell conducted. At the concert and on the recording that followed, Milt Hinton and Osie Johnson also played in the ensemble. Two records were later released on Columbia. *Music for Brass* included J. J. Johnson's "Poem for Brass," John Lewis' "Three Little Feelings," featuring Miles Davis, and Giuffre's "Pharaoh," as well as Schuller's "Symphony for Brass and Percussion." *Modern Jazz Concert* featured all of the pieces from Brandeis. [26]

If Katz's comments were full of foresight, Nat Hentoff's article in *DownBeat*, "Jazz's Third Stream," had the benefit of hindsight. Expressing his own initial reservations about the potential for a "durable" new music of this kind, Hentoff allows that some composers—he cites John Lewis, Schuller, Russell and Mingus—have the potential to develop such ideas without disservice to either jazz or classical music. Discussing the Brandeis disc, it is Russell's "All About Rosie" that Hentoff singles out for praise. He calls it "brilliant" and says that it convinced him "more than any modern jazz extended form piece I had heard until then" that "a fairly long composed Jazz work could actually enhance and intensify the improvised solos within it, as in the case of Bill Evans' startling explosion in 'Rosie'" Ralph J. Gleason was similarly enthusiastic in a piece for the *San Francisco Chronicle*, though he singled out Mingus's *Revelations* for the highest praise. Again, one gets the sense from Gleason's article that the mould had been broken. [27]

In the first edition of this biography, *George Russell: The Story of an American Composer*, I described Russell as "one of the most obviously 'Third Stream' composers to come out of jazz." [28] I will clarify this more fully in the final chapter when I review the Lydian Concept and Russell's approach to composition in more detail. It is important to say here, that Russell was primarily and saw himself as a "jazz composer." It is true that he drew on a wide range of musical influences, not least from European art music, including its post-Darmstadt developments. With hindsight, what I should have stressed in this context was, not that Russell could be seen as a "Third Stream' composer by virtue of such influences from classical music, but rather because of the way he used these to develop his own singular approach to jazz composing and its relationship to improvisation.

Lewis and Schuller had formed the Jazz and Classical Music Society with the aim of enhancing the status of jazz as a composed music and promoting its credibility as an art form. The aim was laudable but, as Katz noted in his piece, however far the music might have been changing jazz was far from equal in terms of financial support, academic respectability or access to rehearsal, recording and performance opportunities. The real significance of Brandeis and Lewis and Schuller's valiant efforts lay not just in what it would lead to but in the way it predicted the dilemma that would face jazz for the next fifty years and beyond. The very possibility that it might be a unique form in its own right does not appear to have been under consideration. Rather the questions posed were - is jazz an art music for the concert stage, one that can be taught academically alongside classical music—or is it a popular form allied to show business that is at its most potent through its connection with a pop vernacular culture and best confined to and learned on the club stage?

Of course, it is quite arbitrary to say that it cannot be both. The classical repertoire is performed in small venues, churches and village halls by jobbing musicians and amateurs, as well as by the virtuoso professionals of the major orchestras in the grand cathedrals of culture like Carnegie Hall and the Royal Opera House. It begs another question, as well, namely how much of that repertoire has been rendered trite by overperformance and unambitious programming? The classical audience can often be remarkably unadventurous in its tastes. Yet its support by governments, record companies and paying public continues despite this. The difference between this reality and the world of jazz, where its major writer-composer-performers form one progressive strand, while another relies largely on re-treading the past of bebop, swing and trad, is perhaps more imagined than real. In a sense, those local and small venue gigs, like their classical counterparts, keep the language alive, while the grander works extend and revitalize it. The difference, perhaps, lies in the scale and variety of the classical repertoire and in the respect in which it is held by the cultural establishment.

While some European countries have permanent big bands, often attached to radio stations, performing works by established jazz composers and newly commissioned works, the same is not true of the United States, Britain and many other developed countries. It may be that this is the way forward for jazz and a way of realizing Schuller and Lewis's dream that would allow for regular performance of important jazz compositions and new works that would serve an existing audience, while developing a new one. Certainly, the fossilization of a jazz tradition that presents jazz as a museum exhibit and allows only space for those new works that fall within a canonical style will never advance its cause.

In fact, without wishing to dispute the desirability of more equitable funding for jazz and other non-classical 'art' musics, I would question whether such attempts to locate jazz in relation to classical music do not do disservice to both. Jazz needs to be valued for itself, on its own terms. Achieving that must involve a far more radical challenging of ideological, cultural and racial assumptions than that suggested by Schuller and Lewis' approach. It is that approach and argument midwifed by Schuller and Lewis in the mid-fifties onwards that has continued to dominate debate around such access and funding issues across differing national jazz scenes ever since. However, at least Schuller and Lewis raised the issue. How we respond in the present is another matter.

The other by-product of Brandeis would be the jazz education movement and, again, Gunther Schuller and John Lewis would be prime movers in that cause.

Lawrence Berk, a dance band composer and arranger, had already established the Berklee School of Music in 1945. Berk had studied with Joseph Schillinger and was one of only twelve pupils, often referred to as "the twelve disciples," authorized by Schillinger to teach his system. Called originally Schillinger House—"Boston's Progressive School of Music"—the school offered a four-year diploma course based on Schillinger's principles with a curriculum "designed for a broad range of interests." As the school's prospectus promised, "From the writer of popular songs to the symphonist, from the arranger of tunes for dance bands to the orchestrator of television and moving picture scores, from the composer of radio jingles to the creator of tone poems." [29] As this makes clear, Berk intended his school to be broad-based and within the mainstream of popular music rather than concerned with jazz. That said, Berklee has since become associated with the music of jazz and, fairly or not, with a particular style of jazz education.

Lewis and Schuller's aims, however, focused specifically on the teaching of jazz rather than Berk's more-broad-based musical educational intentions. 1957 was an important year for American jazz. Not only was the Brandeis concert a milestone, the year saw a number of important record releases, including Russell's and McKusick's Workshop dates. [30] It was also the year of the first of four annual summer schools—the Lenox School of Jazz. Lewis and Schuller wanted to provide the opportunity for students to study jazz and be taught by some of the leading names active on the scene. It was in every sense a continuation of their goal to raise the profile and stature of jazz. Jazz was being put forward as a music of the concert hall, one to be taught in the conservatory and, in those respects, their aim was quite different from that of Lawrence Berk.

According to researcher Michael Fitzgerald,

> The School was an outgrowth of a lecture series that had been in existence in Lenox since 1950. These roundtables were started by Dr. Marshall Stearns, a professor of English at Hunter College. Stearns, who later was the founder of the Institute of Jazz Studies, now housed at Rutgers University, brought the greatest minds in music together to discuss jazz in all of its many aspects and intricacies. Their goal was to show that "Jazz is a significant contribution to American culture." [31]

As Gunther Schuller explained, "No one was teaching jazz, and though that didn't prevent the great ones from being great—they learned self-taught— but the time came when John [Lewis] thought we should have a real kind of academy where themes about jazz are taught to talented young people." [32]

In its March 6, 1957, issue, *DownBeat* printed a news item, "Jazz School's First Session at Lenox," promising a three-week jazz summer school in the Berkshire Mountains taught and staffed by "top-ranking" musicians. Planned guest lectures included Duke Ellington, George Russell, Gunther Schuller, African-American author Langston Hughes and promoter/impresario Norman Granz. [33]

Though not announced at the time, faculty members that first year included Dizzy Gillespie, guitarist Jim Hall, Jimmy Giuffre, Max Roach, John Lewis (who was executive director), MJQ drummer Connie Kay, Percy Heath and MJQ vibraphonist Milt Jackson. The school was aided by the provision of funds and premises on the estate of patrons of the arts Stephanie and Phillip Barber. Now an executive housing estate and luxury hotel, Wheatleigh Hall and its surroundings provided an astonishingly lovely setting for the school over the next four years. During that time 122 students passed through the school, including several later figures of significance in jazz and jazz education such as Jamey Aebersold, Dave Baker and Larry Ridley; producer Arif Mardin; journalist Don Heckman; and musicians Ran Blake, Mike Gibbs, Attila Zoller, Ian Underwood (later of the Mothers of Invention), Don Ellis, Steve Kuhn, Bob Dorough, Steve Marcus, Gary McFarland and J. R. Monterose.

Gunther Schuller was invited by Lewis to assist in developing the course.

> John and I were very close and I had all kinds of connections that he didn't have in the managerial world and the classical world in general. So he invited me to kind of co-organize the thing with him, which we did. But it turns out that the idea was too far ahead of its time and it only lasted three years, mainly because financially it could not be supported enough. The Barbers gave a lot of their own personal wealth, not that they were all that wealthy, and income, but they finally had to give it up. But while it lasted it was about thirty, forty years ahead of its time. [34]

Russell did not teach the first year as a faculty member but gave a lecture titled "Techniques in Jazz Composition." An article in *DownBeat* in October 1957 reported that he would be on the faculty the following year. Clearly his profile in the jazz world had risen to the point where this was considered significant in itself. According to Schuller, he and Lewis had always intended to involve Russell.

> So John and I both immediately had the idea when the Lennox School of Jazz came around that—my god, here's a man who's a wonderful musician, composer, pianist and he's a theoretician of jazz. We've never had anything like that. So it was a unique opportunity to bring that kind of thinking and that kind of a concept that we've had for hundreds of years in the field of classical music and to bring that to the school. I represented, along with Martin Williams, the teaching of the history of jazz. George was in charge of teaching his Lydian Concept to the young students and creating a theoretical consciousness and the others were the instrumental teachers. [35]

Russell taught composition from 1958 to 1960, and the school, though planned to continue in 1961, was cancelled that year due to lack of finances. It did, however, establish a model that has fostered and informed jazz summer schools, not least those run by Jamey Aebersold's organization and permanent college-based jazz courses ever since.

Reading comments from students who attended the school in 1957 on Mike Fitzgerald's website, the two most striking points made about Lenox were its democratic ethos and how the school experience served to demystify jazz and its musicians. If anything it was the access to established artists that seems to have inspired students, whilst also helping to counter some of the myths about these once-exotic creatures, who proved nothing like the stereo-types so loved of the media. [36]

Composer and trombonist Mike Gibbs echoed some of this in his comments at interview for the first edition. His main point, however, concerned how Russell's lectures helped him gain a new perspective on jazz composition. Gibbs had arrived in Boston from what was then Rhodesia in 1959 to study at Berklee College of Music and enrolled at the Lenox School in 1960. He recalled both what he learned from attending Russell's classes and how this contrasted with the musical education that he was receiving at Berklee. For Gibbs, already developing as a composer, the Lydian Concept had seemed more concerned with improvisation than composition. However, as Russell discussed his approach to scales with the class, an important insight struck Gibbs.

> He had about seven scales all with the name Lydian in there. They all started from the Lydian scale, but the last scale was chromatic, with all the twelve notes. He even called that the Lydian Chromatic Scale, something like that and it just suddenly hit me. Throughout my life I've always maintained that all the notes are available in a tonal situation. It doesn't have to be atonal. I just liked that as a concept and I came away from George's classes with that. It was how I was understanding what he was doing and then I decided to devise my own way to do it. In a way what I do is to devise my own way for each piece that I write. It's not really a method. It's just a concept but all the notes are available because we were learning at Berklee that you can't use this note in this tonal situation. You mustn't have a Flat 9 here. All these "must-nots." I kind of rebelled against that and was always looking for a way to do that. Then George comes up with this scale with all the notes in it and you could use all the notes in a harmonic situation. I'm really simplifying what he's saying but this was very thrilling for me. I was in awe of him because he was a name even then. [37]

Perhaps the most famous Lenox incident occurred in 1959, when Ornette Coleman and members of his group attended the school—officially, at least—as students. As Schuller put it forty-five years later, "The great thing was to have Ornette Coleman, who was already a fully developed genius on the frontier of jazz, and he was a student there—technically speaking." [38]

According to legend, John Lewis, already a fan of Coleman, wanted to introduce him to a wider and discerning public. Interviewed in 2005, Coleman remained unclear as to what the deal was. "I didn't know it was a school. I guess maybe it was. I thought it was a retreat. I didn't really have an idea what it was." And as he noted, "I really didn't have any idea what I was doing there. But I thought it was something to do with me having to meet more musicians because I had just gotten to New York." [39]

It seemed to him at the time that "I guess what they were trying to do was analyse the quality of improvised music, [whether it] was eventually going to open up or to reveal what could be done with a different way of writing music. It was very enjoyable to be there. There wasn't a lot of things you could discover because I was already playing the way I was playing before I got there." Coleman liked the atmosphere, however, which he also described as "very democratic." [40]

Hearing Coleman play for the first time that summer at Lenox is one of Russell's strongest memories of the school.

> I had heard that there was a madman coming to the school who was sensational. Jimmy Giuffre and I were sitting on a Sunday afternoon, sitting in that wonderful garden on the grass, and we suddenly heard coming from the music bar this music. He looked at me. I looked at Jim. We'd never heard music like that. It was Ornette. We'd all been expecting to hear him because John Lewis discovered him. Giuffre and I looked at each other and said, "Whoa! That's something." [41]

Russell also remembered that Coleman put him on the spot in one class with a question he asked. "I had heard about the kind of vacuous questions this fellow from the coast used to ask. So Ornette got up and begins talking. He said, 'What is the tonic?' *(laughing)* I said, 'What?' He said, 'What is the tonic?'" To make matters worse, friends and musicians like Lewis, Connie Kay and Percy Heath were in the room. "I'm with all these guys. I don't know how I got out of that. I don't think I did. I didn't get out of it. I just felt like closing up the book and going off, you know." [42]

Hearing Coleman was important to Russell for another reason as well. At this point, Russell had codified his theory of tonal gravity in terms of two categories or levels – vertical and horizontal. [43]

> I thought I had things pretty categorized until one very quiet, very beautiful Sunday afternoon, I hear this wild music coming out of the Music Inn up there and it's Ornette's music. It was the first time I really heard it. Then, I realized I didn't quite have all the categories. I'd left one category out. And largely through him I incorporated that. I called it Supra-Vertical Tonal Gravity—all and everything. So it was exchange on that level where you suddenly were blown into a new dimension. [44]

Also, attending Lenox in 1959 were two young musicians from Indiana—trombonist Dave Baker and trumpeter Al Kiger. Gunther Schuller had met them while playing with the Metropolitan Opera in Indianapolis and had written an article he called "The Indiana Renaissance" about Baker and a then-unknown guitarist named Wes Montgomery. The next year Schuller ensured that Baker and Kiger were offered scholarships to Lenox. Both were students at Indiana University at the time and played together in Baker's group. Baker and Kiger got on well with Russell and he befriended the two musicians, keeping in touch after the summer school ended. As Baker explained: "And when I got [to] the School of Jazz, of course, I was in George's theory class—I mean, his Lydian Concept class. We got to be friends at that time, even though I was hard-headed and always arguing with him about something or another." [45]

Russell went out to Indiana and began working with these very green musicians. His intention was quite clear—they were to provide the nucleus of the group he now planned to form. From Baker's group, he took Kiger, Baker and an exceptional tenor player called Dave Young, and, from Baker's big band, he took drummer Joe Hunt. Perhaps prompted by the success of Coleman's unveiling at the school in 1959, the intention was that they would play at Lenox in 1960. All four were given scholarships by John Lewis. Dave Baker remembered that Russell did much more than simply hire the four of them.

> We were all at the School of Jazz. So when he decided to form his sextet, he came out to Indianapolis and took the group that I had been leading and then began teaching us how to play, how to make music and he wrote arrangements and things and really just mentored us for the next . . . I don't know . . . for a month or so, before we then became the George Russell Sextet. [46]

Up to that point, Russell had shown little interest in leading a group, let alone playing piano except to compose. As we will see, his decision was largely pragmatic.

Meanwhile, Russell's career was not standing still, as Dom Cerulli's article in *DownBeat* in May 1958 had made clear. Cerulli's article was one of the first pieces, if not the first, to cover Russell's history and his Lydian Concept in detail. Russell also tried his hand as a critic and wrote several album reviews for the *Jazz Review* around this period.[47]

Cerulli's article was also an indication of Russell's status amongst certain critics. In fact, by 1958, Russell was sufficiently well-regarded to warrant inclusion in the final programme of the National Broadcasting Company TV series *The Subject is Jazz*. In that programme, entitled "The Future of Jazz", Russell was interviewed by presenter Gilbert Seldes on the Lydian Concept while the house band with draftees Bill Evans, Barry Galbraith and Art Farmer performed Russell's "Ballad of Billy the Kid" and "Stratusphunk".

His heightened profile in the music no doubt contributed to the opportunity to record two LPs for Decca under the auspices of Milt Gabler. I will discuss *Jazz in the Space Age* (1960), one of Russell's major releases, in the next chapter but Russell's second LP, *New York, N.Y.* (1959), though less significant in terms of his work, is not to be underestimated. Both records were big band albums and both would feature some of New York's finest musicians.

Quite how Milt Gabler came into Russell's life is unclear. In the notes for the 1998 CD reissue of *New York, N.Y.*, Russell told the story in this way.

> Years of struggle and several jazz albums later, I found myself in the towering offices of one of the truly great recording executives of all time, the legendary Milt Gabler, president of Decca Records.

Noting all the great musicians Gabler brought to Decca and worked with, Russell added,

> He was dedicated to jazz in a meaningful way which helped to expand its potential while securing its foundation.[48]

Russell is referring here to a meeting with Gabler where they were discussing a recording contract with this prestigious label. This was at the point when Russell was planning his tribute to New York, *New York, N.Y.* The likelihood is that Gabler had initiated the contact and was keen to sign the now thirty-five year old composer. From Russell's comments, it is apparent that he felt he had found a kindred spirit in Gabler. Russell's notes suggest that Gabler gave him *carte blanche* for the project.

*New York, N.Y.* is a tone poem and tribute to the city and to its place in jazz. It is also an expression of personal gratitude to New York and its musicians which and who had given him the opportunity to express himself as an artist and composer. Russell recalled later,

> In 1934, my sixth-grade teacher gave the class an assignment to write an essay on our favourite subject; it could be a fantasy or real life, whatever we chose. I selected New York because of its glamour and sophistication and for what resonated in me, at that time and at eleven years of age, a tolerance for things new. I wouldn't have been able to articulate my feelings about New York then but it was the Apple's life-positive energy which impressed me, and, eventually, magnetized me to it. The essay earned me an A+ (one of the few in my academic life). [49]

Where *Jazz Workshop* featured a series of vignettes or miniatures, *New York, N.Y.* gave Russell the opportunity to explore one subject from different angles. Both *New York, N.Y.* and *Jazz in the Space Age* offered large canvases and involved extended compositional ideas and structures. As he explained to writer Burt Korall in an interview for the original liner notes for the release,

> My Lydian Concept has changed my whole mode of life. It took years but I now feel that I function logically. At least, I'm organized and ready. I realize that music, like life, must have an inner logic. George Endrey, a scientist friend of mine, taught me how mathematics relates to life and music. Without him, I would never have understood logic for what it is. [50]

George Endrey appears to have exerted quite an influence on Russell. It seems plausible that Russell derived his notion of the relationship between gravity and tones, even if as a misunderstanding, from Endrey. As well as referring to him in several interviews, Russell asked him to write the "Historical Perspective" section of the Concept, which appeared in the first and second editions of the work. [51] In the Dom Cerulli interview mentioned above, Cerulli wrote,

> From a scientist friend, George Endrey, Russell learned that "even mathematics has a soul. Endrey gave me a scientific language without which I could not have begun to follow the logic of logic." [52]

Endrey seems to have been a rather intriguing, if shadowy figure on the jazz scene. Stephanie Stein Crease in her biography of Gil Evans describes him as "a fellow musician and counsellor/mentor to Gil, George Russell, and others on the scene . . ." [53] Russell explained to J. "Hepcat" O'Brien in *Panache* magazine,

> George was on the scene in the early days. I probably met him at Gil's. We were all fascinated with George and his venturesome mind; he had inner knowledge which drew people to him. I believe he emigrated from Hungary. He was the one who first got us up to Juilliard. George was into the Schillinger System of music. The great gift he imparted to me was to respect an alternative way of thinking about things, in going for the 'outer view'. [54]

In 1965, Endrey wrote an article on Gil Evans in the short-lived magazine, *Sounds & Fury*. That aside, he would seem to be one of those individuals known only through the comments and recollections of others.

In the sleeve-notes for *New York, N.Y.*, Russell also acknowledged his debt to "the Gil Evans composer enclave of 1949–50," Gil, John Lewis, John Carisi and Gerry Mulligan—and to classical composers Alban Berg, Bela Bartok, Igor Stravinsky and Stefan Wolpe. These composers, he noted, "helped shape my thinking," and, admitting that his output between 1947 and "Cubano Be, Cubano Bop" and the completion of the Lydian Concept was slim, he told Korall, "I felt I had to finish my thesis before I could say what I wanted to." [55]

Following Max Harrison, I was somewhat lukewarm in my comments regarding this record in the first edition of this biography. [56] My mistake, and Harrison's, has been to view *New York, N.Y.*, solely, in terms of its musical content. I now realise that one needs to consider it as whole. Significantly, and even controversially, Russell chose to frame the tunes with poetry specially composed by jazz singer Jon Hendricks. Moreover, in some respects, in the process of its making, *New York, N.Y.* also offers insights into what was happening in jazz and into the nature of the jazz scene in New York, in terms of its relationships both between the musicians themselves and between musicians and the music business. In several senses, the story it tells of New York and jazz is then echoed in the story of its making. The story it tells is also is its own story.

I have no evidence that Russell was aware of the poetry and jazz movement that began in the mid-fifties. However, it seems highly unlikely that he was not aware of such events. Jack Kerouac had performed at the Village Vanguard with Zoot Sims and Al Cohn in December 1957. [57] Lawrence Ferlinghetti, Kenneth Patchen and Kenneth Rexroth had all recorded LPs with jazz accompaniment that same year and there were also readings with jazz at the Five Spot in the late fifties. Of perhaps more importance in this context is the fact that African-American poet and Harlem Renaissance figure, Langston Hughes had made and released an album for the MGM label, *The Weary Blues with Langston Hughes* in 1958, prior to the first session for *New York, N.Y.* in September 1958. That record featured amongst others Charles Mingus, Osie Johnson and Milt Hinton. Russell knew Mingus and had, of course, used both Johnson and Hinton on the *Jazz Workshop* sessions. It is more likely than less that Russell would have known of these collaborations, even if he had not heard them himself. Indeed, Jon Hendricks references, rather dismissively, the poetry and jazz movement, in his opening poem on *New York, N.Y.*.

> A while ago there were cats reading, while cats played jazz behind them, but there was nothin' happenin', so the musicians just cooked right on like they didn't even mind them. [58]

Russell's conception for *New York, N.Y.* was undoubtedly his own. More than that, with this record, he continued to push the boundaries of jazz in terms of subject matter, musical content and manner of presentation, just as he would for the rest of his career. Yet, the record must also be seen in the context of wider experimentation in jazz and cultural activity in general at that time.

The second point concerns the way the record came about and the circumstances of its recording. These processes reveal both the informal contacts that brought musicians and new ideas together in performance and the more formal aspects of business in particular those relating to the session work that was a crucial mainstay for jobbing musicians.

*New York, N.Y.* featured three standards, all clearly associated with the city —Rodgers and Hart's "Manhattan" and Vernon Duke's lovely "Autumn in New York" in a medley with Lane and Freed's "How About You"—alongside a number of original tunes – "Big City Blues," "Manhattan-Rico" and "A Helluva Town". However, even the three standards become extended and transformed in the composer's hands.

As for the band, for all three sessions between September 1958 and March 1959, it was made up of some of New York's finest—Max Roach on drums; Doc Severinsen and Ernie Royal on trumpets; John Coltrane, Phil Woods and Benny Golson on saxes; and Bob Brookmeyer on valve trombone, alongside Bill Evans, Art Farmer, Barry Galbraith, Hal McKusick and Milt Hinton from the *Jazz Workshop* dates. Russell clearly chose musicians with whom he was familiar, whom he trusted and whose work he admired. Such informalities ease and facilitate while reducing the difficult and unpredictable aspects of the working lives of musicians, including the need to manage the costly and time-consuming process of recording.

With regard to the libretto, Jon Hendricks recalled Russell approaching him in the Turf Bar, which was part of the Brill Building and a gathering point for songwriters, both aspiring and already successful. Though unfamiliar with Russell's music, the singer was immediately taken with Russell's manners and respectful attitude, unusual in his experience among jazz musicians working New York. Russell was quite clear regarding what he wanted for the album and Hendricks was hooked when he heard who was to be on the record.

> To get to the point, he asked me, "I hear you write lyrics?" I said, "Yes, I do." He said, "Do you also write poetry?" I said, "Well, lyrics are poetry. So, yes, I do write poetry." He said, "Because I'm working on a project called *New York, N.Y.* and I've assembled a dream band." None of them were that famous but everybody in the jazz world knew them. They were famous in the jazz world. And when he named me the band, I said, "Whoa! What would you want me to do on something with those guys?" He said, "The album is going to be called *New York, N.Y.* So I want a poem running through it that tells verbally about New York, that complements the music. Could you do that?" I said, "Sure." [59]

Hendricks attended the sessions but cut his contribution later.

> When George got through with the album he made me a tape of the entire album and he told me he wanted an intro for each segment. So that's where I got the feel of the album from, because Max breaks it up with brushes *(imitates sound of Roach drumming)*. I just put words to that. "Think you can lick it, get to the wicket, buy you a ticket"—boom! I kept repeating that from time to time, and that gave me the theme for it. Then for each segment I conformed to the musical flow. If it was slow and languid I wrote a slow and languid lyric about the East Side. I called it—"The East Side, the beauty and the beast side." *(laughs)* It was one of the finest things I've ever written and it was all inspired by the music and the musicians. [60]

Apparently, Milt Gabler tried to censor Hendricks's line about the NYPD—"New

York's finest/The finest money can buy"—but that and his comment on the city's "cabaret card restriction" were allowed to stand. Russell himself felt the remarks to be entirely justified, and, as Hendricks says, "Besides, when you make people laugh you can say things you couldn't if you were serious." [61]

Not everyone appreciated Hendricks's contribution. Writing in the *Jazz Review*, Max Harrison—British critic and Russell advocate from early on—described the spoken commentary as "superfluous and, with repeated hearing, annoying," and found the album as a whole disappointing—"Only [Russell's own] *Big City Blues* is really worthy of him, and it would be unfortunate if people heard this record and thought it represented the best of his powers." [62] By contrast, *Cash Box* chose *New York, N.Y.* as one of its "Jazz Picks of the Week" and called Hendricks's narration "the hippest" and the album "one of the most explosive jazz sets in a long while." While the *New Yorker*, using words like "pretentious" and phrases such as "precooked, frozen jazz," agreed with Harrison's verdict, *DownBeat* awarded the record five stars and a French committee presided over by Jean Cocteau gave it the prestigious Oscar du Disque de Jazz. [63]

In *DownBeat*, reviewing it as a Jon Hendricks/George Russell disc, critic Ralph Gleason called it "the most important album Decca has made in a decade." "The music," Gleason noted, "is excellent, a triumph of indigenous feeling and a concept that is bold, intuitive and soft with love all at once." He continued, "This is music for a real life, contemporary musical cultural expression," and, noting that music without narration and vice versa would make the record "incomplete," he spent the rest of the review extolling Hendricks's virtues. [64]

Decca ran an excellent and upbeat advertising campaign in the trades.

> George Russell's *New York, N.Y.* is today and a little of tomorrow, drawn with rare craftsmanship and originality. It is a showcase for such major jazz soloists as Art Farmer, Bob Brookmeyer, John Coltrane, Bill Evans, Benny Golson and Max Roach; the probing wit and intelligence of Jon Hendricks; and a large star-filled jazz orchestra. This album will not soon be forgotten. [65]

In reality, *New York, N.Y.* is one of the most accessible of Russell's records and perhaps also one of his most atypical. In one sense, it is more famous for an incident that occurred during the September date than for the music itself. It was also an incident that defines the formal/informal dichotomous nature of relationships between musicians on the New York jazz scene. There was off the clock but also on the clock, as well.

That session only produced one piece—Rodgers and Hart's "Manhattan"—and was interrupted by John Coltrane. When the band reached the place for Trane's solo, he floundered and called for a break, taking his part over to a corner of the studio, studying it intently. The rest of the band, several of them with gigs or other dates to go on to, and the producer became angry and accusations began to fly around the room that the tenor player could not read the chord changes.

Russell has written about the episode in his book [66] and in the sleeve notes for the CD reissue of *New York, N.Y.* However, in an interview for this volume, he gave a concise but elaborated account of the event.

It was in that period Coltrane was melodicizing each chord to the nth degree. I had a beautiful song, "Manhattan." I had already worked with the chords in a way that I thought Coltrane had enough to work on but he probably wanted to take every opportunity to bring the chord of the moment out. His brain was tied to the chord of the moment and it was a little too much because when he was in the studio he hadn't seen the music. So he goes over into a corner [and] probably cost a couple of thousand dollars in New York musicians' time. Bob Brookmeyer said, "I heard about him, but this guy doesn't even know his chords." That wasn't the case; he wanted to know how to . . . he wanted to apply his way of projecting that chord. That involved a lot of notes. That took time.[67]

Brookmeyer acknowledges that he was angry at the time.

Coltrane was there because we had to wait about half an hour while he learned the chords to "Manhattan." *(laughs)* Well, George and I were standing in the corner and he'd written some altered chords for "Manhattan." And John wanted to know really how the chords worked. He didn't want to just play on the top and get by. So he and Bill were over on the stage playing and playing and George and I were going, "Oh, man! That's been about a half an hour already." So, Coltrane was right. He wasn't being practical but he was being musical.[68]

As Ralph Gleason noted, Hendricks' poem and role are crucial elements on *New York, N.Y.* and, I think, best understood in terms of African/African-American folklore. Hendricks' remarks about how one could say things as a joke that would provoke a different response if said in more obvious seriousness is important. Hendricks does joke but he also makes a number of serious points as well, points the musicians and audience would understand. In a way, his role is that of the trickster archetype of African-American folklore, the trickster that Henry Louis Gates Jr. refers to as the "Signifyin' Monkey." Gates relates this to the Yoruba Orisha, Esu Elegbara who "dwells at the margins of discourse, ever punning, ever troping, ever embodying the ambiguities of language . . .".[69] The "Signifyin' Monkey" subverts through that ambiguous use of language and that defines Hendricks' role perfectly.

This is beautifully illustrated on "Manhattan" and "Big City Blues." With the former, Russell took a trifling, if lovely, tune and turned that trifle into something that is witty, affectionate and modern. It opens with the narration set to Charlie Persip's drums, as Hendricks describes New York – " a cold town but a soul town/ and it ain't a bit hard to find/ someone who's lonesome and forlorn . . ." Towards the end, he adds, "There's one thing that New York city has/And that's jazz" before puckishly dismissing the poetry and jazz efforts of others to conclude, "I wrote the shortest jazz poem ever heard/nothin' about huggin' or kissin'/one word/Listen!"

The remarks that Milt Gabler apparently wanted to sensor about New York's finest and the iniquitous cabaret card system controlled in practice by the NYPD follow Russell's noir-ish introduction to "Big City Blues." Hendricks continues:

So, cat's keep on strugglin'/To say their say/But between them and the audience/Sits the

DJ/And unhip lack of acceptance is a drag/People not diggin' the only thing that's their own/That's really in another bag/But lack of acceptance is less something to hide from/And more like somethin' (pause)/Bird died from . . .

Perhaps best of all are his insightful words that link Russell's percussion-led "Manhattan-Rico" to the migration of so many Puerto Ricans to New York, their contribution to the city's music and the welcome that awaits. More significantly, Hendricks draws attention to the deeply felt connections felt by African-American musicians and jazz fans to the Afro-Cuban/Afro-Latin rhythms that these people brought with them,

> A quick look around will tell you what's going on/You dig who's livin' high on the hog/And who's the underdog/And you dig what shape the underdog is in/'Cos you're living where he just bin/So, you dig him/And you dig your host/And you dig the one/who it is/You resemble the most/Right on down to the rhythm that moves him/There might be some slight difference/In the way you say the word/But Machito didn't have any trouble/Cuttin' some sides with Bird/They probably had some trouble/Pronouncing each others' names/But they showed/How two things could sound/Altogether different/And yet have a familiar ring/Because they're the same thing.

Hendricks' narration is full of contrasts. Jokey remarks slip into darker asides. Apparent resignation, a shrug at the way things are, masks the complex negotiations contained in the verb "to scuffle" and its gerund, "scuffling". The sub-text is 'this ain't right.'

Given that the music was recorded prior to Hendricks adding his poem, this has allowed him to respond to the music. However, it seems that Russell had left the spaces for Hendricks to fill – Persip's drums on "Manhattan", the bluesy solo piano from Bill Evans on "Big City Blues" and Al Epstein's bongos on "Manhattan-Rico." This is an artfully constructed and beautifully conceived record.

*New York, N.Y.* also established a pattern that would define Russell's big band compositions and arrangements for the rest of his career. He would use a limited number of carefully chosen and trusted soloists. This did not mean that the other band members were not of great importance. They would be essential to the creation of the colours, textures and dynamic effects Russell would create in his music.

Here, the three standards feature in very different arrangements from those written for other artists – trumpeter Harry James and Ella Fitzgerald and "Manhattan", Charlie Parker and Billie Holiday and "Autumn in New York," Frank Sinatra, Chet Baker and the Sauter-Finegan orchestra and "How About You." "Manhattan" opens with a fanfare before sliding into a fox-trot that is continually broken up by the horns. Solos – from the trombones of Bob Brookmeyer and Frank Rehak, Bill Evans, Coltrane and Art Farmer – are initially accompanied only by Milt Hinton's bass before the whole rhythm section joins, while a brass chorus intervenes before the next solo. The lead out with Coltrane improvising over a band vamp diminuendo is masterful.

Intriguingly, there is virtually no gap between "Manhattan" and the opening of the next track, "Big City Blues," with its nourish introduction before Bill Evans piano blues accompanies Hendricks' narration. Russell's intentions are clear – he is painting a picture in words and music of New York and the episodic nature of these opening injections whether by Hendricks or by the band act as a kind of anacrusis. The music has a filmic quality with Russell at his most Ellingtonian. Subtle changes of pace and use of diminuendo and crescendo mark the fact that the first half of the track's twelve minute duration are orchestral, albeit with some fine guitar interpolations from Barry Galbraith. The soloists Benny Golson on tenor, Art Farmer and Bill Evans – are then shadowed by sotto voce horns before an orchestral coda with brass and woodwinds playing two different melodies. Even Max Harrison pointed out that "Big City Blues" is most definitely worthy of Russell's talents.

"A Helluva Town" closes the record and is primarily a feature for Max Roach set against a brass fanfare with a counter melody from the woodwinds. The pace is frenetic, recalling the noise of a working city, of traffic and people at play – a city that never sleeps. And with Max Roach on drums, you could not sleep even if you wanted to.

But the most important track here, and the one that reveals a consistent and coherent thread in Russell's oeuvre is "Manhattan-Rico." In his narration, Hendricks points up the way jazz musicians such as Charlie Parker, Dizzy Gillespie, Russell and others connected with the Afro-Cuban music of singer and band-leader Machito (born Francisco Raúl Gutiérrez Grillo) from the forties onwards. That connection was through a shared African heritage. One can trace Russell's awareness of this from "Cubano Be, Cubano Bop" through "Manhattan-Rico" and the orchestral *Electronic Sonata for Souls Loved by Nature* from 1970 (on which drummer Jon Christensen and conga player Rupert Clemendore duet with a pre-recorded tape of African percussion) to Russell's other magnum opus *The African Game* from 1983. For Russell, such connections were essential, that is part of his essence and of all our essences. He would in later life point out that we are all Africans, having our biological origins in the Great Rift Valley and he continually sought to express those connections in his art.

Here, Hendricks' poetry leads into a percussion trio with Don Lamond on kit drums, Al Epstein on bongos and Russell on Boo-Bams. Whether consciously or not, the use of three different percussion instruments echoes the three sacred Batá drums of the Santería/Lukumí religion practised in Cuba and Puerto Rico. Iyá is the largest and is referred as 'mother drum'. Itótele, the middle one, and Okónkolo, the smallest, are called 'father' and 'baby.' Though the correspondence is not exact, the deeper tones of the Boo-Bams would be the mother drum, with the kit the father and bongos the baby. There is also, here a musical link back to Russell's duet with Ossie Johnson on "Fellow Delegates" from *Jazz Workshop*. The next (two minute section) is purely orchestral with Russell using both unison passages and competing riffs, vamps and motifs distributed to different sections of the band for contrast. Brookmeyer solos first, then Evans against fills from the band and over Latin percussion. Farmer's contribution is as elegant as always but the surprise here is alto saxophonist Phil Woods. Woods had played with and toured with Dizzy Gillespie in 1956 but his playing here makes one wish Russell had used him again. Somehow he seems to grasp Russell's intentions and, though his sound is very different, the way he plays against the rhythm recalls Charlie Parker. While it may not be as adventurous or as ground-breaking as "Cubano Be, Cubano Bop," in some ways,

"Manhattan-Rico" represents a consolidation of Russell's use of Afro-Latin rhythms and static harmonies in his writing.

*New York, N.Y.* is less immediately striking than and not as dramatic as either *Jazz Workshop* or Russell's next album, *Jazz in the Space Age*. That distinctive strangeness or even eeriness sometimes apparent in Russell's compositions is absent but it is, as I have said, one of the composer's most approachable recordings and is deserving of a warmer critical appreciation than has often been the case, hence the attention given here. It reflects and connects with many of the developments within jazz at the time and is truly a warm, affectionate tribute to a city and its music.

*New York, N.Y.* is an excellent place for a newcomer to Russell's music to begin. That said, with *Jazz in the Space Age* Russell would start to aim for the stars.

## Notes

1. Interview with Juanita Giuffre, June 2004.
2. Interview with George Russell, October 2003.
3. Interview with Jack Reilly, October 2003.
4. Interview with G. Russell, October 2003.
5. See M. Hinton and D. Berger, *Bass Line: The Stories and Photographs of Milt Hinton* (Philadelphia: Temple University Press, 1988).
6. Ian Carr, interview with Art Farmer for BBC Radio 3 Broadcast *George Russell—The Invisible Guru*, July 1994.
7. Ibid.
8. Interview with Paul Motian, June 2006.
9. E-mail to the author from Norbury-Russell, July 2005.
10. Nat Hentoff, Review of *The RCA Jazz Workshop—Hal McKusick* (RCA 1366), *DownBeat*, May 16, 1957; Paul Sampson, Review of *The RCA Jazz Workshop—Hal McKusick, Washington Post*, May 5, 1957; Fred Sherman, "McKusick Album Is Best Thing to Come out of Jazz Workshop," *Miami Herald*, June 23, 1957; C. H. Garrigues, Reviews of *The RCA Jazz Workshop—George Russell and His Smalltet* (RCA LPM1372) and *The RCA Jazz Workshop—Hal McKusick* (RCA LPM 1366), *San Francisco Examiner*, August 25, 1957.
11. Don L. McIver, "Hal McKusick's Performance Is Good, But—," *Fort Lauderdale Sunday News*, April 28, 1957. See also "Chords and Discords," *DownBeat*, June 26, 1958. A letter from one Larry Townsend took both the magazine and Russell to task for claims made on behalf of the Lydian Chromatic Concept. Its author questions its originality and in particular refers readers to the work of Joseph Schillinger. Russell replied in the same issue in typically feisty form without really stating the differences between his approach and Schillinger's.
12. Review of The RCA Jazz Workshop—Hall McKusick. Metronome, June 1957.
13. Bob Reisner, "Jazz Composition," *Village Voice*, July 10, 1957; Nat Hentoff, "The Jazz Mainstream," *Saturday Review*, June 29, 1957; Review of *The RCA Jazz Workshop—George Russell and His Smalltet* (RCA Victor LPM1372), *Jazz Today*, September 1957. See also "1199er Wins Acclaim as Jazz Composer," *RWDSU Record*, September 15, 1957; "Drummer to Composer," *Cincinnati Post*, July 13, 1957; "Adventuring with George Russell," *Jazz Today*, June

1957. The *RWDSU* (Retail, Wholesale and Department Store Union) article features a marvellous photo of Russell handing over a copy of *Jazz Workshop* to 1199 president Leon J. Davis. Russell never forgot who he was or where he came from. Davis was an important labour leader on the East Coast who built the organization into a progressive force in city and American politics.

14. Polly Cochran, "Workshop Creates Learned Jazz," *Indianapolis Star*, May 5, 1957.
15. Garrigues, Reviews; Feather, Review of *The RCA Jazz Workshop—George Russell and His Smalltet* (RCA Victor LPM1372), *DownBeat*, August 17, 1957.
16. Review of The RCA Jazz Workshop—George Russell and His Smalltet (RCA Victor LPM1372), Cash Box, June 15, 1957; Billboard, May 17, 1957; Review of The RCA Jazz Workshop—George Russell and His Smalltet (RCA Victor LPM1372), Hi-Fi Low-Down, October 1957; Memphis Commercial Appeal, July 21, 1957.
17. I.F. Stone, Oct 7th, 1957. "The United States as Three Nations, Not One," in *The Best of I.F. Stone's Weekly*, ed. N. Middleton (Harmondsworth, UK: Penguin, 1973), p. 106. Not for nothing did Charles Mingus write and record his The Original Faubus Fables around that time. See Charles Mingus Presents Charles Mingus Candid 9005.
18. Ernest Green went on to obtain a master's degree and eventually to become an assistant secretary of labor in the Clinton administration. He became embroiled in the so-called Chinagate investigation and pleaded guilty to a matter of income tax evasion. See entry "Ernest Green" in Wikipedia.org, http://en.wikipedia.org/wiki/ Ernest Green.
19. Leonard Feather, Review of Moody Marilyn Moore, Bethlehem LP BCP-73, *DownBeat*, March 6, 1957.
20. Intriguingly, the Russell- and Evans-arranged numbers feature very different instrumentation and personnel with only Russell on drums and flautist/cor anglais player Romeo Penque common to both.
21. Bob Reisner, "Jazz Composition," *Village Voice*, July 10, 1957.
22. Carr, interview with G. Russell, June 1992.
23. "Six Works of Jazz Commissioned by Brandeis University," *DownBeat*, April 4, 1957.
24. Norman J. O'Conner, "Jazz at Brandeis—Some New Areas Are Opened for Jazz by the Work of a Noted Institute of Culture and Learning," *DownBeat*, July 25, 1957, p. 18.
25. Richard Katz, "Music Festival at Brandeis University," *Jazz Today*, August 1957.
26. *Music For Brass* Columbia CL941; *Modern Jazz Concert* Columbia WL127. Reissued in 1996 as single CD with All Set and On Green Mountain omitted as The Birth Of The Third Stream, Columbia 485103 2.
27. Nat Hentoff, "Jazz's Third Stream," *DownBeat*, May 29,1958; Ralph J. Gleason, "An Album That Couldn't Have Been Made at All Ten Years Ago," *San Francisco Chronicle*, July 13, 1958.
28. Duncan Heining, *George Russell: The Story of an American Composer*, (Lanham, MY: Scarecrow 2010), p.47.
29. 1946 brochure Ed Hazell, *Berklee: The First Fifty Years* (Boston: Berklee Press, 1995). p.22
30. Other records released that year included, Sonny Rollins' *Way Out West* Contemporary C3530; Miles Davis' first release on Columbia, *Round Midnight* Columbia CL949 and, with Gil Evans, *Miles Ahead* Columbia CL1041; John Coltrane *Coltrane* Prestige 7105; Thelonious Monk *Brilliant Corners* Riverside RLP12-226; Charles Mingus *East Coasting* Bethlehem BCP6019 and *The Clown* Atlantic 1260; Duke Ellington *Such Sweet Thunder* Columbia CL1033.

31. M. Fitzgerald, "The Lenox School of Jazz," JazzDiscography.com, November 1, 1993, www.jazzdiscography.com/Lenox/lenhome.htm. Quote in quotes from R. A. Niccoli, "Stearns Conducts Jazz Panel Series," *DownBeat*, September 7,1951, p. 18.
32. Interview with Gunther Schuller.
33. "Jazz School's First Session at Lenox," *DownBeat*, March 6, 1957. See also "The School of Jazz," *DownBeat*, October 3, 1957.
34. Interview with Gunther Schuller.
35. Ibid.
36. Michael Fitzgerald, "Lenox School of Jazz" at https://jazzmf.com/category/lenox-school-of-jazz/
37. Interview with Mike Gibbs, June 2005.
38. Interview with Gunther Schuller.
39. Interview with Ornette Coleman, July 2005.
40. Ibid.
41. Interview with G. Russell, October 2003.
42. Ben Young, broadcast devoted to George Russell in celebration of his seventy-fifth birthday, WKCR Radio, New York, June 23, 1998.
43. For levels of tonal gravity see , Ingrid Monson. "Oh Freedom—George Russell, John Coltrane and Modal Jazz." In *In the Course of Performance*, edited by B. Nettel and M. Russell. London: University of Chicago Press, 1998. "The improviser, in Russell's view, can choose to relate to tonal gravity (the chords of the composition) in three general ways. The musician may (1) allow each chord as it passes to determine his or her choice of scales ("Vertical Tonal Gravity;" see Russell 1964, 22); (2) impose a single scale on a sequence of chords that resolve to a tonic ("Horizontal Tonal Gravity"); or (3) improvise his or her chromatic melody in relationship to the overall tonic of the entire piece ("Supravertical Tonal Gravity)" The examples Russell gives in respect of each level are – Vertical – Coltrane's "Giant Steps"; Horizontal – Lester Young "Dickie's Dream"; Supravertical – Ornette Coleman's "Lonely Woman."
44. Young, broadcast devoted to George Russell.
45. Interview with Dave Baker, April 2004.
46. Ibid.
47. Dom Cerulli, "George Russell," *DownBeat*, May 29, 1958. For Russell's reviews, see the *Jazz Review*, November 1958, for the Jimmy Giuffre 3's Travelin' Light (Russell liked it); and the *Jazz Review*, June 1959, for Johnny Mandel's I Want To Live soundtrack for the film of the same name and Henry Mancini's Music from Peter Gunn. While he enthused about the Mandel score, Russell savaged the Mancini record. Russell's writing style is heavy and ponderous, yet he does bring in elements of social criticism into the review of Mandel in commenting on the subject matter of the film, i.e., capital punishment.
48. Notes to *New York, N.Y.* CD reissue Impulse IMP 12782.
49. Ibid.
50. Korall, Burt. Original sleeve notes to *New York, N.Y.* Decca DL-9216.
51. George Russell, *The Lydian Chromatic Concept of Tonal Organization* (New York: Concept, 1959).
52. Cerulli, op cit.
53. Stein Crease. *Gil Evans: Out of the Cool*. (Chicago: A Cappela. 2002), p. 172
54. J. "Hepcat" O'Brien. *Panache* magazine 18, Issue 5.

55. Notes to New York, N.Y.
56. See Max Harrison, Reviews of *The RCA Jazz Workshop—George Russell and His Smalltet* (RCA LPM1372) and *George Russell—New York, N.Y.* (Decca DL9216), Jazz Review, November 1960, p. 30; Max Harrison, "George Russell—Rational Anthems (Phase 1, 2, 3)," *Wire* (Autumn 1983): 19.
57. Howard Smith, H. "Jack Kerouac: Off the Road, Into the Vanguard" *Village Voice* December 25, 1957, Vol. III, No. 9
58. Liner notes *New York, N.Y.* CD reissue IMP12782
59. Interview with Jon Hendricks, April 2006.
60. Ibid. Hendricks refers to track 5, "A Helluva Town" rather than the opening to track 1 "Manhattan." Charlie Persip is the drummer on track 1.
61. Ibid.
62. Max Harrison, *Jazz Review*, op cit.
63. *Cash Box* (no date available); Ralph Gleason, Review of *New York, N.Y. DownBeat*, September 3, 1959; *New Yorker*, Autumn 1959 (no other information). Russell's Oscar was awarded on January 15, 1962.
64. Gleason, op cit.
65. See *DownBeat*, August 20, 1959.
66. George Russell, *Lydian Chromatic Concept of Tonal Organization* (Brookline, MA: Concept, 2001), pp. 177–78.
67. Interview with G. Russell, October 2003.
68. Interview with Bob Brookmeyer, October 2003.
69. Henry Louis Gates, Jr. "The "Blackness of Blackness": A Critique of the Sign and the Signifying Monkey," *Critical Inquiry* Vol. 9, No. 4 (Jun., 1983), pp. 687-689. The term seems to derive from the Cab Calloway/Mort Dixon song "The Jungle King: You Ain't Done a Doggone Thing" (1947), which was recorded by Willie Dixon that same year as "The Signifyin' Monkey" and in 1960 by Oscar Brown Jr. in a slightly different version with that title.

CHAPTER SEVEN

# Space Music

It could be argued that, *Jazz in the Space Age* is perhaps the first genuinely "modern" big band album. To use the language of the advert Decca placed in the trades papers for *New York, N.Y.*, it is a little of today and a whole lot of tomorrow.

Unusually for the time, in jazz at least, Russell produced music that featured two pianists as its main soloists. Russell noted that Milt Gabler initiated the recording—as he had *New York, N.Y.*—and the idea was to do something that anticipated the new decade. "Milt was behind that too. I think that followed *New York, N.Y.* It was reaching for the space age."[1]

The two pianists—Bill Evans and Paul Bley—with their contrasting approaches, feature on four of the six tracks. Evans and Bley play with a combination of courage and confidence, as Russell leads them into what is for both, though for different reasons, unfamiliar territory. Bley had been developing his own approach over the years that allowed him considerable freedom rhythmically, melodically and harmonically, so the panchromatic and rhythmic elements of Russell's music were, in principle, comparatively straightforward. The writing, however, with its long and complex passages that were through-composed, drew the young Canadian into less familiar areas of form and structure. In Evans's case, by contrast, Russell was again pushing him in the direction of abstraction and free playing that were outside his favoured mode of operation. Needless to say, Evans had little or no problem in meeting Russell's demands.

Of at least as much significance in the longer term—for Russell's music and for jazz in general—were the ideas and devices the composer was deploying, which would be developed and extended in his later work. Firstly, one can hear that this is definitely the same man who wrote "Cubano Be, Cubano Bop," *All About Rosie*, "Similau,"

"Livingstone I Presume," and "The Day John Brown Was Hanged." Secondly, with repeated listening, one realizes that the writing has also reached a whole new level. The quality of the through-composed sections is *sans pareil* in jazz but they retain all the spontaneity and intensity of improvisation. The use of solo voices (as on *New York, N.Y.*) is highly selective, with Russell's recent recruits from Indiana University - Dave Young on tenor, Al Kiger on Trumpet and Dave Baker on trombone - getting much of the remaining space after Evans and Bley. Both the use of through-composition and the selective deployment of soloists would continue to be strong features in Russell's works such as *Othello Ballet*, *The African Game* and *Living Time*. Finally, and perhaps most significant of all, *Jazz in the Space Age* sounds "modern" in the fullest sense. It belongs in a whole new universe or category. It does not sound like Duke Ellington or Fletcher Henderson or Claude Thornhill or even Gil Evans. It is jazz that is orchestral in the fullest sense of the term, with its resources organized less like a symphony orchestra and more like a large chamber ensemble. It is here, perhaps, that the influence of Stefan Wolpe is at its strongest.

Six tracks make up the suite. Three are titled "Chromatic Universe"— parts 1, 2, 3. These are separated by three other pieces—"Dimensions," "The Lydiot," and "Waltz from Outer Space"—this being at Russell's request, as he felt it would provide for greater variety.[2] In practice, each piece glides into the next, creating a long suite of performances. The contrasting approaches of Evans and Bley are used to powerful effect and these then contrast magnificently with the wide harmonic and rhythmic variations of the orchestra—less a symphony perhaps and more a double concerto.

The title certainly raised eyebrows in some quarters. Nat Hentoff in *Jazz Today* put it down to "someone in the advertising department."[3] Drummer Joe Hunt, who was to join Russell's sextet, interviewed in 2004, still felt that titles like this might have put some musicians and fans off.

> I mean, *The Stratus Seekers* and this idea of . . . back then, it was like even before they'd gone to the moon, you know, and this idea of space-age jazz—*Jazz in the Space Age*. I think those kind[s] of titles and things put some people off because, on the one hand, it meant that we were stretching the limits and going to the edge and pushing ourselves as musicians, but I think for the average listener it sort of put them off. Even some other musicians didn't like us because of this "space music" they'd call it and it kind of had a bad reputation among some of the musicians. Some of the really good beboppers, they didn't like George and they still don't like Ornette or George. I mean these are like really great players too, who—I won't name names—but some of them are my colleagues and people I've played gigs with. You mention Ornette Coleman and they'll put him down. Of course, I think Ornette's a genius. So what can you do, but I also admire these guys, but they were very opinionated and I think the "space" thing, that title was detrimental in hindsight maybe. It was pretty catchy at the time, I guess. It probably got some of the curiosity seekers into the club to hear "space jazz" to see what it was like. *(laughs)*[4]

Hentoff was, however, impressed, as ever, with Russell's music. "In contrast to the arranging clichés of nearly all contemporary jazz big band writing (Duke Ellington excepted), Russell's scores are considerably more variegated and surprising. Moreover, he continually pushes his soloists into stretching their imagination beyond the familiar signposts of much jazz improvisation."[5]

Russell recalled that he was quite clear about his goals with *Jazz in the Space Age* and they were quite different from those for *New York, N.Y.* "I wanted to do a new thing, something that would make one think of the approaching era and how things might feel in that particular space-time condition and give a hint of where the music was going."[6] And to Burt Korall, Russell noted,

> Jazz is changing; the 60's could well be a crucial decade. One thing is certain. A variety of sounds and rhythms, many of which are alien to what audiences are used to, will find their way into jazz. Unaccountably, things we hear around us every day, very human things, have either disappeared or been left out of jazz as we know it. Progress is inevitable. Today's musical palette is just not adequate. ALL feelings relative to life and beauty cannot be validly expressed with techniques now in vogue. What is more, Jazz is an evolving art; it is not meant to be restricted. The very nature of the music and its history indicate this.[7]

This was a statement of both principle and intent. More than any of his previous works to date, *Jazz in the Space Age* exemplifies the application of his Lydian theory in practice. It is also a prophetic statement in its anticipation of immediate and future opposition to new developments in jazz. Russell's position has always remained unaltered in this regard. He has consistently opposed any attempts to confine the music or turn it into a standardized repertoire or museum piece.

It is interesting to reprogram the tracks and play "Chromatic Universe"—parts 1–3 as one continuous suite. In fact, the rest of the orchestra enters only briefly on two occasions in part 2. For the rest, only Evans, Bley, bassist Milt Hinton, and drummer Don Lamond are heard. On part 1, Evans and Bley improvise freely around and against the tonality and 5/2 rhythm provided by the bass and drums. Part 2 opens with a free improvisation from the two pianists, with the remaining two and a half minutes being entirely scored. Part 3 is freely improvised against a pattern and rhythm similar to that on part 1.

Interviewed by Burt Korall for the sleeve notes at the time, Russell described part 2 as "probably my most ambitious piece of music yet." His comments on part 1, which would also apply to part 3, are particularly illuminating in terms of his ideas and approach.

> Bill and Paul were free to come close to the tonality—sum total of the bass notes—relate to the 5/2 gravitational pull or not. Tonality and rhythmically out in space, they were not victim to the tyranny of the chord or a particular meter. In essence, this is musical relativism. Everything can be right. The idea takes over. They worked in the realm of ideas, projecting one upon the other. This is panchromatic improvisation.[8]

With regard to his comments on "musical relativism," his concern was not with the imposition of a rigid system but rather with how the musician or musicians related to the music they are playing. This notion underpins Russell's Lydian Concept, and indeed it is in the actual practice of musicians in relating to chords, scales, melodies, harmonies, rhythms, and so on that the Concept has its origins.

Russell remembered an initial problem with Paul Bley's playing of part 2. "I was mad at Paul because he hadn't studied it. I'd written out a whole huge part of that piece for the two pianos to play, the two pianos [part], he hadn't studied it at all. I was really mad. I said, 'Go home and don't come back until you . . .'".[9]

Bley's recollection is different.

> When George invited me to do the date he said, "I've got a lot of music. I want you to take the music home, learn it and come back in thirty days and play it for me. If you make one mistake you don't get the gig." There were pages and pages and pages of orchestral music. Not solo parts, these were extra things. Also, some of the duets that Bill and I were to play were all written out. So, like a monk I went into a room and I said to Carla, "Just put a tray under my door for the next thirty days. That's it. No phone calls, I don't want to see you, I don't expect anything." That was it. I *became* that written music *because* I wanted that date. You couldn't have made me make a mistake if you had sat on my lap or smacked me in the head. So, I went to George's house and I played the damn thing perfectly. He said, "You've got the date."[10]

According to Bley, he was not fazed by the prospect of playing with Evans, despite the pianist's reputation and involvement with Miles Davis and Russell. After all, Bley had played with Ornette Coleman and was himself familiar with a range of improvisational approaches. What bothered him was how to relate to his opposite number. Should he meet him halfway, adapt himself to Evans's style? "He was a sweet guy and a good friend. I said, 'Fuck him! Everybody loves him; he already owns 99.9% of the music piano business. I'm going to throw the kitchen sink at him from the get go."[11]

> So, I threw the kitchen sink at him and then I thought I heard what was an echo in the room because the same mode, feeling comes back at me in his phrase. I thought, "Well, it must be a lucky phrase on his part. This next one he definitely won't get." He was so "on it," he played my stuff better than I played my stuff and I got mad. It's one thing to have someone play as well as you but he played my stuff better than me! Well, George was ecstatic after the first take with the rhythm section. He said, "No-one has ever played my music like this before!"[12]

Bley and Evans also perform on "The Lydiot," this time with a full big-band arrangement, from the session recorded in May 1960.[13] Here Russell uses the orchestra almost as a Greek chorus, warning and commenting on the solo action from Evans and Bley, who swap choruses throughout the first five minutes. Two contrasting trombone solos follow from Frank Rehak and then Dave Baker, with Baker's J. J. Johnson–influenced double-tonguing trumping Rehak's more conventional approach. Al Kiger follows with a fast series of trumpet choruses before Dave Young enters on tenor. There is something of Coltrane in his playing, what one critic called Coltrane's "sheets of sound," but any such influences are highly personalized in the maturity of Young's delivery, timing and warm sound. Again, the piece reiterates many of the musical ideas used in "Chromatic Universe."

"Dimensions" and "Waltz from Outer Space" were recorded on August 1, 1960, without Bley and with Bob Brookmeyer on trombone and Hal McKusick on alto added to the ensemble, along with a few other changes, most notably Charlie Persip, one of the drummers from the *New York, N.Y.* album dates. In some ways, these two pieces are the meat and drink of *Jazz in the Space Age*: Beautifully crafted arrangements, complex but accessible with the solos emerging naturally out of the ensembles with Young, Kiger and Baker complementing Evans's wonderful playing. In fact, Evans brings to *Jazz in the Space Age* some of his best and most adventurous performances. In fact, there is more of an angularity in his attack and an oblique quality to his note choices here that compliments Russell's compositions very well. But despite the availability of seasoned musicians like Rehak, Brookmeyer, McKusick and Ernie Royal, Russell gives second billing—after Evans—to the trio from Indiana. For these young men, it was their first real experience in a recording studio and they play with all the technique of the veteran and the fire and enthusiasm of the understudy seizing their moment. Dave Young is particularly astonishing.

Asked in an interview if he found the music difficult, Young replied, "Well, I guess for an accomplished musician it wouldn't be, but for me it was. *(laughing)* It was a good experience. I was around twenty-three and there I was with all these experienced New York session guys. There I was, I couldn't run and I couldn't hide but I had to go on and face it. It was awe inspiring—all those musicians and how sharp they were." [14]

As to Bill Evans' view of the experience, the pianist was interviewed by Dan Morgenstern a few years later and talked about how different this was from his usual approach.

> The only way I can work is to have some kind of restraint involved—the challenge of a certain craft or form—and then find the freedom in that . . . I have allowed myself the other kind of freedom occasionally. Paul Bley and I did a two-piano improvisation on a George Russell record that was completely unpremeditated. It was fun to do but there was no direction involved. To do something that hadn't been rehearsed successfully, just like that, almost shows the lack of challenge involved in that type of freedom. [15]

Keith Shadwick, from whose biography of Evans this quote is taken, comments that Evans was being slightly unfair, noting that Russell was engaged in "a controlled experiment, not a formless, open-ended free-for-all." Shadwick's point is well made and distinguishes Russell's approach from others in the jazz avant-garde. For Russell, free improvisation or freedom in music is a means to express a musical idea, not an end in itself, just as atonality has a musical function but can become wearisome if that is all that a composer has to offer. [16]

*Metronome* gave *Jazz in the Space Age* a rating of 10 and described it as "[f]ar-out funkiness that is a must for lovers of music." The reviewer focused on the music's internal coherence and cohesion, noting, "In this album, George Russell has presented an integrated product of genius" and calling Russell "a modern jazz giant." *DownBeat* gave it four and a half stars, feeling that the record showed Russell's potential but that the composer had yet to come "to full bloom."

The latter review, which also covered *George Russell Sextet at the Five Spot*, is extremely perceptive in its examination of Russell's skills and working methods. First, it notes Russell's analytical approach, his "thinking" about the music he is making, and the creation of a form that retains its links with the past but to which the composer has added new levels of rhythmic complexity, chromaticism and unusual choices of notes and intervals. Second, and more important for the listener, is Russell's capacity to create "a musical atmosphere so pervading that most of the players he selects—and on these records he selects carefully and wisely—subordinate their own musical personalities to his." It is ironic to note here that Russell has throughout his career sought out musicians with their own distinctive sound and yet the comment remains valid. Their sound becomes enveloped within Russell's musical world to the extent that it is given new depth and meaning in his sonic universe. [17]

In the October 26, 1961, issue of *DownBeat*, pianist-conductor André Previn was the magazine's guest for its "Blindfold Test," and one of the pieces he reviewed was "Waltz from Outer Space."

> Is that George Russell? I have heard better things by him but over-all he is by far the most interesting of all the guys attempting this kind of writing. I found this fascinating. It's controlled and organized and it really has something new to say within the realm of jazz. I have never studied that modal conception of his . . . that again is a label I don't think it needs. Contrary to the others you have played, here you don't have to have anything explained or pointed out. This is an attractive piece, very well played and orchestrated. I have never had the pleasure of meeting George Russell but I admire him greatly. Five stars. [18]

Perhaps the crucial promise *Jazz in the Space Age* foretold was that in Russell's hands, jazz was being reforged and, perhaps for the first time, aside from Ellington, was becoming a music with a wholly new place within it for the composer-arranger. It also secured, for better or ill, Russell's position as a figure of the emerging avant-garde.

Russell's developing skills as a composer and arranger could certainly have opened up other doors, potentially lucrative ones, to him. Whether other choices could have led to Russell's crossing over into broader areas of popular taste seems highly unlikely. Given the filmic quality of Russell's writing, one possibility might have been that of composition for film and TV. In an interview with Ben Young, Russell remarked upon an offer from Milt Gabler to help him get into film and TV work. It was certainly something Russell fantasized about. He told Young how he had hoped one day to get a call from Cecil B. DeMille and how he had learned that director Robert Wise had used his piece 'Jack's Blues' to explain to composer Johnny Mandel what he was looking for from the soundtrack to the film *I Want To Live!* by way of mood. However, when the chance came to consider working "on the lot," Russell turned it down.

> I had an opportunity to deal with it because when Milt Gabler had hired me to do the *New York, N.Y.* album and he liked it, after it was finished he said, "George you know I can get you a job on the lot if you want but you gotta do all kinds of music." I said, "Thanks, Milt. I don't think it's for me." So I could have done it and probably wanted to be asked at least

once to do it. Fortunately, I didn't become a career Hollywood person. It wouldn't have lasted. [19]

*Jazz in the Space Age* was the last recording Evans made with Russell until 1972, when Evans invited Russell to write and arrange a big-band album for him and his new label, Columbia. [20] Though Evans is forever associated with Miles Davis because of his contribution to *Kind of Blue*, even here Russell had played a part in his early career, in suggesting to Davis that he offer Evans a job.

> I was with Miles and he said, "George. you know of a piano player?" He was at the height . . . one of his heights . . . he said, "Red [Garland] and the junkies in the band are fucking up." I said, "Yeah, I know a piano player who could really take the place of anybody." He said, "Is he white?" I said, "Yeah, he's white but he can play, you know. He wears glasses." He said, "He wears glasses? I know that muthafucker!" *(laughing)* So he says, "Bring him over to Brooklyn. We're playing a club." He told me the name of the club and I told Bill, and Bill, Barry Galbraith and I, in a little German car—a VW Beetle—we take off for Brooklyn. Big town, confusing town driving but we did get to the nightclub and the band was Coltrane, Miles, Philly Joe Jones, Paul Chambers—all heavy on junk. In fact, that was what was worrying Miles was what irritated him. And during the intermission or something he asked Red to get up and let Bill play and that was it. Miles said, "You're going to Philadelphia with us on Saturday." That was it. It happened that way and I read books on that and they didn't get it right at all. Books that deal with history and what's happening. That's the way that Miles and Bill struck it up. [21]

Evans's period with Miles was quite short but it added the final lustre upon his developing reputation and made him one of jazz's more bankable stars. In reality, throughout the fifties Evans's career had been assisted by Russell's use of the young man on a number of records and performances. Evans had played Russell's compositions and arrangements with Lucy Reed, Hal McKusick and Helen Merrill, as well as playing on *Jazz Workshop*, *All About Rosie*, *New York, N.Y.*, and *Jazz in the Space Age*. Yet Evans never studied with Russell. Nor did he ever read *The Lydian Chromatic Concept of Tonal Organization*. Rather he was an extraordinarily open-minded musician familiar with many styles of jazz piano and with classical music and was already engaged in his own harmonic explorations by the time he met Russell.

Pianist Jack Reilly's comments are particularly perceptive with regard to the nature of the creative partnership between Russell and Evans: "I think Bill was so knowledgeable and he had worked out his own horizontal approach and he came from the history of jazz piano music, that he fitted George's music like a glove and elevated it to a higher level, I think, and made it something very special." [22]

There was certainly a meeting of minds between Russell and Evans and they kept in touch over the years, with Evans often sending postcards to Russell signed "Liberace." Evans probably did more than any other musician in the period, after Davis and Coltrane, in bringing Russell's ideas to a wider public. But this was not as a proselytizer on Russell's behalf but by virtue of his interpretation of Russell's work on those fifties recordings and by his essential role in the *Kind of Blue* sextet. Had it not been for the latter, Evans probably would not have been saxophonist Oliver Nelson's piano choice for another highly influential modal jazz album, *Blues and the Abstract Truth*.[23]

One further—and valuable—comment regarding Russell's supposed influence on Evans is found in Shadwick's biography of the pianist. Referring to Evans's arrangement of Richard Carpenter's "Walkin'" for Tony Scott's *The Complete Tony Scott*, Shadwick notes,

> In conception and method, Evans' work on "Walkin'" is strongly reminiscent of George Russell's thematic dissections and linear writing. Initially stressing the blues element of the melody's intervals, he quickly begins weaving counterpoint lines between band sections and intensifying the mood of the music by modulations and such typically Russell methods as contrary movement and imitation, even as accompaniment to the brief solos. A busy three minutes of music![24]

It is true that by the time this track was recorded that Evans had already begun working with Russell. However, his first sessions with Russell took place in October 1956 and that with Scott less than two months later in December. Shadwick is clearly talking about a complementarity of approaches between Evans and Russell, something deeper than words such as influence can convey. Jack Reilly put this very well when he commented to me, "Just hearing the music, I think they all fed each other. It was a wonderful creative period of discovering things. They just wanted to contribute to each other."[25]

George Russell could look back on the fifties with some satisfaction. He had completed his *Lydian Chromatic Concept of Tonal Organization* in 1953 and it had been reissued in amended form in 1959. Its publication was greeted by the *Jazz Review* in February 1960 with a full-page dissertation on the Lydian Concept by Russell's friend, composer John Benson Brooks.[26] In practice the 1959 issue was really the first commercially available edition. Russell's original mimeographed copy had barely sold at all but this was a fine-looking ring-bound manual complete with exercises for the student to explore.

No mainstream publisher had been interested in putting out the book and Russell did not have the resources to issue it himself. However, around this time, guitarist David "Bucky" Wheat joined the Kingston Trio and, like many of the younger musicians on the East Coast folk scene, his musical interests extended to blues and jazz. Wheat had met Russell (Russell had used Wheat's Boo-Bams on *Jazz Workshop* and *New York, N.Y.*) and Wheat had heard about his Lydian Concept. Knowing that Russell was looking for a backer, Wheat showed some of the material to Dave Guard, founder of the trio.

> Somehow through a friend I had met one of the people who was a part of the very successful folk band—it was the folk band of the day. Dave Guard was the guy that put the band together. He saw the book and he freaked out. Bucky [Wheat] had shown him—not the full copy because it wasn't quite finished . . . So Bucky showed it to David from the Kingston Trio. He fell in love with the Concept. One day he came over with a check for $5,000.[27]

Tom Guard, David's son and also a successful guitarist, recalls how his father enthused over Russell's ideas.

> I always thought that the book was a new thing in 1959 since Dad gave it the financial assistance. But, like most good things that are ahead of their time, I guess it needed a push. Dave "Buck" Wheat was a godsend for the Kingston Trio. His playing and knowledge really kept my father's composing and arranging at its best. It only figures that the Lydian Concept would be shared with Dad. Neither my mother or I really know the details of when or how Russell received the $5,000 but in my mind it wasn't just a contribution. Dad bought a good number of the books from George, knowing it was a truly good investment. Our family toted around a hundred or so copies of the book. [28]

In fact, Dave Guard drew heavily on Russell's ideas in developing his own *Colour Guitar* manual for teaching guitar students. "A lot came from the latter, which was about 90 percent influenced by the Lydian Concept." Tom also acknowledges Russell's influence on his father's writing and playing. "After studying with George, all of Dad's writing involved a whole lot of chords that only jazz guys care to learn. So there is no denying it. All those wheels were turning in his head and giving his songs a lot of verve. I look at later arrangements of his Kingston Trio songs and the moving lines are just incredible." [29] But Dave Guard did more than adapt Russell's ideas; he even included in his book a complex diagram designed around the guitar fret board that paralleled the slide rule of scales Russell included in the 1959 edition of the book. Furthermore, in his approach he changed the standard tuning of the instrument so that the intervals were all in perfect fourths. As guitar players will know, in standard tuning the interval between the third and second strings is a major third. According to Tom Guard,

> This allowed the student to move a chord or scale template across the field of notes and examine how various notes change within chords/scales. It also made it easy to learn the chord inversions. If the board were designed in standard tuning with the inconsistency, the movable template would not have functioned. *Colour Guitar* was more basic than the Lydian Concept but I can guarantee the similarities I mentioned advanced my understanding of musical theory in a big way. [30]

Given Dave Guard's place on the folk scene at that time and his later role as a guitar teacher, there is an argument to be made that Russell's ideas about modes as a way of relating chords and scales entered the arena of folk music as well as jazz. This may seem quite a leap to some readers and, yet, ideas often cross disciplines in the sciences, social sciences and philosophy without it being easy to trace their trajectory. New ideas spread through the arts in a similar way. Dave Guard provides an example of Russell's direct influence and through him a source of influence on other musicians outside jazz. And many on the folk scene were interested in jazz. In his autobiography Bob Dylan refers to listening to and enjoying Russell's music and players like Dave Van Ronk were well versed in jazz, ragtime and blues. Modal ideas also entered the British folk music scene in the early sixties, in particular through the music of Davy Graham, who in turn influenced guitarists like Bert Jansch, John Renbourn, Paul Simon and Roy Harper. [31]

It is also worth remembering that rock music in America saw a different process of development from that in Britain. In Britain, it started with aspiring musicians who listened to R&B and rock and roll and with players already familiar with traditional and modern jazz, not least through the localized phenomenon of skiffle. In America, it was heavily influenced by the famous "British Invasion" of groups such as the Beatles and the Rolling Stones but found favour in particular with musicians involved in folk music. The Grateful Dead, Jefferson Airplane, Tim Buckley and the Byrds are excellent examples of this. It is no accident that American rock music often had a distinctively folk-modal flavour to it that was enhanced but not initiated by the increasing interest in Indian and Eastern music of the late sixties. It is perhaps not too great a leap to suggest that Russell's ideas might have had some influence, indirectly, at least.

Such thoughts aside and thanks in no small way to Wheat and Guard, Russell was even able to take out a few advertisements in the trade papers early in 1960.

---

Now available as a correspondence Course

GEORGE RUSSELL'S
LYDIAN CHROMATIC
CONCEPT FOR JAZZ
IMPROVISATION

"The first important theoretical innovation to come from jazz."—John Lewis, musical director of the Modern Jazz Quartet.

"Important for every serious jazz musician."—Art Farmer.
Taught at the School of Jazz, Lenox, Mass.

For information write to:

Concept Publishing Company
121 Bank Street, N.Y. 14, N.Y

---

Having addressed the thorny issue of Russell's influence on Bill Evans above, it is worth, for a moment, trying to pinpoint more clearly Russell's impact upon on Coltrane, Miles Davis and others who spearheaded the modal period of modern jazz. Indeed, "impact" may be a much more useful term here than "influence."

We can, of course, infer this from comments by the musicians themselves. However, as Russell himself noted, everyone learned from everyone else. In such a milieu, it is hard to trace an exact lineage between an idea and its subsequent appearance in other places, by which point it has often been altered somewhat by other inputs.

It is better, easier and more helpful to note processes, events and timings as a way of mapping how Russell's ideas might have spread across the New York jazz scene and beyond. In that regard, it is clear that Russell was a significant figure in this world, one noted for his new and interesting ideas and the music he was creating. Conversations and discussions obviously did take place but we are not privy to those. Events and timings do themselves, however, tell a story.

"Cubano Be, Cubano Bop" came out in 1947 and other recordings, such as Lee Konitz's version of "Ezz-Thetic," followed. And even though unreleased, Buddy DeFranco's take on "A Bird in Igor's Yard" was played regularly on Symphony Sid's show. *Jazz Workshop*, Russell's own album of modal jazz, and the music he wrote and arranged for Hal McKusick were also out there by 1957. "Milestones" was recorded in April 1958, the sessions for *Kind of Blue* began in March 1959 and Coltrane recorded his *Giant Steps* album in April 1959. In jazz as in life, timing is everything. *New York, N.Y.* appeared later that Summer, while Russell had also lectured for three years at Lenox by that point. Over the intervening years, several articles on Russell had appeared but that by Dom Cerulli from *DownBeat* in 1958 seems particularly significant in the scope it gave Russell to outline his theories. In a way, the appearance of the *Lydian Chromatic Concept of Tonal Organization* in 1959 closed the circle. The Lydian Concept might not have captured the jazz mainstream but it had, by the late fifties, found its audience, a fact shown by *Jazz Review*'s commissioning of Benson Brooks' article.

A couple of points might be added with specific regard to Russell's "influence" on Coltrane. In an article for the French *Jazz* magazine, Benoit Quersin asked Coltrane how he liked Russell's music. Coltrane's reply is instructive.

> He has some good music. He has what is the type of music that seems to be coming to the fore nowadays. I've heard a few records of his, one that Eric Dolphy was on, that I heard, that I—several things on there I like very well. And he [Russell] understands quite a few of the problems that musicians are running across today and he's probably going to do a great deal to contribute to solving of such things. [32]

Coltrane's familiarity with Russell's ideas is also illustrated in Lewis Porter's article "The Atlantic Years." Referring to a piece written by Coltrane in 1958—"Coltrane on Coltrane"—Porter noted the saxophonist's comments on Miles Davis's new modal approach. The sentence he draws attention to reads, "He used tunes with free-flowing lines and chordal direction. This approach allowed the soloist the choice of playing chordally (vertically) or melodically (horizontally)." Porter's point is that Coltrane is using terminology taken from Russell's manner of describing this distinction. He added, "(The words in parentheses reflect Coltrane's having been exposed to the music and terminology of jazz composer George Russell)." [33]

In terms of Miles Davis himself, three authorities cite Russell's influence on the trumpeter during this period. Ian Carr noted that the composer and Davis had "spent some time together and Russell's great theoretical (and profoundly) practical work *The Lydian Chromatic Concept of Tonal Organization* had, among other things, examined the scales appropriate to certain chords. The translation of chords into scales paved the way for this later modal thinking." [34] Ashley Kahn quotes Davis discussing scalar approaches in an important 1958 *Jazz Review* article by Nat Hentoff (also referenced earlier in this book). Of particular relevance here is, "And look at George Russell. His writing is mostly scales. After all, you can feel the changes." [35] Finally, Eric Nisenson, discussing the track

"Milestones" in his biography of the trumpeter *Round about Midnight—A Portrait of Miles Davis*, has written, "The simple melody was an experiment inspired by an evening Miles had spent with the jazz composer and arranger George Russell, who at the time was working on his theoretical 'Lydian Concept of Tonal Organization.'" He continued, "Miles was fascinated by Russell's approach. Here was a means of breaking free from tonal clichés—while maintaining some amount of restraint." [36] There is always a slight problem with proof via reference to "higher" authority. However, it is fair to note that Russell's impact on Davis is broadly accepted. However, in relation to Russell's influence on and within the wider circle of musicians around Davis, Coltrane and Gil Evans, this was essentially indirect. Here, the issue of timing, and in particular the timing of Russell's own recordings and compositions, and spread by word of mouth would seem to be the key factors.

At the beginning of the fifties, Russell had felt that his career had plateaued with the Carnegie Hall performance of "Cubano-Be, Cubano-Bop." However, by the end of the decade he had clearly become a figure of some importance in jazz. There was a lot of goodwill toward him from musicians and others involved in the music. It was, after all, quite a small, even insular world, which might have extended up and down the East Coast, while the West Coast had its own scene and the hinterland remained largely unexplored and uncolonized by the new music.

At the same time, there was a lot of interaction across the arts in general in and around New York. Any individual with any pretensions to being remotely hip or cultured would be expected to know about jazz, literature, theatre and art. And indeed, jazz musicians mixed with their peers in other fields. George and Juanita's apartment at 121 Bank Street saw its share of parties, as Bob Brookmeyer recalled,

> Socially we spent a great deal of time together. We had parties back and forth. One of the jobs at parties was trying to get Bill Evans out of a corner. He would seek the first available corner and stay there for the party. We would attend each other's concerts—be together a lot. I don't recall us talking a great deal about music because people in those days didn't talk a great deal about music, not in my group anyway. [But] Gil Evans was there and John Benson Brooks. It was for those days one of the "in" parties. We had a group of very happy people who enjoyed each other a lot. They were, in my memory, very mellow occasions. [37]

Juanita Giuffre also remembers the time with a lot of fondness.

> Oh, God yes. We gave a couple. We didn't have a lot because he was really busy and I was working and money was not all that, you know, but we did have parties. One of them was with Manny Albam and Barry Galbraith and I think Ray Nance was there and Gerry Mulligan, Gil Evans and his wife were there. I mean, just stardom without our thinking about it as stardom. Cecil Taylor was at one of the parties, and so was . . . who was the author? Robert Graves was there and he followed me around all night long trying to figure out what nationality I was. Everywhere! He kept naming names and I kept saying, "No." Finally, he said, "Well, it's gotta be" and he looked at me and said, "I know what it is—

Canton-Greek." *(laughs)* They used to be crazy parties, a lot of fun. I was trying to think who else used to be at those parties—Bobby Brookmeyer, Jim Hall, all those people we hung out with.[38]

Russell's career might well have been on the up but, at the same time, all was not well within the marriage. Probably because of everything he had experienced in his childhood, youth, and young adulthood, Russell could seem distant and emotionally reserved. Although Juanita clearly understood why he was like that, it sometimes left her feeling, as she put it, "I needed more."

She acknowledges that Russell could be hard to get close to "sometimes but at other times he was extremely open and vulnerable. Let's put it this way. The preoccupation with music theory and the music business and what he had to accomplish kind of was a dominating factor."

She even tolerated his indiscretions, as she explains: "It's not something that you say, 'Well, I'm going to go out and I'm gonna . . .' Although there may have been instances when he might have been a little indiscreet, George. I mean to him it was just nothing. *(laughs)* So I had no problems with pursuing my own happiness."[39]

The event that led to the marriage breakup was that Juanita met saxophonist Jimmy Giuffre. Their paths first crossed at the sessions for *New York, N.Y.*, which Giuffre attended but it was at the Lenox School of Jazz that their relationship blossomed. While Russell was angry and felt hurt at the time, he remained good friends with Juanita and Jimmy. "Yeah, that puts a new light on it because I can see back where it happened. It came out of the School of Jazz and she and Jimmy Giuffre got along real well and it really was not a disaster kind of thing. And as I say, we're very close today, closer to people than back then."[40]

For her part, Juanita found in Giuffre someone she could more easily relate to and feel closer to. "When I finally met someone, you know, the two of us were really mutual because it's hard to read George sometimes in terms of his feelings of affection. Even though he might show them here and there, he just has a certain reserved quality in that regard. Nothing bad about it. It's just what the person is." She adds, "I think there was more anger than sadness about it on his part."[41]

The only really awkward moment either George or Juanita can recall occurred when Russell appeared at the Five Spot opposite Giuffre's group. As Russell told Ian Carr, "He and Juanita were then going together, you know. That was . . . *(pause)* . . . a little sparky there, you know? *(laughing)*"[42]

## Notes

1. Interview with G. Russell, October 2003.
2. Stan Britt, notes for Affinity reissue of *Jazz in the Space Age* (1986), AFF152; Burt Korall, original sleeve notes to *Jazz in the Space Age*, Decca DL-9219.
3. Hentoff, "Jazz's Third Stream," p. 10.
4. Interview with Joe Hunt, June 2004.
5. Hentoff, "Jazz's Third Stream," p. 10.

6. Interview with G. Russell, October 2003.
7. Korall, sleeve notes to Jazz in the Space Age.
8. Ibid.
9. Interview with G. Russell, October 2003.
10. N. Meehan, *Time Will Tell—Conversations with Paul Bley* (Berkeley, CA: Berkeley Hills Books, 2003), p. 63. Paul Bley repeated this story in an interview with the author for Jazzwise magazine on June 14, 2007.
11. Ibid, p. 64.
12. Ibid.
13. I have three different sets of dates for *Jazz in the Space Age* – May and August 1960; January 1960; and December 1959 and January 1960. The May/August dates seem to have most support, so I have gone with these. Moreover, This accords most clearly with Dave Baker and Russell's recollections of the chronology of their meeting and coming to work together.
14. Interview with Dave Young, January 2007.
15. Dan Morgenstern, "The Art of Playing," *DownBeat*, October 22, 1964. Quoted in Keith Shadwick, *Bill Evans: Everything Happens to Me—A Musical Biography* (San Francisco: Backbeat, 2002), p. 84.
16. Shadwick, *Everything Happens to Me*.
17. *Metronome*, 1961 (no other information available); Dom DeMichael, "Spotlight Review of Jazz in the Space Age (Decca9219) and George Russell Sextet at the Five Spot (Decca9220)," *Down Beat*, June 8, 1961.
18. "The Blindfold Test—André Previn," *DownBeat*, October 26, 1961.
19. Young, broadcast devoted to George Russell.
20. There are rumours that Evans and Russell took part in a project, perhaps with Gunther Schuller as well, for Riverside featuring arrangements of jazz standards. According to Steve Swallow's recollections, other members of the George Russell sextet were involved, as well as pianist Jaki Byard. Gunther Schuller remembers something of this ilk, but nothing was ever released and the current owners of the Riverside catalogue can find no trace of any tapes that might be from the session.
21. Interview with G. Russell, October 2003. See also Hentoff, Nat, "An Afternoon with Miles Davis," Jazz Review, December 1958.
22. Interview with Reilly, October 2003. It is sometimes pointed out that Evans had recorded a modal piece, "Aeolian Drinking Song," with clarinettist Tony Scott prior to his work with Russell. In fact, he had already played on sessions with Hal McKusick performing Russell's compositions and with Russell himself by the time this was recorded. Tony Scott, *The Touch of Tony Scott*, RCA Victor LPM1353.
23. Oliver Nelson, *Blues and the Abstract Truth*. Impulse A-5.
24. Shadwick, *Everything Happens to Me*, p. 57.
25. Interview with Reilly, October 2003.
26. John Benson Brooks, "George Russell," *Jazz Review*, February 1960, p. 38. Though Brooks was rather under-recorded, among his albums are *Alabama Concerto* and *Folk Jazz USA*, Lonehill JazzLHJ10275. Both come recommended. Brooks also wrote the lovely "Where Flamingos Fly," which Gil Evans recorded—*Gil Evans, Out of the Cool* HMV CLP1456 and *Where Flamingos Fly*, A&M 390831-2.
27. Interview with George Russell, June 2004.
28. Interview with Tom Guard, May 2005.
29. Ibid.
30. Ibid.
31. Bob Dylan, *Chronicles, Volume One* (London: Simon & Schuster, 2004), pp. 94 and 74. See also C. Harper, *Dazzling Stranger: Bert Jansch and the British Folk and Blues Revival* (London: Bloomsbury, 2001).

32. B. Quersin, (1963) *La Passe Dangereuse* in Woideck, C. (ed) *John Coltrane Companion* (Shirmer, New York, 1998)
33. L. Porter, L. (1995) *The Atlantic Years* in Woideck, C. (ed) *John Coltrane Companion*.
34. Carr, I. *Miles Davis – The Definitive Biography* (Harper Collins, Hammersmith, 1999)
35. Kahn, A. *A Kind Of Blue* (Granta, London, 2000).
36. Nisenson, E. *Round About Midnight – A Portrait of Miles Davis* (Da Capo, New York, 1996)
37. Interview with Bob Brookmeyer, October 2003.
38. Interview with Juanita Giuffre, June 2004.
39. Ibid.
40. Interview with George Russell 2003.
41. Interview with Giuffre.
42. Ian Carr, interview with George Russell, June 1992.

CHAPTER EIGHT

## You Are My Sunshine

Russell's decision to form a working group came at the turn of the decade. From Indiana, he had recruited Dave Baker on trombone, Al Kiger on trumpet, Dave Young on tenor – all of whom had played on *Jazz in the Space Age* – and a fine, confident young drummer in Joe Hunt. In fact, Russell would later recruit saxophonists Paul Plummer and John Peirce from Indiana through Baker. The group's first bassist was Ted Snyder, who was shortly to be replaced by Chuck Israels.

Russell had shown no real interest up to that point in playing live or leading a band, let alone playing piano except to compose. By his account, his reasons for doing so were largely pragmatic. As he put it, it was simply "[t]o stay alive and play music. But my main interest was in writing music, not playing it."[1]

Exactly how the idea originated is unclear. In fact, it is not a question Burt Korall found necessary to ask in a February 1961 piece for *DownBeat*. The sense that the article does convey is that it was time, as its closing quote from Gil Evans makes clear,

> George is finally out there, playing fine piano, writing for immediate situations, living in music every day. Now he can relax a bit more and make contact and more important be as diversified as he wants. Recognition . . . it has to happen for him and probably will before you know it. I don't see anything but better and better things for him. He's on the threshold.[2]

Russell has attributed the original suggestion that he form his own group to Riverside Records boss Orrin Keepnews but has on other occasions said that it was he who approached Keepnews with the idea for a record with the musicians he had played with at Lenox.

They were all very, very talented. It was Orrin Keepnews that suggested that I make a . . . that I should record. I think Orrin came to the School of Jazz as many people did. They came up just for the day. It was a very relaxed environment. A nightclub on campus, wonderful food, beautiful weather in that open natural environment, it was conducive to people fraternizing and socializing and having a good time. So out of that came a contract with Riverside. I never played piano in my life. So the first time I played piano was on the first date. I never really played piano.[3]

However, in an interview with Ben Young, Russell said,

When I convinced Orrin Keepnews to record *Stratusphunk*, the first album with my personal group, I hadn't played piano before. But I did play the Concept. I played the Concept, I didn't play piano. So when you're hearing me accompany Eric Dolphy, that's the first time I ever played piano on a record at all. I never had really focused on playing piano, I just played it enough to put a composition together.[4]

Russell's recollections are out of sync; Dolphy plays on *Ezz-Thetics* from 1961, not on *Stratusphunk*. However, the actual recording sequence is quite confusing. The first album Russell made with his own sextet and with him on piano is *George Russell Sextet at the Five Spot*, which was recorded on September 20, 1960, for Decca. Orrin Keepnews then produced *Stratusphunk* for Riverside on October 18, just four weeks later. To add to the confusion, *George Russell Sextet in Kansas City*, Russell's fourth and final album for Decca, was cut on February 21, 1961, followed by *Ezz-Thetics* for Riverside on May 8, 1961. This was obviously a very concentrated period of activity for the sextet since its formation in the summer of 1960. The two final albums for Riverside—*The Stratus Seekers* and *The Outer View*—were both recorded in 1962.

This means that these six albums were made in the space of twenty-three months. Moreover, listening in sequence, one has the sense that each one was planned as a complete statement. As well as using his own compositions and jazz standards by Charlie Parker, Miles Davis and others, tunes by Carla Bley, Dave Lahm, Dave Baker and Al Kiger are also featured. Baker, Lamb and Kiger all studied with Russell. So, it is not surprising that their pieces fit with Russell's own extremely effectively. In Carla Bley's case, one suspects that Russell chose her tunes to fit an overarching conception for each record. Certainly, Bley's compositions, such as "Dance Class" and "Bent Eagle", already reveal her precocious talent and unique voice.

Neither the *Five Spot* nor *Kansas City* dates were live; both were New York studio recordings. The reason for their titles seems to be an attempt on Decca's part to capitalize on the group's live performances at the Five Spot and in Kansas City. In terms of live work, the group debuted at the Museum of Modern Art on July 28, 1960,[5] prior to the first of two three-week engagements at the Five Spot, which came either side of the band's residency at Lenox as "group-in-residence." This was followed not long after by two weeks of dates in Kansas City. A brief residency at Birdland aside, that was pretty much it in terms of gigs for the sextet for the next twelve months. Drummer Joe Hunt remembered,

Our work sort of trickled down. In the beginning, we had this wonderful job at the Five Spot. I guess all in all we must've played there about six weeks. We had a very good run. Toward the end—they changed bands anyway there and, toward the end, I think the business was falling off a little and from then on we really didn't have much work in New York. We had a gig at Birdland, I think maybe that same year or maybe 1961. I remember we played at Birdland for a week. They didn't like us at Birdland. We even got some boos there.[6]

When the band first played the Five Spot, prior to their residency at Lenox, Ted Snyder was on bass, but after Lenox, Chuck Israels had joined the group. According to Hunt, Snyder had come with them from Indiana and "wasn't real crazy about being in New York." Hunt had met Israels at Lenox. They had become friends and enjoyed playing together, which made Israels the obvious choice to replace the homesick Snyder.[7]

The Five Spot was quite a legendary New York club that had opened in the late fifties in a bar close to the Bowery. Tenorist Dave Young described the venue, "The physical experience of it was like a local tavern but it wasn't at all rowdy. People came in there to hear some music."[8] In fact, being close to the Village, it attracted a crowd drawn from the Apple's intelligentsia— musicians with a night off or coming down after their own gigs, artists like Willem DeKooning and Larry Rivers, journalists, and writers. Joe Hunt was amazed and horrified to see Max Roach, Ornette Coleman, Horace Silver and Roy Haynes in the audience for opening night.

Oh, it scared me man! *(laughs)* I was scared but we had to play. The other guys were . . . we were intimidated on the one hand but we realized we had rehearsed well and so we had to give it our best shot, so we did and we were well received. The people liked us, you know. Ornette had already broken in the free music there.[9]

According to Hunt, the first time they played opposite Jimmy Giuffre. Money for the gig was not great, but, as he added, it was just enough to live on.

Well, we played opposite Jimmy Giuffre's trio the first time. He had a really good trio with Jim Hall, Buell Neidlinger and Billy Osborne, a really good drummer. Most of the clubs in New York at that time had two bands. This might be interesting for you. I recollect that we made $89 a week. That was New York scale for a week's work, six nights a week. That comes down to less than $15 a night! In 1960 that would be pretty decent. You added it up and you could eat and live.[10]

Dave Young remembered Coltrane turning up one night.

On the first one, that's when I met Trane. He came in with Eric Dolphy, who I had met at Slide Hampton's house. We had stayed at Slide's house the first few days there; in fact, it was when we were getting ready to do the *Jazz in the Space Age* album. Eric Dolphy brought John in. It was a very pleasant experience—he was so down-to-earth. I had admired him for a long time.[11]

George Hoefer in *DownBeat* was impressed by the group's performances of Russell's complex arrangements, noting that "[t]he playing of the Russell sextet narrows the gap between free-blowing jazz and written chamber jazz." Hoefer closed with the comment, "I believe that the Russell sextet will be a source of enjoyment and satisfaction for some time to come." [12] And *Playboy* told its readers, "We caught the nifty new George Russell Sextet at the Five Spot in New York and dug the meaty, modern jazz that came tumbling out." The unnamed writer was hugely impressed by the young band, concluding,

> In all, it's a serious set of jazzmen capable of essaying fresh material like Russell's "Stratusphunk" and Baker's "Stone Nuts" and "Kentucky Oysters" with stunning style and excitement and also able to turn a jazz standard like "Woody 'n' You" inside out and back again with such dazzle and verve that even the Five Spot's waiters had to shake their heads to regain focus. Go listen. [13]

According to Kirk Silsbee's notes for the *Five Spot* CD reissue, Miles Davis, Charlie Mingus and J. J. Johnson were also in the audience. As Chuck Israels, the group's bassist, told Silsbee, it was not unusual to see people from the other arts turn out for these gigs. "People were paying a lot of attention to us but remember, jazz at this time was connected to intelligent society, just as the work of writers and painters was. This was perfectly normal." [14]

With *George Russell Sextet at the Five Spot*, like its "live" twin *George Russell Sextet in Kansas City*, the aim seems to have been present the group as a working unit, as it would have sounded live on stage at these two residencies. According to Leonard Feather's original sleeve notes, *Kansas City* featured "compositions that the sextet was asked to play in the course of a two-week engagement at a club called The Blue Room in Kansas City." [15] These are really dynamic, highly charged sets that on first hearing impress with their virtuoso playing and powerful, driving swing. They bear comparison with Art Blakey's band of the time and even with Miles Davis's group for their dynamism and commitment to the music.

Another thing that strikes the listener is the quality of the sound production, even on the original vinyl. It is bright, clear and immediate. It is only on repeated plays that one becomes aware that the writing and arranging is of a different order from much of the jazz of the period and, indeed, since.

Even Davis's "Sippin' at the Bells" from the Five Spot disc opens with an extended scored section where the horns play variations on the theme in unison, not unlike the way the frontline might have been used in early jazz. It closes in similar fashion but also uses a favoured Russell technique of having the soloist play out of tempo and then playing briefly *a cappella* before the next section or solo. Russell's own piano solo—his first on record—is highly chromatic and polyrhythmic, with the closest comparison being Thelonious Monk. But it is the originals rather than the "standards"—the record also includes Coltrane's "Moment's Notice"—that stand out. Carla Bley's evocative "Dance Class" utilizes radical shifts in tempo, stop-start passages and polytonality, in particular from the piano, where Russell's accompaniment is unusually free harmonically. Bley's "Beast Blues" is slightly more conventional, with a lovely opening where the horns play against each other. Yet it is also quite an unsettling blues with a slightly eerie atmosphere, again because of the unusual harmonies that are used. Russell's own "Swingdom Come" stretches the use of polytonality even further and its rhythmic shifts are rapid; both these aspects give the piece a free-sounding quality not that different from early Ornette Coleman and Cecil Taylor. In fact, Russell's piano, though not as virtuosic as Taylor's, has similar chromatic and multi-rhythmic characteristics. The playing from the frontline is astonishing and there is no doubt that this is an uncompromisingly professional unit. As bassist Chuck Israels told Kirk Silsbee, "It was swinging music. We were all going for that."[16] And as Dave Young explains, "I felt if I could just keep up with Al and Dave, everything would sound alright. It wasn't easy, especially playing lines in different keys at the same time."[17]

If one listens now, this music does not sound so "far out," and one wonders for a moment what all the fuss was about. But one needs to play these records alongside Coleman's *Tomorrow Is the Question* and Taylor's *Looking Ahead!* They do not sound that radical anymore precisely because the way we hear jazz has adjusted—because of these albums and what followed. In 1960 we were still five years away from the "New Thing at Newport" and the likes of Archie Shepp and Marion Brown. Coltrane had only just released *Giant Steps* and the far more radical *Ascension* was not recorded until April 1965. Russell's sextet albums for Decca and Riverside were, nevertheless, pushing jazz into whole new areas of exploration, demonstrating how composition and improvisation can be allied without detriment to either spontaneity or art.

In contrast to the two 'live' records, with *Stratusphunk*, and with the other 'studio' albums, Russell's aim was different. The impression left is of a desire to make a complete statement presenting pieces that, taken together, offer a coherent narrative rather than simply a collection of tunes or otherwise present the group as it would sound on stage. In this respect, *Stratusphunk* is less successful than *Ezz-thetics*, *The Status Seekers* or *The Outer View*. The problem with the record lies in its pacing and specifically with the second track, "New Donna" based on Charlie Parker's "Donna Lee." If one programmes the disc to exclude that track, coherence of narrative is restored, also in respect of Russell's closing piece "Things New," which otherwise sits awkwardly on the record. The title track and Carla Bley's precocious "Bent Eagle" meet Russell's objectives more successfully and David Lahm's "Lambskins" seems to push the soloists—Al Kiger, in particular—in more interesting directions than several of the leader's compositions. The same can also be said of Dave Baker's gospel-influenced "Kentucky Oysters," which has a freshness that would have suited Cannonball Adderley's groups of the time, with Dave Young again shining on tenor.

John S. Wilson, writing in *DownBeat* on March 3, 1961, gave the record three and a half stars and concluded: "In view of the imagination that has gone into some of the writing (Carla Bley's 'Bent Eagle,' for instance), it is disappointing to find so much of this record devoted to essentially the same old thing that already has contributed many aimless LP's to the library of jazz records."[18] Wilson's comments may be a bit strong—the record is certainly better than that—but I do understand his frustration and he is certainly correct about "Bent Eagle."

By the time, the K.C. disc was recorded, trumpeter Don Ellis had replaced Al Kiger. According to Joe Hunt, "Kiger didn't like New York much either. These guys were all from Indiana and they weren't city people."[19] Kiger missed home, so he left. Fine player though Kiger was, Ellis brought a different dimension to the group's sound.

Something that dogged Russell's career was the suggestion that his bands had often been reliant on student musicians as opposed to the seasoned pros called upon by the likes of Art Blakey, Miles Davis and Cannonball Adderley. He would react very testily to a later comment from DJ Ben Young during their radio interview for WKCR. I also recall a discussion I had about jazz composers with a well-regarded British jazz journalist. When I asked about his opinion of Russell as a composer, his response was that perceptions of Russell in that regard had suffered due to his need to employ such apprentice musicians.

Such cavils are remarkably misplaced. One only needs to listen to the playing of Young, Kiger, Hunt and Baker or to hear how mature Dave Baker's compositions sound on these records to consign such views to the critical waste bin. It is true that Al Kiger and Dave Young both returned to the mid-West a couple of years after joining Russell's group. Alto saxophonist John Peirce,[20] who played on *The Stratus Seekers* and tenor player Paul Plummer, who appears on that album and *The Outer View*, would also head back to Indiana later. They did so for their own reasons and, given the perils associated with the jazz life in the New York (addictions, broken relationships, constant struggles for work, rip-off agents and club-owners), one can hardly blame them.[21]

Dave Baker's decision to return home was different. Recurring problems with an injury to his jaw brought an end to his playing of the trombone. He needed to retrench to establish a new direction in his musical career.

Nor did these 'students' disappear entirely from the world of jazz. Dave/David Baker became one of the most important figures in jazz education at Indiana University, where he adopted *The Lydian Chromatic Concept of Tonal Organization* as a core text. Musicians of the calibre of Michael and Randy Brecker and Freddie Hubbard passed through his studio. He also continued composing and playing cello. He later led the 21st Century Bebop Band (in which he played cello) and was also leader of the Smithsonian Jazz Masterworks Orchestra and was a noted composer of contemporary music.

Drummer Joe Hunt would go on to play in groups led by Stan Getz and Bill Evans, as well as Hal McKusick and Red Rodney and record and perform with the likes of Dexter Gordon, Charles Mingus, Chet Baker and others.

Al Kiger continued to work in music in Cincinnati and Indiana. The main outlet for his talents from the eighties onwards was the Blue Wisp Big Band, for which he also wrote and arranged. John Peirce taught and continued to play jazz. In 2012, Cadence Jazz Records released a collection of his performances from 1956-1982 under the title *Memorial Album* (Cadence Jazz CJR 1226).[22] Paul Plummer recorded several albums with Indiana/Cincinnati-based drummer Ron Enyard, while Dave Young worked with such diverse figures as Lionel Hampton, saxophonist Sam Rivers, Nigerian drummer Olatunji, Frank Foster and Brother Jack McDuff. He made one album under his own name for the Mainstream label in 1971. (MRL 323). Though this might not have received general release, it was reissued on CD in Japan in 2017. It is well worth seeking out with a line-up that includes Sonny Fortune on baritone and flute, Virgil Jones on trumpet, Harold Mabern Jr. on piano with bassist Richard Davis and drummer Idris Muhammad making up the rhythm section. For students, these guys kept pretty heavy company.

However, the addition of Don Ellis certainly added a dimension to Russell's group that is already evident on the Kansas City record. There is a wit and confidence to his playing on Dave Baker's "Lunacy" and a lightness to his solo on Clifford Brown's "Sandu," an unusual choice for this group, that Kiger might have struggled with. That said, Kiger was arguably a more interesting player in the context of Russell's group and certainly had a greater sense of Russell's aims than Ellis. Russell contributed only one tune to this record, "Theme." Described by Feather as "every man for himself in F minor," [23] it is about the closest Russell has ever written to a straight-ahead jazz theme—hence the title, no doubt. Even then, the contrapuntal effects he obtains from the horns are quite typical of his style. "Tune Up," one of two tunes Eddie "Cleanhead" Vinson donated to Miles Davis, is given a fluid and breakneck reading, while Baker's "War Gewessen" demonstrates a point that Russell has always been quick to emphasize. The function of the Lydian Concept is to open up the individual's creativity, not to produce Lydian clones or soundalikes. Baker's piece is a tricky, slippery and episodic blues that moves through changes in time, yet with an almost burlesque quality to it. [24]

Dave Young again makes one wish he had recorded more. Though he does sound like Coltrane, every time he solos it is with authority and elegance. What is more, the sense is that he is on the way to achieving a sound both personal and distinct. It is, however, Carla Bley's "Rhymes" that stands out on the album. It is certainly the most "modern"-sounding tune on *Kansas City*. Modal in form and in its solos, it would not have been out of place on Davis's *Kind of Blue* and, compositionally it is at least as interesting as the tunes Davis used. "Rhymes" is marvellously atmospheric and quite lovely.

As to how the band was received in Kansas City, Russell is quoted by Feather, "The musicians in K.C. really come out to dig you," noting that Eddie "Cleanhead" Vinson, among others, turned up several times. [25] Joe Hunt also remembered the Kansas City gigs as a highlight from his time with the group. "The only place they really liked us after the Five Spot was out in Kansas City. We played at a black club in the black part of town and these people were used to hearing Kansas City Blues, right? That was a real perk for us the Kansas City gig. It was really a good gig." [26]

Dave Young's memory of the experience is different, however. "They weren't ready for our kind of music. The crowds were very slim, especially after the first night. *(laughing)*" [27] The clarity of Hunt's recollection of this and of other events perhaps gives his account the edge. Yet it is worth noting that the music this group was making was at odds with the prevailing style of the day. As Hunt had noted, the group were booed at their week's engagement at Birdland.

Musicians from the Midwest must have dreamed of playing a gig like Birdland and one can imagine what it felt like to see that dream realized—but instead of applause to be met with catcalls. However, not everyone who saw the band at the club hated it. One fan who enjoyed it was Ran Blake, the brilliant pianist-composer. Blake is one of those people who, when he likes something, he really likes it, "I went every night to Birdland. He had a one-week gig. My fifth night, he said, 'Is that you again?' You could get right up front at the old Birdland, and I tried to get as close to his piano as possible. It would have been around '61 or '62, when the first Riverside came out." [28]

Blake's enthusiasm aside, it was not a triumphal homecoming for Russell to the club where he used to hear Bird and Diz in the forties and fifties. As to why the band was met with such a response, Hunt's comment is both succinct and pertinent: "I think it was mostly the sound of the Lydian harmony. It was a pretty free band. It was new. It was different." [29]

By that time, with obvious exceptions (such as Ornette Coleman, Charlie Mingus, Cecil Taylor, Miles Davis and Dave Brubeck, for example), hard bop was the dominant style of jazz. Even though these six albums share some elements stylistically with the music of other small groups of the period—records like *Five Spot* push and swing just as hard as albums by Horace Silver, the Adderleys and Blakey—they are quite different in feel and approach. Kenny Mathieson in *Cookin'—Hard Bop and Soul Jazz 1954-65* excludes the Russell sextet from his survey. [30] There are reasons why jazz fans are many times more likely to hear at their local jazz club a band delivering their version of Nat Adderley's "Work Song," Horace Silver's "Song for My Father," or Benny Golson's "Blues March." Of Russell's tunes, only "Blues in Orbit," "Stratusphunk" and "Ezz-Thetic" have achieved anything like standard status. The first two probably owe their relative popularity to the Gil Evans' versions rather than Russell's own and "Ezz-Thetic" is best known through the Lee Konitz–Miles Davis recording.

As for the reason the recordings for Decca and Riverside overlapped, Russell was unable to recall why this was. He got the opportunity to record and was paid for it and that kept him going. He had no agent at the time and, as long as he could survive and work on the Concept, that was all he asked. The answer, if there were one, is probably about cost, timing and opportunity. Even then there were limitations. Asked by WKCR's Ben Young if he considered at the time working with a larger group, Russell replied,

> It wouldn't have been practical. I had to go to a sextet because largely the budget of the record company couldn't tolerate anything bigger. Of course, on the road it's absolutely important—a sextet is a luxury. I wasn't a strong instrumentalist in being like a superstar pianist or something. I was a background player. I did that well and I think I was hired by the record companies because of my . . . I think Orrin liked my compositions. Sort of rare. [31]

On one level, this was quite a satisfying period for Russell. He made a series of six records in a very short space of time, keeping a sextet of musicians fairly intact through that period. He taught privately and generally kept body and soul together. Live work was infrequent, however, and Russell clearly felt he was not getting his due acknowledgment. His frustration surfaced occasionally in various ways and would eventually result in his leaving the United States for Scandinavia for five years in the mid- to late sixties.

These records were, as Russell said, made both as a way to earn a living and keep a group together but also as experiments within the Lydian Concept. However, as noted above, Russell was always open to the inclusion of compositions by other group members. Dave Baker, in particular, valued the opportunity to hone his compositional skills.

> Everybody didn't take the time to write but he encouraged us to write because he had Carla Bley writing and David Lahm, who was a student of his at the time, too. It was a wonderful

experience for me as a neophyte, somebody who's not really tasted much in the way of success as such because I had been here in Indiana and it was very thrilling when George encouraged me to write and on about all the albums I did with George I wrote at least one piece. It was so gracious to choose a piece to record of mine and not only could we record it but we had a chance to really internalize it because we were playing the things on the job. So by the time we record[ed] it, it was a piece which we were familiar with, it was a piece which we also felt comfortable playing and that makes a world of difference.[32]

As for Carla Bley, she had come out to New York with her husband, Paul Bley, and had been struggling to gain any recognition as a composer in her own right. Though Paul Bley had recorded one of her tunes and played others live, with no other validation or support she was about to give up her hopes of making it in the male-dominated music business, as she told Ian Carr.

So I was going to a psychiatrist at that time and the psychiatrist said to me, among other horrible things like maybe I should try shock treatment, that I should give up trying to be a composer. Because that was obviously the silliest thing he had ever heard, that somebody like me would be a composer. He said, "Is there anything else you can do?" So I said, "Well, I can sew a little bit." He said, "Well, get a job sewing." So I went home and looked in the paper for jobs as a seamstress and I applied for three of them and while I waited to hear back I happened to take a piece of music to George Russell and he looked at it and he said, "This is fantastic. I want to record it." So he saved my life. At that moment, I was about to become a seamstress. I actually went to one of the designers and sat in his office watching that scene and wondering how I could be a part of it but thinking I should learn to be a part of it and give up music, since the psychiatrist had told me to but George at that moment interfered and said, "I'll record that piece." I think it was called "Bent Eagle." And so I didn't take the job as a seamstress and my whole life changed.[33]

In an interview for this book, Bley recalled,

I knew that George had this theory about the Lydian Scale, so I made sure to put a sharp 11th in all the pieces. Like a tip of the hat, you know. So I went over to his house and I brought the tunes with me and I showed them to him and he liked them and he recorded a couple of them. Oh, "Dance Class"—that's the piece I wrote after I met George and that was the one with the sharp 11th. Because I think that "Bent Eagle" was written a long time before that and so was "Zig-Zag." "Dance Class" was written for George's band. I think I liked that one more. I didn't think "Zig-Zag" was a very good piece; I didn't know why he liked it. I don't even know why he recorded any of them. He had plenty of good music of his own. I've no idea why he recorded me and Dave Lahm. I mean, he was much better than us.[34]

It has been said that Carla Bley was a student of Russell's. For example, Leonard Feather describes her in that way in his sleeve notes to the Kansas City record.[35] However, she is adamant that she never studied with him.

**DH:** Did you study with George Russell?
**CB:** No. What does study mean? You mean like take lessons?
**DH:** Yes.
**CB:** No.
**DH:** So nothing formal like that?
**CB:** No. I never paid him any money, that's for sure. [36]

Later in the same interview, she explains that she did transcriptions for Russell. "Yes, and that could be called study because I had a good ear, so I was able to just listen to the records and make lead sheets, you know, write out what people were playing. That was fascinating and I caught mistakes that he made and everything." [37]

One number in which she found an error between the recorded version and the sheet music was "Ezz-Thetic." Her answer goes on to clarify the nature of her relationship with Russell, which at most might be described very loosely as that of mentor. Bley, like Russell, is *sui generis*.

> Maybe it was the old lead sheet that had the mistake, I don't know ... But also then he wrote some new pieces and I would be the copyist—this went on for a couple of years and I went over to his house quite a bit. He lived near me on Bank Street. I would go over to his house and I think once he did loan me the big book about the thing. I think he did loan it to me once and I leafed through it but I couldn't understand it because I was absolutely an unschooled musician, so I really didn't understand modes or chord changes or anything. [38]

The tunes on these small-group albums made between 1960 and 1962 are highly personal, reflecting both the character of their composers and the group that would perform them. They are episodic, with unusual time signatures and changes of tempo. Soloists often play against the rhythm section rather than along with it. Key centres shift and the music is pan-tonal and pan-rhythmic. Often the arrangements present a little drama and will contain a variety of moods. Indeed, this heightened sense of drama and dramatic presentation of his music seems to have been a continuous thread in Russell's work from the first performances of "Cubano Be, Cubano Bop," through pieces such as "The Day John Brown Was Hanged" and "Ballad of Hix Blewit," albums like *New York, N.Y.*, *Electric Sonata for Souls Loved by Nature* and *The African Game* to later performances of his Living Time Orchestra.

These performances present complete compositions with structured introductions, a middle section that is distinct from the beginning, though it follows logically from it and a final section that is both a development and an extension of the composition. Effectively, they are performances in three or four definite and identifiable movements. This is clearly to be heard on Russell tunes like "Swingdom Come" and Carla Bley's "Beast Blues," both from the Five Spot record and Dave Lahm's "Lambskins" from *Stratusphunk*. Further, if one considers Monk's "'Round Midnight" from *Ezz-Thetics* and "You Are My Sunshine" from *The Outer View*, Russell's ability to deconstruct and transform other writers' compositions is uncanny.

In fact, Russell's reworking of jazz standards appears to fall into two categories. These range from more or less straight reworkings drawing extensively on the structure of the original tunes, albeit reflecting the more open harmonic possibilities discovered by Russell, to recomposition and deconstruction. For example, the Russell sextet covered Charlie Parker's "Donna Lee" on *Stratusphunk*. This is largely a straight reading, albeit reflecting the opportunities for extended solos offered by the LP format against the original three minutes available when Parker and Miles Davis made the original 78rpm disc in 1947. The same can be said of Miles Davis' "Sippin' at the Bells," which appears on the Five Spot album. However, with "Au Privave" from *The Outer View*, Russell begins the piece with a unison section featuring the three horns and reminiscent of early New Orleans jazz. More significantly, each soloist is introduced by a rubato section before their solo proper backed by the rhythm section playing time.

Seen in this way, examples of Russell's more conservative – or conservationist (!) – approach to arranging jazz standards from this period would include Clifford Brown's "Sandu" and Eddie "Cleanhead" Vinson's "Tune Up" (here, the Miles Davis' 1956 version is the reference point) both from the Kansas City record, and John Coltrane's "Moment's Notice" from the Five Spot disc. In this respect, they contrast well with freer, more open original pieces such as Dave Baker's "War Gewessen," Carla Bley's gorgeous ballad "Rhymes", Russell's own "Theme" from Kansas City and Bley's angular "Dance Class" and Russell's "Swingdom Come" from the Five Spot record. Perhaps, the straighter reading of these standards was intended as just such a contrast and as a way of leading more bop-oriented fans and critics into Russell's musical universe.

However, by May 1961 when *Ezz-thetics* was recorded, Russell seemed to have begun to adopt a more radical, deconstructionist approach to standard material. The record featured an extraordinary reimagining of Thelonious Monk's "'Round Midnight" and an intriguing version of Miles Davis' "Nardis," written for Cannonball Adderley and recorded on the *Portrait of Cannonball* LP (1958 Prestige). The latter departs from the Riverside take by using the horns to play a highly chromatic counterpoint to the melody at several junctures to heighten dramatic and emotional effect. Where the Adderley recording is sad and reflective, Russell's succeeds in expressing that sense of sadness but adds an ironic, questioning undertone. "Round Midnight," however, offers a more drastic re-examination of that tune. It opens with Russell playing the inside of the piano and Steve Swallow striking and plucking the strings of his bass randomly, bearing comparison sonically and compositionally with the opening of "Chromatic Universe, Part 1" from *Jazz in the Space Age* with its use of beads on tuned drums and with the beginning of "Event 1" from the later *African Game*. The entry of the horns and drums is entirely free and rubato, lasting just over one minute before Eric Dolphy states the theme and begins his extended solo. Dolphy's tone, vocalizations, choice of notes and the way he plays against the rhythm contrast well with the gentle accompaniment from the rhythm section with its subtle shifts of pace behind the soloist and are essential to the success of the performance and to Russell's reworking of the piece. At several points Don Ellis and Dave Baker add oblique comments, while at the end the whole edifice fractures around Dolphy.

Russell would continue to rework standard material. *At Beethoven Hall: Volume 1* (1965) features Milt Jackson's "Bags Groove," Charlie Parker's "Confirmation" and "'Round Midnight" within the context of a Lydian Chromatic suite. The *New York Big*

*Band* album (1978) featured a version of the Billie Holiday staple "God Bless the Child." And, of course, Miles Davis "So What" was a concert favourite from the mid-eighties onwards. In the so-called post-modern era, Russell's approach to jazz standards - less marked by irony and more by curiosity and even mischievousness – may seem less radical. However, it is worth suggesting that in this regard he was a forerunner of later such practices. I would in no sense describe him as a 'proto-post-modernist.' Instead, I would propose that what he was doing with these reworkings is a core element in jazz practice, namely the creation of new narratives based upon existing material or on using that material to tell the story afresh.

Russell's role as pianist in these group recordings is also an interesting one. Russell has always been quite disparaging about his piano playing. It is hard to assess Russell's qualities as a pianist because he has played piano only in the context of his own group. As he told Ben Young, "What I did was, I played the Concept. So the Concept pulled me through that and being a drummer I could very . . . my talent was accompanying a soloist. It turned out to be my meagre pianistic talent being able to accompany them and challenge them with unique environments." [39]

Referring to the Monk tune that had brought him to New York, he said, 'I think that the first piece I played because I learned the chords was "Round Midnight' with the sextet. I told Monk, I said, 'I think I've messed up one of your tunes.' He said, 'Oh, you wouldn't mess it up.' I'm not a piano player. I mean I can do something on it but I'm not a pianist." [40]

However, Russell does bring to his accompaniments and solos both a percussive, hard-driving quality and a wildness that suits his music and creates its own sense of excitement and, once again, drama. Joe Hunt certainly enjoyed this aspect of his involvement in the sextet.

> One thing I can say too is that as a drummer that George is lots of fun to play with. He's a drummer, right? He's a great feel when he plays the piano. It's just really fun for a drummer to work with him. He's just got a great rhythmic feel. It was fun for me just to play with him as the piano player. That was good. He didn't have piano technique at all in the usual sense but his phrasing and his feel was tremendous, kind of like Horace Silver in a way. It was like playing with another drummer. That was really fun. I just loved playing with him. [41]

And Ran Blake lists Russell as one of his favourite pianists, as he explained in his rather unusual, elliptical syntax: "I think that he would be the first to say that he doesn't pretend to have a pianistic sound à la Monk, and I know there are all those speed freaks, but Tatum doesn't speak to me. It's Thelonious that does. And I remember in the sixties feeling that George was, with Ray Charles or Mary Lou when she would do blues, maybe George is . . . I find his piano playing very rich and wonderful." [42]

Bassist Chuck Israels was the next group member to move on. He had played on the K.C., Five Spot and *Stratusphunk* discs. The opportunity came to join Bill Evans' trio and was too good to miss. Going by his comments to me in an email, his remarks to Kirk Silsbee notwithstanding (see above), Israels seems, anyway, to have been less than enamoured with Russell's music,

> I was not interested in what seemed to me to be self-conscious and perhaps pretentious efforts at sounding avant-garde. I know that I have participated in and been identified with a few things that are thought to represent this kind of musical point of view; George's band, an Eric Dolphy recording and a Coltrane recording (with Cecil Taylor—that was originally issued as Cecil's date) but they were all simply work opportunities and I would have made other choices, given the chance. [43]

Israels was replaced by Steve Swallow, who made his recording debut on *Ezz-Thetics*.

> I was working in a coffee shop on Bleecker Street in Greenwich Village with Don Ellis and Paul Bley and one Sunday Don Ellis said to me, "George Russell is looking for a bass player. You should call him up." That was something I had never done. I'd never solicited a gig and was very nervous and awkward about making the call but I wanted to play George's music. So I did. I called him up fully expecting him to flunk me off. But he didn't, he paused after I'd done a little overture speech and said, "Yeah, okay. Come on by. Bring your bass." So I did, I went to his apartment on Bank Street. And we played through several of his tunes and then he said, "Fine. You're hired," which I thought was just remarkable and I was thrilled. [44]

According to Swallow, the group rehearsed in Russell's one-room apartment, and he recalled meeting Ornette Coleman there for the first time. "I remember also one day going there to get some music from George to study and he and Ornette were just sitting around talking and I joined them for a couple of hours and that was one of the most memorable hangs I can recall. I was in awe of both of them and thrilled to be sitting with them." [45]

*Ezz-Thetics* introduced two new players—Swallow and Eric Dolphy on alto and bass clarinet in place of Dave Young. This was Dolphy's only session with Russell and followed not long after the altoist had recorded *Blues and the Abstract Truth* with Oliver Nelson.

Steve Swallow remembered how supportive Dolphy was of the other musicians at the *Ezz-Thetics* session.

> Eric was extremely gracious and assumed a kind of leadership role on that date, a kind of secondary to George leadership role. I remember Eric kind of going around from one to the other of us during the making of the date and calming us down or eliciting energy from us, as was needed. He was extremely gracious and helpful. That's my primary memory of that date, was just the remarkable social skills that Eric had and I think they were a great factor in the success of that album, which I think is a very, very good album. [46]

And, as the bassist told Ian Carr, "George tended to be quite nervous in performing and recording situations as well. So Eric was the cool head in the studio and he was tremendously gracious and graceful that day." [47]

*Ezz-Thetics* is an excellent example of how new ideas meet with tradition to produce an effective synthesis. Russell, as with other pioneers such as Ornette Coleman and John Coltrane, never eschewed the jazz tradition. Rather, his pride in the origins of his music encouraged him to foster its development. Russell seems to have had a clear understanding that jazz is a syncretic musical form. His own theoretical ideas took in not only jazz but, according to Russell at least, the whole history of equal temperament in music. In developing and expanding the range of jazz, any source was both valid and viable.

Interviewed in 1959 by Burt Korall [48] for a collection of essays and articles published as *The Jazz Word*, Russell identified the key question for jazz as the relationship between the composer and the improviser. Here, Russell is actually framing the issue in a new way, locating it in the dynamic human context of writer versus performer as opposed to the abstracted process of composition versus improvisation. He defines jazz history to date in terms of a shifting equilibrium from a position of reciprocity between writer and soloist pre-bebop to a point where the soloist (post-Bird) became the dominant figure in moving the music forward. In this later period, Russell argues, the level of compositional sophistication and technique had fallen behind the standard of improvisation.

A further distinction made by Russell in the interview concerned the differences between the composer who provides a framework for the improviser to say what he wishes to say and the composer who forces the improviser to say what the composer wants him to say. Russell does not give an example of the former, probably because these would include the majority of jazz composers. He does, however, cite Thelonious Monk, Benny Golson and Gerry Mulligan as examples of the latter. For Russell, the improviser deals with melody and the reason why jazz composers have not influenced the improviser is simple, "There have been hardly any writers with enough melodic equipment to be able to take hold of the improviser and have the improviser investigate the writer for what he is doing; so that the improviser can emerge with that new thing that the writer has." To many readers, Russell's citation of Monk in this context will be easily understood.

In the interview, Russell predicted a turning away from atonality toward what he calls "pan-tonality," noting jazz's roots in folk, scalar forms. Pan-tonality is a highly chromatic musical approach but one that does not negate the use of key centres or scales. Russell continued saying that it was essential that jazz retain its intuitive, improvised feel even where the music is through-composed, if it is to preserve its "intuitive, earthy dignity." He also suggests that complexity in jazz will increase rhythmically with composition "which utilizes many different meters . . . all kinds of rhythmic feelings, with music weaving a pattern over this fabric of various meters." [49] Russell is describing his own contribution and influence on jazz very precisely and presciently here. However, it is in the previous paragraph that he articulates most clearly the role of composer in jazz and their relationship with their colleagues in classical music.

> As for jazz and classical music coming together, it depends on how you define classical. If you define it as meaning music which is art, music that is intellectually developed; music that is treated intellectually and thematically—then I'd say that jazz will become a classical music and that there will be writers who will write in the jazz idiom, using all the dowry that jazz has to bring to this new music. And there will also be writers who will not use the

jazz idiom. But the musics will certainly be equal. Equally good or equally bad . . . that depends on the composers.[50]

Of all the sextet recordings from the early sixties, *Ezz-Thetics* arguably best illustrates Russell's intentions. While Russell has always maintained that each record demonstrated the best that he could achieve at a given point with available resources, he could also be quite dismissive of those early sixties albums.

**GR:** I'm not crazy about those records at all.
**DH:** Why is that?
**GR:** It doesn't reflect anything profound to me. *Stratusphunk* I like.[51]

In the same interview he was also quite ambivalent about the tune "Ezz-Thetic."

It's an old-time goody for me. It was good for the time but it wasn't ahead of them. But there's a delicate interval between what is good in different periods. If I make a record and then listen to it and it says, but you can do better, you could do more, you could explore more . . . and furthermore a lot of pieces like "Ezz-Thetic," as really most jazz is, it's lifting music from Broadway, Broadway redone.[52]

These comments reiterate that, for Russell, the groups and big bands he has led also serve as his laboratory for testing his theories. The product is always secondary to the Lydian Chromatic Concept. Learn from it and move on. That said, he had every reason to see *Ezz-Thetics* as a tribute to both theory and practice. There are few albums to match it—from the period or since—for its bravura playing, for its complex but fluid arrangements and compositions or for the way its authentic jazz feel is expressed within a new and fresh context.

"Ezz-Thetic" opens the record played at an incredible lick and ends with a delightful series of trade-offs between the horns. Miles Davis's "Nardis" is transformed from a nice ballad with a Middle Eastern flavour into an event rooted in the blues and Monk's "'Round Midnight" becomes a piece of high drama full of an almost Shakespearean tension with an exceptional alto saxophone solo from Dolphy. In between, "The Lydiot" from *Jazz in the Space Age* is given a spare, loose reading for small group, while David Baker's "Honesty" is full of wit and great good humour and sounds as if the whole band were having a ball. "Honesty" also echoes the earlier point about Russell's roots in the jazz tradition with Ellis's New Orleans–inspired trumpet and Baker's use of the plunger mute. A similar point can be made about Russell's "Thoughts," which typifies certainly qualities of Russell's compositional style. It is episodic, with changes of tempo and solos played against the prevailing rhythm. Yet it also stresses Russell's idea that the composer can and should not only frame the soloist's melodic lines but shape their direction. But if there is one track here that ensures the record's status as a classic, it is "'Round Midnight." Russell was overwhelmed when he first heard Monk's tune and he creates in this setting the most perfect tribute. It is art by any standard, from its surreal, ghostly beginning to Dolphy's beautiful opening statement of the theme and then his lyrical solo set simply by Russell and punctuated by occasional and sometimes bizarre choruses from the other horns. Even Russell's unfussy piano accompaniment is perfect.

Russell maintained that although Dolphy did not study the Concept with him in any formal sense, they discussed it together and Dolphy took a copy of the book to read. By this account, Dolphy was very enthusiastic about what it had to offer and even wrote to Russell while the altoist was on tour in Europe to that effect, noting in regard to the Concept, "it gives you so much more to work with." [53] Dolphy holds a rather unusual position vis-à-vis "The New Thing"—he is often seen as a part of the avant-garde without actually having that much in common with it stylistically. In a sense, it seems entirely likely that he would take to the Concept because of the way it discusses and views tonality; it suggests that the combining of old and new is possible and desirable and that it is possible to be "modern" without embracing atonality.

Despite the status *Ezz-Thetics* now enjoys, it was not that well received at the time. Don Heckman, who had been a student at Lenox, wrote in *Metronome*, "This version of the group (with Ellis, Dolphy and Swallow replacing Al Kiger, Dave Young and Chuck Israels) is the best so far but, with the exception of Russell's new composition 'Thoughts,' they are better than the material they have to work with." [54]

Frank Kofsky gave the album three and a half stars in *DownBeat*. Kofsky located Russell firmly in the radical camp of "The New Wave," albeit as "more of a reformer than a revolutionary," then proceeded to damn the whole enterprise for its lack of any new "intellectual and/or emotional sensation their predecessors could not have done." As performers, only Russell and Ellis are singled out for any degree of praise. Though the "Record Notes" column in the *Reporter* was more encouraging, there was scant enthusiasm for Russell's project. [55] With little to show in the way of gigs, the Russell group had become a rehearsal ensemble, coming together when they had a performance or a record date. As Steve Swallow explained,

> At the point I joined it, the band ceased working weeklong engagements, ceased touring for more than two or three gigs at a shot. We were really kind of reduced to the isolated sort of prestige gig. Like, I remember playing in the courtyard at the Museum of Modern Art and, you know, an art centre in Long Island, that kind of stuff. But it was essentially a band that just rehearsed a lot and made a recording and nobody seemed to mind rehearsing without pay for long hours. [56]

That Russell was struggling to keep a regular group going in terms of work is illustrated by trumpeter Bill Dixon. According to Dixon, Russell asked him to join the sextet. He told the trumpeter that he wanted him, Don Cherry, Thad Jones and Al Kiger to be on call for jobs. Dixon had been introduced to Russell by mutual friend pianist-composer John Benson Brooks. While not averse to the idea of playing with Russell, Dixon had made a decision to play his own music from that point on and turned Russell down. [57]

There had been a whole series of personnel changes in 1961. It is not clear why Russell dropped Dave Young. Young himself put it down to the composer's desire to try out another tenor player, Paul Plummer. Though Dolphy had worked on *Ezz-Thetics*, this was just a one-off and that group never played live. Judging by his comments to WKCR's Ben Young, Russell viewed the group as being a fluid entity in terms of its personnel.

> It was a recording band mostly. We worked two or three times and I know that a couple of times I used John Gilmore from Sun Ra's group, who I respected a lot, a very nice man and very talented. So I'd meet these different players—like, I'd use Dolphy on that famous "'Round Midnight" recording he did with us—and I'd meet these different players and that kind of interaction was wonderful. [58]

Other changes were dictated by circumstance. Drummer Joe Hunt got his callup in 1962 and was replaced by Pete La Roca. Paul Plummer came in for Dave Young but then he too joined the army. Don Ellis left to do his own thing and, along with Steve Swallow, proved the most successful of this generation of Russell alumni in recording terms. Ellis made a number of small-group albums and then returned to his native Los Angeles, where he established a hugely successful big band. Ellis, who had an interest in Eastern music, specialized in compositions with unusual time signatures and used electronics to powerful effect. Anyone interested should hear his *Electric Bath* and *Live at Monterey* records. How much he picked up from Russell is impossible to say—perhaps only a sense of what was really possible within the form. However, it is fair to say that his first groundbreaking music was made with the composer.

Ellis was obviously an ambitious and self-assured young musician, and Russell heard something vital in his playing even back then.

> He always seemed a little cocky to me. I hired Don because I wanted to . . . after I heard Ornette, I wanted guys that played differently. The guys that were available wouldn't have been into that kind of thing because they weren't following Don Cherry. Don and Ornette were just something else. So the nearest to me who was an adventurous trumpet player at the time was Don Ellis. [59]

Asked about Ellis, Steve Swallow laughed at the recollection: "Well, he was a bit of a martinet, but that being said, he was a fiercely dedicated and directed and disciplined young man. What I found instructive and inspiring about him was his extraordinary self-discipline and at an extremely early age." [60]

According to Swallow, while he and other young musicians saw practice as being about all-night sessions rehearsing or being on the bandstand, "Don would do that but also get up four hours later and practice for three or four hours. I was kind of remiss in the practicing area." [61]

Dave Baker remembered Ellis as being "a little egocentric at times," but adds a number of very pertinent points.

> Wonderful player. He had original ideas and was a good playing mate because he worked hard to learn the music and understand the music, even though he was already experimenting with his adventures in time and moving that way. I think the thing that attracted

him to George, and I found attractive about him, he had a good historical sense of where he came from. You know, he knew the music and playing of Rex Stewart and Bubba Miley and, of course, of all of his contemporaries, so that when he formed his own big band, he drew on a vast storehouse of historical knowledge. [62]

After Ellis, the great Thad Jones—one of the three Jones brothers, along with drummer Elvin and pianist Hank—joined the group. Both John Gilmore and Joe Farrell filled the tenor spot at different times, and Garnett Brown and Brian Trentham took over from Dave Baker on trombone at various points. Baker's story is a sad one but also an inspiring and transcendent one. Badly injured in a car accident in the fifties, Baker had had to endure reconstructive surgery on his jaw. As he put it, "1962 was when my physical apparatus broke down from an accident I'd had ten years before. I spent, like, in and out of the hospital for eighteen months while I had all kinds of therapy and tried different ways to try to solve the problem." [63]

He was already experiencing problems when the group recorded *Ezz-Thetics* but managed to keep going and played on *The Stratus Seekers*. Though he did get some respite in the early seventies and was briefly able to play trombone again, [64] his career as a horn player was effectively over from 1962, though not as an educator, cellist, composer and band-leader. Baker was a remarkable musician and individual and an inspiration to the many students who passed through his classes at Indiana University.

Nineteen sixty-one had proved quite a good year, in terms of publicity at least. Gerry Mulligan had recorded *All About Rosie* with his Concert Band in a beautiful new arrangement by Russell. Mulligan noted in Dom Cerulli's sleeve notes, "The way George wrote it for us, Rosie's grown up!" [65] There had also been a number of articles on him, and he had been given his own "Blindfold Test" in *DownBeat*—he praised Duke Ellington's "Dance of the Floreadores" and J. J. Johnson's piece from the Brandeis disc but was critical of Shorty Rogers, Quincy Jones and Stan Kenton, while being tactful about a Gunther Schuller composition performed by the MJQ. In November Russell took part in a *DownBeat* round robin panel that also included Bob Brookmeyer, Don Ellis and Hall Overton. Its tone seems rather portentous now and in content it seems worthy without really have much to say. Russell's participation did, however, speak loudly about his standing in jazz, on the East Coast at least.

Perhaps best of all that year was his placing in the *DownBeat* Critics Poll. He came top in the "New Stars" arranger/composer section and his sextet came second in the "New Stars" combo section, behind Coltrane. [66] In general, Russell fared quite well in *DownBeat* polls and reviews and articles in that magazine and others, such as *Jazz Today*, have been fair and broadly favourable. The failure of publicity to translate itself into regular and consistent gigs was, however, a constant feature of his Stateside career.

Despite such critical favours, the new year of 1962 would see the end to this phase in Russell's recording career with his last two albums for Riverside – *The Stratus Seekers* and *The Outer View*. The group continued to perform when opportunity arose. For *The Stratus Seekers* the sextet became a septet with the addition of alto player John Peirce, a fine player with an attractively forceful style somewhere between Charlie Parker and Eric

Dolphy. The rest of the group comprised Joe Hunt on his final session with Russell, Paul Plummer, Don Ellis, Dave Baker and Steve Swallow.

*The Stratus Seekers* is a beautifully balanced record with Russell taking four of the compositions with Al Kiger's "Kige's Tune" and Baker's "Stereophrenic" making up the other two. Russell's compositions have, as noted, attracted few cover versions from other artists. With tunes such as "Concerto for Billy the Kid" or "The Day John Brown Was Hanged" or extended works like *Jazz in the Space Age* that is perhaps unsurprising. However, with numbers such as "Ezz-Thetic" and "Stratusphunk" this does surprise and on *The Stratus Seekers* three tracks – "Pan-Daddy", "Blues in Orbit" and "A Lonely Place" – really deserve the attention of other jazz musicians.

The title track, on the other hand, contains several of Russell's more personal compositional tricks – stop-start breaks, solo cadenzas, discordant and out-of-time passages, dramatic shifts of tempo. Yet, for much of its seven minutes, the group perform at a furious pace. The ensemble sections are particularly fine with the three horns trading phrases or weaving lines around each other. Both "Kige's Tune" and "Stereophrenic" show how much Kiger and Baker gained from their studies or contact with Russell. Indeed, they could pass for his own work. "Kige's Tune" has so many different moods to its six minutes – booze-drenched blues, ragtime filtered through Stravinsky, other sections recalling Ornette Coleman, while others have a filmic quality that seem to suggest the Far-East. "Stereophrenic" opens with a strong piano solo from Russell set against a much slower fanfare from the horns. The piece threatens to fall apart but builds in tension mixing fairly straight-ahead, bebop-oriented moments with looser, more out playing.

"Pan-Daddy" and "Blues in Orbit" offer two of the most approachable of Russell's compositions. The former is a fast-paced bebop tune with the occasional twist with strong rhythm playing from Hunt and Swallow. It is unclear whether "Blues in Orbit" owes anything to Ellington's tune of the same name but it is certainly Russell at his most Ellingtonian. A loping, swinging blues with unusual accent placings, it is just great fun. However, it is "A Lonely Place" that offers the biggest surprise. A very slow, bluesy ballad, "A Lonely Place" is one of the saddest and most poignant pieces in Russell's catalogue. It would certainly not have been out of place on *Jazz Workshop*. Russell's own performance is beautifully weighted and the horns, often *sotto voce*, are hugely atmospheric. Ellis, in particular, plays with great sensitivity and tenderness,

Don Ellis is the stand-out soloist here, contributions to the ensembles also adding considerable character. However, altoist John Peirce is the surprise turn here. His solos on "Pan-Daddy," "A Lonely Place" and the title track are quite stunningly fresh and acerbic. The album also offers some of the leader's finest piano playing on record to this point. It may have been the case that the band had had little on-stage experience but it does not show. This is an excellent, well-drilled jazz group mastering and delivering some very tricky material.

Joe Goldberg's sleeve notes talk of the kaleidoscopic qualities of the music and the range of colours to be heard. There is, nevertheless, a slightly apologetic tone to his comment,

And although Russell's music is experimental, often difficult, and based on considerable technical theory, it is definitely full of just such vivid, electric and appealing qualities. [67]

*DownBeat*'s Harvey Pekar liked the record a lot giving it four stars and commenting,

His work abounds with such devices as polyphony, polytonality, and changing tempos and time signatures. He is also a brilliant orchestrator ... producing constantly varying sonorities and textures. [68]

By contrast, British jazz journalist Les Tomkins played selections from *The Stratus Seekers* for members of the Modern Jazz Quartet as part of a 'blind date' article for *Crescendo* in 1964. Suffice it to say that they, including one-time Russell supporter John Lewis, were less than impressed, indicating just how Russell's work could polarize opinion. [69]

It was around this period that the wonderful singer Sheila Jordan came into Russell's life. "I met George at the Page 3, this club that I sang at. That was down in Greenwich Village and he came down because a student of his was playing on Monday nights. Monday nights was session night at the Page 3." [70]

The student was Jack Reilly. Reilly had told Russell about Jordan and Russell stayed to listen for the whole evening, as the singer remembered,

It was quite "out" and so George came and then he came up to me afterwards and he introduced himself and he said, "Where do you come from to sing like that?" He said he was really moved by what I was singing. So I told him. So we became friends. And I, of course, was legally married to Duke Jordan at the time. So George paid for my divorce in Mexico. At that time you couldn't get divorced in New York City unless you could prove adultery, which I could very easily have done. *(laughing)* I didn't want to. I just didn't want to go through all that. George paid for my divorce. I went to Mexico—I guess New Mexico— and got a divorce and came back. I had a wedding dress and everything made. Were going to get married but it never worked out. [71]

As Jordan put it, "in the long run we were better friends than lovers," but for a time they were very close and their one performance together on record, "You Are My Sunshine," has its own place in jazz history.

Russell had wanted to see where Jordan came from, so they drove up to Pennsylvania to meet her family. The main industry in the area had always been coal mining but now the mines were beginning to close and many of the miners were out of work. With Jordan's grandmother in tow, they went to a local social club, where the singer was pressed into performing "You Are My Sunshine". [72] At first Russell accompanied Jordan but her grandmother soon pushed him out of the way because he was not "playing it right." Jordan says that afterward he joked with her, saying, "Your grandmother sounds like Thelonious Monk." [73]

About a month later, Russell called her and showed her his arrangement of "Sunshine," telling her he wanted her to sing it on his next album.

Then we went into the studio and that's how "Sunshine" was born. But it was a dedication to the coal miners of Pennsylvania. He wanted to call it "A Drinking Song," because we were drinking and we knew the miners all drank because that was their form of recreation and they were all out of work. It was a really sad kind of . . . in the introduction you hear that, you know. But it was like a little documentary for the coal miners and, unfortunately, we couldn't call it "A Drinking Song." They wouldn't let us change it.[74]

Jordan explained what she meant in calling the song a "documentary,"

George wanted to see the mines, even though they were closed up. He saw the towns, the poverty. He saw the whole thing where I grew up, and he associated all that with the coal mines and the miners going down into the mines. You know, I had told him about the explosions, the mine explosions where miners were trapped in the mines and never got out and wrote their wills in coal dust on the walls. It was terrible. So he knew all that and George was very much into people and how they lived and that all came out in his music. That's why his music is so great. That's why I always thought of it as a documentary, a musical documentary on the coal miners. Because you can hear it, you know. You can just hear it.[75]

Recorded on *The Outer View*, the last album Russell made in the States until 1972, this performance still takes one's breath away on hearing it. It is another example of Russell's ability to transform a trite, over-familiar tune into something infinitely more dramatic and special. But it would be something far less singular were it not for Jordan's vocal, as Steve Swallow recalled.

Sheila has an extraordinary ability to move me when she sings. The take of "You Are My Sunshine"—and I can only recall one or two takes of that—was a devastating emotional moment for me. At the end of the take I was shattered, and, as I say, this is something that Sheila has always been able to do to me.[76]

If "Sunshine" is the standout track on *The Outer View*, there are also strong versions of Carla Bley's "Zig-Zag" and Bird's "Au Privave." The title track has really strong piano from Russell and the frontline of Ellis, Paul Plummer and Garnett Brown blend particularly well. Russell's trademark stop-start and out-of-time passages and use of different key centres mask just how far the piece is centred in the blues. However, after "Sunshine," it is "D.C. Divertimento" that most impresses. In this piece—commissioned for the First International Jazz Festival in Washington, D.C., in the summer of 1962, promoted by President John F. Kennedy's Music Committee—Russell pulls out all the stops. Stravinsky is once again a reference point but "Divertimento" is definitely jazz. The complex arrangement never gets in the way of the drama Russell seeks to create and his band push and challenge each other to splendid effect. It is one of Russell's finest works and it is surprising that its potential has not been grasped by an imaginative modern choreographer. It cries out for dancers.

Interviewed more than four decades later, Garnett Brown still found the complexity of

Russell's music remarkable and surprising. However, he also emphasised how important each individual's contribution was to the music and to ensuring that its diverse elements held together.

> I'd never heard music like what he was writing. George had such a command over everything that he did. The music was loose but still precise in certain areas and the stretching of the harmonicness of it and the freedom to do what you wanted to do but there were times when it was left to you to bring it all together. Each individual had that responsibility in the music. That was just unheard of. Everything was so cut and dried and what we perceive as the approaches to music that everybody just knows what to do all the time. Well, we didn't know that. It was just kind of left out there and the responsibilities became paramount upon each individual to direct the traffic so to speak but everybody knew at some point where we were going to go. We just didn't always know how we were going to get there.

And Brown added, "It was all thoroughly satisfying and exciting, kind of scary all at the same time." [77]

*The Outer View* received fine reviews just about everywhere. *Billboard*, *Cash Box*, and *Music Vendor* all liked it, though *Jazz Review* for once was not convinced. Nat Hentoff in *Hi-Fi/Stereo Review* singled out "Sunshine" for particular praise and noted Russell's continued growth as a composer. *DownBeat* called it "essential listening" and awarded it five stars, but Russell must have found *Time* magazine's applause especially encouraging. [78] The album's release also coincided with the latest *DownBeat* poll, which saw Russell's sextet in strong second place in the "Talent Deserving of Wider Recognition" category and saw him third, equal with Thelonious Monk, in the arranger/composer section, behind Gil Evans and Duke Ellington. [79]

Jordan's vocal performance is one of the most striking and spectacular in jazz. She also sang "You Are My Sunshine" with the sextet at the Philharmonic Hall, Lincoln Center for the Performing Arts, on August 22, 1963, when the group played opposite Jimmy Giuffre's trio. The group at the time was Paul Plummer on tenor, Thad Jones on trumpet, Garnett Brown on trombone, Russell on piano, Steve Swallow on bass and Pete La Roca on drums. Swallow also played the second set with Giuffre and Paul Bley. But the song's most famous performance was at Newport the following summer.

It was an incredibly windy, wet day, and the group's sheet music kept blowing off the stand. The rain was at its heaviest when Jordan came on stage. "I started to sing it and it was raining. I think the music started blowing around too and, of course, we got the music back but it started to rain. Oh, it was Max Roach and Abbey Lincoln. Max said, 'Who did your lighting and your sound?' Because we started out and it was raining and when we finished the sun came out. Isn't that amazing?"

With a mixture of whimsical humour and romantic fantasy, Jordan continued, "All those dead miners that had been trapped in the mines. They wanted us to know they were all right." [80]

In fact, a bootleg recording finally surfaced that includes, alongside the original Russell sextet's 1960 performance at Lenox, four numbers from the Newport gig, including "You Are My Sunshine." The sleeve notes credit Don Ellis as the trumpeter, when in fact it would have been Thad Jones and Dave Baker as the trombonist, when it was probably Garnett Brown. The tenor player was John Gilmore with Russell on piano, Swallow on bass and Pete La Roca on drums. The sound quality is not good but the band sounds a lot further out than the studio recordings might suggest.

Though Russell "left her standing at the church door," as he put it, for the daughter of his friend, composer John Benson Brooks, there were no hard feelings, and it was his intervention that kick-started Jordan's career.

> But in the meantime he did a lot for me. He was the reason I ever recorded. So it was way beyond "so, like, you jilted me" or whatever. I never felt that way about George because he was so good to me. As I said, we just weren't compatible. It would've been a disaster if we ever married but in the meantime I got a divorce from Duke Jordan and he had also made a demo of me. He loved the way I sang and he made a demo of me, paid for a demo and took it around to all the record companies. He took it to Mercury—and Quincy Jones was the A&R man at the time—and he took it to Blue Note and Blue Note bought it up right away. Then Quincy sent a letter over. He was interested to record me. [81]

That demo, which apparently featured Kenny Burrell on guitar, opened the door and led to *Portrait of Sheila*. Jordan was the first singer to record for Blue Note and for a long time was one of only two singers on the label (the other was Dodo Greene). With Barry Galbraith on guitar, Steve Swallow and Denzil Best on drums, it was almost a family affair. It remains a definitive example of the singer's art.

But Russell's involvement went beyond that of midwife, as Swallow explained.

> Alfred Lion brought Denzil Best into it. That was Alfred's choice. But Barry and me were chosen by George and I remember too that the chord charts that we were playing were in George's hand. I know damn well he was responsible for the harmonization for at least most of those tunes and he was there at the rehearsals. I don't recall that he was there at the actual recording. I have a feeling he wouldn't have been because there would have been conflict between him and Alfred, who ran a kind of tight recording ship, and Rudy Van Gelder as well, for that matter. They looked most unkindly on any visitors during their recording sessions and I think that in particular they would have found George meddlesome but he was guiding the harmonic content of that recording beyond a doubt and I think that he must have had a hand in choosing the repertoire too, just because he and Sheila were together and talking about all these things a lot. [82]

Their romantic attachment may have been a factor behind Russell's motivation. However, as Jordan points out, such behaviour was unusual in the jazz world but not untypical of Russell.

> So the thing with George was that he really went to bat for me. I think he's known for doing that. I think he did that with Bill Evans too. He did that with a lot of young musicians but for a musician still to go to bat for you, that was really special. I don't know

if I would have ever recorded if I hadn't met George and if he hadn't paid the money—he paid for this tape—and God, I was pleased that I knew somebody that closely that was such a genius because he writes unbelievable stuff. We always remained friends even though the romantic thing didn't work out. I got a free divorce. I have a wedding dress that I've never used and I have some beautiful memories. [83]

Writer Francis Davis tells a lovely and instructive story about Russell. The writer D. Antoinette Hardy was speaking at a colloquium on jazz at Temple University in Philadelphia in 1984. Russell was due to deliver a lecture on the Lydian Concept at the conference and was sitting in the audience during a panel discussion on women in jazz. Handy spoke about a dictionary of black women instrumentalists that she was compiling and when the discussion was opened to the floor Russell suggested that she had missed two very important women. Handy asked who these were and Russell mentioned Billie Holiday. Handy pointed out that the dictionary referred to instrumentalists and Russell mumbled that Holiday had influenced more musicians than any of the artists Handy had spoken about.

Handy then asked who the other woman was that she had not included.

"Sheila Jordan," Russell replied—to embarrassed laughter from the audience, because, as Handy quickly pointed out, "Sheila Jordan is white."

Russell, who is black but has often been mistaken for white (including by Wilfrid Mellers in *Music in a New Found Land* and, I would conjecture, by many in the audience that day), grinned devilishly and paused before delivering the punch line: "Well, that depends on how you define it, doesn't it?" [84]

## Notes

1. Interview with Russell October 2003.
2. Korall, B, "Who Is George Russell?" *DownBeat*, February 16, 1961.
3. Conversation between George Russell and the author, June 2004.
4. Ben Young, broadcast devoted to George Russell in celebration of his seventy-fifth birthday, WKCR Radio, New York, June 23, 1998.
5. Reviewing the gig for the *New Yorker*, Whitney Balliett was not impressed by Russell's orchestrations, which he contrasted negatively with those of Gil Evans: "[U]nlike those of Gil Evans, which are done in subtle oils, they appear to be fashioned out of strands of colourless lucent plastic." He was, however, impressed with the group, in particular Al Kiger, and described the performance as "a full-bodied blowing session." Review of George Russell Sexted, Jazz in the Garden, MoMA, New York, "Musical Events—Jazz Concerts," *New Yorker*, July 1960.
6. Interview with Joe Hunt, June 2004.
7. A press release from Mildred Fields regarding the Five Spot dates gives different personnel. According to this, Larry Ridley was on bass and Paul Partridge was on drums. This may have been for the opening couple of nights only. None of the other participants recalls these changes.
8. Interview with Dave Young, January 2007.
9. Interview with Hunt.

10. Ibid.
11. Interview with Young.
12. George Hoefer, "Caught in the Act (Review of *George Russell Sextet at the Five Spot*)," *DownBeat*, September 15, 1960.
13. *Playboy* (no date available but likely September 1960).
14. Kirk Silsbee, sleeve notes to reissue of *George Russell Sextet at the Five Spot* (2000), Verve 088112287–2.
15. Leonard Feather, sleeve notes to *George Russell Sextet Live in Kansas City*, Decca DL 4183
16. Silsbee, op cit.
17. Interview with Young.
18. John S. Wilson, Review of *George Russell Sextet—Stratusphunk* (Riverside RLP-341), *DownBeat*, March 2, 1961.
19. Interview with Hunt.
20. This is the correct spelling, not 'Pierce' as listed in *The Stratus Seekers* album.
21. Indiana/Ohio drummer Bill Enyard, who worked and recorded with Al Kiger, Paul Plummer and John Peirce for Cadence Jazz commented in an interview for Cadence magazine: "Kiger and John Peirce, and Plummer had recorded with George Russell. . . .. They made the New York scene, but they're not New York dudes. If they had stayed, they'd have played with Miles and all of them, but they'd have wound up dead! (Laughing)"
22. See Bill Donaldson CD review John Peirce *Memorial Album* (Cadence Jazz CJR 1226) *Cadence* October 2013, Volume 39, No. 4.
23. Feather, sleeve notes to *George Russell Sextet Live in Kansas City*.
24. Russell would return to the piece in the eighties on his second album for Blue Note, *So What*.
25. Feather, op cit.
26. Interview with Hunt.
27. Interview with Young.
28. Interview with Ran Blake, October 2003.
29. Interview with Hunt.
30. K. Mathieson, *Cookin'—Hard Bop and Soul Jazz 1954-65* (Edinburgh: Canongate, 2002).
31. Young, broadcast devoted to George Russell.
32. Interview with Dave Baker, April 2004.
33. Ian Carr, interview with Carla Bley for BBC Radio 3 broadcast *George Russell—The Invisible Guru*, July 1994.
34. Interview with Carla Bley, February 2004.
35. Feather, sleeve notes to *George Russell Sextet Live in Kansas City*. This error is repeated by Chris Albertson in his sleeve notes to *Stratusphunk* Riverside RLP 9341.
36. Interview with C. Bley.
37. Ibid.
38. Ibid.
39. Young, broadcast devoted to George Russell.
40. Ibid.
41. Interview with Hunt.
42. Interview with Blake.
43. E-mail interview with Chuck Israels, August 2004.
44. Interview with Steve Swallow, February 2004.
45. Ibid.
46. Ibid.
47. Ian Carr, interview with Steve Swallow for BBC Radio 3 broadcast *George Russell—The Invisible Guru*, July 1994.
48. Burt Korall, "Where Do We Go from Here?" in *The Jazz Word*, edited by D. Cerulli, B. Korall, and M. Nasatir (New York: Ballantine, 1960). See also Korrall, "Who Is George Russell?"
49. Korall, "Where Do We Go from Here?" p. 188.

50. Ibid.
51. Interview with G. Russell, October 2003.
52. Ibid.
53. Postcard from Dolphy to Russell in Russell's personal papers.
54. Don Heckman, "Review in Depth—George Russell," *Metronome*, November 1961.
55. Frank Kofsky, Review of *Ezz-thetics* (Riverside 375), *DownBeat*, November 9, 1961; *Review of George Russell Sextet—Ezz-thetics* (Riverside 375), "Record Notes," *Reporter*, September 28, 1961.
56. Interview with Swallow. Such as the Jazz in the Garden concert at the Museum of Modern Art on August 23, 1962.
57. Ben Young (ed), *Dixonia: A Bio-Discography of Bill Dixon* (Westport, CT: Greenwood Press, 1998). See p.68. Interestingly, the Archie Shepp-Bill Dixon Quartet regularly played "Stratusphunk" in their live sets. Apparently Russell attended one of the group's performances at the Café Avital, New York in December 1962, leaving "rather obviously" in the middle of the second number "reflecting his dislike of the proceedings." p.49
58. Young, broadcast devoted to George Russell.
59. Interview with G. Russell, October 2003.
60. Interview with Swallow.
61. Ibid.
62. Interview with Baker.
63. Ibid.
64. Baker played on *Living Time*, the album Russell made with Bill Evans in 1972.
65. Gerry Mulligan and the Concert Band, *A Concert in Jazz*, Verve V/V6-8415.
66. See "Blindfold Test," *DownBeat*, January 5, 1961; "Afterhours—A Jazz Discussion with Clark Terry, Don Ellis, Bob Brookmeyer, George Russell," *DownBeat*, November 9, 1961; "9th Jazz International Critics Poll," *DownBeat*, August 3, 1961.
67. Joe Goldberg, Sleevenotes to *The Stratus Seekers*.
68. Harvey Pekar, Review of *The Stratus Seekers DownBeat*: August 16, 1962 vol. 29, no. 22
69. Les Tomkins, "Disc Discussion," *Crescendo* p.22 June 1964
70. Interview with Sheila Jordan, May 2004.
71. Ibid.
72. "You Are My Sunshine" was written by country singer Jimmie Davis. Davis was later state governor of Louisiana. While Davis is known for his support for poor whites, he was also an arch segregationist. The original sleeve notes make no mention of this and it is unclear whether Russell was aware of Davis' racist politics.
73. Interview with Jordan.
74. Ibid.
75. Ibid.
76. Interview with Swallow.
77. Interview with Brown.
78. Reviews taken from Russell's private collection and papers. No dates for *Billboard*, *Cash Box*, or *Music Vendor*. Nat Hentoff, "Way Out Front with George Russell," *Hi Fi/Stereo Review*, October 1963; Review of *George Russell Sextet—The Outer View* (RLP440), *Time*, May 22, 1964; Review of *The Outer View* (Riverside 440), *DownBeat*, July 18, 1963.
79. "Critics Poll Results," *DownBeat*, July 18, 1963.
80. Interview with Jordan. See also D. DeMichael, "Newport Report," *DownBeat*, August 13, 1964.
81. Interview with Jordan.
82. Interview with Swallow.
83. Interview with Jordan.
84. Francis Davis, *Jazz and Its Discontents* (Cambridge, MA: Da Capo, 2004), p. 82.

*Nannie Kathaleen George—Class of 1920. George Russell's mother is fourth from the left sitting in the front row.*

*George Russell—Withrow High Class of 1939 home room picture. Russell is squatting in the left-hand corner.*

# The Wilberforce Collegians

BUD JENKINS

Often termed "America's Greatest College Orchestra," the Wilberforce Collegians have this year enjoyed one of the most successful years since their organization. This orchestra is unique in the fact that all of its members are majoring in the School of Music. This year the Collegians have travelled extensively throughout the Southern states and have earned an enviable reputation for their inimitable renditions.

At present the orchestra is smaller than usual, but in spite of its size it still possesses some of the best musicians in the country. Feature men for the orchestra are: Ernest Wilkins on tenor, Oliver McLean on alto, Jesse Hart and Clifford King on trumpet. The rhythm section is composed of George Russell on drums, Joseph McRae on bass, and John Cotter on piano. James Wilkins plays a fine trombone, Hibonza Gray and Louis Transue compose the rest of the sax section. Flozell Fleming ably handles the vocals.

The orchestra is managed and directed by Bud Jenkins, who also plays trumpet. He is looking forward to a very promising season next year.

The Wilberforce Collegians, 1942, with the "handsome" George Russell on the drums.

*George Russell in Scandinavia, 1967. Photographed by Tom Hoeg.*

*George Russell at New England Conservatory, mid-1970s.*

*George and Norbury-Russell outside the Village Vanguard with Russell's son, Jock, and club founder Max Gordon, 1978. Photographed by Ray Ross.*

*George Russell with manuscript of African Game, 1984. Photographed by Maje Waldo.*

*The NEC Jazz Big Band, conducted by George Russell, premiering Russell's Timeline (March 4, 1992). Photographed by Jeff Thiebauth.*

*Alice and George Russell in Belgium, 1989.*

*George at his home in Boston with various album covers, 2003. Photographed by Hiro Honshuku.*

*George Russell and the Living Time Orchestra, 2008.*

CHAPTER NINE

## Norwegian Blues - Pining for the Fjords?

George Russell's profile in the jazz and other press continued to be quite strong. The French *Jazz* magazine interviewed him at length for its February 1963 issue in a piece entitled, "Le Philosophe de Greenwich Village." It treated Russell as the elder statesman of the jazz avant-garde, asking his opinions of Ornette Coleman, John Coltrane and Cecil Taylor. In respect of the latter, Russell acknowledges a lack of personal enthusiasm, though he enthuses about Coltrane and Coleman.[1] That Russell was now seen as a figure of some significance is confirmed by invitations to take part in panel discussions for both *Playboy* and *DownBeat* in February and June of the following year. Intriguingly, given *Playboy*'s other function, its panel seems the more interesting and challenging than *DownBeat*'s, perhaps because of the calibre of its participants, which included Charlie Mingus and Dave Brubeck, among others.[2] However, by 1964 Russell had become increasingly frustrated at the lack of work and recording opportunities for his group. In July a duodenal ulcer had perforated and this had been followed by a bout of pneumonia. In October *DownBeat* ran a news item, "George Russell Sends Call for Blood Donors," about his illness, noting that as a result, Russell had needed to cancel his first European tour.[3] In fact, the magazine was a little late in its call for blood donations to assist the composer's recovery and had underestimated Russell's recuperative powers and determination. By the time the item appeared, Russell had embarked on his first trip to Europe with his sextet, as part of promoter George Wein's Newport Festival All-Stars tour. It had, however, been touch and go as to whether he would make the trip, as Garnett Brown, the sextet's trombonist, remembered.

Before that European trip with George Wein, George had had an operation, a surgical procedure. We were rehearsing and he was recuperating. We had a point where he felt that he might not be able to make it and he was really doubting if he was going to make the tour. We were all sad about that because how could we do it without him? He felt that Hank Jones could do it and he always brought up Hank's name, saying, "If I can't make it, Hank'll do it." But in the end he ended up able to make it and he got stronger as the time went on because we were over there for months. [4]

Packed with stars, often in unusual and quite artificial combinations, George Wein's annual Newport Festival All-Stars trips were the ultimate jazz package tour and one of the hottest jazz tickets in Europe. Given his health, Russell was unable to undertake the work of putting a group together and Juanita and Jimmy Giuffre had come to his aid. While most of the players had already played with him, Steve Swallow could not make the tour. At the suggestion of the Giuffres, Russell auditioned a young bassist from the West Coast named Barre Phillips, who had recently arrived in New York. This was quite a leap forward in Phillips' career.

For me it was quite a rush. There I am, a young free jazzer and improviser playing contemporary music and then to be hired by a band like that with people like Thad Jones in it was very exciting for me. It was my first trip to Europe. So the whole trip was exciting to be with the big boys and play at the big halls. [5]

The rest of the band comprised Joe Farrell on tenor, Thad Jones on trumpet, Garnett Brown on trombone, Russell on piano and Albert "Tootie" Heath on drums. As Phillips remembered, all the bands on the tour played at the Berlin Festival and then toured Europe together and separately.

Miles's quintet was on that tour. I remember hanging out with them. I remember there was an organ trio—I think it was Richard "Groove" Holmes. The plane coming over there were forty-four jazz musicians on this plane, the same plane and all played at the Berlin Festival. Everybody played and then everybody had their tour. Some bigger than others. [6]

On several dates, the "avant-garde" George Russell Sextet was on a bill with the Chicago All-Stars—Ruby Braff, Pee Wee Russell, and Bud Freeman—and the Uptown All-Stars—Coleman "Bean" Hawkins, Harry "Sweets" Edison and Jo Jones. Of course, the musicians got on just fine. In fact, Phillips found himself depping for Ellington alumnus Jimmy Woode at some concerts due to the bassist's unexplained absences. A friendship with Bean and Sweets was cemented on a long train journey from southern France to Brussels with large quantities of the cognac Hawkins always carried with him to "cut my cold." When the musicians arrived at the venue that evening, the promoter presented a local bass player who had been hired as a stand-in. Hawkins was having none of it. He told the promoter, "No! I want Bass to do it." The tenorist had taken to calling Barre by the name of his instrument. "Bass" pointed out diplomatically that he had not brought his instrument to the hall, as he was not playing that night. At that point, Hawkins turned to the Belgian stand-in and said, "Lend Bass your bass, man." The Belgian, with typical Old World good manners, obliged. [7]

Joe Boyd, one of the tour managers employed by George Wein, recalls that he had been very impressed with Russell's sextet and with Thad Jones in particular. He adds that "Russell's band were the surprise stars of the tour."[8] The billing was, however, not a match made in heaven, in one certain and important respect. Some nights it attracted audiences that were split between fans of the mainstream and the modern. The former were sadly not impressed by Russell's take on jazz and frequently showed their displeasure. One of the concerts in Paris, at the Salle Pleyel on October 1, 1964, was recorded for radio broadcast and came out both on a bootleg recording on an Italian label and more recently on the Spanish imprint Gambit Records.[9] Both performances suggest that live, the band sounded much further "out" than was the case on record. Everyone plays with real fire and aggression and Russell's ability to lead and direct from the piano is really clear in this setting. While in Bremen the audience are enthusiastic and demand an encore, in Paris half the audience was cheering but the other half sound as if they wanted blood.

With booing greeting the ending of "The Outer View," Russell walked to the microphone and said, "The next composition some of you may like even less." Then he laughed and added, "It's called 'Volupte.'" For Garnett Brown, it was the high point of his time with Russell.

> So what happened was we played a couple of concerts in Paris in a big hall, I can't remember what it was but I just remember it being large and wondering how comfortable it was going to be on the stage, as far as hearing was concerned. That wasn't really a problem but what happened was that after we had played one or two numbers, Miles was off in the wings watching. When we finished this first tune, the people started booing George, our group. They sat there for a minute then all of a sudden the other half of the audience started applauding. So you had this interaction of boos and applauding going on simultaneously at a raucous level. Now, George was still recovering from the surgery he'd had in New York, so we were all wondering how that was playing on him. George got up walked to the front of the stage took a very determined stance, wide-legged and with his fists clenched and on his hips. He just stood there staring at the audience—I think he was soaking it in, loving what was going on. We never really discussed that but that to me was one of the more interesting, unpredictable but rewarding things that happened with George.[10]

It was also quite a shock for the young Barre Phillips.

> In Paris it was the strongest because they actually threw things at us. They threw mostly pennies, which were not going to hurt you because they were almost like cardboard. It was some very light kind of metal, some kind of pot metal. I never got hit. Nothing fell down a saxophone bell or anything like that. And it was incredible because people started to hoot and holler, "No! No! No!" Then the people who were for it were saying, "Shut up! Shut up! Shut up!" At one moment, it was just a huge roar that we were playing to. At least that was the impression I had. It was the first time I had played on a stage where people were shouting, "No!" *(laughs)* "Get off! Get off!"[11]

One of Russell's favourite anecdotes concerns the premiere of Stravinsky's *Rite of Spring* with Diaghilev's Ballet Russes on May 29, 1913, at the Théatre des Champs-Elysées in Paris, where the performance was met with catcalls and fights broke out between rival factions in the audience. Given his sense of the dramatic, it seems a reasonable assumption that this story was not far from his thoughts that night at La Salle Pleyel. [12]

The group went on to Sweden, where they were offered a residency at a Stockholm club, as Phillips recalled.

> There was two weeks of touring and then there was two weeks at the Golden Circle in Stockholm. We had played at Stockholm at a festival and the club said, "Can you guys stay?" So everybody checked with home and everybody could do it. So everyone stayed for an additional two weeks and played at the Golden Circle and went home from there. [13]

Everyone except Russell himself, that is. Russell's frustration with the lack of work for his group had bubbled to the surface before in an interview for the *Louisville Times* in Kentucky in April 1960. "'You can't play jazz in New York,' says brilliant composer-arranger George Russell. 'There is no opportunity to play jazz other than in the studio and I think that is really forcing the music out into the other communities of the country.'" [14]

Talking with Ian Carr, Russell recalled how rarely the group had worked live but that he had made ends meet through the opportunities to record in the studio. It seems that Russell's decision to stay in Scandinavia was essentially made on the spur of the moment.

> Well, I know that we wound up that European tour with the Newport All-Stars in Stockholm and I decided to stay there and I was offered a two-week engagement at the Golden Circle. And I took it and stayed. You know, and it was the right move because I began to work again to get . . . you know, the work just happened, working with Swedish Radio, the Danish Radio Jazz Orchestra. [15]

The reception his music had received there was obviously a factor. The calibre of the Scandinavian musicians he had heard was extremely high and he was accorded the same respect African-American musicians like Louis Armstrong, Miles Davis, Dexter Gordon, Kenny Clarke and others had found in Europe. Speaking to Carr, Russell's friend and sometime lover Marit Jerstad contrasted what he was feeling about America with his reception in Scandinavia.

> There, you know, it was everybody should be black Negro. You had to be black and he was very white. He had tried to become white in a way. It was very difficult, you know. Imagine. He was so light he didn't really look Negro at all. He looked like a Jew or mid-European. That alienated him from the milieu in America, which was, naturally, wanted to be fighting and very militant. Then he had no space there because he was a theoretician and you shouldn't be that, being a jazz musician. He had written a book. That was very suspect. Coming here he was given space. He was given room for everything. Especially in Norway; in Sweden it was with jazz on the radio, here it was the new music milieu and new music composers. [16]

Speaking with Vivian Perlis, Russell acknowledged that the political situation in America in the mid-sixties was a further factor in his decision to leave America.

> **GR:** Yeah, I think that had something to do with it. Things began to get rather mean, I thought, and forces were coming into the music that were non-musical forces and musicians and especially those who had lent themselves to various causes. I found it an ugly scene that didn't have much to do, really, with aesthetics. The art being . . . the anger being used as a kind of justification, maybe the justified anger. Anyway, anger being used as the justification for art, actually. But for an art that—what can I say—an art that was being . . . anger was being used as a commodity, as a commodity that one could believe was justified but at the same time behind that was a drive to power. Do you understand what I'm saying?
> **VP:** Yes, power in the wrong sense . . .
> **GR:** It was basically, the anger was being used by people to ride on, to get into positions of power and not as a justifiable anger out of injustice and wanting to see justice done. Bring about a certain shift in power.
> **VP:** Was there more appreciation for jazz in general, more respect and more opportunity for you in Europe during that time, more understanding of what you were . . .
> **GR:** Oh yes. Enormously much more.[17]

Russell saw much of the so-called avant-garde jazz as sloppy and lazy and lacking in the values and virtues he looked for in music. He was also concerned about what he saw as the aggressive and confrontational stance taken by some African-American musicians toward their white counterparts and to the jazz scene. After all, Russell counted many of those musicians as personal friends. Further, he was horrified by what he considered to be the infiltration of jazz by communist elements in America and outside. This may sound extreme or even paranoid but he outlined his reasons for this view in an interview for *Avant* magazine in 1998.

> When I left, it was a different kind of conservatism because it was people who might have been very Avant-garde but who insisted that their way was the way music was going and I never saw it that way. I always saw even the most radical serialist or so-called free players as playing in a zone—identifying a zone of music but it was merely a zone. I didn't want my music to be simply Serial or the New Thing. I wanted it to have many different colours. So, when that became politicised I left America.

Asked what he meant by the latter statement, Russell replied:

> Well, actually at the time, Communism was coming in and beginning to try to exert control over the far out people and it did to a certain extent. I mean in terms of world youth conferences, that they had in Finland or wherever, and certain musicians would be there and I began to feel really oppressed by that. *(Wry smile)*[18]

On a return to New York in May 1965 on business, Russell was interviewed by

*DownBeat*. He talked about teaching his Lydian Concept to a group of Swedish musicians and of forming a sextet with Swedes Bertil Lövgren on trumpet, Eje Thelin on trombone and Bernt Rosengren on tenor, along with Polish bassist Roman Dylag and Tootie Heath on drums. The group had played in Copenhagen, Brussels and Zurich, was due to play the Norwegian Molde Festival that summer and also in Baden-Baden in Germany. He also talked about a possible State Department/Swedish government–sponsored tour behind the Iron Curtain.

However, it was his other comments that provoked controversy. Noting the interest in Europe for new developments in jazz, he distinguished work that he saw as being of merit from what he saw as fraudulent. "'There's a lot of nonsense involved,' he explained. 'In some ways, the avant-garde is the last refuge of the untalented.'"

The article continued, with Russell leading with his chin:

> Many of the new players, Russell said, have "an over-evaluated sense of their ability to become instant composers. Composing is different from playing and always will be. The composer must take time to plan, to build structures and forms that will sustain interest. Much of what I hear is boring; there is a sameness to it all."

Furthermore, the New Thing indicated that the composer was needed more than ever, "The era of the idiocy of endless improvising is coming to an end: we need greater control in the hands of people who have an understanding of improvisation and its importance."[19]

Such comments in mid-sixties America would not go unanswered. It was Archie Shepp, a fine musician and at other times an articulate polemicist, who went into print to respond to Russell's castigation of the New Thing. In "An Artist Speaks Bluntly," which appeared in *DownBeat*'s December 16, 1965, issue, Shepp leaves no target unbloodied or unscarred. It is actually a striking "period piece" that draws Cuba, South Africa, Vietnam, racism in America and ghetto riots, along with white critics and George Russell, into its invective. Russell is singled out in the second paragraph, not least because critic Leonard Feather had used Russell's "last refuge of the untalented" tag approvingly in a festival review: "I address myself to George Russell, a man whose work I have always respected and admired, who in an inopportune moment with an ill-chosen phrase threw himself into the enemy camp."

Russell had, in Shepp's eyes, given succour to the enemy—white America, who has murdered "Bird, Billie, Ernie, Sonny" out of "a systematic and unloving disregard." In the only direct reference to the music, Shepp stated,

> Some of you are becoming a little frightened that we—niggers—ain't keepin' this thing simple enough. "The sound of surprise"? Man, you don't want no surprises from me.
> How do I know that?
> Give me leave to state this unequivocal fact: Jazz is the product of the whites—the ofays—too often my enemy. It is the progeny of the blacks—my kinsmen. By this I mean: you own the music, and we make it. By definition, then, you own the people who make the music. You own us in whole chunks of flesh. When you dig deep inside our already

disemboweled [sic] corpses and come up with a solitary diamond—because you don't want to flood the market—how different are you from the DeBeers of South Africa or the profligates who fleeced the Gold Coast. All right, there are niggers with a million dollars but ain't no nigger got a *billion* dollars. [20]

At this point, it might have been better to leave well enough alone. Russell, however, wrote a long open letter to *DownBeat*—"Popular Delusions and the Madness of Crowds." Russell appeared hurt and frustrated at the way his comments were received, comments he stated were certainly not directed at all musicians who were or saw themselves as part of the jazz avant-garde. Unfortunately, he accused the author of the original piece, Dan Morgenstern, of orchestrating his remarks into "a cantata of conservatism." Morgenstern and *DownBeat* obviously disputed the accusation, replying at some length to the charge. Whatever the truth—and one suspects it lies somewhere other than in the perceptions and misperceptions of the participants—it is a shame that a more intelligent debate could not have resulted from Russell's original remarks. Perhaps that has to be the preserve of hindsight, such were the inflamed passions of those times. If ever there were a time to talk about the relationship between art and politics, it surely was then. It was just so hard to be heard above the clamour. [21]

In fact, it seems unlikely that Shepp was not indeed one of the musicians Russell was thinking of when he was interviewed by Morgenstern. The Norwegian saxophonist Jan Garbarek, who worked extensively with Russell in Scandinavia, was surprised at the suggestion that Russell might have directed his ire toward Shepp.

> I'm very puzzled by this information because I think he was a huge fan of Archie Shepp's. Because Archie Shepp was also for us one of the leaders and I certainly tried to comprehend as much as I could as a young man. I would say George was really behind that. He wanted to put that freedom into some larger form. It could be used alongside organized things and then came his ideas about various strata in music and also different music going on at the same time. I think free playing was certainly one of these aspects. I'm sure he had a symbol for that kind of playing in his compositional tool kit. [22]

These exchanges between Russell and Shepp were more than just a case of "spit and feathers." They came on the heels of a series of disputes and debates within the American jazz scene. In the early sixties, there was a widespread belief amongst white jazz musicians and critics that that white players were being 'discriminated against' by black band leaders. [23] The insulting and grossly insensitive term bandied about at the time was "Crow-Jimism," a reversal of Jim Crow, the name given to the formal and informal segregation practised in the American South. Whatever the truth or not of this accusation, the very notion that the accusation that African-American musicians were excluding their white colleagues could be compared to the oppression and indignities of segregation beggars belief. More than that underpinning these issues on one side was the sharpness and bitterness of the struggle of African-Americans for civil rights, while on the other the underlying assumption on the part of white liberals was one based on a desire to see and represent jazz as a world free of such racial tensions. The latter was, unfortunately, far from the reality for African-American jazz musicians, many of whom felt with justification that they were not receiving their due in terms of critical acclaim or financially, in the context of a society that continued to deny them full civil rights in practice, if not in law.

As I noted in the introduction to this biography, this debate prefigured later controversies in the 1990s around Wynton Marsalis and his views on avant-garde jazz, views held by and pronounced upon with vehemence by his supporters, Stanley Crouch and Albert Murray. That too would prove to be a debate into which Russell would be dragged somewhat unwillingly. If history repeats itself, as Hegel suggests, then, as Karl Marx added, the first time might be tragedy but the second is surely farce! [24]

However, Russell did make a number of points very articulately in the interview and in his open letter, which set out his views on music and on politics. It is clear that Russell had no desire to locate himself either with the reactionaries or revolutionaries. His faith and hope lay with America and its people and those of the rest of the world rather than governments. In his open letter, he castigated America for preaching democracy at home but failing to practice it abroad, while he singled out Russia and China for preaching democracy abroad but failing to implement it at home. It is, however, no Jeremiad—naive, his comments might be, but Russell genuinely believed there are better ways for human beings to conduct their affairs. For Russell, however radical his music or ideas about music might have seemed to some jazz critics or fans, politics and art were deeply personal issues, not to be subsumed by ideology or theory. As a result, he could not ally himself with African-American musicians such as Archie Shepp, Charles Mingus, Bill Dixon, Marion Brown, Cecil Taylor or even his old friend Max Roach who would insist 'Freedom Now!' His response was one that sought to emphasise his right to independence and his own individuality.

I will discuss Russell's political beliefs later but in his remarks upon the musicians of the 'New Thing,' he did more than just call into question the more bogus aspects of the current jazz scene. He was criticising the aesthetic stance, and this in this context this was inseparable from the political stance, of many radical African-American musicians. What is more, he was commenting from a position of stature and reputation within the community of musicians. That is why Shepp reacted as he did and probably also why Feather latched onto Russell's choice of phrase. Among Russell's papers is a letter from critic and writer Martin Williams thanking him for writing the article, commenting, "and how much what it said needed saying." [25] Russell was certainly not alone in feeling as he did but he was very much speaking for himself in his comments.

In the BBC Radio 3 series on Russell, "The Trail Blazer", musician and broadcaster Ian Carr commented about this period in Russell's life,

> Also, he did not seem to belong anywhere in the current American musical landscape. This was a time of militant black music, expressing itself often in passionate free improvisation. Russell was a composer and a very light-skinned black man, who had written a major theoretical work on music. All of which was very suspect in the prevailing climate because it smacked of the white academic world. [26]

Carr is clearly drawing here on Marit Jerstad's remarks (see quote above). There is no doubt a certain amount of truth in what Carr (and Jerstad) have to say but there is another explanation that relates more directly to Russell's personality. In this regard, Garnett Brown offered an interesting insight into Russell's character and how this might have related to the shortage of work opportunities for his group in New York. "I think George was not that aggressive," Brown told me, "because I think the way he was he could have ended up like a prominent composer. He just wasn't a terribly assertive person in those days." Put bluntly, the jazz scene in New York and elsewhere was a competitive business. Musicians have to hustle or better, if they can afford it, pay someone to hustle on their behalf. [27]

Interviewed by Carr for the programme, Russell spoke eloquently of his concerns and dissatisfactions with the situation in jazz in the States at the time. He goes on to speak of how accepting he found Scandinavia.

> When I left America, I felt that the prevailing mechanism here was based on coming up with a gimmick, whatever kind of a gimmick would propel you in front of the public eye and then on into the heights of recognition, you know. People were almost bending over backward to just be anything. They were willing to just take on a role and play a role, even if it had to with dressing or a manner of speech or putting on a certain kind of thing. And this was so widespread, this feeling that for me had poisoned the whole atmosphere in America. It was like nothing genuine would ever come out of this place anymore and there was a great deal of hostility I felt here at the time I left and I didn't fit into any of that. So, Europe was, for me, an oasis of neutrality from this because when I did go to Scandinavia it was open arms and I was accepted and for the first time I really felt like an individual and I really felt that I had some individual value and felt, in terms of being a man and as an artist, I got respect for the first time ever. There was no role playing in that either from me or from anyone else. [28]

The phrase, "oasis of neutrality," is an interesting one, Sweden being historically a neutral country, in that it is not a member of any military alliance. In an interview with Bob Daughtry for Smithsonian Jazz Oral History Program in May 2004, this exchange took place with Russell making the following remarks,

> GR: ... chaos, complete chaos. You'd have people that never held a horn in their mouth coming to you and saying, "Just show me how to play. I don't want to know anything about music. Just, how do you get sounds out of this?" So I said, I can't – and furthermore, they – on a political side, there was a movement into supposedly a free society, but at that time, to me the communists didn't have a free society. It was – festivals and everything were promoted by communists in Russia. I didn't – I didn't join in on that thing.
> BD: What made you decide on Sweden?
> GR: Sweden was neutral and has always been neutral and always will be neutral.
> BD: Wasn't communist or capitalist.
> GR: No, not at all. They usually – it's their style to stay away from things that would identify them with this or that way. [29]

These two quotes help to provide a context for Russell's comments to *DownBeat* and his disagreement with Archie Shepp. More than that, they reveal (respectively twenty-seven and forty years after those events) the depth of feeling and emotion that Russell was experiencing at the time. These remarks also offer an insight into Russell's own political views and, given Sweden's history of social-democracy, one would position him as a left-of-centre liberal.

In terms of the pursuit of his musical goals, Russell certainly saw Europe as offering more fertile and productive ground for his ideas, as he explained in the article in *Avant* magazine in 1998.

> Musically I was very interested in the new music that was going on in Europe and so Stockhausen's *Momente* was very influential. Later pieces by Norwegian composer Kåre Kolberg, as well. He's not very well known but he is a fantastic composer and there was my need to free up the jazz score, free the musicians from the notes and also free up the tempos and stack tempos and aleatory writing. So, musically that was the reason. I felt choked in the USA because at the time I think there was what I would call a pretty conservative thing going on, that I didn't care for much. I thought Europe would give me freedom, which it did—Scandinavia particularly. [30]

There are a couple of points here that require elaboration. First, the regard between Russell and Scandinavia has always been a mutual one. Russell has continued to be honoured in Sweden, Norway and Denmark. He expressed his gratitude to a group of journalists in an interview for Swedish Radio in 1995.

> I can say that America has given me a chance to develop my musical ideas, with Sweden... Sweden gave those musical ideas a chance to blossom when I came here in 1965. I feel very much a part of the Swedish jazz cultural life because Sweden opened its doors very widely to me and that was primarily due to the efforts of one of your really truly great jazz musicians and that was Bosse Broberg, who at the time was director of jazz at the Swedish Radio and who had the good sense to hire Ulla Leksamda as his assistant. So, between them, I made out very well in Sweden. [31]

The second point concerns Stockhausen and in particular his so-called "moment form" and specifically *Momente*, to which Russell referred in the *Avant* magazine interview. In the next chapter, I will examine certain parallels between how Russell's musical approach developed in this period and the work of Stockhausen and others.

Russell's decision to move to Sweden was fairly momentous (no pun intended), and it proved to be a life-changing one. Russell had made some remarkable music in America—pieces like "Cubano Be, Cubano Bop," "Jazz in the Space Age" and "All About Rosie" that still shock and surprise and albums like *Jazz Workshop* that remain unparalleled in jazz. But Russell's music changed again in Scandinavia and he produced two of the finest extended works in jazz—*Othello Ballet Suite* and *Electronic Sonata for Souls Loved by Nature*—during his time in Sweden and Norway. Add to that the gigantic, sprawling oratorio *Listen to the Silence*, which was recorded two years after his return to America and it is evident that this period of six or so years was incredibly rejuvenating and revitalizing for the composer. All of Russell's subsequent work owes much to those years.

Critics, from America in particular, have misunderstood the importance of these years for Russell, seeing them as almost a holiday away from the main action Stateside. [32] Indeed, Russell's absence from the American scene goes some way to explain his subsequent difficulty in gaining acceptance with American jazz fans for his music. The sound quality of the records that resulted is not the best. They often sound muddy and with insufficient differentiation between the instruments. But somehow this detracts from neither the music itself nor the astonishing musicianship of the players. But more than that, Scandinavia offered access to facilities for Russell that America never had, as Russell explained to WKCR's Ben Young,

> A young man who was head of jazz at the Swedish Radio, Bosse Broberg, commissioned everything I had ever written, recommissioned it for Swedish Radio broadcast. It was an experience, a very positive experience being there. They gave me all the time I needed to work in an electronic music studio to build the electronic tape foundation for *Electronic Sonata for Souls Loved by Nature*. I'd never worked with electronic music. They opened the doors for me. Miles Davis, bless his heart, in the pop music of the time, he saw a direction for jazz and I saw it too. *Electronic Sonata* was an expression of what I saw. [33]

When Russell returned from his New York business trip in the spring of 1965 he was crippled with stomach pains. He arrived in Stockholm in a wheelchair and was again admitted to hospital. The Swedish surgeon removed a swab that his American counterpart had left in Russell's stomach after the earlier operation for ulcers and cleaned up the mess that had been left. Without this surgery, Russell might well have died. By the summer, however, he was well enough to tour Europe and Scandinavia.

It seems that Russell had two overlapping groups at the time—one with the personnel outlined in the *DownBeat* article, which prompted the spat with Archie Shepp, and another that had Americans Ray Pitts on tenor, Brian Trentham on trombone, Cameron Brown on bass and Don Cherry joining Bertil Lövgren on trumpet. It was this group that made the recording at Stuttgart's Beethoven Hall in August 1965.

This record, originally released against Russell's wishes as two separate LPs on the German MPS label, came out as a single edition on the CD reissue in 1998. It is an amazing group performance that deserves to be heard in its entirety. The first part of the concert—comprising the first LP—features a long suite built around Russell's compositions and Milt Jackson's "Bags Groove," Charlie Parker's "Confirmation," and Monk's "'Round Midnight," with Russell using the Lydian Concept to connect and unify the music. The second original LP includes "You Are My Sunshine," "Oh Jazz Po Jazz" (split over two sides of the record), and "Volupte." Produced by Joachim Berendt, this is one of the most "out" recordings Russell made. [34]

The opening track, "Freein' Up," contains some of Russell's finest piano playing, finding the composer occupying space somewhere between Thelonious Monk and Cecil

Taylor, driving the piece through furious tempo changes and using some wonderfully rich tone clusters. The four horns create a constant internal dialogue within the music, while Russell's use of counterpoint and counter-rhythms is complex and masterful. But it is not just his arranging skill that integrates these themes into one whole. Rather it is, with no pun intended, his conceptual ability. Russell is able to bring the disparate and diverse together. The live version of "You Are My Sunshine" is a case in point. It is perhaps less breathtakingly challenging than the original with Sheila Jordan and lacks the high drama of that performance. Yet it is almost as emotionally affecting. There is a delightful moment when Cherry finishes his solo in mid-cadenza where the audience reacts with laughter that conveys the humour and irony in Russell's use of the old warhorse, without detracting from its genuine sentiment. In several senses, this is Russell's master class in arranging, and many a student arranger could do much worse than start their studies here. "Oh Jazz Po Jazz," which always sounds like a title Gershwin might have used, is beautifully played, with the musicians achieving a looseness in their performance that just slips by with a loping stride. Obviously, of the horns the great Don Cherry stands out and, as a long-time admirer, Russell loved playing with him. But Pitts, Trentham and Lövgren also acquit themselves well. However, it is the playing of the rhythm section that is perhaps the most striking aspect of the record. Heath and Brown work so well together in this context and leave Russell enormous scope to move between the horns and drums and bass. It is almost as if Russell has invented a new category of jazz, one that absorbs its history and projects its potential at the same time.

There are too many marvellous moments on the record to cover them in their entirety here. The opening brooding section of "Volupte," the almost New Orleans–like interlocking of the horns on "Confirmation" and elsewhere, the shock at the way Russell opens up still further "'Round Midnight," the wittiness of "Sunshine," and the liberties he takes with "Bags Groove"—these are a few such highlights. Sadly, this is the Russell album that is most often overlooked. It certainly deserves better than *DownBeat*'s grudging three-and-a-half-star review, which argues that the record falls down in the final analysis due to "the unwillingness of his [Russell's] players to give themselves completely over to him—to his design." The reviewer's reaction is one thing; however, his ignorance of Russell's post-Brandeis music is another altogether. It is as if the reviewer lost all track with the composer's music after the late fifties. [35]

After Russell's group played the Stuttgart concert, they performed in Koblenz. When they began "Sunshine," some of the audience laughed, according to Joachim Berendt, good-naturedly. Then someone whistled. Russell stopped the performance, went to the microphone and said, with anger in his tone, "If you know it better, why don't you finish the concert?" Memories of Paris the previous year, or just Russell's occasional spikiness? Or maybe the tune and its origins simply meant a great deal to him. [36]

Prior to the German dates, Russell and his group played at Molde on July 29. Molde was to prove one of the most significant events of his time in Scandinavia—in more ways than one. The tenor player he was using for the date was Swede Lennert Åberg, who had met Russell the previous year when Russell had worked with the Emanon Big Band. That, apparently, had been quite an occasion, with the leader of the sax section, Lennart Jansson, dead drunk and the whole section falling apart during the faster numbers. Tenor saxophonist Bernt Rosengren, who was in the sextet prior to Molde, had left the group and the inexperienced Åberg was surprised to get the call.

> We went to Molde to play at the festival there, July 1965. I was totally paralysed by nervousness and, at the airport in Oslo, I succeeded with the impossible thing to just drop the saxophone on the floor. In Molde I checked it and the small round ring between the body and the bell was like an egg so I had to very carefully try to adjust it to be able to play it. I thought I almost did it, just a few millimetres left, and I made a last effort and the Bell just was bent out in a nanosecond and the saxophone looked like a smoking pipe! The Bell did not point up but straight out! In Norway, they did not have any Selmer saxes, so one was sent for from Denmark! Meanwhile, we had to rehearse and I borrowed a sax from Booker Ervin but I could hardly get a sound out of it. I had heard the rumours about Don Byas having so hard reeds that only he could play it and so on, so I thought this was something similar. G had always been nice to me but this time he lost his temper and screamed, "Blow Man Blow!" Maybe even, "Blow Motherfucker!" When the rehearsal was over and I unpacked the sax something fell out and it turned out that it was full of packages of cigarettes that Booker had smuggled! Probably some of them prepared too!
>
> I thought the concert was a nightmare and I just wanted to disappear but G and "Tootie" Heath told me to follow to the control booth for the Norwegian TV to have a look at the result and I remember we looked at "'Round Midnight" that was a feature for tenor sax and they both said, "Great!" and were very nice to me. Other musicians there were Donald Byrd and Dexter Gordon and G made a small speech for Dexter just before our concert. We also heard two very young unknown musicians from Oslo at a jam session, Jan Garbarek and Jon Christensen.[37]

Russell's ten or so months in Sweden had certainly proven exceptionally eventful. He had married a young Swedish artist and had also had a child, his son Jock, by another young woman.[38] At Molde, he met Marit Jerstad, who had just separated from her husband. They soon became lovers and began a stormy relationship that lasted six years. Jerstad was involved with the Norwegian new music scene and its organization nyMusikk, as well as with the theatre. She had developed what she describes as visual compositions to accompany music and would later create one of these for Russell's *Electronic Sonata*, which was performed with the piece at various festivals. Through her Russell got to know most of the new composers on the Scandinavian scene, and they, along with Stockhausen, Ligeti and Penderecki, were perhaps the last new influences on Russell's music.

However, after his concert at Molde, Russell went along to a session where a group of young Norwegian musicians were playing and sat in on piano. The group included a very young Jan Garbarek on tenor, Arild Andersen on bass and Jon Christensen on drums. Andersen spoke for all of them when he recalled the event. "I remember he came up to a jazz club where we were playing with Garbarek and Christensen and I'm not sure if Terje was on that gig. George came up and sat in on piano and it was incredible. I still remember it. We played 'Just Friends' and the energy just got up to the ceiling."[39]

It seems unlikely that guitarist Terje Rypdal was present, as he remembered meeting

Russell for the first time on a later occasion.[40] More prosaically, Jon Christensen recalled how Russell was so taken with their playing, he immediately wanted to hire them.

> We played a concert at Molde Jazz Festival in the summer of 1965 with Jan Garbarek and George Russell was sitting in at a jam session that evening and he liked very much what he heard and so he invited me and Jan to come over to Stockholm, where he was living at the time. Jan was still at school but I was finished, so I could go and meet George in Sweden.[41]

As for Garbarek, his strongest memory is of how it felt to receive the older musician's affirmation for what he and his peers were trying to create.

> I think I would have to go back to the very first meeting with George, because—I don't know if you are at all familiar with how that happened—it's enough to say that it was all about a release of energy. We had plenty of that, of course, being young free jazz musicians into everything like Coltrane and so on. So it was all about energy anyway. But George had a tremendous fire in him and when he played with us, we seemed to reach yet another gear, another level. So it was opening up a freedom and a freedom that was accepted by others at the time. It was a little bit difficult because we were the first generation in Norway that took up this really free-energy playing and this free-associative creation. But George was fully into it and he backed it and he was a part of it and he accepted it.[42]

Some fans and critics may bemoan the absence in more recent times of artists and innovators of the stature of Louis Armstrong, Duke Ellington, Charlie Parker, Miles Davis and John Coltrane. But such thinking perhaps results more from nostalgia regarding their own first discovery of jazz and from the security that history can have when bestowing the mantle of greatness. There are at least a few who have changed the way the music sounds since then. One would be Keith Jarrett. Another would be John McLaughlin. Others might with justification argue on behalf of Wayne Shorter, Michael Brecker and Pat Metheny, in which case Jan Garbarek would deserve more than a mention. He is not just an astonishing improviser with a huge, wide-ranging sonic palette but the records he has made for ECM have defined a whole sound and genre. It is too easy to rely on the certainties of hindsight in making our judgments and critical evaluations.

Marit Jerstad, who was also present, saw something else. In all the interviews for this book—with men and women, colleagues and lovers—each person has offered his or her own insights into Russell, his motivations and his character. However, it seems that it is often the women in his life who have been most keen in their perceptions of him.

> I came to a jam session after the concert and George was playing. And I got so struck by his music. It struck me very deeply and when I saw him sitting at the piano, I felt very strongly his loneliness. We are all uniquely alone and I felt that very strongly about George—those two things, the man and his music.[43]

Her comments echo something that Sheila Jordan has said about Russell.

I watched him one time when he would come by and pick me up at my office when we were still going together. And I was in the building and he was standing outside the car— and I'll never forget that image—and he was standing there and there was an aura about him that was like he didn't even belong here. He was displaced. He was standing there but he looked like, "I don't belong here," and I'll never forget that look. I can't explain it but it was like a very lonesome . . . I got a very lonely feeling when I saw him. I'll never forget that. [44]

Jerstad and Russell lived together for much of his time in Scandinavia and though they stopped being lovers in 1970, they remained friends. As Jerstad told Ian Carr, Russell had liaisons with other women, invariably white, while they were together, and she had affairs as well. "When he had all his affairs, I had some, which infuriated him." [45]

At the same time, they shared common interests in music, food and philosophy—both had discovered the ideas of G. I. Gurdjieff. Jerstad told Carr that Russell helped her develop more self-confidence but it was certainly a relationship characterized by its share of fights and arguments. Jerstad recalled that on one occasion in Italy, she threw a chair at Russell that missed and went through a window. It seems, however, that it was an important relationship for them both, not least, for Russell, in opening the world of Scandinavian new music. They went to concerts together and socialized with many of the musicians and composers involved in that world. It ended when Russell had moved back to the States and when "he fell in love with a mutual friend." [46]

Jerstad also noted that Russell arrived in Scandinavia with a certain sense of bitterness and "a very strong rage" inside him. [47] These characteristics were also part of the man and his music—and, however much age and maturity may have impacted upon him, continued to be an aspect of his personality.

Just before he played at Molde and jammed with Garbarek, Andersen and Christensen, Russell began writing a letter to his old friends Peggy and John Benson Brooks. The letter gives a strong insight into his thoughts and feelings at the time, not least in light of Jerstad's comments. It is an unusual letter that mixes the personal with Russell's political observations. When he began the letter, he was at Molde, due shortly on stage with his group. There is a slight discrepancy here over dates. Russell's letter is dated July 31, yet elsewhere the date of his performance was given as July 29. He noted that Dexter Gordon, Jimmy Cleveland, Booker Ervin, and Donald Byrd were also appearing at the festival and that both Brian Trentham and Cameron "Cam" Brown were with the band. He wrote, "Brian and Cam are here to stay—both would be fed to the Viet Nam meat grinder if they remained there. That shit is ridiculous."

Adding that Al "Tootie" Heath was on drums—Russell spells it "Tutti"— he writes that the "two Swedish cats" in the band on trumpet and tenor were "promising but just not up to the music we play or rather not up to the demands of the music." Russell then outlines his thoughts on America and its stance over Vietnam, contrasting America's sense of itself as the supporter of democracy and freedom while at the same time supporting some of the worst dictators on the planet: "[A]nd look at the 'anti-communist' mothers that have used our dough to degrade their own—Diem, Trujillo, Batista, Chiang [Kai-shek], Franco, Duvalier. We'll support any son of a bitch who says he's against godless communism."

Russell resumed the letter on September 2 and commented on how he felt *DownBeat* had misrepresented his views (see above) and talked of the birth of his son, Jock. He then wrote briefly about his recent German tour and the Stuttgart date with Don Cherry and mentions a concert the group was doing for German Radio and a big-band gig at the Konserthuset in Stockholm opposite Dexter Gordon. Then came an interesting and amusing postscript: "Had an interview with AFN in Stuttgart [armed forces network] and expressed my views on Viet Nam. I was pretty stoned but I did get the impression that the interviewer was constantly try [sic] to change the subject."[48]

Unfortunately, it seems that any tape, if the interview was ever broadcast at all, no longer exists unless there is one in private hands. It would certainly be interesting to hear a "stoned," hip African-American jazz musician bemoaning American foreign policy to a member of the U.S. armed forces. Russell was never unwilling to speak his mind.

## Notes

1. Benoit Quersin, "Le Philosophe De Greenwich Village," *Jazz*, February 1963.
2. "The Playboy Panel: Jazz—Today and Tomorrow," *Playboy*, February 1964; "Tangents," *DownBeat*, June 18, 1964.
3. "George Russell Sends Call for More Blood Donors," *DownBeat*, October 22, 1964.
4. Interview with Garnett Brown, July 2004.
5. Interview with Barre Phillips, March 2007.
6. Ibid. See also Joe Boyd, *White Bicycles* (London: Serpent's Tail, 2006), p. 46. Boyd, the producer and sometime impresario, worked on the tour and recalls in his autobiography that the tour included Davis; Brubeck; the Charlie Parker All-Stars with Sonny Stitt, J.J. Johnson, and Howard McGhee; Roland Kirk; Sister Rosetta Tharpe; the Original Tuxedo Brass Band; the Coleman Hawkins/Harry Edison Swing All-Stars; and the George Russell Sextet—eight bands, six different itineraries, and four tour managers.
7. Interview with Phillips.
8. Boyd, *White Bicycles*, p. 53.
9. *George Russell Sextet, Live in Bremen and Paris*, Gambit Records 69293; *Chicago All Stars— George Russell Sextet—Uptown All Stars 1964 Live*, BJ036CD. It is unclear what the provenance of these two discs is or whether any payment will go to the musicians, who are still alive. I hesitate to recommend what may be a "bootleg" recording, but the Gambit disc features some truly fantastic playing from all concerned—from saxophonist Joe Farrell and trumpeter Thad Jones in particular. It also contains some of the finest examples of Russell's talents as a pianist. What is more, the company have made a real effort to provide accurate information and reasonable sleeve notes. You pay your money and you take your choice.
10. Interview with Brown.
11. Interview with Phillips.
12. This story has acquired mythical status over the decades. It is probable that it was less Stravinsky's music that inspired the "riot" than other features of the performance by the Ballets Russes. Kevin Elyot, author of the television play Riot at the Rite, writing in the *Guardian* on March 2, 2006, suggests that it was Serge Diaghilev, the founder-manager of the Ballets Russes, who in part engineered the incident through provocative publicity and invitations to those he knew would detest the performance as well as those who would champion it. It was also arguably Vaslav Nijinsky's choreography and its sexual and barbaric subject matter that provoked the most outrage. Indeed, the performers could not hear the music above the din and Nijinsky resorted to standing on a chair in the wings, his coattails held by Stravinsky to stop him

falling, shouting the calls to the dancers. It seems unlikely that the audience could actually hear the music either. Sometimes, interpretation is more important than historical fact.
13. Interview with Phillips.
14. William Peeples, "Top Jazzmen Move into Hinterlands," *Louisville Times*, April 6, 1960.
15. Ian Carr, interview with George Russell, June 1992.
16. Ian Carr, interview with Marit Jerstad for BBC Radio 3 broadcast *George Russell—The Invisible Guru*, July 1994.
17. Vivian Perlis, interview with George Russell, American Music Series, December 8, 1993, Oral History Project of American Music, sponsored and supported by the National Endowment for the Arts Special Jazz Projects.
18. Duncan Heining, "A Meeting with a Remarkable Man," *Avant* 7 (Summer 1998).
19. "Random Thoughts from George Russell," *DownBeat*, July 29, 1965.
20. Archie Shepp, "An Artist Speaks Bluntly," *DownBeat*, December 16, 1965.
21. George Russell, "Popular Delusions and the Madness of Crowds," *DownBeat*, April 7, 1966.
22. Interview with Jan Garbarek, July 2004.
23. See Ingrid Monson, *Freedom Sounds: Civil Rights Call Out to Jazz and Africa*, (Oxford: OUP, 2007), pp. 238-251.
24. Karl Marx, *The Eighteenth Brumaire of Louis Bonaparte* (Moscow: Progress, 1972), p. 5 "Hegel remarks somewhere that all great world-historic facts and personages appear, so to speak, twice. He forgot to add: the first time as tragedy, the second time as farce." For discussion of Jazz at Lincoln Center and related matters, see S. Nicholson, *Is Jazz Dead? Or Has It Moved to a New Address?* (Abingdon, UK: Routledge, 2005).
25. Martin Williams, letter to George Russell, March 25, 1966.
26. Ian Carr, *The Trail Blazer* BBC Radio Three 8th August 1994
27. Interview with Brown.
28. Carr, *The Trail Blazer*.
29. Bob Daughtry interview with George Russell for Smithsonian Jazz Oral History Program, May 2004.
30. Heining, "A Meeting with a Remarkable Man."
31. Swedish Radio Panel interview with George Russell, 1995.
32. See, for example, Sy Johnson, "Interview: Bill Evans & George Russell," *Changes*, Spring 1972. For an alternative view on the same issue see Brian Priestley, Review of *The London Concerts Volumes 1 & 2* (Label Bleu LBLC65278), in *Gramophone Jazz Good CD Guide*, ed. K. Shadwick (Harrow, UK: Gramophone, 1995), p. 450; Max Harrison, "George Russell—Rational Anthems," *Wire* (1983): 19–21.
33. Ben Young, broadcast devoted to George Russell in celebration of his seventy-fifth birthday, WKCR Radio, New York, June 23, 1998.
34. Joachim Berendt was a renowned jazz critic and producer and wrote *The Jazz Book—From New Orleans to Jazz Now* (New York and Westport, CT: Lawrence Hill, 1974).
35. W. Russo, Review of *George Russell at Beethoven Hall* (Saba MPFS 15059), *DownBeat*, October 20, 1966.
36. Wolfram Knauer, sleeve notes to reissue of *George Russell Sextet at Beethoven Hall* (Complete Recordings), MPS 539084-2.
37. E-mail interview with Lennart Åberg, July 2007.
38. According to a letter from Russell to John Benson Brooks and his wife, Peggy, written between August and September 1965, he met Jock's journalist mother when she was visiting the States and just after his relationship with Wendy Brooks had ended. It seems that Jock might have been conceived in America rather than in Sweden.
39. Interview with Arild Andersen, November 2005.
40. Interview with Terje Rypdal, November 2005.
41. Interview with Jon Christensen, September 2005.
42. Interview with Garbarek.

43. Quote taken from Ian Carr's notebooks made from interviews for The Invisible Guru and Trailblazer programs for BBC Radio 3, broadcast July and August 1994.
44. Interview with Sheila Jordan, May 2004.
45. Carr, notebooks for The Invisible Guru and Trailblazer.
46. Ibid.
47. Ibid.
48. Letter from Russell to John Benson Brooks, July 1964.

CHAPTER TEN

## Listen to the Silence

It is hard to know just what it must have felt like for Russell to find himself and his music in such demand in Europe compared with his experiences in his homeland. Essentially, he worked regularly throughout Sweden, Norway and Denmark, with occasional forays into the rest of Europe, during the five years he spent in Scandinavia. He toured and recorded with a new sextet but much of his work came from Swedish Radio and involved new works and recommissions of older material. As noted, Bosse Broberg was the person at Swedish Radio responsible for commissioning jazz projects.

Broberg met Russell when he was working with the Emanon Big Band, a grouping that was beginning to explore areas outside more established lines of writing and arranging for large jazz ensembles. Russell's arrival in Scandinavia in 1964 proved very timely, as Broberg told me,

> He sort of opened our minds to new ways of thinking with his theory of the Lydian scale as combining element or dimension. Also, he brought in philosophical ideas about music being a means of release. From early on he was making the case for synthesising different musical traditions, for example Afro-American with European (not to forget the tinge of Latin American).[1]

It was Russell's "audacious and unconventional writing techniques" that impressed Broberg, in particular the way Russell combined different sections of his groups and big bands in unpredictable ways. He noted Russell's role as a teacher in Scandinavia and described him as, in effect, Swedish Radio's "composer-in-residence" during that period. As well as the records that resulted from Swedish Radio commissions, the radio station commissioned twenty-four performances by various Russell groupings between 1966 and 1983, of which fifteen performances took place between 1966 and 1969.

In terms of Russell's impact on Swedish jazz, Broberg was unequivocal.

> Russell's ideas of anchoring improvisation with a scale or a central note over extended periods was of great importance. The method aims at opening the way for freer exploration. I regard this as important for the development of Swedish (then) contemporary jazz music. The study of his theoretical work in which he is discussing the relationship between vertical and horizontal forms and courses served as an inspiration for many practitioners—players as well as writers. [2]

That Russell had a huge influence on Scandinavian jazz during his stay in Sweden and Norway is evident. However, Danish trumpeter-composer Palle Mikkelborg told a story regarding Russell's reception in Denmark that is well worth consideration.

> I remember the first session where we played *All About Rosie*. It did not go well. We were too scared to give it . . . .. we were good musicians but the copyist had done a terrible job. So, the saxophone players had to turn the page and it irritated George so much. There were these phrases and when they got there they had to turn the page. So, we all had to stop there all the time. I remember he said, 'Where were you guys in fifty something?' We were really scared but the day ended with a really good version of it. You know how he can be. He made some of them very scared. [3]

For Mikkelborg, this was a clash of personalities and expectations. Noting that, in Denmark, Russell was "not the most popular conductor there for big band," the trumpeter distinguished between the different responses of the Danish Radio Jazz Group and the station's big band, "The Radio Jazz group loved him but the Big Band was something else. They were very conventional-thinking musicians. Very good but there were some of them that didn't like his way of wanting what he wants. 'I want this!' They couldn't fulfil it, so they turned around and became angry with him." [4]

One might be tempted to suggest that this difference was partly a cultural one – New World/New York jazz scene versus Old World/Publicly subsidised jazz scene. There might well have been some aspect of that involved here. However, the Norwegian and Swedish musicians - and not just the younger generation of players, either - seemed to have reacted very favourably to Russell, his music and ideas. Mikkelborg's anecdote serves to illustrate that Russell's Scandinavian years were not always a honeymoon. Nor was his approach to jazz without its detractors in Northern Europe. It is also intriguing that the issue of the copying of Russell's musical scores was once more an issue!

By this point, Russell had already begun to recruit the musicians he had jammed with at Molde and incorporate them into his sextet. As noted, Garbarek was just seventeen and needed to finish high school, so was not able to join immediately. Jon Christensen, who was four years older, joined Russell fairly immediately and Arild Andersen came in as soon as he had completed his compulsory military service.

One of Christensen's first experiences with Russell was at a remarkable concert in

Denmark in December 1965. It featured Russell with a big band, which appeared in the middle of two performances of Stockhausen's *Gruppen* for three orchestras.

> For me it was a learning process to be part of that thing but there was one special concert in Copenhagen which was arranged by Danish Radio at the Tivoli Concert Hall featuring the music of George Russell and the classical composer Karlheinz Stockhausen. That was nice because Stockhausen had this famous composition where he used three bands on three different stages. We were there with the big band and George and Stockhausen were talking together and it was nice to be part of a concert with him. He was very nice also. I think it was the late sixties. So many things happened.[5]

The way the music scene was set up at that time in Scandinavia must have been quite a pleasant surprise for Russell. There were many more opportunities for work and direct and indirect state sponsorship, both through public broadcasting stations and through organizations like nyMusikk in Norway. Russell and his various groups performed at the Golden Circle in Stockholm, played at various schools and performed two major concerts arranged by nyMusikk at the University of Oslo in March 1966 and August 1967.[6]

At the time he had signed with the Swedish company Sonet Records and much of the Scandinavian material came out first on that label. The actual recording sequence of the music released and dates when albums came out is rather complicated and is really a matter of interest only to jazz historians. The records actually released while Russell was in northern Europe or in the process of returning to the United States, were *Othello Ballet* (which includes Russell's *Electronic Organ Sonata No. 1*), *Electronic Sonata for Souls Loved by Nature—1968* (the sextet version), and *The Essence of George Russell* (which contained the big-band version of *Electronic Sonata for Souls Loved by Nature*, *Now and Then*, and "Concerto for Self-Accompanied Guitar"). It makes sense—artistically and critically—to treat *Trip to Prillarguri* from 1970 and *Listen to the Silence* from 1971 as being part of that same sequence of albums. Not only did they include much the same personnel, but they spring from the same source, both in terms of commissioning and inspiration.

The first piece Russell recorded in Sweden was *Now and Then*. It was premiered at Konserthuset, Stockholm, in autumn 1966 and was finally released on Sonet in 1970 along with a big-band performance of *Electronic Sonata for Souls Loved by Nature*, with sleeve notes by the Norwegian composer Kåre Kolberg. It clearly indicates how far and how fast Russell's thinking about big-band composition had moved since *Jazz in the Space Age*.

There's a quote from Leonard Bernstein that seems very apt here: "We have reached that supra-level of musical semantics... where those apparently mismatched components can unite—tonal, non-tonal, electronic, serial, aleatory—all united in a magnificent new eclecticism."[7] Bernstein's words can fairly be applied to Russell, and "unity" is a word Russell used often in conversation, particularly in terms of what he calls "chord-scale unity." One aspect of Russell's search has been to try to discover a point of shared origin for all music, in an emotional and philosophical rather than strictly historical sense. Another has been his desire to achieve a theoretical understanding that incorporates all music, Western and non-Western, composed and improvised. His ideas about tonality—or, as he puts it, "tonal gravity"—and of "time," in its musical and broader philosophical senses, provide places where these forms can be found, explained and explored. His compositions are his research laboratories and the place where his theory is most articulately expounded. In that respect, the music Russell began to make in Scandinavia epitomized his mature output.

Famously, *Now and Then* was one of Jan Garbarek's first performances with a Russell band. Though Garbarek was still in school, Russell suggested that he might still be able to undertake some recordings in Stockholm.

> My reading wasn't that good but he offered to send me the music a couple of months before, which he did. He sent me all the parts, I think, for tenor saxophone for his big-band music. That's how I learned to read music, basically, getting those parts and learning them for my trip to Stockholm, which went not brilliantly from my point of view but I survived. I sat next to some of my real heroes, Swedish professional top musicians that I admired very much and I was really in awe I would say of the whole situation. As I said, I barely survived but I did survive. In a way that was a good thing for me. [8]

With his love of the music of Archie Shepp, Coltrane and Albert Ayler, the young man must have felt in his element. This was a huge, Mingus-like piece in which different musical elements collide and combust. It is polyrhythmic, polytonal and panstylistic, to use the terms utilised by Russell in his earlier interview with Burt Korall, and he uses different musical strata working simultaneously and often pulling in completely different directions. In lesser hands, it would sound like chaos. In fact, ironically, it is the composer himself – playing piano - who seems to lose focus briefly at the end, when he continues playing after the band has finished. With Russell's skill as a musical architect, it embodies jazz past, present and future. It is not Russell's greatest work, by any means, but certainly one that augurs in a new chapter in his music.

Stockhausen is certainly one of the influences that one begins to hear on *Now and Then* and also on *Othello Ballet*, which was Russell's next major work. "Influence" often feels too strong a word in such a context. The composer's voice that the listener hears is still Russell. It is just that his scope as a composer has expanded to incorporate what has been newly discovered. The word "parallel" often feels more useful because it suggests a separate exploration of similar ideas and musical language. In that sense, the listener may hear Russell exploring similar musical territory to Ligeti, Penderecki, Stockhausen and also Edgar Varèse but filtered through African-American musical traditions, sensibilities and practices.

An article by composer Malcolm Ball on Stockhausen that appeared in *Avant Magazine* in 1998 is instructive here and readers may detect certain parallels with Russell's own ideas and work.

> The work that took "moment form" to its limits is *Momente* which Stockhausen worked on and off during the period 1961/70. The work uses three different kinds of "moments": K-moments (*klang*, sound or timbre), M-moments (melody) and D-moments (duration).

Apparently it is no coincidence that these moments bear the initials of key people in Stockhausen's private life at the time where considerable personal conflict had arisen. D is Doris, Stockhausen's first wife and mother to four of his children, M is Mary Bauermeister, an artist who Stockhausen met in 1960 and resulted in a relationship developing with two more children, and K is obviously Karlheinz. (It is perhaps interesting to note that years later, the super-formula of *Licht* also is based around three characters: Eve, Michael and Lucifer.)

From 1963 through to 1970 Stockhausen began to give his performers less and less fixed musical notation using instead symbols such as plus, minus and equal signs, so the interpreter is to use his own musical skills to transform events using these signs and relating them to various parameters such as dynamic levels, duration, pitch etc. So plus (+) would be louder, higher, longer and minus (–) could be shorter, lower, slower, broadly speaking. This period also saw the introduction of live electronics in performance in works such as *Mixtur* for orchestra, sine-wave generators and ring modulators (1964), *Mikrophonie I and II* (1964/65), *Prozession* (1967) and *Kurzwellen* (1968). Throughout this period events in Stockhausen's life were taking dramatic changes and turns. One such event was his trip to Tokyo in 1966 and the realisation of *Telemusik* in the NHK studio. Stockhausen has said that he lived in a kind of dream world and was fascinated by all things Japanese and soon became "more Japanese than the Japanese."

His longest studio based work up to now (1965/67) was *Hymnen* for electronic and concrete sounds. That favourite musical "buzz" word of the 1980's "world music" really starts here with *Hymnen*. Here Stockhausen weaves about forty national anthems from all around the world with electronic sources discovered throughout his time at WDR and concrete sounds such as breathing and the sounds of short wave radio waves which adds an almost extra terrestrial quality to the near two hour long piece. *Hymnen* exists in three versions: 1. *Hymnen* Electronic and concrete music; 2. electronic and concrete music with soloists; and 3. *Hymnen* electronic music with orchestra (third region). Each of its four "regions" has key "centres": region 1 has the Internationale and Marseillaise as its centres, region 2 has West Germany and several African anthems, region 3 is centred around the American, Russian and Spanish anthems and the 4th region has two centres, one being the Swiss anthem and the other is a hymn associated with the Utopian realm of Hymunion in *Harmondie unter Pluramon*.[9]

I have questioned whether I might have over-emphasised the connections between Russell's music and European Art music in *George Russell: The Story of an American Composer*, though hopefully not at the expense of the more important African-American elements – blues, gospel and jazz. I would, however, suggest that during his period in Scandinavia, Russell was absorbing and exploring the new musical ideas and approaches he was discovering through nyMusikk. Russell certainly knew of Stockhausen's work already and it is unlikely, given his studies and contact with Stefan Wolpe, that he would not have been aware of other twentieth century composers such as Edgar Varèse or Penderecki. But what Russell did with these ideas was more than a recycling of textures, techniques or colours. We noted earlier Russell's comment that he felt the need "to free up the jazz score, free the musicians from the notes and also free up the tempos and stack tempos..."[10] Such ideas were a means to an end. For example, if one were to think of the phrase – "Free up the tempos and stack tempos..." and then listen to the first part of *Othello Ballet Suite*, between about four minutes in to approximately seven minutes, the listener will find several examples of Russell doing precisely that.

Russell was always fascinated by the possibilities of tempo and time in jazz. Musician/composer, Roger Dean, for example, noted that on "Ye Hypocrite, Ye Beelzebub" from the *Jazz Workshop* album, Russell has the soloists play in 4/4 against a rhythm in 6/4. As Dean also notes, this practice would be considerably extended in later works such as *The African Game*.[11] Such polyrhythmic approaches certainly owe something to the African-American or even African musical heritage of jazz. Here the analogies of the African-American Gospel choir and African drum choir, to which Russell would often later refer, seem apposite.

I have, however, wondered whether Russell might also have derived inspiration from Edgar Varèse in this regard. The French-American composer was unusual as a classical composer in his strong interest in rhythm and was also one of the first to experiment with the potential of electronics as a compositional tool.[12] It is worth listening to the opening sections of both parts one and two of *Othello Ballet Suite* and comparing these with the Varèse composition *Déserts*. They share a brooding, solemn intensity and there are certainly parallels between the way both composers deploy percussion and brass and woodwinds against each other (Russell used four percussionists, including Jon Christensen in his suite). The use of bells, presumably tubular, on both is further suggestive of a possible link between the two. On *Déserts*, each of the four episodes bracket an "interpolation of organised sound," that is an electronic tape, a technique Russell would use on his *Electronic Sonata*. Again, however, as Russell's piece develops the use of rhythm, including any new rhythmic devices he may have discovered, are utilised very much in the service of jazz and not as some kind of 'third stream', musical hybrid or fusion.

By now Russell was using what was also the Jan Garbarek Quartet as part of his own sextet and as the core for the big-band work he was doing for Scandinavian radio. *Othello Ballet* was written at the suggestion of Walter Nicks, the African-American dancer and choreographer who was at the time a consultant at the University of Stockholm. One of the most successful dancers of his generation, it seems possible that Nicks had met Russell through Harry Belafonte, for whom Nicks had worked in the States and whom Russell knew through mutual friend, the songwriter Jack Segal. According to Max Harrison,[13] Russell did not collaborate closely with Nicks and, perhaps for that reason, the music works very much on its own terms. The ballet, called *The Net*, was televised by various European TV stations during 1968. As it happens, Russell's music had been used in a ballet before, in 1963, when the Warsaw Opera Ballet Company used the "Chromatic Universe" sections of *Jazz in the Space Age*.[14] *The Net* was, however, the only occasion when Russell wrote directly for the stage, as he explained to WKCR's Ben Young.

> That's the only experience I've ever had with doing music for ballet and I did the music... I mean, I had an idea of what the choreographer is wanting to bring out at certain places. *Othello*—it's pretty obvious that it's building up to a tension and the moods that it

insinuates are pretty easy to follow. So I made mood my chief aim in the various areas of it because I know what's going to go on in those areas. Whether it's Othello getting a bit antsy because the antagonist was putting ideas in his head about his wife—Iago. So the moods were implied and I like to include mood in all my writing.[15]

A further comment Russell makes in the interview in relation to *Othello Ballet* and other extended works is also instructive.

I write longer compositions because I consider a piece as a piece of theatre, really, and I think in terms of acts and events taking the listener on a trip down a ... telling a story. Furthermore, I automatically rebel against this sort of unwritten law with most media that if you want to be heard you stay within a six-minute boundary. I'm never going to conform. If I want to write something six minutes I will but I don't want to write it, so I'm trying to make the hit parade. So I feel like, as I said, that our music can represent music on a very high level and be a truly classical music and is in many instances, or was at least. Until this recent period when innovation became a bad word.[16]

He continued in the interview to stress that he is not suggesting that a profound piece of music cannot be written that is a few minutes long and popular, citing Ellington's "Sophisticated Lady" and Steely Dan's "Aja" as examples. He adds, "So that's a big challenge. But so is writing a forty-five minute work. Lots of people say that jazz composers can't write extended works. That made me mad."[17]

*Othello Ballet* comprises a series of events and is perhaps Russell's first work using this approach. Despite its diversity and the shortness of some episodes and their abrupt endings, the coherence of the work is maintained throughout. What is more, Russell uses the whole orchestra of twenty-three musicians to the fullest extent. The electronic instruments used—guitar, bass, organ, and possibly electric piano—add textures that could not be achieved any other way and create contrasts with the acoustic instruments. Garbarek is again the primary soloist. The *Othello Ballet* session took place barely twelve months after the recording of *Now and Then*. One presumes that the saxophonist's reading skills were still developing. Nevertheless, here his instrument fashions blocks and sheets of sound that offset the finer detail that emerges from the ensemble. *Othello* is a dark, often unsettling work, rich in emotion and mood.

When it was eventually released in the States, *DownBeat* gave *Othello Ballet* five stars, and the review's author wrote:

*Othello* is a ballet in every sense of the word. It is danceable, with rhythms and polyrhythms playing against each other. Rather than being programmatic, Russell lets the dancers tell the story. His music is pure music that will stand alone, devoid of any associations with Shakespeare's tragic hero.[18]

The author singled out Garbarek for praise, describing him as "a complete gas." He was also impressed with Russell's *Electronic Organ Sonata No. 1*, which completes the LP but saw it as the "work of a composer in transition," being Russell's first exercise within the form of electronic music. In fact, though the reviewer might not have known this, Russell had for some time been working on the tape that would be used within the context of *Electronic Sonata for Souls Loved by Nature.*

*Electronic Organ Sonata No. 1*, performed at Grorud Church in Oslo on October 1, 1968, is essentially an improvisation by Russell; it was recorded by Bjornar Andresen and Kåre Kolberg, both avant-garde composers in their own right. The recording was then taken into the electronic music studio of Radio Sweden, where engineer Gøte Nilsson worked with the tape. One hesitates to use the word "spontaneous" in this context, for Russell is clearly drawing heavily on the Lydian Concept here and there is a lingering influence of Stockhausen about the whole project. What emerges has a certain fugue-like quality. Ideas are developed and returned to by the composer and then explored in a different way. There is little sense of linear progress, as is the case with much electronic music but Russell creates an intense, controlled and mood-laden work. These qualities are clearly further enhanced through its treatment in the studio. If only Russell had pursued this approach rather than leave it ostensibly behind him in Scandinavia. He has continued to use electronics in his music; however, the creation of a solo performance that was then treated electronically is not an experiment he has repeated. That said, his brief dalliance with the form is vital and exciting and one could argue that *Electronic Organ Sonata No. 1* is the distilled essence of George Russell.

It is not entirely clear exactly when Terje Rypdal joined Russell but it was probably soon after the recording of *Othello Ballet*. As Rypdal remembers it, he was playing in a rock/jazz group called the Dream, with whom Garbarek had also played for a time.

> Then they asked me to join his new quartet. Arild had been in the military and George was having these courses on the Lydian Concept in Oslo. So I started with Jan. I was desperate to learn anything that was more serious about improvisation. I had been improvising long before. I almost got fired from one band for not playing the same solo every night. So the interest was there. So I took this course and it was very important. It was a case of how you wanted to use the course, in a way. There were all sorts of possibilities.
>
> Then we started Jan's quartet and I was asked to join his [George's] sextet. I got the old valve trombone part from some recordings and it was so difficult. *(laughs)* So I spent several months rehearsing and trying to learn it and it was probably one of the hardest things I have done [at] any time. We did quite a few gigs. A couple of gigs, like Prillarguri, were recorded. So it was a real learning period. It was extremely important. Later on he got into this freer stuff, *Electronic Sonata*, that was very interesting. I could use some of the older rock things in that. I liked that time very much.[19]

The first recording of *Electronic Sonata for Souls Loved by Nature—1968* was by Russell's sextet. The sense of temporal distortion is even more evident on this version than on its big-band sibling, recorded in 1970. With the blues-drenched playing of Garbarek and the way the electronic tape melds with and changes the group's performance, this is a genuinely spooky, otherworldly experience. These are the places that jazz-rock could have and should have gone – and certainly did so in Miles Davis mid-seventies recordings. It continues to surprise on repeated listenings. Yet the sense of continuity with Russell's early work remains. Russell has always liked to have the band drop out and leave the soloist alone. Here, not only does he do this to create dramatic tension or presage a change of mood or direction, but he uses the electronic tape to accompany and challenge the soloist. With bassist Red Mitchell maintaining a steady pulse, Rypdal's Hendrix-inspired guitar and Christensen's powerful drumming combine to make this record a tour de force. As the music moves in and out of time, it is a summation of the stop-start rhythms and tempo changes Russell has used throughout his career. Arguably, this music is further out than even Miles Davis's forays into jazz-rock at that time. But there are also straight-ahead passages with a solid groove that slip into spikey, almost Monk-like moments, with some fine blues piano from Russell. This version more than complements its big-band sibling; it also shows how the composition could be refashioned and refocused.

The whole performance is over fifty minutes long and is a fascinating and disorienting ride across the terrain of different world musics. It opens with an almost rock-soul groove underpinned by Mitchell and Christensen. Russell adds a simple ostinato pattern on piano. Then the horns – Garbarek and trumpeter Manfred Schoof – plus Rypdal play a melody line over the top that runs counter to the two different rhythms provided by Russell, and by Christensen and Mitchell. Throughout the electronic tape creates eerie, dislocating effects. The music then breaks up into a long rubato section that begins with just bass, drums and the tape. Horns and guitar join offering fragmentary comments and asides responding to the tape. Occasionally, one can identify the original source of a sound emanating from the tape – an organ or a cymbal – but the overall impression is of space and of sounds rising and falling. The next phase or event has a strong north African feel with Schoof playing freely over conflicting rhythms and against a unison melody line from Garbarek and Rypdal. This again dissolves as the tape again comes to the fore with the saxophone improvising in response along with Christensen's drums. It is only slowly that one realises that Red Mitchell's bowed bass rather than the tape is responsible for some of the strange noises one hears. Every time a more regular pulse starts to emerge, it is disrupted by the musicians and tape in combination. Russell simply refuses to let the music settle.

This effectively sets the structure of the piece – short pulse-driven sections, followed by sections were the musicians respond to the tape and rubato sections featuring the group with the tape backgrounded. En route the musical journey takes some unusual detours – Christensen duetting with African percussion, out-of-kilter blues and even passages with a Latin feel. Ironically, in this context, it is those shifts into more straight-ahead playing that seem most odd, as if one has become so immersed in this world to have lost all bearings. On the record, the musicians' contributions - whether soloing, shadowing or accompanying each other – seem indivisible from the whole. This is jazz as group music, as far away from soloist plus rhythm as one can imagine. Pianist Joe Zawinul once commented of Weather Report, "We never solo, we always solo."[20] Such a claim would have been at least as true of as at least as true of *Electronic Sonata for Souls Loved by Nature—1968*.

If Jan Garbarek is the most strikingly dramatic contributor to the big-band *Electronic Sonata*, recorded in 1970, the record also features some excellent Miles-ish trumpet from

American exile Stanton Davis. Rypdal is an absolute asset to the piece throughout and his main solo is quite stunning, while Jon Christensen and percussionist Sabu Martinez—echoing Chano Pozo—provide the music's heartbeat. Here the piece opens out into a massive outpouring of emotion that is truly exhilarating.

Both versions of *Electronic Sonata* came out in America quite a while after they were recorded, which lessened their impact. By that time Miles Davis had released both *In a Silent Way* and *Bitches Brew* and Weather Report's first album had also been issued. Trumpeter Stanton Davis recalls hearing Miles's *Bitches Brew* and speaking to Russell about it.

> So we've done *Electronic Sonata*, it wasn't released pre-Miles *Bitches Brew* but it was pre-Miles Davis *Bitches Brew*. George knew that the universe and the world were going in that direction. When *Bitches Brew* came out, I was like calling George and saying "George, they're doing our stuff." He said, "I know. Miles knows what's going on," and just laughed. [21]

Stanton Davis is quite correct. The timing of Russell's Scandinavian releases did little to advance his cause or status. *Othello Ballet* was made in 1967 and appeared three years later. The sextet *Electronic Sonata* was recorded in 1969 and released on record two years afterwards, while the big band version came out at least eighteen months after it was performed. Those in Scandinavia who heard his music might have known about Russell's ground-breaking work but the rest of the world had to wait. In the meantime, others such as Miles Davis, John McLaughlin, Herbie Hancock and Weather Report had claimed this space as their own.

To place *Electronic Sonata* further in its rightful context, Davis notes the range of music and musicians he came into contact with through Russell while in Norway and confirms the kinds of influences that Russell was exploring.

> A lot of musicians I met through George, like Don Cherry and composers who were living in Scandinavia, they were writing very experimental kinds of things, aleatory types of things similar to Ligeti and Klaus Egge, who was a composer from Norway. I got involved in all those types of classicism that I probably would never have been connected with just playing jazz. [22]

*Electronic Sonata* is a remarkably coherent piece that seems to embrace musical styles from across the planet and exemplifies Russell's command of a variety of musical idioms. One section draws on North African music, another on Afro-Cuban and Latin music and elements of the blues also surface. Russell's palette is the whole world, but now it seems to want to include deep space as well. If his *Get Down with It* double album, recorded between 1970 and 1974, was "Miles' first attempt to make Ellington dance with Stockhausen," *Electronic Sonata* was Russell's, and it is arguably one of the finest attempts to merge jazz and contemporary music influences. Here, the link is primarily to *Hymnen* and Stockhausen's use of recordings of different national anthems, then treated electronically. This is echoed, indeed more radically, with Russell's multi-layered tape of different world musics. Where Stockhausen's work on *Hymnen* seems to attempt to transcend nationalisms, Russell's integration of the taped sounds on *Electronica Sonata* offers a counter to Western-dominated assumptions about music and art. [23]

Russell is forced to integrate sources and influences. He and Miles Davis have been among the few in jazz to grasp the rhythmic potential of Stockhausen's ideas. It is not just the elisions and abrupt changes of rhythmic emphasis or the collision of different rhythms; these were in large measure already present in Russell's music. But from now on, there is a much greater sense of how these can be used by the composer to create whole new shapes, textures and rhythms within the music and yet still, as he put it years before, "*You can retain the funk.*" [24] It is that lesson he took from Stockhausen – and transformed for his own purposes.

The electronic tape Russell created in the Swedish Radio sound lab is never used just to colour the work; the musicians improvise with it and respond to it. For example, one of the most dramatic sections of the big-band *Electronic Sonata* occurs when the African drumming on the tape is joined by the two drummers, Jon Christensen and Egil Johansen, and percussionist Sabu Martinez. Elsewhere, Garbarek responds directly to the electronic sounds in his improvisation. The tape changes the musicians' contributions, just as a written line might. This in itself is a hugely interesting development. There is music made in real time and, with the tape, music already created at different points in time. In every sense, musical and philosophical, Russell is playing with time. If he chooses, he can change when the tape is used in the music and thereby change the composition and the way his musicians play it. Music from other times and places can be used to create a kind of temporal schism. A quote from Stockhausen from a 1972 lecture at the Oxford Union seems very apt here,

> New means change the method; new methods change the experience and new experiences change man. Whenever we hear the sounds we are changed: we are no longer the same after hearing certain sounds and this is the more the case when we hear organized sounds, sounds organized by another human being: music. [25]

At one point the band members chant, "You can learn to live another way. Go inside and you'll awake anew someday. You can really change the world if only you believe it." The text is derived from Russell's involvement with the ideas of G. I. Gurdjieff, the Russian mystic who had taught extensively in France and Western Europe. As noted, Russell had been introduced to "The Work" in Norway in 1966 and had joined a "circle" there led by American expatriate Brenda Tripp. Gurdjieff, and even more so his follower Maurice Nicoll, had certain ideas about time that in an age of quantum physics might now seem (slightly) less outlandish than might once have been the case, though theirs is the world of metaphysics and not science. Russell would use the title of one of Nicoll's books, *Living Time*, for his all his big bands from the seventies onwards. It is to these ideas that Russell is making specific reference and he is even illustrating them in the work itself by literally playing with time.

The tape also advances the composition and adds new levels of thematic coherence. This is incredibly complex music, but, on the big-band version, it is essayed by the orchestra with such skill, enthusiasm and ease that it swings and drives with both great passion and a sense of mystery. With towering performances from Russell's core sextet, this is one of his greatest works and one of the few completely successful extended works in jazz. What is more, it has surely one of the greatest finales in jazz.

It is well worth contrasting the two sextet albums, *Electronic Sonata for Souls Loved by Nature—1968* and *Trip to Prillarguri* from 1970. In some ways, *Prillarguri* is the least satisfying of all these records. Recorded live at Estrad in Sweden in March 1970, it featured what had become Russell's core group of Jan Garbarek, Terje Rypdal, Arild Andersen and Jon Christensen, along with the African-American trumpeter Stanton Davis. Its shortcomings lie not in the performances or material but in the impression of incompleteness it leaves. It feels as if the listener has walked into a club halfway into the performance and has to leave before the end, never quite able to make sense of the whole. That said, it features powerful playing from Garbarek on his own "Theme," in practice a "head" arrangement and Russell's "Souls," an extract from *Electronic Sonata*. With Russell's percussive piano in the background and some lovely guitar from Rypdal, these two tracks alone reveal what an exciting, visceral jazz-rock group this was—and what a pity it was that they did not record more together.

The performance then seems to lose some of its structure as it slips into a more abstract phase with Russell's "Event III" and Garbarek's "Vips." Again, the playing is fine—from the rhythm section and Garbarek, particularly so—and the rather retrospective, in this context, "Stratusphunk" has some very nice trumpet from Stanton Davis. Yet the dynamic built up by the first two numbers has been lost. The record recovers with Garbarek's loose, meandering "Esoteric Circle," with its Miles-inspired trumpet solo from Davis, before launching into a powerful take on Ornette Coleman's "Man in the Moon," with some bravura guitar from Rypdal.[26] Arild Andersen and Jon Christensen provide assured support throughout but, here, combining with Russell behind Rypdal they provide one of the record's high spots. But, again, the listener is left wanting more, as the track is phased out before the end. One suspects that it is a case that what worked effectively live just allows too many longueurs on record. *Prillarguri* remains an album with some fine moments but without a finale: a case of what might have been.

*Electronic Sonata for Souls Loved by Nature—1968* and *Trip to Prillarguri* certainly do give a sense of what the group was like live. Compared to Russell's earlier American bands, it was wilder, looser, and more spontaneous—occasionally guests like Don Cherry might sit in with the group. Russell continued to encourage his musicians to contribute to the band's book, just as he had with Dave Baker and Al Kiger. Perhaps the key difference, however, between this group and his earlier sextet lay in the use of electronic instruments and textures in the music. It is surprising that Russell himself did not use organ or Fender Rhodes in place of an acoustic piano but then he has always been unduly modest about his abilities as a performer. And if Russell rejected free playing and atonality in jazz as an end in itself, it seems that with his Scandinavian sextet he found ways of incorporating such elements into his music. Garbarek remains proud of the group's prowess as a live act.

Don Cherry was living in Scandinavia and, whenever he was around, if we played with George's big band or sextet, he would invite him on stage to play, which was a great boost as well. That was very free, what he did. We just opened up and let him go for as long as he wanted. Absolutely fantastic! Inspiring! So George was always open for leaving room for that sort of approach in his music. There was always room for anything there that he found valuable. It didn't have to be his own but it created yet another "strata", you might say.[27]

*Listen to the Silence* was recorded two years after Russell returned to the States to commence what proved to be a long teaching career at New England Conservatory. Its inspiration and commissioning lie within his Scandinavian period and, for these reasons, it should be considered within the context of the other recordings made in Sweden and Norway. Though this was not the only time Russell wrote for a choir, sadly, it was the only time his work in this area has been recorded and released. *Listen to the Silence* reveals a remarkable potential in this respect.

Commissioned by the Norwegian Cultural Fund for the 1971 Kongsberg Jazz Festival, *Listen to the Silence: A Mass For Our Time*, to give it its full title, was premiered on June 26 of that year. Not only had Russell composed and arranged the music, he had created the libretto, supplying both his own written material and also texts from Maurice Nicoll; Rainer Maria Rilke's *Duano Elegies*; Dee Brown's seminal lament for the Native American, *Bury My Heart at Wounded Knee*; and further texts from *Newsweek* and the *New York Times*. The orchestra comprised Russell's sextet from *Trip to Prillarguri*, plus Bjornar Andresen on Fender bass (who had helped with the recording of the electronic tape for *Electronic Organ Sonata*), Webster Lewis on organ, Bobo Stenson on electric piano and Russell himself on timpani. The work also featured the chorus of the Musikk Konservatoriet of Oslo and eight additional singers from New England Conservatory, including the exceptionally gifted Dan Windham as bass solo voice. It is his voice that adds both great pathos and gravitas to the text.

However, in a jazz context, Russell's work goes far beyond Ellington's *Black, Brown and Beige* and predates Anthony Davis's *X, The Life and Times of Malcolm X* by fifteen years and Wynton Marsalis' *Blood on the Fields* by twenty-two.[28] It shares with these works a certain didactic aspect. Russell's primary target is American imperialism and. in citing its treatment of the American Indian alongside its involvement in Vietnam, he draws parallels between American internal and external expansionism. Taken from a *Newsweek* review of Dee Brown's book, Russell quotes:

The motive force for our theft of land and identity from the Indians was Manifest Destiny—the belief that white men were ordained to rule this continent.

And later:

Manifest Destiny was a simple instrument to operate, once we got the hang of it.

The libretto also confronts the crimes against freedom perpetrated by communist regimes, with Russell singling out Soviet use of psychiatric labels and institutionalization as a means of silencing its critics. Russell had been due to play the International Jazz Festival in Prague in 1968. The festival was cancelled because the country was invaded by several of its "allies." Russell kept the letter he received from the organizers apologizing for the cancellation. Given the circumstances, in which it was written, it is a masterpiece of calm understatement and quiet optimism, something Russell would understand and appreciate. [29]

In his commentary, Russell's analysis is both trenchant and sophisticated, far more so than many artistic-political statements of the time. But Russell's didactic purposes with *Listen to the Silence* are not just political. He also seeks to address spiritual concerns. Here, his use of Maurice Nicoll's work *The Mark*, specifically in "Event IV," puts forward the concept of "Metanoia," or self-transformation through spiritual growth. Nicoll's book focuses on what he argues is the true message of the gospels and of Jesus Christ, namely, that it is about spiritual rebirth and the liberation of the unborn, latent person inside each of us. Nicoll's—and Russell's—message is that it is inside us that we can discover our essence. Halfway through this last section, a narrator quotes from *The Mark*,

> The inner teaching of Christ's teaching is not sentimental. It has nothing to do with comforting weak or useless people or in encouraging slave morality. The sentimental liberties taken in literature and art and poetry that have grown up around the teaching of Christ are merely an example of the complete misunderstanding of what this tremendous and ruthless teaching meant. Christ's teaching is about a possible individual evolution in a man. [30]

Here, Russell is contrasting human potential that can be found inside us with the cruelties and destructiveness of goal-seeking, exploitative behaviour.

Stanton Davis had a number of very valid musical points to make about *Listen to the Silence*, even if his other remarks perhaps exaggerate the threat posed to American foreign policy by the music.

> We did *Listen to the Silence*. What I really liked about it was that it had really classical and aleatory techniques of voice, which I thought was great, the chanting and all that. There was a political reason that it wasn't released because it had some anti-war statements in it and it was really a political message from that time. I guess coming up through the Vietnam War, I didn't think about it as being that serious, which is odd, but I guess some countries like the States, they stopped it so that record didn't come out too soon. When it did come out it opened up some doors about aleatory music again. [31]

Musically, Russell opts for quite a simple accompaniment for the voices at times. Sometimes, it is just percussion or Arild Andersen's bass. However, elsewhere the music is more complex. For example, in "Event I" a scored but free-sounding orchestra clashes with a chaos of voices. At times, some of the techniques that Russell uses recall Krysztof Penderecki's work, in particular *Threnody for the Victims of Hiroshima for 52 Stringed Instruments*, which, though scored for strings, creates highly vocalized effects. [32] Also, Penderecki's use of glissandi is mirrored in certain of the vocal techniques Russell uses, for example, the fade at the end of "Event II."

*Listen to the Silence* is best heard as a jazz oratorio. The piece, along with *Vertical Form VI* (1977), can be reasonably characterised as "third stream" works – an epithet perhaps unhelpfully attributed more widely to Russell's compositional output. It would seem to owe its conception, at least in part, to the work of Berio and Stockhausen. Its use of prose extracts from newspapers, books and like sources is not original to Russell—both Berio and Stockhausen used such material and, of course, the use of spoken text in music is found in the baroque, classical and modern eras. However, comparison of *Listen to the Silence* and Luciano Berio's *Sinfonia* (1968), a work making extensive use of sung and spoken texts, raises the significant possibility that the latter might have informed certain of Russell's compositional choices.

Firstly, there is the issue of timing. *Sinfonia* was first performed and recorded in 1968 in four movements with an additional, more expansive fifth movement premiered in Donaueschingen in 1969 and in New York in 1970. *Listen to the Silence* was written in 1970 and performed and recorded the following year. Secondly, in terms of length, Berio's piece lasts thirty-three minutes long through its five movements. Though, the four events of *Listen to the Silence* last forty-five minutes, the first three, which reveal the closest comparison with *Sinfonia*, are of a length similar to Berio's work. Russell's final event is quite different from the rest of his composition, structurally and stylistically.

Most important of all, however, are the parallels between the ways both composers structure their compositions, in the pacing of the first three movements of *Sinfonia* and of Russell's first three events and in the way that voices and instrumental accompaniment work together. The idea that Russell might have been influenced by Berio's *Sinfonia* does not in any way suggest copying on Russell's part or diminish the achievement but rather the intriguing possibility that he might have sought to use certain of the aleatory techniques applied by Berio but within a jazz context. Rather it would illustrate and confirm Russell's abilities as a composer.[33]

*Listen to the Silence* also features one of Russell's most popular themes that opens and is repeated across "Event IV" and he regularly used it to powerful effect in concert and recorded it on three other albums.[34] However, on this version, Stanton Davis's solo is one of the record's high points, revealing the trumpeter's wonderful grasp of the dramatic.

A comment from Bobo Stenson, who plays piano and keyboards on *Listen to the Silence*, is instructive and perhaps indicates why the Scandinavians took Russell so much to their hearts. Acknowledging Russell's influence on Scandinavian jazz, Stenson noted,

> He opened up a new way of writing music and he involved a lot of people. He stayed there. He was there for quite some time. He had a sextet and different bands they put together and leading these big groups. He was busy there. He meant a lot to a lot of people. Also with Palle Mikkelborg in Denmark, who was one of his favourites, I guess. He meant a lot, especially in Norway and Sweden, I would say.

He continued, referring specifically to *Listen to the Silence*,

> But that's what I'm saying. He opened up a new way of thinking and writing. When you write like that, I've always also been into classical music, and for me there was nothing

strange about that. I like those kind[s] of things. He was very strong in those days. He had also the American tradition in the background. He had those heavy rhythms and bluesy phrases that can come in. As you say, it's kind of a mixture.[35]

Here, Stenson suggests, with some justification, that it was the marriage of the blues and jazz, coupled with his respect for and understanding of European art music, that defined Russell's approach and his appeal for northern Europeans, especially at a time when musicians in Europe were increasingly looking to develop their own ways of playing jazz.

While *Listen to the Silence* is not a completely successful work—specifically, "Event III" seems over long and its didactic purpose takes over from aesthetic considerations—it is a highly unusual and significant work to come from a jazz composer. Its strengths lie in the sense of mystery and otherness that its elements—voices, orchestra, and text—create for the listener.

By this time, of course, Russell had returned to the United States and was living in Boston and teaching at New England Conservatory. Talking to Ian Carr in 1992, Russell explained that despite his strong and positive feelings toward Scandinavia and the people who had befriended him, by 1969 it had become time to go home. He had come to feel that Swedish society, though less than that of Norway, was an emotionally inexpressive one.

> Then this feeling of being in an isolated, you know, in a culture that was emotionally mute, coupled with what was going on in America and that was the kids like Alice [Russell's third wife] were coming up. They were protesting, you know. They were [protesting] and I think protesting about some very important things. Not just the Vietnam War but the way of life and the whole thing, you know. And, of course, many of them were not sincere, you know, because they ended up being on Wall Street and stuff and stockbrokers. But it seemed like a sincere movement—people going down South and the buses and things and America was looking at itself, having a good look at itself, you know.[36]

Russell had worked consistently in Scandinavia, more so than at any time in his career. His group had played festivals and gigs in northern Europe. He had recorded for radio stations and was fêted throughout the period he lived in Norway and Sweden. In an act of typical generosity, before he returned to America Russell helped Jan Garbarek record his first album with his own quartet, called *George Russell Presents The Esoteric Circle*. The title was obviously Russell's and is another reference to Gurdjieff. It is a marvellous debut, with impressive writing from Garbarek and playing from all four musicians—Rypdal, Andersen, Christensen and Garbarek himself. Russell's assistance in the recording, which was made sometime in 1969, went far beyond mentorship, as Garbarek remembers.

> It was a quartet album but George was kind enough to offer to pay for the recording expenses, which was done here at the museum of modern art. They have recording facilities. So he was sort of [the] behind-the-scenes guy there, financially. So we had this master tape, which I tried to sell to ECM Records, which I later joined. They turned that

down and said they would like to do their own recording. I think then George sold it to Flying Dutchman in the States. So George had no part in it in a musical sense. It was strictly our own material we were playing at time.[37]

The album was eventually released, as Garbarek correctly recalls, on the American Flying Dutchman label in 1971. Though Manfred Eicher of ECM did not take up the record—he has always had an executive preference for producing his artists himself—the futures of Garbarek, Rypdal, Andersen and Christensen with the label were assured. In fact, it was at one of the Russell sextet gigs in 1969 in Bologna that Eicher first heard the group and it was there that a series of very productive and creative partnerships were formed.

A comment about Russell's Scandinavia sojourn from Kåre Kolberg, the Norwegian composer who knew Russell well, is quite telling. As Kolberg pointed out, influence is often a two-way street.

To me, Scandinavian jazz and also Scandinavian contemporary music might have been important for him. It was absolutely important for us to meet him. I showed him what I had done and how I had made a system for one piece, and he said, "Well, it's okay, it's interesting, but it is as far from the Lydian Concept as it could come." It shows that he's open-minded and certainly not dogmatic. So he is [a] creative person and active and creative in finding new ways but he also has a very strong theoretical background. He's a very systematic person. This combination may be rather radical for jazz musicians and for serious composers.[38]

It was not just Russell's music that developed while he was in Scandinavia, but also his theoretical ideas. Quite when, where, and how these new ideas came into play is unclear. For example, in the 1959 edition of *The Lydian Chromatic Concept of Tonal Organization*, Russell refers to horizontal and vertical polymodality, but does not use the terms "vertical tonal gravity," "horizontal tonal gravity," or "supra-vertical tonal gravity." It seems that he began to use this new terminology early in his teaching career at NEC.[39]

It, therefore, likely that Russell also used his period in Scandinavia—and not least the teaching opportunities it provided—to refine his ideas in these respects. The other two important developments in his thinking concerns his concept of "vertical form" as an approach to composition. This will be discussed later at some length. Here it suffices to note that this was perhaps the final refinement in his oeuvre. The second development was philosophical or rather theosophical. Increasingly, Russell found in the ideas of Gurdjieff and Nicoll the spiritual underpinning of his music and of the Lydian Concept.[40] Far from being a holiday from the main action Stateside, Russell had used his years in Sweden and Norway to produce some important works but he had also revitalized and rejuvenated himself, his art and his intellectual curiosity.

## Notes

1. E-mail interview with Bosse Broberg, May 2007.
2. Ibid.
3. Interview with Palle Mikkelborg, June 2003.
4. Ibid.
5. Interview with Christensen.
6. Interview with Broberg.
7. Leonard Bernstein, *The Unanswered Question: Six Lectures at Harvard* (Cambridge, MA: Harvard University Press, 1976), pp. 421–22. I am indebted to Michael Tucker's *Jan Garbarek: Deep Song* for this insight and quote.
8. Interview with Garbarek.
9. Malcolm Ball, "Licht aus Stockhausen," *Avant* 5 (Winter 1998): 6–11.
10. Duncan Heining, "A Meeting with a Remarkable Man," *Avant* 7 (Summer 1998).
11. Roger Dean, *New Structures in Jazz and Improvised Music Since 1960*, (Milton Keynes: Open University Press.1992), pp.146-147.
12. For Edgar Varèse, *The Complete Works*, Decca CD 475 487–2.
13. Harrison, "Rational Anthems," pp. 19–21.
14. Ibid.
15. Young, broadcast devoted to George Russell.
16. Ibid.
17. Ibid.
18. J. Klee, *DownBeat*, April 29, 1971.
19. Interview with Rypdal.
20. John L. Walters, obituary for Joe Zawinul, *Guardian*, September 13, 2007. https://www.theguardian.com/news/2007/sep/13/guardianobituaries.jazz
21. Interview with Stanton Davis, June 2003.
22. Ibid.
23. R. Cook and B. Morton, *The Penguin Guide to Jazz on CD* (Harmondsworth, UK: Penguin, 2000), p. 380. Davis was introduced to Stockhausen's music by the British cellist, composer, and conductor Paul Buckmaster. See Ian Carr, *Miles Davis—The Definitive Biography* (Hammersmith, UK: HarperCollins, 1999), p. 304; also Miles Davis with Q. Troup, *Miles: The Autobiography* (London: MacMillan, 1989), p. 312.
24. D. Cerulli, B. Korall, and M. Nasatir, *The Jazz Word* (New York: Ballantine, 1960), p. 191.
25. Karlheinz Stockhausen, Lecture on Electronic Music, Oxford Union, May 6th, 1972.
26. This tune was actually released as a 45 rpm single by Impulse, for which label Ornette was recording at the time, no doubt to coincide with the first manned space flight to the moon. Strangely, it did not chart. Pop fans preferred David Bowie's Space Oddity.
27. Interview with Garbarek.
28. Various versions of the Ellington piece are available. For the Anthony Davis this is available as Gramavision R2–79470.
29. Letter from management of the 5th International Jazz Festival, Prague, September 1968.
30. Maurice Nicoll, *The Mark* (Utrecht: Eureka Editions, 1998), p.97.
31. Interview with S. Davis.
32. See D. J. Grout and C. V. Palisca, *A History of Western Music* (New York: Norton, 1996), pp. 751–53.
33. Luciano Berio, *Sinfonia/Eindrücke*, Erato 2292-45228-2.
34. George Russell and the Living Time Orchestra, The 80th Birthday Concert Concept; George Russell's Living Time Orchestra, The London Concert, Label Bleu LBLC 6527/8; George Russell—New York Big Band, Soul Note SN 1039.
35. Interview with Bobo Stenson, March 2007.

36. Carr, interview with G. Russell, June 1992.
37. Interview with Garbarek.
38. Ian Carr, interview with Kåre Kolberg for BBC Radio 3 broadcast *George Russell—The Invisible Guru*, July 1994.
39. These comments draw both on George Russell, *Lydian Chromatic Concept of Tonal Organization* (Brookline, MA: Concept, 2001) – see p. 197 and on George Russell, *The Lydian Chromatic Concept of Tonal Organization* (New York: Concept, 1959), See pp. xviii–xix in the 1959 edition.
40. The most obvious reference to the Fourth Way teachings of Gurdjieff, Ouspensky and Nicoll can be seen in the title of the 1972 LP with Bill Evans, Living Time. However, for explicit reference to such ideas see George Russell, *Lydian Chromatic Concept of Tonal Organization*, pp.235-237.

CHAPTER ELEVEN

# Living Time at New England Conservatory

Gunther Schuller had already played an important part in George Russell's early career. He had commissioned Russell to write a piece for the Brandeis concert and hired him to teach the Lydian Concept at the Lenox School of Jazz. He had also been a friend and source of support throughout the fifties and sixties. The part that he would now play was, if anything, even more significant because his offer of a post at New England Conservatory was to shape the rest of Russell's working life.

NEC, the oldest independent music school in the United States, was founded in 1867 by organist Eben Tourjée. Patterned on the European *conservatoire* model, the whole concept was quite revolutionary in America at that time and proved to be a significant success with budding classical musicians and singers. For many years, the school grew and thrived, seeing the building of its prestigious and elegant Jordan Hall in 1903 and its community ties develop through its connections with the Boston Symphony Orchestra and the promotion of low-cost concerts open to all. However, by the time Schuller took over as president of the conservatory in 1967, the school was facing major difficulties. In recent times, the school, once one of the top music colleges in North America, was in a state of financial and educational decline, as Schuller explained: "The enrolment, which is supposed to be around 250, was down to 75. This school was dying and, financially, they had something like $78,000 left in the till when I arrived. I mean, the sheriff was about to put the padlock on the door."[1] Schuller had no idea how bad things were when he took the job but set about transforming an institution mired in an earlier time and bringing it into the reality of the late twentieth century.

It took a couple of years to get a grant from the Ford Foundation—$2.5 million, which we had to match then—but what I did was revolutionize the whole curriculum and the first act of my presidency was to create the Jazz Department, in respect of which many on the board and the faculty were horrified, but I said to myself, there was no doubt in my mind, "1967? A major conservatory in the United States doesn't have a Jazz Department? The music that was created on this soil sixty, seventy years ago?" So to me, this was absolutely automatic that I would do that.[2]

Just as Schuller and John Lewis had fostered the whole notion of "jazz education" in America with the Lenox summer school, so his efforts bore fruit in terms of college-based degrees in jazz. Other conservatories and schools soon followed suit, though at the time, as Schuller noted, many music educators considered his decision little short of heresy. Schuller's connections in the jazz community were such that he was able to bring in some of the best and brightest minds in jazz and, although he left his post as president in 1977, his influence remains. Any school that can number among its staff over the years musicians of the calibre of Russell; pianist Jaki Byard; bassists Miroslav Vitous and Dave Holland; trombonist/arranger Bob Brookmeyer; saxophonists Jimmy Giuffre, Joe Maneri, Joe Allard and Steve Lacy; and composer/pianist Ran Blake can be remarkably proud. But Schuller went even further by reaching out to the poorer, socially disadvantaged areas of Boston through offers of scholarships to pupils of ability.

[T]he other thing I did was I went personally into the black communities here—Roxbury and Dorchester—and brought kids from there, who felt that the NEC was some white establishment they could never get into and they weren't welcome there. I went there and reached out and brought them in.[3]

Additionally, Schuller soon established the Third Stream Department (now the Contemporary Improvisation Faculty), created the Ragtime Ensemble, the Duke Ellington Orchestra, a swing band, a country fiddle orchestra and even a Klezmer ensemble. NEC became a school that offered a fully rounded musical experience to its students with a curriculum that celebrated American music in its diverse forms.

But first Schuller needed a major jazz composer for his new department. There were two choices for Schuller. As he told Ian Carr in 1992, one of these was Charles Mingus. However, "Charles was still so busy playing bass and traveling around. George had more or less given up playing—he played the piano occasionally—but mostly he was composing, so that seemed to me the ideal choice."[4]

Russell not only offered his abilities as a composer and arranger; he was also jazz's leading—possibly only—theoretician and had led his own bands.

George was the one who was already composing in these new directions, and the uniqueness of George is that he then was able to formulate that into a theoretical concept which can be used both in a practical way as a way of performing and improvising but also as an intellectual concept. To this moment, I think he's the only one who's achieved that.[5]

As Schuller also pointed out to Ian Carr in 1992, the breadth and scale of Russell's work was hugely impressive and, perhaps, unique in jazz.

> He is one of the few composers who has managed and dared to write an hour-long ballet or some things that are almost like operas, gigantic suites that go beyond anything that Ellington did. So I admire him very much for taking up that particular cudgel, because that, to me, is still the one area where jazz has, by and large, not gone very far—in the extended form.[6]

Asked how Russell fit in to the school, Schuller's comments tell us a lot about his own iconoclastic nature.

> He was famous enough as a composer and a performer and a theoretician that he was, I would have to say, he was rather readily accepted, except by some old diehards who thought this was pure heresy. They began with the idea that jazz shouldn't be allowed in the school. When I got here, the saxophone was not allowed as an instrument to be taught here—and I'm not even talking about jazz saxophone, even classical saxophone. That's how hostile it was.[7]

With regard to how student's received Russell as a teacher, Schuller acknowledged that some found his classes a challenge.

> [I]t's true that some people went to his classes expecting to learn some kind of easy, tricky way to learn how to improvise or something like that, to get some kind of a formula for their careers, which of course is not the idea at all. They were disappointed and they couldn't connect up with George's way of presenting this material. This is a musical concept and what it does, it puts into formal verbal intelligent, intellectual forms what is already happening, was already happening in jazz.[8]

As Marit Jerstad told Ian Carr, Schuller's offer was extremely important for Russell as an affirmation of his achievements.

> George has always wanted to do everything himself—print it himself and distribute it. He felt very antagonistic toward big institutions—record companies and all that. All his life he's had a problematic relationship with the establishment. It was very important to him when he got the offer to be a teacher at New England Conservatory. It meant a lot to him and he's an excellent teacher because he has such a deep knowledge of music.[9]

Jerstad's assessment of Russell's abilities as a teacher is a fair one. However, no one who knew Russell well—or indeed at all—would have described him as an easy man. He had high expectations and standards and suffered those he saw as fools with difficulty. However open he was to new ideas or the suggestions and contributions of others, he could be stubborn once set on a course of action and would remain resolute about what he felt he had to offer, to the point of intractability. What you saw, with Russell, was what you got and that could be hard on those struggling with those aspects of his character.

Carl Atkins, who conducted the orchestras for two albums Russell worked on—*Living Time* with Bill Evans and *Vertical Form VI*—was chair of the Jazz Department for several years during Russell's long tenure. Atkins, Jaki Byard and Russell took turns teaching the school's large ensemble. Whereas Atkins and Byard did their own and music by other composers, Russell had his own way of doing things.

> George would only do his music. So I said to George one time, "You know you've had such a wonderful experience with this music and you've known Dizzy and you've known Bird, you've known all of these people, it would be great if the kids could hear and could experience some other music with you, with the years of knowledge you've had about this music in general." His answer was pretty straightforward: "I don't do anybody else's music." That was the end of that conversation. [10]

Russell's tendency to concentrate on "his stuff" created another difficulty for the administration, as Atkins noted. It meant that, by year three, some students in his classes were finding the learning experience somewhat repetitive.

> Well, by the third year, George is starting to recycle stuff. So then you kind of have to say that this kid now has gone through that experience and you got to find another place for the kid. So it makes it a little bit of a logistic problem. You sort of generally only recycle freshmen and sophomores and first-year graduate students but George wouldn't bend. [11]

As far as the petty political squabbles that went on in NEC, Russell largely avoided these. According to Atkins, he and Schuller took turns to act as a "buffer to keep George from having to deal with a lot of that." There were also comments about Russell's sometimes non-politically correct language.

> I heard stories when I came back here about how some of the bands had women in them who didn't like playing for George because George used language that sometimes certainly sounded misogynistic or didn't sound at least PC. One of his favourite sayings used to be, in the days when we had the band, was "Let's play the bitch." And he would say that to the kids. He'd say, "Let's play this bitch." Then there'd be a girl trumpet player standing there and she'd kind of take umbrage at the use of the word "bitch." George didn't mean anything by it. That ain't George. He's old-school on a lot of levels but that's not him. [12]

Among the many students Russell has taught and affected at NEC are musicians like Don Byron, Bill Urmson, Pat Hollenbeck, Marty Ehrlich, John Medeski, Ricky Ford, Marc Rossi, Andy Wasserman, Satoko Fujii, James Falzone, Gregory Burk and Ben Schwendener, who now teaches the Lydian Concept at the conservatory. Their comments are both intriguing and insightful.

Ingrid Monson, trumpeter and now Quincy Jones Professor of African-American Music at Harvard, was a student at NEC and became a personal friend of George and Alice Russell. Her comments suggest a balanced assessment of Russell as a teacher.

It wasn't that people wanted to avoid the classes. They wanted to be a part of it but they were afraid of being humiliated and they were afraid of having George point to them to solo and have him say something negative. [13]

Ironically, as one of the few female students, Monson felt she could stand outside that "kind of competitive thing among the guys".

[T]hey probably just didn't take me seriously at all. *(laughs)* So they were much more sensitive about whether they got called on to solo or corrected by George than I was. I figured I was going to take whatever criticism he has to say and I found that he didn't have that much to say that was critical. [14]

Monson also remarked on Russell's use of language.

I recall when he taught the course that he would sometimes say something off-colour about sex or something like that, that would make some people uncomfortable. It wasn't like he cursed a lot. I remember one time—and I just have to laugh thinking back on this—but we were sitting in the Lydian Chromatic Concept course and somehow he was talking about male and female principles, yin and yang, some Chinese stuff, active and submissive, and the women in the class, of course, we weren't buying this. [15]

On another occasion, Russell made a comment about *Hustler* magazine that shocked some of the students.

[I]t was all part of George as this image of perhaps a rakish, sexually intimidating person perhaps. I think that it was kind of student lore. It's not like George did anything. It's like people are like nineteen, twenty years old. They're not real together with who they are in this dimension and I never found anything he did . . . let me say that I had far more sexist experiences at the conservatory than from George. George was not real bad on that score in my opinion. [16]

As she got to know Russell as a friend later on, Monson came to see this as "a kind of persona, of an exterior," that contrasted with the Russell she got to know as "a very sensitive guy, very thoughtful, warm."

I look back and I think about some of the discourse of that, and there was this extra nervousness about it was way beyond what was real, in my opinion. So he talked about maybe going out some times and maybe drinking too much or something. Big deal. [17]

Bill Urmson, who played bass guitar with Russell's Living Time Orchestra, confirmed that Russell demanded high standards. "He definitely gave us the message that what was happening in New York was the standard. He was really proud of his time in New York and he taught us a lot about how the New York standard was a very high ideal at the time." As he added, "He definitely instilled that into us." [18]

Urmson appreciated and valued his studies with Russell, noting that it was clear in all his courses that the students were there to study the Concept and he was there to teach it. Not all students were comfortable with his approach, as Urmson explained.

> At the time there were some issues—some students really felt that they wanted more of a personal touch with him. They wanted him to be more interested in what they were doing. But George was definitely there to explain his story and, if you were interested in that, it was a good situation. If you weren't, then you wouldn't get much out of the situation. [19]

That Russell could also be quite dogmatic and that his expectations could appear to be paradoxical if not downright contradictory for some of his students, is evident from a story pianist Fred Hersch provided.

> Certainly, we sort of came to blows over *All About Rosie*, where I deliberately did not listen to the original recording with its famous unaccompanied four choruses by Bill Evans. Because I didn't want to play it the same way. He got annoyed that I hadn't listened to the recording and that I wasn't playing that way, and I mouthed off. I said, "You want Bill Evans? Call him. I'm supposed to be here as a creative jazz musician. Here are the chord changes. I'm going to interpret them the way that I interpret them and I would think that you would encourage me, as someone who talks a lot about freedom in music, to interpret them in a personal way." He didn't want to hear that. He got very angry. [20]

At the same time, Hersch added that he "sure enjoyed playing that music." Russell was, and remains, in his opinion, "a really significant composer." [21]

Ricky Ford was one of the few students who failed Russell's Lydian Concept class at NEC.

> He told me that I was the only guy he ever flunked but I still worked with him. In '78 I made a CD with him. I did a few more gigs with him here and there. Even though that happened, I always think about what he taught. [22]

Ford realised that he was not at that point ready to deal with that degree of theoretical complexity and he readily accepted Russell's assessment. "And George, I felt, was more advanced for what I was trying to do at the time," he told me.

However, with maturity and more experience behind him, Ford discovered that he had gained more from Russell's class than he had believed at the time.

> Now, in retrospect, we can balance these things out and sit back and intellectualise what we are doing as well introject our creative functions also. But as I said, a lot of things that he taught me at that time really stay with you throughout your career. It's more of a subliminal thing. [23]

Moreover, Ford was able to give a very specific example of his own application of Russell's teaching.

In 1999, I wrote a blues that used two chords, it used Dm and Aflat7. And no-one has ever done that in Jazz before just to do a blues using those two chords . . . I really thought about George when I wrote that blues, it's called "Blues Work" and it's on an album of mine called *[balaena]* and features George Cables, Ed Thigpen and Cecil McBee. He was dealing with the Lydian scale and we never did touch on minor and the relationship to the Flat 5 and minor as a tonal function, chordal function. So, I felt really good to have discovered this little thing that you could put in the blues. Some of it is George's influence but the other part is my persistence to explore it musically. [24]

The clarinettist and composer Don Byron who was also one of Russell's students, remains a supporter of Russell and acknowledges his own debt to him as a teacher in various ways. He made two points, however, that reflected how students in general, but in particular African-American students, might have experienced Russell's classes.

I couldn't say that I enjoyed the big class so much. There were a lot of other people around. I always felt that George was a little uncomfortable in front of the class. He was always kind of trying to prove things were right. There was a lot of pressure to answer a question exactly the way that he wanted a question answered. It was a bit like playing *Jeopardy* . . . . It was kind of a feeling in the class of being on edge and being tested. It was not the greatest feeling. After I took it for a while, I wanted to interact with him in a different setting. [25]

The second-year class was much smaller, more intimate and clearly more comfortable, as Byron noted.

It was different, because if you brought something in you could really get a sense of how he listened through the system that he'd devised, how he actually heard things. It was always interesting. At the time I saw him as someone who was a little cut off from developments that were happening. If you were interested in something and you brought that in he'd have some kind of analysis for that too, that would be surprising. [26]

As an African-American student at the conservatory, Byron recalled that "the atmosphere at the school—it wasn't very Afrocentric. There was about half a dozen of us black students who would be in the position to take his class at any one time and he was the only person for a period that we could look up to." [27] Now a teacher himself, Byron's perspective has changed somewhat. Yet there was still a sense that his own contact with Russell was lacking for him at a personal level and, perhaps, was more one-sided than he would have hoped.

You know, he was the only black teacher at New England Conservatory a lot of the time that I was there. He was certainly the only black teacher in the Jazz Department or Third Stream. That's always incredible to me but it happens a lot in academic settings. As a teacher now, I can see that when that happens and there are students of colour around, they kind of look up to you in this kind of puppy-dog way. You try not to show too much favouritism in public. Yet you want them to do well but you kind of get like "this is your bag/this is your stuff," and there's always this feeling that you should be better at it because you're black. You don't want to show favouritism. You're teaching for everybody. At the time I really didn't like him for it. Now I can see what the difficulty of the position is with my students. [28]

The pupil-teacher relationship, even in adult education, can be an ambiguous one that can reawaken childhood anxieties. We rarely experience our teachers until much later as fully-rounded human beings with human flaws as well as human virtues. A good teacher can help us reach our goals. A bad teacher will leave us despairing of our own inadequacy. The problem is that the teacher who is "good" for one student may not be so marvellous for another. As Bill Urmson noted, "I think George sizes you up pretty quick." He added that Russell wanted to hear his music played well by the students and, as a result, "if a student was really having a tough time I think it might not have been the most comfortable thing for the student. It may not have been a great thing for them to be there until they had it more together and could take on the challenge."
He continued,

I've seen him be confrontational but I've also seen him be very supportive. For me, he was very supportive in the beginning. I wasn't a virtuoso or anything but I learned his music. I did the homework and I paid attention to it, so I didn't have any real confrontations in that sense. I think he was probably right in the middle. I could see him go both ways. [29]

He added that Russell demanded a high level of commitment.

He's sending a message that there's a very high level out there. I remember my first concert with him, he dedicated it to the level of excellence that John Coltrane had achieved. He was really trying to send the message that it was a serious business and we should be shooting for a higher level and not settle for the mediocrity that we see in the modern music around us every day. [30]

The woodwind virtuoso and multi-instrumentalist Marty Ehrlich remembered getting on well with Russell and recalled his enthusiasm.

He was passionate about the Concept. It intrigued me from the start as a way to start getting a handle on the materials of music, one that I could readily use. There seemed to always be a student or two who wanted to argue with George about how the Concept would help them play jazz. I think that they wanted to learn a style and the Concept doesn't teach a style, it teaches possibilities. Often though, George would take these arguments pretty personally. [31]

And the brilliant Japanese composer/pianist Satoko Fujii valued the sense she got from Russell of her own potential.

I have learned I can do anything I want. There is nothing that we cannot do when we compose. He showed [how] to analyze all pieces we compose by Lydian Concept and this means we can do anything but we are still in a law of the cosmos. I was so released from everything by this class. Some other theory has many rules that we cannot do and [the] more we study [the] more we get the things we cannot do. But his concept is opposite. I felt good to try something I want to do. This idea help me a lot to be a musician including my big band writing. [32]

Ehrlich recalled one other incident that illustrated for him a rather unique perspective and an unusual lesson.

For some reason, George had sat in on the Afro-American Music History class taught by Carl Atkins. On that day, Carl does an interesting listening example. He plays two versions of "Amazing Grace" both sung in rural churches from the South, one black and one white. The white church is singing in what is called shape note singing. Carl asks us to define the difference. Students are descriptive but not much more. Finally, George joins in and says emphatically, "The Blues Scale! The Black singers are using the Blues Scale!" Then Carl reads from the liner notes for the white shape note singers, how one listener, surely of a different class, called their singing "similar to the braying of asses." George gets clearly upset and says in no uncertain terms to us, "This is ethnocentrism of the worst order." It was a defining artistic/moral lesson for me. [33]

Pianist/composer John Medeski was one student who clearly enjoyed Russell's classes and who responded positively to his exacting standards.

He was really funny. He had lots of stories. He was a character, very feisty. I loved it. He had no problem breaking the balls of the students, which he did a lot. Look at the people he played with and worked with and the kinds of bands he had and records he made, then be at a school with these little punks? He definitely reminded us that we were punks. That was one of the things I loved about his big band [class]. It was hilarious to see him. He also knew how to rehearse a band—but the drummers! I felt so sorry for every drummer that ever played with him because he was just brutal. That's how and what I learned from George. It was like picking up on his whole spirit, really respecting what he did and where he came from, and trying to just absorb everything I could from him. [34]

As Schuller, Urmson, Ehrlich and Medeski suggest, Russell's influence came both through his theoretical ideas and also through the sense that his students had of him as a musician and embodiment of jazz history. Another former student, clarinettist James Falzone, noted, "I think anyone at NEC came under George's influence, you know, even if not a direct student. His concepts float through there quite strongly." [35] And pianist Greg Burk commented in similar fashion:

George Russell the man certainly had as much if not more of an impact on me than the LCC. That is not to say that the Concept did not profoundly change the way I looked at harmony, melody and rhythm (and their inter-relationships). Through the four semesters of classes I had with George and the year of Big Band, I came to understand something fundamental about being a jazz musician. It is the depth of relationship between the creator and his creation or the musician and his material in this case, that makes a master musician. [36]

And he added, "This kind of commitment was very inspiring to me as a student. George reminds me, in some ways, of a benevolent gunslinger from the old west, prepared to defend his territory, for which he has fought and rightfully owns." [37]

Russell had, after all, known Bird, Diz, Miles, Trane, Bill Evans, Dolphy and Mingus. Some students may have found him intimidating, but others clearly gained a great deal from him.

A comment from bassist/composer Dave Holland, who taught at the school for a time when Russell was there and who is still a visiting lecturer, gave credit to both Russell's and Schuller's achievements there.

He's done something which a lot of musicians aspire to, which is create a world of his own within the music. He defines it in his own way and so on and he brought that idea into the school. One of the great things about New England Conservatory is that it's not a totally integrated curriculum where everybody's marching to the same step. It's a very independent attitude there, where each person that teaches there is given very much their own freedom to pursue their approach, so you get a wide diversity of concepts being presented within the program. Along with the normal staple kind of issues that need to be considered—of rhythm, harmony, and arranging and things like that, which are ongoing aspects of the program—the individual teachers are very much left to pursue their own method of teaching and their own concepts with the students that study with them and I think that's a very good thing. [38]

If Russell avoided the political game-playing of the school, he was nevertheless active as a teacher and in its program of concerts and events. Like all music schools, NEC encourages its staff and students to give regular performances, many of which take place in Jordan Hall. Many of these performances have been recorded and can be heard in the school's sound archive. Perhaps the most significant of these concerts was *Time Line*, which Russell created and curated in 1992 to celebrate 125 years of the conservatory.

This huge three-hour collage was a musical depiction of American and world history from the Civil War through two world wars, economic depression, civil rights struggles and anti-Vietnam protests. It took in Russell's own *Listen to the Silence*, *American Trilogy* (which was commissioned by the Glasgow Jazz Festival in 1990 and involved rearrangements of "Battle Hymn of the Republic," "You Are My Sunshine," and "Ballad of Hix Blewitt"), "Stratusphunk," *All About Rosie*, "Ezz-Thetic," and a new work, *Dialogue with Ornette*. To this were added American popular songs, jazz standards and various classical music pieces, along with carefully chosen narrative sections.

*Dialogue with Ornette* requires some elaboration. It came from a tape that Russell had made with Coleman in his apartment in New York in the sixties, just after the saxophonist had bought his first violin. Much later, Russell decided to use elements from the music they played together to produce a piece based on their improvised dialogue. It became both a small ensemble work and, orchestrated brilliantly by arranger and musician Pat Hollenbeck, a symphonic work.

Featuring at various times a full symphony orchestra and chorus, a big band and Klezmer ensemble, Russell layers *Time Line* with one piece fading into another, sometimes even using several pieces simultaneously. For example, one section involved three flautists: one improvising, another playing Ravel's *Bolero* and a third Varèse's *Density 21.5*.[39] It may sound like a mess but in Russell's hands the approach works. It is intriguing given earlier comments regarding Joseph Russell's piano playing that Russell also used Charles Ives's "Country Band March." (See pp 35-36) Ives wrote the composition in recollection of his bandmaster father, who would have two or more marching bands playing different tunes parade around their hometown, to then emerge in the town square because he liked the cacophony this would create.[40] Russell also included works by Stockhausen and Cage (both fellow collagists) and drew upon Debussy's *Fêtes* (a composition that had Russell had used upon early in his career while writing and arranging for Earl Hines), Schoenberg's *Pierrot Lunaire* and Stravinsky's *Le Sacré Du Printemps*, all works that had affected and influenced him. Add to these "Ol' Man River," with its civil rights associations with activist Paul Robeson, an African drum section, "Milestones" (his friend Miles Davis's first application of Russell's ideas), Monk's "'Round Midnight" and a recording of the King Oliver Band and the impression is that Russell is presenting the audience with a history of his own musical development. Even Penderecki's *Threnody* does not surprise, as it is suggested anyway by *Listen to the Silence*.

Over the concert's three hours, the performers and audience seemed to have a ball. It was truly a marvellous celebration of history and of music.[41]

Schuller had recruited Russell as a working composer/musician and it was accepted that his career would continue alongside his teaching commitments. Of course, recordings and concert tours by faculty members serve to enhance the conservatory's reputation and attract new students. Russell continued to play in Scandinavia and elsewhere in Europe and, though performance opportunities became less common in the United States, his sextet performed at the prestigious Tanglewood concert series in the Berkshire Mountains in 1970, an appearance that was probably due to Schuller's support. Stanton Davis recalled that they had had problems there that contrasted with their experiences elsewhere.

> We'd just done a great concert and got back to New York and then went to Tanglewood and they didn't have the right equipment. They didn't have speakers big enough for *Electronic Sonata*. The guy who was talking to the engineer, he said, "Well, I don't really like this music anyway." So George was furious but it was that kind of ignorance really.[42]

By contrast, two things happened in 1971–72 that had the potential to give a focus to Russell's profile in his home country. First, he received a Guggenheim Fellowship. Second, his old friend Bill Evans commissioned him to write an album-long suite for his second record for his new label, Columbia. The John Simon Guggenheim Memorial

Foundation paid Russell a grant for $10,000 for "music composition" for twelve months from April 1972. In the same period, he also received a similar award from the National Endowment for the Arts. Unsurprisingly, asked why he had returned stateside, Russell told Ken Linden in a 1969 interview for *Jazz & Pop* magazine that with these two awards, "I felt like they finally said, 'Yes, George come on back.'" [43]

According to Evans's biographer, Peter Pettinger, signing with Columbia was, for Evans, "a childhood dream come true." [44] Clive Davis, the company's president, seemed keen to give the pianist every opportunity to explore new directions. As Davis told *DownBeat*, "Bill Evans—how do you get him out of what he's doing for the last few years and say, 'use your genius and start communicating to new audiences, get into exciting areas, use other instrumentation, bring your musical ideas to new people?' If the artist is not interested in doing that, then I'm not interested in having that artist record for us." [45] Evans' first album for Columbia, *The Bill Evans Album*, was a fairly straightforward trio set, though its troubled background and birth are detailed well by both Pettinger and Keith Shadwick. [46] Evans's second—and it turned out, final—record for Columbia was to be everything Davis claimed he wanted - and more. This was, after all, now the label of electric Miles Davis, John McLaughlin, Weather Report and Ornette Coleman.

Brian Hennessey, a friend of Evans and keeper of the Bill Evans Archive, questioned whether the pianist actually initiated the recording of *Living Time*. Instead, he suggested the pressure came from the Columbia hierarchy. If Hennessey is right, then the company's handling of the album and its treatment of Evans' and Russell's work is all the worse.

> I don't think he initiated it. *(laughs)* I don't think so. It was part of the pressure of trying to do something different rather than just carry on with a trio or even solo but he'd been all through that. Solo, duo, trio, quintet and he also needed the payments from the record companies, especially the down payments. So I don't think he really instigated that. I don't even think George did either. [47]

According to Hennessey's impression, Evans was not "particularly enamoured with it."

> I mean, he'd always be respectful of it, how much he respected the musicians that were on it and the composer and all that sort of thing. He wouldn't say anything about how terrible it was. But he would dismiss it fairly quickly and get on with the next thing. [48]

Comments from Evans' drummer Marty Morell from a 2005 interview would seem to echo Hennessey's view. Morell is scathing regarding the music and its whole conception. He was of the opinion that Russell had already written the piece prior to Evans' commissioning, merely using "the opportunity to have his already- written composition recorded."

He continued, "[A]nd I don't believe that he really had the trio in mind for it at all. In my opinion, it's evident when you listen to it. That is, if you can get through it all! Eddie and I - and even Bill -- kept looking at each other during the date with confused expressions as if to say "what is going on?" [49]

It is unclear now whether Russell already had some material written that he could utilise for the project. This may even be likely. However, both Morell and Hennessey seem to have reached their conclusions by inference rather than evidence.

Set against their impressions, we must consider first of all Evans' and Russell's own comments in a two-part interview with arranger Sy Johnson for *Changes* magazine before the release of the record. [50] According to that article, Evans and Russell had spoken while Evans was doing some New York dates in 1971 about the possibility of doing a project together. Then Evans talked further with Columbia sales executives and was given the go-ahead for the project. Secondly, the sleevenotes are by Evans producer and Riverside Records founder Orrin Keepnews. Keepnews quotes both Evans and Russell on the project's origins, as follows,

> Bill asked him [Russell], but there was no immediate response. As Evans (who, incidentally, is one of the world's great unrecognized deadpan comics) insisted to me: "I figured he must have thought I wanted straight romantic backgrounds for twelve standard tunes, that he didn't want to have to turn me down – but if he didn't answer I'd just go away." George admits he did hesitate, but for rather different reasons. "Bill and I are both involved with modal music, but we have sort of gone off at right angles from each other over the years. Bill is more into tonal playing. I haven't stayed there; I've been working in extensions, the outer reaches of modal things. But I love and respect Bill's playing so much that I really couldn't resist the challenge. As I saw it, the task would be to create a mode that enhanced his work without inhibiting my own." [51]

Later in the notes, Keepnews also quotes Russell regarding what he saw as the "strength of this musical union" – "neither of us is capable of even considering making 'compromises' – or of expecting compromises from the other." [52] The implication of Morell's and Hennessey's comments is just the opposite, namely that Evans was, in fact, willing to compromise.

Thirdly, neither of Evans' biographers, Keith Shadwick and Peter Pettinger, offer even the slightest hint that Evans was an unwilling participant or that his dissatisfactions focused on the recorded outcome. His later comments on the matter address his treatment at the hands of Columbia Records and its boss, Clive Davis. [53] Indeed, Evans was to perform the piece with Russell conducting largely the same orchestra at Carnegie Hall in 1974. It seem unlikely, therefore, that he was so dissatisfied with the result. Finally, as will be seen from Carl Atkins remarks, Evans was an active participant throughout including with the "mix-downs."

Either way, it was to be a major undertaking—Russell planned a suite comprising eight movements or events featuring an enormous jazz orchestra. The band contained some of the finest musicians in America. As well as Evans's current trio of Eddie Gomez on bass and Marty Morrell on drums, the ensemble featured other rhythm players, with drums, percussion, guitar, electric bass and two electronic keyboards alongside a full horn section. Tony Williams played drums, while Ron Carter and Stanley Clarke featured on Fender bass on several events. The woodwind section included Howard Johnson, Jimmy Giuffre, Joe Henderson and Sam Rivers. Dave Baker, with a brief respite from the jaw problems that had brought a premature end to that aspect of his career, was in the trombone section with Garnett Brown and Dave Bargeron (then with Blood, Sweat & Tears) and Snooky Young, Richard Williams, Ernie Royal and Stanton Davis were on trumpet. With Evans playing Fender Rhodes and acoustic piano, this should, by any standard, have been one of the greatest jazz summit meetings of the seventies.

What exactly went wrong is now unclear but to quote Keith Shadwick, "If any major jazz album of the past 30 years or so needs a sympathetic remix, then this is the leading candidate." [54] Dave Bargeron, who continued to work with Russell in the Living Time Orchestra, remembered that it was a truly ground-breaking experience but one that was very challenging for all involved.

> As a jazz project and as a project to be done in a recording studio, this was revolutionary in the fact that there was George with essentially a double orchestra, two rhythm sections, Bill Evans as featured pianist and this music organized in such a way that none of us had ever seen before and the pieces separated into events with Roman numerals, subset of that, areas, subset of that, ABC within the areas. And coordinating all of these various functions for the very first time, George developing a technique of conducting this way, random events that would last a time span rather than a certain amount of measures. He had a little stopwatch with him or he had an assistant timing a section for him. It was an unbelievable experience, you know. It was a total immersion in George's genius from the get[-go]. And there I was and I enjoyed it so much. *(laughs)* [55]

And Bargeron added, "It was so memorable, and the band we travel with now is called the Living Time Orchestra. I think I'm the only one that was involved on that first record from which the band's name comes from." [56]

According to Carl Atkins, Russell had decided to use his concept of vertical forms for the recording and the musicians in the orchestra were struggling to understand his aims and expectations. As a result, he got a call to come to New York right away.

> They had had a session with George's music and it wasn't going very well. The musicians just didn't know quite what to make of all these cards that George was holding up with Roman numerals on it and cycles here and cycles there.
>
> And it was an unusual mix of players.
>
> He had [..] veteran players and younger players and players who were out of a traditional playing bag and players like Sam Rivers, who were out of a more modern bag. So it was a real funny mixture of players and so evidently they weren't taking to the music very well. They just didn't understand how to make it happen. I had done some things with George here [at NEC] with the school bands. I guess he remembered that we made some of those things work. So he asked me to come down and try to make this work. That's how I got the call. Then we did it and in two more sessions we put that album together. [57]

Atkins took on the role of conductor and this enabled the session to be completed successfully. Atkins remembers that after that the only difficulty they had with the recording process concerned getting the musicians back from their breaks to continue the session. It was like herding cats of a different kind!

> So I asked Tony Williams if he had a whistle, a police whistle, in his kit. He said, "Yeah, I got one." I said, "Let me have it." I said, "What I'm going to do from now on, is I'm going to go outside the studio door on the street and I'm going to blow this whistle and wherever these cats are they'll hear the whistle." And that was the running joke. I'd go outside and blow the whistle and they'd come from all manner of places doing whatever they were doing. [58]

Atkins said that Evans was fully involved throughout.

> As we did the mix-downs, for example, he was very much involved in that and had some very good things to say about our ideas and what I remember too after that was that he was very kind to me and had some very kind things to say about the things that we did and about a week after the session he sent me a beautiful leather briefcase with just a little note in it, saying, "Thanks, Bill." I've still got the briefcase and I still got the note. [59]

However, Atkins added that there was a marked difference between the record that Evans, Russell and he finished and the one that was released. "When we did the mix-down, we left the product in one state, as I remember it. When the record came out it was in a different state. It was in a different acoustic state." Atkins puts this down to Columbia, who he believes made changes to put Evans out front in the mix and mask many of the things Russell had written. "I know when I've listened to it and I haven't listened to it in a while, I've always said, 'That line didn't come through. Where is that line?'" [60]

Russell's third wife, Alice, however, offered a simpler explanation. "It was a terrible recording due in large part to substance abuse in those days by the people who were actually engineering the album. I'm afraid so. It seems so. The mix is appalling. You can't hear most of the horn parts on that record and that's unfortunate because I think it's an amazing piece of music." [61]

The sound is very muddy. Russell's writing is quite dense anyway and benefits from the maximum possible separation available for analog technology. In fairness, side 2 of the original LP sounds better than side 1 but so much detail has still been lost. What remains is, by any standard, an astonishing record. There is some fabulous drumming from Tony Williams on "Event II" and "Event VI," along with a beautiful half-valve trumpet solo from Snooky Young. Elsewhere there are fine performances from Sam Rivers, a really outgoing solo on Event II and from Joe Henderson on Event V, set against Evans on electric piano. As for Evans, he performs some way outside his usual style, matching himself against the complex and multi-layered orchestral environment Russell created for him. His playing on Event V is genuinely soulful and funky on Fender Rhodes and he swings with a joyous freedom on acoustic piano. Keith Shadwick commented, "He plays with concision and force, often using phrases that are found nowhere else in his recorded output." [62] Evans had shown in all the projects he had undertaken with Russell an ability to adapt to the composer's harmonic idiom and *Living Time* is no exception. This was the record Columbia had asked for—a modern Bill Evans record that took no prisoners and would sit well alongside Miles Davis's *Bitches Brew*, Mahavishnu Orchestra and Weather Report. As Max Harrison suggested, *Living Time*, like its peers, located its soloist or soloists wholly in the musical fabric, "Evans is not really a soloist: he is firmly embedded in the boiling complexity of, for instance, Events II and IV." [63]

Shadwick made another telling point about the record's lack of success. "This is a terse and extreme harmonic idiom, especially in the jazz world—and perhaps this was the biggest reason for the piece's general failure to make a popular mark." [64] Not only did Bill Evans's fans stay away in droves but, according to Alice Norbury-Russell, "That's the one that lost Bill Evans so many fans. They were furious with him for playing that way. He got threats in the mail, 'If you ever, ever do anything like this again, I'll never buy another record.'" [65]

Russell re-recorded the piece in November 1995 with his Anglo-American Living Time Orchestra and additional musicians from various French *conservatoires* for Label Bleu. The clarity of the writing finally emerges but also adds to the regret that the Bill Evans version had not fared better.

In 2010, and again in 2013, Sony Japan reissued *Living Time* on CD. The reissue certainly sounds clearer and sharper and the quieter sections are much improved. As Boston-based critic Steve Elman noted,

> My first impressions of the piece back in the 1970s were of how varied and diverse it seemed; now I hear how carefully knit together it is, how thematic material appears and reappears, and how sensitive Bill Evans is to every ebb and flow in the music. [66]

Sadly, however, we can never know what Russell, Evans and Atkins heard on the playback in the control booth to compare it with the CD releases.

Columbia did little to promote the record and, after leaving Evans pretty much to his own devices, decided against renewing his contract. Evans was uncharacteristically forthright about the experience in an interview with Len Lyons some years later, "I thought I'd finally arrived at a company that had the money and the interest. Clive Davis and I just didn't hit it off. I never even talked to the man and he was already directing my career, making me 'creative,' 'communicative,' whatever." It seems likely that it is that sense of frustration which Brian Hennessey picked up from Evans. [67]

Like many on the jazz scene, Russell had stuck with Evans through his ten or more years of heroin addiction. Evans had finally kicked the habit thanks to methadone treatment. His life was on the up by this point, after years of quiet degradation. His long-term partner, Ellaine, was herself an addict and a fragile individual. In the spring of 1973 Evans met another woman while on tour on the West Coast and he told Ellaine of the affair. No sooner was Evans on his way back West when Ellaine threw herself under a subway train. Russell was one of the friends in whom Evans sought solace. Though Russell's recollection was hazy on some of the details, his account revealed their closeness.

About the saddest time with him was when the woman he married . . . I remember being in the house at the time and she made a remark in front of Bill. She said, "I think if Bill left me I'd kill myself." Bill looked strangely surprised by that. Later on, he was going to St. Louis, I guess . . . I get a call that she jumped in front of a subway train. Bill was crying on the phone. He said, "Please come up." I go over to New York and to the church, he met me and gave me a hug, a tearful hug. I couldn't get that out of my mind for months and months and months. It seemed like such a horrible thing. He was on his way down. What a painful way for a beautiful man like that . . . [68]

In 1974 MCA reissued *Jazz in the Space Age* and *New York, N.Y.* as a twofer double package. Russell had often commented that he could not understand why the latter was out of the catalogue, being a favourite work of his, so he was understandably happy when Leonard Feather wrote to him to advise of the reissue.[69] Bill Evans also appeared at Carnegie Hall with Russell for a performance of *Living Time* with a full band in 1974. Promoted by George Wein's organization, the event fared poorly in attendance, despite a double bill that also included Gary Burton performing music by Mike Gibbs. In his autobiography Wein used the phrases "downright shameful" and "especially embarrassing" to describe the turnout—or, rather, lack thereof. It was, Wein noted, "a bold and terrific concert"—but one that only sold two hundred tickets.[70]

Surprisingly, the following year the performance was repeated, without Evans. Russell again played the hall, this time as part of the New York Jazz Repertory Company's series of concerts, on March 10, 1975, with pianists Alan Pasqua and Stanley Cowell and a band that included Tony Williams, Sam Rivers, Jimmy Giuffre, Stanton Davis, Howard Johnson, guitarist Sam Brown, bassist Herb Bushler and John Clark on French horn, all of whom had been on the original session. Attendance seems to have been much better second time around.

However, *DownBeat*'s Arnold Jay Smith, writing in the June 19, 1975 issue, complained about the poor sound and noted that "where *Living Time* made complete sense," the second half's performance of *Electronic Sonata* "made complete noise." And John S. Wilson in the *New York Times* was even more dismissive, writing, "The electronic sonata, which used a tape of swoops and chatters as an interlude between 'events' was filled with strong intense rhythms. But not even the spurts of excitement could entirely overcome the monotony of this long, meandering, repetitious work." It is quite possible that managing a reasonable sound balance in Carnegie Hall at that time for such a mix of instrumentation might have been beyond the capacity of the engineers. However, one is more tempted to comment that it is hardly surprising that Russell has spent so much of his career performing his music in the more open and sympathetic environments of European audiences.[71]

Gary Giddins took a very different view from Wilson and Smith in his "Weather Bird" column in the *Village Voice*. Contrasting an apparently bland performance of Michel Legrand the previous night, Giddins described the concert as "a personal triumph for the composer-theorist" but a flop in terms of public relations. Comparing Russell's "peripatetic career and the reluctance of major American labels to finance his recording projects" with that of film director Orson Welles, an inspired and apt comparison,

Giddins mounted an assault on the conservatism of the jazz community. His analysis of Russell's theories and the music he heard provides an insightful response to both Smith and Wilson's criticisms.[72]

## Notes

1. Interview with Gunther Schuller, October 2003.
2. Ibid.
3. Ibid.
4. Ian Carr, interview with Gunther Schuller for BBC Radio 3 broadcast *George Russell—The Invisible Guru*, July 1994
5. Interview with Schuller.
6. Carr, interview with Schuller.
7. Interview with Schuller.
8. Ibid.
9. Ian Carr, interview with Marit Jerstad for BBC Radio 3 broadcast *George Russell—The Invisible Guru*, July 1994.
10. Interview with Carl Atkins, October 2003.
11. Ibid.
12. Ibid.
13. Interview with Ingrid Monson, November 2005.
14. Ibid.
15. Ibid.
16. Ibid.
17. Ibid.
18. Interview with Bill Urmson, June 2003.
19. Ibid.
20. Interview with Fred Hersch, January 2007.
21. Ibid.
22. Interview with Ricky Ford, October 2003.
23. Ibid. *[balaena]* JFP005.
24. Ibid.
25. Interview with Don Byron, July 2005.
26. Ibid.
27. Ibid.
28. Ibid.
29. Interview with Urmson.
30. Ibid.
31. E-mail interview with Marty Ehrlich, April 2005.
32. E-mail interview with Satoko Fujii, January 2005.
33. Interview with Ehrlich.
34. Interview with John Medeski, October 2003.
35. E-mail interview with James Falzone, April 2007.
36. E-mail interview with Greg Burk, April 2007.
37. Ibid.
38. Interview with Dave Holland, September 2006.
39. The inclusion of *Density 21.5* offers an indication of how interconnected the world of jazz. Russell's friend Eric Dolphy had performed this piece at the Ojai Contemporary Music Festival in 1962 and had been tutored for the performance by Gunther Schuller. See Duncan Heining, "Vintage Dolphy", https://www.allaboutjazz.com/vintage-dolphy-eric-dolphy-gm-recordings

40. Charles Ives, Symphony No. 3, Naxos CD 8.559087
41. These observations derive from several sources, including a DVD and tape made by NEC, program notes, a press release, and review data.
42. Interview with Stanton Davis, June 2003.
43. Ken Linden, "George Russell," *Jazz & Pop*, Autumn 1969.
44. Peter Pettinger, *How My Heart Sings* (New Haven: Yale University Press, 1998), pp. 203 and 212.
45. *DownBeat*, September 16, 1971.
46. Pettinger, *How My Heart Sings*; K. Shadwick, *Bill Evans: Everything Happens to Me—A Musical Biography* (San Francisco: Backbeat, 2002).
47. Interview with Brian Hennessy, April 2004.
48. Ibid.
49. Jan Stevens, interview with Marty Morell 2005. https://www.billevanswebpages.com/images/2morellintvue2.htm
50. Sy Johnson, "Interview: Bill Evans & George Russell," *Changes*, Spring 1972.
51. Orrin Keepnews, sleevenotes to *Living Time* KC31490
52. Ibid.
53. Pettinger, *How My Heart Sings*; Shadwick, *Bill Evans: Everything Happens to Me—A Musical Biography*.
54. Shadwick, *Everything Happens to Me*, p. 154.
55. Ian Carr, interview with Dave Bargeron for BBC Radio 3 broadcast *George Russell—The Invisible Guru*, July 1994.
56. Ibid.
57. Interview with Atkins.
58. Ibid.
59. Ibid.
60. Ibid.
61. Ian Carr, interview with Alice Norbury-Russell for BBC Radio 3 broadcast *George Russell—The Invisible Guru*, July 1994.
62. Shadwick, *Everything Happens to Me*, p. 154.
63. Max Harrison, "George Russell—Rational Anthems (Phase 1, 2, 3)," *Wire* (Spring/Summer/Autumn 1983).
64. Shadwick, *Everything Happens to Me*, p.154.
65. Carr, interview with Norbury-Russell.
66. Steve Elman "Commentary Drill Down: George Russell's *Living Time*", *Arts Fuse*, February 1st, 2012
67. Quoted in L. Lyons, *The Great Jazz Pianists* (New York: Da Capo, 1983), p. 226.
68. Interview with George Russell, October 2003.
69. Leonard Feather, letter to George Russell, March 21, 1973. Not everyone feels as Russell does about *New York, N.Y.* Max Harrison has never liked it. See earlier citation.
70. G. Wein, *Myself Among Others* (Cambridge, MA: Da Capo, 2003), pp. 394–95.
71. Arnold Jay Smith, "The Music of George Russell," *DownBeat*, June 19, 1975; John S. Wilson, "Russell Presents His Episodic Jazz," *New York Times*, March 10, 1975.
72. Gary Giddins, "St. George and the Chord," *Village Voice*, March 24, 1975

CHAPTER TWELVE

# Playing the African Game

Following the making of *Living Time*, the 1975 Carnegie Hall performance aside, Russell withdrew from performance and recording to focus on his teaching commitments and on further research into the Lydian Concept. The following year, he received two further awards – a second grant from the National Endowment for the Arts (the first was on his return to the USA in 1969) and recognition by the National Music Award. The latter was particularly important coming as it did in America's bicentennial year. The award named Russell as one of 121 people who had made substantial and significant contributions to American Music from 1776 to 1976.

1976 was also an important year for Russell at a personal level. It was then that he met Alice Norbury, who was director of the Midtown School for the Arts in St. Louis, which was a legacy of the American community school movement. New England Conservatory visited such projects across America each year to audition potential students. Russell came along on that particular visit and invited Norbury to dinner that first night. They spent the next year meeting in various cities where they both had business dealings and, at the end of the year, Russell asked her to move to Boston to live with him. They lived together for four years and married in 1981. Alice Norbury-Russell proved to be a major stabilizing influence on Russell but also has helped him organize and structure his working life in ways that proved hugely beneficial. A former actress, model and arts administrator, she was able to bring a clearer business emphasis to her husband's career, while ensuring that Russell's creative energies were given free rein. As she put it, "My background melded well with George's in that we could speak a similar language."[1]

When Norbury moved to Boston, she had intended to seek a position in the arts but Russell asked if she would instead consider working with him.

George said, "It would be helpful if you would work with me because I have this idea of starting an orchestra again." Of course, he was at that time working on finishing volume 1 of this edition of the Concept. So I just gradually worked into doing what I do, which is basically acting as a sort of manager, tour manager, book publisher, CD producer and also taking care of the business and secretarial side, which is a scream because, of course, I never learned to type because I never wanted to be anybody's secretary. *(laughs)*

She added,

For a lot of couples, working together can be hellish, and it can be now and then with George and I because we get on each other's nerves because I think we're both very much individuals and sort of loners but for the most part I think it's been good. We've had an amazing life together and we've done some amazing projects when I look back on them.[2]

Norbury-Russell has helped Russell take things to a different level in the world of jazz, because, as she noted, "We never gave in to that sort of compelling mission that the jazz business has to make a musician feel like he's worthless—George never allowed that to happen to him." Russell, she said, has always insisted on doing things his way, "even when it was the wrong way, which wasn't often."[3]

To the lay jazz or classical music fan, the creation of a handful of new works over a period of twenty-five or thirty years may not seem that productive. The quality of Russell's output, however, speaks volumes in itself. Between 1976 and 1996, Russell produced eight major extended works—*Vertical Form VI* (1977); *Time Spiral* (1982); *African Game* (1983); *Uncommon Ground, Six Aesthetic Gravities, Centrifugue*, written for The Relâche Ensemble for New Music, and *La Folia: The Rocella Variations* (all 1989, the latter written together with Ben Schwendener); *American Trilogy* (1991); *Dialogue with Ornette* (1992); and *It's About Time* (1995). This list excludes the *Time Line* project for NEC's 125th anniversary in 1992.

As a rule, Russell wrote when he had a record date, concert tour or commission. Norbury-Russell pointed out that when he did so, it was a painstaking and drawn-out process.

George is not a prolific composer. Everything is written, even the things that sound improvised, as you know. He does a master plan for each composition and that is where he determines what will happen in each measure for each instrument. The master plan is the thing that takes him the longest time. He can spend months on that, years on that if he's given that luxury. Thankfully he isn't, so he has to push on. Once the plan is in place, the actual writing of the composition is the easy part.[4]

After five years' absence from recording, Russell made *Vertical Form VI*, with Carl Atkins as "principal conductor" and a crack orchestra specially assembled by Swedish Radio for the commission. When it was eventually released in the States, John Diliberto in *DownBeat* gave it an encouraging four and a half stars, while Bob Blumenthal, writing in *Boston after Dark*, was also favourably impressed.[5] Describing the idea of "vertical forms" in the record's sleeve notes, Russell wrote,

If you were standing in the middle of New York City on a typically busy day or night, focusing on all the patterns of sound around you, without attempting to identify their sources, you would be experiencing "vertical form"—layers or strata of divergent modes of rhythmic behaviour. This one huge mass of sound is always there, holding linear time captive, and therefore going nowhere but up or down the scale of vertical density and complexity.[6]

Later, Russell would use the analogy of the African choir to describe the idea. The music it creates is cyclical. Its level of intensity, density and complexity may change but it has no sense of forward movement. It is more as if it breathes, expands and contracts and holds time suspended. This is a good description of the music on the record. In the notes, Russell went on to state that he considered *Now And Then* his first essay in vertical form, *Othello Ballet* his second, *Electronic Sonata* the third, *Listen to the Silence* the fourth and *Living Time* the fifth.

The most remarkable aspect of *Vertical Form VI* is that, with the exception of a short interlude involving pianist Vlodek Gulgowski and Bertil Lövgren in Event IV, the entire piece is composed. This includes the apparently free improvisations in Events I and III. The writing is, like that in *Living Time*, dense and compressed. Its two most impressive aspects are its dark forests of concentrated rhythms and its architectural structure. Within these the music flows smoothly and with, at its best, a filmic quality. It is a demanding work, but, with the exception of an all too brief finale and, arguably, Event II's rather repetitive closing section, it is a hugely rewarding piece. Perhaps best seen as an experiment or work in progress.

As far as forming a big band was concerned, Russell got his wish. At club owner Max Gordon's suggestion, Russell began rehearsals for a series of dates at the Village Vanguard in New York scheduled for April 1978. As usual, Russell's expectations in preparing a band for performance was that the musicians would play his music as if they were on the stand and, as usual, he met a degree of understandable resistance from the band and from the brass players in particular. Marty Ehrlich had not long finished his studies at NEC when Russell asked him to play in his band.

> I was the youngest guy in the band, I believe, and I probably wasn't on that [same] page. I was in NYC to do exactly what he was doing. Even at NEC, George would get right up to you if he felt you weren't really playing hard on a part or a solo. It wasn't just accuracy; it was a vibe he was going for. This is something he shares with many composer/ensemble leaders I've had the fortune to work with. I tried my best to make the rehearsal have the intensity of a performance.[7]

In Russell's defence, his music is unusually difficult and it is not enough for the players to read it and play it. He relies on them to make it come alive and make it swing.

Despite Russell's difficulties in getting his music across in his home country and the debacle of his 1975 Carnegie Hall performance, expectations of the New York dates were unusually high. Musicians, critics and fans turned out in force and the audience on one night included Donald Fagen and Walter Becker from Steely Dan. Critic Gary Giddins wrote a long piece in the *Village Voice* for his "Weather Bird" column,[8] and Stanley Crouch reviewed the gigs at length for the *Soho Weekly News*.[9] Russell presented a retrospective of his music for the engagement, which is captured in part by the *New York Big Band* album on Soul Note, recorded four months later. Giddins commented that "his themes are luminescent, and they fully engage heart, mind and body. The orchestra played the music so forcefully and with such abandon that Russell actually did boogie." He continued, "The impact of his works depends on the exacting rhythmic and structural transitions; these reflect Russell's training as a drummer, but also the accomplishment of his musicians." He then singled out Stanton Davis and Terumasa Hino on trumpet, Janice Robinson on trombone, Ricky Ford and Roger Rosenberg on tenors (the article actually refers in error to Bob Handlin), Warren Smith on drums, Cameron Brown on bass and the twin keyboards of Goetz Tangerding and Kikushi Masabumi for special mention.[10]

In the Stanley Crouch piece, the author bemoaned a tendency among black musicians to ignore innovators from their own community because they are "sometimes so caught up in the hip convention of the moment." In so doing, they miss "a fresh aesthetic thrust—when it becomes hip—then attack the black artist with a new conception for using 'white boys.'" Crouch continues,

> The upshot of it all, though, is that much of Russell's recorded music suffers from a timbral dilution and a lack of rhythmic juiciness because so many of the players he used in the past, however, skilled at reading and execution or intellectually committed, lacked the *cultural* guts in their respective buckets to make the music stand up and shout the sophisticated folk message that is so central to Russell's art.[11]

A few lines further on he noted, "George Russell is, however, a man of great integrity and the integrated band he leads seems far above the kind of racial politics so many New York musicians work form at the behest of club owners, promoters and record companies. He has even been able somehow to inspire the notoriously tasteless Japanese trumpeter Hino to play fine Fats Navarro lines."[12]

As far as poor Hino is concerned, it was a case of damned if you do and damned if you don't. Crouch's comments succeeded in proffering praise and taking it back in the same breath. In fairness, Crouch's article made a number of interesting points and he came to praise Russell, not to bury him. One just wonders why he felt the need to bring the shovel.

Crouch's piece has the inspirational title "From the Cottonfields to the Cosmos." A better description of Russell's music is hard to imagine. As an individual African-American growing up in a racist society, Russell had more reason to feel aggrieved and bitter than many of his fellow citizens. Yet, however much racism might have angered him, Russell never seems to have seen the world in simplistic, binary terms. His music is open to the whole earth and the cosmos, without bias, and the same was true of the musicians with whom he chose to play. One feels that that is how one should write about his music.

Marty Ehrlich recalled thirty years later, that various musicians were unhappy with

Crouch's comments. "I recall only vague things about that review. I remember that it was intellectually dishonest and inconsistent as much of Crouch's writing was becoming and would become. (I was a fan of him in earlier years.) Yes, I remember certain players he singled out being hurt." [13]

The *New York Big Band* album gives a good representation of what the band must have sounded like those nights in the Vanguard. It adds a fine version of "Cubano-Be, Cubano-Bop" from the Swedish session that produced *Vertical Form VI*, with Sabu Martinez on congas and strong trumpet from Bertil Lövgren and Americo Belotto. With modern production and recording, "Cubano-Be, Cubano-Bop" seems just as impressive but now its true subtleties emerge.

With no Janice Robinson or Kikushi Masabumi, but with the addition of Stanley Cowell on the opening, "Living Time Event V," the studio band differs slightly from the live ensemble. However, with the exception of a strained vocal from Lee Genesis on "Big City Blues," this is a fine set of performances and an interesting retrospective of Russell's music. Any issues relating to Genesis' contribution are more than compensated for by Ricky Ford's freewheeling tenor solo. Ford had studied with Russell at NEC and had struggled in the class. However, just a few years later he was pleased to be asked to join Russell's New York Big Band.

> It was great, I mean, to work with George after flunking. I was very honoured that he called me to work with him because at that point I'd been in New York, I'd already worked with Mercer Ellington. I worked with Charles Mingus. I had a little bit of name recognition.

Asked how it felt to play Russell's music on the stand compared to studying it in at NEC, Ford replied insightfully,

> I related more to playing his music than the classroom situation but his music is very eclectic – we played *All About Rosie*, it's like playing Handel's *Messiah* in some ways. Everybody knows it, so they hear you play it and reflect about how Coltrane might've done it in his own way, certain themes in there that are very popular. I really would like to play more of George's music. I guess that's a special project that I have to think about to do on my own. [14]

There is also a nice version of Billie Holiday's "God Bless the Child" and a sharp take on Stanton Davis's "Mystic Voices." Davis plays beautifully throughout and particularly so on "Listen to the Silence," as do Roger Rosenberg on tenor and Gary Valente on trombone.

In 1980 Russell took a sextet to Italy that featured (in addition to himself on piano and organ) Lew Soloff on trumpet, Robert Moore on tenor and soprano, Victor Comer on guitar, the fine French bassist J. F. Jenny-Clark on bass and Keith Copeland on drums. In the sleeve notes for the new version of *Electronic Sonata* the group recorded in the studios in Milan, Russell noted that he had disbanded the New York Big Band "because most of our music was old music, although it wasn't old to the people who came to hear it." He then talked about his intention to form a new big band to do new material and considerably reworked versions of older tunes. [15]

Moore had studied with Russell and, as a little known musician even around Boston, was surprised to get the gig. It was a fairly short tour but included performances at Tasso's Oak, Rome, and Venice. There was also a concert with the RAI Big Band that was to be broadcast, which Moore learned about only when they got to Italy. The strain of rehearsing for two weeks took its toll on Moore, whose lips started to bleed and blister.

> I really didn't know what to do and what concerned me so much was that in the rehearsal with the big band, whenever it came time for me to solo, George wanted me to put 100 percent into it and I was just suffering. I remember in the midst of one solo I was just fumbling along trying to save myself, he came up to me and said, "Play like Trane! Play like Trane!" Oh my goodness, in fact there were several musicians who came up to me in the course of that tour—Ornette Coleman and some others—and they said, "Don't let George kill you, man!" *(laughs)* Somehow I made it through that and we did the record at the end, which I can't listen to anymore because all I can think of is the pain. I told a number of people that I remember reading a review of that recording, and one reviewer said, "Moore's solo is good . . ." and so forth and so on, ". . . but he climaxes too soon." *(laughs)* And I was thinking to myself that I wanted to climax at the start because it was so painful. [16]

Probably only the most devoted fan will check out this third version of Russell's opus. Extracts from the composition feature on two later Russell records as well. That is unfortunate because it is quite different from the Swedish sextet with Stanton Davis recording. In a way, it is tighter and more inward-looking but the playing of Moore and Soloff is really quite beautiful and both depart sonically and even timbrally from the approach of Davis and Garbarek. And Comer, Jenny-Clark, and Copeland contrast dramatically with Rypdal, Andersen and Christensen. Even the way the electronic tape is used is changed from the original version.

It was the next project, however, that created the mould that would shape Russell's future career. In 1979 Russell had again been commissioned to write a piece by Swedish Radio. The piece, *Time Spiral*, provided the impetus for him to launch a new big band, though it was again called George Russell's New York Big Band. This band was, if anything, even better than its predecessor. *Time Spiral* was recorded in July 1982 at the Vanguard in New York for the Italian Soul Note label. It may not be from the top drawer of Russell's compositions but it is a fine extended work, perhaps more traditional in structure and in the greater degree of freedom it gives its soloists. The performance is a touch slow to get started but, from Marty Ehrlich's flute solo on, the band plays with great force and majesty. With the contrasting styles of Jack Reilly and Mark Soskin on pianos, excellent guitar work from Jerome Harris and ecstatic ensemble work, this is excellent big-band jazz. Side 2 of the LP features two versions of older tunes. Russell uses Jerry Coker's big-band arrangement of "Ezz-Thetic" for this version, while Goetz Tangerding, who played on *New York Big Band*, arranged "D.C. Divertimento." Ehrlich's alto really comes into its own on "Ezz-Thetic." As he explained, it was important to put the Dolphy version to one side and find his own way through the piece. "I wasn't thinking of Dolphy's solo so much as using this amazing melody as my jumping off point, more than the changes to 'Love for Sale.' It was a challenge I was only partly ready for at that age, as the tempo George took on the piece was fierce. I tried." [17]

As for the flute solo on *Time Spiral*, Ehrlich recalled, "I felt particularly good about the flute solo and it might have been my idea to play flute there, one that George went for. I was glad to have a context to add some of the textural and sonic stuff I had been improvising with at that time into the context of George's music." [18]

Ehrlich also toured Europe that year with a Russell big band, with a memorable performance at the North Sea Festival in Holland, though two Italian dates had to be cancelled when Italy's soccer team made first the World Cup semi-final and then the final. "Italy won that year! Both concerts were cancelled but I remember that George got paid and I think without a fight, as the promoters themselves said, 'No one will come, not even us; the whole country will be watching these games!'" [19]

Jack Reilly, who played keyboards on the *Time Spiral* session, noted that by the time of the recording, the band was really playing at its best.

> Well, it was done from live performances at the Vanguard. We had done three weeks of concerts, so it was really bedded down great. There was only one substitute; Ray Anderson came in on trombone and he was unbelievable. I couldn't believe what was coming out of the trombone. We played strong bebop stuff. It was just George took the tapes home and decided what to put out. It was a thrill to play with them. There were no talk-overs at the end of the night, where something wasn't working. He never did say much, either, at the initial rehearsals before the tour. [20]

Preparation had, as always, been demanding, but Reilly highlights another problem, one which can be traced back to the Chicago rehearsals with Earl Hines' band.

> He was upset when I couldn't read "D.C. Divertimento" right off. I said, "George you wanna read it?" It was the way he wrote it. I almost wanted to have it copied over for him. Boy, that was horrendous and he had no patience with that. That was no excuse. I don't mean the musical part. No, the music was hard enough. Not really technically hard. It was just that the treble for the bass clef, the left-hand part was not lined up with the downbeat of the beats in the bar. The downbeat in the right hand was on the second and half the beat and you knew it was supposed to go to the left hand, and vice versa. And it was in a terrible script. [21]

A sad event occurred around this point – the loss of and old friend. Barry Galbraith, Russell's guitarist from the Jazz Workshop and other sessions, died on January 13, 1983. Galbraith had also taught at the conservatory with Russell and they had been friends for almost forty years. Russell was the obvious choice to write Galbraith's obituary, and wrote in *NEC Notes* in the summer of 1983, "From 1950 to the late 1960s, I relied most heavily on Barry to make my music 'come off.' His guitar became a lead trumpet, or part of a saxophone section, or doubled in octaves with the bass and, at times, the whole orchestra. He was a professional in the true sense of the word." And he continued, "In inestimable ways, he continues to colour my life, as well as my music. It is, therefore, impossible for me to conceive of him as having departed." [22]

If the interest provoked in the United States by his 1978 Vanguard dates was encouraging, Russell must have been truly touched by the response his music was beginning to receive. It might not have been the second coming but it certainly was not a case of "the prophet without honour." Several things seemed to happen in the space of a few months.

The first event was a concert in Russell's honour in March 1983 for the Boston Globe Jazz Festival at the Berklee Performance Centre. Members of NEC faculty and student body contributed, with a student ensemble led by Pat Hollenbeck and performers that included the original George Russell Sextet drummer Joe Hunt, trombonist Gary Valente, saxophonist Ricky Ford, pianist Fred Hersch and guitarist Mick Goodrick. Governor Michael Dukakis even proclaimed it "George Russell Day" in the Commonwealth of Massachusetts. [23]

The second event was the commissioning by the Boston Jazz Coalition, from a grant from the Massachusetts Council on the Arts and Humanities, of a new work, *The African Game*, for a performance in Boston in the summer of 1983. The tape of that concert was sent to Blue Note label boss Bruce Lundval. Lundval listened to the tape on a flight to the West Coast, and, liking what he heard, signed Russell as the first artist on the revived Blue Note label. This was in 1984. This should have been the honour to match them all. If that did not turn out to be the case, it did lead to one of Russell's finest recordings and to a very good companion album from the same concert.

Recorded live at Emmanuel Church in Boston on June 18, 1983, and credited for the first time to George Russell and the Living Time Orchestra, *The African Game* is the record Russell was destined to make and the one that sums up man, music and mind. As he told Francis Davis,

> People assume *The African Game* is about black evolution but it's not. It's about *human evolution* because we're all Africans at the core, when you trace these things back. It's ironic in a way that I'm playing the Afro-American Museum because there are so many white players in my band, it'll probably look like Buddy Rich's band to some people. But I've never bought that theory that says only black people have soul or essence of whatever—that does nobody any good. I don't care where a musician comes from or what he looks like. I listen for that electricity you get from certain players. [24]

Coming some five years later, this makes an entirely apt riposte to Stanley Crouch's *Soho Weekly News* piece.

The band at Emmanuel Church featured a mix of experienced and younger players. Among the older pros were the exceptional George Garzone on tenor and soprano and Keith Copeland, who had played with Russell in Italy in 1980 and 1982. The younger musicians included a very young Bill Urmson on electric bass, Mark Rossi on piano and Mark White, now a professor at Berklee, on guitar. For Urmson in particular, it was a baptism by fire.

> I remember I was taking my last final exam at the conservatory, it was Jazz Studies and Mark Harvey, a trumpet player in Boston was the instructor, and I went to hand in my test

and I was thinking, "That's it, I'm passing my last final. I'm done." And he says, "I've got to talk to you about something." He says, "George is doing this thing." So I'm literally hired. I was asked to play as I was handing in my final exam. What a segue. Right into George's band from class.[25]

Russell has always bridled at the oft-repeated suggestion that his music has suffered due to his reliance at times on student bands. Interviewed by Ben Young for WKCR, his response to Young's innocent comment seems quite acerbic and unduly defensive.

**BY:** It's a large list of players, mainly from New England Conservatory or Boston area.
**GR:** They're mainly players from the Boston area but... they're... sometimes if you mention the term "students" it definitely tends to diminish any effort that you're involved in. People forget that Miles was a student. He was a student at Juilliard, where he used to use the little practice rooms to work out what he'd learned with Bird the night before. George Garzone is a legend. He was a student at one time. We all were students. This is a pro band from the Boston area.[26]

*The African Game* was one of Russell's first commissions in some time in the United States. For the work, Russell chose to compose nine events, each one representing a period in human evolution, giving each titles such as "Consciousness" (III), "African Empires" (VI) and "Cartesian Man" (VII). The remainder of the concert featured performances of *Time Spiral*; Russell's arrangement with Tim Engels of Miles Davis's "So What," using Goetz Tangerding's transcription of Miles's own solo as the basis for the theme; Dave Baker's "War Gewessen"; and Carla Bley's "Rhymes." These four pieces were later issued by Blue Note under the album title *So What*.

Pianist Marc Rossi said the first thing he did when he was asked to do the gig was to clear his week.

So I could make sure I could practice my butt off. I wasn't going to take any chances on this. I saw some of the horn players at the rehearsals looking like they'd never looked at the part before. Not me, pal! My recollection of it was the amazing focus and the intensity of the music, putting this mammoth thing together with all these people, and the enormous sense of respect people had for George's music and the great joy of working at that very high level. It was absolutely one of the two or three most highest-level things I've ever had the privilege to do in my life. When you play with George, you go beyond yourself. You transcend.[27]

He found Russell inspiring to work with in this context. "George is very cool under all that fire. He's a lot of fun to work with. Very focused and very liberating at the same time. I think that everybody just plays at their best."[28]

There were some corrections to be made in the studio afterward due to leaks on some parts but *The African Game* is essentially a very live recording. Rossi describes the album as one of Russell's two or three greatest works. He also did some U.S. dates with the Living Time Orchestra and says that Russell helped him manage his performance nerves.

You're not going to want to print this. George helped me get over some of my nerves. I remember asking him. He said, 'What are you nervous about?' I said, 'I'm afraid I might make mistakes and the audience will hear.' He goes, 'Fuck the audience! Play the music!'[29]

Several things impress immediately about *The African Game*. The first is Russell's vision for the piece and its inspiration in human evolution. This is clearly expressed in the notes Russell wrote for the release. Russell has often used his compositions to express philosophical ideas but, here, he references Africa as the cradle of humanity. As he often remarked, we are all Africans.

The second aspect that impresses is the architecture of the work. It is highly unusual and nonlinear in structure. It seems simultaneously episodic and yet it coheres over its forty minutes very successfully. There is a density and intensity to the writing, as always, and the different parts of the work shift constantly. Again, percussion and rhythm are key features in the architecture of the work and Russell incorporated into the performance five Cuban Batá drummers. Everything about *The African Game* is unexpected. The final aspect that impresses is the way the solos reflect Russell's ideas and yet are also so expressive. The listener is drawn to Mark Rossi's synthesizer solo on the final event, "The Future?" and Gary Joynes's tenor on "African Empires" (VI), and Mark White's guitar solo on "The Survival Game" (IV), which stand as models of how effectively writing and improvisation can combine in the right hands.

But there is also a strong sense of history about *The African Game*, both in terms of its subject matter and in relation to Russell's own musical history. The fractured, fragmented sounds from the guitar and electric pencil-sharpeners (!) at the beginning of "Event I – Organic Life on Earth Begins: Uni-celled Beings to Amphibians" refer back to the use of beads on tuned drums for effect on the opening of "Chromatic Universe – Part I" from *Jazz in the Space Age* and again on "Event I" from *Living Time*, to Russell's scraping of the inside of the piano at the outset of "'Round Midnight" on *Ezz-Thetics* and, perhaps, also the Boo-Bams he uses on "Fellow Delegates" from *Jazz Workshop*. It also bears comparison with the use of the pre-recorded tape on *Electronic Sonata*. The music here emerges organically, as in the event's subtitle. This use of odd, otherworldly sounds is partly about the creation of drama, tension and expectation. But it is also about how non-musical sounds can be used to create intriguing musical effects as an end in their own right. Is it too fanciful to suggest that this echoes African musical practices in the way that found objects are utilised or transformed into musical instruments? The use of five Cuban drummers refers back directly to "Cubano-Be, Cubano-Bop," "Manhattan-Rico" and the dialogue between Jon Christensen, Egil Johansen, Sabu Martinez and the drumming on the pre-recorded tape on *Electronic Sonata*.

Alongside these references one hears those same concerns with interlocking rhythms and melodies of earlier works. The musicians are grouped in odd combinations and play in different time signatures. The music is layered and cyclical. It is here that Russell's analogy of the African choir is most apt. And, by George, does it retain the funk! There are also some quite exquisite passages. "Event VI – African Empires: Spiritual Consciousness – The Age of Light Intelligence of the Heart, Illuminating the Unity of the Cosmos Why and How" offers just one example in the way Gary Joynes' lyrical tenor solo is shadowed by other instruments before this gentle opening expands into a more assertive and expansive mode and mood.

The subtitles for each event that Russell uses strongly suggest programmatic intentions on the composer's part. Each event can be seen to reflect and represent its subject musically. So, the sounds of synth and electronic keyboards and clattering percussion punctuated by brief and longer brass interruptions heard on "Event VII – Cartesian Man: The Ascent of Technocentricity and Its Division of Man and Nature, The Fragmentation of All and Everything" echo the age of industrial and technological production. Though there are similarities in the way that Russell uses the horns to the way he used brass on *New York, N.Y.*, the difference here is both ethical and aesthetic. The latter was paean to the modern city. Here, this is no utopian vision of modern life but its opposite. The same can be said of "Event VIII - The Mega Minimalist Age: Style Over Substance, The Decline of the Spirit." I almost wonder whether the opening few minutes with the marimba-like sounds of percussion and keyboard are not a satirical reference to the minimalist music ethic of Steve Reich, John Cage et al. As Wim Mertens has argued in *American Minimal Music* (1983), American minimalism can be read as representing a musical and political nihilism that denies history, which venerates form as style over content and, here referring specifically to Cage, a denial of value – the kind of ethical and aesthetic values Russell would deplore. [30]

And the contrast of such values with *The African Game* could not be more marked. The final section, "Event IX – The Future?: The Collective Level of Being Attracts the Common Future" illustrates this perfectly. The pace is quite frantic, a planet driven by a single species is being led to a future increasingly beyond the capacity of that species to control. Rhythms and riffs collide. Repeating motifs intersect with discordant melodies. There is no single key centre but many and yet a central pulse, provided primarily by Bill Urmson, holds the piece together. It fades rather than concludes, leaving a musical question mark to echo the one in its subtitle.

In his sleevenotes, Russell wrote,

It is said that Albert Einstein once remarked, "God doesn't play dice with the universe." Perhaps he did, once, in Africa during the Miocene epoch some 5 to 20 million years ago when the African Game began.

As the cradle of humanity, Africa is our common home; we are all Africans – white, yellow, red, brown or black. Great Nature is on our side. We feverishly pursue the game of *how* to conquer nature, while failing to understand *why* it needs us to join her in a state of unity. Nature responds by sending signals to tell us we are outpacing her capacity to adjust to our technical innovations. These signals are everywhere; they cannot be missed. Entropy is accelerating.

The African Game says something of a positive nature about this. It says that God (Great Nature) is on our side. It wants to win the game it began millions of years ago. But in order to win it needs the awareness and cooperation of each of us descendants from the Miocene epoch now inhabiting Planet Earth. (original italics) [31]

Yet, if the work refers back to earlier compositions, *The African Game* is also definitely a post-Scandinavian work. There is the greater confidence in handling the extended form and the way Russell manages the dichotomy between freedom/control here is quite masterful. But there is also a normative aspect at play here. This is expressed very clearly in the titles and sleevenotes. As we have seen in earlier chapters, Russell sought to base the Lydian Concept scientifically and philosophically quite early on in its life. Here, he links art, music, science, history and, what I can only call, the dimension of the spirit - each being inseparable in his schema. In many ways, *The African Game* is a summation of his life and work to that point. It is a programme work but to understand it fully, one must appreciate it as a normative work as well. Moreover, it is a work built upon a coherent aesthetic and ethical philosophy that has its roots in Russell's Fourth Way studies in Scandinavia and after. [32]

*The African Game* did not hit the stores until 1985. However, in October 1983 Russell embarked on what was, shockingly, his first ever full American tour. The Living Time Orchestra were actually touring in support of *Live in an American Time Spiral* but given the artistic success of *The African Game*, Russell devoted a large section of the concerts to the work. The tour took Russell's music to the San Diego Kool-Aid Festival; Tempe, Arizona; Albuquerque; Houston; and New York, among other places.

On the whole the band was well received, though one review was quite dismissive of the soloing abilities of Russell's young musicians. Of the LTO's performance at the Entermedia Theatre in Greenwich Village, John Pareles wrote in the *New York Times*, "The band's soloists didn't add much to the music." He concluded, "Apparently, Mr. Russell is willing to pay that price in order to get his music played so precisely." [33] Whether this comment was justified or not is, without personal experience, hard to say, though Stanley Crouch reviewing a Sweet Basil performance in February 1984 suggested the band was "full of musicians who were full of more enthusiasm than authority." However, Crouch was full of praise for Russell's music, and *The African Game* in particular, and granted that "Russell is far from trapped by the limitations of the players he can afford. In fact, by closing night the ensemble was showing impressive potential." [34]

Two things do seem to have really assisted Russell's career from the late seventies onward. The first of these, as noted, concerns Alice Norbury-Russell's role as his business manager. The second was that Russell was taken on as a client by Marty Khan and Helene Cann and their agency, Outward Visions Inc. Having professional management and organization finally left Russell to work on his music and on the Concept and let others take care of business.

Russell had been getting good press coverage in the States since his return. *DownBeat* had been particularly supportive, the occasional and inevitable nay-saying episode aside. Newspapers local to NEC, such as the *Boston Globe* and the *Boston Phoenix*, were also in his corner, with Bob Blumenthal a very strong advocate. In fact, it is unfair to be too critical of the media in terms of Russell's career. Certainly there seems to have been a rather chauvinistic downplaying of Russell's period in Scandinavia in some quarters. [35] However, it has to be said that the records Russell made in Europe were only haphazardly available until the early 1980s, when the Italian label Soul Note reissued them and improved their distribution Stateside. *DownBeat* certainly did its bit from this point on. In its April 1982 issue, John Diliberto gave *Electronic Sonata for Souls Loved by Nature—1980* a fair four-star review, but gave *Vertical Form VI* four and a half. In December 1983 Bill Shoemaker, reviewing reissues of *Ezz-Thetics*, *The Essence of George Russell*, and *Live in an American Time Spiral*, awarded all three five stars and revealed a genuine appreciation of the continuities in Russell's work over time. He did, however, suggest that Jan Garbarek's work on the big-band *Electronic Sonata* represented the apex of his career. Here one merely notes the continuing quality of the saxophonist's music. *DownBeat* even gave Michael Cuscuna, the writer/producer/archivist who had worked extensively on the early eighties Blue Note reactivation, two pages to review the launch of Russell's own Concept label and the reissuing of *Othello Ballet*, *The Essence of George Russell*, *Electronic Sonata for Souls Loved by Nature—1968*, and *Listen to the Silence*.[36]

And Blue Note could not have asked for better press in response to the release in 1985 of *The African Game*. The *Houston Post* described it as "a vast, sprawling work that is also utterly compelling and thought-provoking." Robert Palmer called it "one of the most significant new album releases of the past several years," in a long *New York Times* piece entitled "A Jazz Visionary Eyes the Evolution of Life on Earth." J. D. Considine raved, "Masterpiece may be too modest an accolade" in the April 1985 issue of *Musician*, and the ever-reliable Bob Blumenthal wrote in another long article in the *Globe* that it was "the only new Blue Note we are likely to play over and over."[37]

However, more significantly in terms of the next phase of Russell's career, *The African Game* was beginning to cause ripples across the Atlantic.

## Notes

1. Interview with Norbury-Russell, October 2006.
2. Ibid.
3. Ibid.
4. Carr, interview with Norbury-Russell.
5. John Diliberto, Review of Electronic Sonata (SN1009) and Vertical Form VI (SN1019), *DownBeat*, April 1982.
6. George Russell, sleeve notes to Vertical Form VI, Soul Note 121019-1
7. Interview with Ehrlich.
8. Gary Giddins, "George Russell Boogies," *Village Voice*, April 17, 1978.
9. Stanley Crouch, "From the Cottonfields to the Cosmos," *Soho Weekly News*, April 20, 1978; the gigs were also reviewed by John S. Wilson (*New York Times*, May 4, 1978) and Don Nelsen (*Daily News* [New York], May 9, 1978). See also "Russell Storms the Vanguard," *DownBeat*, June 1, 1978.
10. Giddins, "George Russell Boogies."
11. Crouch, "From the Cottonfields to the Cosmos." My copy of the piece came via critic Ian Carr, who had written "Bullshit" by the quote.
12. Ibid. Again Carr has written "Rubbish" in the margins.
13. Interview with Ehrlich.
14. Interview with Ford.
15. L. Jeske, sleevenotes to *Electronic Sonata for Souls Loved by Nature—1980* Soul Note 121009-1.
16. Interview with Robert Moore, July 2004.

17. Interview with Ehrlich.
18. Ibid.
19. Ibid.
20. Interview with Jack Reilly, October 2003.
21. Ibid.
22. George Russell, "Barry Galbraith—Obituary," *NEC Notes*, Summer 1983.
23. See "By George," *DownBeat*, July 1983, p. 12; *Jazz Times*, June 1983; Bob Blumenthal, "A Tribute to a Local," *Boston Globe*, March 23, 1983; Drago, C. "Boston Globe Festival—Safe but Sound." *Jazz Times*, June 1983.
24. Francis Davis, "George Russell: Intellect of the Heart," *Jazz Times*, December 1984.
25. Interview with Urmson.
26. Ben Young, broadcast devoted to George Russell in celebration of his seventy-fifth birthday, WKCR Radio, New York, June 23, 1998.
27. Interview with Marc Rossi, October 2004.
28. Ibid.
29. Ibid.
30. Wim Mertens, *American Minimal Music* (London: Kahan & Averill, 1983). See pp.113-124.
31. George Russell, sleevenotes to *The African Game* (Blue Note BT85103)
32. I think I should make clear that I do not share Russell's spiritual beliefs. Here, and elsewhere, it is for me to outline his thinking not my own on such questions.
33. John Pareles, "Russell Big Band in Two Showpieces," *New York Times*, November 11, 1983.
34. Stanley Crouch, "George Russell's Victory," *Village Voice*, February 21, 1984.
35. Sy Johnson's comment is the most extreme example. In general, it is mentioned *en passant* or not at all.
36. Diliberto, Review; Bill Shoemaker, Review of Ezz-thetics (Riverside Original Jazz Classic OJC-070), The Essence of George Russell (Soul Note 1044/5), and Live in an American Time Spiral (Soul Note 1049), *DownBeat*, December 1983; Michael Cuscuna, Spotlight review of reissues of Othello Ballet, The Essence of George Russell, Electronic Sonata 1968, and Listen to the Silence, DownBeat, February 13, 1975.
37. Bob Claypool, Review of *The African Game, Houston Post*, June 4, 1985; Robert Palmer, "A Jazz Visionary Eyes the Evolution of Life on Earth," *New York Times*, April 28, 1985; J. D. Considine, Review of *The African Game, Musician*, April 1985; Bob Blumenthal, "Captured by the Game," *Boston Phoenix*, May 14, 1985. See also *DownBeat*, October 1985 for review of Sweet Basil residency.

CHAPTER THIRTEEN

## Live in a European Time Spiral

John Cumming, then director of British independent producers Serious, had worked on a number of projects for the Arts Council of Britain's Contemporary Music Network. CMN promoted and helped fund tours by important British, European and American artists and composers, mainly from jazz and new music. Cumming had recently managed a Carla Bley tour and had worked with Gil Evans, Steve Reich and others, as well as organizing the Camden Jazz Festival. In 1985 Annette Morreau, the founder of CMN, contacted him with the suggestion of a UK tour with George Russell.

> I said, George Russell would be fantastic but the problem is you've got to find a way of doing it because trying to bring a full band over from the States and I was aware that the last band I'd seen—I'd never met George—but I knew it was an unhappy experience. It was a touring band that I'd bumped into when I was tour-managing Carla Bley's band. I bumped into them at a couple of festivals here, there and everywhere, and I knew some of the guys in the band and it was clearly not a happy experience, partly because the business side was being very badly handled in Europe and partly because it was a pickup band, really, and there were some people that he trusted and others that he didn't get on with. And I said, I think you've got to be really careful because apart from the fact that it's going to be an expensive operation, maybe the thing to do is to talk to George in a different way. Let's find out what he wants to do. Let's find out if he's interested in forming a band that takes players that he does trust from America and build British artists around it, select some of the young musicians that are coming through that will respond well, that might give something back to the music, so that there'll be a real dialogue.[1]

Cumming had used this approach with other artists, and, on a business trip Stateside, approached Russell.

> George came and picked me up and took me to Anthony's Pier 9, which is a famous seafood restaurant full of pictures of Mafiosi on the wall. There's all these pictures of Frank Sinatra with dodgy Italians and we sat and talked and drank, not getting pissed or anything, but we sat and drank wine for about two hours and talked about the scene in general and what might happen. Then he drove me to the airport because I had to fly on somewhere else. So he drove me to the airport and we continued to talk on the way and that's really how it started. He was really interested in the idea, told me what he needed for rehearsal time, told me the kind of players he wanted to have in the band and we worked it from there.[2]

Russell's first UK tour took place in February and March 1986, and the Anglo-American Living Time Orchestra played ten dates covering virtually the whole of England. Of the players who made that tour, one or two proved with hindsight to be wrong for the music and, while saxophonist Courtney Pine had proved an excellent choice, his own career was just taking off and he was unable to play with Russell again. Russell brought with him keyboardist Brad Hatfield, bassist Bill Urmson and drummer Keith Copeland. Serious' success in selecting the right players is illustrated by the fact that a fair number of those chosen would play on Russell's subsequent European tours. Trumpeter Stuart Brooks, saxophonists Pete Hurt and Chris Biscoe, and Danish trumpeter Palle Mikkelborg would all continue their association with Russell into the twenty-first century. Trombonist Pete Burchill would also play on Russell's next European tour in 1989, while bass trombonist Ashley Slater played with Russell on two further tours.

The experience of playing with Russell was to prove particularly important to the young Courtney Pine. He describes it as a marvellous apprenticeship that taught him a lot about being a bandleader, like how to rehearse a band, how to get the best out of his musicians, how to conduct and how to relate to an audience. As he said, "At that time it was just what I needed."

As well as his own band, Pine had been instrumental in forming and directing the Jazz Warriors big band.

> We had some really deep conversations and out of that the things that were played by the Jazz Warriors came out of that whole experience. He's got this Lydian Chromatic Concept that Steve Williamson showed me first and I got a copy of it and read it inside out and played it inside out but just checking his scores, I based my writing for the Jazz Warriors on that experience. All the African cross-rhythms, where you get three or four drums playing, he's not just done that but put it on brass instruments, so you get that kind of cross-rhythm thing happening. So when I looked down the score and saw how George did it, I thought, "That's exactly what I'm going to do," and I did.

And he added, "Yeah, a lot of those tunes are George Russell inspired."[3]

Chris Biscoe had heard, via trombonist Rick Taylor, who was helping Serious put the band together, that the tour was happening. Biscoe was a fan of Russell's sixties sextet records, in particular *The Outer View*, and asked Taylor to consider him for the tour. "I said, I'd be really interested in that because I really liked the music. I really love that format of the sextet because you can get very interesting colours and a bit of orchestration but you still get the sort of small-band feel with it as well."[4]

Rehearsals were exacting, as Biscoe recalled, and it was not easy for the players new to Russell's music. "The first rehearsal, we did an enormous amount of material in three days. It was very hard material and it was very intense—in physical circumstances that were extremely difficult because it was extremely cold and rather dank in the place we were rehearsing in. It was pretty tough because he's quite a hard taskmaster."[5]

As a relative newcomer, Pine was surprised by the amount of written material that they were to cover. "I remember loads of sheet music and turning loads of pages over and thinking, 'Is this right?' I'd never seen so much music for a jazz gig. I mean, I'd done other big bands but there were just reams and reams of stuff. And it was very complex music." Pine said Russell used the big band arrangement of "So What" as "a way of finding out who in the band could do what and to bring the American rhythm section he'd brought from the States and the British horn players together."

"He wanted to get the feel right first," Pine remembered, and though the band struggled through the piece at first, it became easier from there on. "After that I realized that this guy wasn't just wanting us to play what was on the paper. He was after something special."[6]

Pine's comments are important. What he is saying is that musicians who have played with Russell over protracted periods may not have studied with him but they still absorbed much of what he has to say musically and theoretically.

Pete Hurt played baritone and bass clarinet on Russell's first tour and on subsequent tours. He was primarily a tenor and soprano player and it was his reputation as a musician that got him the gig. He played the initial rehearsals on borrowed instruments, using Courtney Pine's rather ancient bass clarinet and a baritone borrowed from a friend.

> So George can look a bit fearsome sometimes and he'd never heard us play before and we started playing and I thought, "Oh, God. He hates us." But after a bit he seemed to think to himself, "Actually, they're not too bad," and everyone began to relax a bit. But personally, I was very nervous but after the first rehearsal I started to enjoy it. Playing most of George's music, you have to rehearse fairly intensely. You need a road map really. Apart from some of the earlier things, which are quite straightforward, you can't just sit down. It's not like someone counts in and you're off. I've done Carla Bley's big band and that's a lot more straightforward. I think George's music is, in the end, more rewarding because you have to work a lot harder at it and you get more out of it.[7]

Hurt explained further:

Some of his music is fairly straightforward, but some of it is like, "What on earth do I do here?" because he has such a unique way of writing. He may have one rhythm going, say, in the rhythm section, and he has a group of instruments, not necessarily written sections, like a saxophone, a keyboard, and a trombone who do something completely against the rhythm. It might be completely out of tempo, and there might be several other groups of instruments doing other completely different things, and you've got to try and coordinate all this. If you're playing out-of-tempo lines against a fixed rhythm, trying to ride that can be very difficult. Sometimes the parts can be a little confusing and it takes a lot of rehearsal to coordinate all these different layers going on. [8]

British-based Canadian trumpeter Kenny Wheeler was also on that tour and remembered Russell's stagecraft and skill at communicating with both band and audience.

We played some of the old pieces, like "All About Rosie." I must admit that I liked them much better than the newer pieces. The newer pieces kind of had a lot of different things happening at once, so much so that when I played my part I didn't feel it was all that important somehow. But I did like his actual compositions. They were very good. As for the audience, I think they loved the music. As I said, George was very good at communicating to an audience, and to the band also, but the audiences seemed to like it very much. [9]

Bearing in mind that Russell had not toured Britain before, the tour was a major success. Cumming was particularly pleased and was determined to continue what had proved a very successful partnership with George and Alice Russell. "We had a lot of fun on the tour, as you do when you start to feel comfortable with people. You get away from that sort of thing where it's, 'Oh, god, I hope that's all going to work.' You get to the point where you can see the tour growing night by night and the music growing night by night." [10]

Reviewing the opening date of the tour at London's Logan Hall, John Fordham's piece in the *Guardian* confirmed a mixture of first night nerves and bravura playing. "For a pick-up band," wrote Fordham, "it was a spectacular first night with some of the most demanding compositions in Jazz." [11] Richard Williams in the *Times* was quietly enthusiastic about the gig and seemed to enjoy the first set's back catalogue of "Cubano-Be, Cubano-Bop," *All About Rosie*, and *Electronic Sonata* more than set two's *The African Game*. He noted in respect of the latter, "Between bouts of therapeutic rowdiness, several memorable events occurred." [12] By the time the tour hit Southampton's Mountbatten Hall, however, Derek Eaton's review in the *Southern Evening Echo* began with the words, "Electrifying, riveting, immaculate" and ended, "The hall reverberated to incredible gargantuan sounds." [13] In fact, the tour went so well overall that Russell was back the following year to play festivals in France and Austria and also the Bracknell Festival in the UK.

Russell had worked well with both his audiences and his musicians, who appreciated his democratic style, as Chris Biscoe noted.

In fact, in a way it's surprising and not surprising, in view of what I said about him being a taskmaster. I think he's a very nice person, and, for instance, he always travels with the band. We've done some terribly tough schedules for someone his age because he's not a young man. I thought he would certainly have been justified in saying, "I want a limo" or "Put me on a plane," instead of going on the coach with the other people or something like that. He wants to travel with the band—and I've seen other examples of that—not to have special treatment. In the way he treats people, he's a very sort of democratic person. [14]

The warmth of the response Russell had received in the UK was clearly reflected at the time in an article by Stan Woolley. Woolley produced a full and detailed profile of Russell for British magazine *Jazz Journal* that proved the beginning of a love affair between the British jazz press and the composer. [15]

In autumn of 1987 and back in America, Russell played a prestigious concert at Washington's Baird Auditorium in the Museum of Natural History. The concert, one of a series of avant-garde big-band performances promoted by the District Curators and Smithsonian Resident Associates, was preceded by a long feature from Howard Mandel in the *Washington Post*. [16] The program featured *The African Game*, *Electronic Sonata* and "Cubano-Be, Cubano-Bop," which included a tape recording of Sabu Martinez's 1977 performance in Stockholm. Reviewing the concert, also in the *Post*, Geoffrey Himes wrote, "Not only were the harmonics, melodic and dynamic shifts in the extended suites often astonishing but the rollicking, joyful rhythms often tempted one to flout the Smithsonian's decorum and get up in the aisles and dance." [17]

That November, Russell toured the United States with a sextet that included himself on piano, Mingus alumnus John Stubblefield on saxes, Graham Haynes on trumpet, Brad Hatfield on keyboards, Bill Urmson on bass and Keith Copeland on drums. Compared to the difficult experiences of the sixties, Russell was, in comparison, having some success in getting his music out there to the American public.

The following spring Russell was invited to play in Japan for the first time at the end of the 4th Tokyo Music Joy Festival, with a version of the Living Time Orchestra that featured a number of Japanese musicians. Kuniharu Akiyama, reviewing the concert in *Komei Shimbun*, commented, "Responding to the prism of emotions, we, the audience, feel the throbbing in our hearts and enjoy a feeling of being musically satiated; this was the effect of Russell's performance that night." The concert was recorded and released as *New York—Live in Tokyo* in Japan on Electric Bird, featuring strong performances of "Cubano-Be, Cubano-Bop," *All About Rosie*, *Electronic Sonata* and "Pan-Daddy" (from *The Stratus Seekers*), as well as extracts from *Listen to the Silence* and *New York, N.Y.* A video was also made of the performance and issued in Japan, although both remain very hard to obtain. [18]

In fact, Russell's visit provoked a lot of interest in Japan, not only in his music but in his Lydian Concept. Japanese composer Toru Takemitsu had already expressed his admiration for the work and as a result of the TMJ concert Russell was invited back in 1993 to give a two-day seminar at the Epicurus Studio in Tokyo. William Penn Montgomery, writing in the *Japan Times*, noted, "Russell was pleased with the turnout and said that it was encouraging to see his work taken seriously in Japan. The price tag of ¥20000 for the clinic and ¥13000 for the Japanese version of the book was worth the chance to spend two days studying with the master." [19]

Back in Boston, Russell premiered another new piece on March 18, 1988, at NEC's Jordan Hall as part of the Boston Globe Jazz Festival. Intriguingly, *Six Aesthetic Gravities* was commissioned by Boston Musica Viva, an ensemble devoted to twentieth-century composition, and was Russell's first commission by a "classical" music group. According to *DownBeat*, Russell's piece stole the show from Kurt Weill's one-act opera *War Play* and "manifested Russell's typically vivid textures and dance-like momentum." [20] Then, at the end of June, another Russell work, *Centrifugue*, was given its first and only performance in Philadelphia as part of the Freedom Week celebrations. Performed by the contemporary music ensemble Relâche and commissioned by Bell Atlantic, Daniel Webster of the *Philadelphia Inquirer* raved about the piece and Relâche's "purpose and authority" in its execution. [21]

Such varied opportunities to compose and perform must have seemed very encouraging. Yet, though hardly overnight, a gradual shift had begun around 1988 that would see a change in Russell's area of operation. Russell again toured Europe in the spring of 1988 and was now becoming a regular feature on the European jazz scene. The relationship with John Cumming and his team had become increasingly important, especially when gigs in his homeland again became less frequent. Without the kinds of packages of support, funding and organization offered by a company such as Serious, the economics of touring a big band can be prohibitive. Nor at that time in the States was there a network of producers capable of piecing together a realistic tour schedule.

Apart from three dates in 1999 with the full Anglo-American Living Time Orchestra on the East Coast, Russell was to make his last major U.S. tour in 1988. Sponsored by the New England Foundation for the Arts, the Living Time Orchestra visited five New England states, playing ten colleges and universities, including Wesleyan, Lowell, and Dartmouth. Russell had also been commissioned by New England Presenters to write a new work, which he called *Uncommon Ground*.

Around this point, work prospects for big bands became increasingly bleak in the United States. American jazz artists, including those writing for and leading large ensembles, looked more and more to Europe for gigs and a process began where Europe's festivals began to be dominated by American performers.

It was not that Russell stopped being honoured and acknowledged in America. Ironically, just before embarking on his 1989 European tour, Russell was contacted by Kenneth Hope of the John D. and Catherine T. MacArthur Foundation and told that he had been awarded a fellowship. The sum involved was $375,000, paid over five years and followed a similar award to Russell's friend and NEC colleague Ran Blake. The press statement from the foundation noted that *The Lydian Chromatic Concept of Tonal Organization* was "one of the first major theoretical contributions by a jazz musician. It stands as a pioneer work in the investigation of contemporary modal harmony." [22]

Russell's 1989 Living Time Orchestra included Brad Hatfield, Bill Urmson, Chris Biscoe, Stuart Brooks, Pete Hurt, Pete Burchill, and Ashley Slater, who had toured with him in 1986. Russell had been very sorry to lose Courtney Pine but accepted that Pine had to avail himself of the chances that were coming his way. His replacement, who had joined the Living Time Orchestra in 1987, could not have been better. Andy Sheppard had begun his playing career with a group called Sphere featuring Geoff Williams on piano, Pete Maxfield on bass and Tony Orrell on drums, with Trevor Taylor occasionally depping for Orrell. Signed by Island Records alongside Pine in the mid-eighties, Sheppard is the only British musician to have played with the "Big Three" American big-band leaders—Gil Evans, Carla Bley and George Russell. Sheppard was the only British member of the band Russell took to Tokyo in 1988. He had been introduced to Carla Bley by Steve Swallow, who had recommended him along the lines: "You're going to love this tenor player. He doesn't sound like anyone else." [23] Sheppard recalls his first rehearsal with Russell very clearly indeed. He had already listened to *The African Game* but when he got to the first rehearsal,

> All the stuff I thought was improvised was all written. It was just a nightmare. I was really struggling. So I knew George was into scales, and the music had a scale written on it from the previous sax player. It's my tenor solo, so I'm sticking on this scale, thinking that's what he wants, just to improvise using these notes. Anyway, he came over and, he's a bugger is George, and he says, "It's no good just playing a blues scale, man!" but really heavy! So I thought, there's two ways here. Either leave and don't come back or say, "Fuck you!" and I just went mad when I played and got the gig! [24]

Also joining the Living Time Orchestra in 1988 was pianist Steve Lodder. Lodder replaced Django Bates, who was unable to make that year's tour and who, with hindsight, was perhaps not the best choice in the first place. Bates's approach is not only distinctive but idiosyncratic, or even eccentric, characteristics that are not easily accommodated in Russell's music world. Lodder was, however, an excellent replacement. As it was for Sheppard and others before them, the first rehearsal in a basement in Clerkenwell was highly demanding. Not only was the noise deafening but the bigger problem was the adjustment required by Russell's music.

> There was no looking at it beforehand and of having to get into this man's way of thinking. Just sitting there, reading and reading. You can't really do that. I remember going home after the first day, thinking that this was the tiredest I'd ever felt, simply because there was so much information being chucked at me because the music is so dense, so you're trying to find your way around aurally and trying to find your way around on the page, which is hard. Not an easy day. [25]

Making aural sense of things is itself a problem initially, as Lodder explained. This is partly because of the way Russell organizes the music: in cycles that compete and interlock in different ways at different times. However, it is also because of the way the internal arrangement of musicians into pairs, trios, and quartets within the whole varies within and between numbers.

> Rehearsals can be tricky as well because he knows exactly what he wants; if he's not hearing it, you can spend a long, long, long time trying to get [him] to hear it. So it can be a drum pattern or particular synth sound or anything that—if it's not as he's heard it in his head or

heard it before in performance—the rehearsal will just stop and it could be twenty minutes and that's a very uncomfortable twenty minutes if you're the person on the receiving end not coming up with the goods for some reason or because you don't understand or it's not possible or whatever. [26]

Nor is it easy for a keyboard player in the band working with three other chordal instruments—perhaps a synth, guitar, and vibes—especially when you are not merely doubling a part, as Lodder noted. "The keyboard's very much there for colours and power and harmonic complexity because he likes that. There'll be two internal areas sometimes going on in the keyboards and another one in the vibes. Then the guitar will take a line over the top." [27]

That it produces music of such power despite its complexity is, as Lodder pointed out, due to Russell's grasp of harmony, "I think because he's got a really good understanding of the way things stack up harmonically, with things on top of other things. So that what for somebody is a full conventional jazz chord, that's kind of the starting point for George and then other things just get put on top." [28]

Others joining the band in 1989 included trumpeter, author and broadcaster Ian Carr, who would later make two BBC Radio 3 documentaries on Russell—*The Trailblazer* and *The Invisible Guru*. Steve Johns had by now replaced Keith Copeland on drums and the other important new arrival was guitarist David Fiuczynski. Russell has always had a strong affinity for guitarists from Barry Galbraith onward and had been immediately taken with Fiuczynski's guitar playing.

The band played dates in the UK that included the Brecon and Edinburgh festivals, Snape Maltings in Aldeburgh (the venue associated with Benjamin Britten), and four nights at Ronnie Scott's Club, where the band recorded a two CD album for Label Bleu. They also played dates in Belgium, Germany, Luxembourg and Portugal. Press coverage was excellent, with features in the *Guardian*, *Times*, *Sunday Times*, *International Herald Tribune* and *Time Out*. [29]

*The London Concert* was recorded between August 28-31 at Ronnie Scott's Club. Recording at the club is not easy, as the control booth itself is—or at least was—located in another building a few doors along Frith Street. Though the album is essentially a live recording, the difficulty of some of the material coupled with the usual problems involved in obtaining a good sound balance of a large ensemble in a small club meant that some parts were recorded or overdubbed during the day. Keyboardist Brad Hatfield remembered it as an amusing but challenging experience. Those pieces that had been played extensively on the road were working really well but some others needed additional rehearsal.

> So it took its toll, on the horn players especially. Also, being in that club and the band being at the dynamic level we were, we had horns at the back, so the rhythm section's in front, which we do because that keeps the rhythm section from getting too much into the horn mikes but it doesn't keep the horns from blasting in to the overheads of the drum mikes. So it was an engineering nightmare, further confounded by the fact that the control booth was down the street. So you actually had to leave the club, walk down a couple of buildings, go

up a couple of staircases, through somebody's office and, finally, you arrive at the control room. So going and checking out playbacks and communicating with the engineer in a normal fashion was ridiculous. So we had a lot of telephone conversations. *(laughs)* [30]

Russell had recognized the talent of guitarist David Fiuczynski when he was a student at NEC. Fiuczynski struggled somewhat in his first year at the school due to tendonitis and had been unable to take Russell's ensemble class. He had heard, however, stories from classmates of "what an awkward character he was in terms of his music and personally." His first real contact with Russell was far more positive, however.

> I was rehearsing with a trio and he came down to the room where we were rehearsing and he had a locker there and was putting some music away. He heard us playing and he started listening. We were all really intimidated but kept on playing until he was like, "Wow! Where have you been hiding?" *(imitates Russell)* He invited us to play a piece at his annual concert at the school and I think that's probably one of the few times he's ever had someone do a piece that wasn't his music. A great introduction. We were scared when he left. We were scared when we played. It was great. From then on I started taking his classes. He was really supportive. [31]

Fiuczynski's comments about Russell as a teacher and bandleader provide a real insight into the composer's priorities. Acknowledging that he still uses Russell's perspective on, and distinction between, the vertical and horizontal approaches to improvisation and composition in his own work, Fiuczynski saw Russell's personality and charisma as being highly significant in terms of his ability to communicate his ideas and expectations.

> Besides the fact, he was just a very inspiring person and there was just so much there as soon as he walked into the room and just by being there and being with him and interacting. Even though he's a no-bullshit kind of guy, he didn't have any patience if you didn't do your homework, but he didn't have any patience if you did all your homework and weren't saying anything. He didn't have any time for that either. He didn't care about correct notes. He wanted flavour, groove, soul, happiness, pain, lyricism. That was very important to him. [32]

Now a teacher at Berklee, Fiuczynski understands Russell's impatience in this respect only too well. While still at NEC, Fiuczynski began playing in the Living Time Orchestra. The Ronnie Scott's Club gigs and recording were the highlight of his involvement with Russell.

> It was intense. It was, like, my first really big thing. We'd played the music inside and out but even if you know the music, it's work—great work, if you can get it—but it's a lot of concentration and focus. There was also a lot of pressure to get it done. We'd record during the day, do a couple of shows at night and record again during the day. It must've been really hard on the lead trumpet players. [33]

Beginning, as usual, with three days of intense rehearsal, the demands were certainly severe, but as Fiuczynski reveals, there are clear reasons why Russell's musicians are prepared to put up with his demands.

> As much as he wanted from you, you received twice back, if not more. Just in terms of the support or the criticism you would get. It was always there for you to grow. And when he gave you a spot to do your thing, he always wanted you to shine. He encouraged you to speak in your own voice. It was always very exciting for him to hear something creative, new and different. The last thing he wanted to hear was something that had already been done. He could be very hard if something was played incorrectly but I'll never forget that when we were playing things correctly and he was frustrated, he was like, "You've got the notes together. Screw the notes. I can care less about the notes. You have to say something." [34]

Brad Hatfield was very much involved in remixing the record back in Boston and the sound on *The London Concert* is quite exceptional given the problems its making involved. Ian Carr had been asked to do the tour in the absence of Japanese trumpeter Tiger Okoshi. He was not playing that much at the time, concentrating instead on his writing and broadcasting. One of Britain's finest musicians, Carr began the tour struggling with his embouchure.

The tour had taken the Living Time Orchestra to Italy, where Carr was quite well known due to his work with Nucleus and with the pan-European United Jazz and Rock Ensemble. Before one of the Italian dates, he was recognized by some Italian fans on the street. "I was with the trumpets and we were just getting ready and three Italians came 'round the corner, and one said, in a very loud voice, 'That's the legendary Ian Carr.' And the other trumpeters looked at me in complete disbelief." Disbelief turned to dismay later, however.

> [O]n the first day, I could see these young guys saying, "God, this is the 'great' Ian Carr. What the hell's going [on]?" So in the interval, I went up to George and said, "George, would you really rather like me to drop out and get somebody else?" He said, "No, no. I want you." So I stayed and, of course by the third rehearsal, my chops were really strong and so it was okay. But I really liked him for that. I would have gone, you know, because he could have got several other trumpet players. [35]

Carr was in fine form by the time they got to Ronnie's and plays beautifully on *The London Concert*'s versions of "So What" and "Electronic Sonata," which also features the 'rap' Russell had added on a previous tour. Amusingly, Carr had been banned from Ronnie's following a disagreement with its other owner, Pete King, eighteen years before. Fortunately, bygones were allowed to be bygones and Carr's ban was lifted.

As Andy Sheppard remembered, the band was really hot by the time they played Ronnie's. "It was a good band actually; the balance of personalities, I thought, were really strong—Chris Biscoe, they [the rest of the band] really kind of rose to the occasion. I think that's what George liked about the British band was that they all wanted to get it right and play the music and give it that 100 percent." [36]

*The London Concert* features fine performances of "So What" and *Electronic Sonata* but it is also very much a new record. It contains the only recordings of Russell's two 1988 commissions, *Six Aesthetic Gravities* and *Uncommon Ground*. The band also performs "Struggle of the Magicians," by sometime Living Time Orchestra member Mark White, and "La Folia: The Rocella Variations," a joint composition with Ben Schwendener, Russell's assistant/deputy.

*Uncommon Ground* is a highly dramatic piece, with dense electronic synth passages and powerful bass lines from Bill Urmson. Soloists emerge from the sound and punctuate the music briefly rather than dominate it with extended choruses. "La Folia," on the other hand, is one of the more atypical pieces in Russell's repertoire, suggesting that Schwendener's influence on the piece was quite significant. Its opening has an almost madrigal feel to it but it opens out beautifully, with strong playing from Andy Sheppard and David Fiuczynski, into what might be described as "funky baroque." But perhaps the most important piece on the double CD is "*Six Aesthetic Gravities*," which betrays its origins as a piece for a non-jazz ensemble, its sections fitting together subtly but building section by section. Though it has its moments of drama and release, the impression it leaves is one of quiet intensity. An excellent record, *The London Concert* makes a good entry point to Russell's late period work.

On both sides of the Atlantic, 1990 proved to be a good year for Russell. Back home in Boston in January, Russell was one of the three recipients of a Jazz Master Fellowship awarded by the National Endowment for the Arts. The other recipients were Cecil Taylor and trumpeter/composer Gerald Wilson. The award of $20,000 was again given without strings.[37] Then, in July in Britain, the Living Time Orchestra was in Glasgow for the city's first International Jazz Festival. In fact, Russell was composer-in-residence for the week, which he and the band spent working with school and college students, as well as performing a concert at the Theatre Royal on Friday, July 6. There were a few changes in the band from 1989. Tiger Okoshi was back, Teese Gohl took over briefly from Steve Lodder, Pat Hollenbeck made his first European trip with Russell and saxophonists David Mann (who had been in Japan with Russell) and John Purcell were in for Chris Biscoe and Pete Hurt. Russell was also commissioned to write a new work for the festival. In fact, he produced something quite exceptional. In *American Trilogy*, he took two earlier pieces, "You Are My Sunshine" and "The Ballad of Hix Blewitt," to which he added "The Battle Hymn of the Republic" to create a three-movement work. The piece became a concert favourite following this first appearance.[38]

The Glasgow concert was broadcast on November 5, 1990, on BBC Radio 3. Derek Drescher, then a producer at the BBC and a tireless supporter of jazz throughout his period at the station, was the architect behind the program and also behind Ian Carr's two documentaries on Russell. It is perhaps hard for music fans in countries without a well-established and well-funded public service broadcasting network to appreciate how essential this is for minority interest music to get exposure and access to audiences. Radio 3 is a jewel in the UK's media. Its support for classical music, new music, world music and jazz, though constantly threatened by governments of neo-liberal philistines, is *sans pareil*, and has been so for decades. There is simply nothing to touch it anywhere in the world.

Introduced by veteran broadcaster Charles Fox, the program also featured a long interview with Andy Sheppard about his experiences working with Russell. The band plays *Listen to the Silence*, *American Trilogy*, and *Uncommon Ground*, closing, as always, with "So What."

Russell returned with the Living Time Orchestra in 1991 to play the Town & Country Club in London as part of the Camden Jazz Festival. There had been good pre-gig publicity. Martin Gayford had written a good piece in the *Telegraph* prior to the festival, and even Tower Records in Piccadilly was plugging the concert.[39]

Reviewing the gig in the *Financial Times*, Garry Booth was full of praise for both Russell and Jimmy Giuffre, who had played the Jazz Café with Paul Bley and Steve Swallow as part of the festival. His review carried mixed encouragement for the Jazz Warriors, noting that they only really came alive when American trombonist Craig Harris joined them and he all but ignored Cassandra Wilson's support slot for the Living Time Orchestra gig. Booth wrote, "The sight and sound of the Living Time Orchestra is far removed from the image of Russell as jazz theorist and provides the best possible opening to the 'outdoor' season ahead and close to a Camden fest of mixed blessings."[40]

By way of complete contrast, trumpeter-photographer Roland Ramanan's review in the *Wire* put the opposite case. The Warriors' performance, he wrote, "clearly demonstrated the potential that can be unleashed from the Jazz Warriors if they only had a strong conductor and a writer with imagination and courage." Cassandra Wilson, however, "bewitched and beguiled with her marvellous voice." The Living Time Orchestra, on the other hand, got short shrift. Ramanan refers to Russell's "over-stuffed rhythm section," which "came equipped with concrete over-shoes," and described *Uncommon Ground* as "fairly typical: simple motifs being added to, layer by layer, until I was being pushed back by the wave of sound." He concluded, "I was grooved but not moved."[41]

The May 1991 European release of *The London Concert* from the band's 1989 Scott Club residency brought, however, a glowing review from the *Guardian*'s John Fordham:

> The recording catches Russell's characteristic mix of mid-tempo rockers, baroque classicisms that turn into funk, misty abstract passages illuminated by sudden flares, wry outbursts of jazz tempo. The sheer quantity of musical events behind the solos (slabs of ensemble horn sounds colliding, slewing guitar effects, percussion cross-rhythms) makes Russell's band an ensemble of compelling intensity and depth whilst sustaining a rock group's rhythmic earthiness.[42]

There was a further spring date in Paris that year, plus a couple of gigs in France and Belgium that autumn. By contrast, 1992 seems to have been a comparatively quiet year for Russell, with just one gig for the Living Time Orchestra in Virginia. There was also quite a delay between the European release of *The London Concert* and its American release on Stash Records and it was not until March 1993 that Gary Giddins reviewed the album in the *Voice*. Giddins's only complaint was that Stash issued *The London Concert* as two separate discs. Otherwise, it was a "stunning entertainment, brash and vigorous and swinging, sometimes eerily beautiful, frequently ebullient."[43]

A couple of months after the U.S. release, Russell was elected to the Hall of Fame in *DownBeat*'s 2nd Annual Achievement Awards for Jazz Education. Bearing in mind that Russell was now seventy and had been teaching at NEC for a quarter century, it was an honour richly deserved. MacArthur Fellowships, Guggenheim Awards, NEA Awards—no one could suggest that Russell was without honour at home. Periods of public neglect aside, however, the most sorry occurrence in Russell's long and distinguished career took place between the spring of 1992 and August 1993.

It all began with a casual lunch between Marty Khan, Russell's American manager, and Rob Gibson, director of the Lincoln Center's jazz program. There are differing accounts of what did and did not happen and of what was and was not said. Because of these differences, the matter has never really been put to bed. It went on to become the focus of disagreement within New York's jazz community and indirectly produced one of its strangest tales.

Khan remembered that Gibson at one point mentioned that "he was tired of trying to tell his children that all of the great jazz musicians were dead and that there were no living great jazz musicians." Khan asked him, "What about George Russell? That's certainly one of the giants of modern music, not just jazz. What about him? He'll be turning seventy years old shortly and I think he'll be an ideal person." According to Khan, Gibson agreed and suggested that they put the prospect of a Russell concert at the Lincoln Center in motion. A meeting followed between Alice Norbury-Russell, Khan's partner Helene Cann, and Gibson, which seemed to indicate a strong intent on the part of the Lincoln Center team to go ahead with the project. A fax from Norbury-Russell to John Cumming dated March 26, 1992, notes that the meeting had taken place the previous week. Her fax confirms her strong impression that Gibson was committed to the idea. She even noted two sets of dates offered—"August 4 through August 14 for a week of rehearsal and a concert," and later another date in the following March. Norbury-Russell added that the latter would be better due to plans to tour Europe in August 1993. Again according to Khan, from June 1992 onward he and Cann tried to contact Gibson by phone to follow up on the suggested concert but were not able to speak with the director. By the tone of Khan's fax to Gibson dated December 23, 1992, Khan was not only justifiably frustrated but had also been quite rudely treated by some junior Lincoln Center staff. [44]

Gibson's letter dated January 4, 1993, is conciliatory and apologetic. While one could not conclude from it that anyone was getting cold feet about the project, one sentence seems, with hindsight, prophetic, if not indicative in that respect. Noting that the Centre had not completed its planning for the forthcoming season of concerts by the time intended, Gibson wrote, "While we understand that we may have missed out on an opportunity to produce some programs because of our delays, this is something we must accept." [45] The rest of his comments certainly indicated an intention to continue to try to promote Russell at the Centre. Further attempts to achieve any progress with this on the part of Outward Visions foundered. The concert never went ahead and the Russells remained in the dark as to why this was the case.

In such circumstances, rumour and supposition often fill in the gaps. According to Marty Khan, he was contacted in the summer of 1993 by a New York journalist who had been at a meeting with a number of other journalists and Lincoln Center staff at Gibson's home. It transpired that this had taken place on July 13, 1993 and the purpose was to try to improve relations between the Lincoln Center and the New York and jazz press. A report of the meeting appeared in the *Village Voice* more than a year later in the context of a longer article by Richard B. Woodward about "the missteps that have dogged jazz at Lincoln Center." [46] Titled "Jazz Wars: A Tale of Age, Rage and Hash Brownies," the article included the allegation that the journalists were fed brownies for dessert laced with hashish. This was, of course, vehemently denied by Rob Gibson.

> We invited eight to ten guys over just to talk. I actually thought it was a nice dinner and I thought we had a good time. But at the end of the night the publicist at Jazz at Lincoln Center (Marilyn Laverty), who had made dessert, served brownies. Somebody said, "What'd you put in the brownies?" She said, "Wouldn't you like to know!" Two weeks later a cover story appeared in the *Village Voice* called "A Rage Supreme" where they claimed we had put hash in the brownies—hashish in the brownies—which was of course a total and utter lie... this is the kind of stuff that goes on. [47]

Russell's connection with the discussions was a small one, but has, in the context of the debacle, assumed more prominence. Khan stated that the journalist who contacted him told him that "one of the things that was brought up was the issue of what had happened to the George Russell event that was supposed to occur." Khan continued, "At that time, Stanley Crouch told them that the reason why George was not... why the date was not going to happen is that after numerous phone conversations between Stanley and George, George adamantly refused to use an acoustic rhythm section for the performance of his earlier works like *All About Rosie* and the classic works that he had done in the early fifties." [48]

However one reads this, the fact that the Russells were left unclear why the planned or proposed concert did not go forward resulted from the fact that they have never received a clear response from the Lincoln Center. Certainly, as far as they were concerned, no such conversations between Russell and Crouch ever took place. The reason the Russells, Khan, band members, friends, colleagues and associates believe the concert discussed did not go ahead was due to Russell's use of electric instrumentation. The outcome is that Russell was unable in later life—and indeed during what was his most active and successful period as a performer—to perform his music at the Lincoln Center, which had become one of the most prestigious in America in presenting jazz to the public.

In September 1998 the *New York Times* ran its own story on Jazz at Lincoln Center. The author covered many of the areas of dispute, and quoted Russell at one point: "They've done a lot to take the essence of jazz and distort it; they've put a damper on the main ingredient of jazz, which is innovation. I think that whatever happens at Lincoln Center, history will have to correct it because it does need correcting terribly." [49] In fairness to all concerned, this was a measured and dignified comment, especially in light of Russell's own experiences.

A while later, after Gibson left Lincoln Center, Alice Norbury-Russell received a further approach regarding a possible concert at the venue around Russell's eightieth birthday in 2003. Money was apparently discussed but, according to Khan and Norbury-Russell, the sums involved would have seen the Russells partly funding the concert. Russell himself decided that, in any event, he was unwilling to have anything to do with Jazz at Lincoln Center and the proposal went no further. Ironically, in April 2020, JLCO with Wynton Marsalis were due to perform "some of the most masterfully structured pieces of the jazz canon written by musical architects such as Jelly Roll Morton, Charles Mingus, Thelonious Monk and George Russell" at the venue. The concert was cancelled due to the Covid-19 pandemic. [50]

As a codicil to the Lincoln Center saga, Russell did get to play New York with his Anglo-American Living Time Orchestra in 1999. The band played in Boston, Washington, and New York. The Washington gig at the Smithsonian was high profile with a good fee and this allowed a certain amount of flexibility for the New York date. Sadly, the venue was less prestigious than Russell deserved. It was also very poorly publicized by the firm the Russells were using, which resulted in Khan and Cann taking over late in the day to try and improve the situation. Ben Ratliff of the *New York Times* provided a generally favourable review, though he was not overawed by the sound of the synths, which he deemed "jazzanachronisms." [51] That said, the concert on May 8 at the Tribeca Arts Centre garnered a fine review from John Szwed in the *Village Voice*.

As Szwed wrote in a highly perceptive conclusion about a program that featured *American Trilogy*, *It's About Time*, *All About Rosie* and the Gil Evans arrangement of "Stratusphunk,"

> It's also obvious now that those reassuring rock rhythms make Russell's compositions seem more innocent than they really are: underneath lie shifting moods and tone centres, overlapping contrapuntal figures and riffs which skip across the beat and erode tonality. Even deeper yet, there are his serpentine, rumbling 5/2 bass lines: perhaps subsonic representations of a musical world to which jazz—whatever that is—is still afraid to commit. [52]

Writing on his Web site three years later, Marty Khan commented:

In 1999, we had the wonderful opportunity to hear George's *real* Living Time Orchestra (the one that Europeans have had the benefits of hearing for years) in its first (!?!) American appearance. We traveled from Tucson just to be at these concerts in New York City and at the Smithsonian in Washington, D.C. [53]

Russell's problems in sustaining a consistent audience for his music in America seem to have little to do with either proper acknowledgment of his talents or of his contribution to jazz, the Lincoln Center debacle aside. Although his ability to tour regularly with musicians of his choice at appropriate recompense certainly resulted in a switch of focus of operations to Europe, Russell played quite a number of concerts in the United States following his return from Scandinavia. While these were less frequent than they might have been, Russell is not the only jazz artist of stature who has found work in Europe easier to come by from the eighties to the present. The problem for Russell seems in part the costs of touring a big band coupled with lack of funding support, and what might be seen as the innate conservatism of American audiences. If the latter remark seems a little unfair, American readers might ask themselves why so many of their more adventurous jazz musicians have found Europe more welcoming of their talents from the fifties to the present. [54]

## Notes

1. Interview with John Cumming, May 2003.
2. Ibid.
3. Interview with Courtney Pine, May 2005.
4. Interview with Chris Biscoe, February 2006.
5. Ibid.
6. Interview with Pine.
7. Interview with Pete Hurt, June 2003.
8. Ibid.
9. Interview with Kenny Wheeler, August 2004.
10. Interview with Cumming.
11. John Fordham, "George and the Geometry," *Guardian* (Manchester), February 28, 1986.
12. Richard Williams, "Patterns of Relish," *Times* (London), February 28, 1986.
13. Derek Eaton, "Band Strikes High Note," *Southern Evening Echo* (Southampton), March 3, 1986.
14. Interview with Biscoe.
15. Stan Woolley, "George Russell," *Jazz Journal* 39, no. 10 (October 1986).
16. Howard Mandel, "The Mathematical Musician," *Washington Post*, September 27, 1987.
17. Geoffrey Himes, "Russell: In the Mood for Modes," *Washington Post*, October 3, 1987.
18. Kuniharu Akiyama, reviewing the concert in *Komei Shimbun*, March 5, 1988; George Russell and the Living Time Orchestra—New York—Live in Tokyo, Electric Bird 6488/89.
19. William Penn Montgomery, "Theorist Proposes a Scale Harmonious with All Music," *Japan Times*, August 6, 1993.
20. Fred Bouchard, Review of Boston Musica Viva performance of Six Aesthetic Gravities, *DownBeat*, June 1988.
21. Daniel Webster, "Relâche Presents Flashes of Americana," *Philadelphia Inquirer*, July 1, 1989.
22. F. Gonzalez, "Russell Will Finish My Life's Work," *Boston Globe*, July 19, 1989.
23. Duncan Heining, "Carla Bley," *Independent* (London), November 16, 1999.
24. Duncan Heining, "Learning to Wave," *Avant* 9 (Autumn 1998).
25. Interview with Steve Lodder, February 2003.
26. Ibid.
27. Ibid.
28. Ibid.
29. C. Davis, "The Week Ahead (Preview of Brecon Jazz Festival," *Times* (London), August 12, 1989; R. Cook, "Old Hand Who Gets a Kick out of the Big Band," *Sunday Times* (London), August 27, 1989; J. Fordham, "King George's Gold Blend," *Guardian* (Manchester), September 1, 1989; P. Urpeth, "George Russell (Preview of LTO at Ronnie Scott's Club, London," *Time Out*, August 30–September 6, 1989; M. Zwerin, "Probing the Dialectics of Chords," *International Herald Tribune*, August 10, 1989.
30. Interview with Brad Hatfield, June 2003.
31. Interview with David Fiuczynski, February 2006.
32. Ibid.
33. Ibid.

34. Ibid.
35. Interview with Ian Carr, April 2003.
36. Interview with Andy Sheppard, April 2003.
37. J. P. Kahn, "Names and Faces: Russell Named Jazz Master," *Boston Globe*, January 2, 1990.
38. K. Mathieson, program notes for Glasgow International Jazz Festival; Press release for GIJF, June 1989.
39. Martin Gayford, "Ignoring the Sirens," *Weekend Telegraph* (London), March 16, 1991; N. Hadsley, "George Russell: Don't Kick Sand at This Theory with Muscle," *TOP*, February 1991.
40. Garry Booth, Review of Camden Jazz Festival, *Financial Times*, March 26, 1991.
41. Roland Ramanan, Concert review of Cassandra Wilson, George Russell at Town & Country Club; Jazz Warriors, Tony Remy at Shaw Theatre, *Wire*, May 1991, pp. 18–20. As a general rule, I avoid commenting on other writers' work. This deserves some response, however. Sadly, it is an example of an inexperienced writer his own lack of knowledge and understanding with slick and gratuitous comment. Myth debunking and icon smashing are often seen by young writers as ways of building a reputation, while the insertion of the odd clever phrase or *mot juste* is believed to be a substitute for critical insight. The jazz community should expect better.
42. John Fordham, "Lazy Rocking Russell," *Guardian Weekly* (Manchester), May 12, 1991.
43. Gary Giddins, "Making It New," *Village Voice*, March 30, 1993.
44. Interview with Marty Khan, February 2004; Alice Norbury-Russell, fax to John Cumming, March 26, 1992; Marty Khan, fax to Rob Gibson, December 23, 1992.
45. Rob Gibson letter to Marty Khan, January 4, 1993.
46. Richard B. Woodward, "Jazz Wars: A Tale of Age, Rage and Hash Brownies," *Village Voice*, August 9, 1994.
47. Quoted in S. Nicholson, *Is Jazz Dead? Or Has It Moved To A New Address?* (New York: Routledge, 2005), p. 60. Nicholson provides a very complete and thorough discussion of issues involving Jazz at Lincoln Center.
48. Interview with Marty Khan, February 2004.
49. P. Applebome, "A Jazz Success Story with a Ting of the Blues," *New York Times*, September 22, 1998.
50. E-mail correspondence between Marty Khan and Lincoln Center. For 2020 concert, https://wyntonmarsalis.org/news/entry/the-music-of-charles-mingus-and-thelonious-monk-andy-farbers-usonian-structures
51. Ben Ratliff, "Rock, Funk and Electronics in a Splashy 80s Sound," *New York Times*, May 12, 1999. According to Marty Khan, the representative of the *Times* asked for the volume to be turned down! Interview with Khan.
52. J. Szwed, "Still on His Own Page," *Village Voice*, May 25, 1999.
53. Marty Khan [writing as George Lane], "George Russell & Anglo-American Living Time Orchestra Perform in USA for First Time," GMN.com, 7.12.02.
54. Readers wishing to accuse me of Eurocentrism might wish to note Francis Davis's comments in "George Russell: Intellect of the Heart," *Jazz Times*, December 12, 1984: "If as robust and stimulating work as The African Game fails to arouse jazz listeners, one will be forced to share its composer's concern for the survival of jazz. But one will also be forced to conclude that it is the complacency of the Jazz faithful, rather than the indifference of the mass media, that may ultimately plant the seeds of destruction."

CHAPTER FOURTEEN

## It's About Time

In 1993 Russell toured Europe once again, playing in France, Italy and at London's Jazz Café. The Paris date at the Banlieues Bleues Festival included a performance with students from the Conservatoire National Supérieur de Musique et de Danse de Paris in what would prove an interesting and new development for Russell. The concert at the Jazz Café, though well received, was perhaps less successful in terms of the size of its audience.

John Cumming's view was that the problem actually had more to do with the size of the venue and the expanded stage required for the band than the turnout itself. However, Andy Sheppard recalled being disappointed on Russell's behalf. He had experienced similarly small audiences elsewhere in Europe when on tour with Russell and he compared this with touring with Gil Evans.

> Gil certainly had this kind of charisma in himself and was ... he was kind of successful when I was touring with him. In Italy especially, places would be packed and I toured with George and there would be very few people. I remember doing a gig in the Jazz Café, which was a fantastic gig and there was, like, a handful of people and I just couldn't understand that. Here was this major figure in twentieth-century music, and most people just couldn't get up to speed with it. People who were there really loved it because, of course, it is a challenging and full-on experience or it was with that band.[1]

Russell seemed to take this in his stride, as if he expected little else. For him, the Concept was the most important thing in his life and his major contribution to jazz and music in general. Yet at the same time, his response to an audience was invariably warm and open, especially when people reacted positively to him and his music.

In 1994 Russell played the Umbria Jazz Festival for the first time and also the North Sea Jazz Festival in the Hague, as well as gigs in Newcastle in the UK and Pori in Finland. Guy Barker, one of Britain's most charismatic musicians and veteran Henry Lowther, who had played at Woodstock with the Keef Hartley Band, had come in on trumpets to replace Ian Carr and Tiger Okoshi. Guitarist Dave Fiuczynski had also left and, though Adam Rogers had filled in during 1993, there was a need to find a long-term replacement. Thanks once again to John Cumming, Mike Walker, the musician chosen to fill Fiuczynski's shoes, proved perfect for the band. As Cumming put it, "George loves Mike Walker and with good reason. He's dead right for George because George likes to hear a screaming rock guitar in there." [2]

The following year, Swedish saxophonist Lennart Åberg and John Cumming of Serious jointly commissioned Russell to write a new piece, *It's About Time*, with funds from the Swedish Rikskoncerter and the Arts Council of England. Prior to its performance in Stockholm in November, Russell and the Living Time Orchestra were able to present the work, complete with a small symphony orchestra drawn from various French music schools at La Cité de la Musique as part of the Paris Banlieues Bleues Festival. This project had been painstakingly put together with the help of Serious and had been orchestrated by Living Time Orchestra member Pat Hollenbeck. In fact, later that year Russell was able to record the new work for the French company Label Bleu, along with a new version of the work he had written for Bill Evans, *Living Time*, this time featuring a fifteen-piece string section.

Russell again toured the United Kingdom in November 1995, once more with Arts Council support, playing a date at London's Queen Elizabeth Hall as part of the London Jazz Festival and another in Huddersfield for its Contemporary Music Festival. As John Cumming recalled, Russell was invited to give a lecture at Huddersfield as part of the festival program, something he had done at other festivals during the later phase of his career.

> I mean, I once heard him do a lecture on the Lydian Concept in Huddersfield where you could hear the sound of jaws dropping on the floor as he managed to combine the African Diaspora and the Ottoman Empire in one sentence as part of the touching points of the Lydian Concept. [3]

Russell liked to shock, though never as an end in itself.

A few dates in France, including one at La Maison de la Culture in Amiens, were sandwiched in the middle and the band was able to record both *It's About Time* and *Living Time* for Label Bleu in a local studio. The band was a powerful mix of the tried and trusted. The tour went exceptionally well, with good pre-tour publicity encouraged in Serious' usual efficient fashion. Ronald Atkins wrote in the *Saturday Guardian Guide*, "It took us long enough to get George Russell over here. Now, his Living Time Orchestra has become a welcome fixture." It is a fair description of the reception that greeted Russell when he and his band came to Europe. Phil Johnson's comments in his review of the Bath leg of the tour in the *Independent* were typical, beautifully capturing the power and internal dynamism that the band had developed, "George Russell gave his musicians their heads, pointing at soloists, as if lighting the blue touch paper and then standing well back."[4]

*It's About Time* was released on Label Bleu in Europe in March 1997. John Fordham made the record his jazz CD of the week in the *Guardian*, while the Scottish newspaper the *Herald* noted that *It's About Time* was "Russell at his most mobile and punchy." The album was not, however, issued until May 1999 in the States. This did at least coincide with the three-date Living Time Orchestra tour of the East Coast that year and John Szwed did draw the public's attention to it in his *Village Voice* review of the Tribeca gig.[5]

*It's About Time* is a fine latter-day Russell work and has, if anything, improved with age. Its interlocking parts slide together like a well-oiled machine. At times, some of the synth sounds do sound a bit like they were left over from the previous decade but it is the way that Russell builds sounds, textures and rhythms upon each other and yet is still able to afford his soloists remarkable degrees of freedom, that surprises. In fact, Stanton Davis, Mike Walker and Andy Sheppard are all given incredible latitude within a piece that is so clearly and carefully structured. There is also some forceful playing from Dave Bargeron and Brad Hatfield but it is the magnificent edifice Russell creates—or has his orchestra create—that really impresses. The power and energy that is delivered by the band in the final five minutes of the second section of the piece is quite staggering.

By contrast the first section, teases from the outset with its koto-like sounds at the beginning to brief interventions from Walker, Sheppard and, most notably, Bargeron, whose braying trombone succeeds in being both joyful and witty. There are hints of the full-on release to come throughout, in particular in Walker's rock guitar solo and Davis' growling trumpet chorus. But this is, after all, a love letter from its composer to his wife and it is that emotion that comes across most strongly in the orchestra's performance. At its heart, this is music rooted in gospel and the blues and, yes, it retains the funk.

The second section is a slow burn that increases in emotional intensity with the baton passed from one soloist to another and back. When it finally lets rip, the outpouring of passion is palpable. Even here, Russell refuses to just let the music rip. He keeps pulling the band back into collective but scored rubato passages that repeat to build to its final emphatic close.

What is more, the version of *Living Time* is everything the Bill Evans' version was not allowed to be due to its awful mix. Young French pianist Paul-Christian Staicu takes many of the solos Evans covered on the original Columbia LP. Staicu is not Evans, obviously; however, there is a quality to his performance and something about his pianistic touch on the keys that is hugely effective and affecting. His lines are crystalline and beautifully defined. Bargeron, his second time around on this one, gets a lot of room on Event V and has that tailgate sound that truly grabs the gut and Stanton Davis constantly surpasses expectation. In turn, Mike Walker, Andy Sheppard and Brad Hatfield provide some of the work's finest moments of tension and release.

The sound on the record is excellent, with the strings and other horns clearly audible in the mix. Again, Russell's vertical form structure is the defining feature. It seems constantly on the verge of either exploding or imploding and yet it really swings and rocks and sounds as if the musicians are genuinely having a great time. All things considered, Russell has succeeded in continuing the modern big-band work that had begun with *Now and Then* in 1966 and has developed and honed his writing into an intricately balanced world of melody and countermelody, rhythm and counter-rhythm, all emerging from some of the widest and richest harmonic textures in jazz.

In 2012, critic Steve Elman wrote a piece for online magazine, *Arts Fuse*, comparing the two versions of *Living Time*. Describing the work as a "piano concerto", he draws attention to the way that Paul-Christian Staicu "gets Bill's parts right without imitating him". In particular, he noted that Staicu's performance of the now-expanded theme of the final Event VIII improves on Evans' original take and allows the piece a greater coherence.

However, Elman made one other important point about the composition as a whole, which could equally apply to other long works by Russell, "The music is not intended to flow from point A to point B but rather to create a series of impressions that make a whole when they all have been explored." The problem of the long form is one often highlighted in relation to jazz composition. Here, Elman neatly outlines Russell's solution to the dilemma.[6]

By now Russell was seventy-four years old, but he was far from resting on his laurels. He enjoyed the companionship of musicians, as he always had. If anything, he had become more enthusiastic about being on the road with his music, at least for part of the year. Teaching commitments at NEC continued and, as ever, he was working on a new edition of *The Lydian Chromatic Concept of Tonal Organization*, which would be published in 2001, though a second volume planned by Russell focusing on rhythmic modes of musical behaviour would never be completed.

In early spring 1998, Russell and Serious embarked on their most ambitious project to date. In fact, outside the confines of NEC, it is hard to imagine the idea coming to anything at all Stateside. At one point, John Cumming was pushing for a performance of *Time Line*, Russell's three-hour celebration that premiered at the Conservatory in 1992. In reality, this proved impractical even on an abridged basis, much to Alice Norbury-Russell's relief.[7] The project that replaced it was, however, almost as ambitious and almost as difficult to realize.

As well as other European dates, the plan was for Russell and the Living Time Orchestra to perform concerts in both Paris and London, using musicians, jazz and classical, from the Paris Conservatoire and the London Guildhall School of Music and Drama. The program was to feature three sets. The first would present Stratusphunk, *All About Rosie* and *Dialogue with Ornette*, the latter performed in an extended version by the student classical players conducted by Pat Hollenbeck. The second set would feature the whole of *Vertical Form VI*, using professional and student jazz players as well as various classical students. Finally, the Living Time Orchestra was to perform *American Trilogy* and an extract from *It's About Time*, closing, as always, with "So What."

The British program notes list Pat Hollenbeck and Hiroaki Honshuku as assistant musical directors, which fairly described the roles that both, and Hollenbeck in particular, were now taking on. Hollenbeck, something of a Renaissance-like musical figure in the diversity of skills he brings to any project, had worked for some time on orchestration in the film industry, with actor/director Clint Eastwood and others. In addition, he performed on a regular basis as percussionist for the Boston Pops. His assistance to Russell since joining the band had proven immeasurable, according to Steve Lodder.

> Pat [has] been an incredible addition in terms of the orchestration side and also in terms of the rehearsal side. He takes a lot of work off George. Pat's used to rehearsing Hollywood Bowl orchestras, so he's immediately comfortable with a large party of musicians and complexity as well. It doesn't faze him at all. He's got incredible ears. In fact, he'll often pick up something that George might not in terms of wrong notes or whatever.[8]

Hollenbeck had been very active in working on the *It's About Time* recording and he was carrying much of the load for this project as well. The French rehearsals and performance went quite smoothly, despite the fact that some seventy people, many of them musicians, were involved. Generally, organizing musicians is never easy. However, it was not until the circus arrived in London and began rehearsals at the Guildhall that problems really began. Essentially, it seems that a combination of obstruction on the part of some teaching staff at the Guildhall and what can only be described as an absence of any efficient administration system dedicated to the project was to blame. Even the list of the names of students from the Guildhall traveling to France did not arrive till very late in the proceedings, while the French had their end tied up well in advance. There had been plans to use singers from the Guildhall but, in John Cumming's words, "we had to drop the choir at one stage because they didn't get it together—nobody could quite work out why." Cumming continued,

> We were finding that students weren't turning up when we thought they were. They were being fitted around rehearsals of other things. There was a big problem internally at Guildhall attached to this between the Jazz Department and the Classical Department, as it were. One senior member of staff at the Guildhall who had basically helped to set the project up and who was the enthusiast left it because George had a go at him.[9]

It was clearly far from a happy or satisfactory situation, as was evident when I interviewed Russell for a magazine article during a break in rehearsals. Russell was, frankly, furious. Cumming acknowledged this:

> Within all that there was a lot of tension. We were having to move rehearsal rooms into unsuitable spaces and students were actually coming up to people throughout that project saying, "We wish we'd known more about this because actually we're doing an opera in the evening. We're not actually able to devote the time we should be to this, but this is much more interesting music." Some of this is quite boring, but it doesn't help; it meant that George felt that he'd been undervalued actually.[10]

Of course, this cannot and should not be compared with the events five years earlier (and again circa 2001–2002) involving Jazz at Lincoln Center. This was simply a case of chronic inefficiency rather than bad manners. Fortunately, for once, the series of communication and other failures that dogged the London end did not affect the final performance at the Barbican in London. It was a triumph and both the Living Time Orchestra and the students from both sides of the channel rose boldly to the challenge. Cumming's view of events prior to the performance did not change but he clearly felt that what happened that night at the Barbican made it worthwhile.

> I think, to be honest, there are two things or three about that project. The first thing is that despite all the problems, we came out with a triumph, I have to say. I think we've all listened to the music, one way or another, of it, and people who were there, the critics who were there—it actually was remarkable. I think that sometimes out of complicated practical issues the art comes shining through at the end of the day. [11]

John Fordham, who had written a long piece in the *Guardian* prior to the concert, [12] wrote, without exaggeration:

> In a storm of sound that lasted almost three hours, the mix of American, British and French musicians resembled a vast Rock n' Roll band, a Moroccan Folk ensemble, a symphonic band playing a hoe-down, a Free-Jazz group, a jostling crowd of Dixieland street-stompers, a scholarly Schoenbergian tone-row outfit whose drinks had been spiked and plenty more besides. [13]

It really was that good and, though sadly it remains unreleased, the symphony orchestra's performance of *Dialogue* was simply wonderful.

As late as 2002–2003, Russell's passion remained undiminished, though his energy could not always keep pace with his enthusiasm. In 2002 he took up an offer from Umbria Jazz to carry its *'Round Midnight* slot at the Teatro Morlacchi for the week. Unfortunately, some key players were unavailable. Andy Sheppard was touring with the Carla Bley Very Big Band and Chris Biscoe was unable to make the tour. George Garzone and Steve Slagle took their places. Despite the fact that he was now less than a year from his eightieth birthday, Russell was keen to use the residency to cover his entire catalogue, as Steve Lodder recalled.

> George was charged for it, no doubt about it, and the list of music that he wanted to play over that week went back across his career, including things this band has never looked at. He came up with all this music and he wanted to play it all. He wanted to play a different set every night. There were actually things that mitigated that, because there were different saxophone players, as Andy and Chris couldn't make it. They were having trouble enough with the regular material, let alone stuff the band hadn't looked at before. George's energy, even though he is amazing, completely amazing, it's fallible. So in the end the list got whittled down, but, yeah, he came with very high expectations of what we would do that week, which in the end we didn't get anywhere near. But we did a slightly different gig most nights. [14]

One of the finest gigs was the band's early evening show on Monday, July 15, again at the Teatro Morlacchi. The atmosphere in the rococo, eighteenth-century theatre was electric. It was thundery, humid weather, and the hall has no air-conditioning but something happened that night: the music succeeded in bringing the band and audience together in a communal celebration of jazz and its representative in the person of George Allan Russell. Looking around the theatre, even in the boxes, people were leaning forward, willing the band on, finding it impossible to be still with the excitement that was generated from the stage. The Living Time Orchestra delivered on every count. I have to say I have rarely experienced anything quite like it at any gig or concert whether jazz, world, rock, reggae, soul or classical music. Steve Lodder remembered that this night felt special.

> **SL:** I think the real feeling that night... and I remember that particular night... of wanting to play for George because he was struggling...
> **DH:** In what sense?
> **SL:** In the sense of he was struggling with the idea that we wouldn't be able to get through all the material he wanted to get through. He was looking... the phrase "retrospective" comes to mind. I think he was looking on it as a sort of retrospective, but obviously very present, but wanting to trawl back to hear things that he hadn't heard for a long time. Then, when that wasn't happening, the frustration about it, and then that built a bit before we got that release. [15]

It was evident nonetheless that it was getting harder for Russell to make these transatlantic trips, let alone play week-long residencies 'round midnight. Although he missed these dates, Andy Sheppard was in Perugia for some of the concerts and recalled that band members were concerned for Russell.

> I thought that was a tough gig for George because he's seventy-nine. He flies over from the States, he rehearses the band as George is wont to do, and, of course, instead of concentrating on six pieces of music, he'll want to play his entire back catalogue. So things get half rehearsed, and all the guys in the band were exhausted in the restaurant at eight o'clock, as they'd been rehearsing all day, and then they'd be on stage at midnight. I just thought this is a really tough gig for a man of that age. [16]

In fact, at the end of the week, Russell and the band had to travel to the other end of Italy for one more concert. This was exhausting for the younger, fitter members of the band, but for Russell, often determined to be there with his musicians, sharing their company, it can take weeks to recover. It was also a colossal strain on his wife, Alice Norbury-Russell. It was clear that week in Perugia that there would not be many more tours.

There was, however, one more shake of the tail to be had. It came about once again with the assistance of John Cumming and, as tour manager, Martel Ollerenshaw. Russell celebrated his eightieth birthday with concerts at the Moers Festival, Royal Northern College of Music in Manchester and, one again, the Barbican. For several band members, the Moers gig was one of the best they had experienced with the orchestra. This was despite the fact that there was little time between their arrival and the evening show.

Danish trumpeter-composer Palle Mikkelborg was back in the band. He noted with fondness how the success of the Moers' concert had affected Russell, "You could see the man going from eighty to seventy to sixty-five to fifty-nine, ending up like this glint in the eyes like a seven year old boy on Christmas Eve because it went so well. It was such a gift to see." [17]

For Pat Hollenbeck, it was a defining moment, despite the need to break in a new drummer, Richie Morales. Hollenbeck's comments also explain something essential about this band and jazz in general.

> **PH:** It was just that everything was right. The audience was with us the whole time. The sound was good for both the band and the audience and everything just seemed to be right. This was an interesting experience, because this is a new drummer and that was his first concert with the band. The band is really affected by any changes in personnel because all of a sudden that person's personality and their playing makes it different. It's fascinating actually.
> **DH:** It's like a family, people have said.
> **PH:** It's a scary thing when there's a new adopted child in there but when you get a great musician and plug them in they bring a special something and it's really excellent. We're unlike a classical or symphonic orchestra; if you change a violinist or somebody in another section you're not going to really know the difference. But here everybody has a key part in this, so it's not a situation like that, where certain people are like the rank-and-file people just playing their parts. It really affects the whole thing. [18]

Russell noted with almost fatherly approval that trumpeter Stanton Davis was in no way put out by Palle Mikkelborg's presence and was genuinely welcoming, despite the fact that the Dane took over solo spots that Davis had made his own. Again, there was a feeling within the band of "doing it for George." Even new member Richie Morales could sense it and felt he had gelled fine within the band.

> I mean, if I did something that was totally out of the realm of possibility, they'd let me know. *(laughs)* But we had a concert in Germany on Monday and they—Alice and George—were very complimentary and said that they felt it was one of the better, if not the best, performances the band had done. I don't know how much of that is just trying to make me feel comfortable, but it felt really good, and you can tell when the band gets the right groove and the atmosphere is right, then everybody plays better and the whole band levitates, because with an ensemble this size—most of my background is in small-group work—it's the difference between driving a sports car and a bus in terms of performance. It can get very unwieldy and awkward if things aren't synced up. [19]

Manchester was also a fine performance, albeit with a poor turnout due to an almost total absence of pre-concert publicity. In fact, the band and Russell had worked earlier in the day with some students from the college and the tour's sound engineer made a point of getting them free tickets for the gig, much to the apparent annoyance of box office staff. There were moments of great drama, with Palle Mikkelborg's entrance playing the theme from *Listen to the Silence*, followed shortly after by Russell. There were fine performances of *Electronic Sonata, It's About Time* and "So What," and an unusual small-group arrangement of "Dialogue with Ornette" featuring a guest appearance by violist Christopher Jenkins. But the meat of the evening came with the performance of *The African Game*. Mike Walker on guitar was incandescent and Andy Sheppard in particular seemed to pick up on his energy, while Mikkelborg, Bargeron, Biscoe and Lodder seemed determined to seize every opportunity they were given as well.

The Barbican gig was even better and, fortunately the Russells and Cumming, had the foresight to ensure it was recorded for posterity. The lengthy applause at the end says everything. There was a sense across the auditorium that the band had given everything and that this was probably the last time the audience would see this jazz legend—one of the last remaining links to Bird, Diz, Gil, Miles, 'Trane and Mulligan—on a British stage. As Norbury-Russell said, "We wondered about letting the applause go on that long at the end of the record. But then I said, 'Oh, hell! Why not?[20]

*The 80th Birthday Concert* is Russell's last record and a fine valediction. In the absence of the Blue Note version of *The African Game*, it puts a very significant musical work back in the catalogue and in a form that is the equal of—though in places quite different from—the original. Most importantly, it features a great big band playing music that has come to matter to them personally with the utmost commitment. But one writer felt otherwise. Paul DeBarros found it "pompous" and "melodramatic," noting that "Russell favours structure over lyricism, a liability he shares with modern architecture."[21] I would disagree with DeBarros about modern architecture as well.

But music and work had to continue. Russell prepared the Conservatory big band for a special concert to celebrate one hundred years of the Jordan Hall in October 2003. He continued teaching until he took a sabbatical in 2004, after which, at age eighty-two, he retired. The honours continued. There were trips to Stockholm and Copenhagen for concerts of his music. For the latter, he was able to take Brad Hatfield, Stuart Brooks, Richie Morales and Pat Hollenbeck with him, though it certainly was not "touring" like in the old days. Then, on March 5, 2007, Russell was one of thirty-four jazz legends honoured at the Kennedy Centre in Washington. His peers included Dave Brubeck, Clark Terry, Chick Corea, Gerald Wilson, Phil Woods, Marion McPartland, Toshiko Akyoshi, Curtis Fuller and Freddie Hubbard. Closer to home for Russell and his own history in the music, Buddy DeFranco, Jon Hendricks, Dave Baker, Ornette Coleman, and Benny Golson, who played on *New York, N.Y.*, were also being honoured at the gala.[22] If only Miles, Gil and 'Trane could have been there.

George Russell and the Living Time Orchestra would have one more outing. On September 20, 2008, at the new Institute for Contemporary Art, Pat Hollenbeck and Alice Norbury-Russell brought a version of the LTO together for what proved to be their last concert with Russell at the helm. Performing as part of the Ditson Concert Series, British guitarist Mike Walker and pianist Steve Lodder joined a number of Boston-based musicians to pay tribute to George Russell and celebrate his eighty-fifth birthday. Joining them on stage for "You Are My Sunshine" was, of course, the great Sheila Jordan.

Lloyd Schwartz reviewed the concerts for the *Boston Phoenix* on September 25 and said of the LTO's performance,

The most roof-raising was the evening with the George Russell Living Time Orchestra. Perhaps the festival's most poignant moment came when the legendary master of avant-garde jazz, now 85, got up from his first row seat and, a bit shaky, began to dance and conduct extended sections of his 1983 through-composed *The African Game*, which alternates sounds of the jungle (lion-roaring trombones) with the cacophony of modern technology, and his love letter to his wife, Alice, the ballad *It's About Time*. Jazz singer Sheila Jordan wailing *You Are My Sunshine* created another sensation. [23]

Finally, after a long illness, on Monday, July 27, 2009, at around 9 p.m. Eastern Standard Time, with his wife Alice, his son Jock and one or two close friends at his bedside at Mass General, George Russell left town. As always, the plaudits have followed. Some of these came from critics like John Fordham, who knew Russell's music well and who championed it. From others, the words rang less true and their eulogies mixed half-remembered anecdotes and all too hastily checked details. It often seems that we forget people when they are alive but fall over ourselves to acknowledge their passing.

Perhaps none of this truly matters because, as Alice Norbury-Russell once said to me, "People can dismiss George's ideas all they want but the evidence is there in the music." Russell had a wonderfully rich, full life packed with great achievements and success. Having known the man, I think he will rest content with the legacy he leaves behind.

## Notes

1. Interview with Sheppard, March 2003.
2. Interview with Cumming.
3. Ibid. See also, Huddersfield Contemporary Music Festival Program Notes. November 1995.
4. Ronald Atkins, "The Guide—Preview of LTO at Queen Elizabeth Hall," *Guardian* (Manchester), November 11, 1995; Phil Johnson, "Music—Review of Russell & LTO at the Forum in Bath," *Independent* (London), November 21, 1995.
5. John Fordham, "A Time to Live," *Guardian* (Manchester), March 21, 1997; *Herald* (Glasgow), March 15, 1997. Szwed, J. "Still on His Own Page." *Village Voice*, May 25, 1999.
6. Steve Elman "Commentary Drill Down: George Russell's *Living Time*", *Arts Fuse*, February 1st, 2012
7. Fax correspondence between Alice Norbury-Russell and John Cumming.
8. Interview with Lodder.
9. Interview with Cumming.
10. Ibid.
11. Ibid.
12. J. Fordham, "Send Off the Clones," *Guardian* (Manchester), March 5, 1998. See also A. Shipton, "Play What You Mean," *Jazzwise*, March 1998; S. Oliver, "George Russell," *Jazz Express*, February 1998; Phil Johnson, "Lydian Modes and All That Jazz," *Independent* (London), March 7, 1998.
13. J. Fordham, "Stars in the Eye of a Storming Sound," *Guardian* (Manchester), March 9, 1998.
14. Interview with Lodder.
15. Ibid.
16. Interview with Sheppard.
17. Interview with Mikkelborg.
18. Interview with Pat Hollenbeck, June 2003.

19. Interview with Richie Morales, June 2003.
20. Interview with Norbury-Russell, October 2006.
21. Paul DeBarros, Review of The 80th Birthday Concert (Concept), *DownBeat*, November 2005.
22. W. Jenkins, "Living History," *Jazz Times*, May 2007.
23. Lloyd Schwartz, *Boston Phoenix*, September 25, 2008

CHAPTER FIFTEEN

# On Conceptual Thinking

Russell's conception assimilated modal writing to the extreme chromaticism of modern music. By converting chords into scales and overlaying one scale on another, it allowed improvisers to work in the hard-to-define area between non-tonality and polytonality. Like all great theoreticians, Russell worked analytically rather than synthetically, basing his ideas on how jazz actually was, not on how it could be made to conform with traditional principles of Western harmony. Working from within jazz's often tacit organizational principles, Russell's fundamental concern was the relationship between formal scoring and improvisation, giving the first the freedom of the second and, freeing the second from being literally esoteric, 'outside' some supposed norm.[1]

The circumstances leading to George Russell's "discovery" of the Lydian Concept have been described already. Those events provide a context for Russell's research and even furnish and people his social and cultural milieu. Russell tended to play down his earlier formal musical studies and experience as a musician. However, we know from his friend Nadi Qamar that he had begun writing, arranging and even leading his own groups in Cincinnati by his late teens. That he was far from an *ingenu* by that point is further indicated by his work in the forties with Benny Carter and Earl Hines and by his ready acceptance into the circle of musicians around Gil Evans a few years later.

There was always a degree of mythologization by Russell concerning his own background and his 'discovery' of the Lydian Concept. It is necessary to cut through that to develop a clearer picture of Russell's theories and their broader context and relevance. There are a number of ways of understanding the way Russell approached his researches in the TB sanitorium as he puzzled the conundrum that Miles Davis had posed for him. These are both more interesting and more illuminating than any attendant myth-making.

My aim here is not to provide a depth analysis of the Lydian Concept, though reference needs to be made to its tenets and implications, to criticisms of it and arguments in its support. Instead, I want to look at the Concept, firstly, as a body of ideas that emerged from Russell's studies not just as an individual musician but as a member of "Gil Evans's Church of the Aesthetic." Secondly, in the longest section here, I want to examine, through the comments of students and musicians, the Concept as a practical tool for composers, improvisers and educators. This will inevitably this will raise the issue of the terminology Russell developed to explain and describe the Concept. Thirdly, I will look at the Concept as science and as a system (after all, Volume One is subtitled *The Art and Science of Tonal Gravity*). Fourthly, we will consider the Concept as a reflection of a personal psychology and philosophy; and, finally, we will look at the Concept in terms of Russell's career as a composer.

The one area I do not intend to address here is that of the historical origins of the Lydian scale and Concept beyond necessary explanatory mention. This is, as I wrote in the first edition of this biography, a subject in great need of further exploration and clarification.

To suggest that Russell's Lydian Concept might be in some sense the property of the group around Gil Evans in no way detracts from its theorist's achievement. New ideas do not simply spring fully formed from the brow of their creator, they arise at particular times and in particular circumstances. The 55th Street set were a highly literate, articulate and curious bunch. Gunther Schuller has noted, following his entrée into the group, his surprise at how knowledgeable the members, including Russell, were about classical music. As we have seen, the group often attended pre-concert rehearsals by Hindemith and Stravinsky at Juilliard. These musicians – Evans, Miles Davis, Max Roach, John Lewis, Gerry Mulligan, Charlie Parker, Russell – were at the very centre of the new music of bebop and its subsequent developments in New York. That group also intersected with the circle around Stefan Wolpe and several of the musicians, including Russell, studied with Wolpe.

It is a point that Andy Wasserman, a former student and friend of Russell's, expressed beautifully.

> It always seemed to be his neighbours and his friends were Dizzy Gillespie and Max Roach and Gil Evans and Bill Evans . . . it was all camaraderie and all community. There wasn't any conservatory. It wasn't about money. It wasn't, "Oh, I'm going to make friends with Max Roach so I can make money." They were all basically poor. You hear about the prejudice. They were doing this because of where they were at that point in time. All of that is the conjunction of him as a theoretician and the Lydian Chromatic Concept is based on his life in the culture of jazz.[2]

Russell described the group as "an esoteric school" with Evans its "school master", where "the key thing to come out of it was that we were all encouraged to reach for the impossible."[3] And, while Gerry Mulligan always referred to Russell as the "group's resident innovator", one of the group's main shared concerns was the finding of new ways of relating composition and improvisation, "of a different kind of relationship between the improviser and the ensemble."[4] This is, after all, a primary feature of the Lydian Concept.

But more than that, as the quotation at the head of this chapter clearly states, Russell's research focused on what the new jazz musicians were actually doing on stage at clubs like the Royal Roost, Birdland and Minton's. Not only did Miles Davis' response to Russell's question as to his musical aims – "To learn all the changes" – trigger Russell's quest, his fulfilment of that quest grew out of observation of these musicians' musical practice. It is worth repeating a quote used earlier from John Lewis. Asked by Ian Carr whether he saw the Lydian Concept as a "significant breakthrough", Lewis replied,

> It was, but not for me and not for the same generation that he and I both belonged to because the things he was using were the way we both played and thought. This was really for the next generation of people.[5]

Lewis' point is an important one. However, to clarify it slightly, this was a group of forward-thinking musicians who clearly engaged in wide-ranging discussions about the music they were making and the music beyond jazz they listened to. Russell's description of the circle around Gil Evans as a school speaks volumes. Those involved learned from each other and Russell developed his theories, in part at least, from inductive research into their musical practice. In this regard, the Concept was theirs as well.

As to the Concept as a practical tool for improvisers and composers, from the outset, Russell presented the Lydian Concept in book form as both a theoretical outline of his thesis and as a series of examples and exercises that allowed the student to explore the practice implications of the Concept. From 1953, and its first edition, to 2001, and its final edition, the work has expanded both in attempts to ground the theory historically in earlier musical practices and in providing a wider range of musical examples for students to consider. From the outset, its whole format and mode of presentation offered both a tool for improvisers and composers and, at the same time, present the case for the Lydian Scale against the Major/Minor Scale of traditional music theory. My concern here, is primarily with the former aspect. As noted already, this will inevitably raise questions about the terminology Russell used in his writing on and in his teaching of the Lydian Concept.

One recurring comment, at least from those who have found Russell's ideas of value, concerns the permissive and motivational character of the Concept. This is something which British pianist Howard Riley, who studied with David Baker in Indiana after the trombonist left Russell's group, emphasised.

> What I got out of it was that it made me think a lot about the notes you can use against chords. I had just begun to play a lot of music that was without chord sequences and it opened my ears for that as well because I realized the kind of harmony you can get in a non-functional harmonic situation. In other words, the kind of notes you can put against chords where the harmony isn't functional. I seem to remember that George Russell

stresses that it's not a system but more a philosophy of tonality and everybody can find their own identity via that. And that's exactly what happened with me because through reading it, it made me think about different things and eventually it got translated into my playing and it freed up a lot of my note choices when I was playing, so I did actually get further toward my own identity. [6]

This is something Riley has since sought to communicate to his own pupils in order to help them expand their own range of note choices in relation to the chords they are playing. "I try to get over to my students that there are limitless possibilities, as long as you're hearing it and you know what you're doing, it can only add to the interest of your playing. That's the long-term thing I got out of the Concept." And he added, "It could get to be a real doctrinaire thing but Dave, and George Russell as well, they're not doctrinaire about it. They just hope it will help you get toward your own identity, which indeed it did help me at that time."[7]

That the Concept is non-prescriptive in this way is something Russell always stressed.

I think the Concept tells me that music has a living, natural organization that is totally objective and non-invasive with small laws and that tonal organization is based on the principle of tonal gravity."[8]

And elsewhere,

It's not a theory that demands that you go from the two to the five to one. It's a theory that opens up choice for musicians. There are no rules but there are laws, but [because] the laws are big, there are very few laws."[9]

Using this approach does not eradicate the "hit-and-miss" of trial and error or the surprise of serendipity. Instead, it teaches the student about musical relationships in a new way and provides a map for their exploration and elaboration. It does not prescribe the journey, so much as offer a range of different possible routes, as Andy Wasserman suggested,

Like, here's a map. You want to go from Cincinnati to West Stockbridge. You can go via Florida or Senegal, West Africa. You can take a rowboat. You can walk. You can take a moped. You can take a jet plane. You can go up via Montreal. You can take a rocket ship, orbit the earth a few times and then come down to West Stockbridge. He says, "All of those ways I'm going to show you are possible, but however you want to go from Cincinnati to West Stockbridge, that's up to you." [10]

Of course, not all musicians accept the value or need for such theorizing. Chuck Israels, who played on *Stratusphunk*, took such a position in an e-mail interview for the first edition of this biography.

George's theories seem to me to result in complex ways of looking at things that have been understood in simpler ways for hundreds of years. It's more obfuscation than revelation to musicians who are well educated in traditional analysis—like going from London to Paris by way of Buenos Aires. You can make the trip, but it's not the most efficient route. In the nine-year history of the National Jazz Ensemble, only one composition provoked criticism from the band members. When we played *All About Rosie*, Greg Herbert (the great saxophonist who had worked with Thad and Mel, and Woody Herman) said that it was the only thing in our entire repertoire that rang false to him. He felt it was full of what he called "fake blues licks." [11]

As will be seen below, pianist Jack Reilly was one interviewee for this book who certainly felt that Russell's use of his own terminology obfuscated ideas that could be incorporated in traditional music theory. And, of course, it must be acknowledged that jazz musicians have made music before and after the appearance of the Lydian Concept drawing upon the major scale and traditional music theory.

Nevertheless, if Russell's approach derived from observation of the musical practice of beboppers does offer a more accurate means of understanding and describing those practices than traditional music theory, then it is must also be valid in those terms. Jazz is as an African-American music based in whatever degree on African music traditions. Therefore, while it can be analysed according to tradition Western music theory, the danger of shoe-horning jazz into a music theory framework which it does not necessarily fit must surely be a real one. Israels' comments would seem to fail to acknowledge this possibility. Additionally, he failed to take into account how far Russell's ideas had by the early sixties become part of the tonal repertoire of jazz, regardless of whatever he and others might think.

Trumpeter Randy Brecker, who studied jazz and the Lydian Concept with David Baker privately and at Indiana University was clearly of a different point of view. He had also had quite a bit of experience on the bandstand prior to his studies with Baker. Brecker stated that he drew extensively on Russell's ideas both as an improviser and composer.

> They're very closely connected and I think everyone has adapted modality and the Lydian Concept that George has mapped out so well into their playing. It goes without saying that it's part of the jazz repertoire and vocabulary that one needs to know. Particularly when, around that time, Miles's *Kind of Blue* had really exposed that modal way of playing to the wider public. I think a lot of what I play is based on those teachings. The book is hard to get through. I had to take it very slowly, I remember, at the time, because a lot of it was over my head. But I still go back and refer to it. [12]

Brecker continued, emphasizing the value of formal study in jazz as a lifelong process,

> Also, just the fact that I've continued to kind of educate myself, because other than studying with David at Indiana they didn't have a full-fledged jazz department yet. So pretty much I had to pick up everything on my own and I still kind of study out of books to shorten the gaps in my own education and I still used [it], and particularly in my writing

back then, unbeknownst to me, because I didn't know how to codify things. I quite often used minor modality and I'd play a triad with one hand and a bass note with the other hand and then move the bass note with the same triad and notice that it changed the tension but I didn't know how to connect the two. Now I do and it's all still based on modes, still based on a lot of things that George discussed in his book, melodic minor modes.[13]

The contrast in terms of "traditional" musical education, in relation to jazz or other styles, is in part a question of permissiveness. Though the Concept is a "system," despite Russell's own arguments to the contrary, it is not rigid or deterministic but instead based upon the development of an understanding of how musical elements are organized. As Ben Schwendener, now teacher of the Lydian Concept at NEC, noted,

My understanding is that, when learning music theory in the traditional Western way, you are taught to write in many different styles using the "rules" or accepted conventions of whatever style or period you're trying to be in. For instance, a sonata or fugue, or eighteenth/nineteenth-century counterpoint, or even when in jazz theory you learn about II, V, I progressions and transcribe and learn solos on your instrument and learn about different chord substitution techniques and ways jazz musicians have traditionally used to navigate through the changes [chord progression] of a piece.

By contrast,

The Concept is not a "paint by numbers" sort of concept. It ultimately puts 100 percent responsibility for creativity on you. That's not to say that analysis of what's already been done doesn't play an important role in learning the Concept—it's that conceptual analysis uncovers the tonal resources a composer/improviser employed in his or her work and how tonal gravity is being manifested. Any system can be identified, if one chooses, after that. All systems and methodologies, within equal temperament, are embraced in the Lydian Chromatic Concept. The Concept simply offers an objective organization of all the tonal resources (melodic and harmonic) available. It's up to the musician to arrange or combine any selection from these elements in a way that fulfils the creative aim of whatever music is trying to be created.[14]

However, Russell's departure from traditional terminology is clearly an issue for some students. Marc Rossi, a former student and now a teacher of the Concept, recalled other students struggling with this aspect of Russell's ideas. "A lot of kids in the class were always, 'What do we need the Lydian scale for? What's wrong with the major scale?' Always trying to say, 'Well, what is good about this?' But for me, a new way of looking and a new way of thinking was very comfortable."[15]

And Ben Schwendener also acknowledged that some students do struggle with the language and with the defining of music as a science, here as the science of tonal gravity.

I think it's because George redefined what he felt music theory should be, which is a science—as he puts it—"the Art and Science of Tonal Gravity." Understanding music should first and foremost be accessing the natural objective elements that are available. It has nothing to do with how people feel about it—good or bad, right or wrong, happy or sad, or a methodology or a stylistic consideration. It has simply to do with how tonal gravity behaves. [16]

For pianist and composer Jack Reilly, the problem in terms of his studies in the fifties with Russell lay in the terminology that Russell used more than the ideas underpinning the Concept. In particular, he found Russell's use of the term "chordmode" confusing.

Yes, the Concept made more sense when I related or, better yet, translated the terminology back into traditional theoretical teachings. To recap and give one example simplifying the above: Traditional theory says the V chord is always a dominant seventh of any major scale and of any ascending minor scale. The Lydian Chromatic Concept of Tonal Organization says the II is a dominant seventh of any Lydian scale. To reiterate, by using the same Roman numeral symbols to name his chordmodes, George clashes head on with traditional classical theory. Solution? Don't study classical theory, if you want to really understand and apply the Lydian Chromatic Concept of Tonal Organization to your jazz playing! Or do what I did; apply George's seven principal scales to your jazz playing, omitting the chordmode theory. Only then I was able to dialectically fuse and conflate his theory with my classical theoretical training! [17]

Reilly, though broadly supportive of Russell's ideas and aims, is clearly questioning here how far such new terms mask ideas that can be accommodated within more traditional musical theory and its terminology.

One of the most balanced critiques of Russell's ideas can be found in Darius Brubeck's article "1959: The Beginning of Beyond." Its title summarises Brubeck's argument that jazz changed dramatically in that year. Within the article, he builds a case that four highly influential records—Miles Davis's *Kind of Blue*, John Coltrane's *Giant Steps*, his father's *Time Out* and Ornette Coleman's *Shape of Jazz to Come*—provided a series of portents for where jazz could go. In the article, he also noted the significance of the Lenox School of Jazz, Gunther Schuller and John Lewis's pioneering of the notion of Third Stream music and George Russell's Lydian Chromatic Concept. For Brubeck, the importance of these ideas lay in their influence on musicians who encountered them directly at Lenox and indirectly through these four classic albums.

In his analysis of Russell's book, *The Lydian Chromatic Concept of Tonal Organization*, Brubeck noted, "Unfortunately, his attempt to present and prove such an audaciously comprehensive theory sometimes resulted in unreadably turgid discourse burdened with jargon, yet the work's influence has spread far beyond those who have actually read it." [18]

In these remarks, Brubeck echoes both Randy Brecker's comments above about how the Concept influenced other musicians but also my earlier remarks about how the Concept grew out of and influenced the milieu of musicians around Gil Evans and through them others. However, he also clearly questions Russell's "special terminology," citing the terms "vertical polymodality" and "auxiliary diminished scale" specifically. [19] Just to take the former example, Ingrid Monson has expressed this idea very succinctly,

> When Russell speaks of "vertical polymodality," he is referring not only to a parent scale but also to a group of scales, a family of possibilities for the musician to explore. [20]

And in an article comparing the compositional and improvisational approach of guitarist Frank Zappa and Russell's Lydian Concept, quoting from the 1959 edition of *The Lydian Chromatic Concept of Tonal Organization*, Brett Clement noted,

> The LCC is directed toward the vertical conception (Russell's "vertical polymodality"), as it seeks to demonstrate the various melodic possibilities that are open to the improviser when faced with a chord symbol. This is achieved through the process of converting a chord symbol into "the scale which best conveys the sound of the chord," thereby "greatly free[ing] the improviser from the vertical limitation of arpeggiated playing." Therefore, once the correct scale has been determined, any note within the chosen scale may be applied "freely" over the given chord. [21]

I claim no great expertise or knowledge, but, as someone with some formal grounding in traditional music theory, the idea of "vertical polymodality" seems quite clear and quite useful, With regard to Russell's use of other terminology, it is easy to see that some students trained more traditionally might find this confusing. For example, Russell used the term "chordmode" over "chord" and departed from the use of words such as "free" and "freedom" (both with strong positive and negative associations), "atonal," and "dissonant" and replaced these with the terms "ingoing," "semi-ingoing," "semi-outgoing," and "outgoing" to suggest both the distance from the parent scale but also the relationship to it. But, despite any such difficulties these might present, these terms do seem to fulfil their purpose as explanatory concepts.

Take "chordmode" as one example. Russell's point, as he noted in his book is,

> In this vertical sense, the term refers to that scale which is ordained by the nature of tonal gravity – to be chord's source of arising, and ultimate vertical completeness: the chord and its parent scale existing in a state of complete and indestructible chord/scale unity – a CHORDMODE. (emphasis in original) [22]

Granted the prose lacks elegance but the idea that the chord is in unity with its scale does seem both clear and helpful and the term, "chordmode" does perhaps convey this relationship in ways that justify its coinage. Though this is outside my scope here, I do, however, have some sympathy with Brubeck when he notes that Russell's "justifications, precedents and far-reaching claims" for the Concept "complicate rather than clarify."

In his article, Brubeck made great efforts to offer an even-handed view of the Lydian Concept and praised Russell as a composer, describing him as "a daring and rigorous experimentalist" with "unusual technical skill at manipulating structure, harmony and balance, affecting the usual concerns of jazz composition, which are the interplay of improvised solos and ensemble passages."²³ Brubeck's article, sometimes seen as critical of Russell and the Concept, also credits Russell with a valuable insight into why we have a major scale with a perfect fourth rather than a Lydian scale and its derivatives, quoting directly from the 1959 edition of the Concept to demonstrate the point.²⁴

As Brubeck rightly suggested, "This is original, brilliant, even self-evident, but no one had quite said it before. The practical implications are indeed far-reaching and amount to a theory that works for playing and teaching jazz."²⁵ Given Brubeck's own status as an important jazz educator, this last point is praise indeed. Acknowledging that Russell's innovations have been widely adopted in jazz education in the teaching of chord-scale relationships,²⁶ Brubeck continued that, despite certain reservations, "the Lydian Chromatic Concept meant liberation from the obsolete concerns and dictates of 'legit' academic theory which is based on a different tradition of tonal organisation."²⁷

There have been a number of other attempts to assess and evaluate Russell's ideas theoretically. Mark S. Haywood, in the *Annual Review of Jazz Studies* in 1991, suggested that Russell's theories need updating to account for new developments in jazz, in particular what Haywood calls "melody-based harmony," in other words, that harmony is implied by the melody line rather than by the chord or tonic station.²⁸ While this may be a point worthy of further study, it does seem that Haywood might just be putting the cart before the horse and that, in most instances at least, the melody line has already been suggested by pre-existing harmony in some form. Others might also suggest that this notion was accommodated anyway by Russell's vertical-horizontal tonal gravity distinction between melody and harmony.

In *Jazzforschung—Jazz Research*, the journal of the Graz Institute of Jazz, Alfona Michael Dauer provides a very thorough analysis of Russell's work that is satisfyingly free of jargon.²⁹ And in 2002, in *Contemporary Music Review*, Peter Burt provides a similarly intriguing assessment of Russell's influence on the Japanese composer Toru Takemitsu. Noting the latter's frequent references to his reading in 1961 of the 1959 edition of the Concept, Burt explores in detail, albeit tentatively, similarities in their harmonic practices. Both articles are broadly supportive of Russell's ideas. As is, Pierre-Emmanuel Seguin's intriguing article from 2014, in which he explores the influence of Russell's ideas on Antipodean jazz musicians through the Australian jazz pianist, Bryce Rohde.³⁰

However, André Jeanquartier's article in *Jazzforschung* offers perhaps the most thorough critique of Russell's theories. Many of the points he makes are beyond the scope of this book (or my own grasp of musical theory). Briefly, however, Jeanquartier argues that Russell fails to prove the dominance of the Lydian scale or its value against the major scale. Its only advantage, according to the author, might be within the realms of modal jazz. In his opinion, it is otherwise too static and undynamic as a means of accommodating most modern music. He adds that there are significant deficiencies in the formation of Russell's scales, which he says are unbalanced, inconsistent and arbitrary in their use of non-Lydian scales. Most significantly, Jeanquartier argues that there is nothing in Russell's system or in his scales that could not have been produced within the traditional system of major-minor tonality.³¹ It is an article of depth and substance that is well researched and argued. This is the article to which advocates of the Lydian Concept must apply themselves, for its conclusions are potential quite damaging to the credibility of the Concept.

The article is, however, not without its own flaws and some brief points may be made here. First, within any system, musical or otherwise, one's starting point is important. How the universe will look and be experienced is greatly affected by things like perspective and trajectory. All systems are accommodations with reality. It seems unfair to criticize Russell in this regard without exploring the universe from his point of origin. If Russell's system does not sustain its own logic, then so be it, but it should also be evaluated on its own terms. That said, in claiming that his ideas take in the whole world of equally tempered music, Russell clearly invites challenges such as those of Jeanquartier. A second issue relates to whether Russell's system can better accommodate musics based on non-Western forms and concepts. This is not a simple point. To claim that Western musical ideas can best or even adequately account for music as diverse as that of Islam, the blues, gamelan and so forth, smacks of ethnocentrism.

Third, and most importantly, there is the issue of what kind of theory the Lydian Concept actually is. Russell's claims for it aside, it sits most easily within the terms of "practice theory," "praxis" or "theory for use;" that is, theory that guides and informs action. In these terms, Russell's ideas also need to be judged in terms of their utility. In fairness, Jeanquartier does credit Russell in terms of the way his ideas have opened up our understanding of the relationship between chords and scales and also credits him with influencing the development of both modal and free jazz. Either way, his article deserves to be read by proponents and opponents of Russell's ideas.

With regard to the Lydian Concept as a science and as a system, I have already addressed in an earlier chapter Russell's misunderstanding and misapplication of theoretical concepts from physics. As I suggested, the term "tonal gravity" works well as a metaphor but not as science. [32]

Russell, as Howard Riley noted above, disapproved of reference to the Concept as a system. Quite why is not entirely clear, though one suspects this had something to do with the widespread distrust in the fifties and sixties of "The System," as represented by dominant political, economic and cultural authority. After all, for Russell, it was that system that forced the separation of his natural parents – "the kids", as he called them. More than that, Russell disliked comparisons of the Lydian Concept with the Schillinger Method and appears to have felt that the very idea of a "system" in music represented something rigid and formulaic.

However, the Lydian Concept is most definitely a system and one that does seem quite internally consistent and coherent. I come from a social science rather than musical background and one that draws extensively on General Systems Theory. From that perspective, it seems to me that beginning with the Lydian Scale at the centre linked through the concept of the chordmode, it would not be hard to draw a systems map of the Lydian Concept. [33] Related scales would be located in the map at closer or greater distance from the parent scale using Russell's terms "ingoing," "semi-ingoing," "semi-outgoing," and "outgoing". At the same time, within the map, different levels of tonal gravity could be positioned either within quadrants or better at different levels. If this seems a little arcane to some readers, I apologise. Simply, my point is that the very fact that such a map, describing graphically Russell's schemas and the relationships between them, is possible demonstrates that the Lydian Concept has quite a high degree of internal consistency and integrity. It works.

The other issue in relation to the scientific aspect of the Concept lies in the way Russell reached his initial conclusions and developed these subsequently. Whether he was aware at the time that this was what he was doing, it seems clear that he approached his research very scientifically. The scientific method, which has guided research since the 17th century, is based on a clear and sequential series of processes. Briefly, it involves careful observation, scepticism about those observations, formulation of hypotheses via induction, experimental testing of deductions from any hypotheses and later refinement based on experiment. As we saw in Chapter Four, this is a very good description of how Russell conducted his experiments in the New York T. B. sanatorium.

He has described his methodology to various authors including Dom Cerulli, Ian Carr, Vivien Perlis, Ben Young and myself. Moreover, Russell refused to accept his "discovery" at face value; rather, he consciously sought to test it. The process, known in the philosophy of science as "falsification," [34] seems very apt in this context. Recognizing that any new theory would immediately meet resistance, Russell told Kirk Silsbee in an interview for *Cadence*, "So I became its chief challenger and tried to destroy the logic of it and what stood up, I then built on that. In fact, I think that's the only way theories should really be tested. I don't think a theory should be released or let go of or enforced on other people until it's been through that process." [35]

Certainly, one reviewer of *George Russell: The Story of an American Composer* could not see the importance of this point and perhaps I was less clear on this than I might have been in the first edition. [36] It is precisely the systematic and scientific way Russell went about researching his ideas that gives the Lydian Concept a greater validity than say Lennie Tristano's approach, Ornette Coleman's Harmolodics or other chord-scale approaches.

Turning to the Concept and Russell's own personal philosophy and psychology, the first thing to note is that until the mid-sixties, he would have counted himself as an atheist. As we have seen, during his *sojourn* in Scandinavia, Russell came into contact with the writings of G. I. Gurdjieff, P. D. Ouspensky and Dr. Maurice Nicoll – a belief system sometimes referred to as the Fourth Way. As he wrote to me on the subject in 2005,

> I would avoid Americans in Europe when I could, but one day I met an American musician who I had seen around Stockholm. I tried to ignore him but he approached me, and said, "Man, you have to read this book," and shoved it between my arm and sensing my coldness, said, "It's about all and everything in life," while walking away. I never saw him again and I don't recall his name but I hope we meet again on this or whatever planet, so I can tell him how grateful I am that he introduced me to Gurdjieff. He's always there when you need him; he always has answers for whatever situation or puzzlement you find yourself in. His is the only philosophy/practice, which has ever seemed to me to be objective. I have read and reread his books, as well as the books of Dr. Maurice Nicoll, whom I believe worked with Jung until he "discovered" Gurdjieff. In any event, whatever road leads to a psychological pathway for one's life is the right one. [37]

At risk of repetition, there are constant references throughout interviews with Russell, in the titles of his compositions and in sleevenotes to his records. "*Living Time*" and "*Live in An American Time Spiral*" refer directly to Nicoll's work, notably his 1952 book, *Living Time and the Integration of the Life*. Russell's references to "essence", including the record title *The Essence of George Russell*, derive from Gurdjieff and Ouspensky's division of the individual into three parts – personality, essence and consciousness. Two quotations from Russell, one from the sleevenotes to *Electronic Sonata for Souls Loved by Nature— 1968* and the second from the last paragraph in the 2001 edition of the *Lydian Chromatic Concept of Tonal Organization*, clearly indicate how deeply such ideas were ingrained in his own personal belief system.

"Duality and its side effects, they [philosophers such as Gurdjieff] claim are the chief causes of suffering on Earth." [38]

And even more so:

"I hope this knowledge will light your way, inspiring and empowering your essence to express its truest, most unique self—not only musically, but also daring to venture into music's womb, that unseen philo-spiritual world which is music's seminal source and foundation connecting it—and you—to the stars." [39]

The Concept, certainly according to George Russell himself and to some of its advocates, seeks to say something about the natural order of things but in ways that owe more to metaphysics than physics. Russell clearly did not see that there was any divide between the natural world and its scientific study, on the one hand, and the "philo-spiritual world", on the other.

I have to say that as an atheist (albeit one not unsympathetic to religion as a guide to human conduct) I do struggle with this aspect of Russell's work. However, for those such as myself who neither follow Fourth Way belief systems or more mainstream religions, there maybe a couple of ways of understanding such ideas and their relationship to the Concept both on their own terms and as metaphor.

Firstly, in an incredibly insightful discussion of the non-Western religious beliefs of Coltrane and Russell, Ingrid Monson considered how Russell's spiritual beliefs derive from Gurdjieff's ideas about nature, gravity, harmony and unity. As she points out, Russell's theory is "essentialist" in its most exact meaning. [40] That is, it is about essence and the individual's pursuit of the goal of enlightenment in allowing full expression of his or her essence. It does not matter that Russell did not discover Gurdjieff until he was living in Scandinavia, by which time *The Lydian Chromatic Concept of Tonal Organization* had reached its second edition. Like many "seekers" after universal truths, when Russell discovered Gurdjieff it was for him the realization of a search and 'The Work', as it is called in Fourth Way terminology, made sense in terms of his own existing artistic and spiritual goals.

Expressed in this way, George Russell is functioning intellectually according to a different definition of science, that of "science as knowledge." In the terms that he is concerned with, that knowledge base can equally include Platonic, Pythagorean, Buddhist, Hindu, mystical-Christian or, indeed, any philosophical belief system. The test of those beliefs owes little to Western "scientific" models of proof but lies instead in the existential and experiential. It is necessary to understand this to fully appreciate George Russell's philosophical position rather than simply dismiss it out of hand. As Monson has noted,

> A number of terms that Russell employs can be found in Gurdjieff's series of books titled *All and Everything*. Russell, for example, refers to the concept as the "all and everything of tonality" and the "all and everything of music." Indeed, Gurdjieff's talks about gravity, harmoniousness, space travel, the planet Saturn, unity, and the idea of spiritual essence seem to have provided a fertile means for Russell to combine his interests in tonality, philosophy, modernity, the non-Western world, and self-awareness."

And:

> Russell's identification with international spiritual ideas underlies his assertion that the concept is "the first theory to unite the music of the East and the West and be applicable to both of them." [41]

Monson is quite correct in identifying how Russell found in the totalizing philosophy of Gurdjieff, answers to many, if not all of the questions that concerned him. The philosophy helped Russell to integrate all aspects of his world – the Concept, his music, his relationships, his life history, his feelings about himself and the world – within a frame of reference that was uniquely personal. It worked for him.

But there is, I think, a much more specific, practical application of these ideas to be found in Russell's work. The source in this respect is in Maurice Nicoll's book, *Living Time and the Integration of Life* (1952/1998). It has taken me a long time (no pun intended) to grasp how the term 'living time', as the name of his album with Bill Evans of that title and of his orchestra actually related to the music itself. To me, the Fourth Way and all religions function by mystifying the natural world and the place of human beings within it. They confuse illuminating metaphor with revelation and human consciousness with the idea of soul or essence. At the same time, they simultaneously elevate and, paradoxically, devalue sensory experience over cognition. There is a philosophical dualism at play here. Sensory experience is, within this schema, both revelatory but, in other respects, illusory and a distraction. The truth, it is argued, lies within.

But there is also what I would describe as an ecological aspect to all this, one that relates the ecology of the individual to the ecology of the species and nature, albeit within the context of belief and faith rather than science. In *Living Time and the Integration of Life*, Nicoll quotes Ouspensky, on whose ideas he draws,

> It is necessary that the centre of gravity of everything shall lie for man in his inner world, in self-consciousness and not in the outer world at all. [42]

Nicoll is talking about a "higher consciousness," which, in his terms, allows the individual "to become an object of study to himself," and, so doing, reach beyond "merely sensible knowledge and even rational knowledge." [43] As to the purpose of this "reaching," it is "the integration of life," which I take to mean the integration of the individual in their life and in the natural world beyond mere sensual experience in the "transcending" of "the major illusion of the senses." As Nicoll wrote,

> We must think beyond time, out of time, and unless we question our temporal existence, unless we begin to think differently about everything and give quite a new interpretation to our lives, we cannot change our standpoint, which is the standpoint of illusion. To think Time itself brings us near the sense and meaning of Eternity. The rushing movement of passing-time ceases. There comes, from an indefinable direction, and intermittently, the sense of now . . . A new action of the mind begins - a rethinking of everything in terms of all the life and now. [44]

Now listen to *Living Time* (either version) or *The African Game* with the idea of "living time" as all time happening now in your mind. The music is not about thematic development. Its motion is not linear. There are multiple rhythms, riffs and melodies all taking place at the same moment. The music is multi-layered and multi-coloured. It is polyrhythmic and polytonal. It is incredibly rich texturally and harmonically. To use another very different composer's dictum, "Jazz happens in real time – once!" [45] In a sense, this is perhaps how Vertical Tonal Gravity, in particular, connects with Nicoll's idea of "living time". For Russell, the orchestra and the music it makes is the musical embodiment of what Nicoll is writing about.

My remarks on how Russell related to the Concept psychologically will be brief. I think, that this can best be understood in relation to his own origins and his reaction to those origins and in relation to his religious-scientific ideas. In terms of the former, he was the product of a liaison between Kathleen George, a music student at Oberlin, and an unidentified white man and was the adopted son of Bessie and Joseph and. In terms of Russell's musical theories and beliefs about science and nature, several years of reading, researching and hours of talking with George Russell sometimes left me wondering where George Russell ended and the Lydian Concept began – and *vice versa* – the two seem so intertwined.

On the one hand, Russell continually described the Concept as something he had discovered or perhaps rediscovered in the sense that this was ancient, even esoteric knowledge going back to Pythagoras and the early Church Modes. [46] On the other, he often seemed to want to protect the Concept from dilution to the point that its very dissemination was inevitably restricted. It was as if its essence were also his own. It was, perhaps, not for nothing that he called the Lydian Scale the "Parent Scale". I think it was both his baby and his parent. It rooted him in the natural world in certain ways and, perhaps, met a need that the circumstances of his birth and adoption could not.

In the course of my career in social work, and in my personal life, I came across a number of people who had been adopted who struggled to form strong attachments with others. That was never the case with Russell. In fact, the quality of his relationships with others – including, the musicians in his band – always impressed. I suspect that his parents Bessie and Joseph and the experience of growing up in the community of Walnut Hills fostered that capacity in him. But that does not mean that the experience of being given up for adoption, of never knowing one's birth parents, of never having that sense of biological connection would not leave a mark psychologically. If so, perhaps the Concept gave Russell that sense of deep connection and rootedness.

That Russell drew to a huge extent on the Lydian Concept as a composer states the obvious. However, any limiting notion of Russell as a "Lydian Composer" must be rejected. Similarly, any idea that those who draw upon the Concept in their compositions might in some ways sound similar is equally wrong.

Researching this book, I listened at NEC to several tapes of compositions by students studying the Concept with Ben Schwendener. Each one was completely distinct and different in both organization and execution. As Russell – and his students – have repeated – this is not a "'paint by numbers' sort of concept" and "it ultimately puts 100 percent responsibility for creativity on you." [47]

In the first edition of this biography, *George Russell: The Story of an American Composer*, I perhaps overemphasised the idea of Russell, as I put it there, as "one of the most obviously 'Third Stream' composers to come out of jazz." [48] I also went to some lengths to talk about influences upon Russell from European art music, perhaps taking for granted the more important influences from African-American and African music. With hindsight, both points require clarification and qualification.

Coined by John Lewis and Gunther Schuller, the term "Third Stream" quickly came to define the bringing together of jazz and European art music. More recently, at NEC the name of the Third Stream department has changed to "Contemporary Improvisation." In a recent article, its previous head of department, Ran Blake described the approach somewhat differently from its earlier definition,

> I would say it's "third streaming". It's an act of combining two radically different approaches to music. So, for me it might be early Schoenberg, Olivier Messiaen, whom I adore, mixing that with Howlin' Wolf or Chris Connor or Abbey Lincoln. [49]

Leaving aside any potential difficulties with so broad a definition, what Blake is reaching towards is something that goes beyond genre-bending or stylistic mixing. Instead, it requires the conscious and deliberate creation of dialogue within a composition between differing musical traditions, a dialogue that is then continued and expanded through improvisation. Clearly, what Russell set out to achieve in his music would sit well with such a definition.

However, in relation to the original definition proposed by Lewis and Schuller, we can certainly point to a few works where Russell appears to have set out with the aim of bringing jazz and European art music together. Those would be *Vertical Form VI* (1977), *Six Aesthetic Gravities* (1988), *Centrifugue* (1988), *Dialogue with Ornette* (1992) and, maybe, *All About Rosie* (1957).

There is, I feel now, a better way of understanding how Russell might be seen as a 'third stream' composer and that is through Ran Blake's description above. George Russell's music clearly represents a conscious attempt to extend the use of compositional techniques in jazz that did involve significant reliance on written forms and on the location of improvisation within those formal structures. It is more in that sense that Russell can or should be considered a third stream composer, than in terms of the Lewis/Schuller definition.

Russell's approach to the use of compositional material is described well in the following remarks by Andy Sheppard:

> George's music is very dense, so that a lot of the written stuff is very hard to play, and he'll have different rhythms happening at the same time, where the bass player's "one" is different to the drummer's "one," which is different to my "one" when you're reading the part. So that time cycles are happening simultaneously and the band will be playing in different keys, and then there's the whole Lydian Concept. It's a very dense, intricate world.[50]

When Sheppard prepared himself to play with George Russell the first time, he listened to *The African Game*. "I thought the whole first section sounded fairly improvised to me. It sounds like the band are pretty free there." When he sat down at the rehearsal and saw the music, however, "All the stuff I thought was pretty free and improvised was actually written and the system of cues is incredibly complex." Additionally, Ricky what he as the tenor player was playing at a given point could be "wildly different to what the saxophone player next to you is playing. It makes you question the music you play. You think am I right here?"[51]

Some players and composers have questioned the amount Russell wrote. Keyboardist Masabumi Kikuchi, who played briefly with Russell but more extensively with Gil Evans, contrasted the two experiences for Stephanie Stein Crease: "After the first night, I couldn't do it. His [Russell's] music is all very scored and you can't do anything else." With Gil Evans, "He wanted the orchestra to play beyond notation." After being with Russell, "I realized how much freedom Gil gave me," he explained to Evans's biographer.[52]

And the British composer and bandleader Graham Collier has made a similar point. Despite acknowledging Russell's significance in expanding the potential for the big band, Collier told me, "I'm not an enormous fan of George's work, and, like a lot of people, I find he writes too much. He has a tendency for that." He told a story about Gil Evans to explain the kind of model he prefers.

> I'll tell you a funny story. Do you know John Ellson [then a director of Serious Music]? He told me he went to pick up Gil from the airport for some London Festival commission and he said to Gil, "Have you finished the piece yet? Is it all done?" Gil said, "Yeah, I've got it in here somewhere." And he pulled out this scrap of paper and that was it. Yet they made a magnificent concert out of it.[53]

It is no more necessary to agree with Kikuchi and Collier than it is to choose between Evans and Russell. Both composers had in common a desire to expand the possibilities in terms of how jazz composition could be made to affect and work with improvisation in new ways.

However, both Kikuchi and Collier make a valid point that the two found their own ways of achieving this end. Evans was increasingly more concerned with creating open, impressionistic musical settings that allowed all members of his orchestra, not just his soloists, latitude in their contributions. Russell was clearly much more focused on providing a fully-fledged compositional frame than was Evans. Yet, both composers produced music rich in tone colours and, from the early seventies onwards, made significant use of electric instruments. I sometimes imagine that had he been a painter Evans might have been a Matisse-like figure, a fauvist, simultaneously modernist but reaching for something wilder and uncontained. Russell, on the other hand, might have been an artist such as Peter Brueghel the Elder, if one thinks in terms of the detailed way Russell's musicians populate his landscapes/soundscapes. Whether such somewhat idiosyncratic comparisons mean anything to fans of both or either is another matter.

Both composers were, also, highly chromatic in their use of tones and textures. From his period with Thornhill onward, Evans used the horns, in particular the lower range brass instruments, to create soft, vibrating colours. Later, in his own bands, those same colours became less definite and more impressionistic as they emerged from the washes - sometimes in pastel tone colours but at others more jarring - of electric instruments and percussion. Musical time hangs suspended and there is no definite tonal centre anchoring the music.

Yet time, according to the principles of tonal gravity—or, to use Russell's own favoured philosophical metaphor, "living time"— was more important in Russell's music. Time is about rhythm, dance and pulse —essential ingredients in Russell's art - with the energy in the music deriving from these sources. Where Evans realised that musical colouration could derive from minimizing writing, Russell took the message that you could actually produce these effects through notation. Both Evans and Russell started with similar aspirations but arrived at different—but equally justifiable—conclusions.

Further, while some musicians might have found a lack of freedom in performing Russell's music, this was certainly not a universal response. Andy Sheppard's remarks above clearly indicate that Russell sought individuality in the musicians he hired. Palle Mikkelborg made a similar point to me in which, comparing Miles Davis and Russell, he likened Davis to a painter and designer and Russell to an architect, "George has already .. … the house is ready but there's no furniture in it. But the house is there. In that sense, George is free and he loves people to furnish their apartments in their own way, as long as they are strong." [54]

Mikkelborg played with both Russell and Evans and enjoyed both experiences. For him, the difference was one of precision versus looseness.

> There is the obvious one that Gil was very, very loose, while George is very precise. He wants a certain thing. With Gil it could go any way. Maybe something completely different than you thought. Yes, very, very different. How can I describe it better? Yin and yang in a

way. Without them this music would never exist, without these two beautiful ways of looking at the same thing. [55]

Both men also thought very deeply, certainly when it came to music but Mikkelborg makes another distinction that relates to Russell's frequent use of his work to express social or philosophical concerns. Evans was, perhaps, more focused on the music as his primary concern.

[T]here's also something very philosophical about them both but Gil was like a wise man. Of course, George is very much associated with creating a system finding out where human beings were born in Africa. *The African Game* is about that. I don't know if Gil would ever think like that. He was in a way much more vertical in a way. He was very much about now. Let's see what we can do now? [56]

It should also be clear that Russell used a range of musical techniques in his compositions. He was, once again, not just a "Lydian composer." His music is often strongly contrapuntal both melodically and rhythmically. His compositions are often cyclical, or fugue-like in form. For Russell, the fugue does not seek resolution. It grows upward in ever-ascending spirals. As Andy Wasserman recalled from his studies in composition with George Russell,

The very first thing he said was, "Man, I don't care what you write . . ." —because I would write pieces and bring them in and he would critique them—the only thing he ever said was, "Funky fugues, man. I don't care what you do. I want it to be a funky fugue." And when you listen to his music, that's what it is. [57]

Also, compared to Evans, Russell was more interested in exploring the possibilities of long form in jazz composition. On the whole, longer pieces in jazz have relied on a series of solos in place of thematic development. Russell, as a composer uses, in addition to the jazz solo, a number of other devices. The first of these, as we have suggested, involves a complex layering of rhythmic patterns using a range of instruments, not just drums and bass. These polyrhythms interweave like an African drum choir, to use Russell's own analogy, and on a piece like *Living Time Event II*, the effect is like that of swirling winds in a vortex. The second derives from way he used different pairings of instruments within the orchestra to create intriguing and complex rhythmic and harmonic effects.

That Russell was influenced by certain composers of the European, post-war *avant-garde* is evidenced by his association with nyMusikk in Norway, through his studies with Stefan Wolpe and by his own admission. In 1978, interviewed for one of the chapters in *The Black Composer Speaks*, he cited both Karlheinz Stockhausen and György Ligeti as influences. [58] He might also have added Krzysztof Penderecki, whom he mentioned in a 1974 interview with Olive Jones for the journal, *The Black Perspective in Music*. [59]

However, what needs to be understood is how Russell incorporated such influences and how he viewed these. To take the first point, in *The Black Composer Speaks*, when Russell referred to Ligeti and Stockhausen, the full quote reads,

I listen to everything and everybody, who has a new musical law to offer. I repeat: I have no style. But I might add that I am particularly interested in those artists who change the musical aesthetic, such as Charlie Parker, Thelonious Monk, Louis Armstrong, and Ornette Coleman. You might add György Ligeti and Stockhausen to that.[60]

During the interview, there are other answers that seem important. In regard to his writing, he is asked which genres he preferred. He replied, "Black music. Just black music." Earlier in the same article he noted,

> Jazz, or Afro-American music (as it should be known), is the only serious music that is at the mercy of fans (old and new) who have the nerve to criticize an art music without "knowing do from re," as a friend of mine has explained. This is all because of the American attitude toward the Negro as a relaxed, happy fellow. Still, there are some people who take their jobs as critics seriously and are artists in their own right.[61]

Asked how he viewed "the role of the black artist in contemporary society," Russell replied: "To show a new path to human evolution based upon his high African heritage."[62] Indeed, throughout the interview, he makes references to the Concept as a higher law and relates this specifically in response to one question as one of "uniquely black (in terms of both musical and philosophical considerations)."

Russell clearly saw himself as a black composer, saw himself as operating within the field of jazz (albeit, that his preferred term would be "Afro-American music") and saw the Concept as being directly connected to this heritage. As Gerhard Kubik and David Evans have argued jazz was never a remotely straightforward marriage of western forms and African rhythms. What those descendants of slaves stolen from their home and families achieved was something far more remarkable. That they took from western music a great deal is obvious. The question is more what they did with this new musical information and technology and how they used this in their music practice. The key words are, as Kubik notes, "Retention, Resilience, Reinvention."[63] Essentially, Kubik and Evans argue that African-Americans took into their musical culture aspects of western music, the folk song and ballad forms and western instruments for example, but reinvented them within their own retained and developing musical practice. The vocalisation used by black musicians on woodwinds, trumpet and even guitar offers one illustration of this, as does the use of blue notes.[64]

The taking of a technique or way of making music from one tradition and reinventing it in one's own context and tradition is much more than mere exoticism or musical colouration. It involves the conscious reimagining of how that technique might sound and might feel and what it can be used to express in its transplanted state. Instead of common-place understandings of syncretism as the cross-cultural equation of apparently similar traits, Kubik and Evans propose that that which is taken from the dominant white culture here becomes something wholly different once transplanted, even if certain resemblances remain. They suggest that a series of cultural, psychological and spiritual processes are involved that, in the case of jazz, "Africanized" (my word) those elements taken from western music.[65]

This is directly relevant to what Russell was doing in terms of whatever he might have learnt from Wolpe, might have heard in the music of Scriabin or Stravinsky or Debussy or discovered in the approaches of Ligeti and Stockhausen. Moreover, he reframed such ideas and approaches through the Lydian Concept, which he saw as representing a much more ancient, non-western "world of music." Russell was not only transforming and reshaping such influences within the context of jazz or, as he preferred, "Afro-American music." He was doing so through the medium of the Lydian Chromatic Concept of Tonal Organization. More than that, his use of the Concept as a composer cannot be separated from his position as an African-American composer in the musical world of jazz or from the philosophical beliefs that informed his understanding of the Concept.

This is, arguably, best demonstrated in relation to the question of pantonality and pan-stylism. Despite studying with Stefan Wolpe, who himself studied with Schoenberg's pupil Webern, Russell never embraced atonality. He has always favoured polytonal or tonal approaches as a composer and, indeed, this sits more easily with the Concept's notion of chord-scale unity. Russell was very clear on what he learned from the composer in his contribution to Austin Clarkson's *On the Music of Stefan Wolpe*. As he noted, "The rate of chromatic circulation and the thirdless sound were big ideas." [66]

Readers will recall, Russell's remark on the future jazz in *The Jazz Word* (1963). In that interview, Russell argued that jazz would "bypass atonality" and would be "pan-Rhythmic and pan-tonal," a "Big Bill Broonzy sound" that retained "the funk." [67]

A decade later, in his sleeve notes for *Electronic Sonata for Souls Loved by Nature—1968*, Russell further defined his own ideas in terms of what he called "pan-stylism.

> The essential concepts which inspired the creation of the *Electronic Sonata for Souls Loved by Nature* lay in philosophical and socio/musical areas. Its socio/ musical objective was to create a pan-stylistic electronic tape; a tape consisting of fragments of many different styles of music, avant-garde jazz, ragas, blues, rock, serial music etc. treated electronically. And to have this tape serve as a palate upon which non-electronic musical statements of a pan-stylistic nature could be projected. The wedding of non-electronic pan-stylism to electronic pan-stylism was meant to convey the cultural implosion occurring among the earth's population, their coming together. Also it is meant to suggest that man, in the face of encroaching technology, must confront technology and attempt to humanize it. [68]

Readers will note the continuity of concern between what Russell wrote here and the notes he provided for *The African Game*.

Whether or not one accepts the validity of the Lydian Concept, Russell's ideas have clearly been significant in their influence upon jazz. Those ideas and Russell's own work as a composer have anticipated many of the later developments within the music, from modal jazz to jazz-rock and, even, to what is lazily referred to as "post-modern" jazz. Russell, I am sure, would prefer the term "pan-stylistic." Moreover, as theory, Russell's Lydian Concept does appear to be internally consistent and logical and does appear to describe and explain certain aspects of jazz, not least the jazz harmonic and rhythmic practices that emerged with and after bebop.

In terms of his influence on jazz as a theorist, Russell is the only musician-composer to have produced a written and original body of ideas. Those ideas have had an impact on the development of modal jazz and on musicians from Miles Davis, John Coltrane, Eric Dolphy, Art Farmer, Dave Baker, Oliver Nelson, Steve Swallow and others. Subsequent generations carry that influence forward in the continuing and extensive use of modes in the music. Although not always credited, Russell's ideas have surely informed the prevalence of chord-scale theory in jazz since the 1970s and in jazz education. That said, this seems to have been at the expense of certain more profound aspects of the Lydian Concept, musically as much as philosophically. It appears to me that study of the Concept, as opposed to more limited variations on chord-scale theory, requires of the student a far greater and deeper understanding of the relationship between chords and scales. Furthermore, using (as just one example) Russell's terms "ingoing," "semi-ingoing," "semi-outgoing," and "outgoing," surely presents a wider perspective on what is possible compositionally or improvisationally. As Eric Dolphy wrote to Russell, while on tour in Europe with Charles Mingus, "It gives you so much more to work with."

As to the future influence of the Lydian Concept on musicians, in jazz education and on students, it is hard to say. The Lydian Concept is still taught at NEC and other musicians and educators such as pianist-composer Hans Koller, Head of Jazz at Trinity Laban in London, and saxophonist John O'Gallagher are active supporters of Russell as a theorist and composer. Neil Leonard, saxophonist and composer and ex-student of Russell, has also been involved at the University of Gothenburg teaching students about the Lydian Concept and exploring its uses in improvisation. [69]

In terms of Russell's music its dissemination continues. Hans Koller has plans for a recording dedicated to Russell's work, while Ran Blake released *Ghost Tones: Portraits of George Russell* (A Side Records) in 2015. Pianist-composer Diane Moser has also performed Russell's *Jazz in the Space Age* in concert, while French pianist Philippe Seignez has released records of his own compositions dedicated to Russell of his own compositions. As I write, the wonderful Portuguese Orquestra Jazz de Matosinhos have just released their own live recording of *Jazz in the Space Age* with pianists João Paulo Esteves da Silva and José Diogo Martins. Other tribute gigs to Russell's music have taken place recently in New York by the Juilliard Jazz Ensemble and in Moscow with Aleksandra Mumurashkina's Sextet. [70] A few swallows, if not yet a full-blown summer heatwave.

As to the future of the Concept as a continuing influence on jazz practice, this will probably be through the various online tutorials available on sites such as *YouTube*. [71] This may not be the equivalent of actually studying with Russell himself or accredited practitioners but the Lydian Concept is kept alive and disseminated by such processes. In some ways, such processes seems to have more in common with the way jazz evolved and developed through informal channels rather than in the setting of the academy. The fact that these sites have thousands of views allows for a certain cautious optimism.

And Russell's importance continues through younger players and composers—musicians such as Randy and the late Michael Brecker, John Medeski, Don Byron, Courtney Pine, Ricky Ford, Jan Garbarek, Terje Rypdal, Jon Christensen (now sadly deceased), Satoko Fujii and Marty Ehrlich.

There have long been signs in the work of both younger and older jazz composers such as Satoko Fujii, Jon Balke, Colin Towns, Christian Wallumrod, Tim Berne, mathias rüegg, Graham Collier, Roberto Bonati and Keith Tippett that extended form is now the territory for jazz to conquer. In this case, George Russell led the way and can surely look down from his pinnacle, smile and reflect on his own pioneering days. Works from *All About Rosie* and *Jazz in the Space Age*, through *Electronic Sonata for Souls Loved by Nature* and *Living Time*, to *The African Game, Six Aesthetic Gravities, Uncommon Ground* and *It's About Time* provide a marvellous, rich legacy and library for younger explorers.

Anyone who remains to be convinced that Russell does deserve his place in the pantheon should simply listen to Russell's sixties sextet records. Whether it is *Jazz Workshop*, *Ezz-Thetics*, or *Stratusphunk*, this is as good as small-group jazz gets. What more is there to say? George Russell has been a jazz composer, theorist, drummer, pianist, bandleader, teacher, innovator and pioneer. Many of the best and brightest of several generations of jazz musicians owe him a greater or lesser debt. Let's hope that wherever he goes next, he takes the sounds of that last standing ovation from the Barbican with him, ringing in his ears.

## Notes

1. Richard Cook and Brian Morton. *The Penguin Guide to Jazz On CD.* pp. 1282-1283
2. Interview with Andy Wasserman, June 2004.
3. Stein Crease 2002, p.133.
4. Ibid, p.138
5. Ian Carr, interview with John Lewis, The quote is taken from Carr's notebooks.
6. Interview with Howard Riley, December 2005.
7. Ibid.
8. Interview with George Russell, June 2004.
9. Interview with George Russell, March 2003.
10. Interview with Wasserman.
11. E-mail interview with Chuck Israels, August 2004.
12. Interview with Randy Brecker, August 2006.
13. Ibid.
14. Interview with Ben Schwendener, October 2003.
15. Interview with Marc Rossi, October 2004.
16. Interview with Schwendener.
17. Interview with Jack Reilly, September 2005.
18. Brubeck, "The Beginning of Beyond," p. 191.
19. Ibid.
20. Ingrid Monson, *Freedom Sounds: Civil Rights Callout to Jazz and Africa* (New York, NY: OUP. 2007) p.289
21. Brett Clement, "A New Lydian Theory for Frank Zappa's Modal Music," *Music Theory Spectrum*, Vol. 36, No.1 (Spring 2014), p.147
22. George Russell, *Lydian Chromatic Concept of Tonal Organization* (Brookline, MA: Concept, 2001), p.10

23. Brubeck, "The Beginning of Beyond," p. 190.
24. Russell, *The Lydian Chromatic Concept of Tonal Organization*. New York: Concept, 1959, p. iii-iv.
25. Brubeck, "The Beginning of Beyond," p. 192.
26. Ibid., p. 192.
27. Ibid., p. 193.
28. Mark S. Haywood, "The Harmonic Role of Melody in Vertical and Horizontal Jazz," *Annual Review of Jazz Studies* 5 (1991).
29. Alfona M. Dauer, "Das Lydisch-Chromatische Tonsystem Von George Russell Und Seine Anwendung," *Jazzforschung/Jazz Research* 14 (1982).
30. Peter Burt, "Takemitsu and the Lydian Chromatic Concept of George Russell," *Contemporary Music Review* 21, no. 4 (2002). Pierre-Emmanuel Seguin, "Lydia in Oz: The reception of George Russell in 1960s Australia," *Jazz Research Journal*, Vol. 8, No. 1-2 (2014), pp. 238-256
31. André Jeanquartier, "Kritische Anmerkungen Zum 'Lydian Chromatic Concept,'" *Jazzforschung/Jazz Research* 16 (1984).
32. Ibid. M. Nelkon, *Principles of Physics* (Harlow, UK: Longman, 1981), chaps. 22 and 23; I. S. Grant and W. R. Phillips, *The Elements of Physics* (Oxford: Oxford University Press, 2001), pp. 245–72. The difference between "sound" waves and electromagnetic wave phenomenon, such as light and radio waves, relates to mass. Sound has no mass upon which gravity can act. This is why sound requires another medium, such as air or water, through which it can travel. Unlike light waves, which consist of tiny particles called photons, sound cannot travel where there is no atmosphere. By contrast, light and radio waves can travel through space. See also J. Gribbin, *Get a Grip on the New Physics* (London: Weidenfeld & Nicholson, 1999), pp. 82–90.
33. Debra Hammond, *The Science of Synthesis: Exploring the Social Implications of General Systems Theory* (Boulder, CO: University of Colorado Press, 2003)
34. See, for example, R. G. A. Dolby, "The Sociology of Knowledge in Natural Science," *Science Studies* 1, no. 1 (1971); and K. Popper, *The Logic of Scientific Discovery* (New York: Basic, 1959).
35. Kirk Silsbee, "George Russell," *Cadence*, June 1996.
36. Grego Applegate Edwards, Review of *George Russell: An American Composer*, *Cadence* July 2010, pp. 60-63.
37. George Russell, e-mail to the author, April 12, 2005.
38. George Russell, sleeve notes to *Electronic Sonata for Souls Loved by Nature— 1968*. Soulnote 121034–2.
39. Russell, *Lydian Chromatic Concept of Tonal Organization*, p. 39.
40. Ingrid Monson, "Oh Freedom—George Russell, John Coltrane and Modal Jazz," in *In the Course of Performance*, ed. B. Nettle and M. Russell (London: University of Chicago Press, 1998). pp. 154-156.
41. Monson, *Freedom Sounds*, p.293
42. Maurice Nicoll, *Living Time and the Integration of Life*, (Utrecht, NL: Eureka Editions 1998), p.47.
43. Op cit.
44. Nicoll, *Living Time*, pp.277-278.
45. Duncan Heining, *Mosaics: The Life and Works of Graham Collier*, (Sheffield: Equinox Publishing, 2018)
46. George Russell, *Lydian Chromatic Concept of Tonal Organization*, pp.226-234; Reed Gratz, "An

Historical Perspective of the Lydian and Major Scales" in *Lydian Chromatic Concept of Tonal Organization*, pp.239-244.

47. Interview with Ben Schwendener, October 2003.
48. Heining, *George Russell: The Story of an American Composer*, Lanham, MY: Scarecrow 2010, p.289.
49. Duncan Heining, "The Very Singular Mr. Ran Blake" https://www.allaboutjazz.com/the-very-singular-mr-ran-blake-ran-blake January 23, 2020
50. Interview with Andy Sheppard, March 2003.
51. Ibid.
52. Stephanie Stein Crease, *Gil Evans—Out of the Cool* (Chicago: A Cappella, 2002), pp. 279–80.
53. Interview with Graham Collier, November 2004.
54. Interview with Mikkelborg,
55. Ibid.
56. Ibid.
57. Interview with Andy Wasserman.
58. David Baker et al, *The Black Composer Speaks*. Metuchen, NJ: Scarecrow Press, 1978, p.281.
59. Olive Jones. "George Russell—A New Theory for Jazz." *Black Perspective in Music*, Vol. 2, No. 1 (Spring, 1974), p.67.
60. David Baker et al, *The Black Composer Speaks*, p.280.
61. Ibid, p.279.
62. Ibid, pp.279-280.
63. Gerhard Kubik, *Jazz Transatlantic: The African Undercurrent in Twentieth Century Jazz Culture*, Jackson: University of Mississippi, 2017. pp.134-137
64. See Kubik, op cit; David Evans, "The Reinterpretation of African Musical Instruments in the United States," in Isadore Okpewho, Carole Boyce Davies and Ali a. Mazrui, eds. *The African Diaspora: African Origins and the New World Identities*, Bloomington: Indiana University Press, pp.379-390.
65. David Baker et al, *The Black Composer Speaks*, p.276.
66. Austin Clarkson, ed., *On the Music of Stefan Wolpe—Essays and Recollections* (New York: Pendragon, 2003).
67. George Russell, "Where Do We Go From Here?" in *The Jazz Word*, ed. D. Cerulli, B. Korall, and M. Nasatir (London: Ballantine, 1960), p. 190.
68. George Russell, sleeve notes to *Electronic Sonata for Souls Loved by Nature— 1968*.
69. See https://www.youtube.com/watch?v=QPzgc_os23U&feature=emb_logo, for Hans Koller/John O'Gallagher; for Neil Leonard - https://www.gu.se/english/about the university/news-calendar/Calendar/Event_Detail/?&eventId=3175155200
70. For Diane Moser https://www.trumpetsjazz.com/event/diane-mosers-winter-solstice-concert-music-of-george-russell-2/; for Ran Blake https://ranblake.com/; for Phillipe Seignez https://www.philippeseignez.com/hommage-george-russell; for Juilliard https://www.juilliard.edu/news/140761/juilliard-jazz-announces-2019-20-season; for Aleksandra Murashkina https://www.jazzmap.ru/afisha/2019-11-05-klub-alekseya-kozlovasekstet-aleksandra-murashkina-tribute-to-george-russell.php
71. For example, https://www.youtube.com/watch?v=T2wyXL36PDQ&has_verified=1; https://www.youtube.com/watch?v=uXMjqlq99zo.

# Bibliography

"Adventuring with George Russell." *Jazz Today*, June 1957.
"Afterhours—A Jazz Discussion with Clark Terry, Don Ellis, Bob Brookmeyer, George Russell." *Down Beat*, November 9, 1961.
Akiyama, K. "The Joy of Listening to Music—The George Russell Performance," *Komei Shimbun*, March 5, 1988.
Albertson, C. Sleeve notes to *Stratusphunk*. Riverside RLP 9341.
Anderson, K. Sleeve notes for Debussy, *La Mer, Nocturnes*, Naxos CD 8.550262.
———. Sleeve notes to Scriabin, *Piano Concerto, Prometheus, The Poem of Fire*. Naxos CD 8.550818.
Applebome, P. "A Jazz Success Story with a Tinge of the Blues." *New York Times*, September 22, 1998.
Applegate Edwards, Grego. Review of *George Russell: An American Composer, Cadence* July 2010, pp. 60-63
Atkins, Ronald. "The Guide—Preview of LTO at Queen Elizabeth Hall." *Guardian* (Manchester), November 11, 1995.
Austerlitz, Paul. *Jazz Consciousness: Music, Race and Humanity*, Middletown, CT: Wesleyan University Press. 2005
Baillie, M. Sleeve notes to *The Artistry of Artie Shaw*. Fresh Sound FSR-CD397.
Baker, D. "Jazz: The Academy's Neglected Stepchild." *Down Beat*, September 23, 1965.
Baker, D., L. B. Baker, and H. Hudson. *The Black Composer Speaks*. Metuchen, NJ: Scarecrow Press, 1978.
Ball, M. "Licht aus Stockhausen." *Avant* 5 (Winter 1998).
Balliett, Whitney. Review of George Russell Sextet, Jazz in the Garden, MoMA, New York. "Musical Events—Jazz Concerts." *New Yorker*, July 1960.
———. Review of George Russell—*New York, N.Y.* (Decca DL9216). *New Yorker*, December 1959.
Becker, H. S. *The Outsiders Studies in Sociology of Deviance*. New York: MacMillan, 1966.
Benson Brooks, John. "George Russell." *Jazz Review*, February 1960.
Berendt, Joachim. *The Jazz Book—From New Orleans to Jazz Now*. New York and Westport, CT: Lawrence Hill, 1974.
Berger, P., and T. Luckmann. *The Social Construction of Reality*. Harmondsworth, UK: Penguin, 1981.
Bernstein, Leonard. *The Unanswered Question: Six Lectures at Harvard*. Cambridge, MA: Harvard University Press, 1976.

Blangger, T. "George Russell." *Coda*, December 1990/January 1991.
"The Blindfold Test—André Previn." *Down Beat*, October 26, 1961.
"The Blindfold Test—George Russell." *Down Beat*, January 5, 1961.
Blumenthal, Bob. "A Tribute to a Local." *Boston Globe*, March 23, 1983.
———. "Captured by the Game." *Boston Phoenix*, May 14, 1985.
———. "George Russell—Stratus Seeker." *Down Beat*, October 1983.
———. "George Russell Finds Music's Missing Link." *Boston Phoenix*, April 24, 1973.
Booth, Garry. Review of Camden Jazz Festival. *Financial Times*, March 26, 1991.
Bouchard, Fred. Review of Boston Musica Viva performance of *Six Aesthetic Gravities*. *Down Beat*, June 1988.
Boulding, K. 1956 "General Systems Theory: The Skeleton of Science," Management Science, 2, 3 (Apr. 1956) pp.197-208)
Bowlby, John. *Attachment and Loss*. Vols. 1–3. London: Pimlico, 1997.
Boyd, Joe. *White Bicycles*. London: Serpent's Tail, 2006.
Britt, Stan. Sleeve notes for Affinity reissue of *Jazz in the Space Age* AFF152.
Brubeck, Darius. "1959: The Beginning of Beyond." In *The Cambridge Companion to Jazz*, edited by M. Cooke and D. Horn. Cambridge: Cambridge University Press, 2002.
Burford, Mark. *Mahalia Jackson and the Black Gospel Field*, New York, NY: Oxford University Press, 2019.
Burt, Peter. "Takemitsu and the Lydian Chromatic Concept of George Russell." *Contemporary Music Review* 21, no. 4 (2002).
Burton, Nelson. *My Life in Jazz*. Cincinnati, OH: Clifton Hills Press, 2000.
"By George." *Down Beat*, July 1983.
Campbell, Joseph. *The Hero with a Thousand Faces*. London: Fontana, 1993.
Carr, Ian. Program notes for a Contemporary Music Network tour (1992).
———. Interview with George Russell for BBC Radio 3 broadcast *Invisible Guru*.
———. Interview with George Russell for BBC Radio 3 broadcast *The Trailblazer— George Russell*.
———. "The Invisible Guru" BBC Radio Three July 1, 1994
———. *The Trail-Blazer* BBC Radio Three (eight half-hour programmes broadcast July 4 – August 22, 1994)
———. *Miles Davis—The Definitive Biography*. Hammersmith, UK: HarperCollins, 1999.
———. Notebooks for BBC Radio 3 Broadcasts *Invisible Guru* and *Trailblazer*, broadcast July and August 1994.
Carr, Ian; Fairweather, Digby; and Priestley, Brian, *The Rough Guide to Jazz: The Essential Companion to Artists and Albums* (London: Rough Guides, 2004),
Cerulli, Dom. "George Russell." *Down Beat*, May 29, 1958.
Cerulli, D., B. Korall, and M. Nasatir. *The Jazz Word*. New York: Ballantine, 1960.
Chilton, J. *Song of the Hawk*. London: Quartet, 1990.
Chinen, N. "Wynton Marsalis: The Once and Future King of Jazz at Lincoln Center," https://www.nytimes.com/2006/08/27/arts/music/27chin.html
"Chords and Discords." *Down Beat*, June 26, 1958. Cincinnati City Directory, 1923.
Cohen, Brigid. *Stefan Wolpe and the Avant-Garde Diaspora*. Cambridge, UK: CUP, 2016.
———. "Diasporic Dialogues in Mid-Century New York: Stefan Wolpe, George Russell, Hannah

Arendt, and the Historiography of Displacement." *Journal of the Society for American Music*, Volume 6, No. 2, 2012. p.144.

Clark, K. B., and M. P. Clark. "Racial Identification and Preferences in Negro Children." In *Reading in Social Psychology*, edited by Maccoby, Newcomb, and Hartley. New York: Holt, Rinehart & Winston, 1958.

Clarkson, Austin., ed. *On the Music of Stefan Wolpe—Essays and Recollections*. New York: Pendragon, 2003.

———. Interview with George Russell at www.wolpe.org

Claypool, Bob. "Blazing the Fusion Trail." *Houston Post*, October 8, 1983.

———. Review of *The African Game*. *Houston Post*, June 4, 1985.

Clement, Brett. "A New Lydian Theory for Frank Zappa's Modal Music," *Music Theory Spectrum*, Vol. 36, No.1 (Spring 2014), pp.146-166

Cochran, Polly. "Workshop Creates Learned Jazz." *Indianapolis Star*, August 4, 1957.

Considine, J. D. Review of *The African Game*. *Musician*, April 1985.

Cook, Richard. "Old Hand Who Gets a Kick out of the Big Band." *Sunday Times* (London), August 27, 1989.

Cook, R., and Brian Morton. *The Penguin Guide to Jazz On CD*. Harmondsworth, UK: Penguin, 2000.

Cosgrove, Stuart. "The Zoot-Suit and Style Warfare." *History Workshop Journal* 18 (Autumn 1984).

"Critics Poll Results." *Down Beat*, July 18, 1963.

Crouch, Stanley. "George Russell's Victory." *Village Voice*, February 21, 1984.

———. "From the Cottonfields to the Cosmos." *Soho Weekly News*, April 20, 1978.

Cuscuna, Michael. "Spotlight Review of Reissues of *Othello Ballet*, *The Essence of George Russell*, *Electronic Sonata 1968*, and *Listen to the Silence*." *Down Beat*, February 13, 1975.

Dabney, Wendell P. *Cincinnati's Colored Citizens*. Cincinnati, OH: Dabney Publishing, 1926.

Dauer, Alfons M. "Das Lydisch-Chromatische Tonsystem Von George Russell Und Seine Anwendung." *Jazzforschung/Jazz Research* 14 (1982).

Daughtry, Bob. Interview with George Russell for Smithsonian Jazz Oral History Program NEA in May 2004.

Davis, C. "Structuralist of Free Form." *Times* (London), November 10, 1995.

———. "The Week Ahead (Preview of Brecon Jazz Festival)." *Times* (London), August 12, 1989.

Davis, Francis. "George Russell: The Intellect of the Heart." *Jazz Times*, December 12, 1984.

———. *Jazz and Its Discontents*. Cambridge, MA: Da Capo, 2004.

———. *Tonight, A Rare Treat in Music*. Philadelphia Inquirer, June 22, 1984.

Davis, Miles, with Q. Troup. *Miles: The Autobiography*. London: MacMillan, 1989.

Dean, Roger, *New Structures in Jazz and Improvised Music Since 1960*, Milton Keynes: Open University Press.1992.

DeBarros, Paul. "Review of *The 80th Birthday Concert* (Concept)." *Down Beat*, November 2005.

de Bedts, Ralph F. *Recent American History: 1933 Through World War II*, Homewood, IL: Dorsey, 1973.

DeMichael, Dom. "Newport Report." *Down Beat*, August 13, 1964.

———. "Spotlight Review of *Jazz in the Space Age* (Decca9219) and *George Russell Sextet at the Five Spot* (Decca 9220)." *Down Beat*, June 8, 1961.

———. "Vortex: The Dave Baker Story." *Down Beat*, December 17, 1964.
Diliberto, John. Review of *Electronic Sonata* (SN1009) and *Vertical Form VI* (SN1019). *Down Beat*, April 1982.
DiNardo, R. "Jazz Prophet." *Boston Globe Sunday Magazine*, June 12, 1983.
Dolby, R. G. A. "The Sociology of Knowledge in Natural Science." *Science Studies* 1, no. 1 (1971).
Donaldson, Bill. "John Peirce *Memorial Album*." CD Review. *Cadence* October 2013.
Drago, C. "Boston Globe Festival—Safe but Sound." *Jazz Times*, June 1983.
Driggs, Frank. Liner notes in *The Fletcher Henderson Story*. (Columbia CL419). "Drummer to Composer." *Cincinnati Post*. July 13, 1957.
Duncan, S. R. *The Rebel Café: Sex, Race, and Politics in Cold War America's Nightclub Underground* Baltimore, MD: John Hopkins, 2018
Dylan, Bob. *Chronicles, Volume One*. London: Simon & Schuster, 2004.
Eaton, Derek. "Band Strikes High Note." *Southern Evening Echo* (Southampton), March 3, 1986.
"1199er Wins Acclaim as Jazz Composer." *RWDSU Record*, September 15, 1957.
Elman, S. 2012 "Commentary Drill Down: George Russell's *Living Time*", *Arts Fuse*, February 1st, 2012
Elyot, K. "Riot at the Rite." *Guardian* (Manchester), March 2, 2006.
Evans, D. "The Reinterpretation of African Musical Instruments in the United States," in Isadore Okpewho, Carole Boyce Davies and Ali a. Mazrui, eds. *The African Diaspora: African Origins and the New World Identities*, Bloomington: Indiana University Press, pp.379-390.
Fanon, F. *Toward the African Revolution*. Harmondsworth, UK: Penguin, 1970.
———. *The Wretched of the Earth*. Harmondsworth, UK: Penguin, 1969.
Feather, Leonard. "Dance Biz Needs Younger Leaders: DeFranco." *Down Beat*, March 9, 1951.
———. Letter to George Russell. March 21, 1973.
———. Review of *Moody Marilyn Moore*, Bethlehem LP BCP-73. *Down Beat*, March 6, 1957.
———. Review of *The RCA Jazz Workshop—George Russell and his Smalltet* (RCA Victor LPM1372) *Down Beat*, August 7, 1957.
———. Sleeve notes to *George Russell Sextet Live in Kansas City* (Decca DL4183).
Fitzgerald, M. "The Lenox School of Jazz." JazzDiscography.com, November 1, 1993. www.jazzdiscography.com/Lenox/lenhome.htm.
Fordham, John. "George and the Geometry." *Guardian* (Manchester), February 28, 1986.
———. "King George's Gold Blend." *Guardian* (Manchester), September 1, 1989.
———. "Lazy Rocking Russell." *Guardian Weekly* (Manchester), May 12, 1991.
———. "Send Off the Clones." *Guardian* (Manchester), March 5, 1998.
———. "A Time to Live." *Guardian* (Manchester), March 21, 1997.
———. "Stars in the Eye of a Storming Sound." *Guardian* (Manchester), March 9, 1998.
Gamble, P. "George Russell the Lydian Pioneer Takes Stock with Peter Gamble." *Jazz Journal*, July 1992.
Garrigues, C. H. Reviews of *The RCA Jazz Workshop—George Russell and His Smalltet* (RCA LPM 1372) and *The RCA Jazz Workshop—Hal McKusick* (RCA LPM 1366). *San Francisco Examiner*, August 25, 1957.
Gates, Henry Louis Jr. "The "Blackness of Blackness": A Critique of the Sign and the Signifying Monkey," *Critical Inquiry* Vol. 9, No. 4 (Jun., 1983), pp. 685-723
Gayford, Martin. "Ignoring the Sirens." *Weekend Telegraph* (London), March 16, 1991.
*George Russell—A Jazz Portrait*. WGBH Radio, Boston.

"George Russell, Le Retour D'Un Grand Du Jazz." *Le Courier Picard*, November 13, 1995.

"George Russell Sends Call for More Blood Donors." *Down Beat*, October 22, 1964.

Gibson, Rob. Letter to Marty Khan. January 4, 1993.

Giddins, Gary. "George Russell Boogies." *Village Voice*, April 17, 1978.

———. "Making It New." *Village Voice*, March 30, 1993.

———. "St. George and the Chord." *Village Voice*, March 24, 1975.

Giglierano, Geoffrey J., and Deborah A. Overmyer, with Frederic L. Propas. *The Bicentennial Guide to Greater Cincinnati: A Portrait of Two Hundred Years*. Cincinnati, OH: Cincinnati Historical Society, 1998.

Gillespie, Dizzy (with Al Fraser). *To Be or Not To Bop* (Minneapolis, MN: University of Minneapolis Press. 2009)

Gleason, Ralph J. "An Album That Couldn't Have Been Made At All Ten Years Ago." *San Francisco Chronicle*, July 13, 1958.

Goffman, E. *Stigma*. Harmondsworth, UK: Penguin, 1968.

Gold, D. "Aaron Copland: The Well-Known American Composer Finds Virtues and Flaws in Jazz." *Down Beat*, May 1, 1958.

Goldberg, Joe. Sleeve notes to *The Stratus Seekers* Riverside RLP9412

Gonzalez, F. "From Blue Note, a George Russell Tone Poem." *Boston Globe*, May 3, 1985.

———. "Russell Will Finish My Life's Work." *Boston Globe*, July 19, 1989.

Grant, I. S., and W. R. Phillips. *The Elements of Physics*. Oxford: Oxford University Press, 2001.

Gratz, R. "An Historical Perspective of the Lydian and Major Scales." Appendix 1 in *Lydian Chromatic Concept of Tonal Organization*, by George Russell. Brookline, MA: Concept, 2001.

Gribbin, J. *Get a Grip on the New Physics*. London: Weidenfeld & Nicholson, 1999.

Grout, D. J., and C. V. Palisca. *A History of Western Music*. New York: Norton, 1996.

Hadsley, N. "George Russell: Don't Kick Sand at This Theory with Muscle." *TOP*, February 1991.

Hakim, S. "Reflections of an Era: My Experiences with Bird and Prez," *Jazz Journal International* [London], Vol. 49, No. 8, August 1996, pp. 16-18, 35.

*Hal McKusick Quartet—The Complete Barry Galbraith, Milt Hinton and Osie Johnson Recordings*. Sleeve notes. Lonehill LHJ10176.

Halliwell, M. 2007 *American Culture in the 1950s* Edinburgh: Edinburgh University Press, 2007.

Hammond, D. 2003 *The Science of Synthesis: Exploring the Social Implications of General Systems Theory* Boulder, CO: University of Colorado Press

Harper, C. *Dazzling Stranger: Bert Jansch and the British Folk and Blues Revival*. London: Bloomsbury, 2001.

Harrison, Max. "George Russell—Rational Anthems (Phase 1, 2, 3)." *Wire*, Spring/ Summer/Autumn 1983.

———. "Gerry Mulligan." *These Jazzmen of Our Time*, edited by R. Horrocks. London: Jazz Book Club, 1959.

———. Reviews of *The RCA Jazz Workshop—George Russell and His Smalltet* (RCA LPM1372) and *George Russell—New York, N.Y.* (Decca DL9216). *Jazz Review*, November 1960.

———. ed. *Modern Jazz: The Essential Records*. London: Hanover Press, 1975.

Haywood, Mark S. "The Harmonic Role of Melody in Vertical and Horizontal Jazz." *Annual Review of Jazz Studies* 5 (1991).

Hazell, Ed. *Berklee: The First Fifty Years*. Boston: Berklee Press, 1995.

Heckman, Don. "The Changing Face of the Large Jazz Group." *Down Beat*, April 25, 1963.
———. Review of *Modern Jazz Concert: Six Compositions Commissioned by the 1957 Brandeis University Festival of the Arts* (Columbia WL127). *Jazz Review*, November 1959.
———. "Review In Depth—George Russell." *Metronome*, November 1961.
———. "Sheila." *Down Beat*, May 9, 1963.
Heining, Duncan. "Bley's Way." *Jazzwise*, September 2007.
———. "Carla Bley." *Independent* (London), November 16, 1999.
———. "Learning to Wave." *Avant* 9 (Autumn 1998).
———. "A Meeting with a Remarkable Man." *Avant* 7 (Summer 1998).
———. *George Russell: The Story of an American Composer*, Lanham, MY: Scarecrow 2010
———. *Mosaics: The Life and Works of Graham Collier*, Sheffield: Equinox Publishing 2018
———. "The Very Singular Mr. Ran Blake" https://www.allaboutjazz.com/the-very-singular-mr-ran-blake-ran-blake January 23, 2020
Hentoff, Nat. "An Afternoon with Miles Davis." *Jazz Review*, December 1958, pp.9-12.
———. "The Birth of the Cool." *Down Beat*, May 2, 1957.
———. "George Russell." *Broadcast Music Inc.*, 1960.
———. "George Russell: Emergence of a Jazz Composer," *HiFi Stereo Review*, October 1962.
———. "Introducing Bill Evans." *Jazz Review*, October 1959.
———. Review of *The RCA Jazz Workshop—Hal McKusick* (RCA 1366). *Down Beat*, May 16, 1957.
———. "The Jazz Mainstream." *Saturday Review*, June 29, 1957.
———. "Jazz's Third Stream." *Down Beat*, May 29, 1958.
———. "Way Out Front with George Russell." *Hi Fi/Stereo Review*, October 1963.
Himes, Geoffrey. "Russell: In the Mood for Modes." *Washington Post*, October 3, 1987.
Hinton, M., and D. Berger. *Bass Line: The Stories and Photographs of Milt Hinton* Philadelphia: Temple University Press, 1988.
Hodeir, A. *Jazz: Its Evolution and Essence*, London: Jazz Book Club, 1958.
Hoefer, George. "Caught in the Act (Review of *George Russell Sextet at the Five Spot*)." *Down Beat*, September 15, 1960.
Huddersfield Contemporary Music Festival Program Notes. November 1995.
"Jazz School's First Session at Lenox." *Down Beat*, March 6, 1957.
Jeanquartier, André. "Kritische Anmerkungen Zum 'Lydian Chromatic Concept.'" *Jazzforschung/Jazz Research* 16 (1984).
Jenkins, W. "Living History." *Jazz Times*, May 2007.
Jeske, L. Sleeve notes to *Electronic Sonata for Souls Loved by Nature—1980*. Soul Note 121009-1.
John, G., and D. Humphrey. *Because They're Black*. Harmondsworth, UK: Penguin, 1971.
Johnson, Marjorie S. "Noah Francis Ryder: Composer and Educator." *The Black Perspective in Music* 6, no. 1 (1978), pp.19-31.
Johnson, Phil. "Lydian Modes and All That Jazz." *Independent* (London), March 7, 1998.
———. "Music—Review of Russell & LTO at the Forum in Bath." *Independent* (London), November 21, 1995.
Johnson, Sy. "Interview: Bill Evans & George Russell." *Changes*, Spring 1972.
Jones, O. "George Russell—A New Theory for Jazz." *Black Perspective in Music*, Vol. 2, No. 1 (Spring, 1974), pp.63-74.

Kahn, Ashley. *A Kind of Blue*. London: Granta, 2000.

Kahn, J. P. "Names and Faces: Russell Named Jazz Master." *Boston Globe*, January 2, 1990.

Katz, L. "All That Jazz Theory." *Boston Herald*, May 5, 1999.

Katz, Richard. "Music Festival at Brandeis University." *Jazz Today*, August 1957.

Kendall, P. M. 1973 *The Art of Biography*, London: George Allen & Unwin.

Kendall, P. M. 2013 Biography entry in Online Encyclopedia Britannica at http://www.britannica.com/EBchecked/topic/65924/biography

Khan, Marty. Fax to Rob Gibson. December 23, 1992.

———  [writing as George Lane]. "George Russell & Anglo-American Living Time Orchestra Perform in USA for First Time." GMN.com, 7.12.02.

Klee, J. Review of *Othello Ballet Suite and Electronic Organ Sonata No.1* (Flying Dutchman FDS-122). *Down Beat*, April 29, 1971.

Knauer, Wolfram. Sleeve notes to reissue of *George Russell Sextet at Beethoven Hall (Complete Recordings)*. MPS 539084–2.

Kofsky, Frank. Review of *Ezz-thetics* (Riverside 375). *Down Beat*, November 9, 1961.

Konitz, Lee. "Blind Date." *Down Beat*, July 11, 1958.

Korall, Burt. Original sleeve notes to *New York, N.Y.* Decca DL-9216.

———. Original sleeve notes to *Jazz in the Space Age*. Decca DL-9219.

———. "Who Is George Russell?" *Down Beat*, February 16, 1961.

———. "Where Do We Go from Here?" In *The Jazz Word*, edited by D. Cerulli, B. Korall, and M. Nasatir. New York: Ballantine, 1960.

Kouwenhoven, J. A. *Made in America: The Arts in Modern American Civilization*, W. W. Norton & Co, 1967

Kramer, A. Sleeve notes to *George Russell—The Complete Bluebird Recordings*. Lonehill LHJ10177.

Kubik, G. *Jazz Transatlantic: The African Undercurrent in Twentieth Century Jazz Culture*, Jackson: University of Mississippi, 2017.

Laing, R. D. *The Divided Self*. Harmondsworth, UK: Penguin, 1971.

———. *Self and Others*. Harmondsworth, UK: Penguin, 1975.

Lawless Jones, Bill. "Diggin' That Joyous Jazz." *NIP*, March 1990.

———. Sleeve notes to *Cincinnati Jazz Collection Volume I* (1998). J Curve Records J71098.

———. Sleeve notes to *Cincinnati Jazz Collection Volume II* (1999). J Curve Records J7005.

Lees, G. *Cats of Any Color: Jazz Black and White*, London: Da Capo, 2001.

Levin, Michael. "Despite Bad Acoustics, Gillespie Concert Offers Some Excellent Music." *Chicago Tribune*, October 22, 1947.

Lincoln Collier, James. *The Making of Jazz—A Comprehensive History*. Basingstoke, UK: Papermac, 1981.

Linden, Ken. "George Russell." *Jazz & Pop*, Autumn 1969.

Lyons, L. *The Great Jazz Pianists*. New York: Da Capo, 1983.

MacDonald, R. "Writing the Galton Case." In *On Crime Writing*. Santa Barbara, CA: Capra Press, 1973.

Macero, Teo. "Blindfold Test." *Down Beat*, March 6, 1957.

———. Review of Teddy Charles Tentet, *Same* (Atlantic 1229). *Metronome*, June 1956.

Management of the 5th International Jazz Festival, Prague. Letter to George Russell. September 1968.

Mandel, Howard. "The Mathematical Musician." *Washington Post*, September 27, 1987.
Marmande, F. "George Russell, celui qui a change la notion de jazz." *Le Monde*, April 1, 1995.
Martin Riches, William T. *The Civil Rights Movement: Struggle and Resistance*, Basingstoke: Palgrave Macmillan, 2010.
Marx, Karl. *The Eighteenth Brumaire of Louis Bonaparte*. Moscow: Progress, 1972.
Mathieson, K. *Cookin'—Hard Bop and Soul Jazz 1954-65*. Edinburgh: Canongate, 2002.
———. Program notes for Glasgow International Jazz Festival.
McIver, Don L. "Hal McKusick's Performance Is Good, But—." *Fort Lauderdale Sunday News*, April 28, 1957.
Meehan, N. *Time Will Tell—Conversations with Paul Bley*. Berkeley, CA: Berkeley Hills Books, 2003.
Mellers, W. *Man & His Music—Romanticism and the Twentieth Century*. London: Barrie & Rockliff, 1969.
*Memphis Commercial Appeal*, July 21, 1957.
Mertens, Wim. *American Minimal Music*, London: Kahan & Averill, 1983.
*Miles Davis—The Complete Birth of the Cool*. Sleeve notes. Capitol 724349455023.
Monson, Ingrid. "George Russell." In *International Dictionary of Black Composers*, edited by S. A. Floyd Jr. Chicago: Fitzroy Dearborn, 1999.
———. "Oh Freedom—George Russell, John Coltrane and Modal Jazz." In *In the Course of Performance*, edited by B. Nettle and M. Russell. London: University of Chicago Press, 1998.
———. *Freedom Sounds: Civil Rights Call Out to Jazz and Africa*. (Oxford: OUP, 2007)
Montgomery, William Penn. "Theorist Proposes a Scale Harmonious with All Music." *Japan Times*, August 6, 1993.
Moore, Robert E. "George Alan Russell: Jazz's First Theorist." *Trotter Institute Review* 2 (Summer 1988), p.15-19.
Morgenstern, Dan. "The Art of Playing." *Down Beat*, October 22, 1964.
Moten, Fred. *Black and Blur*, (Durham, NC: Duke University Press 2017), p.xii.
Murray, Albert. *Stomping the Blues*, New York: McGraw-Hill, 1976.
Nelkon, M. *Principles of Physics*. Harlow, UK: Longman, 1981.
Nelsen, D. *Daily News* (New York), May 9, 1978.
Niccoli, R. A. "Stearns Conducts Jazz Panel Series." *Down Beat*, September 7, 1951.
Nicholson, S. *Is Jazz Dead? Or Has It Moved to a New Address?* Abingdon, UK: Routledge, 2005.
Nicoll, Maurice. *Living Time and the Integration of Life*. Utrecht: Eureka editions 1998.
———. *The Mark*. Utrecht: Eureka Editions, 1998.
"9th Jazz International Critics Poll." *Down Beat*, August 3, 1961.
Nisenson, Eric. "George Russell." *Music Sound Output*, July 1964.
———. "Modes and Modalities." *Jazziz*, April 1994.
———. *Round about Midnight—A Portrait of Miles Davis*. New York: Da Capo, 1996.
———.*Blue: The Murder of Jazz*, New York: St. Martin's Press, 1997.
Notes to *New York, N.Y.* CD reissue Impulse IMP 12782.
Oakley, J. Ronald. 1986 *God's Country: America in the Fifties* New York: W. W. Norton
O'Brien, J. *Panache* 18, no. 5.
O'Conner, Norman J. "Jazz at Brandeis—Some New Areas Are Opened for Jazz by the Work of a Noted Institute of Culture and Learning." *Down Beat*, July 25, 1957.

Okiji, F. *Jazz As Critique: Adorno and Black Expression Revisited*, Stanford: Stanford University Press, 2018.

Oliver, S. "George Russell." *Jazz Express*, February 1998.

Oliver, W. "Black Males and Social Problems: Prevention through Afro-Centric Socialization." *Journal of Black Studies* 20, no. 1 (1989).

Palmer, Robert. "A Jazz Visionary Eyes the Evolution of Life on Earth." *New York Times*, April 28, 1985.

———. "Some Timeless Music by George Russell Band." *New York Times*, February 8, 1984.

Panish, J. *The Color of Jazz: Race and Representation in Postwar American Culture*, Jackson, MS: University of Mississippi Press, 1997.

Pareles, John. "Russell Big Band in Two Showpieces." *New York Times*, November 11, 1983.

Peeples, William. "Top Jazzmen Move into Hinterlands." *Louisville Times*, April 6, 1960.

Pekar, Harvey. Review of *The Stratus Seekers* Riverside RLP9412, *Down Beat*, August 16, 1962.

Perlis, Vivian. Interview with George Russell, American Music Series, December 8, 1993. Oral History Project of American Music, sponsored and supported by the National Endowment for the Arts Special Jazz Projects.

Pettinger, Peter. *How My Heart Sings*. New Haven, CT: Yale University Press, 1998.

"The Playboy Panel: Jazz—Today and Tomorrow." *Playboy*, February 1964.

Popper, K. *The Logic of Scientific Discovery*. New York: BasicBooks, 1959.

Porter, Eric "'Born out jazz . . .but embracing all music': Race, Gender, and Technology in George Russell's Lydian Chromatic Concept" in Rustin, Nichole. T. and Tucker, Sherrie *Big Ears: Listening for Gender in Jazz Studies*. (Durham, N.C.: Duke University Press, 2008)

Porter, Lewis. "The Atlantic Years." In *John Coltrane Companion*, edited by C. Woideck. New York: Shirmer, 1998.

Priestley, B. Review of *The London Concerts Volumes 1 & 2* (Label Bleu LBLC6527/8). In *Gramophone Jazz Good CD Guide*, edited by K. Shadwick. Harrow, UK: Gramophone, 1995.

Quersin, Benoit. "La Passe Dangereuse." In *John Coltrane Companion*, edited by C. Woideck. New York: Shirmer, 1998.

———. "Le Philosophe De Greenwich Village." *Jazz*, February 1963.

Ramanan, Roland. Concert review of Cassandra Wilson, George Russell at Town & Country Club; Jazz Warriors, Tony Remy at Shaw Theatre. *Wire*, May 1991.

"Random Thoughts from George Russell." *Down Beat*, July 29, 1965.

Ratliff, Ben. "Rock, Funk and Electronics in a Splashy 80's Sound." *New York Times*, May 12, 1999.

Reisner, Bob. "Jazz Composition." *Village Voice*, July 10, 1957.

"Report on Lenox." *Down Beat*, October 15, 1959.

Review of George Russell—*Jazz in the Space Age* (Decca DL9219). *Metronome*, June 1961.

Review of George Russell Sextet—*Ezz-thetics* (Riverside 375). "Record Notes." *Reporter*, September 28, 1961.

Review of George Russell Sextet—*The Outer View* (RLP440). *Time*, May 22, 1964. Review of *The Outer View* (Riverside 440). *Down Beat*, July 18, 1963.

Review of *The RCA Jazz Workshop—George Russell and His Smalltet* (RCA Victor LPM1372). *Cash Box*, June 15, 1957.

Review of *The RCA Jazz Workshop—George Russell and His Smalltet* (RCA Victor LPM1372). *Hi-Fi Low-Down*, October 1957.

Review of *The RCA Jazz Workshop—George Russell and His Smalltet* (RCA Victor LPM1372). *Jazz Today*, September 1957.
Review of *The RCA Jazz Workshop—Hal McKusick. Metronome*, June 1957.
Review of Teddy Charles Tentet, *Same* (Atlantic 1229). *Time*, May 21, 1956.
Richmond, M. E. *Social Diagnosis*, Russell, New York, NY: Sage Foundation. 1917
Rilke, R. M. *Duino Elegies*. London: Chatto & Windus, 1981.
"Russell Storms the Vanguard." *Down Beat*, June 1, 1978.
"Russell Writing for Victor Jazz." *Down Beat*, March 21, 1956.
Russell, Alice. Fax to John Cumming, March 26, 1992.
Russell, B. O. Letter to Mr. B. H. Heard, Wilberforce College, March 3, 1941.
Russell, George. Review of Jimmy Giuffre 3—*Travelin' Light* (Atlantic 1282). *Jazz Review*, November 1958.
———. Reviews of Johnny Mandel—*I Want to Live* (UAL4005) and Henry Mancini—*The Music from Peter Gunn* (RCA LPM1956). *Jazz Review*, June 1959.
———. *The Lydian Chromatic Concept of Tonal Organization*. New York: Concept, 1959.
———. "Where Do We Go from Here?" In *The Jazz Word*, edited by D. Cerulli, B. Korall, and M. Nasatir. London: Ballantine, 1960.
———. "Popular Delusions and the Madness of Crowds." *Down Beat*, April 7, 1966.
———. Sleeve notes to *Electronic Sonata for Souls Loved by Nature—1968*. Soulnote 121034-2.
———. Sleeve notes to *Vertical Form VI*. Soul Note 121019-1. 1977.
———. "Barry Galbraith—Obituary." *NEC Notes*, Summer 1983.
———. Sleeve notes to *The African Game,* Blue Note BT85103.
———. Sleevenotes to *New York, N.Y.* reissue. IMP 15782.
———. *Lydian Chromatic Concept of Tonal Organization*. Brookline, MA: Concept, 2001
Russell, R. *Bird Lives*. Aylesbury, UK: Quartet, 1988.
Russo, W. Review of *George Russell at Beethoven Hall* (Saba MPFS 15059). *Down Beat*, October 20, 1966.
Sainsbury, E. 1970 *Social Diagnosis in Casework*, Abingdon: RKP
Sampson, Paul. Review of *The RCA Jazz Workshop—Hal McKusick. Washington Post*, May 5, 1957
"The School at Lenox." *Down Beat*, November 10, 1960.
"The School of Jazz." *Down Beat*, October 3, 1957.
Schuller, G. "The Future of Form in Jazz." *Saturday Review*, January 12, 1957.
———. *Early Jazz: Its Roots and Musical Development*, Oxford: OUP, 1968,
———. *The Swing Era*. Oxford: Oxford University Press, 1989.
Schumach, Murray. Review of *The RCA Jazz Workshop—Hal McKusick* and McKusick *Jazz at the Academy. High Fidelity*, November 1957.
Schwartz, Lloyd. *Boston Phoenix*, September 25, 2008.
Seguin, P-E, "Lydia in Oz: The reception of George Russell in 1960s Australia," *Jazz Research Journal*, Vol. 8, No. 1-2 (2014), pp. 238-256
Sehgal, K. *Jazzocracy: Jazz, Democracy, + The Creation of a New American Mythology*, Mishawaka, IN: Better World Books, 2008
Sengstock, Charles A. *That Toddlin' Town: Chicago's White Bands and Orchestras*, Urbana and Chicago: University of Illinois Press 2004.
Shadwick, Keith. *Bill Evans: Everything Happens to Me—A Musical Biography*. San Francisco: Backbeat, 2002.

Shepp, Archie. "An Artist Speaks Bluntly." *Down Beat*, December 16, 1965.

Sherman, Fred. "McKusick Album Is Best Thing to Come out of Jazz Workshop." *Miami Herald*, June 23, 1957.

Shipton, Alyn. *A New History of Jazz*. London: Continuum, 2001.

———. "Play What You Mean." *Jazzwise*, March 1998.

———. *Groovin' High: The Life of Dizzy Gillespie*. (New York, NY: OUP. 1999)

Shoemaker, Bill. Review of *Ezz-thetics* (Riverside Original Jazz Classic OJC-070), *The Essence of George Russell* (Soul Note 1044/5), and *Live in an American Time Spiral* (Soul Note 1049). *Down Beat*, December 1983.

"Shot to death trying to loot S. Side church," *Chicago Tribune*, April 24, 1951, p.5.

Siclier, S. "Le triomphe de George Russell à la Cité de la musique." *Le Monde*, April 4, 1995.

Silsbee, Kirk. "George Russell." *Cadence*, June 1996.

———. Sleeve notes to reissue of *George Russell Sextet at the Five Spot* (2000). Verve 088112287–2.

"Six Works of Jazz Commissioned by Brandeis University." *Down Beat*, April 4, 1957.

Smith, Arnold Jay. "The Music of George Russell," *Down Beat*, June 19, 1975.

Stearns, M. "Jazz is America", Program notes Newport Jazz Festival 1955, p.56-59

Stein Crease, Stephanie. *Gil Evans—Out of the Cool*. Chicago: A Cappella, 2002.

Stevens, Jan. Interview with Marty Morell 2005. https://www.billevanswebpages.com/images/2morellintvue2.htm

Stone, I. F. "The United States as Three Nations, Not One." *I.F. Stone's Weekly*, October 7, 1957. In *The Best of I.F. Stone's Weekly*, edited by N. Middleton. Harmondsworth, UK: Penguin, 1973.

Stravinsky, I. *Poetics of Music in Six Lessons*, Cambridge, MA: Harvard University Press, 1974

Sulloway, Frank J. *Freud, Biologist of the Mind*. Bungay, Suffolk: Fontana, 1980, p.446.

Swedish Radio Panel interview with George Russell, 1995.

Szwed, J. "Still on His Own Page." *Village Voice*, May 25, 1999.

"Tangents." *Down Beat*, June 18, 1964.

Thomas, P. "The Myth of Jazz, Parts I & II." *Avant* (Winter 1998/Spring 1999).

Tomkins, Les. "Disc Discussion," *Crescendo*, June 1964

Tucker, Michael. *Jan Garbarek: Deep Song*. Hull, UK: East Note, 1998.

Tkweme, W. S. 2008 'Blues in Stereo: The Texts of Langston Hughes in Jazz Music' *African American Review* (AAR) 2008 Fall-Winter; 42 (3-4): 503-512

Ullman, M. "George Russell's Mode of Jazz," *Boston Review*, February 1986.

Urpeth, P. "George Russell (Preview of LTO at Ronnie Scott's Club, London)." *Time Out*, August 30—September 6, 1989.

Vann Woodward, C. *The Strange Career of Jim Crow*. New York: Oxford University Press, 1966.

Walters, John L. "Jazz, the Art of Harmony." *Independent* (London), March 9, 1998.

———, obituary for Joe Zawinul, *Guardian*, September 13, 2007. https://www.theguardian.com/news/2007/sep/13/guardianobituaries.jazz

Wasserman, A. "Tonal Gravity," https://www.andywasserman.com/component/tags/tag/54-tonal-gravity

Webster, Daniel. "Relâche Presents Flashes of Americana." *Philadelphia Inquirer*, July 1, 1989.

Wein, G. *Myself Among Others*. Cambridge, MA: Da Capo, 2003.

Williams, M. Letter to George Russell. March 25, 1966.

Williams, Richard. "Patterns of Relish." *Times* (London), February 28, 1986.

Wilson, John S. Review of George Russell Sextet—*Stratusphunk* (Riverside RLP-*Down Beat*, March 2, 1961.
———. "George Russell: His Big Band and His Big Theory." *New York Times*, November 10, 1983.
———. "Jazz: George Russell." *New York Times*, May 4, 1978.
———. "Russell Presents His Episodic Jazz." *New York Times*, March 10, 1975.
———. Sleeve notes to *Hal McKusick—Jazz Workshop*. RCA Victor LPM1366.
Wilson, P. "George Russell's Constant Quest." *Down Beat*, March 17, 1972.
Withrow High School yearbook, 1939.
Woodward, Richard B. "Jazz Wars: A Tale of Age, Rage and Hash Brownies." *Village Voice*, August 9, 1994.
Woolley, Stan. "George Russell." *Jazz Journal* 39, no. 10 (October 1986).
Wykoff Zapoleon, Marguerite. "Cincinnati Citizens: Elizabeth Campbell (1862– 1945) and M. Edith Campbell (1875–1962)." *Queen City Heritage* 43, no. 4 (Winter 1985).
Young, Ben. Broadcast devoted to George Russell in celebration of his seventy-fourth birthday. WKCR Radio, New York, June 23, 1997.
Young, Ben. Interview with Nadi Qamar. WKCR Radio, New York, 1998.
Young, Ben (ed), *Dixonia: A Bio-Discography of Bill Dixon*. Westport, CT: Greenwood Press, 1998)
Zwerin, M. "Probing the Dialectics of Chords." *International Herald Tribune*, August 10, 1989.

# Interviews

Åberg, Lennart. E-mail, July 2007.
Anderson, Arild. November 2005.
Atkins, Carl. October 2003.
Baker, Dave. April 2004.
Biscoe, Chris. February 2006.
Blake, Ran. October 2003.
Bley, Carla. February 2004.
Bley, Paul. June 2007.
Brecker, Randy. August 2006.
Broberg, Bosse. E-mail, May 2007.
Brookmeyer, Bob. October 2003.
Brown, Garnett. July 2004.
Burk, Greg. E-mail, April 2007.
Byron, Don. July 2005.
Carr, Ian. April 2003.
Charles, Teddy. E-mail, October 2007.
Christensen, Jon. September 2005.
Coleman, Ornette. July 2005.
Collier, Graham. November 2004.
Cumming, John. May 2003.
———. May 2007.
Davis, Stanton. June 2003.
Davis, William. August 2004.
Ehrlich, Marty. E-mail, April 2005.
Falzone, James. E-mail, April 2007.
Fiuczynski, David. February 2006.
Ford, Ricky. October 2003.
Fujii, Satoko. E-mail, January 2005.
Garbarek, Jan. July 2004.
Gibbs, Mike. June 2005.
Giuffre, Juanita. June 2004
Guard, Tom. May 2005.
Hatfield, Brad. June 2003.

Hendricks, Jon. April 2006.
Hennessy, Brian. April 2004.
Hersch, Fred. January 2007.
Holland, Dave. September 2006.
Hollenbeck, Pat. June 2003.
Hunt, Joe. June 2004.
Hurt, Pete. June 2003.
Israels, Chuck. E-mail, August 2004.
Jordan, Sheila. May 2004.
Khan, Marty. February 2004.
Konitz, Lee. April 2004.
Lodder, Steve. February 2003.
Mikkelborg, Palle. June 2003.
McPheeters, Dwight. June 2004.
Medeski, John. October 2003.
Monson, Ingrid. November 2005.
Moore, Robert. July 2004.
Morales, Richie. June 2003.
Motian, Paul. June 2006.
Norbury-Russell, Alice. November 2004.
———. October 2006.
———. Email, August 2020.
Phillips, Barre. March 2007.
Pine, Courtney. May 2005.
Reilly, Jack. October 2003.
———. September 2005.
Riley, Howard. December 2005.
Rivers, Sam. November 2005.
Rossi, Marc. October 2004.
Russell, George. March 2003.
———. April 2003.
———. June 2003.
———. October 2003.

———. December 2003.
———. June 2004.
Rypdal, Terje. November 2005.
Schuller, George. E-mail, May 2006.
Schuller, Gunther. October 2003.
Schwendener, Ben. October 2003.
Sheppard, Andy. April 2003.

Stenson, Bobo. March 2007.
Swallow, Steve. February 2004.
Urmson, Bill. June 2003.
Wasserman, Andy. June 2004.
Wheeler, Kenny. August 2004.
Young, Dave. January 2007.

The author is also indebted to Ian Carr, who furnished his handwritten transcripts of interviews with Jimmy Giuffre, Juanita Giuffre, John Lewis, Art Farmer, Carla Bley, Steve Swallow, Ran Blake, Sheila Jordan, Steve Elman, Don Byron, Gunther Schuller, Mark Harvey, Jan Garbarek, Jon Christensen, Kåre Kolberg, Marit Jerstad, Alice Norbury-Russell, Bill Urmson, Dave Bargeron, Tiger Okoshi, Brad Hatfield, and Robert Moore. Ian also supplied transcripts of his own interviews with George Russell. Even though not all of the above have been quoted, their comments have helped inform this biography.

# APPENDIX A

# Recordings

## George Russell—1950s Recordings

**The Jazz Workshop**
"Ezz-Thetic," "Jack's Blues," "Ye Hypocrite, Ye Beelzebub," "Livingstone, I Presume"
Personnel—Art Farmer (t), Hal McKusick (as, f), Barry Galbraith (g), Bill Evans (p), Milt Hinton (b), Joe Harris (d)
Rec. March 31, 1956.
"Round Johnny Rondo," "Night Sound," "Concerto for Billy the Kid," "Concerto for Billy the Kid (alt version)," "Witch Hunt"
Personnel—Art Farmer (t), Hal McKusick (as, f), Barry Galbraith (g), Bill Evans (p), Milt Hinton (b), Paul Motian (d)
Rec. October 17, 1956.
"Fellow Delegates," "Ballad of Hix Blewitt," "Ballad of Hix Blewitt (alt. version)," "Knights of the Steamtable," "The Sad Sergeant"
Personnel—Art Farmer (t), Hal McKusick (as, f), Barry Galbraith (g), Bill Evans (p), Teddy Kotick (b), Osie Johnson (d). (Russell plays Boo-Bams on "Fellow Delegates")
Rec. December 21, 1956.
Reissued as George Russell, *The Complete Bluebird Recordings*, Lonehill LHJ10177. Released originally RCA Victor LPM1372.

**New York, N.Y.**
"Manhattan" (Richard Rodgers–Lorenz Hart)
Personnel— Art Farmer, Doc Severinsen, Ernie Royal (t), Bob Brookmeyer, Frank Rehak, Tom Mitchell (tb), Hal McKusick (as), John Coltrane (ts), Sol Schlinger (bs), Barry Galbraith (g), Bill Evans (p), Milt Hinton (b), Charlie Persip (d), Jon Hendricks (narr)
Rec. September 12, 1958.

"A Helluva Town," "Manhattan-rico"
Personnel—Art Farmer, Ernie Royal, Joe Wilder (t), Bob Brookmeyer, Jimmy Cleveland, Tom Mitchell (tb), Phil Woods, Hal McKusick (as), Al Cohn (ts), Gene Allen (bs), Barry Galbraith (g), Bill Evans (p), George Duvivier (b), Max Roach (d—"A Helluva Town" only), Don Lamond (d—"Manhattan-rico" only), Al Epstein (bgo—"Manhattan-rico" only), George Russell (chromatic drum—"Manhattan-rico" only), Jon Hendricks (narr)
Rec. November 24, 1958.
"Big City Blues," "East Side Medley," "Autumn in New York" (Vernon Duke), "How About You" (Burton Lane–Ralph Freed)
Personnel—Art Farmer, Joe Wilder, Joe Ferrante (t), Bob Brookmeyer, Frank Rehak, Tom Mitchell (tb), Phil Woods, Hal McKusick (as), Benny Golson (ts), Sol Schlinger (bs), Barry Galbraith (g), Bill Evans (p), Milt Hinton (b), Charlie Persip (d), Jon Hendricks (narr)
Rec. March 25, 1959.
Released originally as Decca DL9216.

*Jazz in the Space Age*
"Chromatic Universe (pts 1–3)," "The Lydiot"
Personnel—Al Kiger, Ernie Royal (t), Dave Baker, Frank Rehak (tb), Jimmy Buffington (frhn), Walt Levinsky (as), Dave Young (ts), Sol Schlinger (bs), Barry Galbraith or Howard Collins (g), Bill Evans, Paul Bley (p), Milt Hinton (b), Don Lamond (d)
Rec. December 29, 1959.
"Waltz from Outer Space," "Dimensions"
Al Kiger, Ernie Royal, Marky Markowitz (t), Dave Baker, Frank Rehak, Bob Brookmeyer (tb), Hal McKusick (as), Dave Young (ts), Sol Schlinger (bs), Barry Galbraith (g), Bill Evans, Paul Bley (p), Milt Hinton (b), Charlie Persip (d)
Rec. January 27, 1960.
Released originally as Decca DL9219.

*At the Five Spot*
"Sippin' at Bells" (Miles Davis), "Dance Class" (Carla Bley), "Swingdom Come" (Russell), "121 Bank Street" (Dave Baker), "Beast Blues" (Carla Bley), "Moment's Notice" (John Coltrane)
Personnel—Al Kiger (t), Dave Baker (tb), Dave Young (ts), George Russell (p), Chuck Israel (b), Joe Hunt (d)
Rec. September 20, 1960.
Released originally as Decca DL9220.

*Stratusphunk*
"Stratusphunk" (Russell), "New Donna" (Russell), "Bent Eagle" (Carla Bley), "Kentucky Oysters" (Dave Baker), "Lambskins" (Russell), "Things New" (Russell)
Personnel—Al Kiger (t), Dave Baker (tb), Dave Young (ts), George Russell (p), Chuck Israel (b), Joe Hunt (d)
Rec. October 18, 1960.
Released originally as Riverside RLP-341.

## *George Russell Sextet in Kansas City*
"War Gewessen" (Dave Baker), "Rhymes" (Carla Bley), "Lunacy" (Dave Baker), "Sandu" (Clifford Brown), "Tune Up" (Miles Davis), "Theme" (Russell)
"Mardi Gras," "Vamp" also recorded but unissued
Personnel—Don Ellis (t), Dave Baker (tb), Dave Young (ts), George Russell (p), Chuck Israel (b), Joe Hunt (d)
Rec. February 23, 1961.
Released originally as Decca DL4183.

## *Ezz-Thetics*
"Ezz-Thetic" (Russell), "Nardis" (Miles Davis), "Lydiot" (Russell), "Thoughts" (Russell), "Honesty" (Dave Baker), "'Round Midnight" (Monk-Williams)
Personnel—Don Ellis (t), Dave Baker (tb), Eric Dolphy (as, bcl), George Russell (p), Steve Swallow (b), Joe Hunt (d)
Rec. May 8, 1961.
Released originally as Riverside RLP-375.

## *The Stratus Seekers*
"Pan-Daddy" (Russell), "The Stratus Seekers" (Russell), "The Stratus Seekers" (alt. version not issued), "Kige's Tune" (Al Kiger), "Blues in Orbit" (Russell), "A Lonely Place" (Russell), "Stereophrenic" (Dave Baker)
Personnel—Don Ellis (t), Dave Baker (tb), John Peirce (as), Paul Plummer (ts), George Russell (p), Steve Swallow (b), Joe Hunt (d)
Rec. January 31, 1962.
Released originally as Riverside RLP-412.

## *The Outer View*
"Au Privave" (Charlie Parker), "Zig-Zag" (Carla Bley), "The Outer View" (Russell), "You Are My Sunshine" (Jimmie H. Davis), "D.C. Divertimento" (Russell)
Personnel—Don Ellis (t), Garnett Brown (tb), John Peirce (as), Paul Plummer (ts), George Russell (p), Steve Swallow (b), Pete LaRoca (d), Sheila Jordan (v—"You Are My Sunshine" only)
Rec. August 27, 1962.
Released originally as Riverside RLP-440.

## *Live in Bremen and Paris*
"'Round Midnight" (Monk), "You Are My Sunshine" (Jimmy Burns), "D.C. Divertimento" (Russell), "Sippin' at Bells" (Davis)
Rec. Bremen, September 1964.
"The Outer View" (Russell), "Volupté (Russell), "You Are My Sunshine" (Jimmy Burns), "D.C. Divertimento" (Russell)
Rec. Salle Pleyel, Paris, October 1, 1964.
Personnel—Thad Jones (tp, c), Garnett Brown (tb), Joe Farrell (ts), George Russell (p), Bare Phillips (b), Albert Heath (d)

## At Beethoven Hall Vol 1
"Freein' Up" (Russell), "Lydia and Her Friends: Lydia in Bags' Groove/Lydia's Confirmation/Lydia Round Midnight/Takin' Lydia Home" (Russell)
Personnel—Don Cherry (cnt), Bertil Lövgren (t), Brian Trentham (tb), Ray Pitts (ts), George Russell (p), Cameron Brown (b), Albert Heath (d)
Rec. August 31, 1965.
Released originally as Saba (G)SB15059ST.

## At Beethoven Hall Vol 2
"You Are My Sunshine" (Jimmie H. Davis), "Oh Jazz, Po Jazz" (Russell), "Volupte" (Russell)
Personnel and date as above.
Released originally as Saba (G)SB15060ST.

# George Russell—Swedish Recordings and After

## Now and Then
Personnel—Palle Mikkelborg, Bertil Lövgren, Palle Boldtvig, Jan Allan (t), George Vernon, Gunnar Medberg (tb), Runo Ericksson (btb), Christer Boustedt, Claes Rosendahl (as), Bernt Rosengren, Jan Garbarek (ts), Erik Nilsson (bs), George Russell (p), Rune Gustafsson (el g), Roman Dylag (b), Jon Christensen (d), Rupert Clemendore (congas)
Rec. Stockholm, September 16, 1966.
Released originally on *The Essence of George Russell* Sonet SLP1411/2.

## Othello Ballet Suite
Personnel—Rolf Ericson, Bertil Lövgren, Lars Samuelsson, Weine Renliden (t), Gunnar Wennberg (frhn), George Vernon, Olle Lind, Christer Torge (tb), Walter Arlind, Aldo Johansson (tba), Bengt Christianson (f), Arne Domnerus (as), Bernt Rosengren, Jan Garbarek (ts), Rune Falk (bs), Knud Jorgensen, Lars Sjosten (p), Nicke Wohrman (g), Lars Blomberg (clo), Roman Dylag (b), Kjell Mattison (el-b), Jon Christensen (d), Rupert Clemendore, Janos Kajlinger, Thore Swanerud (perc), George Russell (cond, org)
Rec. Stockholm, November 3 and 4, 1967.

## Electronic Organ Sonata No. 1
George Russell (org).
Rec. Grorud Church, Oslo, October 1, 1968.
Both released originally as *Othello Ballet Suite* Sonet SLP1409.

## Electronic Sonata for Souls Loved by Nature—1968
Personnel—Manfred Schoof (t), Jan Garbarek (ts), Terje Rypdal (el g), George Russell (p), Red Mitchell (b), Jon Christensen (d)
Rec. Sonjia Henie/Niels Onstad Centre For The Arts, Høvikodden, Oslo, April 28, 1969.
Released originally as Strata East SES-1976/1.

## Trip to Prillarguri
"Theme," "Souls," "Event III," "Vips," "Stratusphunk," "Esoteric Circle," "Man on the Moon"
Personnel—Stanton Davis (t), Jan Garbarek (ts), Terje Rypdal (el g), George Russell (p), Arild Andersen (b), Jon Christensen (d)
Rec. Estrad, Sweden, March 1970. Released originally as Soul Note SN1029.

## Electronic Sonata for Souls Loved by Nature
Personnel—Stanton Davis, Jan Allan, Bertil Lövgren, Maffay Falay, Lars Samuelsson (t), Olle Lind (btb), Arne Domnerus (as, cl), Jan Garbarek (ts), Claes Rosendahl (ts, as, ss, f), Lennart Aberg (ts, ss, f), Erik Nilsson (bs, bcl), Rune Gustafsson, Terje Rypdal (el g), George Russell (p, cond), Bengt Hallberg (p), Berndt Egerbladh (vib, xy), Georg Riedel, Arild Andersen (b), Jon Christensen, Egil Johansen (d), Sabu Martinez (congas)
Rec. Stockholm, October 6, 1970.
Released originally on *The Essence of George Russell* Sonet SLP1411/2.

## Listen to the Silence
Personnel—Stanton Davis (t), Jan Garbarek (ts), Terje Rypdal (g), Bobo Stenson (el p), Webster Lewis (org), Arild Andersen (b), Bjornar Andresen (Fender b), Jon Christensen (perc), George Russell (tym), Sue Auclair, Gailanne Cummings, Joyce Gippo, Kay Dunlap, David Dusing, Ray Hardin, Don Kendrick, Don Hovey, Dan Windham (voices)
Rec. Kongsberg Church, Kongsberg, Norway, June 26, 1971. Released originally as Concept CR002.

## Vertical Form VI
Personnel—Lars Olofsson, Bengt Edvarsson, Jörgen Johansson (tb), Sven Larsson (btb, tba), Ivar Olsen (frhn), Jan Allan (t, frhn), Håken Nyquist (t, flhn, frhn), Americo Bellotto, Bertil Lövgren (t, flhn), Arne Domnerus (as, ss, cl), Ian Uling (as, ts, f), Lennart Åberg, (as, ts, ss, f), Bernt Rosengren (as, ts, ss, f), Erik Nilsson (bs, bcl, f), Rune Gustafsson (g), Bjorn Lind (el p), Vlodek Gulgowski (el p, syn), Monica Dominique (el, p, clavinet, cel, org), Stefan Brolund (el b), Bronislav Suchanek, Lars-Urban Helje (acc b), Lars Beijbon, Leroy Lowe (d), Sabu Martinez (congas)
Rec. Estrad, Sweden, March 10, 1977. Released originally as Soul Note SN1019.

## Cubano Be, Cubano Bop
Personnel—Lars Olofsson, Bengt Edvarsson, Jörgen Johansson (tb), Sven Larsson (btb), Jan Allan, Håken Nyquist, Americo Bellotto, Bertil Lövgren (t), Arne Domnerus, Ian Uling (as), Lennart Åberg, Bernt Rosengren (ts), Erik Nilsson (bs), Rune Gustafsson (g), Vlodek Gulgowski (el p, syn), Lars-Urban Helje (acc b), Lars Beijbon (d), Sabu Martinez (congas, v)
Rec. Estrad, Sweden, March 10, 1977.
Released originally on *New York Big Band* Soul NoteSN1039.
George Russell, *New York Big Band*, Soul Note SN1039
"Living Time Event V," "Big City Blues," "Listen to the Silence Pt 1 and Pt 2," "Mystic Voices" (Stanton Davis), "God Bless The Child" (Billie Holiday–Al Herzog, arr. Ernie Wilkins)
Personnel—Gary Valente (tb), Dave Taylor (btb), Stanton Davis, Terumasa Hino (t), Lew Soloff (t, flhn), John Clark (frhn), Ricky Ford, Roger Rosenberg (ts), Marty Ehrlich (as), Carl Atkins (bs,

bcl), Mark Slifstein (g), Stanley Cowell (p—"Living Time Event V" only), Ricky Martinez (el p, org), Cameron Brown (b), Warren Smith (d), Babafumi Akunyon (congas), Lee Genesis (v—"Big City Blues" only)
Rec. Village Vanguard, August 16, 1978.
Released originally on *New York Big Band* Soul Note SN1039.

*Electronic Sonata for Souls Loved by Nature 1980*
Personnel—Lew Soloff (t), Robert Moore (ts, ss), Victor Comer (g), George Russell (p, org), J.F. Jenny Clark (b), Keith Copeland (d)
Rec. Milan, June 9 and 10, 1980. Released originally as Soul Note SN1009.

*Live in an American Time Spiral*
"Time Spiral," Ezz-thetic," "D.C. Divertimento"
Personnel—Ron Tooley, Stanton Davis, Brian Leach, Tom Harrell (t), Ray Anderson, Earl McIntyre (tb), Marty Ehrlich (as, f), Doug Miller (ts, f), Bob Hanlon (bs), Jerome Harris (g), Jack Reilly (acc p), Mark Soskin (ky), Ron McLure (b), Victor Lewis (d)
Rec. New York, July 30 and 31, 1982. Released originally as Soul Note SN1049.

*The African Game*
Personnel—Mike Peipman, Chris Passin, Roy Okutani, Mark Harvey (t), Peter Cirelli, Chip Kaner (tb), Jeff Marsankas (btb), Marshall Sealy (Frhn), George Garzone (ts, ss), Gary Joynes (ts, ss, f), Dave Mann (as, ss, f), Janus Steprans (as, ss, f), Brad Jones (bs, bcl, f), Mark White (g), Mark Rossi, Bruce Barth (ky), Bob Nieske (acc b), Bill Urmson (Fender b), Keith Copeland (d), Dave Hagedorn (perc), Olu Bata—Joe Galeota, Lazarro Perez, Kuto Perez, Amaro Laria, Enrique Cardenas
Rec. Boston, June 18, 1983.
Released originally as Blue Note BT85103.

*So What*
"So What" (Miles Davis, arr. Russell), "Time Spiral"
Personnel—Mike Peipman, Chris Passin, Roy Okutani, Mark Harvey (t), Peter Cirelli, Chip Kaner (tb), Jeff Marsankas (btb), Marshall Sealy (Frhn), George Garzone (ts, ss), Gary Joynes (ts, ss, f), Dave Mann (as, ss, f), Janus Steprans (as, ss, f), Brad Jones (bs, bcl, f), Mark White (g), Mark Rossi, Bruce Barth (ky), Bob Nieske (acc b), Bill Urmson (Fender b), Keith Copeland (d), Dave Hagedorn (perc), Joe Galeota (congas)
"Rhymes" (Bley), "War Gewessen" (Baker)
Personnel—Mark Harvey (t), Chip Kaner (tb), Janus Steprans (as), Gary Joynes (ts), Mark White (g), Mark Rossi (ky), Bill Urmson (Fender b), Keith Copeland (d)
Rec. Boston, June 18, 1983.
Released originally as Blue Note BT85132.

*Live in Tokyo*
"Listen to the Silence," "Cubano-Be, Cubano-Bop," "All About Rosie," "Manhattan" (Rogers-Hart), "Autumn in New York" (Duke), "Pan-Daddy," "Electronic Sonata for Souls Loved by Nature"

Personnel—Lew Soloff, Palle Mikkelborg, Shin Kazuhara, Nubuo Katoh (t), Ray Anderson, Osamu Matsumoto (tb), Sumio Okada (btb), Andy Sheppard, Kohsuke Mine (ts, ss), David Mann (as, f), Kazutoki Umezu (bs, bcl), Mark White (g), Brad Hatfield, Sohichi Noriki (ky), Bill Urmson (b), Keith Copeland (d), Pat Hollenbeck (perc)

Rec. Gotanda Kan-i Hoken Hall, Tokyo, February 28, 1988.

Released originally in Japan only as Electric Bird 6488/89. Also issued as video in Japan.

## *The London Concert*

"La Folia: The Rocella Variations" (Schwendener/Russell), "Uncommon Ground," "Electronic Sonata for Souls Loved by Nature—Events XI– XV," "Listen to the Silence," "Struggle of the Magicians" (Mark White), "ix Aesthetic Gravities," "So What" (Davis, arr. Russell)

Personnel—Ian Carr, Stuart Brooks, Mark Chandler (t), Pete Beachill (tb), Ashley Slater (btb), Andy Sheppard (ts, ss), Chris Biscoe (as, ss, cl), Pete Hurt (bs, ts, bcl, f), Brad Hatfield, Steve Lodder (ky), David Fiuczynski (g), Bill Urmson (b), Steve Johns (d), Dave Adams (perc)

Rec. Ronnie Scott's Club, London, August 28–31, 1989.

Released originally as Stash STCD560/1. (USA), Label Bleu 65278 (Europe).

## *It's About Time*

"It's About Time," "Living Time"

Personnel—Stanton Davis, Tiger Okoshi, Stuart Brooks (t), Dave Bargeron (tb), Richard Henry (btb), Andy Sheppard (ts, ss), Chris Biscoe (as, ss, cl), Pete Hurt (bs, ts, bcl, f), Brad Hatfield, Steve Lodder (ky), Mike Walker (g), Bill Urmson (b), Billy Ward (d), Pat Hollenbeck (perc). Orchestral musicians: Paul-Christian Staicu (p), Régis Huby, Laetitia Bellanger, Maria Castro Balbi, Frédéric Norel, Johan Renard, Vanessa Urgarte, Cédric Allali, Antoine Ferreyra, Nicolas Maiofiss, Yuri Bessiere (vn), Etienne Cardoze, Grégory Lacour (clo), Nicolas Folmer (t), Laurent Lair (tb), Benoit Fourreau (tba), Lionel Surin (cor anglais), Thomas Savy (ts), Marie Poulanges, Stéphane Ramanantsitohaina, Claire Bobij (as), Cécile Daroux (f), Luc Isenmann (perc)

Rec. Amiens, France, November 1995. Released originally as Label Bleu LBLC6527/8.

## *The 80th Birthday Concert*

"Listen to the Silence," "Electronic Sonata for Souls Loved by Nature," "The African Game," "It's About Time," "So What" (Davis, arr. Russell)

Personnel—Stanton Davis, Palle Mikkelborg, Stuart Brooks (t), Dave Bargeron (tb), Richard Henry (btb), Andy Sheppard (ts, ss), Chris Biscoe (as, ss, cl), Pete Hurt (bs, bcl), Hiro Honshuku (f, elec) Brad Hatfield, Steve Lodder (ky), Mike Walker (g), Bill Urmson (b), Richie Morales (d), Pat Hollenbeck (perc)

Rec. London, June 13, 2003. Released originally Concept 2005.

## Associated Recordings

**Charlie Parker and Dizzy Gillespie, *Diz 'N Bird at Carnegie Hall*, Blue Note CDP 7243**
"Cubano-Be, Cubano-Bop" (Russell-Dizzy Gillespie-Chano Pozo), "Relaxin' at Camarillo" (Charlie Parker; arr. Russell)
Dizzy Gillespie, Dave Burns, Elmon Wright, Raymond Orr, Matthew McKay (t), Taswell Baird, William Shepherd (tb), Howard E. Johnson, John Brown (as), James Moody, Joe Gayles (ts), Cecil Payne (bs), Milt Jackson (vib), John Lewis (p), Al McKibbon (b), Joe Harris (d), Chano Pozo (v, conga), Lorenzo Salan (bongos)
Rec. September 29, 1947.

**Dizzy Gillespie and his Orchestra, *The Complete RCA Victor Recordings 1937–1949*, RCA**
"Cubano-Be, Cubano-Bop" (Russell-Gillespie-Pozo)
Personnel—Dizzy Gillespie, Benny Bailey, Dave Burns, Elmon Wright, Lamar Wright Jr. (t), Ted Kelly, William Shepherd (tb), Howard E. Johnson, John Brown (as), Joe Gayles, George Nicholas (ts), Cecil Payne (bs), John Lewis (p), Al McKibbon (b), Kenny Clarke (d), Chano Pozo (v, conga)
Rec. December 22, 1947.

**Buddy DeFranco and His Orchestra, *1949–52 Studio Performances*, Hep CD77**
"A Bird in Igor's Yard" (Russell)
Personnel—Buddy DeFranco (cl, ldr), Bernie Glow, Paul Cohen, Jimmy Pupa, Jack Eagle (t), Ollie Wilson, Earl Swope, Bart Varsalona (tb), Lee Konitz, Frank Socolow (as), Al Cohn, Jerry Sanfina (ts), Serge Chaloff (bs), Gene DiNovi (p), Oscar Pettiford (b), Irv Kluger (d)
Rec. April 23, 1949.
Released originally as Buddy DeFranco, *Crosscurrents*, Capitol M-11060.

**Charlie Ventura, *Blue Prelude*, Membran 222489-444 (4-CD set)**
"Caravan" (Juan Tizol-Irving Mills-Duke Ellington; arr. Russell)
Personnel—Stan Fishelson, Johnny Mandel, Dale Pierce, Red Rodney (t), Mort Bullman, Benny Green, Bart Varsalona (tb), Bill Barber (tba), Ray Beckenstein, Frank Socolow (as), Charlie Ventura (ts, bs, ss), Al Cohn, Al Epstein (Young) (ts), Manny Albam (bs), Barry Galbraith (g), Lou Stein (p), Curly Russell (b), Ed Shaughnessy (d), George Russell (tamb)
Rec. December 28, 1949.
Released originally as 78rpm Charlie Ventura and His Orchestra, "Caravan" c/w? EP A659.

**Artie Shaw and His Bop Band, *The Artistry of*, Fresh Sound FSR CD397**
"Similau" (Russell)
Personnel—Artie Shaw (cl, ldr), Don Paladino, Don Fagerquist, Dale Pierce, Vic Ford (t), Sonny Russo, Fred Zito, Ange Callea, Porky Cohen (tb), Herb Steward, Frank Socolow (as), Al Cohn, Zoot Sims (ts), Danny Bank (bs), Jimmy Raney (g), Gil Barrios (p), Dick Niveson (b), Irv Kluger (d)
Rec. January 1950.

## Lee Konitz, *Same*, Modern Jazz Archive 221950-306
"Ezz-Thetic," "Odjenar" (Russell)
Personnel—Miles Davis (t), Lee Konitz (as), Billy Bauer (g), Sal Mosca (p), Arnold Fishkin (b), Max Roach (d)
Rec. March 8, 1951.
Released originally as 78rpm Lee Konitz, "Indian Summer" c/w "Odjenar," New Jazz 853; Prestige 753; and Lee Konitz, "Ezz-Thetic" c/w "Hi-Beck," New Jazz 843; Prestige 743.

## Teddy Charles Tentet, *Same*, COL 6161
"Lydian M-1" (Russell)
Personnel—Teddy Charles (vib), Art Farmer (listed as "Peter Urban") (t), Don Butterfield (tba), Gigi Gryce (as), J.R. Monterose (ts), Sol Schlinger (bs), Jimmy Raney (g), Mal Waldron (p), Teddy Kotick (b), Joe Harris (d)
Rec. Jan 17, 1956.
Originally released on Teddy Charles Tentet, *Same*, Atlantic 1229.

## Hal McKusick, *Jazz Workshop* (See George Russell, *The Complete Bluebird Recordings*, Lonehill LHJ10177.)
"Lydian Lullaby" (comp/arr. Russell)
Personnel—Hal McKusick (as, f), Barry Galbraith (g), Milt Hinton (b), Osie Johnson (d)
Rec. March 3, 1956.
"The Day John Brown Was Hanged" (comp/arr. Russell)
Personnel—Hal McKusick (as, f), Barry Galbraith (g), Milt Hinton (b), Osie Johnson, George Russell (d)
Rec. March 3, 1956.
"Miss Clara" (comp/arr. Russell)
Personnel—Hal McKusick (as, f), Art Farmer (t), Jimmy Cleveland (tb), Sol Schlinger (bs), Barry Galbraith (g), Milt Hinton (b), Osie Johnson (d)
Rec. April 4, 1956.
Released originally as Hal McKusick, *Jazz Workshop*, RCA 1366.

## Hal McKusick Quartet, *The Complete Barry Galbraith, Milt Hinton, Osie Johnson Recordings*, Lonehill LHJ10176
"Give 'Em Hal" (Manny Albam), "When the Sun Comes Out" (Ted Koehler-Howard Arlen), "Can't Get Out of This Mood" (Jimmy McHugh- Frank Loesser), "These Foolish Things" (Jack Strachey-Holt Marvell-Harry Link), "Out of This World" (Harold Arlen-Johnny Mercer), "This Is New" (Kurt Weill-Ira Gershwin), "Over The Rainbow" (Harold Arlen-Yip Harburg), "Serenade In Blue" (Harry Warren-Mack Gordon), "Prelude to a Kiss" (Irving Gordon-Irving Mills-Duke Ellington), "Irresistible You" (Don Raye-Gene De Paul)
Personnel—Hal McKusick (as, f), Barry Galbraith (g), Milt Hinton (b), Osie Johnson (d), George Russell (arr)
Rec. November 3, 1956.
Released originally as Hal McKusick Quartet *Jazz at the Academy* Coral 57116.

**Max Roach Quintet, + 4, EmArcy 822 673-2**
"Ezz-Thetic" (Russell)—Max Roach (d), Kenny Dorham (t), Sonny Rollins (ts), Ray Bryant (p), George Morrow (b)
Rec. September 19, 1956.
Originally released as Max Roach Quintet, + 4, EmArcy MG36098.

**Marilyn Moore, *Moody Marilyn Moore*, Bethlehem LP BCP-73**
"Born to Blow the Blues" (George Russell—Jack Segal)

**Lucy Reed, *This Is Lucy Reed*, Fantasy OJCCD 1943-2**
"In The Wee Small Hours of the Morning" (Dave Mann–Bob Hilliard; arr. Russell), "This is New" (Kurt Weill–Ira Gershwin; arr. Russell), "Born to Blow the Blues" (comp. Russell–Jack Segal)
Personnel—Art Farmer (t), Romeo Penque (Ehn, f), Sol Schlinger (bs, bcl), Barry Galbraith (g), Don Abney (p), Milt Hinton (d), George Russell (d)
Rec. January 1957.
"There He Goes" (Jack English; arr. English), "Love for Sale" (Cole Porter; arr. Gil Evans), "A Trout No Doubt" (Philip Kadison-Dan Howell; arr. Evans), "No Moon at All" (Redd Evans–Dave Mann; arr. Evans)
Personnel—Jimmy Cleveland (tba), Tommy Mitchell (btb), Romeo Penque (Ehn, fl), David Kurtzer (bsn), Harry Lookofsky (vn), Gil Evans (p), Bill Pemberton (b), George Russell (d)
Rec. January 1957.
Released originally as Lucy Reed, *This is Lucy Reed*, Fantasy F-3243.

***The Birth of the Third Stream***
"All About Rosie"
Personnel—Louis Mucci, Art Farmer (t), Jimmy Knepper (tb), Jim Buffington (Frhn), John LaPorta (as), Hal McKusick (ts), Robert DiDomenica (f), Manuel Zegler (bsn), Barry Galbraith (g), Bill Evans (p), Teddy Charles (vib), Joe Benjamin (b), Teddy Sommer (d), Margaret Ross (hp)
Rec. June 10 and 20, 1957.
Last CD issue Sony 1996 485103-2.
Released originally as *Modern Jazz Concert*, Columbia WL127.

**Hal McKusick Quintet, *Cross Section Saxes*, Decca DL 9209**
"Stratusphunk" (Russell), "The End of a Love Affair" (Edward C. Redding; arr. Russell), "You're My Thrill" (Jay Gorney-Sidney Clare; arr. Russell)
Personnel—Hal McKusick (bcl, as), Art Farmer (t), Barry Galbraith (g), Bill Evans (p), Milt Hinton (b), Charlie Persip (d)
Rec. April 7, 1958.
Available as Hal McKusick, *Now's The Time*, Decca GRD -651.
Released originally as Hal McKusick, *Cross Section Saxes*, Decca DL 9209.

**Art Farmer, *Portrait*, Contemporary C3554**
"Nita" (Russell)
Personnel—Art Farmer (t), Hank Jones (p), Addison Farmer (b), Roy Haynes (d)
Rec. April 19 and May 1, 1958.

## The Gil Evans Orchestra, *Out of the Cool*, Impulse IMPD 186
"Stratusphunk" (Russell)
Personnel—Gil Evans (p, leader, arr.), John Coles, Phil Sunkel (t), Jimmy Knepper, Keg Johnson (tb), Tony Studd (btb), Bill Barber (tba), Eddie Caine (as, f, picc), Budd Johnson (ts, ss), Bob Tricario (bsn, f, picc), Ray Crawford (g), Ron Carter (b), Elvin Jones, Charlie Persip (perc)
Rec. November 18, 1960.

## Gerry Mulligan and the Concert Jazz Band, *A Concert in Jazz*, Verve MGV 8415
"All About Rosie" (Russell; arr. Brookmeyer)
Personnel—Gerry Mulligan (bs, p), Nick Travis, Doc Severinsen, Don Ferrara (t), Bob Brookmeyer, Willie Dennis, Allan Ralph (tb), Gene Quill (as, cl), Bob Donovan (as, f), Jim Reider (ts), Gene Allen (bs, bcl), Bill Crow (b), Mel Lewis (d)
Rec. July 10 and 11, 1961. Released originally as V/V6-8415.

## J. J. Johnson, *The Dynamic Sound of J.J. Johnson*, RCA 3350
"Stratusphunk" (Russell)
Personnel—J.J. Johnson (tb), Thad Jones, Clark Terry, Ernie Royal, Jimmy Maxwell, Joe Wilder (t), Jimmy Cleveland (tb), Tony Studd (btb), Bill Stanley (tuba), Jim Buffington (Frhn), Harvey Estrin, Jerome Richardson, Jerry Dodgion, Bud Johnson,, Oliver Nelson, Raymond Beckenstein (reeds), Hank Jones (p), Bob Cranshaw (b), Grady Tate (d)
Rec. December 7–9, 1964.
Released originally as RCA Victor LSP-3350.

## The Gil Evans Orchestra, *Blues in Orbit*, Enja 3069
"Blues in Orbit" (Russell)
Personnel—Gil Evans (p, el p, ldr, arr), Ernie Royal, Johnny Joles (t), Garnett Brown, Jimmy Cleveland (tb), Julius Watkins, Ray Alonge (Frhn), George Marge (f, ss), Billy Harper (ts, f), Howard Johnson (bs, tba), Joe Beck (g), Herb Bushler (b), Alphonse Mouzon (d), Donald McDonald (perc)
Rec. 1971.

## Bill Evans & the George Russell Orchestra, *Living Time*, Columbia KC31490
Personnel—Bill Evans (p), George Russell (comp, cond), Carl Atkins (cond), Snooky Young, Ernie Royal, Richard Williams, Stanton Davis (t), Snooky Young, Ernie Royal, Richard Williams, Howard Johnson (flhn), Dave Bargeron, Dave Baker, Garnett Brown (tb), John Clark (Frhn), Howard Johnson, Dave Bargeron (Tba), Jimmy Giuffre, Joe Henderson, Sam Rivers (ts), Jimmy Giuffre, Sam Rivers (f), Sam Rivers (ob), Jimmy Giuffre (cl), Howard Johnson (bcl), Ted Saunders, Webster Lewis (ky), Sam Brown (el g), Eddie Gomez (b), Ron Carter, Stanley Clarke, Herb Bushier, Sam Brown (el B), Tony Williams, Mary Morell (d), Marc Belair (perc)
Rec. New York, May 1972.

## Gil Evans, *Svengali*, Atlantic SD1643 "Blues in Orbit" (Russell)
Personnel—Gil Evans (p, el p, ldr, arr), Tex Allen, Richard Williams (t), Joseph Daley (tb, tba), Howard Johnson (tba, bs, flhn), Peter Levin, Sharon Freeman (Frhn), Dave Sanborn (as), Billy Harper (ts, f), Trevor Koehler (bs, ss, f), Ted Dunbar (g), David Horowitz (syn), Herb Bushler

(el b), Bruce Ditmas (d), Susan Evans (perc)
Rec. May 30, 1973.

**Brecker, Evans, Watts & Turrentine,** *Select Live Sax Workshop*, **Polydor Japan J00J20351**
"Stratusphunk" (Russell)
Personnel—Michael Brecker, Stanley Turrentine (ts) Bill Evans (ts, ss) Ernie Watts (ts, as) Don Grolnick (p, arr) Yoshio Suzuki (b) Adam Nussbaum (d)
Rec. July 29, 1989.

## APPENDIX B

# Tour Dates, 1982–2005

All performances are by George Russell and the Living Time Orchestra, unless otherwise noted.

## 1982

**George Russell New York Big Band**
July 2: Commacchio Ravenna Jazz, Italy; Milan; Bologna; New Morning Clubs, Geneva and Paris; July 17 and 18: North Sea Jazz Festival; The Pori Jazz Festival, Finland (other venues, exact dates unknown)

**George Russell New York Big Band**
July 26–August 1: The Village Vanguard, New York, New York
  Musicians: Stanton Davis, Tom Harrell, Ron Tooley (t), John Clark (frhn), Earl McIntyre (btb), Marty Ehrlich, Doug Miller, Bob Hanlon (saxes), Jerome Harris (g), Ron McClure (elb), Jack Reilly, Mark Soskin (ky), Victor Lewis (d), Lee Genesis (v)

**George Russell New York Big Band**
Sept 2: Chicago Kool Jazz Festival, Grant Park, Chicago, Illinois
  Musicians: Lew Soloff, Stanton Davis, Tom Harrell, Ron Tooley (t), John Clark (frhn), Earl McIntyre (btb), Marty Ehrlich, Doug Miller, Bob Hanlon (saxes), Jerome Harris (g), Ron McClure (el b), Jack Reilly, Mark Soskin (ky), Ronnie Burrage (d), Lee Genesis (v)

## 1983

**George Russell and the Jazz Orchestra**
June 18: The Emmanuel Church, Boston, Massachusetts
  Musicians: Mike Peipman, Chris Passin, Roy Okutani, Mark Harvey (t), Peter Cirelli, Chip Kaner (tb), Jeff Marsankas (btb), Marshall Sealy (frhn), George Garzone (ts, ss), Gary Joynes

(ts, ss, f), Dave Mann (as, ss, f), Janus Steprans (as, ss, f), Brad Jones (bs, bcl, f), Mark White (g), Mark Rossi, Bruce Barth (ky), Bob Nieske (acc b), Bill Urmson (Fender b), Keith Copeland (d), Dave Hagedorn (perc), Olu Bata—Joe Galeota, Lazarro Perez, Kuto Perez, Amaro Laria, Enrique Cardenas

**George Russell and the Swedish Radio Jazz Orchestra**
May 20: Kulturhuset, Stockholm, Sweden
   Musicians: Americo Bellotto, Håkan Nyqvist, Gustavo Bergalli, Ulf Adaker (t), Lars Olofsson, Nils Landgren, Sven Larsson (tb), Krister Andersson, Lennart Aberg, Erik Nilsson, David Wilczewksi (saxes), Henrik Janson (g), Bobo Stenson, Lars Janson (ky), Palle Danielsson (ac b), Teddy Walter (el b), Örjan Fahlström (cond), Lars Beijbom (d), Okay Temiz (p)
Oct 3: San Diego Kool Jazz Festival, San Diego, California; Oct. 6: Gammage Auditorium, Arizona State University, Tempe, Arizona; October 7: New Mexico Jazz Workshop, Kimo Theatre, Albuquerque, New Mexico; Oct. 8: Lawndale Art Annex, Houston, Texas; October 13: New Mexico Jazz Workshop, Kimo Theatre, Albuquerque, New Mexico; November 12: Police Athletic League, Bronx, New York and Entermedia Theater, New York, New York
   Musicians: Mike Peipman, Roy Okutani, Stanton Davis (t), Chip Kaner, Howard Prince (tb), George Garzone, Gary Joynes, Dave Mann (saxes), Mark White (g), Bill Urmson (Fender b), Brad Hatfield, Rick Martinez (ky), Dave Hagedorn (p), Graham Gullian (d)

**1984**
February 7 to February 12: Sweet Basil, New York, New York
   Musicians: Tiger Okoshi, Mike Peipman, Ken Cervenka, Stanton Davis (t), Chip Kaner, Howard Prince (tb), George Garzone, Dave Mann, Dave Finucane (saxes) Mark White (g), Bill Urmson (Fender b), Brad Hatfield, Rick Martinez (ky), Graham Gullian (d), Dave Hagedorn (perc) June 22: "Jazz Live," Afro-American Historical and Cultural Museum, Washington, D.C.; June 23: Kool Jazz Festival, Philadelphia, Pennsylvania; June 30: Kool Jazz Festival, Saratoga Performing Arts Centre, Saratoga, New York Musicians: Tiger Okoshi, Mike Peipman, Ken Cervenka (t), Chip Kaner, Howard Prince (tb), Bill Barron, George Garzone, Dave Mann (saxes) Mark White (g), Brad Hatfield, Rick Martinez (ky), Bill Urmson (Fender b), Graham Gullian (d), Dave Hagedorn (perc)

**1985**
May 22: The Bottom Line, New York, New York; May 23, Walker Art Centre, Minneapolis, Minnesota; June 23: DeCordova Museum & Sculpture Park, Lincoln, Massachusetts
   Musicians: Stanton Davis, Ken Cervenka, Mike Peipman (t), Chip Kaner, Howard Prince (tb), George Garzone, Dave Mann, Gary Joynes (saxes), Mark White (g), Bill Urmson (Fender b), Brad Hatfield, Rick Martinez (ky), Keith Copeland (d), Pat Hollenbeck (Ed Uribe replaces Pat Hollenbeck for June 23)
July 9 to July 14: Sweet Basil, New York, New York
   Musicians: Sonny Fortune, Jimmy Giuffre (saxes—guest artists), Stanton Davis, Mike Peipman, Ken Cervenka (t), Chip Kaner, Howard Prince (tb), George Garzone, Dave Mann, Dave Finucane (saxes), Brad Hatfield, Rick Martinez (ky), Bill Urmson (Fender b), Mark White (g), Keith Copeland (d), Pat Hollenbeck (perc)

September 11: The Boston Arts Festival, The Hatch Shell, Boston, Massachusetts
  Musicians: Stanton Davis, Mike Peipman, Ken Cervenka (t), Chip Kaner, Howard Prince (tb), George Garzone, Dave Mann, Dave Hubbard (saxes), Brad Hatfield, Rick Martinez (ky), Bill Urmson (Fender b), Mark White (g), Keith Copeland (d), Pat Hollenbeck (perc)

## 1986

Feb. 26: Logan Hall, London, UK; Feb. 27: Mountbatten Theatre, Southampton, UK; Feb. 28: Concert Hall, Royal Northern College of Music, Manchester, UK; March 1: Triangle Arts Centre, Birmingham, UK; March 2: Haymarket Theatre, Leicester, UK; March 3: Warwick University Arts Centre Hall, Coventry, UK; March 5: Leadmill, Sheffield, UK; March 8: Arts Centre, Southport, UK; March 9: Civic Theatre, Leeds, UK; March 12: People's Theatre, Newcastle upon Tyne, UK
  Musicians: Stuart Brooks, Kenny Wheeler, Palle Mikkelborg (t) Pete Beachill (tb), Ashley Slater (btb) Chris Biscoe, Pete Hurt, Courtney Pine (saxes), Brad Hatfield, Django Bates (ky), Chris Watson (g), Bill Urmson (Fender b), Keith Copeland (d), Dave Adams (perc)

### George Russell and the Scandinavian Jazzensemble

May 25 & 26: The Bergen International Festival, Bergen, Norway Musicians: Palle Mikkelborg, Bertil Lövgren, Nils Petter Molvaer (t), Eje Thelin (tb), Olle Holmqvist (btb), Knut Riisnaes (ts), John Tchicai (as), Vidar Johansen (bs), Terje Rypdal (g), Bobo Stenson, John Balke (ky), Arild Andersen (ac b), Bo Stief (elb), Alex Riel (d), Marilyn Mazur (perc)

## 1987

July 2: Jazz à Vienne, France; July 4: Bracknell Festival, UK; July 5: Weisen Jazz Festival, Austria; Schwatz, Austria; Stadtgarten, Cologne, Germany; Balzano, Italy; Veneto Jazz, Padua, Italy; North Sea Jazz Festival, The Hague, Netherlands (exact dates unknown)
  Musicians: Stuart Brooks, Dave de Fries, Palle Mikkelborg, Kenny Wheeler (t), Pete Beachill (tb), Ashley Slater (btb), Andy Sheppard (ts, ss), Chris Biscoe (as, ss, cl) Pete Hurt (bs, ts, bcl), Brad Hatfield, Django Bates (ky), Chris Watson (g), Bill Urmson (Fender b), Keith Copeland (d), Dave Adams (perc)

Oct. 2: Baird Auditorium, Smithsonian Museum of Natural History, Washington, D.C.; October 3: Port of History Theatre, Philadelphia, Pennsylvania Musicians: Mike Peipman, Ken Cervenka, Tiger Okoshi (t) Chip Kaner (tb), Howard Prince (btb), Rob Scheps (ts), Dave Mann (as), Dave Finucane (bs), Brad Hatfield, Marc Rossi (ky), Bill Urmson (Fender b), Mark White (g), Keith Copeland (d), Pat Hollenbeck (perc)

### George Russell Sextet

Nov. 7: Grinnell College, Grinnell, Iowa; Nov. 9: Kuumbwa Jazz Centre, Santa Cruz, California; Nov. 10: Great American Music Hall, San Francisco, California; Nov. 14: Kimo Theatre, Albuquerque, New Mexico; Nov. 15: Memorial Auditorium, Ohio University, Athens, Ohio; Nov. 17–22: Sweet Basil, New York, New York
  Musicians: George Russell (p), John Stubblefield (sax), Graham Haynes (t), Brad Hatfield (ky), Bill Urmson (Fender b), Keith Copeland (d)

## 1988

February 28: Tokyo Music Joy, U-Port Hall, Tokyo, Japan

Musicians: Palle Mikkelborg, Lew Soloff, Shin Kazuhara, Nubuo Katoh (t), Ray Anderson, Osamu Matsumoto (tb), Sumio Okada (btb), Andy Sheppard, Kohsuke Mine (ts), Dave Mann, (as), Kazutoki Umezu (bs), Brad Hatfield, Sohichi Noriki (ky), Bill Urmson (Fender b), Mark White (g), Keith Copeland (d), Pat Hollenbeck (perc)

May 7: Newcastle Jazz Festival, Playhouse Theatre, Newcastle upon Tyne, UK; May 9: The 100 Club, London, UK; May 10: New Morning Club, Paris, France; May 11: Coutances Festival, Theatre Municipale, Coutances, France; May 12: Angouleme Festival, France; May 13: Grand Theatre, Maison de la Culture, Amiens, France; May 14: The Bimhuis, Amsterdam, Netherlands Musicians: Palle Mikkelborg, Stuart Brooks, Dave des Fries (t), Pete Beachill (tb), Ashley Slater (btb), Andy Sheppard (ts, ss), Chris Biscoe (as, ss, cl) Pete Hurt (bs, ts, bcl), Brad Hatfield, Steve Lodder (ky), Bill Urmson (Fender b), Chris Watson (g), Keith Copeland (d), Dave Adams (perc)

August 6: Real Art Ways, Trinity College, Hartford, Connecticut Musicians: Stanton Davis, Tiger Okoshi, Ken Dunbar (t), Chip Kaner, Peter Cirelli (tb), George Garzone, Dave Mann, Dave Finucane (saxes), Dave Fiuczynski (g), Brad Hatfield, Teese Gohl (kb), Bill Urmson (Fender b), Steve Johns (d), John Hollenbeck (perc)

Oct. 15: Portland Performing Arts Centre, Portland, Maine; Oct. 21: Mertens Theater, University of Bridgeport, Bridgeport, Connecticut; Oct. 23; Ira Allen Chapel, University of Vermont, Burlington, Vermont; Oct. 25: Arts Centre on Brickyard Pond, Keene State College, Keene, New Hampshire; Oct. 28: Maine Centre for the Arts, University of Maine, Orono, Maine; Oct. 29: Centre for the Performing and Visual Arts, University of Lowell, Lowell, Massachusetts; October 30: Cambridge Multicultural Arts Centre, Cambridge, Massachusetts; Nov. 1: Spaulding Auditorium, Dartmouth College, Dartmouth, New Hampshire; Nov. 3: Jorgensen Auditorium, University of Connecticut, Storrs, Connecticut; Nov. 4: Crowell Concert Hall, Wesleyan University, Middletown, Connecticut; Nov. 5: Palmer Auditorium, Connecticut College, New London, Connecticut

Musicians: Mike Peipman, Ken Cervenka, Tiger Okoshi, Andy Gravish (t), Chip Kaner (tb), Bill Lowe, Peter Cirelli (btb) Dave Mann (as), Rob Scheps (ts), Dave Finucane (bs), Teese Gohl, Marc Rossi, Brad Hatfield (ky), Dave Fiuczynski (g), Bill Urmson (Fender b), Steve Johns (d), Pat Hollenbeck, Doug Lippincott (perc)

## 1989

Aug. 12: Internationales Jazz Fest, Festhalle, Viersen, Germany; Aug: 13: Game Festival, Rossijnol, Belgium; Aug. 15: Middelheim Park, Antwerp, Belgium; Aug. 18: Snape Maltings, Concert Hall, Saxmunden, UK; Aug. 19: Brecon Jazz Festival, Market Hall, Wales; Aug 20: Queen's Hall, Edinburgh, Scotland; Aug. 23 and 24: Amphitheatre, Jazz in August, Lisbon, Portugal; 28–31: Ronnie Scott's, London, UK; September 2: IX Festival Internazionale del Jazz, Roccella Jonica, Italy

Musicians: Stuart Brooks, Ian Carr, Mark Chandler (t), Pete Beachill (tb), Ashley Slater (btb), Andy Sheppard (ts, ss), Chris Biscoe (as, ss, cl) Pete Hurt (bs, ts, bcl), Dave Fiuczynski (g), Brad Hatfield, Steve Lodder (ky), Bill Urmson (Fender b), Steve Johns (d), Dave Adams (perc)

## 1990

May 20: New Music America, Annenberg Centre, Philadelphia, Pennsylvania: May 22: Hartford Festival of Jazz, Bushnell Park, Hartford, Connecticut Musicians: Tiger Okoshi, Mike Peipman, Ken Cervenka (t), Chip Kaner, Bill Lowe (tb), Rob Scheps, Dave Mann, Anthony Paquette (saxes), Dave Fiuczynski (g), Marc Rossi, Brad Hatfield (ky), Bill Urmson (Fender b), Steve Johns (d), Pat Hollenbeck (perc)

July 6: Theatre Royal, Glasgow International Jazz Festival, Glasgow, Scotland; July 9: Amsterdam Jazz Festival, Amsterdam, Netherlands; July 10–15: Umbria Jazz Festival, Perugia, Italy
Musicians: Tiger Okoshi, Stuart Brooks, Tim Hagans (t), Dave Bargeron (tb), Ashley Slater (btb), Andy Sheppard, Dave Mann, John Purcell (saxes), Dave Fiuczynski (g), Brad Hatfield, Teese Gohl (ky), Bill Urmson (Fender b), Steve Johns (d), Pat Hollenbeck (perc)

## 1991

March 18: Teatro Metropolitan, Catania, Italy; March 19: Teatro Communale, L'Aquila, Italy; March 20: Teatro Rasi, Ravenna, Italy; March 21: Auditorium Santa Chiara, Trento, Italy; March 23: Teatro Ariosto, Reggio Emilia, Italy; March 24: Camden Jazz Festival, Town and Country, London, UK Musicians: Tiger Okoshi, Stuart Brooks, Ian Carr (t), Dave Bargeron (tb), Ashley Slater (btb), Andy Sheppard (ts, ss), Chris Biscoe (as, ss, cl) Pete Hurt (bs, ts, bcl), Adam Rogers (g), Brad Hatfield, Steve Lodder (ky), Bill Urmson (Fender b), Steve Johns (d), Pat Hollenbeck (perc)

April 16: Maison de la Culture, Salle Gil Evans, Amiens, France Musicians: Tiger Okoshi, Stuart Brooks, Ian Carr (t), Dave Bargeron (tb), Ashley Slater (btb), Andy Sheppard (ts, ss), Chris Biscoe (as, ss, cl) Pete Hurt (bs, ts, bcl), Dave Fiuczynski (g), Brad Hatfield, Steve Lodder (ky), Bill Urmson (Fender b), Steve Johns (d), Dave Adams (perc)

Oct. 28: Theatre 140, Brussels, Belgium; October 29: Festival d'Automne à Paris, Théâtre des Champs Elysées, Paris, France
Musicians: Ian Carr, Tiger Okoshi, Henry Lowther (t), Dave Bargeron (tb), Rick Taylor (btb), Andy Sheppard (ts, ss), Chris Biscoe (as, ss, cl) Pete Hurt (bs, ts, bcl), Dave Fiuczynski (g), Brad Hatfield, Steve Lodder (ky), Bill Urmson (Fender b), Steve Johns (d), Dave Adams, Pat Hollenbeck (perc)

## 1992

June 27: Filene Centre, Wolf Trap, Vienna, Virginia
Musicians: Tiger Okoshi, Takuya Nakamura, Mike Peipman (t), Dave Bargeron (tb), Bill Lowe (btb) Rob Scheps (ts), Kathy Halverson (bs), Jim Odgren (bs) Dave Fiuczynski (g), Brad Hatfield, Marc Rossi (ky), Bill Urmson (Fender b), Steve Johns (d), Doug Lippincott, (p)

## 1993

March 31: The Arsenal, Metz, France; April 6: Teatro Tenda, Florence, Italy; April 8: Roccella Jonica, Italy; April 10: Banlieues Bleues Festival, Maison de la Culture, Bodigny, France; April 11: The Jazz Cafe, London, UK Musicians: Stuart Brooks, Ian Carr, Tiger Okoshi (t), Malcolm Griffiths (tb), Ashley Slater (btb), Andy Sheppard (ts, ss), Chris Biscoe (as, ss, cl) Pete Hurt (bs, ts, bcl), Adam Rogers (g), Brad Hatfield, Steve Lodder (ky), Bill Urmson (Fender b), Steve

Johns (d), Pat Hollenbeck (perc), with students from the Conservatoire National Supérieur de Musique et de Danse de Paris (Bodigny and Metz only)

**1994**

July 8 and 9: Umbria Jazz Festival, Perugia, Italy; July 10: North Sea Jazz Festival, The Hague, Netherlands; July 13: Newcastle Jazz Festival, Newcastle upon Tyne, UK; July 24: Pori Jazz Festival, Pori, Finland
  Musicians: Guy Barker, Henry Lowther, Stuart Brooks (t), Dave Bargeron (tb), Richard Edwards (btb), Andy Sheppard (ts, ss), Chris Biscoe (as, ss, cl) Pete Hurt (bs, ts, bcl), Mike Walker (g), Brad Hatfield, Steve Lodder (ky), Bill Urmson (Fender b), Billy Ward (d), Pat Hollenbeck (perc)

**1995**

April 2: Festival Banlieues Bleues, Cite de la Musique, Paris, France Musicians: Tiger Okoshi, Stuart Brooks, Guy Barker (t), Dave Bargeron (tb), Richard Edwards (btb), Andy Sheppard (ts, ss), Chris Biscoe (as, ss, cl) Pete Hurt (bs, ts, bcl), Mike Walker (g), Brad Hatfield, Steve Lodder (ky), Bill Urmson (Fender b), Billy Ward (d), Pat Hollenbeck (perc), with additional musicians from the Conservatoire National Supérieur de Musique et de Danse de Paris, Le Conservatoire national de Région d'Aubervilliers-La Courneuve, L'Ecole nationale de musique et de danse de Montreuil, and L'Ecole nationale de musique de Romainville

**George Russell and the Swedish Radiojazzgruppen**
Nov. 4: Berwald Hall, Stockholm, Sweden
  Musicians: Palle Mikkelborg, Bertil Lövgren, Magnus Broo, Peter Asplund, Fredrik Norén, Hans Dyvik (t), Olle Holmqvist, Nils Landgren, Bertil Strandberg, Anders Wiborg (tb), Rolf Nyqvist (horn) Johan Hörlén, Ronny Stensson (as), Lennart Aberg, David Wilczewski (ts), Alberto Pinton, (bs), Johan Norberg (g) Brad Hatfield, Esbjorn Svensson, Bengt Hallberg (ky), Teddy Walter, (b) Jukkis Uotila (d), Pat Hollenbeck, Rene Martinez (perc) Coltrane Magnum Price (v)
Nov. 10: The Maltings, Farnham, UK; Nov. 11: London International Jazz Festival, Queen Elizabeth Hall, London, UK; Nov. 15: Maison de la Culture, Amiens, France, Nov. 17: Turner Sims Hall, Southampton, UK; Nov. 18: The Forum, Bath, UK; Nov. 19: Town Hall, Birmingham, UK; Nov. 20: Lawrence Batley Theatre, Huddersfield Contemporary Music Festival, Huddersfield, UK; Nov. 22: Maison de la Culture, Nevers, France
  Musicians: Stanton Davis, Tiger Okoshi, Stuart Brooks (t), Dave Bargeron (tb), Richard Henry (btb), Andy Sheppard (ts, ss), Chris Biscoe (as, ss, cl) Pete Hurt (bs, ts, bcl), Hiro Honshuku (f), Mike Walker (g), Brad Hatfield, Steve Lodder (ky), Bill Urmson (Fender b), Billy Ward (d), Pat Hollenbeck (perc)

**1998**

March 7: Barbican Hall, London, UK; March 8: Cite de la Musique, Paris, France.
  Musicians: Stanton Davis, Stuart Brooks, Guy Barker (t), Dave Bargeron (tb), Richard Henry (btb), Andy Sheppard (ts, ss), Chris Biscoe (as, ss, cl) Pete Hurt (bs, ts, bcl), Hiro Honshuku (f), Mike Walker (g), Brad Hatfield, Steve Lodder (ky), Bill Urmson (Fender b), Billy Ward (d), Pat

Hollenbeck (perc), with additional musicians from Guildhall School of Music and Drama and Conservatoire de Paris

May 29: The Moers Festival, Moers, Germany; May 30: Verona Jazz 1998, Teatro Romano, Verona, Italy

Musicians: Stanton Davis, Tiger Okoshi, Stuart Brooks (t), Dave Bargeron (tb), Richard Henry (btb), Andy Sheppard (ts, ss), Chris Biscoe (as, ss, cl) Pete Hurt (bs, ts, bcl), Mike Walker (g), Brad Hatfield, Steve Lodder (ky), Bill Urmson (Fender b), Billy Ward (d), Pat Hollenbeck (perc)

## 1999

May 6 and 7: Scullers Jazz Club, Cambridge, Massachusetts; May 8: The Five Spot Jazz Series of Lost Jazz Shrines, Tribeca Art Centre, New York, New York; May 10: The Library of Congress, Coolidge Auditorium, Washington, D.C.

Musicians: Tiger Okoshi, Stanton Davis, Stuart Brooks, Scott Aruda (t, Boston only), Dave Bargeron (tb), Richard Henry (btb), Andy Sheppard (ts, ss), Pete Hurt (bs, ts, bcl), Jason Hunter (as), Hiro Honshuku (f, elec), Mike Walker (g), Brad Hatfield, Steve Lodder (ky), Bill Urmson (Fender b), Billy Ward (d), Pat Hollenbeck (perc)

## 2002

July 15–20: Umbria Jazz Festival, Perugia, Italy; July 21: Pescara Jazz Festival, Pescara, Italy

Musicians: Stanton Davis, Tiger Okoshi, Stuart Brooks (t), Dave Bargeron (tb), Richard Edwards (btb), George Garzone (ts), Steve Slagle (as), Pete Hurt (bs, ts, bcl), Hiro Honshuku (f, elec), Mike Walker (g), Brad Hatfield, Steve Lodder (ky), Bill Urmson (Fender b), Billy Ward (d), Pat Hollenbeck (perc)

## 2003

June 9: The Moers Festival, Moers, Germany, June 12: Manchester Royal Northern College of Music, Manchester, UK; June 13: Barbican Hall, London, UK

Musicians: Stanton Davis, Palle Mikkelborg, Stuart Brooks (t), Dave Bargeron (tb), Richard Henry (btb), Andy Sheppard (ts, ss), Chris Biscoe (as, ss, cl) Pete Hurt (bs, ts, bcl), Hiro Honshuku (f), Mike Walker (g), Brad Hatfield, Steve Lodder (ky), Bill Urmson (Fender b), Richie Morales (d), Pat Hollenbeck (perc), with Christopher Jenkins (vla, UK concerts only)

## 2005

George Russell's Living Time Orchestra October 29: Musikhost 2005, Odense, Denmark

Musicians: Palle Mikkelborg, Stuart Brooks (t), Brad Hatfield (ky), Bo Stief, (b) Richie Morales (d), Pat Hollenbeck (perc), with students from Det Fynske Musikkonservatorium

# Index

Åberg, Lennart, 191, 266.
Amiens, (La Maison de la Culture), 266.
Andersen, Arild, xxii, 194, 238; Molde (jams with Russell) 187-189, 191; *Trip to Prillarguri*, 204; *Listen to the Silence* 206; *Esoteric Circle* 208-209.
Art Music (European), xvii, xx, 34, 107, 197, 208, 291.
Atkins, Carl, on Russell at NEC 216, 221, 225; *Living Time* 226-227, 228; *Vertical Form VI* 230.

Baker, Dave, xxiii, 139, 142, 146, 163, 204, 273, 279, 281, 297; Lenox 109, 112; *Jazz in the Space Age* 126, 128-129, n.13, 138; joins Russell's group 112-113, 141; *At the Five Spot* 144; *Stratusphunk* 145; *Kansas City* 147; "War Gewessen," 147, 151, 241; composes for Russell group 148-149; *Ezz-Thetics*, 155; on Don Ellis 157-158; *Stratus Seekers* 158-159;, *Living Time*, 225 233.
Barber, Phillip, 109.
Bargeron, Dave, 226, 231, 267.
Bernstein, Leonard, 195, 210.
Bertalanffy, Ludwig von, xi.
Birdland, 142-143, 147, 279.
*Birth of the Cool*, 83-84, 86, 91.
Biscoe, Chris, 248, 249, 250, 252, 256, 257, 270, 273.
Blake, Ran, 54, 100, 109, 147, 152, 214, 252, 291, 292, 297.
Blewitt, Hix, 5, 97, 100, 101, 222, 257.
Bley, Carla, xxi, 241, 247, 249, 253, 262, 270; composes for Russell group 142, 144-145, 147, 148-151, 161.
Bley, Paul, *Jazz in the Space Age* 125-129, 138; 149, 153, 162, 258.
Bluefield Colored Institute, xv.
Bowie, Lester, xvii.
Brandeis University (*Modern Jazz Concert* LP), 106-109, 158, 186, 213.
Braxton, Anthony, xx.
Brecker, Michael, xxiii, 188, 297.
Brecker, Randy, xxiii, 146, 281-282, 283, 298.
Broberg, Bosse, 184, 185, 193, 210.
Brookmeyer, Bob, 136, 158, 214; *New York, N.Y.* 116, 117-118, 119; *Jazz in the Space Age* 129.
Brooks, John Benson, 90, 132, 136, 156, 163, 189.
Brooks, Stuart, 254, 274.
Brown, Garnett, *Outer View* 161-162; Newport Festival 163; Newport Festival All-Stars tour 1964 175-177, 177; *Living Time*, 226, 158, 183.
Brubeck, Dave, 148, 175, 273.
Brubeck, Darius, 283-5.
Burk, Greg, 216, 221-2.
Burton, Gary, 229.
Burton, Nelson, 29, 33-36, 38, 44, 48, 55.

Byron, Don, xxiii, 216, 219-220, 297.

Campbell, Joseph (*The Hero with a Thousand Faces*), xiv, xxiv, 49, 50, 56
Carr, Ian *The Invisible Guru/The Trailblazer* BBC Radio 3), xiv, 11, 13, 14, 15, 16, 25, 26, 29, 33, 35, 46, 47, 49, 51, 52, 54, 55, 60, 63, 64, 65, 67, 71, 75, 76, 80, 85, 89, 93, 96, 99, 103, 105, 136, 137, 149, 153, 178, 182, 183, 189, 208, 214, 215, 257, 279; joins Living Time Orchestra/*London Concert* 254-256; 266, 287.
Carter, Benny, 51, 52, 55, 70, 77, 277.
Charles, Teddy, xxii; "Lydian M-1" 91, 92; *Hal McKusick – Jazz Workshop* 92; *This is Lucy Reed* 105; Brandeis/*Modern Jazz Concert* 107.
Cherry, Don, xxi, 34, 156, 157, 185, 202, 204-205; *Beethoven Hall*, 185-186, 190.
Chicago All-Stars, 176.
Christensen, Jon, xxii, 189, 191, 194-195, 238, 297; Molde (jams with Russell) 187-188; *The Essence of George Russell*/big band *Electronic Sonata* 120, 202-203, 242; *Electronic Sonata* 1968, 201; *Esoteric Circle* 208-209; *Othello Ballet*, 198, 203; *Trip to Prillarguri* 204.
Cincinnati music scene in, 28–46; Russell's childhood and adolescence in, xv, 3-21, 23-39.
Coleman, Ornette, xxi, 66, 90, 126, 128, 143, 145, 148, 153, 154, 159, 175, 204, 224, 238, 273, 283, 287, 295; Lenox School of Jazz 111-112; *Dialogue with Ornette*, 222, 234, 268, 273, 291;
Collier, Graham, 292-293, 298.
Coltrane, John, xxi, xxii, 66, 69, 128, 143, 144, 147, 151, 153, 154, 158, 175, 188, 196, 220, 237, 288; *New York, N.Y.* 116, 117-118, 119; Russell's influence on xiv, 131, 134-136, 297; *Giant Steps*, 90, 135, 145, 283;
Conover, Willis (Voice of America), xvii.

Copland, Aaron, 77, 81, 101.
Cosmopolitan School of Music, 33.
Cotton Club (Cincinnati), 32, 36-37, 44, 50, 52.
Crouch, Stanley, xvii-xviii, 182, 236-237, 240, 244, 260.
Cumming, John, 247-248, 250, 252, 259, 265, 266, 268, 269-270, 271, 273, 274.

Davis, Anthony, 205.
Davis, Miles, xiv, xxi, 60-62, 67, 80, 81, 90, 92, 94, 107, 128, 131, 134-136, 142, 144, 147, 148, 151, 152, 154, 178, 185, 188, 200-203, 224, 228, 241, 277, 278, 279, 293; *Birth of the Cool* 83-84, 86, 91; *Kind of Blue* xxii, 100, 131, 132, 135, 147, 281, 283; *Milestones* 89. 90, 135, 136, 223; Russell influence on 61-62, 134-136, 297.
Davis, Stanton, 221, 238; big band *Electronic Sonata* 202; *It's About Time*, 267; *Listen to the Silence* 206-207; *Living Time* 226, 226, 267; *New York Big Band* 236, 237; *Trip to Prillarguri* 204.
Davis, William R (childhood friend), 4-5, 6, 8, 9, 12, 13-14, 15, 17, 24, 27, 29, 30, 31-32, 38.
Decca Records, 82, 106, 113, 117, 125, 142, 145, 148.
DeFranco, Buddy, "A Bird in Igor's Yard" xxii, 51, 80-81, 82, 135, 273.
Dixon, Bill, 182, n.57, 166, 182.
Dolphy, Eric, xxi, 135, 143, 158-159, 222; *Ezz-Thetics*, xxii, 142, 151, 153, 155-157, 238-239; Lydian Concept 156, 297.
Drescher, Derek, 257.
DuBois, W.E.B., xix.

Ehrlich, Marty, xxiii, 216, 235, 236-237, 238, 297; on studying with Russell, 220-221; Time Spiral 238-239.
Ellington, Duke, xx, 32, 54, 70, 77, 81, 83, 91, 93, 102, 109, 120, 126, 130, 158,

159, 162, 176, 188, 199, 202, 205, 214,215; Russell meets Ellington band xvi, 60; and Harold Gaston 33, 48.

Ellis, Don, 145-146, 147, 158, 163; *Ezz-Thetics* 151, 156; *Stratus Seekers* 159; personality of 157-158.

Endrey, George, 65; preface to second edition of Lydian Concept, 114.

Evans, Bill, xxi, 62, 136, 152, 163, 222; meets Russell 97-98, 218; *Jazz Workshop* 98-99, 100, 102, 113; *All About Rosie* 197; *New York, N.Y.* 116, 117, 119-120; *Jazz in the Space Age* 125-129, 131-132; *Living Time* 2216, 223-229, 266, 267-268; Russell influence on 132.

Evans, Gil, xxi, 54, 81, 91, 92, 99, 103, 105, 114, 126, 136, 141, 146, 162, 247, 253, 265; 55th Street enclave xxii, 60, 75, 76, 79-80, 90, 115, 277-299; Stefan Wolpe 68-69; *Birth of the Cool* 83; Russell/Evans compared 292-294; version of "Stratusphunk" 148, 261.

Falzone, James, 221-222.

Farmer, Art, 94, 105; *Jazz Workshop* 97, 99, 101, 103, 113; *Brandeis/All About Rosie* 107; *New York, N.Y.* 116, 117, 119, 120; and Lydian Concept 134, 297.

Farrell, Joe, 158, 176, 190 n.9.

Fitzgerald, Ella, xxii, 71, 88, 119; "How High the Moon" 82-83, 88.

Fiuczynski, David, 254, 255-256, 257, 266.

Folk Music, xx, 101, 104, 133-134.

Ford, Ricky, xxiii, 216, 218-219, 236-237, 240, 297.

Fujii, Satoko, 216, 220-221, 297, 298.

Gabler, Milt (Decca Records), 106, 113, 116-117, 118-119, 125, 130-131.

Galbraith, Barry, 94, 105, 131, 136, 239, 254; Brandeis/*All About Rosie* 107; "The Day John Brown Was Hanged" 92-93; *Jazz Workshop*, 97, 99-100, 113;

*New York, N.Y.*, 116, 129; *Portrait of Sheila*, 163.

Garbarek, Jan, 181, 189, 194, 238; Russell influence on xxii, 97, 297; Molde (jams with Russell) 187-188, 189; *Now and Then* 196; *Othello Ballet* 198, 199; *Electronic Sonata, 1968* 200-201; big band *Electronic Sonata* 201-202, 203; *Trip to Prillarguri* 204; *Esoteric Circle* 208-209, 245. Russell, 208

Garzone, George, *African Game* 240-241; European tour 270.

Gaston, Harold, 31-34; death 48, 50; and Duke Ellington 33-34, 48; teaches Russell musical theory 33-34, 37, 38, 46, 47-48, 51.

Gay, Robert ("Little Diz"), 55, 59, n.60, 56-57.

General Systems Theory, see Bertalanffy, Ludwig von.

George, Kathleen, xv-xvi, 19, 20, 49, 290.

Gibbs, Mike, 109, 110-111, 229.

Gillespie, John Birks "Dizzy," xx, xxi, 52, 53, 60, 61, 63, 84-85, 88, 120, 148, 216, 222, 273, 276; "Cubano Be, Cubano Bop" xxii, 70-72, 75, 85, 91; Carnegie Hall concert 1947 71, 74 n.58, 85; and Lenox School 109.

Gilmore, John, 157, 158, 163

Giuffre, Jimmy, 1, 91, 92, 102, 137, 143, 162,176, 214, 258; Brandeis/*Modern Jazz Concert* 106-107; Lenox, 109, 111; *Living Time*, 225, 229.

Giuffre, Juanita, 1, 75, 84-86, 87, 88, 101, 105, 106, 136-137, 176; on Bill Evans 97.

Gordon, Dexter, 146, 176, 187, 189, 190.

Gordon, Max, 235.

Graves, Milford, xx.

Green, Ernest, 104, 122 n.18.

Guard, Dave, funds second edition of *Lydian Chromatic Concept of Tonal Organization* 132; develops Color Guitar principle based on Lydian

Concept, 132-133.
Guard, Tom, 133.
Gurdjieff, George Ivanovich, influence on Russell 67, 189, 203, 208, 209, 211 n.40, 287-289.

Hatfield, Brad, 248, 251, 252, 273; *It's About Time/Living Time* 267; *The London Concert* 254-255, 256.
Heath, Al "Tootie", 187, 189; *Beethoven Hall* 186; Newport Festival All-Stars tour 1964 176, 180.
Heath, Percy, 88, 119, 112.
Henderson, Joe, *Living Time* 221, 227.
Hendricks, Jon, 273; *New York, N.Y.* 115-117, 118-120.
Hennessey, Brian, 224-225, 228.
Hersch, Fred, 218, 240.
Hindemith, Paul, 79
Hines, Earl, xxii, 28, 37, 53-54, 77, 223, 239, 277.
Hinton, Milt, 105; *Jazz Workshop* 92, 94, 97, 98-99, 100; *Brandeis/All About Rosie* 107; *New York, N.Y.* 115, 116, 120; *Jazz in the Space Age* 127.
Hodeir, André, xvi-xvii.
Holland, Dave, 214, 222.
Hollenbeck, Pat, xiii, 216, 240, 258, 273; assistant musical director for London and Paris concerts 1998 268-269; *Dialogue with Ornette* 223; *It's About Time* 266, 269; on Living Time Orchestra 272.
Honshuku, Hiroaki, assistant musical director for London and Paris concerts 1998 268.
Hubbard, DeHart, 24, 38.
Hunt, Joe, 112, 126, 146, 157, 240; *Jazz in the Space Age* 141; *Five Spot* 142-143; *Kansas City* 142, 146, 147-148; *Stratus Seekers* 159; on Russell as pianist 152.
Hurt, Pete, 248, 249-250, 252, 257.

Israels, Chuck, 141, 143, 144, 145, 156; dismissive of Russell's music 152-153, 280-281.
Ives, Charles, xxiv n.17, 35-36, 54, 101, 223

"Jazzocracy" xvi-xx.
Jerstad, Marit (friend/lover of Russell), 178, 183, 187, 188-189, 215-216.
"Jim Crow"/"Crow-Jimism", xvii-xviii, 8, 70, 77, 180-182.
Johnson, Andrew, 32, 38, 41 n.65.
Johnson, Howard, *Living Time* 225, 229.
Johnson, J. J., 51, 56 n.46, 81, 128, 144; Brandeis/*Modern Jazz Concert* LP 106, 107, 158.
Johnson, Osie, 115; *Jazz Workshop* 92, 94, 100, 101, 120; *All About Rosie* 107.
Jones, Thad, 156, 158, 162, 163; Newport Festival All-Stars tour 1964, 176, 177, 190 n.9.
Jordan, Sheila, "You Are My Sunshine" 160-162, 186, 273-274; at Newport 162-163; *Portrait of Sheila*, 163-164; relationship with Russell 163-164, 188-189.

Kay, Connie, 109, 112.
Kearns, J. Harvey, 11-12, 22 n42.
Keepnews, Orrin (Riverside Records), 141, 142, 225, 231.
Kendall, Paul Murray, xi, xii.
Khan, Marty, Russell as client 244; Lincoln Center negotiations, 259-261.
Kiger, Al, 141, 142, 145-146, 147, 156, 165n.21, 204; Lenox 112; *Jazz in the Space Age* 126, 128, 129; "Kige's Tune" 159; replaced by Don Ellis 145-146.
Kikuchi, Masabumi, compares Russell and Evans, 292, 293.
Kolberg, Kåre, 184, 195, 200, 209, 211.
Koller, Hans, 297
Konitz, Lee, xxii, 81, 84, 86, 92; *Birth of the Cool* 83; "Ezz-Thetic"/"Odjenar" 86-88, 94, 135, 148.

Lawless Jones, Bill, 27-28, 36.
Leonard, Neil, 297.
Lenox School of Jazz, 109-112, 134, 135, 137, 141-142, 143-144, 156, 162, 213, 214, 283.
Lewis, Charles, 32-3.
Lewis, Jack (RCA) 93, 97, 98, 101,
Lewis, John, xxi, 84-85, 134, 160; Carnegie Hall 1947 71; 55th Street enclave 79-80, 90, 115, 276; *Birth of the Cool* 83; Brandeis/*Modern Jazz Concert* LP 106-108; Lenox School of Jazz 109-112, 214; Third Stream 81, 283, 291-292; on the Lydian Concept 89-90, 279.
Ligeti, György, 202, 294-295, 296.
Lincoln, Abbey, xvii, xviii, 162, 291.
Lodder, Steve, 253, 257, 262, 269, 270, 271, 273, 80th birthday tour, 279; joins LTO, 260; last LTO performance, 321; on Pat Hollenbeck, 274; on Russell's music, 260–261; Umbria concerts 2002, 276–27
Lövgren, Bertil, 180, 185, 186, 235, 237.
Lydian Chromatic Concept of Tonal Organization, x, xiv, xx, xxi, 2, 39, 49, 50, 70, 75, 102, 112, 113, 115, 121 n.11, 134, 148, 149, 155, 164, 185, 223, 266, 268; and Miles Davis xxii, 61-62, 131-132, 135-136, ; Russell on 63, 76, 90-91, 114, 127; Dave Guard Color Guitar 132-133; 1953 edition 67, 89; 1959 edition 64, 67, 135, ; Dave Baker/Indiana University 146, 279-281; in Scandinavia 180, 193, 200, 209; and NEC 213, 216-217, 218-219, 220-221; Lydian Concept discussed 63-67, 73 n. 34, 89-90, 110-111, 147, 244, 248, 277-278; and Gurdjieff 287-290; and Russell psychologically 290-291; Third Stream/as composer 291-297; the future 297-299.

Marable, Fate, 26, 28, 40 n.23.
Marsalis, Wynton, xvii-xviii, xx, 182 ;

Lincoln Center 261.
Martinez, Sabu, big band *Electronic Sonata* 202, 203, 243; *New York Big Band* 237, 251.
McKusick, Hal, xxii, 105-6, 132; *Jazz Workshop* (McKusick) 92-94, 97, 98, 109, 135, 138 n.22, 147; *Jazz Workshop* (Russell) 101-102; Brandeis concert/*All About Rosie* 107; *New York, N.Y.* 116; *Jazz in the Space Age* 129.
McLean, Oliver, 32, 38, 46
McPheeters, Dwight (childhood friend) 5, 6, 9-15, 17, 24, 26, 28, 30-31, 43, 61, 72.
Medeski, John, xxiii, 216, 221, 297
Messiaen, Olivier, 291
Mikkelborg, Palle, xxii, 248, 272, ; Russell in Scandinavia 194, 207; *80th Birthday Concert* 273; on Russell and Miles Davis 293–294.
Milhaud, Darius, 77.
Miller, Eli (Dr.), 3-5, 6, 8.
Mingus, Charles, Brandeis University (*Modern Jazz Concert* LP) 106-107; 34, 50-51, 115, 144, 146, 148, 175, 182, 196, 214, 222, 237, 251, 261, 297.
Mitchell, Red, 83; *Electronic Sonata 1968* 201.
Modern Jazz Quartet, 88, 91, 109, 158.
Monk, Thelonious, 55, 100, 144, 154, 160, 162, 201, 261, 295; "Round Midnight" 52, 150, 151, 152, 155-156, 185, 223.
Monson, Ingrid, xviii, 65; on Russell and Coltrane 66-67; on "Cubano-Be, Cubano-Bop" 72; on jazz and Civil Rights 77; on Lydian Concept 123 n. 43, 284; on Russell at NEC 217-218; on Russell and Gurdjieff 288-289.
Moore, Mandy, 105.
Moore, Robert, 83; on Russell early years 7, 14, 21 n.22, 25, 34, 36-37; on Joseph Russell piano playing xxvi n.17, 35; on Russell at Wilberforce 44, 46; *Electronic Sonata 1980* 237-238.
Morales, Richie, 272, 273.

Moser, Diane, 297.
Motian, Paul, *Jazz Workshop* 100.
Mulligan, Gerry, xxi, 91, 101, 136, 154, 273; 55th Street enclave 60, 79-80, 90, 115, 276; *Birth of the Cool* 83-84; records *All About Rosie* 158.
Mundy, Jimmy, 28, 29, 38
Murray, Albert, xvii-xviii, xx, 182.
Murray, David, xvii.
Mumurashkina, Aleksandra, 297.

New England Conservatory, xxiii, 46, 205, 208, 209, 222, 226, 231 n.41, 233, 239, 240, 241, 244, 252, 253, 282, 291, 297; Gunther Schuller on 213-215; 125th anniversary 234; for Russell at NEC see under Russell, George.
Nicoll, Maurice, 203, 205-206, 209, 287-288, 289-290.
Norbury, Alice. See Russell, Alice.
nyMusikk, 187, 195, 197, 294.

Oberlin College, x, xv, 18, 19
Odjenar, Juanita. See Giuffre, Juanita
O'Gallagher, John, 297.
Okoshi, Tiger, 256, 257, 266.
Orquestra Jazz de Matosinhos, 297.

Parker, Charlie, xxi, 52, 555, 60-61, 75, 81, 119, 120, 142, 148, 154, 158, 180, 188, 216, 222, 241, 273, 278, 295; Carnegie Hall concert 1947 71, 74 n.58; 55th Street enclave, 79; "Ezz-Thetic" 88; "Donna Lee"/"New Donna" 145, 151; "Confirmation" 151, 185; "Au Privave" 161.
Penderecki, Krysztof, 187, 196, 197, 206, 223, 294.
Perlis, Vivian, (interview for American Music Series) on life in Cincinnati 6, 9, 16, 24, 53,; music in Cincinnati 25-26, 27, 32-33, 34; on Joseph Russell's piano playing 35-36; on Wilberforce 44-45; on Harold Gaston 50, on Benny Carter 52; on the Lydian Concept 63, 65, 287; on tuberculosis 67-68; on Stefan Wolpe 69; on move to Sweden 179.
Phillips, Barre, Newport Festival All-Stars tour 1964 176, 177-178.
Pine, Courtney, 248, 249, 252, 253, 297.
Pitts, Ray, 185, 186.
Pozo, Chano, "Cubano Be, Cubano Bop" 70-71, 72, 202.
Pryor, Henry ("Little Bird"), 55, 59, n.60, 56-57.

Qamar, Nadi, 29, 34-35, 53, 56 n.38, 277; introduces Russell to classical music 30, 37-38, 41 n.64, 54; on Russell's early music 50-51.

Racism/Race, xi, xv, xvii-xxii, 2, 6-18, 23-24, 36, 38,43, 47-48, 50, 67, 70, 77-78, 93, 104, 108, 180-182, 236, 222, 236, 278. (See also Jim Crow/Crow-Jimism)
Ravel, Maurice, 54, 77, 81, 223.
Reed, Lucy, xxii, 97, 105, 131.
Reilly, Jack, 132, 160; on Bill Evans 98, 131; *Time Spiral* 238-239; on the Lydian Concept 281, 283.
Rhythm Club, 31-32, 38, 47.
Riley, Howard, 279-280, 286.
Rivers, Sam, 146; *Living Time* 225, 226, 227, 229.
Riverside Records, xxii, 76, 138 n.20, 141-142, 145, 147, 148, 158, 225.
Roach, Max, xvii-xviii, 34, 81, 143, 162, 182; replaces Russell with Benny Carter 51-52; Russell befriended by/lives 60, 68, 70; 55th St. enclave, 74,278; *Birth of the Cool* 83; Lee Konitz and "Ezz-Thetic," 86, 88; Lenox School of Jazz, 109; *New York, N.Y.* 116, 117, 120.
Rosengren, Bernt, 180, 187.
Rossi, Marc, 216, 282; *African Game* 240, 241-242.
Russell, Alice, xiii, 1, 2, 19, 61, 208, 216, 233-234, 250, 268, 271, 272, 273-274;

manager 83, 244; Hix Blewitt 100-101; on *Living Time* 227, 228; Lincoln Center, 259-261; working methods, 234; *80th Birthday Concert*, 273.

Russell, Bessie, 10, 17, 20 n.8, 25, 26, 53; adoption of Russell xv, 3-4, 18-19, 38-39, 290-291; as a parent xvi-xvii, 6, 9, 43, 45, 75, 85; marriage 5-6, 20.

George, Russell, George, birth narrative x-xi, xv-xvii, xxi-xxii, 3, 18-20, 49-50, 290-291; childhood in Cincinnati xi, 1-20, 23-39, 43-44; Carnegie Hall concert 1947 71, 74 n.58, 85; at NEC xxiii, 205, 208, 211, 213-223, 233, 237, 241, 255, 259, 265; political views and Vietnam, xxii, 66, 179, 182-184, 189, 205-206, 208, 222;

racism, experience of (see Race/Racism),

in Scandinavia xxii, 178-185, 188-190, 193-209;

tuberculosis xxii, 2, 31, 44-50, 61, 62-63, 67;

Wilberforce University 44-46, 51;

See also Giuffre, Juanita; Jerstad, Marit; Jordon, Sheila; Russell, Alice Russell,

recordings (albums): *The African Game* 120, 126, 150, 234, 240-5, 253, 290, 294; *At Beethoven Hall Vol. I and II* 151, 185-6;

*At the Five Spot* 129-130, 142-145, 147, 148, 150, 151, 152 ;

*The 80th Birthday Concert* 273;

*Electronic Organ Sonata No. 1* 195, 199-200, 205;

*Electronic Sonata for Souls Loved by Nature, 1968* 184, 187, 195, 198, 200-201, 204, 224, 235, 242, 245, 288, 296, 298;

*Electronic Sonata for Souls Loved by Nature, 1980* 237-238;

*The Essence of George Russell/* big band *Electronic Sonata for Souls Loved by Nature* 120, 184, 185, 187, 195, 198, 200, 201-204, 229, 235, 245, 250, 251, 256-257, 273, 298;

*Ezz-Thetics* xxii, 142, 145, 150, 151, 153-154, 155-157, 158, 242, 245, 298;

*In Kansas City* 142, 144, 147, 149, 151;

*It's About Time* 233, 266-268, 269, 273, 274, 298;

*Jazz in the Space Age* xxii, 75, 94, 113, 114, 121, 126-130, 131, 141, 143, 1512, 155, 159, 184, 195, 198, 229, 242, 297, 298;

*Jazz Workshop* xx, xxii, 69, 76, 81-82, 98-105, 114, 115, 116, 120, 121, 131, 132, 135, 159, 184, 198, 239, 242, 298;

*Listen to the Silence* 185, 195, 205-208, 222-223, 235, 237, 245, 251, 258, 273;

*Live in an American Time Spiral* 234, 238-239, 241, 244, 245, 288;

*Live in Tokyo* 251;

*Living Time* 216, 224-228, 229, 233, 235, 237, 242, 266-268, 288-290, 294, 298;

*The London Concert* 254-257, 258;

*New York Big Band* 236-238;

*New York, N.Y.* xxii, 94, 113-121, 125, 126, 127, 129, 130-131, 132, 135, 137, 229, 243, 251, 273;

*Now and Then* 195-198;

*Othello Ballet* 126, 184, 195, 196, 198-200, 202, 235, 245;

*Outer View* 142, 145, 146, 150, 151, 158, 160-162, 249;

*So What* 241;

*Stratusphunk* 142, 144-145, 150, 151, 155, 280, 298;

*The Stratus Seekers* 126, 142, 146, 158-160, 251;

*Trip to Prillarguri* 195, 200, 204-205;

*Vertical Form VI* 207, 216, 234-235, 237, 245, 268, 291;

recordings (arrangements): "Caravan" 81, 82-83, 88; "How High the Moon" 82, 88; "In the Wee Small Hours of the Morning" 105;
recordings (compositions): "All About Rosie",
*American Trilogy* 222, 234, 257-258, 261, 268;
"A Bird in Igor's Yard" xxii, 80-1, 82, 88, 135;
"Born to Blow the Blues" 105;
*Centrifugue* 234, 252, 291;
"Cubano Be, Cubano Bop" xxi, xxii, 51, 67, 70-72, 75, 76-77, 82, 90, 91, 93, 115, 120, 124, 135, 136, 150, 184, 237, 242, 250, 251;
"The Day John Brown Was Hanged" 92-94, 102, 103, 126, 150, 159;
"D.C. Divertimento" 161, 238-239;
*Dialogue with Ornette* 222-223, 234, 268, 273, 291;
"Ezz-Thetic" 87-88, 98,100, 135, 148, 150, 155, 159, 222, 238-239;
"Lydian Lullaby" 92, 102, 103;
"Lydian M-1" 69, 91-92;
"Miss Clara" 92, 93, 98, 102, 103;
"Odjenar" 87-88;
"Similau" 81-82, 125;
*Six Aesthetic Gravities* 234, 252, 257, 291, 298;
"So What" 152, 241, 249, 256-257, 258, 268, 273;
"Stratusphunk" 106, 113, 144, 148, 159, 204, 222, 261, 268;
"This Is New" 105;
*Time Line* 223-234, 234, 268;
*Uncommon Ground* 234, 252, 257, 258, 298;
"You Are My Sunshine" 150, 160-163, 185-186, 223, 257, 273-274;
Russell, Joseph, adoption of Russell xv, 3-4, 18-19, 38-39, 290-291; as a parent xvi-xvii, 6, 9, 15, 17, 43, 45, 75, 85; marriage 3, 5-6, 20; death 15, 37; piano playing xvi, xxiv n.17, 35-36, 223.
Rypdal, Terje, xxii, 187-188, 238, 297; studies Concept 200; *Electronic Sonata 1968* 201; big band *Electronic Sonata* 202; *Trip to Prillarguri* 204; *Esoteric Circle* 208-209.
Russ-Hix, 100.

Schillinger, Joseph, 90, 102, 108-109, 114, 121 n.11, 286.
Schoenberg, Arnold, 79,81, 82, 103, 223, 270, 291, 296.
Schuller, George, 95.
Schuller, Gunther, xvi-xvii, xxv n.21, 138 n.20, 158, 222, 223, 230 n.39; 55th St enclave 90, 278; *Birth of the Cool* 83-84; Third Stream 81, 106-108, 291-292; Brandeis Concert 106-108; Lenox School of Jazz/Jazz education 108-112, 283; NEC 213-214; Recruits Russell to NEC 214-215; on Russell as teacher 215, 26, 221.
Schwendener, Ben, 216, 291; co-composes "La Folia, The Rocella Variations", 234, 257; on the Lydian Concept 282-283.
Segal, Jack, 80, 105, 198.
Seignez, Philippe, 297.
Shaw, Artie, xxii, 77, 81-82.
Shepp, Archie, 89, 145, 166 n.57, 196; dispute with Russell 180-182, 184, 185.
Sheppard, Andy, 252-253, 256, 265, 270, 271, 292, 293; *London Concert* 257; BBC interview 258; *It's About Time* 267; *80th Birthday Concert* 273.
Sissle, Noble, 26-27, 37.
Stein Crease, Stephanie, 92, 114, 292.
Stenson, Bobo, 205, 207-208.
Stockhausen, Karlheinz, 184, 187, 195, 200, 202-203, 207, 210 n.23, 223, 294-295, 296.
Stravinsky, Igor, ix, 77, 79, 80, 81, 82, 115, 159, 161, 178, 190-191 n.12, 223, 278, 296.
Swallow, Steve, 138 n.20, 176, 253, 258,

297; *Ezz-Thetics* 151, 153, 156; *Stratus Seekers* 159; *Outer View* 161; Newport Jazz Festival 162-163; *Portrait of Sheila* 163; on Don Ellis 157.

Tatum, Art, 29, 35, 153.
Taylor, Billy, xx.
Taylor, Cecil, xvi, xvii, xviii, 35, 16, 145, 148, 153, 175, 182, 185-186, 257.
Taylor, Rick, 249.
Taylor, Trevor, 253.
Terry, Anna M., 46.
Terry, Clark, 273.
The Five Spot, 115, 137, 142-144, 147, 164 n.7, 43, 333
The Rhythm Club (Cincinnati), 31-32, 38, 47.
Third Stream, 81, 94, 106-108, 107, 207, 214, 219-220, 287, 291-292.
Townsend, A. B., 50, 53.
Trentham, Brian, 158, 185, 186, 189.

Umbria Jazz Festival, 266, 270-271.
Urmson, Bill, 216, 251, 248, 249; on Russell at NEC 217-218, 220, 221; *African Game* 240-241, 243; *London Concert* 257.

Varèse, Edgar, 196, 197, 198, 223.
Ventura, Charlie, xxii ; arranges "Caravan" for 81, 82-83, 88.
Village Vanguard, 78, 115, 236, 237, 238, 239, 240.

Walker, Mike, 266, 273; It's About Time/Living Time 267; 80th Birthday Concert 273.
Waller, Fats, 29.
Washington, DC, First International Jazz Festival 1963, 161.
Wasserman, Andy, 65, 280, 294; on Lydian Concept 216, 276.
WGBH, (George Russell—A Jazz Portrait), Harold Gaston and tuberculosis 47; Max Roach and own drumming 51-52; Lydian Concept xxii, 89; early days in New York 60.
Wheeler, Kenny, 250.
Whyte, Zack, 27-28, 37, 38, 40 n.21.
Wilberforce University, 44-46, 51. (See also Terry, Anna M.)
Windham, Dan, *Listen to the Silence* 205.
Wolpe, Stefan, 115, 278; Russell studies with 68, 197, 294, 296; influence on Russell 68-70, 76-77, 87-88, 126.

Young, Ben/WKCR, 76, 130-131, 142, 146, 148, 156, 166 n.57, 287; interview with Nadi Qamar 35, 50-51, 56 n.38; Russell on Lydian Concept 76, 89; Russell on 55th Street group 79-80; on arranging for Ella Fitzgerald/Charlie Ventura 82; "Lydian M-1" 91; Russell on own piano playing 152; Russell on move to Scandinavia 185; Othello Ballet 198-199.
Young, Dave, 112, 141, 145,146, 153, 156, 157-158; *Jazz in the Space Age* 126, 128-129; *the Five Spot* 143; *Stratusphunk* 145; *Kansas City* 147.
Young, Snooky, *Living Time* 226, 227.

# About the Author

**Duncan Heining** has been writing about jazz for twenty-five years. In that time he has written for *Jazzwise*, *Jazz UK*, the *Independent*, the *Independent on Sunday* and *Avant Magazine*. He currently writes for the *All About Jazz* website.

Scarecrow Press published the first edition of his biography of George Russell in 2009 under the title, *George Russell: The Story of an American Composer*. His other books are *Trad Dads, Dirty Boppers and Free Fusioneers: British Jazz, 1960-1975* (2012) and *Mosaics: The Life and Works of Graham Collier* (2018), both published by Equinox Press.

Dr Heining's academic background is in the social sciences and he holds honours degrees from North Staffordshire University and the Open University, a master's degree from the University of Leicester and a PhD by published work from Oxford Brookes University.

Until 2003 he worked in the British Probation and Prison Services, both as a probation officer and as a manager. In the course of a rich and varied working life, he has worked in factories and warehouses, on farms, and in offices, and was at one time a long-distance lorry driver. But writing about jazz and the musicians that make is another life entirely.

www.ingramcontent.com/pod-product-compliance
Lightning Source LLC
Chambersburg PA
CBHW080036100526
44584CB00023BA/3221